LAND OF EVERLASTING HILLS

George Masa, Jim Thompson, and the Photographs That Helped Save the Great Smoky Mountains

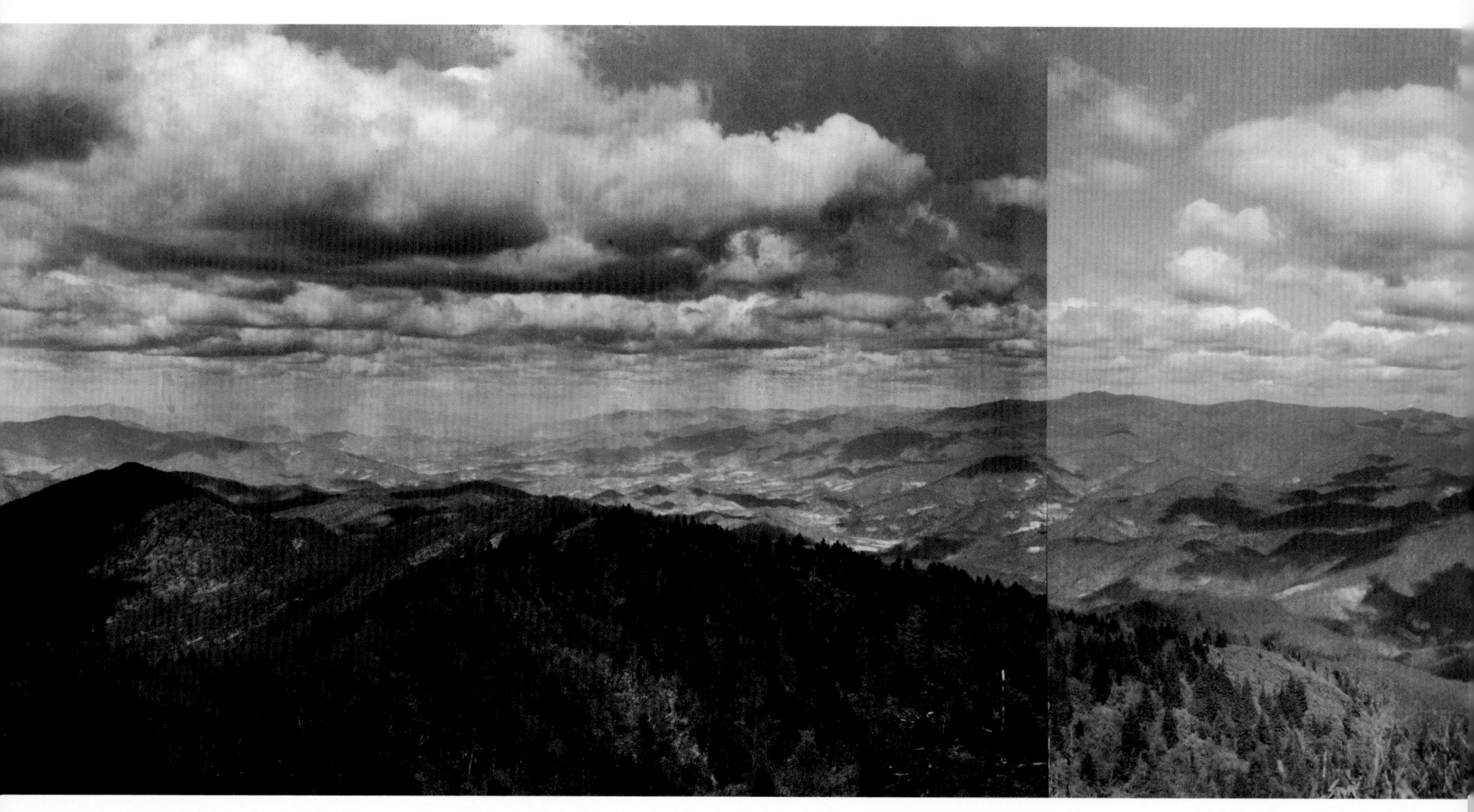

Land of Everlasting Hills

and Blaze the Appalachian Trail

REN DAVIS AND HELEN DAVIS

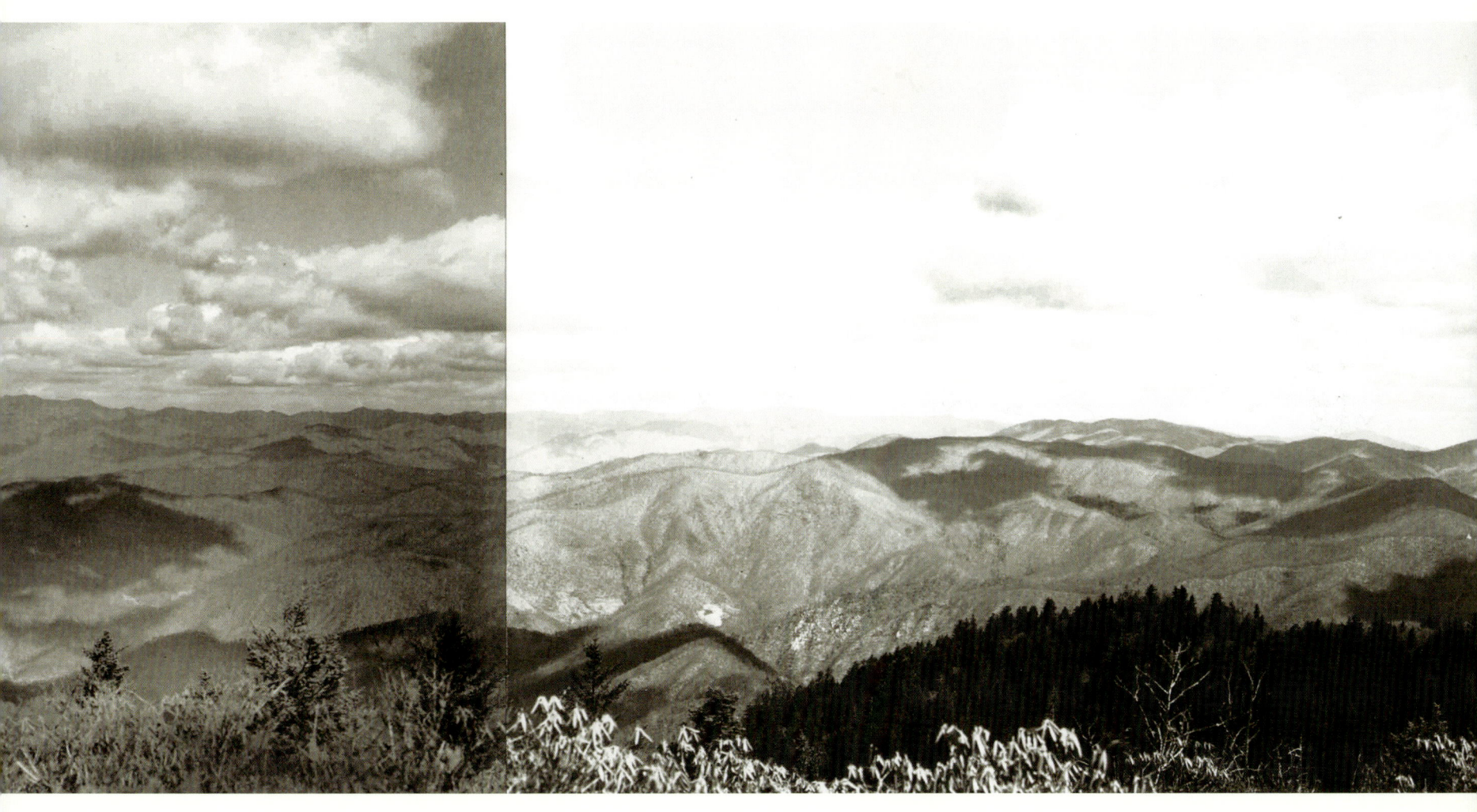

THE UNIVERSITY OF GEORGIA PRESS   ATHENS

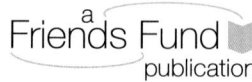

Publication of this work was made possible, in part, by a generous gift from the University of Georgia Press Friends Fund.

Library of Congress Cataloging-in-Publication Data

Names: Davis, Ren, 1951– author. | Davis, Helen, 1951– author.
Title: Land of Everlasting Hills : George Masa, Jim Thompson, and the photographs that helped save the Great Smoky Mountains and blaze the Appalachian Trail / Ren Davis and Helen Davis.
Description: Athens : The University of Georgia Press, [2025] | Includes bibliographical references and index.
Identifiers: LCCN 2025019684 | ISBN 9780820366524 (hardback)
Subjects: LCSH: Masa, George, 1885–1933. | Thompson, Jim, 1880–1976. | Photographers—United States—Biography. | Photography—Appalachian Region—History—20th century. | Appalachian Region—Pictorial works. | Appalachian Region—History—Sources. | Appalachian Trail—History—Sources. | LCGFT: Biographies. | Illustrated works.
Classification: LCC TR139 .D38 2025
LC record available at https://lccn.loc.gov/2025019684

Contents

Photographs

Jim Thompson

GREAT SMOKY MOUNTAINS NATIONAL PARK

WATERFALLS

COLORIZED AND OVERSIZED PRINTS

Preface

"Do you know much about George Masa?"

This question opened our March 2020 conversation with Dr. Nathaniel "Nate" Holly, acquisitions editor at the University of Georgia Press. He shared that the Press was interested in learning if we would work on a book featuring Masa's photography, one that would be similar in format to our award-winning book, *Landscapes for the People: George Alexander Grant, First Chief Photographer of the National Park Service*, published by the Press in 2015.

In our initial response, we said, "We know a little bit about Masa. He was a Japanese immigrant who took photographs in the Great Smoky Mountains. That is about it." Nonetheless, we welcomed the opportunity to learn more about him and his role in the efforts to establish a national park in the Smokies. So we readily said, "Yes."

However, as we dug deeper into Masa's biography, we soon recognized that focusing on his photography alone would create an incomplete story about the Smokies. During our next conversation with Nate, we shared this observation: "George Masa is only half of the story. Living in Asheville, he worked mostly in the North Carolina side of the mountains. There was another photographer working in Knoxville at the same time who produced superb images of the Great Smoky Mountains in Tennessee. His name was Jim Thompson."

The two men were contemporaries, colleagues, and friends. Each made invaluable contributions to the national park effort and, eventually, to blazing the Appalachian Trail through the Smokies and down to Georgia. We believed that combining their stories and photography into a single volume would provide a more complete presentation of the vital roles they played in creating the Great Smoky Mountains National Park.

When we mentioned Jim Thompson to Nate, we actually knew less about him than we did about George Masa. Our introduction to Thompson came from our work on *Landscapes for the People*, which focuses on National Park Service photographer George Grant. In 1934 the Department of the Interior asked Grant to select ten photographs of the national parks that could be adapted for postage stamps to celebrate President Franklin D. Roosevelt's National Parks Year. One of the photographs chosen was of the newly established Great Smoky Mountains National Park, taken by Knoxville commercial photographer James "Jim" Thompson. Over the next four years of research, we delighted in learning more about both Jim Thompson and George Masa.

As we began our research for the proposed book, the world came to a screeching halt with the onset of the COVID-19 pandemic. Libraries and other collections closed their doors to outside researchers, leaving us to make inquiries remotely by telephone, email, and internet searches. Finally, in the summer of 2021, with COVID-19 vaccinations available, libraries began to reopen. Over the next year, we traveled to the archives in the Highlands Historical Society, the Hunter Library at Western Carolina University in Cullowhee; the Calvin McClung Historical Collection at the Knox County Library; and the University of Tennessee Hodges Library in Knoxville. A few months later, we examined documents and photographs at the Ramsey Library at University of North Carolina Asheville and at the Pack Memorial Library Special Collections in Asheville before we made a return visit to Western Carolina. A final trip in July 2022 to the Great Smoky Mountains National Park archives in Townsend, Tennessee, completed our on-site visits. We were also provided digital access to the extensive collection of images from the Horace Kephart Family Collection held by Smokies Life (formerly the Great Smoky Mountains Association).

Additionally, with the help of the Appalachian Trail Conservancy and others, we integrated the work of Masa and Thompson, as well as of their hiking companions, into the yearslong effort to identify a route for the nascent Appalachian Trail through the Great Smoky Mountains. Perhaps the most interesting aspect of this project was our learning of the fundamental disagreements—even heated arguments—between the Tennessee and North Carolina hiking clubs over the preferred route of the trail across the Smokies. In the end, it took the vision of the widely respected outdoorsman and author Horace Kephart, as well as the determination of Appalachian Trail Conference (now Conservancy) chairman, Myron Avery, to bridge the impasse.

While the final route of the trail through the Smokies and into Georgia has been modified a few times over the years, it remains faithful to the vision of these pioneers.

Fortified with digital thumbnails of hundreds of Masa's and Thompson's photographs from the different libraries' online collections and other sources, we undertook the slow process of selecting those we believed to be the most visually outstanding, the most representative of the scope of their work, and the most reflective of their artistic vision. In order to acquire the high-resolution digital copies necessary for publication, we needed to complete the required permissions. Fortunately, the University of Georgia Press provided funding to pay the fees associated with producing the photographs. In the end, we built a portfolio of more than three hundred images for use within the narrative text or as photographic plates.

During this time, we also made a critical connection with filmmaker Paul Bonesteel. His 2003 documentary, *The Mystery of George Masa*, was our introduction to Masa's compelling story. Bonesteel never wavered in his determination to discover the hidden facets of Masa's life—most notably, his early life in Japan and his arrival in the United States, details that Masa never revealed to even his closest friends. For two decades, Bonesteel and his collaborator, Janet McCue, a retired research librarian at Cornell University, pursued the story—both in the United States and in Japan—peeling back the layers of a troubled life and a quest for redemption and rebirth. Their biography, *George Masa: A Life Reimagined*, completed this quest and caused other Masa biographers—ourselves included—to redefine his life story and his relationships to others.

Another goal of our book is to offer a glimpse into the

differing aspects of the work produced by both George Masa and Jim Thompson. Most notably, we sought to convey the influence of Japanese art, spiritual beliefs, and culture on Masa's work while inspiring admiration for the straightforward, natural approach Jim Thompson took when capturing the beauty of the mountain landscapes. We hope that, through these photographic images, the viewer may experience the beauty as captured by the eye of each of these artists.

Finally, we wish to dedicate this book to all of the men and women, from Anne and William P. Davis to Horace Kephart, Colonel David Chapman, Paul Fink, Carlos Campbell, and Myron Avery, who worked tirelessly to create a national park in the Great Smoky Mountains and to blaze a wilderness path through the Appalachians. Their vision, so vividly captured in the photographs by George Masa and Jim Thompson, is a timeless gift to all Americans. For that we are grateful.

Note on the Blue Ridge in 2024

Shortly after completion of this manuscript, Asheville, Chimney Rock, Grandfather Mountain, and many other communities in the western North Carolina mountains were devastated by the winds and rain from Hurricane Helene. In addition, the Appalachian Trail suffered significant damage from downed trees and flash flooding. As they rebuild and restore their magnificent landscapes, the people who love their mountain home display the resilience and commitment that led their forebears to save these mountains a century ago. We further dedicate this book to them.

Acknowledgments

The Land of Everlasting Hills was developed through the collective efforts of librarians, archivists, historians, and others who share a love for the Great Smoky Mountains National Park and for the Appalachian National Scenic Trail, or the AT. Through the generous support of many individuals and institutions, we were able to craft a brief history of the park's origins and the blazing of the Appalachian Trail through the Great Smokies, highlighting the integral role that photographers George Masa and James "Jim" Thompson played in bringing these two projects from vision to reality.

We wish to recognize those whose help was indispensable in telling Masa's and Thompson's stories and in sharing the iconic photographs they had created to support the park and trail. Many of these images are published here together for the first time, allowing the reader to examine the differing approach that each photographer took with his work. As was noted by their contemporaries, George Masa's photographs reflected the art and culture of his native Japan, while Jim Thompson brought the technical acumen of a skilled commercial photographer to his richly detailed images.

First, we wish to thank Nathaniel Holly, PhD, editor in chief at the University of Georgia Press, who has shepherded us through every phase of this project, offering recommendations, suggesting potential resources and individuals to contact, and answering our many questions. He; Lisa Bayer, director of the Press; Laura Price Yoder; Jon Davies; and other dedicated staff have been a joy to work with on this, as well as on our previous books. We are also most appreciative of the careful attention to every detail by copy editor Kate Genn.

Critical to this work was the support of the dedicated archivists and librarians who opened their collections to us and provided high-resolution digital copies of many of Masa's and Thompson's photographs for the book. This group of professionals included Jason Brady, special collections librarian at the Hunter Library, Western Carolina University; Ken Wise, special collections librarian and associate professor emeritus; librarian Laura Romans at the Hodges Library, University of Tennessee, Knoxville; Joanna Bouldin, Eric Dawson, and Steve Cotham (now retired), archivists at the Calvin McClung Historical Collection in the Knox County Library in Knoxville; Kathy Hill, archivist with the Buncombe County Special Collections at the Pack Memorial Library in Asheville; Gene Hyde, head of Special Collections, Ramsey Library, University of North Carolina Asheville; Sarah Carrier, research librarian in the Louis Round Wilson Special Collections Library at the

University of North Carolina at Chapel Hill; Michael Aday, librarian-archivist at the Great Smoky Mountains National Park Collections Preservation Center; Frances Figart, creative services director at Smokies Life; Mieko Palazzo, research service coordinator in Special Collections at George Mason University; Sarah Koontz and Heather South, archivists in the Western Regional Archives at the North Carolina Department of Natural and Cultural Resources; Jennifer Runyon, archivist with the Board of Geographic Names at the United States Geological Survey; Julie Bartlett Nelson, archivist at the Calvin Coolidge Presidential Library and Museum; Marjorie Strong, assistant librarian at the Vermont Historical Society; Renee Papous, archivist with the Rockefeller Archive Center; Anne Merrill, associate vice president at the Appalachian Trail Conservancy; Kelli Fisher, reference assistant in the Special Collections Research Center at Syracuse University; and Phil Potts, archivist at the Highlands Historical Society.

We were also very fortunate to receive invaluable help and support from several historians and authors who generously shared their knowledge and resources, helping us fill many gaps in George Masa's and Jim Thompson's biographies. Among these individuals were Susan Shumaker, historical researcher with Florentine Films, who shared her notes on George Masa and Horace Kephart, which were developed for Ken Burns and Dayton Duncan's film and book, *The National Parks: America's Best Idea*; Paul James and Jack Neely with the Knoxville History Project; Charles Maynard, Knoxville minister and authority on Tennessee history; William A. Hart Jr., Smoky Mountains historian and Masa biographer; and James Casada, Masa biographer and Smoky Mountains historian.

Special thanks must go to Paul Bonesteel, whose 2003 film documentary on George Masa provided an indispensable introduction to this enigmatic figure that would be surpassed only by his determined research, as well as that of his coauthor, Janet McCue, for their groundbreaking new biography, *George Masa: A Life Reimagined*. This book is a must-read for all who seek the full story of George Masa's life.

We were fortunate to speak with Jim Thompson's grandson, also named Jim Thompson, who related the story of his grandfather's meeting with Margaret Bourke White, and for our meeting with Thompson's great-granddaughter, Ann Thompson, who continues to operate the Thompson Photo store in Knoxville. We are also thankful for the generosity of our Atlanta friends: Glenn Kellum, who connected us with Paul James and Charles Maynard in Knoxville, and Mary and Miles Crowder, MD, who opened Miles's childhood home in Knoxville for us to use as our base during our research trip to the city.

LAND OF EVERLASTING HILLS

Introduction

Picturing a Park for the People

In 1871 Civil War veteran and photographer William Henry Jackson was invited to join a geological expedition, organized by Ferdinand Hayden, to explore and document the Yellowstone region of Wyoming and Montana. For years explorers had returned from their travels to the area and recounted tales of amazing natural features, telling of everything from hot springs and geysers to astonishing rock formations and a massive lake surrounded by high mountains. Most who heard the stories discounted them as the ramblings of men too long away from civilization.

Hayden enlisted Jackson to visually document Yellowstone's otherworldly terrain for his team. Large prints of Jackson's photographs were presented to Congress, providing indisputable evidence not only that the stories were true but also that the area needed to be protected from development and exploitation. On March 1, 1872, Congress passed legislation that made Yellowstone the nation's and the world's first national park; this was soon after signed into law by President Ulysses Grant.

In 1890, Yosemite, originally set aside as a California preserve in 1864, was expanded and named a national park. That park was followed by Sequoia (1890), Mount Rainier (1899), Crater Lake (1902), Glacier (1910), and Rocky Mountain (1915). All these parks were created from western

federal lands far removed from the nation's eastern population centers. Creating national parks in the eastern United States would take extraordinary effort and patience from political leaders, visionary conservationists, and even ordinary Americans wishing to share in the national park experience closer to home.

By the 1920s, photography was no longer the new visual medium it had been when Jackson presented his images in the 1870s. Nonetheless, it would prove invaluable in introducing millions of Americans to the majestic landscapes of a proposed national park in the Appalachian Mountains of Tennessee and North Carolina.

Saving Shaconage

> It is in nature's grandeur that mechanized men and women find rest for their souls. True, they don't have to go to the tall mountains, but they are more likely to be impressed with the beauties of nature when presented romantically and dramatically as they are in the Great Smokies.—John A. Livingstone, *Asheville Times*, February 3, 1931

The Cherokee, who settled in the Southern Appalachians centuries ago, called their mountain home Shaconage (Sha-con-o-hey, the "Land of Blue Smoke"). They lived in this sacred landscape of lush coves, fast-flowing rivers,

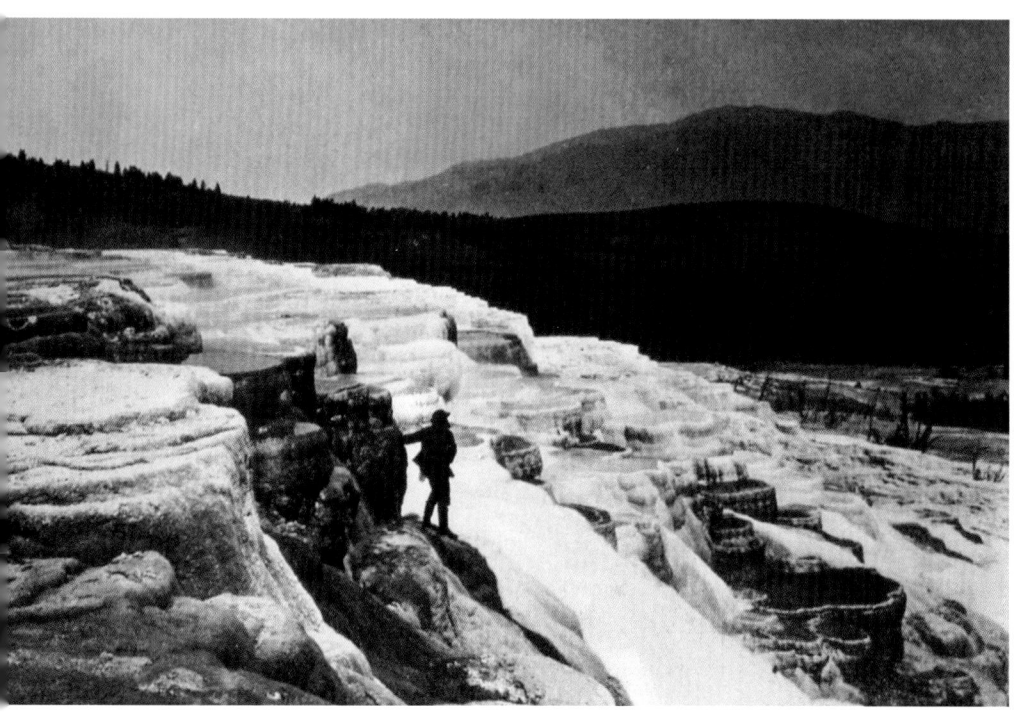

Artist Thomas Moran at Jupiter Terrace, Mammoth Hot Springs, the future site of Yellowstone National Park, 1871. Photograph by W. H. Jackson. National Archives and Records Administration, Record Group 57, still photography. NAID: 517643.

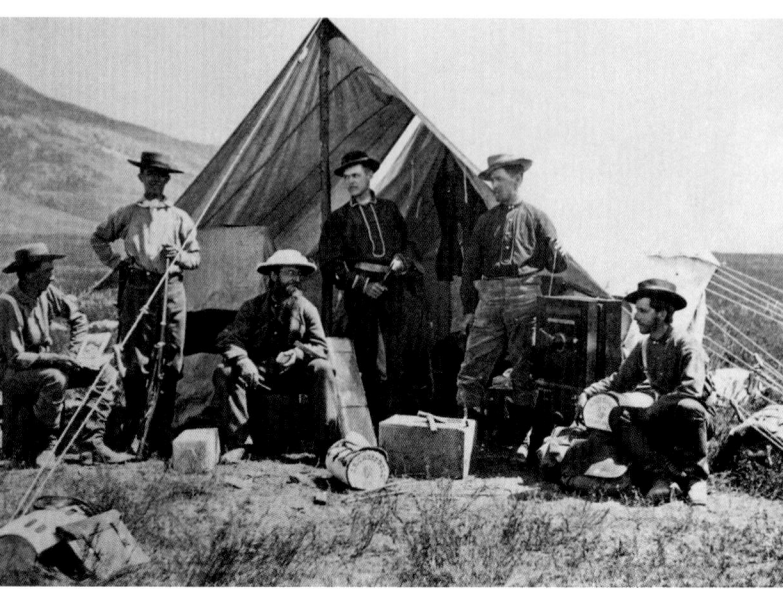

Hayden Expedition in Camp, 1872. William Henry Jackson seated at right. Photograph by W. H. Jackson. National Park Service, Yellowstone National Park Photography Collection.

and primeval forests for generations, until the 1830s, when Scots-Irish American settlers arrived after the forced removal of most of the Cherokee on the infamous Trail of Tears. While the Cherokee legacy lived on in the names of waterways, peaks, and other landmarks, the settlers adapted the name for their new home to English, calling the rugged landscape simply the Great Smoky Mountains.

For the next half century, the remote valleys and high peaks straddling the border of North Carolina and Tennessee remained remote and largely uncharted, with only a few game and hunting trails penetrating the heavy

forest. Those who lived in the area between Cades Cove and the Cataloochee Valley were primarily subsistence farmers (not unlike their Cherokee predecessors) who eked out a living from the soil and the verdant woodlands.

Following the Civil War, daily life and commerce began to change as railroads brought both tourists and industrialists to Asheville, North Carolina, and Knoxville, Tennessee. The first group came to savor the natural beauty and healthful mountain air; the second came to earn massive profits from harvesting the seemingly endless stands of trees feeding the nation's industrial development. Inevitably, these two competing interests clashed in a decades-long effort to preserve an irreplaceable eastern American landscape before it became lost forever. Photography would play a crucial role in bringing the public into the heart of this conflict.

Promoting a New Switzerland

In 1885 Boston physician Henry O. Marcy published an article in the *Journal of the American Medical Association*, suggesting that a national park be created in the Great Smoky Mountains. He compared the area to Switzerland, which had a similar healthy climate, clean water, and clean air. Eight years later, the North Carolina legislature passed a resolution calling for a park and presented a petition for such to Congress, but the proposal failed. The effort was renewed in 1899 by Chase Ambler, an Ohio physician who had moved to Asheville. Familiar with Marcy's efforts, Ambler organized a promotional campaign advocating for a park in the Appalachians. He garnered support from the Asheville Board of Trade and from political leaders in Virginia, Tennessee, North Carolina, Georgia, and Alabama. With momentum building, Ambler and his supporters gathered together to promote the establishment of a "forest reserve or a park somewhere in the Southern Appalachian Mountains."[1]

At that meeting, future North Carolina governor Locke Craig told attendees, "It has been the policy of the government to establish parks from time to time, and it is remarkable that this mountain region of the South has heretofore been overlooked. . . . The government must preserve this valuable gift of nature for the benefit of the people."[2] North Carolina senator Marion Butler joined the call, telling the audience, "If the government is going to have parks for all of us, then there should be one laid out here. . . . There is no place in the Appalachian range where you can find such a favorite region."[3] At the conclusion of the convention, the group voted overwhelmingly to establish the Appalachian National Park Association (ANPA) to pursue the park proposal in earnest.

In 1900 the association garnered congressional support when the Senate approved funds to develop a plan for a national park in the Southern Appalachians. Following visits by forestry experts and representatives from the U.S. Geological Survey (USGS), Secretary of Agriculture James Wilson recommended to Congress a different plan, suggesting that "the idea of a national park is conservation, not use; that of a forest reserve, conservation by use. I have therefore to recommend a forest reserve, not a park."[4]

Almost immediately, North Carolina senator Jeter Pritchard introduced a bill calling for a $5 million appropriation to establish a Southern Appalachian Forest Reserve, a plan that was endorsed by President William McKinley. However, Pritchard was opposed by supporters of western forest reserves, who feared losing funds for their own lands, and by conservatives in Congress, who opposed federal funding for parks. Following McKinley's 1901 assassination, President Theodore Roosevelt pushed forward with a progressive conservation agenda that included forests and parks, such as the one proposed for the Appalachians. In response, Joseph Cannon, Speaker of the House of Representatives and a staunch opponent of Roosevelt's plans, summed up his opposition in a single sentence: "Not one cent for scenery."[5]

Little progress was made on creating such a reserve until the passage of the Weeks Act (36 Stat. 961) in March 1911.

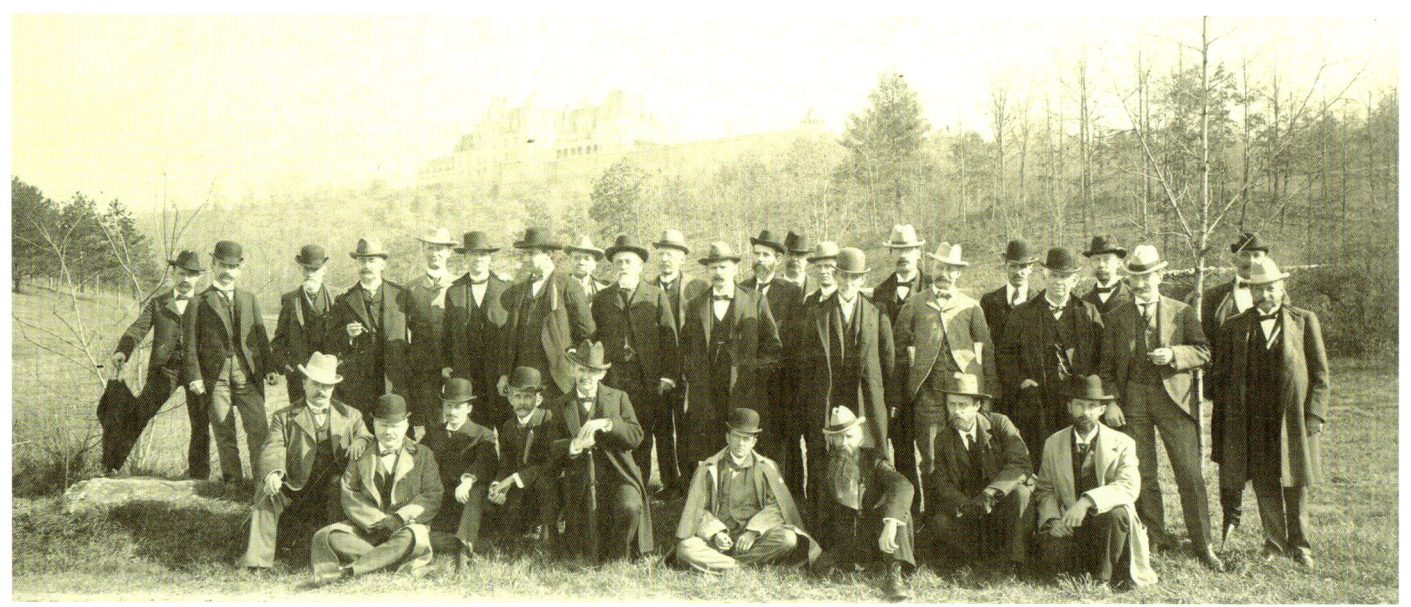

Appalachian National Park Association members at Biltmore in Asheville, 1899. Photographer unknown.
Western Regional Archives, State Archives, North Carolina Department of Natural and Cultural Resources,
State Archives of North Carolina.

The law authorized the federal government to purchase lands for "the protection from fire of the forested watersheds of navigable streams."[6] Notably, of the thirteen potential sites identified for land purchases by Henry Graves, chief of the U.S. Forest Service, the "Smoky Mountain area [of] Tennessee and North Carolina" was not included.[7] The hopes of many park supporters now rested with the recently established National Park Service.

The National Park Service and the Search for an Eastern Park

Industrialist Stephen Mather, a staunch advocate for the national parks, was recruited in 1914 by Interior Secretary Franklin Lane to serve as his assistant in overseeing the national parks. Determined to establish a park system, Mather and his assistant, Horace Albright, were the principal authors of the Organic Act of 1916, which created the National Park Service (NPS), and Mather served as the agency's first director from 1917 until his retirement in 1930. As stipulated in the act, the Park Service would be an independent agency within the Interior Department with the responsibility to "conserve the scenery and the natural and historic objects and the wildlife therein, and to provide for the enjoyment of the same in such manner and by such means as will leave them unimpaired for the enjoyment of future generations."[8] Achieving these objectives would prove to be a longstanding challenge, given both the agency's limited budget and hardened opposition to parks from many powerful political and business interests.

Mather and Albright, superintendent of Yellowstone National Park, recognized the importance of establishing parks in the eastern United States; these would be more accessible to the American people, ensuring support for the fledgling agency. However, unlike the existing parks, most of the potential sites were in private hands, and Congress opposed the use of federal funds to purchase land. The first eastern park, created from donated land, had been established on the Maine coast in 1916: Sieur de Monts National Monument. Later, through generous contributions by philanthropist John D. Rockefeller Jr., the monument was greatly expanded and, in 1929, renamed Acadia National Park. Rockefeller, a powerful advocate for national parks, would later play an indispensable role in the establishment of a park in the Southern Appalachians.

In his *1923 annual report*, Mather wrote, "I should like to see additional national parks established east of the Mississippi, but just how this can be accomplished is not clear. There should be a typical section of the Appalachian Range established as a national park with its natural flora and fauna conserved and made accessible for public use."[9] Park advocates and journalists joined Mather in utilizing a variety of publications to promote a park in the southern mountains. In nearly every case, their articles and essays included vivid photographs illustrating the beauty of the mountains that the nation was being asked to preserve. A number of these images were the work of two local photographers, James "Jim" Thompson in Knoxville and George Masa in Asheville.

Among the proposed sites for a national park were the rugged Great Smoky Mountains of North Carolina and Tennessee. However, from the outset, the Smokies proposal failed to gain support due, in large part, to four significant obstacles. Nearly all the land was privately owned and would have to be purchased, acquired through donations or by other means; the valuable timber there was fueling the nation's growth and industrial expansion; there were strong disagreements over the park's location; and the area was a *terra incognita* (unknown land),[10] as many Americans would be hard pressed to find the Great Smoky Mountains on a map. Despite these challenges, leaders in both states sought support for a national park in the Appalachians.

In North Carolina the state legislature appropriated $2,500 for a commission to explore the possibility of a national park in the Great Smokies. This effort was led by a diverse group of individuals who shared a love of the state's rugged mountain landscapes. Among them were *Asheville Citizen-Times* publisher Charles Webb, North Carolina State College (now University) president E. C. Brooks, and former St. Louis librarian and best-selling outdoor author Horace Kephart, who had sought solace in the Smoky Mountains' "back of beyond" following a mental breakdown in 1903.[11]

A Troubled Visionary

Born in Pennsylvania in 1862, Horace Kephart grew up on a farm in Iowa, where he reveled in stories of western pioneers. After graduating from Cornell University, he worked in the Yale University Library before accepting a position as director of the St. Louis Mercantile Library, the largest library west of the Mississippi River at the time. He and his wife, Laura, had six children, and Kephart was a respected member of the community. However, the unrelenting pressures of work and family, combined with alcohol addiction, led to his depression, during which he threatened suicide and was subsequently admitted to a hospital in 1904 and later discharged to his father's care.

After his recovery, Kephart left his family and settled in a remote cabin in the Smokies, where he could live among and seek to emulate the lives of the frontier pioneers that had captivated his imagination since boyhood. There he would write two notable books. The first, *The Book of Camping and Woodcraft: A Guide for Those Who Travel in the Wilderness*, was published in 1906. A best seller, it introduced many Americans to the joys of camping and outdoor life. The second, *Our Southern Highlanders*, was drawn from his direct observations and served as a narrative of life among the people of the Southern Appalachians—their history and culture. Although criticized by some as stereotyping the mountain people as backward and uneducated, Kephart and his book were accepted by many of his neighbors for fairly representing their lives.

Integral to Kephart's life in the mountains was his growing concern for the devastation wrought by commercial logging of the region and the impact it had on the landscape as well as the people who lived there. By the early 1920s, Kephart was an eloquent and outspoken advocate for protecting the Great Smoky Mountains by establishing a national park.

Through his articles and testimony before government bodies, as well as his travels throughout the mountains, Kephart became known as an expert on the region and the risks to the nation if the area were not preserved and protected. He was also a dedicated friend to many in his adopted hometown of Bryson City, North Carolina, and beyond. Despite his successes, Kephart remained a troubled man who struggled against depression and alcoholism until his

tragic death in an automobile accident in April 1931. His work with George Masa, Jim Thompson, Paul Fink, and many others was critical to establishing a national park in the Great Smokies and the completion of the Appalachian Trail. Sadly, he would not live to see the realization of these goals.

"Why Can't We Have a National Park in the Great Smoky Mountains?"

With support from the Asheville Chamber of Commerce, Webb, Brooks and Kephart established Great Smoky Mountains, Inc. (GSM) to promote plans for a park. Across the state line, parallel efforts were also underway, thanks in large part to the vision of Knoxville couple Anne and William P. Davis.

According to many who were involved in the decade-long and ultimately successful campaign for a national park in the Great Smoky Mountains, the quest began with a simple question. In 1923 Knoxville, Tennessee, business owner William P. Davis and his wife, Anne, took a western vacation trip that included visits to Rocky Mountain and Mesa Verde National Parks. While at Rocky Mountain, Anne purportedly asked her husband, "Why can't we have a national park in the Great Smoky Mountains? They are just as beautiful as these mountains?"[12]

After returning home, Davis began to earnestly explore the possibility of a park in the Smokies. He enlisted the support of friends and business associates, including Col. David Chapman, a druggist and Spanish-American War veteran, and banker and outdoorsman Paul Fink. In December 1923 they organized the Great Smoky Mountains Conservation Association (GSMCA) to formalize their plans. Another group that provided strong support was the

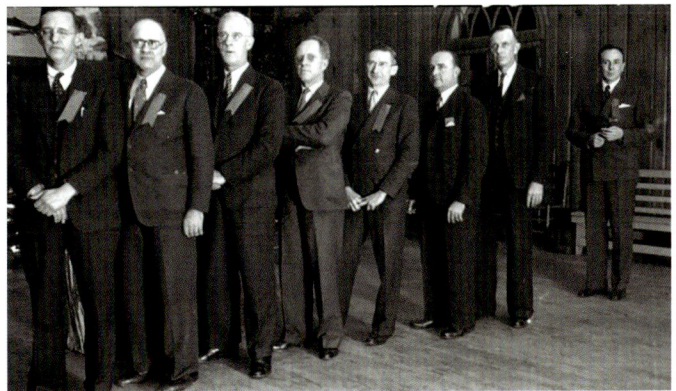

Smoky Mountains Hiking Club presidents, 1924–1937.
Jim Thompson is third from left. Photographer unknown.
University of Tennessee–Knoxville, Hodges Library, Betsy B.
Creekmore Special Collections and University Archives,
Smoky Mountains Hiking Club Collection.

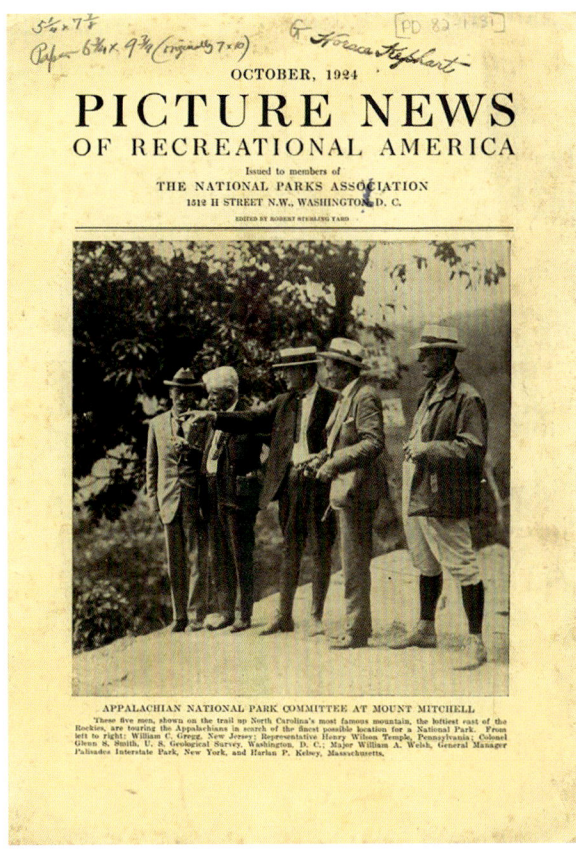

Southern Appalachian
National Park commissioners,
cover photograph from
*Picture News of Recreational
America*, October 1924.
A Publication of the
National Parks Association.
Photographer unknown.
Western Carolina University,
Hunter Library Special
Collections, Horace Kephart
Collection.

Smoky Mountains Hiking Club (SMHC), led by Knoxville commercial photographer and avid hiker Jim Thompson. He would soon become the official photographer of GSMCA, contributing many stunning images to the effort from his years of exploring the Smokies.

In March 1924, Interior Secretary Hubert Work appointed the Southern Appalachian National Park Commission (SANPC) to investigate the region, "with a view of determining whether it included areas suitable for national parks."[13] Interestingly, none of the appointees were from the region to be surveyed. Despite opposition from timber interests calling for the mountains to be designated as reserves, allowing for continued harvesting, the SANPC undertook its work with several visits to sites across the South. In July the commission members met in Asheville with Davis, Chapman, and other GMSCA representatives determined to promote the Great Smokies as a site worthy of a national park. However, divisions among North Carolina park supporters

surfaced. GSM leaders advocated for the Smokies, while others, who were representing Asheville, Blowing Rock, and Boone, argued for an alternative location in the Grandfather Mountain–Linville Gorge area. They were supported by timber company executives, who were claiming that nearly three-quarters of the virgin timber in the Smokies had already been cut, so the area was no longer worthy of park designation. Unless these divisions could be resolved, they would threaten the park project.

Interestingly, it may have been Tennesseans David Chapman and Jim Thompson who helped push the debate in favor of the Smokies. Thompson later recounted that on the morning of the Asheville meeting, Chapman rushed to his Knoxville studio, saying, "Put all the pictures you can in the back seat of this car. I want them all put in the room where we meet."[14] Thompson grabbed several photographs, including large mural prints, and they sped over the mountains, reaching the meeting room while the commission members were visiting Grandfather Mountain. According to Ken Wise, coeditor of *Terra Incognita*, the commissioners, on later seeing the prints, were "suspicious that Thompson's photographs might be fakes . . . [and] insisted on traveling to the mountains and verifying the natural beauty they had seen on display."[15] Needless to say, they were impressed.

In December 1924, the SANPC submitted its initial report to Secretary Work, concluding that, "The Great Smoky Mountains easily stand first because of the height of the mountains, depth of the valley, ruggedness of the area, and the unexampled variety of trees, shrubs, and plants."[16] Ironically, these same characteristics worked against the Smokies, as their remoteness, ruggedness, height, and inaccessibility made development of a recreational park there exceedingly expensive. As a result, the commission recommended the Shenandoah region in Virginia as the first national park in the Appalachians due, in large part, to its proximity to major population centers and accessibility as well as the lower cost of land. However, the report offered hope for a park in the Great Smokies, stating, "We hope that it [Shenandoah] will be made into a national park and that its success will encourage the Congress to create a second park in the Great Smoky Mountains."[17] While supporters of a Great Smokies park were gratified that the mountains warranted selection, they were disappointed that it would likely be deferred to a later time. Edward Meeman, editor

of the *Knoxville News*, urged park advocates to persist in their support, writing, "Let there be only a short interval, or NO INTERVAL AT ALL, between the first and second new national park."[18]

Park advocates worked to persuade the commission to reconsider. North Carolina congressman Zebulon Weaver asked Horace Kephart to "give some salient facts relating to the flora and fauna of these mountains . . . as far as the reasons why this area should be selected."[19] In Kephart's report

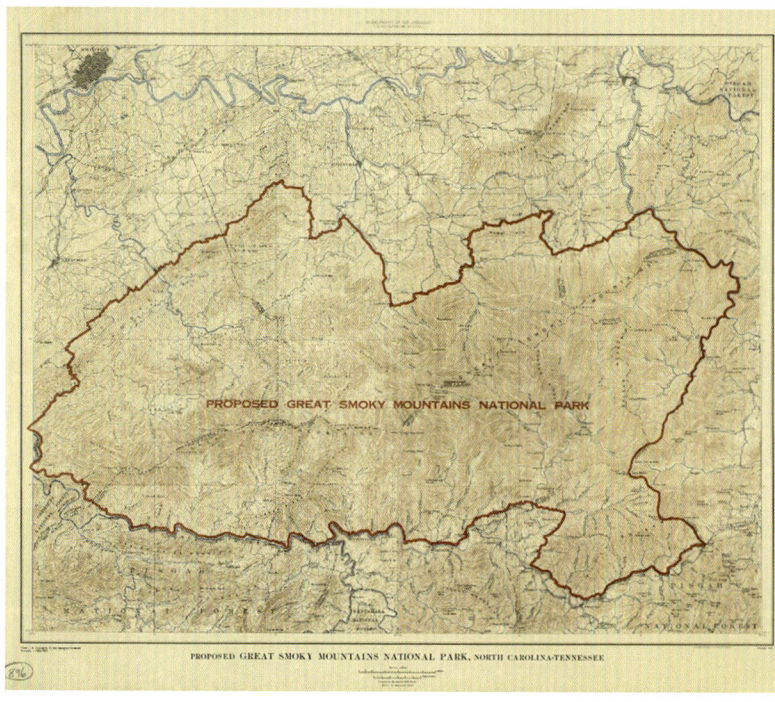

Proposed Great Smoky Mountains National Park, North Carolina–Tennessee, 1926. Often referred to as the Cammerer Map, or "red line map." Drawn by National Park Service cartographers. Tennessee Virtual Archives. Originally published by the United States Geological Survey, 1926, Courtesy of the Tennessee State Library and Archives Collection.

to Congress, he called the Great Smoky Mountains the "dominant range of the entire Appalachian system . . . the most varied forest in the world today and one of the richest collecting grounds for botanists in the United States."[20] He concluded, "For wild beauty and grandeur I have seen nothing in eastern America that equals the Smoky divide and its outlooks."[21]

As the efforts to create the park accelerated, in early 1926, Park Service associate director Arno Cammerer produced a map showing the proposed park boundary across both states. Known as the Cammerer map, or the "red line map," it set the park's size at more than seven hundred thousand acres, creating an ambitious goal for acquiring the required land.

National Parks Association (NPA) executive director Robert Sterling Yard, an early critic of a national park in the Smokies, changed his position following a 1925 visit to the area with Horace Kephart. In the article "A National Park in the Great Smoky Mountains," published in the November 1925 issue of National Parks Bulletin, Yard wrote, "The preservation of this splendid remainder of our original deciduous forest in combination with land features of importance so extraordinary gives the heart of the Great Smokies title to admission to the National Parks system. We must hold it as nearly as possible to perfection."[22]

Secretary Work's Ultimatum

Despite growing momentum for the Great Smokies, support in North Carolina for the Grandfather Mountain–Linville Gorge site remained strong. Frustrated, Secretary Work issued an ultimatum: "Owing to the opposition of certain interests in North Carolina to the original plan for a national park in the Great Smoky Mountains, the Commission may find it necessary to modify its boundary as originally contemplated and consider the advisability of the creation of a national park which will be largely in the state of Tennessee."[23] Recognizing that the state risked losing out on any of the park, park advocates and political leaders in North Carolina finally coalesced to support the Great Smoky Mountains proposal. Horace Kephart wrote optimistically in November 1925: "Everything looks so favorable now, for the park, that one can hardly believe his own memory of the indifference and even hostility with which the park project was met up to a couple of months ago."[24]

A few months later, the April 1926 issue of the periodical World's Work featured a powerful essay by Kephart titled "Last of the Eastern Wilderness." In it he offered a dire warning to readers: "Here to-day is the last stand of primeval American forest at its best. If saved—and if saved at all it must be done at once—it will be a joy and a wonder to our people for all time. The nation is summoned by a solemn duty to preserve it."[25] Notably, the article was illustrated with photographs by Jim Thompson. It would later be included in a twenty-seven-page booklet The Great Smokies, published by the North Carolina Park Commission. In that publication, Thompson's photographs were complemented by images from Asheville photographer George Masa. The challenges set forth by Yard and Kephart were accepted, and the hard work of creating the park could move forward. The work of these two photographers was integral to the eventual success of this endeavor.

Soon Kephart began working closely with Masa, who was earning acclaim for his own artistic impressions of the majestic mountains. The two men became nearly inseparable. Kephart taught Masa the outdoor skills he had learned from years of camping, while Masa shared his photographic and mapmaking talents, as well as his nearly boundless desire to explore the mountains. What began as a professional collaboration evolved into a partnership and deep friendship, with Kephart writing articles and essays complemented by Masa's evocative photographs.

A Bill Is Passed and a Challenge Is Accepted

With Secretary Work's support, a bill was introduced in Congress in early 1926 that called for establishing a national park in the Great Smoky Mountains of North Carolina and Tennessee upon both the acquisition of at least 300,000 acres of land by the two states and its acceptance by the federal government. Col. Chapman expressed concern that this threshold was too high, so the bill was amended to secure

approval once 150,000 acres were acquired. The bill also called for the establishment of Shenandoah National Park in Virginia and Mammoth Cave National Park in Kentucky. It easily passed and was signed into law by President Calvin Coolidge on May 22, 1926.

Supporters celebrated but also recognized that many obstacles remained. It was estimated that $10 million would be needed to acquire the desired seven hundred thousand acres. Park advocates, along with NPS officials Stephen Mather, Horace Albright, and Arno Cammerer, realized that they were in a race against time to secure what remained of the majestic mountain forests, protecting them from the commercial logging that had accelerated in anticipation of the park's creation. Negotiations, sometimes acrimonious, continued with timber companies in both states—most

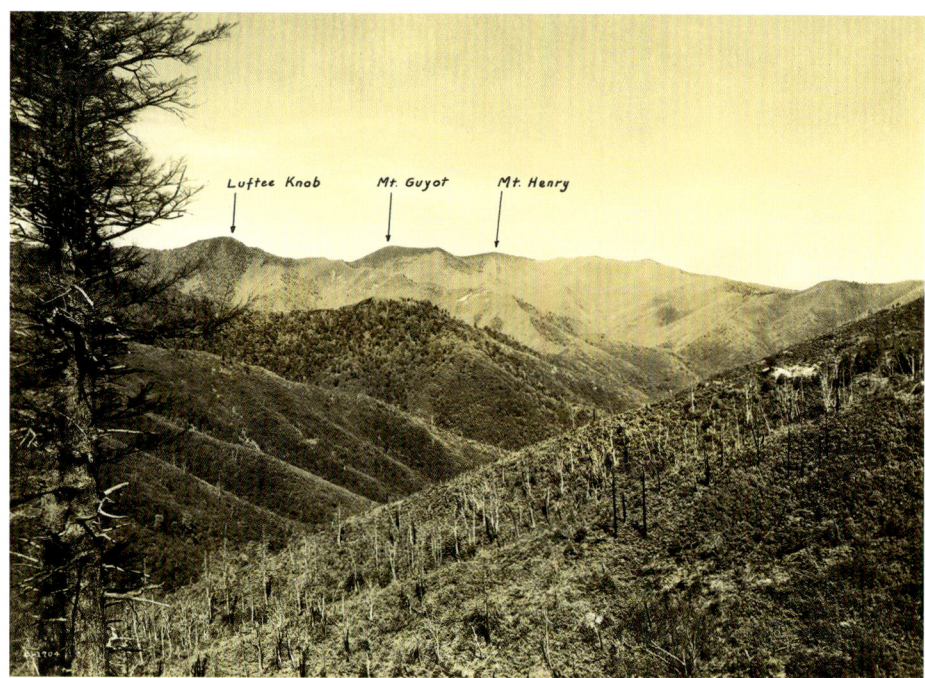

A denuded hillside below Mt. Guyot, Great Smoky Mountains National Park. Photograph by George Masa, 1931. Appalachian Trail Conference Collection, Myron Avery Collection, Special Collections and Archives, George Mason University Libraries.

notably, with the Champion Fibre Company, the owners of the planned park's largest tract (covering more than ninety-two thousand acres across both states). Some of the most notable landmarks in the Smokies were contained within this property, including Kuwohi (previously Clingmans Dome), Mount LeConte, Mount Guyot, and Three Forks. In *Terra Incognita*, Ken Wise wrote, "The formation of Great Smoky Mountains National Park was a highly politicized and contentious enterprise whose business was executed in committee meetings, legal proceedings, and personal correspondence, thus remaining largely out of the public eye."[26]

On at least one occasion, George Masa set out to intentionally document the devastation from logging in the planned park, recounting the following to Appalachian Trail Conference chairman Myron Avery in a letter written on April 18, 1931: "Last week I went to Cataloochee and made trip to Balsalm mountain where Suncrest Lumber has property . . . I made shots worse place in Park area that N.C. Park Commission wants them for evidence."[27] Intentionally or not, both Masa and Jim Thompson produced landscape images that clearly displayed heavily timbered areas of the Smokies. As an example, one photograph attributed to Masa was taken in the Mingus Mill area and shows scattered stumps beneath denuded hillsides.

A Critical Donor Is Found

Even before President Coolidge signed the legislation in 1926, the National Park Service was seeking potential sources for an additional $5 million to supplement existing pledges. Realizing that failure could doom the plan, Director Mather asked Arno Cammerer, who had befriended John D. Rockefeller Jr. during the Acadia National Park

negotiations, to approach the philanthropist regarding the needed funds.

Rockefeller had followed these efforts and informed Cammerer in January 1928 that he was receptive to supporting the project. In a letter written on January 23, 1928, Rockefeller noted, "I am in a position to informally confirm . . . that you are at liberty to say to the proper authorities of the States of North Carolina and Tennessee that if it will be agreeable to them to receive a gift of $4,500,000 to $5,000,000, offsetting the equal sum provided by the two states, thus to make possible the Big Smoky Mountain Park."[28] Rockefeller stipulated two additional conditions. First, the gift would be made in memory of his mother, Laura Spelman Rockefeller, with a suitable public memorial to her to be placed in the park. Second, the funds would be provided if the other pledges were secured by December 31, 1930. In addition, Secretary Work and Director Mather made it clear to park supporters that the government would not accept lands that had been clear cut and the Rockefeller funds would not pay for them.

Secretary Work readily endorsed the proposal, as did the North Carolina and Tennessee Park Commissions. With heightened urgency, the park associations worked to secure the private pledges and arrange for the two states to issue bonds to cover each one's share of the land acquisition costs. Details were finalized, and $9,316,000 was committed to purchasing 427,000 acres, with the Rockefeller gift matching dollar for dollar the funds raised from state and private donations. On March 26, 1928, Secretary Work publicly announced the agreement to the citizens of North Carolina and Tennessee. The hard work of making good on the thousands of individual pledges then fell to the park commissioners, who could share that every dollar donated would be matched 100 percent by Mr. Rockefeller. Through the remainder of the year and into 1929, the funds steadily came in—even pennies from schoolchildren—and all were enthusiastic that the goals would be met.

The situation changed in the fall of 1929 with the collapse of the stock market, which was followed by bank failures, business closures, and rising unemployment. Many park supporters feared that onset of the Great Depression would halt efforts to establish the national park. Remarkably, they were proven wrong. Despite hardships, most pledges were honored, and surprisingly, timber companies, facing slow-downs, proved more willing to negotiate fair prices for the tracts they still held.

In February 1930, a ceremony in Washington, D.C., cele-brated the first land transfers to the federal government for the park. There, Tennessee Governor Henry Horton pre-sented the government deeds for 100,176 acres of land, while North Carolina Governor Max Gardner turned over deeds for 52,000 acres. This met the threshold for the park's cre-ation as negotiated by Col. Chapman in 1926. In his book, *Birth of a National Park in the Great Smoky Mountains*, Carlos Campbell (a longtime member of the Smoky Mountain Hiking Club), wrote of the event: "The importance of the delivery of these deeds for park lands was heralded by news-papers across the nation. It was through this ceremony that many people saw the first fruits of the long battle."[29]

However, negotiations between the park commissions and Champion Fibre dragged on as each party's experts ar-gued over widely differing property valuations. Both sides finally agreed to a meeting in Washington, D. C., in March 1931. After more intense negotiations, the parties settled on a price of $3 million for all of the Champion properties. Of that sum, $2 million would be paid by North Carolina and

$1 million by Tennessee. This was a victory for park advo-cates, but the challenge remained to collect on the pledges for the cost of land and to meet Rockefeller's conditions for his gift. The Rockefeller Foundation expressed dismay that timber cutting on the sold or pending-sale lands would jeopardize the gift. In the end, compromises were reached and properties acquired. By the end of 1931, a total of 287,881 acres had been turned over, just shy of the 300,000 needed to initiate park development.

Optimism turned to concern as anxiety grew that do-nations would fall short of the amount needed to secure the full amount from the Rockefeller Foundation. In 1933 park advocates and congressional representatives from North Carolina and Tennessee appealed to newly elected President Franklin D. Roosevelt for help. Roosevelt en-thusiastically agreed and arranged for an appropriation of $1,550,000 to ensure that the project could be completed.

In the spring of 1930, during the land acquisition nego-tiations, Horace Albright, now the acting director of the National Park Service, made his first trip to the new na-tional park. The experience proved memorable as, accord-ing to writer Steve Kemp, during the visit, Albright and a hiking companion spent a soggy night on a trail in a thun-derstorm, where "getting lost was not on the agenda."[30]

A few months later, J. Ross Eakin, former superintendent of Glacier National Park in Montana, arrived in Maryville, Tennessee, to serve as the park's first superintendent. There, he and his small staff focused on protecting the holdings and planning for future development. An important com-ponent of these plans would be building a road across the mountains.

As early as the mid-1920s, civic leaders, local automobile clubs, and park advocates recognized that a transmountain road would benefit both tourism and commerce. The initial effort, N.C. Highway 28 (now N.C. 28 / U.S. 129), followed the Little Tennessee River from Bryson City to a low ridge in the mountains at Deal's Gap and continued to Maryville, Tennessee. The first automobile trip on this still-unfinished road, led by Horace Kephart, Jack Coburn, and George Masa, was chronicled in a front-page article published on April 21, 1929, in the *Asheville Times*: "Smokies Pierced by Modern Highway." Featured in the article was a photograph by Masa of the group's automobile at the end of the uncompleted road.

While important, the road skirted the heart of the park. Soon state highway planners and the NPS began planning a route that would climb over a higher gap linking Gatlinburg, Tennessee, with Smokemont, North Carolina. In the spring of 1930, with work underway on the road that would eventually cross Newfound Gap, Horace Kephart and George Masa undertook one of their more notable adventures as they attempted to traverse the crest of the Great Smokies by car, an excursion chronicled in an *Asheville Times* article "Find Auto Trip Not Practical in N.C. Section of Smoky Mountain National Park."

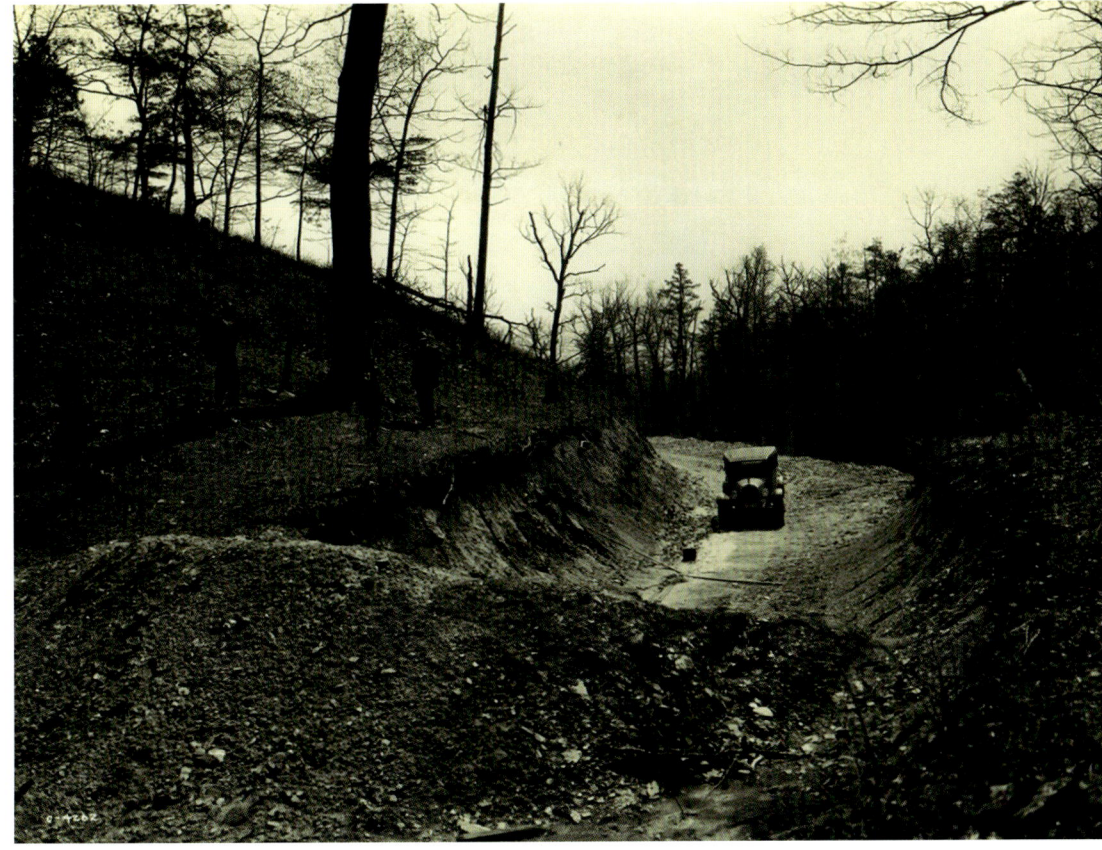

An automobile at the end of an unfinished N.C. Highway 28, near Deals Gap, North Carolina, 1929. Photograph by George Masa. Smokies Life, Horace Kephart Family Collection.

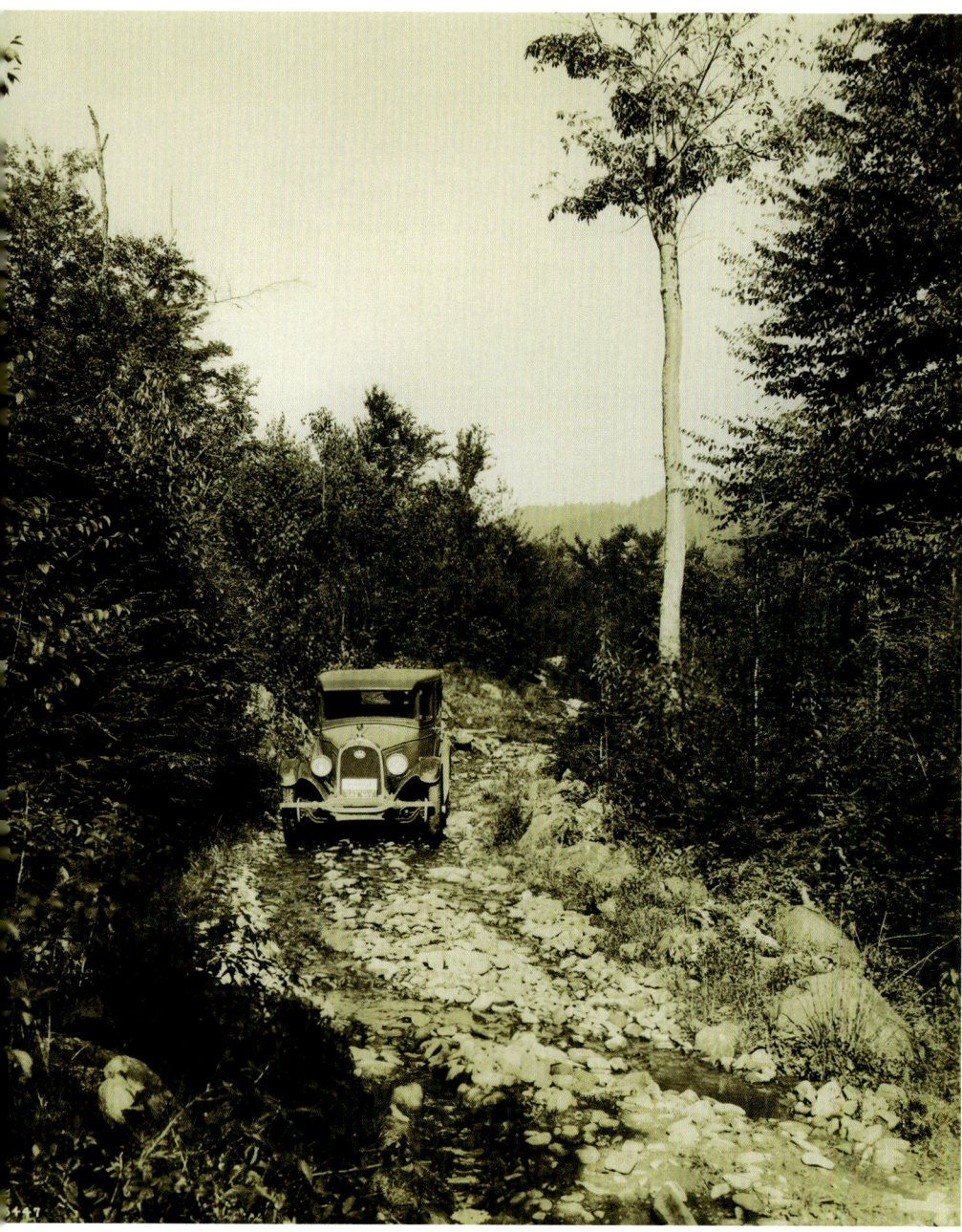

George Masa and Horace Kephart's automobile on the Thomas Road in Great Smoky Mountains National Park, 1930. Photographer unknown, though assumed to be George Masa. Buncombe County Special Collections, Pack Memorial Library.

As described in the piece, the men set out from Waynesville, North Carolina, following the Cove Mountain Road through Cataloochee Valley before ascending to Mount Sterling. Beyond that point, the primitive road climbed to the state line on the Indian Gap Trail (sometimes called the Thomas Road for William Thomas, who had led a group of Cherokee in clearing the path during the Civil War). From there, the route heading north toward Hartford, Tennessee, proved even more rugged, and the automobile became stuck after crossing a log bridge. The two men trekked to a nearby lumber camp and enlisted volunteers to help extricate the car from its predicament. They then turned west along a graded road to Gatlinburg. The return trip on the incomplete Tennessee section of the Newfound Gap Road was smooth going until just short of the gap, where the road abruptly ended. After slowly navigating around large rocks and crossing back into North Carolina, they descended past Smokemont to Bryson City, arriving as darkness fell. Summing up their experience, Kephart exclaimed, "Keep the automobiles out until the roads are improved."[31]

Even as the paved road over the mountains was being built, many issues remained unresolved. State highway engineers were under pressure to construct a basic roadway, while NPS officials envisioned a meandering, scenic route. In his book, *National Park Roads*, NPS historian Timothy Davis noted that "the NPS and BPR (Bureau of Public Roads) went to great effort to transform the utilitarian highway into a bona fide park road."[32] Interestingly, an ugly rock quarry scar left behind by road builders at Newfound Gap, described by park superintendent J. Ross Eakin as "ruined," became the site of the Rockefeller Memorial where President Franklin D. Roosevelt dedicated the park in 1940.

Not all of the planned roads in the park would become reality. Advocates for automobile tourism supported a proposed scenic skyline drive that would follow the high ridges from the eastern to the western boundaries of the park. Opponents condemned the plan, arguing that the project would spoil the high country wilderness. A modified plan for a route west from Newfound Gap was dropped due to lack of support from Interior Secretary Harold Ickes, who, in 1935, noted, "I am not in favor of building any more roads in the National Parks than we have to build . . . I do not happen to favor the scarring of a wonderful mountain side just so we can say we have a skyline drive."[33] Fortunately for wilderness advocates, the only portion of the skyline drive ever built was the scenic byway from Newfound Gap to Kuwohi (meaning "mulberry place" in Cherokee). Today the Appalachian National Scenic Trail follows portions of the never-built skyway route.

What's in a Name?

As the park inched closer to reality, Horace Kephart was appointed to the North Carolina Nomenclature Committee, chaired by Asheville forester Verne Rhoades. The group, along with a similar committee in Tennessee, was charged by the United States Geographic Board (USGB), a division of the United States Geological Survey (USGS), with addressing numerous duplications and establishing permanent names for many peaks, knobs, valleys, and other landmarks within the future park. George Masa was an advisor to the group, and the committee relied heavily on his maps, survey notebooks, and annotated photographs in what was a complex and, at times, stubbornly controversial effort. Masa and Kephart also consulted with Cherokee leaders to preserve native names for peaks, waterways, and other significant geographical features whenever possible. Just across the mountains, Paul Fink (who chaired both nomenclature committees) and Jim Thompson were engaged in the same effort for the Tennessee Nomenclature Committee. The four men corresponded regularly to discuss appropriate names for landmarks and to avoid conflicts and duplications.

Following Kephart's death in April 1931, Masa continued to assist the North Carolina committee, where he worked tirelessly on the many issues that arose. In a letter written on January 1, 1932, to Myron Avery, chairman of the Appalachian Trail Conference, Masa shared, "I had a little celebration (for the New Year) but had to work for completion of Nomenclature and finally finished N.C. side sent them to Mr. [Albert] Pike U.S.G.S. . . . I am sure Paul [Fink] and Tenn. Nomenclature Committee having quite a time to naming, I tell you this is some job."[34]

Similarly, in a letter written on January 15, 1932, to USGB secretary John Cameron, Paul Fink offered details on the challenges confronting the committees:

> With[in] the park boundaries are some eleven hundred names for physical features, with a multitude of duplications, for example: nine Big Branches, eight Long Branches, six Mill Creeks, four Mill Branches, five Deep Gaps, two Laurel Creeks, and four Laurel Branches, and like cases by the score. In endeavoring to work out new names for all these duplications, we have given much thought, to retain the most prominent or the better known, and replace the discarded ones by new titles that will retain the picturesque color of the native nomenclature, or, in other cases, be associated in name with other nearby features.[35]

Fink went on to describe the efforts of committee members in both states to tackle the job: "In addition to personal

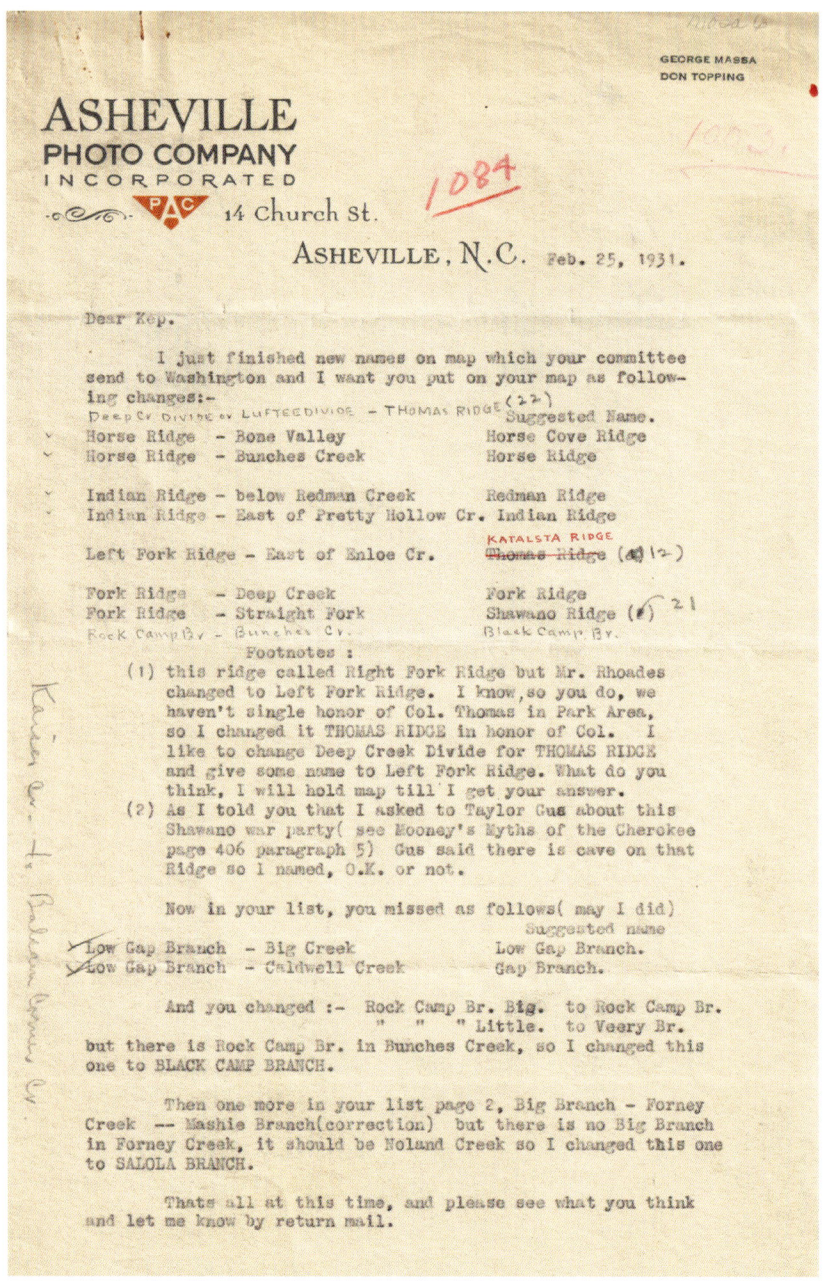

Letter written to Horace Kephart by George Masa, Feb. 25, 1931. National Park Service, Great Smoky Mountains National Park Collections Preservation Center, George Masa Collection.

acquaintance with these mountains, that in some cases dates back twenty years and more, we have collectively travelled some thousands of miles, to familiarize ourselves with the terrain and to interview natives that we might obtain the correct local titles."[36]

Shortly afterward, Fink submitted the detailed information and maps to the government. In June 1932 the agency published its first report, *Decisions of the United States Geographic Board, June 30, 1932: Great Smoky Mountains National Park, North Carolina and Tennessee.* The forty-six-page document listed the names of numerous physical features in alphabetical order, from "Abrams Creek" to "Yonaguska Peak."[37]

One "landmark" that nearly made it onto the list was a peak dubbed Lumadaha. In a letter written on March 8, 1930, to George Masa, Jim Thompson described this as one of the sometimes-humorous challenges confronting the committees: "The name of Mt. Lumadaha I guess we will have to pass up. It is not an Indian name. The name was given by four boys who thought that it had no name, so they took the first two letters of their names, *Lu*-cien, *Ma*-rshall, *Da*-vid, and *Ha*-rvey, making Lu-Ma-Da-Ha."[38] Interestingly, one of the "boys" was Harvey Broome, a twenty-five-year-old Knoxville attorney, smhc member, and active supporter of the national park and the Appalachian Trail. Of this 1927 hike, he shared that the group camped near an unnamed peak and decided to christen it Lumadaha. According to Broome's wife, Anne, "They palmed off the name to a gullible public as Cherokee until some suspicious and studious character announced that one of the syllables was foreign to the Cherokee Syllabary."[39] Despite his "prank," Harvey Broome would become a powerful force behind the creation of the Wilderness Society, later serving as its president, as well as serving as a leader in the Sierra Club and the Appalachian Trail Conference. In the end, that unnamed peak entered the nomenclature committee's final list as Mount Chapman, honoring Col. David Chapman, president of the GSMCA.

Naming Mount Kephart

One notable "nomenclature" effort predated all of these actions. In 1924 I. K. Stearns and other friends of Horace Kephart sought to have a peak in the Great Smoky Mountains named in honor of the man they viewed as a powerful advocate for the national park. Unknown to Kephart, his friends had submitted a recommendation to the U.S. Geological Survey. It was turned down on the grounds that the naming of landmarks should rarely be granted to living persons.

Nonetheless, locals and friends continued to refer to a peak near the Smoky Divide as Mount Kephart, believing that common usage might force the agency to reconsider. Stearns asked Paul Fink to urge Tennesseans to join the effort. On October 3, 1928, the geographic board accepted the name. When informed, Kephart happily wrote to his family, "We Kephart's are now among the higher-ups."[40] While many supported the honor, the chosen peak proved to be a source of acrimony, as many in Tennessee already knew it as "Mount Collins" and did not accept the new name. By 1930 the debate had reached the two nomenclature committees, the park commissions, and the NPS. All agreed to find an amicable solution.

Finally, in November 1930, the Tennessee Nomenclature Committee agreed to return the name Collins to the Tennessee peak and supported naming another for Kephart.

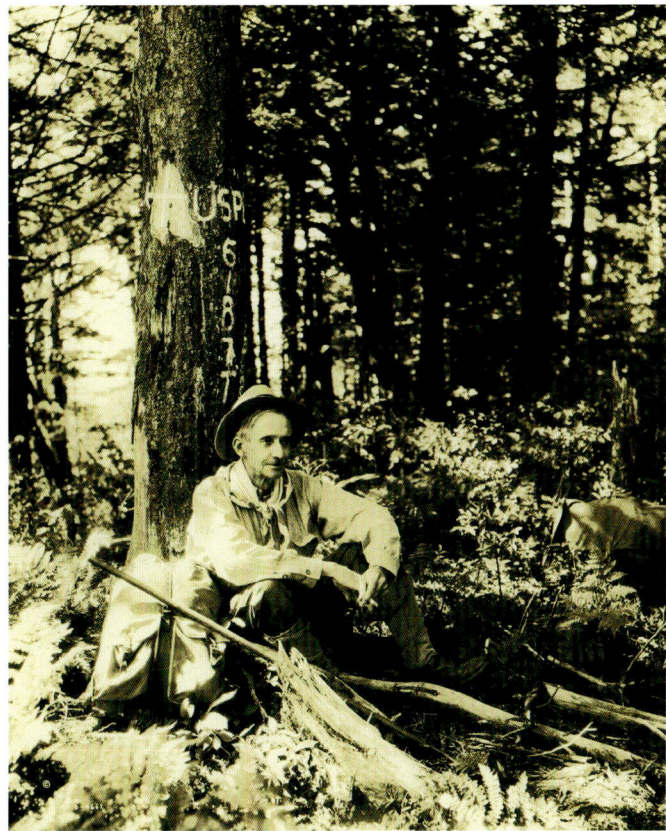

Horace Kephart resting beneath a tree near the summit of the original Mt. Kephart. Photograph by George Masa. Buncombe County Special Collections, Pack Memorial Library.

That new site, a 6,217-foot mountain in North Carolina, was officially designated as Mount Kephart in 1931. Interestingly, Kephart climbed his first namesake peak but died before summiting the second.

On a lighter note, the selection of a permanent name for one site in the Smokies may be attributed to Horace Kephart's sense of humor. One evening in 1929, after a day of strenuous hiking, he and George Masa were relaxing around a campfire with Charlie Connor, a local farmer and mountain guide. Connor painfully removed his boot, complaining, "This bunion feels about as big as that knoll over there," pointing to a nearby rock outcrop locally known as

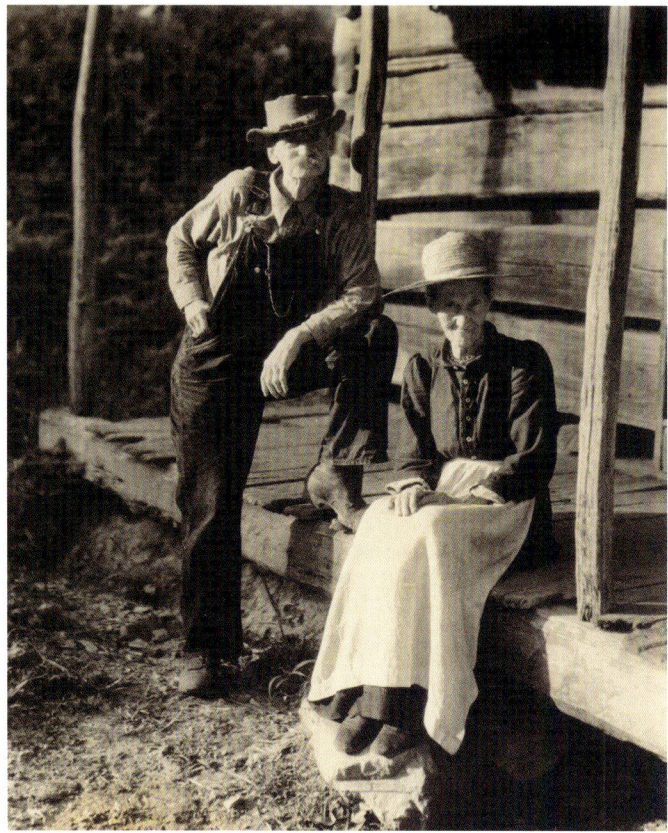

Tom and Sophie Campbell outside their home near Gatlinburg, Tennessee, ca. 1930–31. Photography by Jim Thompson. National Park Service, Great Smoky Mountains National Park Collections Preservation Center, Jim Thompson Collection.

"Fodderstock."[41] Amused, Kephart dubbed the rock "Charlies Bunion."[42] The nomenclature committee later accepted the name, and Charlies Bunion is now a landmark on the Appalachian Trail in the park. (Interestingly, in a 1948 interview for the *Knoxville Sentinel*, Connor admitted that it was "ingrowing toenails," not his bunion, that were the cause of the discomfort.)[43]

Another challenging issue was the number of farm families who lived within the park's planned boundaries in small communities, such as those in Cades Cove and the Cataloochee Valley, and what to do about them. As noted by Margaret Lynn Brown in her book, *The Wild East: A Biography of the Great Smoky Mountains*, "It took more than twelve years to buy the 1,132 farms and 18 large tracts in the Great Smoky Mountains."[44] Some accepted cash compensation for their land, though they did not receive aid in relocation. Others challenged the power of eminent domain that both states had gained, but they were unsuccessful. A few were granted lifetime leases to their property so they could continue to live within the park. Today all the residents are gone, and these pastoral valleys, pioneer homesteads, and historic cemeteries are among the park's most visited destinations.

As land acquisitions continued, park development moved forward. Work on the Newfound Gap road progressed, trails were blazed, nonhistorical structures were removed, and campgrounds were developed. Once much of the work was underway, with some even accomplished, the Great Smoky Mountains National Park was officially established on June 15, 1934. Six years later, on September 2, 1940, President Franklin D. Roosevelt dedicated the park at a ceremony held at the newly completed Rockefeller Memorial, located at Newfound Gap. In his remarks, Roosevelt extolled the unsurpassed value of the surrounding landscape:

There are trees here that stood before our forefathers came to this continent; there are brooks that will run as clear as on the day the first pioneer cupped his hand and drank from them. In this park, we shall conserve the pine, the red bud, the dogwood, the azalea, the rhododendron, the trout and the brush for the happiness of the American people. The old frontier that put the hard fibre in the American spirit, and the long muscles on the American back, lives and will live in these untamed mountains to give future generations a sense of the land from which their forefathers hewed their homes.[45]

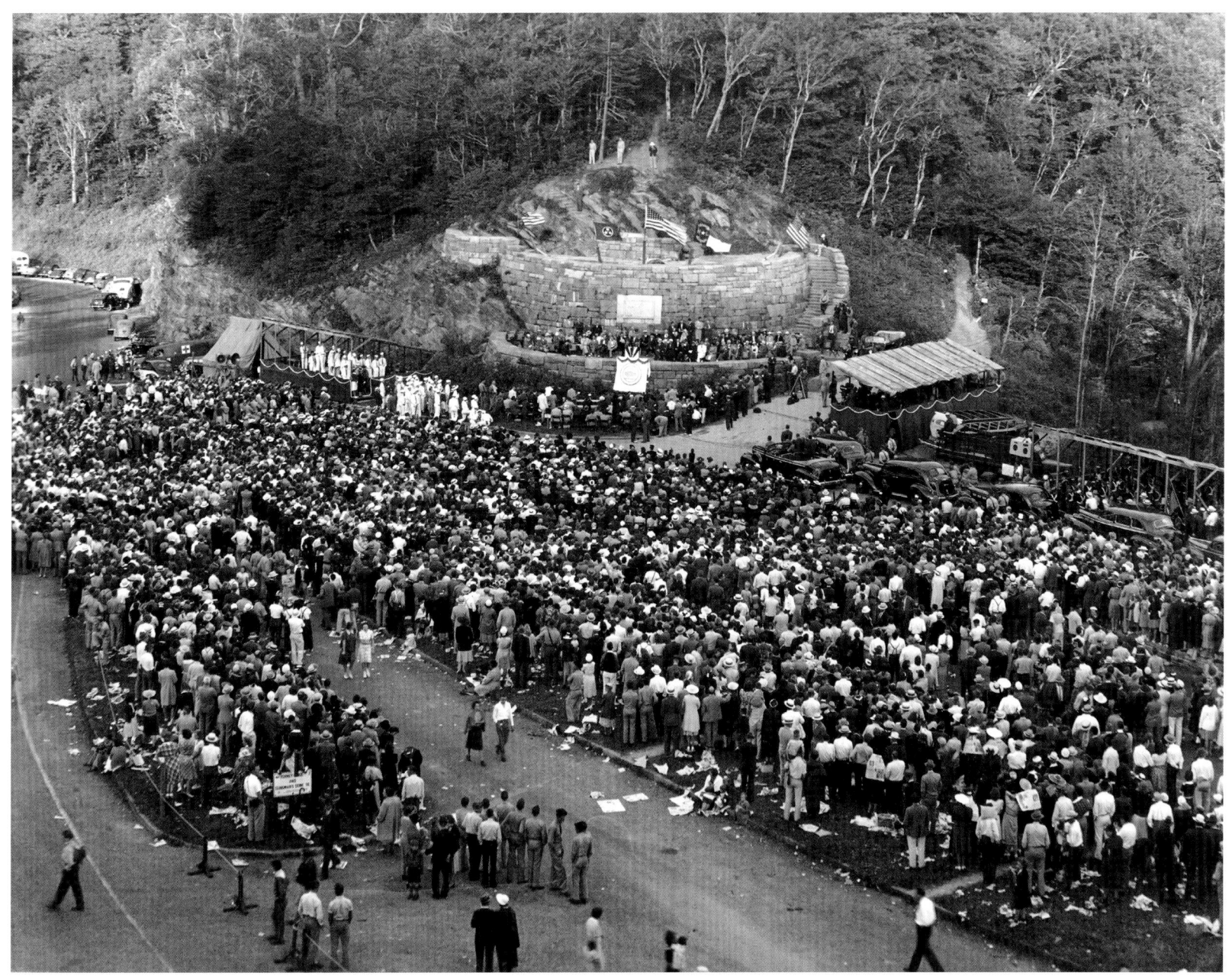

A crowd gathered to hear President Roosevelt dedicate Great Smoky Mountains National Park, Sept. 2, 1940. Photograph by Jim Thompson. McClung Historical Collection, Knox County Public Library, Jim Thompson, Smoky Mountains Photograph Collection, Thompson Brothers.

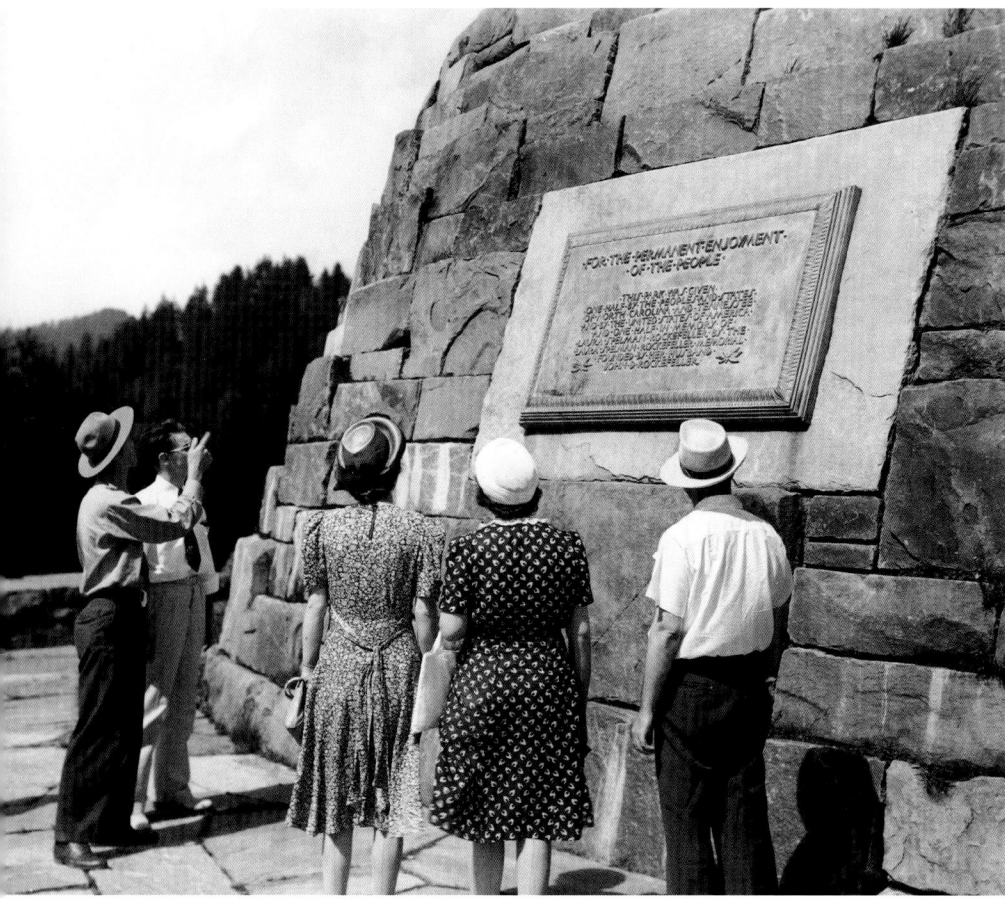

Visitors reading the plaque at the Rockefeller Memorial at Newfound Gap, ca. 1940. Photograph by Jim Thompson. McClung Historical Collection, Knox County Public Library, Jim Thompson, Smoky Mountains Photograph Collection, Thompson Brothers.

During the ceremony, a plaque was unveiled, expressing the gratitude of all Americans for the generosity of those who made the park a reality, especially the state supporters and the Rockefeller family. It read simply,

FOR THE PERMANENT ENJOYMENT OF THE PEOPLE

THIS PARK WAS GIVEN

ONE HALF BY THE PEOPLE AND STATES

OF NORTH CAROLINA AND TENNESSEE

AND BY THE UNITED STATES OF AMERICA

AND ONE HALF IN MEMORY OF

LAURA SPELMAN ROCKEFELLER BY THE

LAURA SPELMAN ROCKEFELLER MEMORIAL

FOUNDED BY HER HUSBAND

JOHN D. ROCKEFELLER.

As they had done with William Henry Jackson's images a half-century before, advocates for a national park in the Great Smoky Mountains recognized the value of photography in advancing their cause. Images captured the viewer's imagination even more than words could by conveying the exceptional beauty and biological diversity of the mountains, which starkly contrasted the examples of the devastation of the irreplaceable forests. Photographers George Masa and Jim Thompson produced large portfolios of images that provided stakeholders with much of this visual documentation.

In October 1933 *Carolina Mountain-Air Magazine* reprinted Horace Kephart's article "Last of the Eastern Wilderness." While the original piece was accompanied by Jim Thompson's photographs, the new edition opened with a panorama of three photographs by George Masa that captured the sweeping majesty of the mountains. This single article perhaps epitomized the influence both men had in

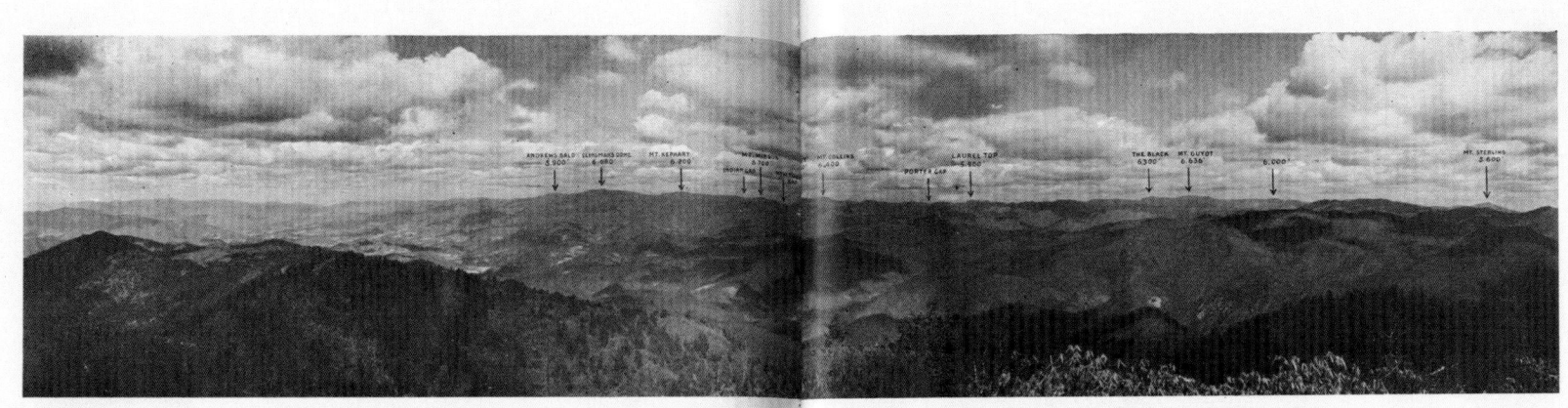

The Great Smoky Mountains   *The* ℒAST *of the* EASTERN WILDERNESS

Panoramic photograph of the northern half of the Great Smokies used on the title page of two articles. Featured in *Carolina Mountain-Air Magazine*, Oct. 1933. Photograph by George Masa. Buncombe County Special Collections, Pack Memorial Library.

capturing the land of everlasting hills that led to creation of the Great Smoky Mountains National Park.

A Vision for an Appalachian Mountains Trail

> Our job is to make an American sanctuary in Eastern America for the birds and trees, yes, but thru them for ourselves.
> —Benton MacKaye remarks for Appalachian Trail Conference, Gatlinburg, Tennessee, 1931

An Appalachian Trail (AT) was first proposed by regional planner and conservationist Benton MacKaye in an article that he penned for the *Journal of the American Institute of Architects* in 1921.[46] MacKaye's plan called for a series of hiking paths to connect along the spine of the Appalachians, which would provide recreation for Americans living in eastern cities. His idea spurred efforts by individuals and hiking clubs to build trails in their regions. Soon more than 350 miles of existing and newly created trails, principally in New England and New York, were incorporated into the nascent Appalachian Trail. At the same time, volunteers laid out trails from Pennsylvania to Virginia. By 1924 the AT planners were envisioning a pathway that would extend from New Hampshire's Mount Washington, with an approach trail starting from Mount Katahdin in Maine, to the Cohutta Mountains of Northwestern Georgia. They also considered including possible side trails to Lookout Mountain in Tennessee and even to Stone Mountain outside Atlanta, Georgia.

MacKaye organized a 1925 meeting of hiking club representatives and other volunteers in Washington, D.C., to

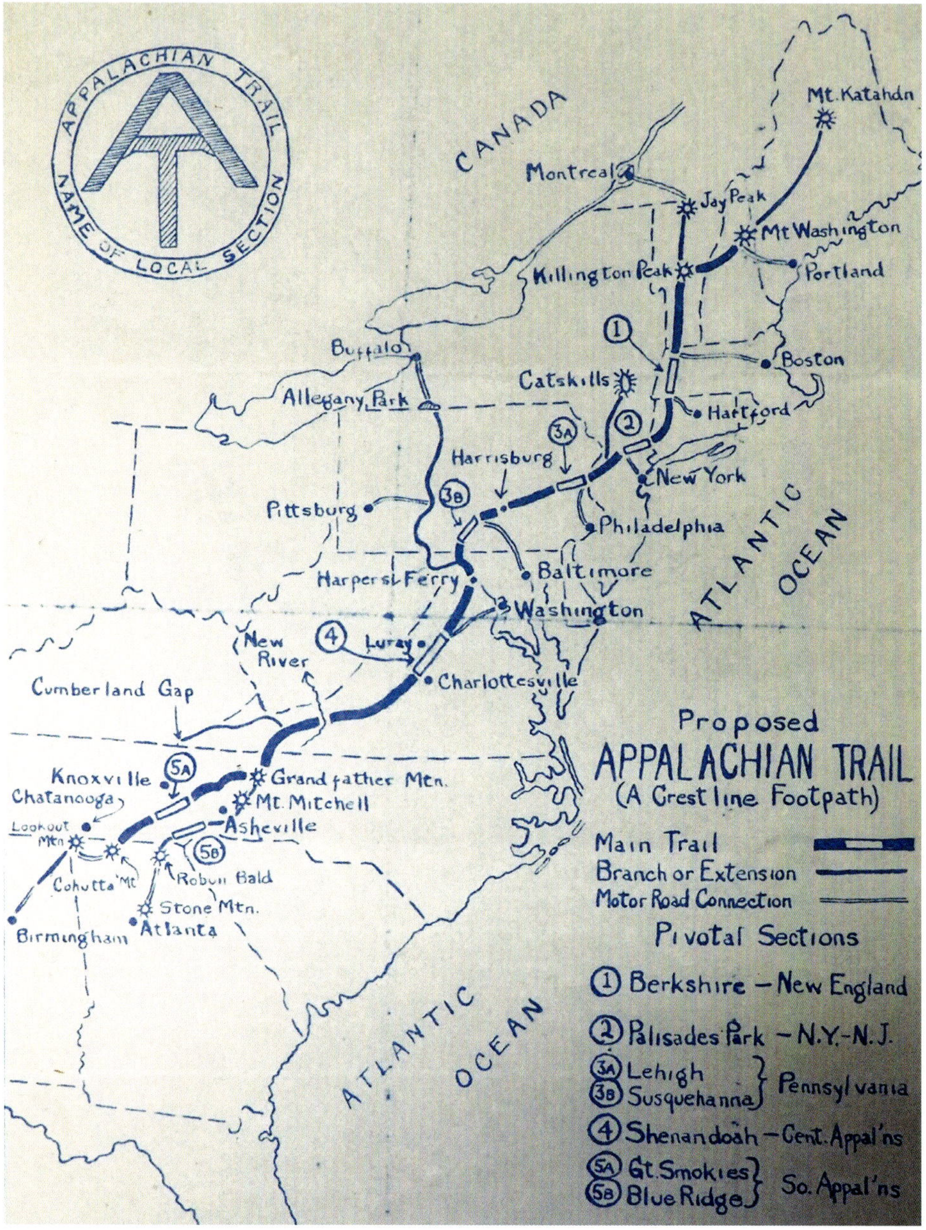

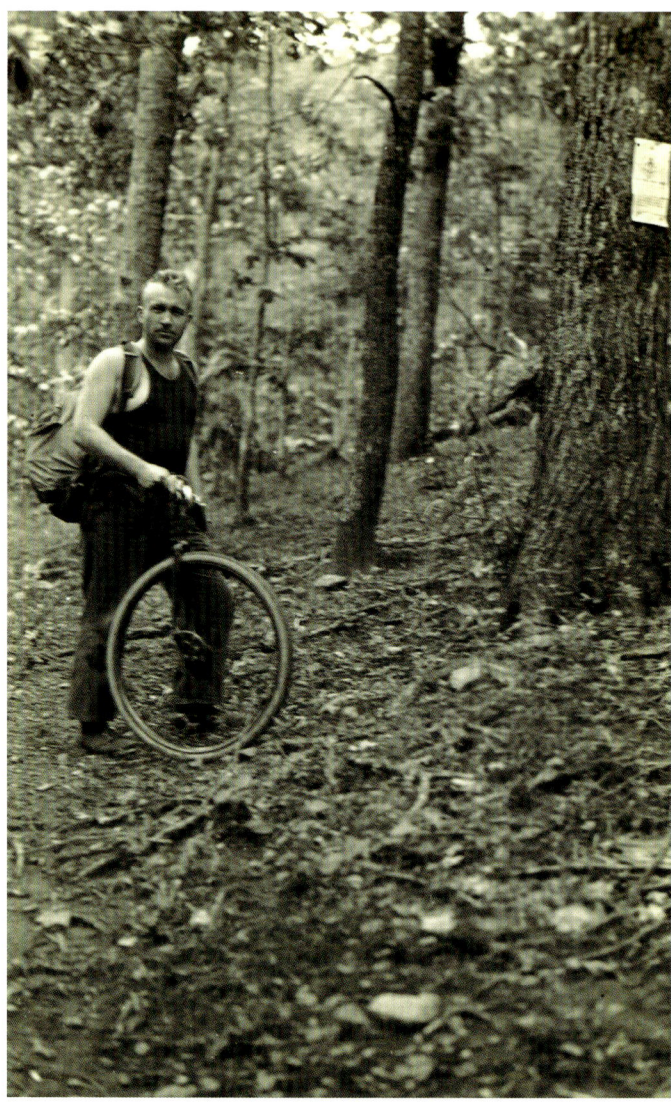

Map of the proposed Appalachian Trail route by the Appalachian Trail Conference, 1924. McClung Historical Collection, Knox County Public Library.

ATC chairman Myron Avery with a measuring wheel in the Great Smoky Mountains. Document scanned by ATC in unknown year. Western Carolina University, Hunter Library Special Collections.

form an Appalachian Trail Conference (ATC; now called the Appalachian Trail Conservancy) to coordinate trail planning and construction by establishing regional sections of responsibility. Major William Welch was elected ATC chairman and was then succeeded by Judge Arthur Perkins in 1927. Perkins was joined by Myron Avery, a fellow member of the recently organized Potomac Appalachian Trail Club (PATC). Avery became chairman in 1931 and was the face of and driving force behind the trail's expansion until his death in 1952. He relentlessly advocated for completion of the AT, from its northern end to its southern terminus—wherever that might be. This would be made evident by his direct involvement in determining the trail's route in the Southern Appalachians, especially in the Smokies, and beyond.

The Appalachian Trail Runs Through It— But Where?

George Masa and Jim Thompson heartily embraced the Appalachian Trail project, and their photographic contributions to it naturally complemented the efforts already made on behalf of the national park. Beginning in the late 1920s, both men, along with many others, became actively involved in completing the trail from Virginia south to Georgia. For nearly three years, they and fellow members of their North Carolina and Tennessee hiking clubs supported, collaborated, and, at times, heatedly debated the appropriate route this trail should follow across the Great Smoky Mountains.

This effort began when Paul Fink was given a copy of MacKaye's journal article in 1921. He was very enthusiastic about the trail idea but knew there was little regional interest around such a path at that time. Later, as a member of the SMHC and an advocate for a national park in the Smokies, Fink, along with fellow club leaders Jim Thompson, Carlos Campbell, Albert "Dutch" Roth, and Harvey Broome, recognized that the Smokies would make an exceptional route for the Appalachian Trail. However, their vision for the trail's route would not always align with those of their fellow hikers in North Carolina.

Across the mountains the Asheville-based Carolina Mountain Club (CMC) was less interested in the park or plans for the AT, focusing instead on maintaining two shelters it had built in the mountains. Despite efforts by Horace Kephart, George Masa, and others, the club's numbers had dwindled. In January 1931 Kephart and Masa, along with forester Verne Rhoades, Barbara Ambler, and others, organized the Carolina Appalachian Trail Club (CATC) to work actively on park and trail projects. Of this club, Masa wrote to ATC president Perkins, "I insist Mr. Kephart preside . . . because I want people quite understanding Appalachian Trail and he is the only man to know about this trail . . . How strong our new Club will go, I can't tell . . . I believe we are quite strong, and I am very glad if you give us some advise to this new organization."[47]

As early as 1927, Kephart and Masa, recognizing that the Smokies would be an ideal pathway for the trail, began scouting potential routes. Their suggested AT path differed significantly from the one proposed by the SMHC leaders. There was consensus on the path making its way through the eastern Smokies, but the selection of a route west from Kuwohi led to nearly intractable disagreements and arguments. The Tennesseans insisted that the AT follow the high ridges to the park's planned southwestern boundary at Deals Gap, located on the state line above the Little Tennessee River. From there it would wind south to eventually reach Georgia's Cohutta Mountains.

Kephart, Masa, and the North Carolinians urged that the trail turn south at Silers Bald and descend toward the Little Tennessee River. From there it would wind through the Nantahala National Forest to northeastern Georgia. It would then follow new and existing trails in the Cherokee (later Chattahoochee) National Forest to Mount Oglethorpe. This proposal was strongly supported by Georgia forester Roy Ozmer, who had been commissioned by the ATC in 1928 to scout potential trail routes from Georgia to Virginia. Ozmer was an assistant to the chief forester, E. B. "Eb" Stone, and both were members of the nascent Georgia Appalachian Trail Club (GATC).

After nearly a year of working to resolve the impasse, Paul Fink hosted a "miniature trail conference" on January 11, 1930, in his home in Jonesborough, Tennessee.[48] In attendance were Kephart, Masa, Jim Thompson, Ozmer, and Hodge Mathes (a SMHC member). After hours of studying maps and notes, each side remained adamant that their route should be selected. Finally, through Kephart's insistence, a compromise was reached: it called for the main AT "trunk line" to descend from Silers Bald, along the route proposed by Masa and Ozmer, while a "branch line" would continue west to Deals Gap, according to the wish of Thompson, Mathes, and the SMHC. Kephart later wrote to Perkins, "I am thoroughly convinced that Mt. Oglethorpe is the natural and most fitting southern terminus of the AT ... Cohutta Mt. is isolated and gets one nowhere. Neither is it the true southern end of the Appalachian Mountain system, which Oglethorpe really is."[49]

Those attending the 1930 ATC meeting at Skyland, located in Virginia's planned Shenandoah National Park, confirmed that Mount Oglethorpe would be the trail's southern terminus. However, Tennessee representatives continued arguing that routing the AT south from Silers Bald would deprive hikers of the extraordinary views atop Thunderhead Mountain, from Spence Field and down into Cades Cove. Additionally, many of the SMHC members were unwilling to work on the trail south of the Smokies, as it was too far to travel there from Knoxville.

Kephart and Masa believed that members of the nascent CATC could carry out this work, but it was a daunting task. In December 1931, following Kephart's death, the CATC and remaining members of the CMC merged to form a larger and more active Carolina Mountain Club. Masa expressed excitement to Roy Ozmer about the new group, writing, "We will have some club in near future. I will do my best to bring our club up to front."[50]

In 1930 Horace Kephart, along with Fink and Jim Thompson, was appointed to serve on the ATC Board of Managers for the southern district. Following Kephart's death and the expansion of the trail into Georgia, Myron Avery appointed Masa, Fink, and S. L. Cole of Virginia as the managers for the Unaka district (the AT section from southern Virginia to the Smokies) and, at the same time, selected Thompson, John Byrne (the supervisor of the Nantahala National Forest), and E. B. Stone to serve as southern district managers. Avery was hopeful that these leaders would be able to overcome their disagreements and complete the trail.

Throughout this process, the ATC and both hiking clubs relied on George Masa's valuable hiking and mapmaking skills to scout the different routes, hoping the impasse could finally be resolved. Following the June 1931 ATC meeting in Gatlinburg, Tennessee, Masa scouted the SMHC's proposed route connecting Deals Gap with the Nantahalas, then offered his analysis in an August letter to Harvey Broome: "At present A.T. from Deals Gap mostly following highway and we don't like the route so far as A.T. concern, we must find out some way to connect these two points."[51]

Avery continued to push the clubs to reconcile over what he called "a most difficult situation," writing on May 17, 1932, that "the connection between Smoky and Nantahala [is] now the major hiatus in the Southern half of the Trail. Were it eliminated, the Southern Appalachians could claim 'Finis.'"[52] He went on to praise Masa, who "has done an extraordinary piece of work in going over the route [Silers Bald to Little Tennessee River]," and concluded by strongly urging "the adoption of this solution," saying, "Otherwise we must frankly admit the impasse will continue for years."[53]

Masa was relentless in his efforts to scout AT routes from Unaka Springs in North Carolina to Mount Oglethorpe in Georgia, providing both club and ATC leaders the details they would need to finalize the trail. Much of this work would be to the detriment of his photography business, which would eventually fail in June 1931. Despite this setback, he did not waver in his determination, as shown in his letter to Myron Avery in October 1932: "Best thing is 'Go and Find' that's my motto."[54] Perhaps all of this strain on Masa, along with the loss of his best friend Kep, contributed to his decline in health and untimely death in June 1933. Sadly, he would not live to see his vision for the Appalachian Trail realized.

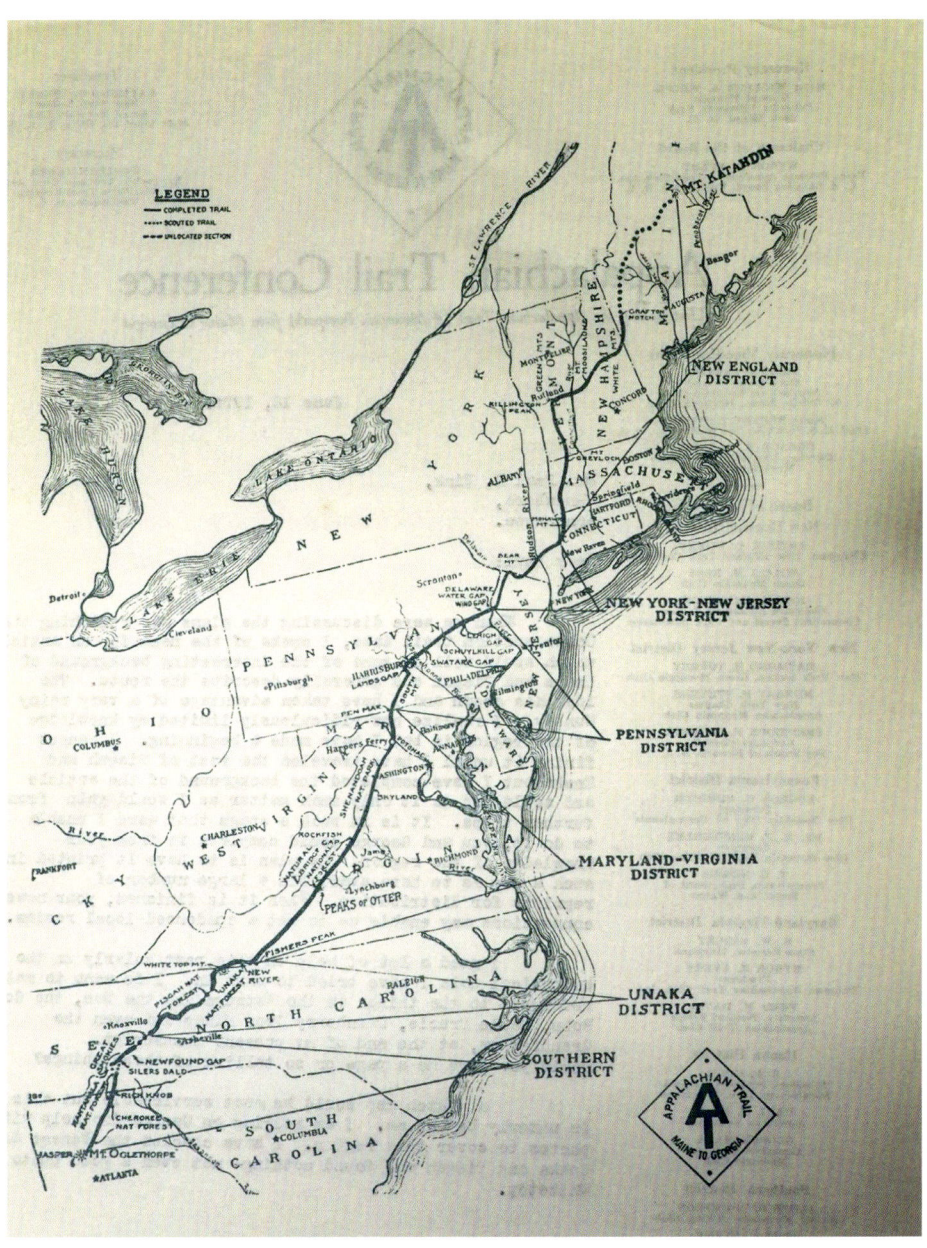

Proposed Appalachian Trail route to Mt. Oglethorpe, 1930. Photograph by Appalachian Trail Conference. McClung Historical Collection, Knox County Public Library.

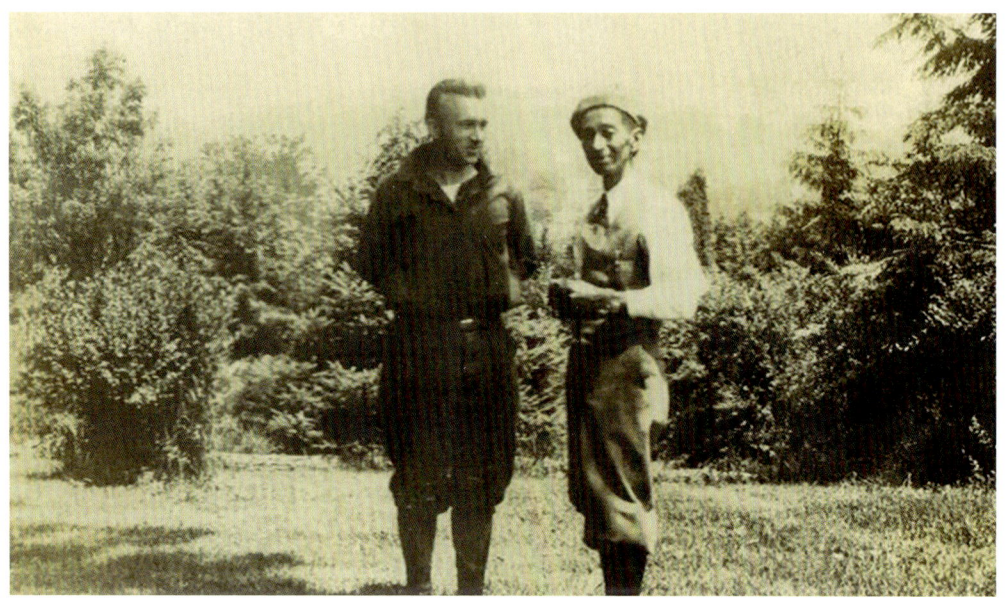

Myron Avery and George Masa. Year and photographer unknown. Myron Avery Scrapbook, Appalachian Trail Conservancy Collection, Fenwick Library Special Collections and Archives, George Mason University.

It would be another several years before a final route for the AT through the Smokies was completed. In the end, the two sides would reach a compromise, as the trail was extended further west to Doe Knob before descending by Shuckstack Mountain and crossing the Little Tennessee River at Fontana Dam (constructed in the 1940s). It would continue south, through the Nantahala Mountains, to northeastern Georgia. Today the century-old Appalachian Trail continues to evolve. In the 1930s much of the trail in Shenandoah National Park was relocated to accommodate construction of the Skyline Drive, and in 1958, the southern terminus was moved to Springer Mountain, Georgia, due to increased agricultural development around Mount Oglethorpe.

To honor their unwavering contributions of time and energy on behalf of the trail, the Appalachian Trail Museum's board of directors inducted Horace Kephart into their Hall of Fame in 2016, followed by George Masa in 2018 and Paul Fink in 2019. Their commitment to Benton MacKaye's vision and Myron Avery's determination were instrumental in creating the trail that continues to be a wilderness oasis enjoyed by millions each year. The Museum and Hall of Fame are located near the midpoint of the trail in Pine Grove Furnace, Pennsylvania.

Masa's and Thompson's Enduring Legacies

While George Masa and Jim Thompson were vastly different in their background and artistic approach, they shared a love for the Appalachian Mountains and a determination that the Great Smokies should be preserved as a park for the benefit of all Americans. Both worked tirelessly to bring the scenic Appalachian Trail from vision to reality. Their photography, appearing in park guides and other publications, introduced this priceless landscape to millions. Thompson lived to see these dreams fulfilled; sadly, Masa did not.

Notes

1. George W. McCoy, *A Brief History of the Great Smoky Mountains National Park Movement in North Carolina* (Asheville: N.C.: Inland Press, 1940), 22.

2. Ibid., 12–13.

3. Ibid., 15.

4. Preliminary Report to Congress by James Wilson, Secretary of Agriculture, July 3, 1901, S. Doc. No. 93 (1901) (56th Cong., 2nd Sess.).

5. Blair Bolles, *Tyrant from Illinois: Joe Cannon's Experiment with Personal Power* (Westport, Conn.: Greenwood Press), 119.

6. The Weeks Act of 1911, Public Act. No. 435, H.R. 11798, *U.S. Statutes at Large, Vol. 36*, Part 1, Chap. 186, March 1, 1911, 961–63.

7. Ann Bridges, Russell Clement, and Ken Wise, eds., *Terra Incognita: An Annotated Bibliography of the Great Smokies, 1544–1934* (Knoxville: University of Tennessee Press, 2013), 80.

8. Organic Act of 1916, U.S.C. §1, 39 Stat. 535 (1916).

9. Stephen T. Mather, *Report of the Director of the National Park Service to the Secretary of the Interior* (Washington, D.C.: Government Printing Office, 1923), 14.

10. Bridges, Clement, and Wise, *Terra Incognita*, xi.

11. Horace Kephart, *Our Southern Highlanders: A History and Narrative of Adventure in the Southern Appalachian Mountains, and a Study of Life among the Mountaineers in Early 20th Century* (New York: Outing Publishing, 1913), 29.

12. Carlos Campbell, *Birth of a National Park in the Great Smoky Mountains* (Knoxville: University of Tennessee Press, 1978), 13.

13. U.S. Department of the Interior, *Final Report of the Southern Appalachian National Park Commission to the Secretary of the Interior* (Washington, D.C., Government Printing Office, 1931), 1.

14. Vic Weals, interview of Jim Thompson 1975 (audio), Calvin McClung Historical Collection, Knox County Public Library, Knoxville, Tenn., hereafter cited as CMHC.

15. Bridges, Clement, and Wise, *Terra Incognita*, 82.

16. U.S. Department of the Interior, *Final Report of the Southern Appalachian National Park Commission*, June 30, 1931, microform, 7.

17. Ibid., 8.

18. *Knoxville News*, December 16, 1924, quoted in Campbell, *Birth of a National Park*, 29.

19. George Ellison and Janet McCue, *Back of Beyond* (Gatlinburg, Tenn.: Great Smoky Mountains Association, 2019), 280.

20. Ibid., 281.

21. Ibid., 281.

22. Robert Sterling Yard, "A National Park in the Great Smokies," *National Parks Bulletin*, no. 46 (November 1925): 8.

23. Ibid., 13.

24. Ellison and McCue, *Back of Beyond*, 289–90.

25. George Miller and Mae Miller Claxton, eds., *Horace Kephart: Writings* (Knoxville: University of Tennessee Press, 2020), 609.

26. Bridges, Clement, and Wise, *Terra Incognita*, 81.

27. George Masa to Myron Avery, April 18, 1931, Appalachian Trail Conservancy Records, Myron Avery Collection, George Mason University Special Collections and Archives, Fairfax, VA, hereafter cited as GMU.

28. John D. Rockefeller Jr. to Arno Cammerer, January 23, 1928, Rockefeller Archive Center.

29. Campbell, *Birth of a National Park*, 96.

30. Steve Kemp, "Lost in the Smokies: Park Service Top Brass Experience Horrible, Awful, Very Bad, No Good Hike," *Smokies Life Journal* 18, no. 1 (Spring 2024): 44.

31. "Find Auto Trip Not Practical in N.C. Section of Smoky Mountain Park," *Asheville Times*, June 15, 1930, Hunter Library Special Collections, Western Carolina University, Cullowhee, N.C., hereafter cited as WCU.

32. Timothy Davis, *National Park Roads: A Legacy in the American Landscape* (Charlottesville: University of Virginia Press, 2016), 179.

33. Ibid., 183.

34. George Masa to Myron Avery, January 1, 1932, CMHC.

35. Paul Fink to John Cameron, January 15, 1932, United States Geological Survey, Board on Geographic Names (BGN NC)_1018241_071, Great Smoky Mountains National Park_cor_1932 Fink, 1.

36. Ibid., 1.

37. United States Geographic Board, *Decisions of the United States Geographic Board, June 30, 1932: Great Smoky Mountains National Park, North Carolina and Tennessee* ([Washington, D.C.]: s.n., 1934).

38. Jim Thompson to George Masa, March 8, 1930, WCU.

39. William A. Hart Jr., "A Voice in the Wilderness: The Miracle of Harvey Broome," *Smokies Life Magazine* 8, no. 1 (2014): 46.

40. Ellison and McCue, *Back of Beyond*, 258.

41. Research suggests that the name "Fodderstack" may have been more commonly used; see Greg Hoover, "The 'Real' Charlies' Bunion," *Go Smokies*, posted August 30, 2010, https//:gosmokies.knoxnews.com/m/blogpost.

42. Ibid.

43. Hugh F. Hoss, interview of Charlie Connor, in Mike Henmbree, "Trailside Talk: Did Charlie Have a Bunion?," *Smokies Live*, accessed November 27, 2024, https://smokieslife.org/2022/06/06/trailside-talk-did -charlie-have-a-bunion.

44. Margaret Lynn Brown, *The Wild East: A Biography of the Great Smoky Mountains* (Gainesville: University Press of Florida, 2000), 97.

45. Franklin D. Roosevelt, "Address at Dedication of Great Smoky Mountains National Park," The American Presidency Project, University of California Santa Barbara, accessed November 30, 2024, https://www .presidency.ucsb.edu/node/209936.

46. Benton MacKaye, "An Appalachian Trail: A Project in Regional Planning," *Journal of the American Institute of Architects* (October 1921): 2–8.

47. George Masa to Judge Arthur Perkins, January 8, 1931, GMU.

48. Paul Fink to Judge Arthur Perkins, January 14, 1930, 1, CMHC.

49. Horace Kephart to Arthur Perkins, February 21, 1930, Pack Memorial Library, Asheville, N.C., hereafter cited as PML.

50. George Masa to Roy Ozmer, January 26, 1931, PML.

51. George Masa to Harvey Broome, August 9, 1931, CMHC.

52. Myron Avery to SMHC, CMC, and GATC, May 17, 1932, GMU.

53. Myron Avery to SMHC, CMC, and GATC, May 17, 1932, GMU.

54. George Masa to Myron Avery, October 5, 1932, GMU.

A Shared Love of the Mountains

Brief Biographies of George Masa and James "Jim" Thompson

During the years of work required to establish Great Smoky Mountains National Park and complete the Appalachian Trail, two photographers stood above the rest in influencing the success of these historically important endeavors. George Masa, a Japanese immigrant who made his home in Asheville, North Carolina, and James "Jim" Thompson, a commercial photographer in Knoxville, Tennessee, provided extraordinary images that captured the imagination of the nation and introduced people to a ruggedly beautiful landscape that truly deserved both protection and preservation.

While Masa died penniless in 1933, he reemerged in the national consciousness with the 2009 documentary film and book by filmmaker Ken Burns and historian Dayton Duncan, *The National Parks: America's Best Idea*. Since that time, his quiet and enigmatic nature has captured the imagination of various biographers, who have sought to reveal the complex layers of his life.

By contrast, Jim Thompson enjoyed a lengthy and successful career as a commercial photographer, studio owner, and retailer. Widely respected as a Knoxville businessman and Rotarian, he was also beloved by his friends in the Smoky Mountains Hiking Club. Unlike Masa, he lived to see the dedication of Great Smoky Mountains National Park and the completion of the Appalachian Trail. Remarkably, the importance of his photographic work in the Smokies has been, to a degree, overlooked. It is time to introduce him to a new generation of national park and trail enthusiasts.

George Masa

> When you look at the pictures which Massa [sic] has made, you will find yourself thinking about the mountains, about their greatness and majesty—about the power which brought them into being, and about the littleness of many of our human endeavors . . .—Lola Love, *Asheville Times*, August 25, 1929

During his renowned career, landscape photographer Ansel Adams visited the Great Smoky Mountains only once, making the trip in 1948. Afterward he remarked that they are "OK in their way, but they are going to be devilish hard to photograph."[1] George Masa would be among the handful of photographers, including Jim Thompson, who would accept that challenge and create a visual legacy of their beloved mountains. Carrying heavy equipment along primitive trails, they captured countless images on film of the exceptional beauty and fragility of the mountain landscapes they loved. Fittingly, Asheville photographer Gil Leebrick, in an interview for Paul Bonesteel's 2003 documentary, *The Mystery of George Masa*, referred to Masa as the "Ansel Adams" of the Southern Appalachians.[2]

Described by friends and hiking companions as a "dear little man" (he was barely five feet tall and weighed only about one hundred pounds),[3] George Masa and how he lived his life were then, as they remain today, enigmas. Only recently have biographers Janet McCue and Paul Bonesteel revealed long-hidden details of his story. The origin of their painstaking research draws from documents and drafts of letters—all in Japanese—left behind in the boardinghouse room where Masa lived until his 1933 death and preserved by the owner's family. The remarkably detailed story, as well as the authors' determined detective work, is chronicled in their book, *George Masa: A Life Reimagined*.

The man who called himself George Masa was born in Japan in 1885 and raised as Shoji Endo. His mother died shortly after childbirth, and he was sent to live with an aunt. At the age of three, he was adopted by other relatives. His adoptive father, Yasushi Endo, was an attorney, while his adoptive mother, an uneducated woman, treated Shoji "coldly as just a stepson."[4]

After high school, Endo realized that his prospects in Japan were limited, so he made plans to immigrate to the United States. With financial help from his father, he departed Japan on December 28, 1904. However, he was denied entry when a routine health inspection at the Port of San Francisco revealed a potentially contagious eye infection.

Forced to return to Japan, he found part-time employment while taking preparatory classes at Tokyo's Meiji University. Unfortunately, Endo found balancing work with school impossible, and he withdrew in September 1905. The following spring, he again boarded a ship with the hope that he could finally make a new life in America. Endo settled in Seattle, Washington, where he lived in a Japanese immigrant community, moving back and forth between there and Portland, Oregon, over the next several years.

During his years in the Northwest, Endo played on several baseball teams, a game he enjoyed as a youth in Japan. After winning a championship in Seattle in 1911, he relocated to Portland to become the captain and star player of the Mikado team. He worked at a variety of jobs to earn a living and, in 1913, met and married Tsuru Iizuka, a divorced Japanese woman. Soon afterward, Endo's life took a dark turn.

In August 1914 the Seattle Nippons, a team for which Endo had previously served as player-manager, departed for a series of games in Japan. While he did not accompany the team, Endo was entrusted with $1,500 to pay for the team's return to the United States. Unfortunately, due to circumstances that were never fully explained, the funds disappeared, and Endo was condemned by his teammates and left humiliated. Unable to come up with the money, McCue and Bonesteel wrote, "Endo must have felt he had no choice but to flee."[5]

Leaving behind a suicide note, Endo traveled to Los Angeles with a plan to disappear into the mountains. In draft letters found after his death, Endo claimed that he had been tricked by unscrupulous business owners and hoped to earn enough to repay the lost funds and redeem his reputation. Realizing he could not raise the money nor return to his community and choosing not to end his life, Endo left Los Angeles on a train bound for the East. While en route, he vowed to "live again and fulfill [his] responsibilities."[6] During the journey Endo practiced writing his new

Leaving Home   *The Japan of George Masa*

George Masa (raised as Shoji Endo) was always reticent to share his family background with friends and/or acquaintances. It is likely that much of what he shared was only a shadow of the truth. According to the most recent research by Janet McCue and Paul Bonesteel, completed for their book, *George Masa: A Life Reimagined*, Endo was born in Japan in 1885 and immigrated to the United States in 1906. His mother had died shortly after Endo's birth, and he was eventually adopted by relatives. During this period in history, Japan maintained a long-standing practice of primogeniture, where a family's wealth and property went to the eldest son, leaving younger (or adopted) sons to find their own way in the world. Since Masa spoke little about his family in Japan; it is likely that he left home to build a new life in America.

Shoji Endo was born following the 1867 restoration of the Meiji Dynasty, which consolidated national power in Japan. Under the rule of the emperor and control by powerful military leaders, Japan sought to form a strong centralized government to prevent domination by European powers that had already carved out portions of China, India, and other Asian countries, as well as Pacific Island nations, as colonial possessions.

The Meiji accomplished this through rapid Western-style industrialization (initially supported by the Europeans), as well as by modernizing and expanding Japan's military, most notably the navy. Integral to this effort was compulsory military service for Japanese males upon turning twenty-one.

To demonstrate its power and deter colonization efforts, Japan won a war against China (1894–95), seizing control of Korea and Manchuria in the process. This victory did not go unnoticed by Western leaders.

A decade later, Czarist Russia, seeking a warm-water port for shipping, sought to wrest Korea from Japanese control. Few European governments believed Japan could defeat a Western power and were shocked when the Japanese Navy decimated the Russian fleet at the Battle of Tsushima in May 1905. Interestingly, this Russo-Japanese War ended with the Treaty of Portsmouth, which was brokered by U.S. president Theodore Roosevelt (for which he received the Nobel Peace Prize in 1906). Despite this victory, Japan continued to fear Western colonialism and further expanded its military, as well as its own territorial ambitions, under the young emperor Hirohito. This expansion led to conflicts that would not end until Japan's humbling defeat in World War II. Given this atmosphere, it is conceivable that Endo would have left Japan to avoid military conscription.

Under the Meiji Dynasty, Japanese citizens were initially prohibited from immigrating to foreign countries. This policy changed in 1884, perhaps due to several factors, including primogeniture and an economic recession in Japan that led to high unemployment. Young men were actually encouraged to leave and seek their livelihoods elsewhere. Many traveled to Hawaii, which, at that time, was an independent country desperate for workers, as

it had recently banned immigration from China. In Hawaii, Japanese laborers earned higher wages working on farms and plantations than was possible back home. In 1893 the Hawaiian government was overthrown by forces supporting annexation to the United States; these forces saw the country as a strategic location for a naval presence in the Pacific and a potential port for commercial shipping to Asia. Despite anti-imperialist sentiments in the United States, Hawaii became a U.S. territory in 1898.

From 1884 until 1900, more than one hundred thousand Japanese men immigrated to Hawaii. Many later moved to California to take jobs vacated by the Chinese as a consequence of the Chinese Exclusion Act of 1882. Despite harsh treatment from White Californians and others, Japanese citizens accelerated their immigration until it was nearly halted by the Immigration Act in 1917, as well as the Johnson-Reed Immigration Act later, in 1924. Due to this dynamic of mistrust, many Asian settlers resisted assimilation, leading to suspicion and xenophobic attacks. Notably, first-generation Chinese immigrants were excluded from U.S. citizenship until 1943 and their Japanese counterparts until 1952.

This would have been the situation when Shoji Endo arrived in Seattle, Washington, in the summer of 1906. One or all of these factors—military conscription, limited prospects for an adopted son, and greater economic opportunities abroad—may have contributed to his choice to leave Japan and, perhaps, his decision never to return.

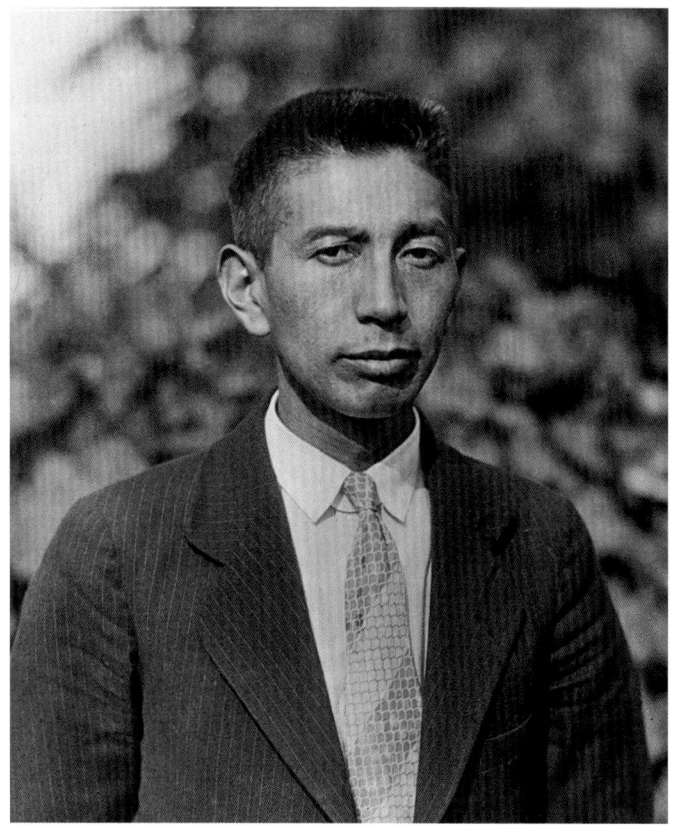

A portrait photograph of George Masa. Western Carolina University, Hunter Library Special Collections, likely ca. 1916–20.

millionaire Edwin Wiley Grove. Fred Seely, Grove's son-in-law and inn manager, hired Masa for a position in the laundry. Excited by his prospects, Masa wrote in his journal, "I visited the Grove Park Inn in Asheville at 11:50 a.m. and had an interview with the manager, Mr. Seely. . . . To make a long story short, they took me. . . . The hotel is huge and true to its claim to be the biggest in the world."[8] In the following day's entry, he continued, "As this is a mountainous area, it will be cool enough to require a blanket in the autumn. No mosquitoes! An excellent place to live; nothing can be better. Now if only I . . . make a lot of money."[9]

Seely found George Masa to be personable, friendly, energetic, and deferential to guests, so he moved him to the valet desk to provide a touch of international ambiance. Soon afterward, Seely loaned Masa his camera to snap photos of guests enjoying the resort's amenities. Masa accompanied visitors on picnics in the surrounding mountains, taking photographs, then processed the film in the evening and provided their prints the following day. Seely was impressed with the quality of Masa's images and allowed him to operate a side business in processing film for inn guests and others. Business grew, and Masa later hired a young friend, Blake Creasman, to assist him by picking up the film after school each day. In retrospect, it is reasonable to consider that Masa's efforts to ingratiate himself to hotel guests and local families were partly cultural and partly a way to counter the suspicions many Americans of that era felt toward Asians, especially those of Japanese and Chinese ancestry.

In 1916 Masa grew tired of his valet position and resigned. While reluctant to lose a popular employee, Seely had grown wary of the secretive Masa. With tensions rising following the outbreak of war in Europe in 1914, Americans

name: George Masahara Iizuka, which he would eventually shorten to George Masa. Perhaps this was a conscious effort to leave behind his old life and begin anew in a place where his past would not haunt him.

In July 1915, while in New Orleans, Masa wrote in his journal, "Now I have to raise money. It can't be helped, for I have just enough money to travel but not [a] penny extra."[7] Seeking employment, he traveled by train to Asheville, North Carolina, arriving on July 10, 1915. The following day, he interviewed for a position at the Grove Park Inn, an elegant resort constructed in 1913 by patent-medicine

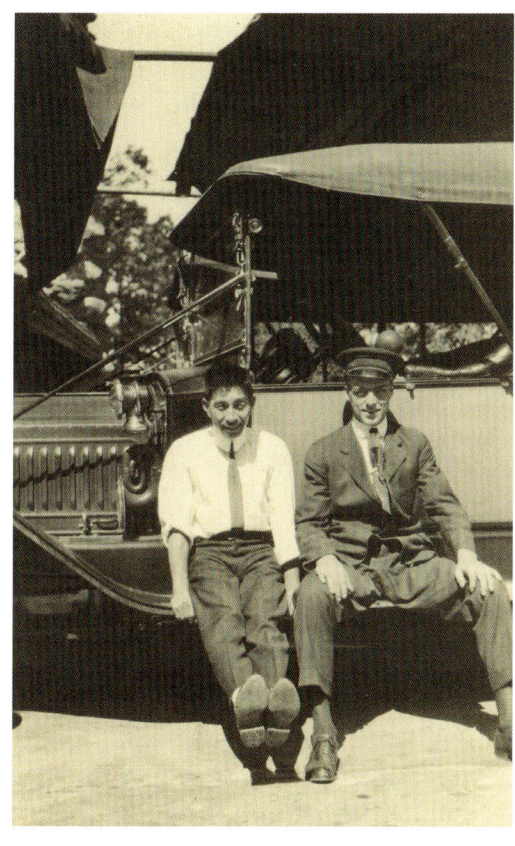

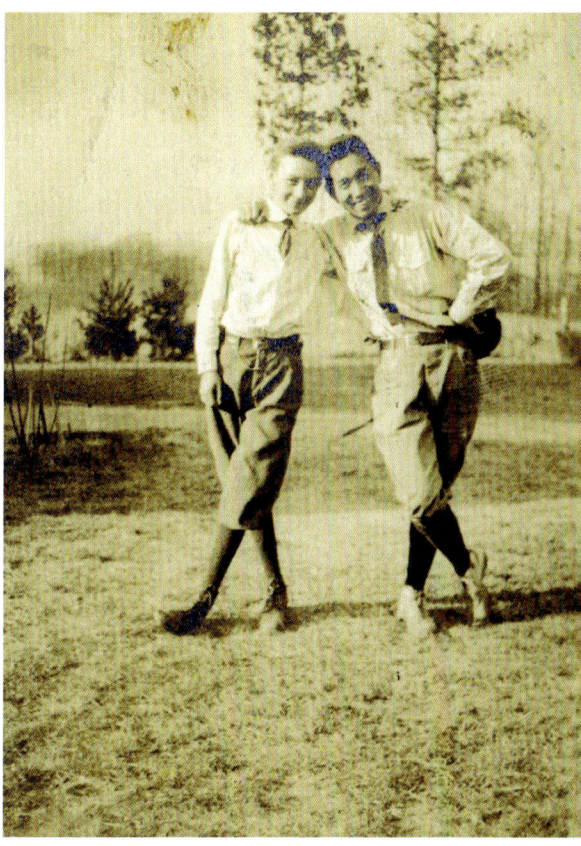

Left: George Masa and a coworker serving as valets at the Grove Park Inn, ca. 1915. Photographer unknown. Western Carolina University, Hunter Library Special Collections.

Right: Blake Creasman and George Masa, likely ca. 1916–19. Photographer unknown, though assumed to be George Masa. Buncombe County Special Collections, Pack Memorial Library.

had become increasingly fearful of foreign immigrants. These sentiments would soon lead to the passage of the 1917 Immigration Restriction Act. The provisions of the act required English literacy tests, which were intended to severely restrict European immigration and prohibit immigration from many Asian and Pacific countries. For this reason, it was alternately known as the Asiatic Barred Zone Act.[10] The restrictions on immigration would be further expanded in the Johnson-Reed Immigration Act of 1924, severely limiting immigration by all nationalities, especially the Japanese.

Unknown to Masa, in November 1916, Fred Seely, acting as president of the local chapter of the American Protective League, wrote a letter to A. Bruce Bielaski, chief of the Bureau of Investigation (later the Federal Bureau of Investigation) at the Department of Justice, requesting an investigation of Masa. Seely expressed concerns about Masa's secretive nature and private activities, suggesting that he was engaged in foreign surveillance or even espionage—concerns that eventually proved to be baseless.

When Masa agreed to continue working at the inn, Seely ceased his queries and persuaded Masa to stay. In May 1917

Masa resigned a second time, announcing plans to travel and perhaps engage in some metals prospecting in the West. He wrote to Seely, "I am awful sorry to say 'Good bye' . . . As you know, I am a student who has ambition, who wishes a good future, and I know I am not the man who [suits] the position as valet, it is so far away from my purpose . . . I made up my mind to go to the Middle West states and get lessons in metal prospecting . . . I never forget your kindness through in my life."[11] (It should be noted that George Masa never mastered English grammar or spelling. Quotations from his writings are verbatim.)

However, within a few months, Masa reached out to Seely from Colorado to inquire about returning: "I had a good time seeing the beauty of nature. . . . I had a fine time hiking, sure the country is wonderful. . . . When you find a position to suit me, except valet, please tell me."[12] Masa closed by requesting forty dollars as an advance on his wages. Seely sent the money and assured Masa he would have a new position on his return. That fall, Masa began work as the inn's head porter, also serving as a wood-carver for nearby Biltmore Industries, which Seely had recently purchased from Edith Vanderbilt. In the fall of 1917, Masa moved in with the family

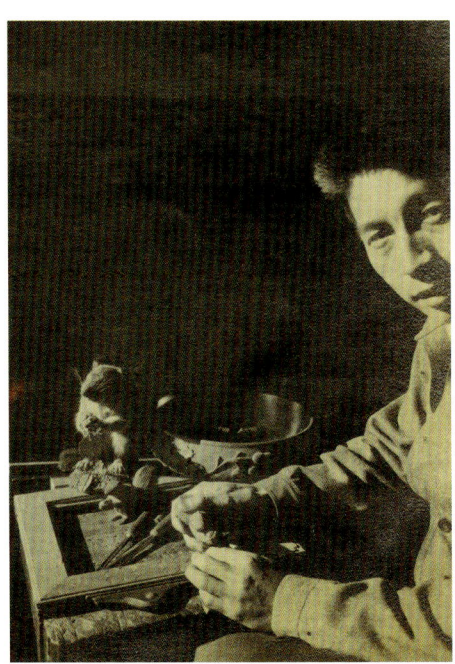

George Masa with a carved squirrel in the Biltmore Industries wood carving shop, ca. 1917–18. Photograph by Julia Brookshire. Buncombe County Special Collections, Pack Memorial Library.

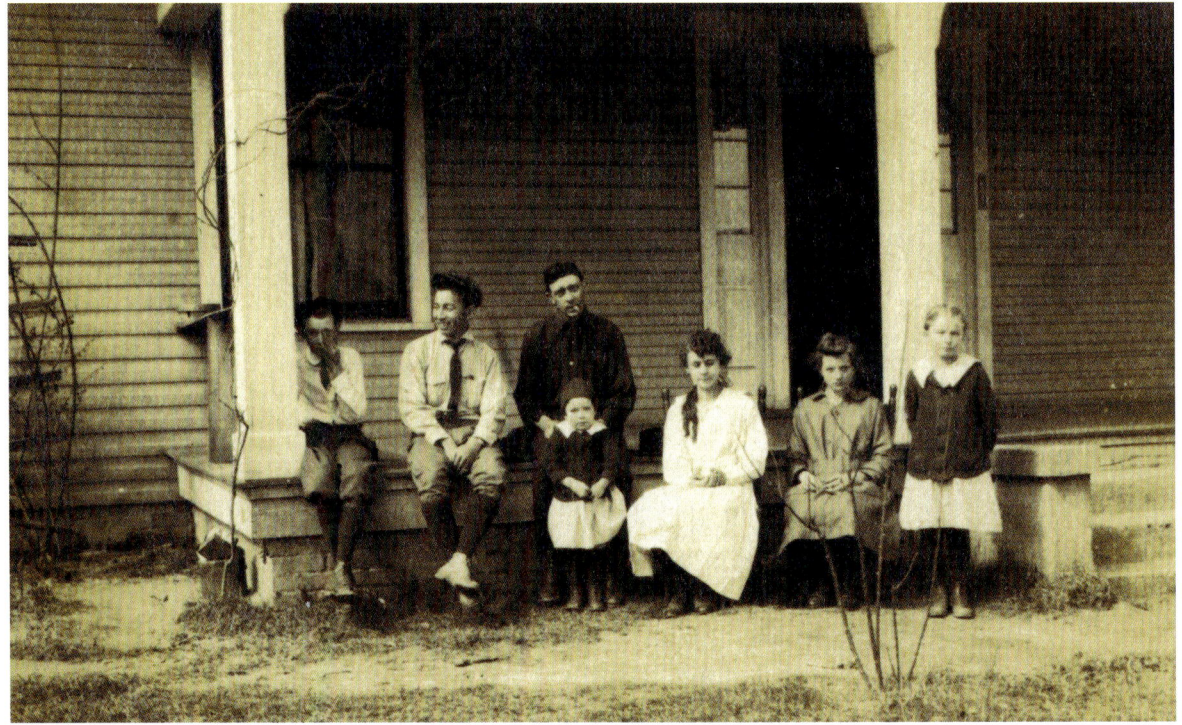

George Masa with the Oscar Creasman family. Masa is second from left. Beside him are Blake Creasman and Oscar Creasman, likely ca. 1917–18. Buncombe County Special Collections, Pack Memorial Library.

of carpenter and coworker Oscar Creasman, the father of his friend Blake Creasman. During this time, Masa continued to produce photographs for Grove Park Inn guests as well as tourists staying at other Asheville hotels.

In May 1918 a wealthy and eccentric guest, Giovanni Emanuele Elia, arrived at the Grove Park Inn with an entourage of aides and employees. Elia presented himself as an officer in the Italian Navy while claiming that he was working with the U.S. Navy on a mine designed to protect the coast from German submarines. Suspicious of the man, Seely again reached out to the Bureau of Investigation, and he was eventually assured that Elia was loyal and a "man to be trusted."[13]

When Elia and his companions left the inn, Masa and another employee chose to go with them to a camp on the Virginia coast. In October Masa accompanied Elia on a trip to Washington, D.C., to meet with the secretary of the U.S. Navy about his project. While there, Masa contracted influenza and was hospitalized for a week. Soon afterward, he returned to Asheville—but not to work at the inn. Instead, he took a job in Herbert Pelton's photography studio while also operating a Kodak film-finishing side business he dubbed Photo Craft. As noted by McCue and Bonesteel, Masa viewed his studio work "like an internship."[14]

Masa wrote to Seely in December 1919, "I am glad inform you that I left Pelton Studios and start business myself, as named Plateau Studios. . . . I ordered a camera about five weeks ago but still it does not come yet!"[15] Masa asked Seely for a loan to help get his business started. If he remained suspicious of Masa and disappointed by his abrupt departure from the inn, Seely set those feelings aside and loaned Masa both a camera and the requested funds.

Masa took on a wide variety of photographic projects, ranging from landscapes and construction projects to local social events and breaking news stories. His work began appearing in newspapers, magazines, and even a silent film. Notably, two of Masa's images were included in the article "Motor-Coaching through North Carolina," featured in the May 1926 issue of *National Geographic Magazine*. At the same time, Masa served as a freelance newsreel photographer for Pathé News and Paramount and even accepted aerial photography assignments. Impressed with Masa's work, the Asheville Chamber of Commerce chose his images to illustrate a 1926 travel and tourism brochure and a documentary film (ca. 1926–27), both promoting the city and region as the "Land of the Sky." Always searching for new ways to generate income, Masa began selling postcards featuring photographs of the Grove Park Inn (some of which he had arranged to have colored by hand) and of the surrounding mountain landscapes.

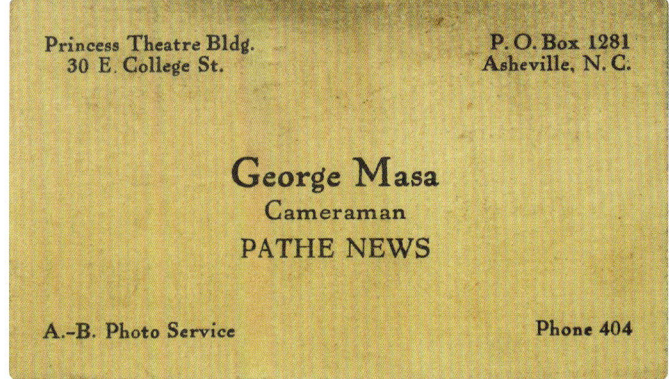

George Masa's Pathé News business card, year unknown. Buncombe County Special Collections, Pack Memorial Library.

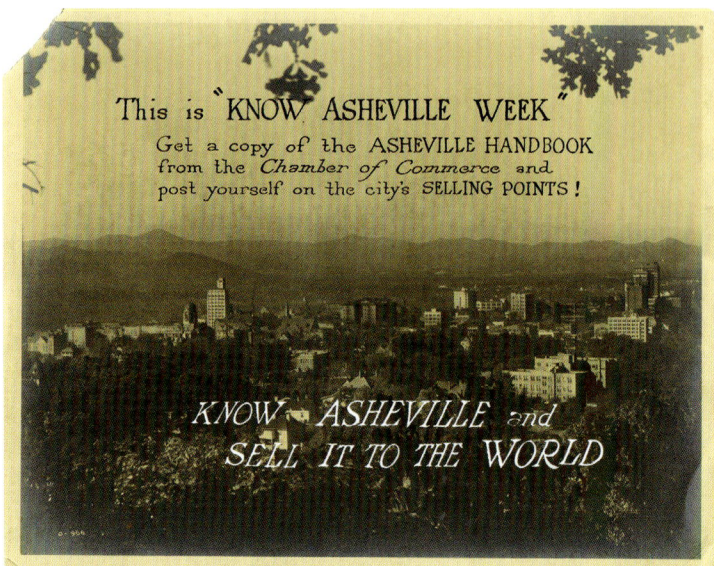

This is "KNOW ASHEVILLE WEEK"

Get a copy of the ASHEVILLE HANDBOOK
from the *Chamber of Commerce* and
post yourself on the city's SELLING POINTS!

*KNOW ASHEVILLE and
SELL IT TO THE WORLD*

Image of the Asheville skyline that was used in the city's promotional campaign, ca. 1926–27. Photograph by George Masa. Buncombe County Special Collections, Pack Memorial Library.

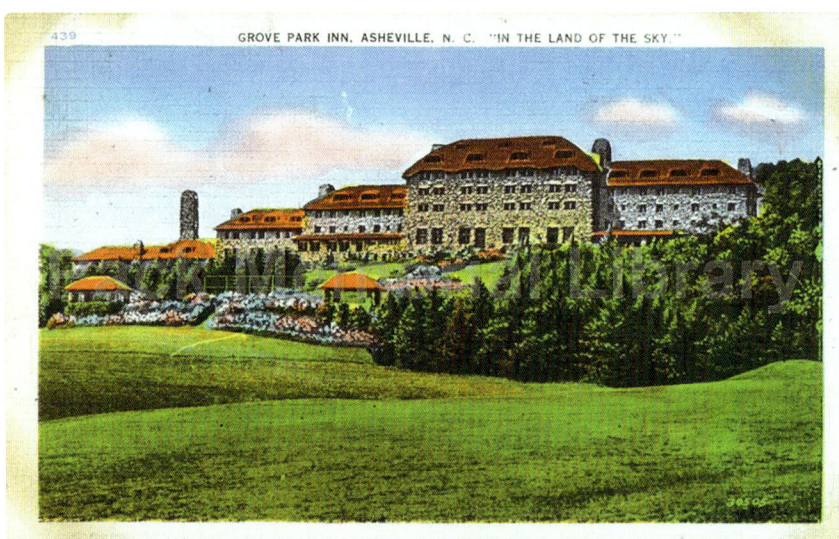

Colorized postcard image of the Grove Park Inn, ca. 1928. Photograph by George Masa, card scanned by Ren and Helen Davis. Buncombe County Special Collections, Pack Memorial Library.

AN UGLY INCIDENT

Masa was well respected in the Asheville community and enjoyed a solid reputation for his photographic work. However, in late 1921, this did not prevent him from being the target of a racist attack fueled by the resurgence of the Ku Klux Klan in the region and, particularly, its infiltration of the local police department. Based on allegations that Masa had taken photographs of nude girls from the local high school, the police raided his studio, and he was arrested. As noted by McCue and Bonesteel in their book, Masa kept silent about the charges, but his attorney, George Pennell, stated that "[Masa] absolutely and positively denies the statement, and states through his counsel that he has never taken the picture of any high school girl, except when dressed in a most becoming, modest manner."[16] Pennell went on to say that the charges were "detrimental and damaging to the character of the defendant."[17]

Interestingly, it was eventually revealed that photographs of older nude women had been processed by an employee of Smith's Drug Store, located below Masa's studio. However, there was no clear evidence to link these pictures to George Masa. Nonetheless, the judge found Masa "technically guilty,"[18] releasing him on a $200 bond, which was quickly paid by several of the most prominent citizens of Asheville. McCue and Bonesteel note, "It would not be the first nor the last time that friends would come to the rescue of this Japanese photographer."[19]

Masa chose to remain in Asheville despite this incident, and his commercial photography business recovered. Over the next several years, it underwent several changes in both name and location as he struggled to make enough money to acquire new equipment and expand. In 1923 Edwin Pepper purchased Plateau Studios, renaming it Plateau Engraving Company, with Masa as his company photographer. A year later, Masa left to establish the Asheville-Biltmore Film Company (later shortened to A-B Photo Service). In 1927, acting on the advice of his friend Don Topping of the Asheville Chamber of Commerce, Masa changed the name to Asheville Photo Service so that the word "Asheville" would appear in any photography credits.

Even as his commercial assignments expanded, Masa ventured farther into the mountains in search of new scenic images to print and sell. Friends recounted that he would often be away from his studio for days, sometimes hiking twenty or more miles over rough terrain or on primitive trails, then waiting for hours to capture what he considered a perfect photograph. On these treks, Masa would often carry little more than a blanket, some food and water, and his heavy camera equipment.

To make extra money, he sold postcard photographs of tourist destinations, including Lake Lure and Chimney Rock. In 1924 he produced a self-funded album, *Mount Mitchell and Views—Along the Mt. Mitchell Motor Road*, which profiled the highest mountain in the eastern United States. In 1929 Masa accepted a commission from Frank Cook, the owner of an inn in Highlands, North Carolina, to produce images of the mountain village to promote it as a resort destination. According to Highlands' historian Randall Shaffner, Cook provided Masa with two complimentary nights' lodging for the assignment, but Masa refused to take photographs unless the lighting was perfect. As a result, he ended up staying for two weeks. However, Masa ultimately gave Cook ninety-seven beautifully composed images (many of which are now in the collection of the Highlands Historical Society).

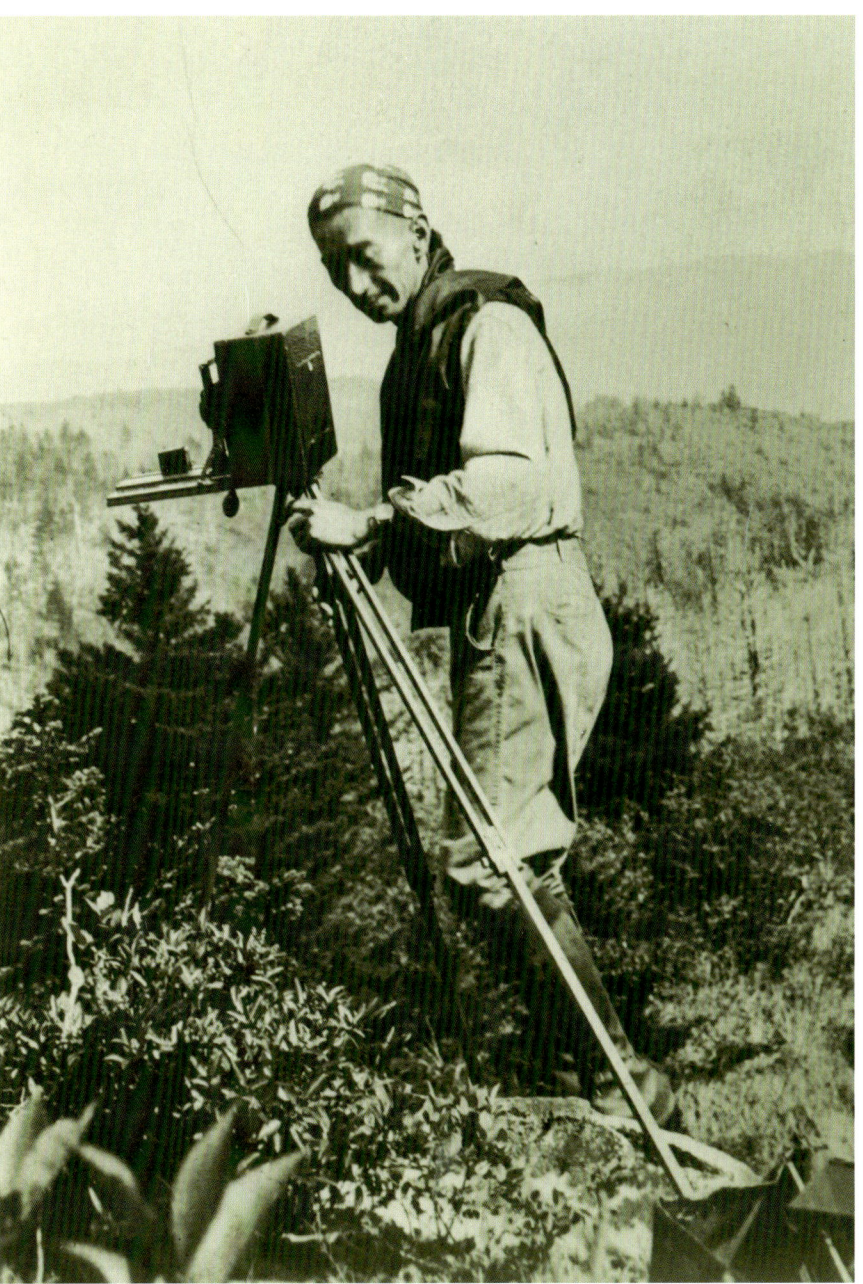

Photograph of George Masa on location with his camera on a tripod, ca. 1931. Photographer unknown. Buncombe County Special Collections, Pack Memorial Library.

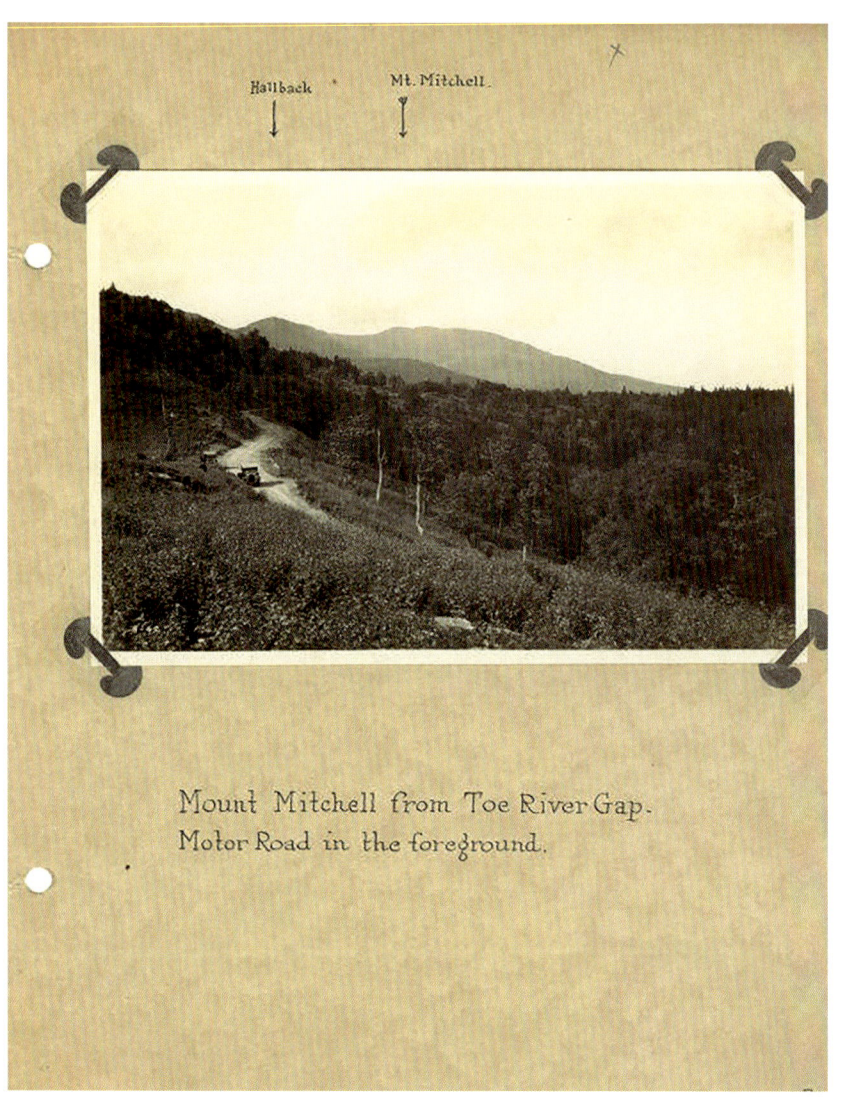

View of Mount Mitchell from Toe River Gap from the
book *Mount Mitchell and Views—Along the Mount Mitchell
Motor Road*, ca. 1924. Photograph by George Masa. Western
Carolina University, Hunter Library Special Collections.

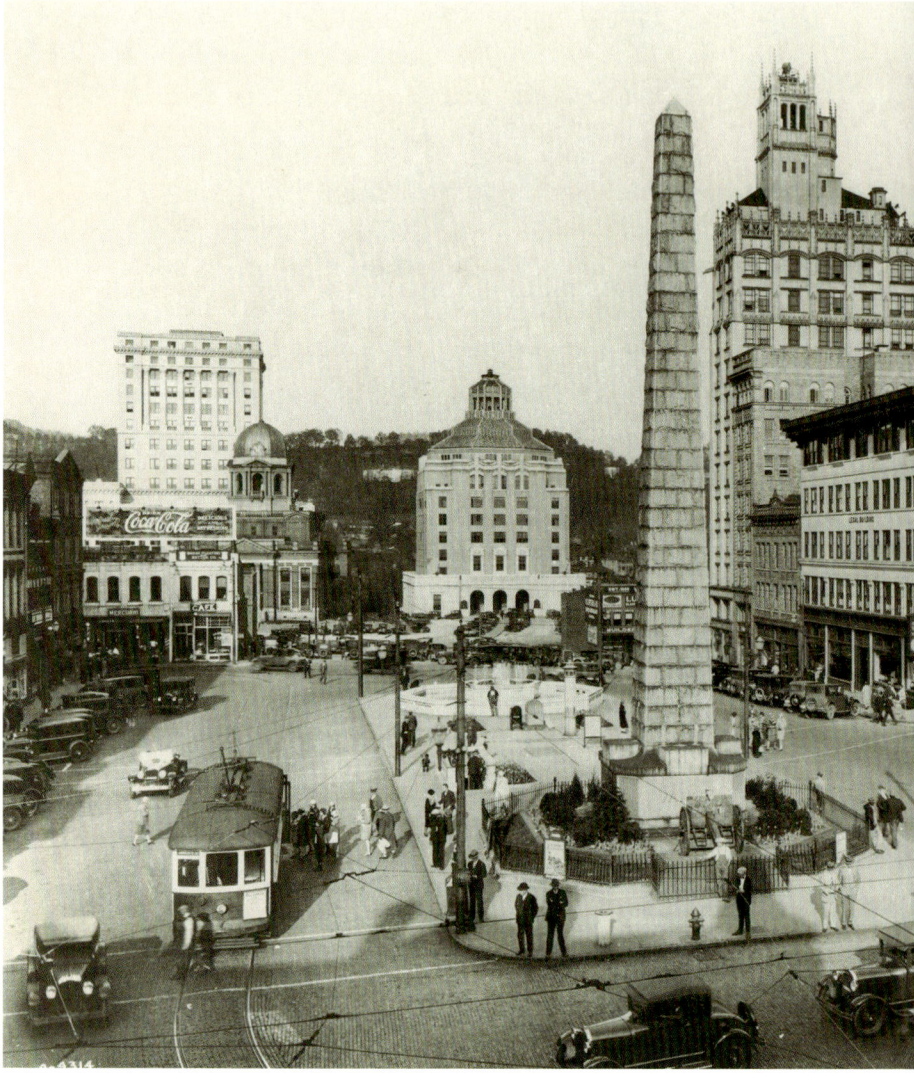

Pack Square in downtown Asheville, 1930. Photograph by George Masa.
Buncombe County Special Collections, Pack Memorial Library.

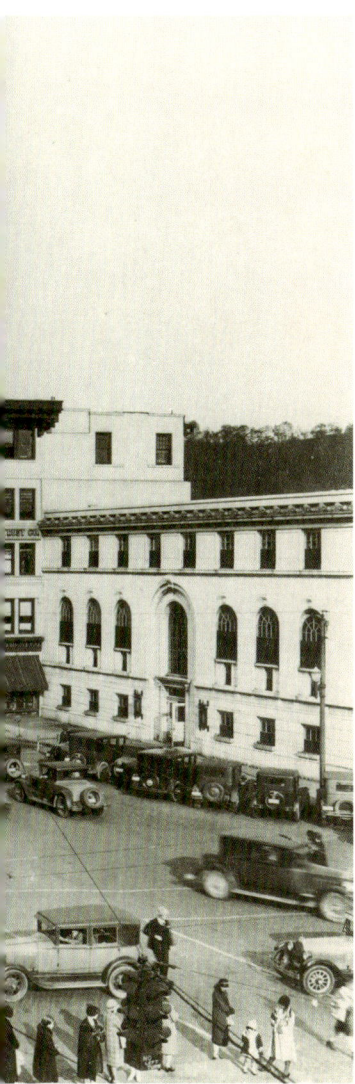

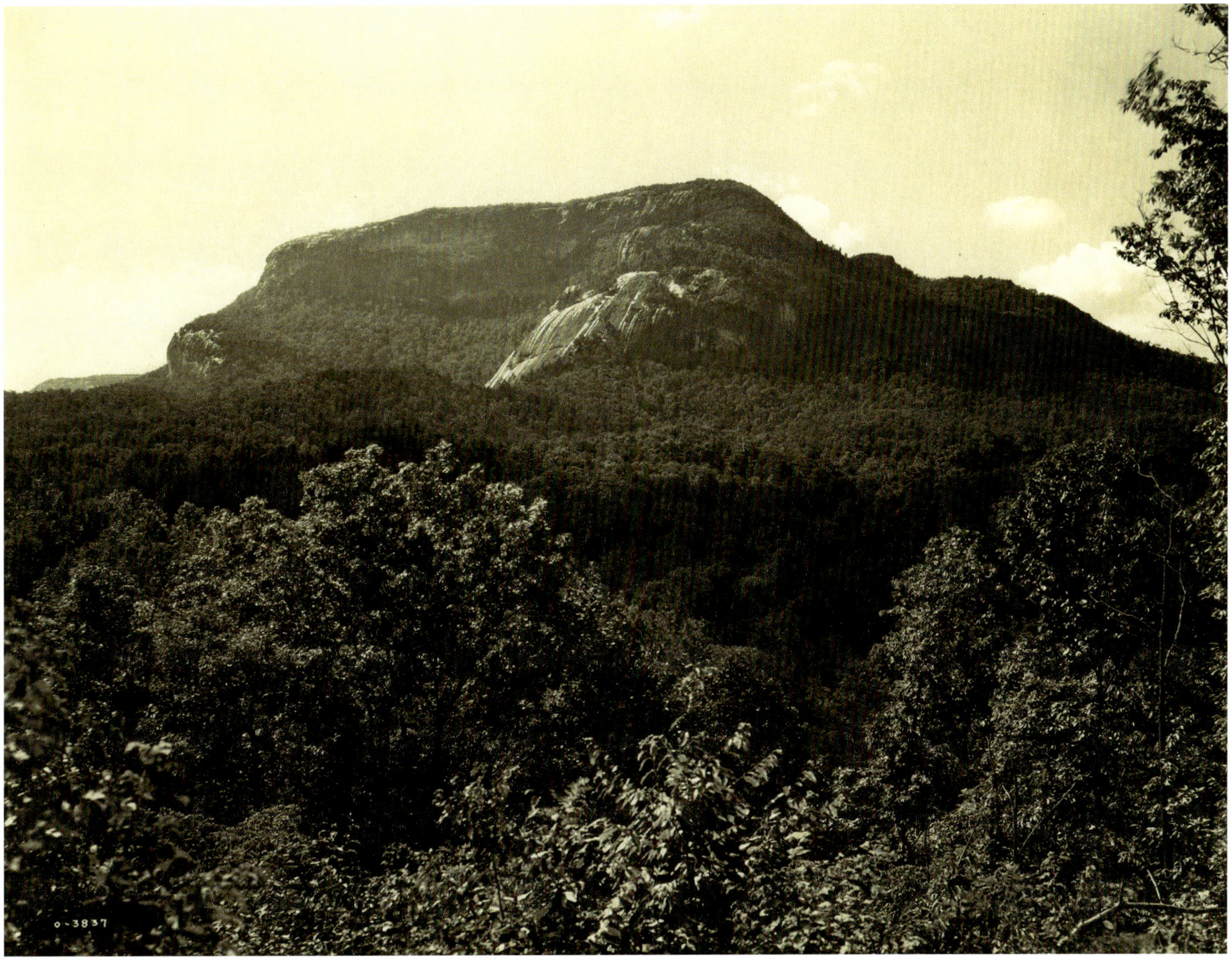

View of Whiteside Mountain near Cashiers, North Carolina, year unknown.
Photograph by George Masa. Smokies Life, Horace Kephart Family Collection.

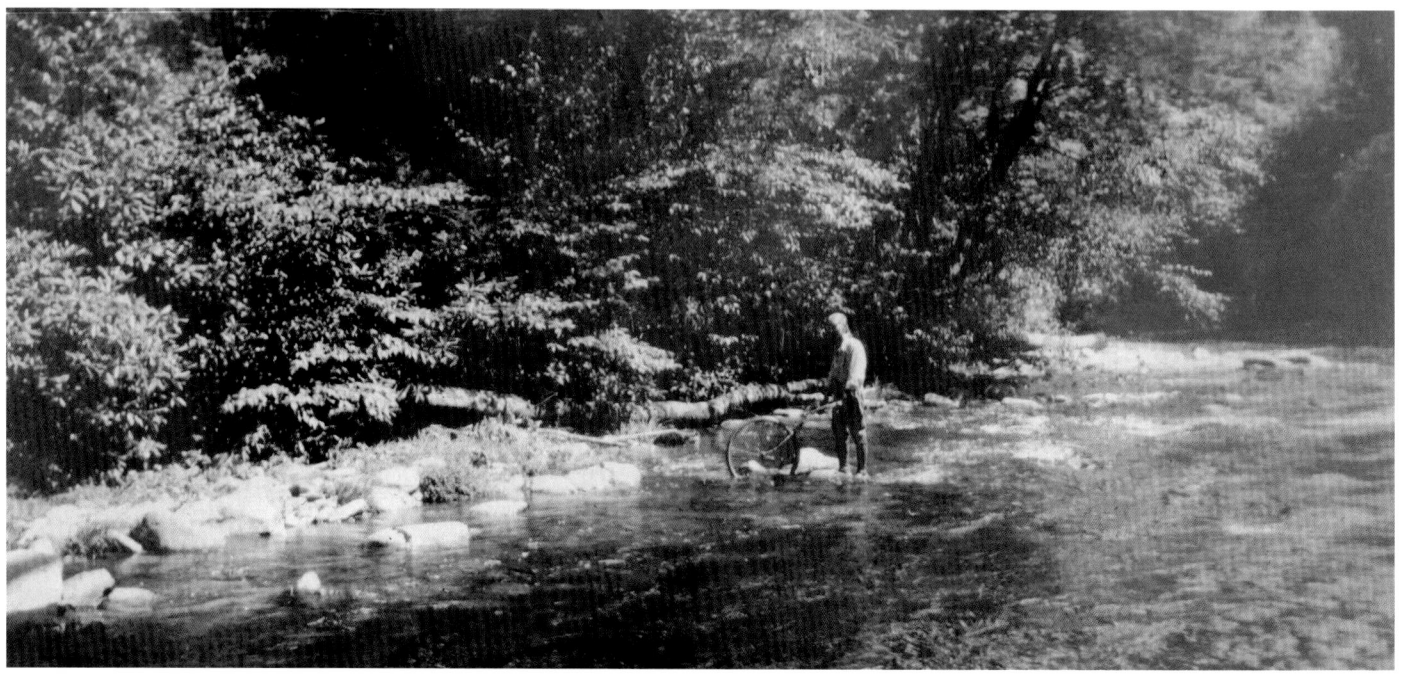

George Masa crossing a river with his cyclometer. Year and photographer unknown. Carolina Mountain Club Collection, North Carolina Collection, Jewel King Collection, Photographic Archives, Wilson Special Collections Library, The University of North Carolina at Chapel Hill.

By the mid-1920s, Masa was becoming widely recognized for the artistic quality of his photography. Bonesteel recorded that "Masa's work expresses both the physical and ethereal aspects of the complex, rolling and undulating landscapes. He was keen on using these layers of mountains, trees, rivers, waterfalls, clouds, and rock features (and occasionally humans) in his compositions, creating images that feel three dimensional . . . or even giving the viewer a sense that you are 'falling' into the scenery."[20]

The diminutive Masa proved to be an unforgettable figure while trekking in the mountains: he was often clad in homespun pants tucked inside his boots and wore a distinctive red bandana. He carried a small pack for basic supplies and a canvas sling for his camera equipment, film, and heavy tripod. Masa also pushed a handcrafted cyclometer (a bicycle wheel with handlebars and an odometer) to measure trail distances accurately. He occasionally startled unsuspecting hikers as he traveled. In one instance recounted by Tom Alexander, the owner of a tourist camp in the Smokies, a young man, who was traveling with him from Smokemont to Raven Fork on a nearly impassable trail, saw Masa approaching through the woods and exclaimed, "My God, yonder comes an Indian riding a bicycle!"[21]

As the efforts to establish a national park in the Great Smoky Mountains gained momentum, George Masa became involved in nearly every aspect of the process. He readily shared his photographs and often eschewed compensation. Writers sought out his images for magazine and newspaper articles, as well as for promotional pamphlets and other materials. He also provided detailed maps and notes chronicling his many travels throughout the Smokies to various park planners.

Along the way George Masa and Horace Kephart crossed paths—a meeting that would profoundly affect both men. While it is uncertain when Masa and Kephart first met, it is speculated that both may have belonged to the Carolina Mountain Club (CMC) in the mid-1920s. By late 1925, they had developed a working collaboration, which would become a nearly unbreakable friendship. Even as "congenial

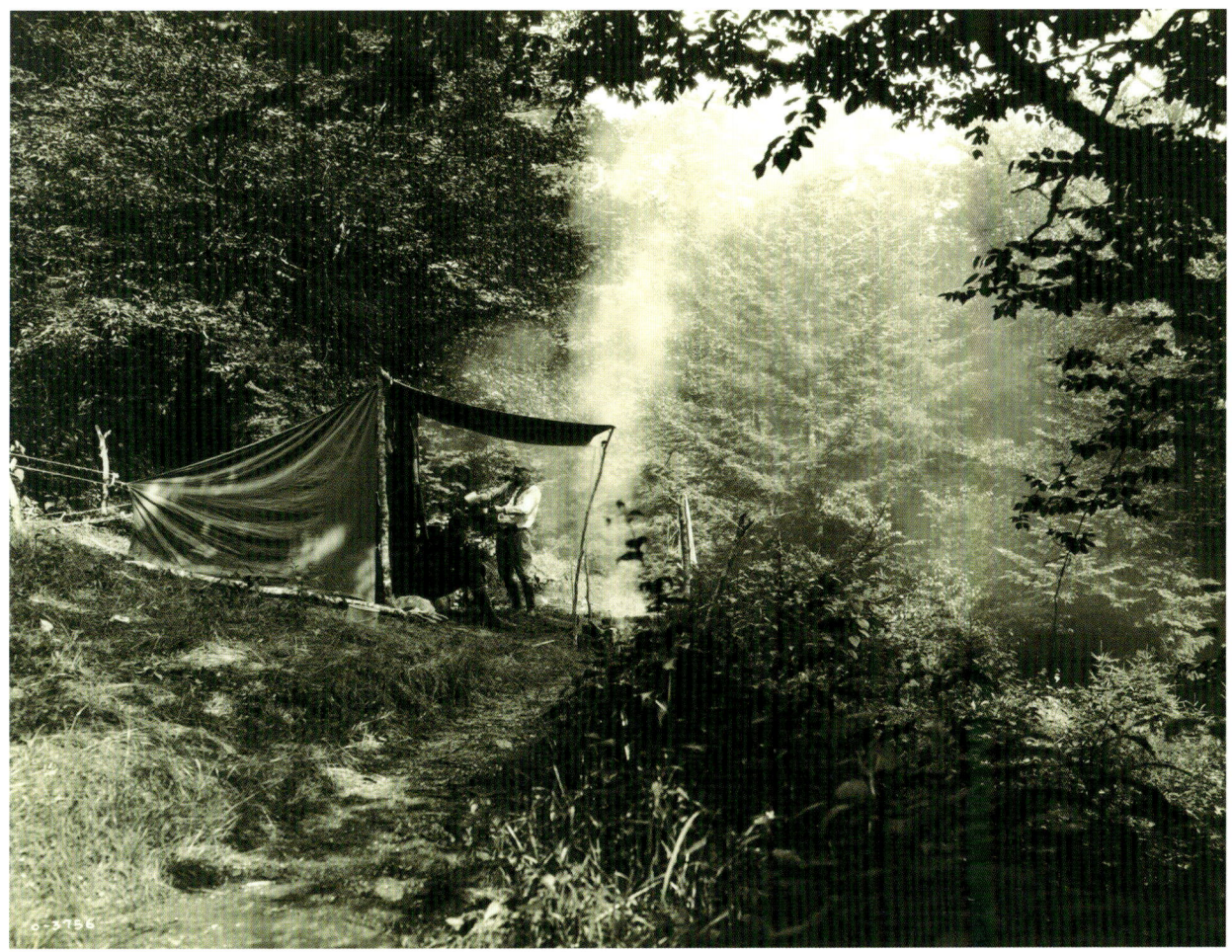

Horace Kephart in camp near Indian Gap, ca. late 1920s. Photograph by George Masa. Buncombe County Special Collections, Pack Memorial Library.

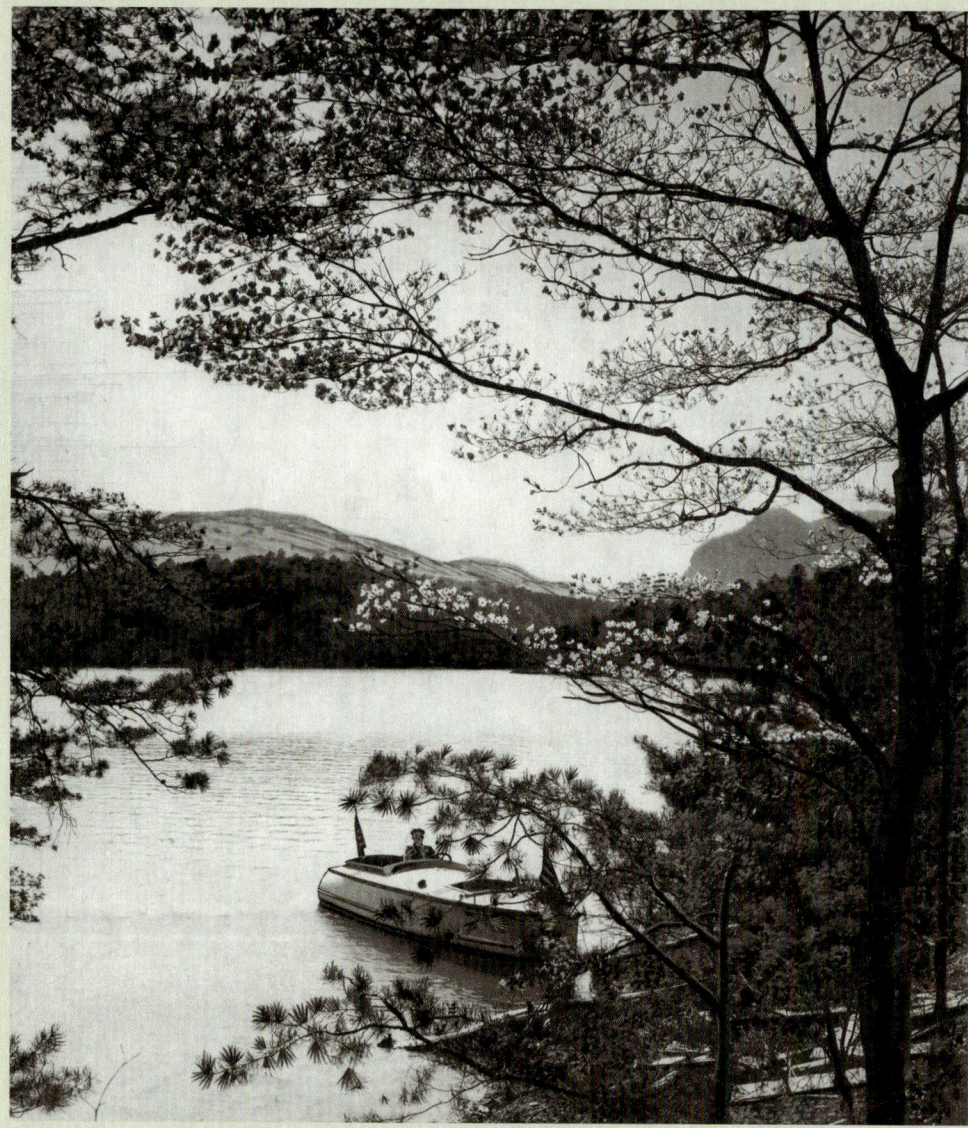

A wooden boat on Lake Lure, North Carolina. Photograph by George Masa, year unknown. Buncombe County Special Collections, Pack Memorial Library.

Massa [*sic*] is an artist at heart—and like the true artist—wants to express by means of his art, something of this feeling of worship which contemplation of nature has inspired in him.
—Lola M. Love, *Asheville Citizen Times*, August 25, 1929

In the article cited above, Lola Love describes George Masa's work as bringing "all the painstaking care and the inward eye for a truly artistic production which made notable the works of the old Japanese painters."[1] More recently, writer Kent Priestly noted that "the better images by Masa—the ones we do have—are tonally complex, full of deep shadows and penetrating light."[2]

George Masa's photography, celebrated for its focus on the fundamental beauty of place and order in the natural world, has been described by both his contemporaries and later historians as reflective of the cultural influences of Japanese art. In an interview with William A. Hart Jr., Asheville photographer Gil Leebrick noted that "Masa was concerned about and had a sense of aesthetic which is apparent in the framing of his pictures, waiting for the light and waiting for the weather effect.... He possessed the Japanese aesthetic that led him to be outdoors . . . searching for trails and trail details."[3] Masa's close friend and hiking companion Barbara Ambler Thorne summed up her firsthand observations of Masa at work, writing, "He would want the clouds a certain way and he waited for clouds to get that way. . . . [T]he man was an artist."[4]

Many viewers have often stereotyped Japanese art as stylized scenes of mountains and trees. In reality, Japanese art—both historical and contemporary—reflects the tapestry of the country's history, cultural traditions, and religious beliefs. It is integral to everyday life, expressing reverence for nature, beauty, simplicity, order, and discipline. Therefore, it is important to consider both the religious and cultural foundations of Japanese art when trying to understand the imagery and its significance.

Shintoism and Buddhism, the predominant religious beliefs of millions of Japanese, contribute to this aesthetic. Shintoism embraces the inherent value of nature, harmony, family, and well-being. In Buddhism all creatures are seen as evolving from or disappearing into nothingness. In art this is expressed as dynamic movement toward nature's or a person's potential—for example, a rising wave is viewed as not yet having reached its peak. Nature itself is always in motion toward a future; at the same time, it is irrevocably impermanent. This perspective is often expressed in the Zen philosophy of mindfulness and the beauty of nature as expressed in growth, death, and simplicity. Components of the Zen aesthetic include the following:

Fukensei: asymmetry, irregularity (不均整)
Kanso: simplicity (簡素)
Koko: basic, weathered (此処 ここ)[5]
Shizen: without pretense, natural (自然)
Yūgen: subtly profound grace, not obvious (幽玄)
Datsuzoku: unbounded by convention, free (脱俗)
Seijaku: tranquility, silence (静寂)[6]

In Japan, art serves a broader purpose than simply being enjoyed. It reveals elements of truth, relationships, and national identity. Many of the characteristics of Japanese culture that are reflected in art draw from *wabi-sabi*, a philosophy that embraces concepts of simplicity, imperfection, and impermanence. In his book, *The Wabi-Sabi Way*, Mike Sturm notes that "wabi [sabi] rejects the idea of the pristine as perfect. In fact, what makes something worthy of our reverence and awe is that it has weathered the storms of life."[7] In his article "Terra Incognita," storyteller Eric NeSmith writes of Masa's vision, "I see Masa's desire to save the scene, to preserve it indefinitely, leading me to think that it may have meant more to him than just saving forests. I'd like to think he knew that saving some natural space, some wilderness, would also help us heal, ultimately offering us a way to save ourselves."[8]

As is often the case, there may be much more to a photograph than the eye can see. Take time to consider this when you are studying George Masa's photographs.

The epigraph is drawn from Lola M. Love, "Japanese Photographer Is Artist with a Camera," *Asheville Citizen Times*, August 25, 1929.

1. Love, "Japanese Photographer Is Artist."

2. Kent Priestly, "Light and Shadow: The Mystery and Legacy of George Masa," *Mountain Xpress*, August 26, 2009, https://mountainx.com/arts/art-news/082609light_and_shadow/.

3. Telephone interview with Gil Leebrick, July 23, 1996, in William A. Hart Jr., "George Masa: The Best Mountaineer," in *May We All Remember Well: A Journal of the History and Culture of Western North Carolina*, ed. Robert S. Brunk, vol. 1 (Asheville, N.C.: Robert S. Brunk Auction Services, 1997), 255.

4. Recorded interview with Mrs. Barbara A. Thorne, June 3, 1996, in Hart, "George Masa," 255.

5. Japanese language reference for Koko is from Scot Gillespie, "Eight Elements of Japanese Aesthetics: To Help You Think Differently," *Medium*, November 17, 2019, https://medium.com/swlh/using-elements-of-japanese-aesthetics-edoc2e07ec0e.

6. Japanese language references (except Koko) are from Garr Reynolds, "7 Japanese Aesthetic Principles to Change Your Thinking," Presentation Zen, posted September 2009, https://www.presentationzen.com/presentationzen/2009/09/exposing-ourselves-to-traditional-japanese-aesthetic-ideas-notions-that-may-seem-quite-foreign-to-most-of-us-is-a-goo.html.

7. Mike Sturm, *The Wabi-Sabi Way: Simple Principles to Bring Calm, Meaning & Authenticity to Your Daily Life* (Emeryville, Calif.: Rock Ridge Press, 2020), 7.

8. Eric NeSmith, "George Masa's Terra Incognita: There's a Tremendous Sacrifice in Making a Photograph a Work of Art," *Bitter Southerner*, October 26, 2021, https://bittersoutherner.com/feature/2021/george-masas-terra-incognita.

comrades,"[22] Kephart and Masa were vastly different. In a 1953 article, Virginia Lathrop, a friend of both men, recalled that they were a curious pair: "Kephart the woodsman who found delight in camping, in sleeping under the stars, challenging nature at its most rugged. Masa, the artist, was content to roll himself in a blanket under the nearest boulder and exist on a jar of caviar in order to sit the day out waiting for a picture."[23] Ultimately, a shared love of the mountains cemented their bond. Masa's passion for capturing the beauty of the landscape in pictures proved the perfect complement to Kephart's gift with words.

As outsiders, Masa and Kephart perhaps shared a search for belonging. Kephart was, in many ways, unmoored from his previous life and family in Saint Louis, while the secretive and deferential Masa revealed very little about his own upbringing in Japan—neither his reasons for leaving nor the scandal he left behind in Seattle. If the two men were seeking an escape from their past lives, it was to America's benefit that they found each other.

Horace Kephart, affectionately dubbed Kep, became Masa's teacher in the ways of the outdoors. Kephart taught him about the animals, plants, and cultural history of the Great Smoky Mountains—from the Cherokee, who had lived in the region for centuries before their removal on the Trail of Tears, to the Scots-Irish pioneers, who had arrived when the land opened for settlement in the 1830s. On a few occasions, they attended Cherokee festivals together, where Masa took photographs while Kephart recorded notes for articles he planned to write. After Kephart's death and with the support of family friend I. K. Stearns, Laura Kephart compiled some of her late husband's pieces in a small book, *The Cherokees of the Great Smoky Mountains*, which she hoped might generate some income to pay his debts.

As early as 1920, Kephart had expressed deep concern for the future of the Smokies. In a letter to Paul Fink, he wrote, "It makes my heart sick to see with what reckless selfishness these gifts of nature are being squandered."[24] As the park movement gained momentum and the lumber and mining companies' opposition grew more strident, Kephart wrote passionately of the inevitable devastation from unchecked large-scale logging and mining. As he captured these concerns in words, Masa continued trekking deep in the mountains, producing landscape photographs, measuring potential trails with his wheel, and occasionally capturing scenes of the devastation detailed in Kephart's essays.

The two became constant companions, taking extended camping trips together, with Masa taking pictures by day and the men discussing plans for a national park around the campfire by night. For several years they explored the mountains on foot, by horseback, and via automobile. As Kephart grew older and his stamina diminished, Masa took on the more arduous hiking trips alone so that he could gather information and capture the images needed for their efforts to save the Smokies; he later did these trips to scout routes for the Appalachian Trail.

In 1927 complicated land acquisitions and a lack of funds from the North Carolina and Tennessee governments put the park's future in jeopardy. Masa took matters into his own hands, sending portfolios of his best photographs of the Great Smokies to the governors of North Carolina and Tennessee, as well as to First Lady Grace Coolidge, in the hope that they might influence efforts to further the cause. Despite determined efforts by Masa, Kephart, and many others, the two states received pledges for only half of the $10 million needed to secure the park's establishment, and many were pessimistic about finding the additional funds.

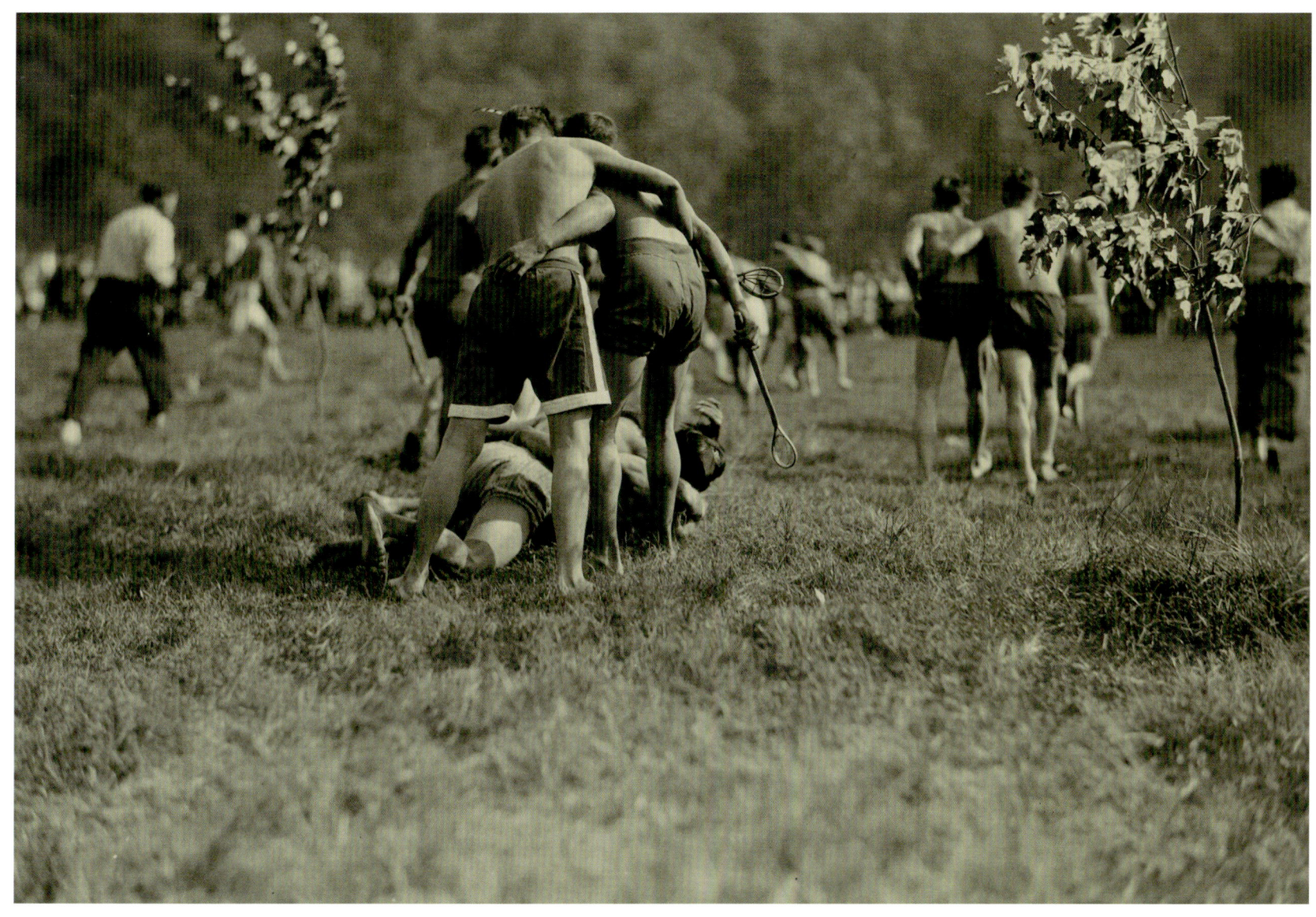

Native Americans playing a ball game at a Cherokee festival, year unknown. Photograph by George Masa. Smokies Life, Horace Kephart Family Collection.

At a meeting in September 1927, Arno Cammerer, in an effort to persuade John D. Rockefeller Jr. to support the park, gave the philanthropist several photographs of the mountains likely taken by both Masa and Jim Thompson. Perhaps the plan worked, as Rockefeller agreed to support the project in January 1928. The influence of Thompson's and Masa's photographs in the decision is unknown, but Cammerer later wrote to Masa, "It seems everybody has been telling me about your fine spirit and your helpfulness and your love of the outdoors. . . . I have admired your photographic work very much."[25] Masa would later photograph

Rockefeller during the philanthropist's 1928 visit to the Grove Park Inn, and the image appeared in the rotogravure section of the *New York Times* on November 25, 1928.

Through the remainder of the decade, Kephart and Masa accelerated their efforts on behalf of the park. Following the election of President Herbert Hoover in 1928, incoming interior secretary Roy Wilbur took an interest in the project as well as the time-sensitive need to proceed with land acquisitions before further logging and mining rendered the region unsuitable for a national park. In the fall of 1930, NPS officials Horace Albright and Cammerer returned to tour the

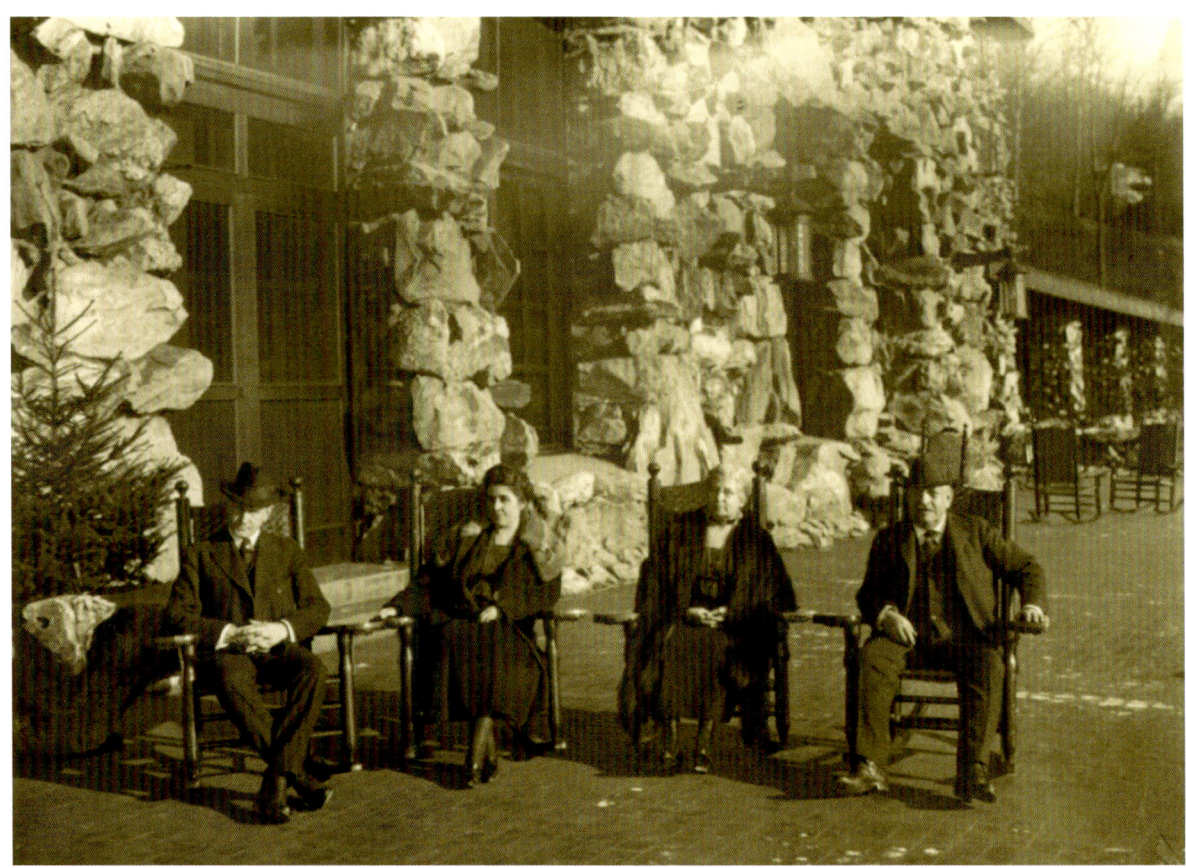

Vice President Calvin Coolidge,
Mrs. Grace Coolidge, and Mr. and Mrs.
Frank Stearns at Grove Park Inn, 1921.
Photograph by George Masa.
Vermont Historical Society.

area and meet with representatives from the SANPC and state park commissions. George Masa participated in these discussions and accompanied a group, which included Albright and Cammerer, into the mountains. There, he snapped a photograph of the group outside a mountain cabin.

In addition to his growing collection of photographs, Masa kept journals filled with details of trail distances, terrain, water sources, landmarks, and more. On the wall of his Asheville studio, he posted a map detailing his treks into the Smokies. Following an interview for a 1929 newspaper article, Masa's friend and hiking companion Lola Love wrote that Masa's map was filled with push pins denoting every place he had photographed, describing it as his "text book … and the visual expression of the plans and dreams which he has made for his work."[26] Of his mapmaking, Paul Fink wrote to Masa on March 15, 1931, "You certainly have done a wonderful job. . . . I wish we had someone on the Tennessee side as capable and willing as you have proved yourself."[27]

In addition to their writing, photography, and work with the Nomenclature Committee, Kephart and Masa devoted countless hours to the ongoing efforts to survey potential routes for the Appalachian Trail. As noted previously, members of the Tennessee and North Carolina hiking clubs held multiple meetings to resolve their disagreements. Also involved in the discussions were Georgia foresters Roy Ozmer and Everett "Eb" Stone, both of whom were knowledgeable about the terrain of the Cherokee (later Chattahoochee) National Forest in Georgia and possible routes for the trail. Prior to the 1931 meeting of the Appalachian Trail Conference in Gatlinburg, Myron Avery and Warren Hall, president of the Georgia Appalachian Trail Club, hiked 170 miles from Mount Oglethorpe to the planned border of the

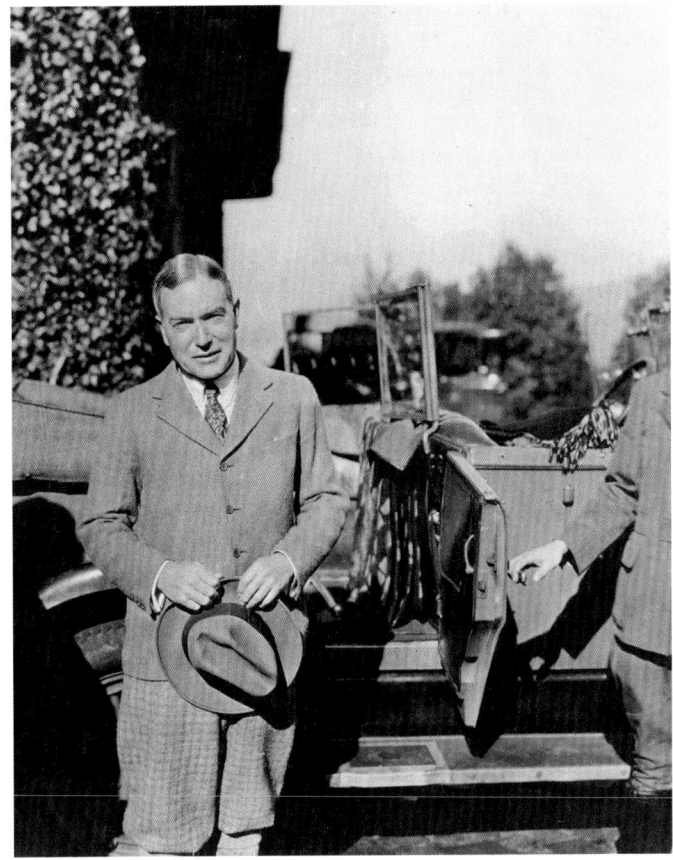

Mr. John D. Rockefeller Jr. at the Grove Park Inn, 1928. Photograph by George Masa. Collection of William A. Hart Jr.

national park at Deal's Gap. There they were met by George Masa, and together, they traveled by automobile to the meeting.

With the decline in his commercial business, Masa turned to his passion for completing the national park and trail projects, increasing his time in the mountains, leading hikes, scouting routes for the AT, and finishing nomenclature work. In an interview years later, Barbara Ambler

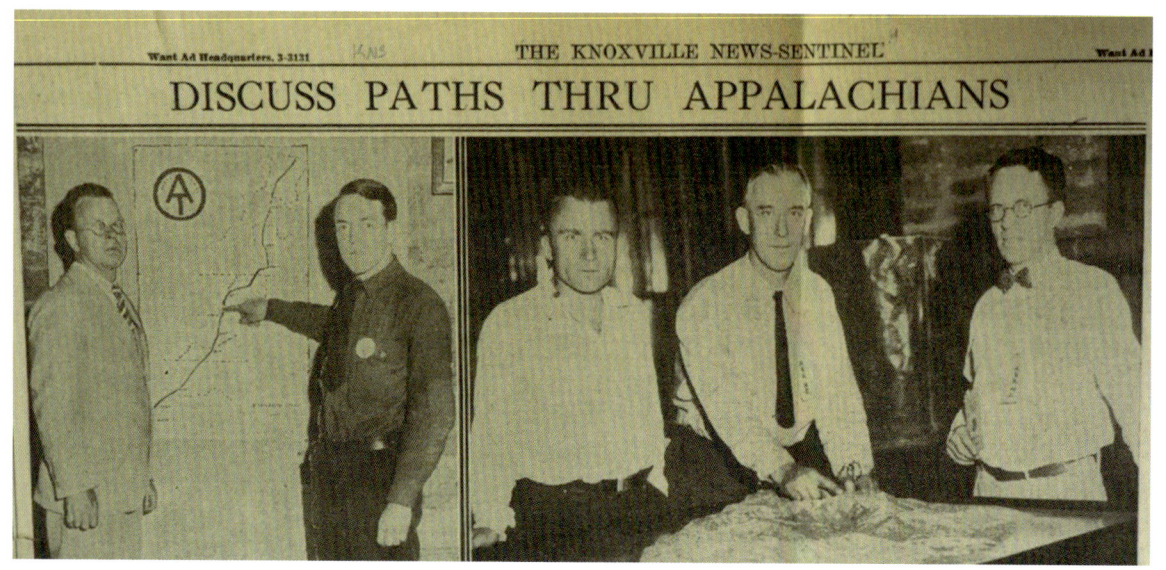

THE KNOXVILLE NEWS-SENTINEL

DISCUSS PATHS THRU APPALACHIANS

Photographs from the *Knoxville News Sentinel* of participants in the ATC annual meeting in Gatlinburg, June 1931. Left photo: Reid Russell and George Stephens examine a map of the AT. Right photo: Myron Avery, Jim Thompson, and Dr. H. M. Jemmison study a relief map of the Great Smoky Mountains. Photograph by Jim Thompson. McClung Historical Collection, Knox County Public Library, Jim Thompson. Smoky Mountains Photograph Collection, Thompson Brothers.

Thorne (daughter of Dr. Chase Ambler, who had proposed a park in the Smokies in 1899) recalled that during this time, Masa urged his hiking companions, saying, "[Get] off your seats and on your feets!" and "More walk, less talk."[28]

In early 1930, George Masa was as busy as ever. Commercial projects, newspaper assignments, and society events (including projects for Edith Vanderbilt at Biltmore House) filled his calendar. But it was not to last. By the year's end, the effects of the Great Depression had reached Asheville. Numerous businesses shuttered, local banks failed, and jobs were lost. In March 1931, after losing his savings when the local bank closed, Masa wrote to his friend Margaret Gooch: "I lost every cents I had in American National Bank, so that's that. But believe me, always my head is up. Never surrender."[29] In another letter to Gooch in June 1931, Masa unburdened himself further, writing, "Local people thinks I am and have plenty money because my customers all rich people or social persons, indeed I worked like hell, studied like hell and got good reputation at present, and I never told any one business 'rotten.'"[30] In an effort to keep his studio open, Masa reached out to friends, hiking companions, clients, park service officials, and others seeking loans. In nearly every instance, he was turned down, as many he had contacted were facing the same situation.

As winter turned to spring in 1931, Kephart and Masa were busy with AT survey work. They also met with Horace Albright, who had returned to the Smokies for an update on park progress. George Masa served as Albright's guide for this trip and provided him with additional photographs for park promotion. As these efforts neared success, Kephart and Masa had several conversations about opening a souvenir shop, studio, and café first in Bryson City and, later, in the national park's proposed Smokemont Campground.

There Kephart could sell his books, and Masa could market prints and postcards while offering refreshments to visitors. They also explored a tour business partnership with Bryson City pharmacist, mayor, and park booster Dr. Kelly Bennett. Kephart and Bennett had previously collaborated on a plan to promote tours of the planned park, for which they had printed brochures advertising the venture.

The men discussed their plans until Kephart's death in April. Afterward, Masa pursued the shop idea in a 1932 letter to NPS acting director Arthur Demaray, who replied, "We have not yet worked out any policy in connection with the establishment of tourist facilities."[31] In the end, the dream would never become a reality.

THE TRAGIC DEATH OF HORACE KEPHART

On April 2, 1931, Horace Kephart and George Masa's friendship came to an abrupt end with Kephart's tragic death in an automobile accident. George learned of the accident from the newspaper the following morning and wrote to Margaret Gooch, "I don't know what I say about death of our Kephart. It shocked me to pieces. This morning I have read the paper, in headline, 'Horace Kephart Killed.' I couldn't believe it."[32] In a note to Paul Fink, Masa lamented, "Kep is gone forever! . . . I never experienced such feeling in my life."[33] Replying to a letter of condolence from Myron Avery, Masa wrote, "Indeed give us great loss in every way,

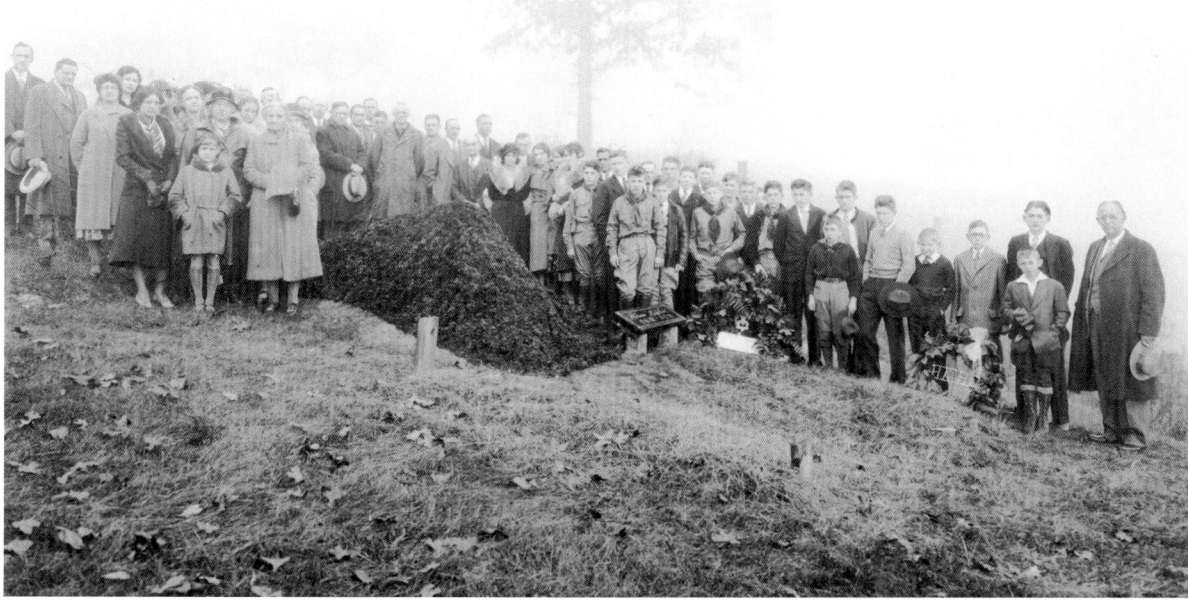

Photograph of group attending the memorial service for Horace Kephart, November 15, 1931. Photograph by George Masa. Buncombe County Special Collections, Pack Memorial Library.

because last few years I am the one who close associate with him personally and his works."[34]

According to Horace Kephart's grandson George, Masa appeared "among the most stricken"[35] of the mourners at the funeral, where he served as a pallbearer and was among the first to arrive and the last to leave. Kephart was interred in a hillside plot owned by his longtime friends Jack and Bland Ball Wiggins Coburn at the Bryson City Cemetery, which overlooked his adopted hometown. On November 15, 1931, Masa attended and photographed a memorial service in the cemetery, where a marker was dedicated to its namesake. Among those attending the ceremony was their mutual friend and park supporter, Tennessee photographer Jim Thompson.

Masa and many of Kephart's friends requested that Kephart's remains be moved to a site on the summit of his namesake mountain, but this was declined by the park service due to concerns regarding precedent. At the same time, Masa, I. K. Stearns, and others reached out to Cammerer and proposed that Kephart's library be placed in the park once it was established and a museum be built to house it. Due to numerous issues associated with Kephart's estate, this, too, was not to be. Today most of Horace Kephart's writings, journals, and other materials are held in the Hunter Library at Western Carolina University.

Determined to move forward with Kephart's work, Masa replaced Kephart on the ATC Board of Managers and on the North Carolina Nomenclature Committee. He went into the mountains for extended periods despite the continued financial decline of his studio. In a letter to Margaret Gooch in October 1931, Masa confided, "Am quite busy attending so many things beside my own business. I am

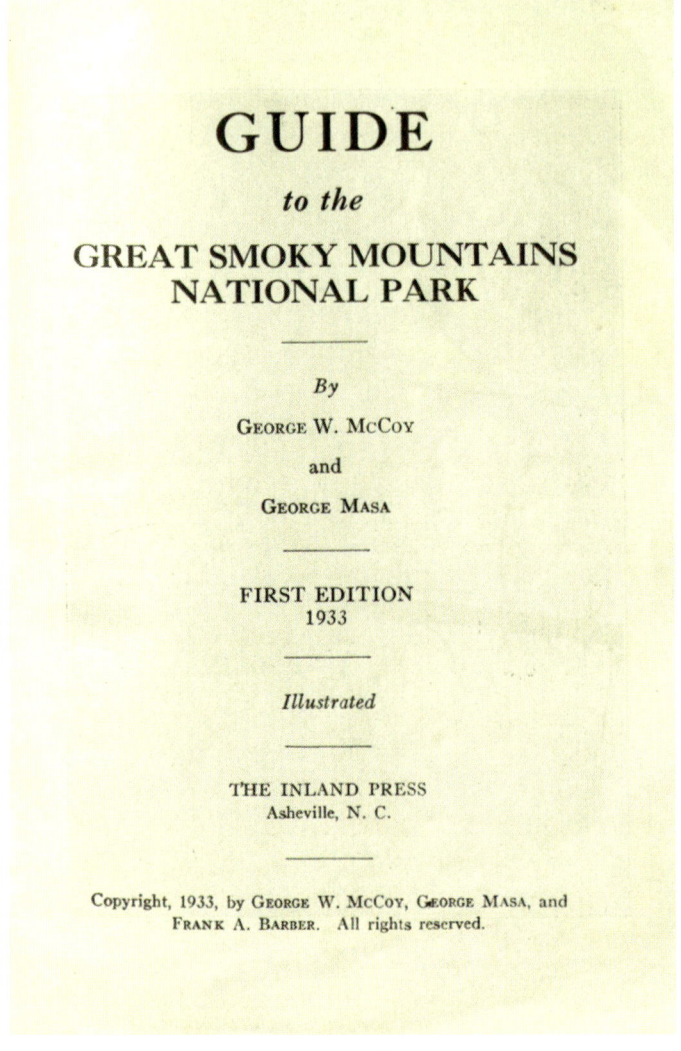

GUIDE

to the

GREAT SMOKY MOUNTAINS
NATIONAL PARK

———

By

GEORGE W. MCCOY

and

GEORGE MASA

FIRST EDITION
1933

Illustrated

THE INLAND PRESS
Asheville, N. C.

———

Title page of *Guide to the Great Smoky Mountains National Park* by George McCoy and George Masa, 1933. Inland Press. Western Carolina University, Hunter Library Special Collections.

making new map of Great Smoky Mountains National Park and Nomenclature and also Appalachian Trail . . . and look after Carolina Appalachian Trail Club. . . . I always cry in my heart 'wish Kep with me.'"[36]

Masa worked tirelessly through 1932 to hike and map the AT in North Carolina and south into Georgia. In a February 1932 report to the ATC Board of Managers, Myron Avery noted that "with the exception of the link between the Smokies and Nantahala, which is being thoroughly scouted, the trail should be completed by August 1932 from Grafton Notch to the southern terminus."[37] Much of that scouting was the work of George Masa.

That same year, Masa began to work with George McCoy, editor of the *Asheville Citizen*, on a book titled *Guide to the Great Smoky Mountains National Park*. Released in 1933, the 142-page guidebook was filled with details from Masa's research and travels, listing him as the coauthor and contributor of nearly all of the guide's photographs. However, when a second edition of the book was published in 1935, George Masa's name was mentioned only in the photography credits. Perhaps this was because it was reprinted after Masa's death.

THE END OF THE TRAIL

During the winter of 1933, George Masa was living in a boardinghouse operated by the mother of his dentist, Dr. Hugh May. While there, Masa's health deteriorated. In early April, even as he organized a hike to commemorate the second anniversary of Kep's death, his friends were growing concerned that he may have contracted influenza. Though he had little money to afford hospitalization, Masa was admitted to the county sanitarium. His decline continued,

and Masa died there on June 21, 1933, likely of tuberculosis. Shortly after his death, the CMC published this tribute to their beloved member and friend: "To those who spent hours on the trail with George, climbing into the less accessible places in the Smokies, discovering or making new trails into territory seldom visited by others, there is left the memory of a genius whose love of beauty was so intense that a hard hike of ten or twenty miles was not too great a price to pay for a photograph capturing some of the beauty to be found at the end of the trail."[38]

Despite Masa's oft-stated wish to rest beside Horace Kephart, his body was interred in an unmarked grave in Asheville's Riverside Cemetery. It would be another fourteen years before club members and friends placed a simple marker at the site.

George Masa died not only penniless but deeply in debt. Members of the CMC sought possession of his photographs, negatives, camera equipment, and personal belongings in order to preserve them for posterity. His friend, *Asheville Citizen-Times* publisher George McCoy, reached out to I. K. Stearns, who was coordinating the preservation of Horace Kephart's papers and artifacts and proposed including Masa's materials.

The two men planned to create a joint collection that could be the nucleus of a proposed museum within the Great Smoky Mountains National Park. However, in a letter to Stearns written on August 5, 1933, McCoy stated, "I had hoped that the Carolina Mountain Club, of Asheville, would take some action to assure the preservation of Masa's collection of mountain photographs intact. . . . The Mountain Club put in a bid for this, but it was too small and unless someone else aids in the matter the collection will

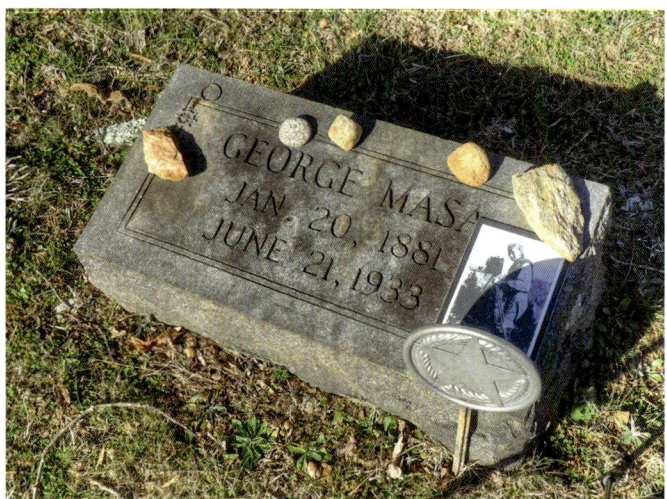

George Masa's grave in Asheville's Riverside Cemetery, 2022. Photograph by Ren Davis. Image from the Ren and Helen Davis Collection.

get into hands where it will be less useful to the public."[39] In the end, the club failed to outbid local photographer Elliott Lyman Fisher, resulting in their loss of possession of more than twenty-five hundred of Masa's negatives. For a period of time, Fisher printed and sold the photographs, crediting them to Masa; he later sold them uncredited. Fisher moved to Florida in the 1950s and died there in 1968. None of the original Masa photographs and negatives that were in his possession have ever been found.

In early 1934, NPS naturalist Arthur Stupka reviewed several thousand of Masa's prints. Of these, he described four hundred as "exceptionally fine,"[40] ordering seventy-five to be made into lantern slides for use by the park. According to biographer Paul Bonesteel, the order went unfilled, and eventually, these images, too, were lost. On June 15, 1934, a week shy of the first anniversary of George Masa's death,

Great Smoky Mountains National Park was formally established by President Franklin D. Roosevelt. Sadly, neither George Masa nor Horace Kephart lived to see this milestone achievement—much of it due to their labors—nor did they witness the park's dedication in 1940.

Through the remainder of the 1930s, Kephart and Masa's friends, led by Stearns, sought to donate their collections of books, photographs, correspondences, and artifacts to the NPS. Initially, park superintendent J. Ross Eakin and historian Hiram C. Wilburn supported the proposal, offering to store and catalog the collection pending a final decision. They were also willing to consider reinterring Kephart and Masa together at a site within the park. However, as time passed, the park service concluded that reburying the men in the park would not be appropriate, as well as that placing their collections in a park museum was not warranted. In order to safeguard the materials, Stearns had them placed in the basement of his Bryson City home until a suitable final destination could be determined.

In November 1940 a recommendation was made to place the collections at Western Carolina Teachers College in nearby Cullowhee. Preliminary discussions with Dean William Bird began in 1941 but were put on hold due to America's entry into World War II. After the war the Kephart family concurred with a plan to offer the collection to the college as a gift, which was accepted. The materials were relocated to the national park in 1948 in anticipation of a museum being constructed to house them. When this was not undertaken, the school (now Western Carolina University) asserted its ownership of the materials. They were permanently returned in 1973, and today, they are located in the Special Collections section of the university's Hunter Library.

As time passed, George Masa's name faded from memory. A notable exception was the CMC, whose members finally secured funds for a marker on his grave in 1947. But they were not done. In 1961, after years of lobbying the park service, the club succeeded in having a rock promontory near Mount Kephart named Masa Knob. In a poignant tribute on the occasion of the naming of the knob, the club issued this eloquent statement: "From the very beginning, George Masa was awed by the grandeur of our mountain ranges and the unique flora of the region. He was seized with the longing to climb along the ridges and mountain tops for the pleasure of viewing the handiwork of God from the high places."[41] Today visitors to Great Smoky Mountains National Park and hikers on the Appalachian Trail may take a short side trip to see this lasting memorial to the man Arno Cammerer dubbed "the best mountaineer."[42]

During a 2011 address in the White House Rose Garden in which President Barack Obama was introducing the Great Outdoors Initiative, the president paid tribute to Masa and Kephart and their roles in the creation of a national park in the Great Smoky Mountains:

> Protecting this legacy has been the responsibility of all who serve this country. But behind that action . . . there's also the story of ordinary Americans who devoted their lives to protecting the land that they loved.
>
> That's what Horace Kephart and George Masa did. This is a wonderful story. Two men, they met in the Great Smoky Mountains of North Carolina—each had moved there to start a new life. Horrified that their beloved wilderness was being clear-cut at a rate of 60 acres a day, Horace and George worked with other members of the community to get the land set aside. The only catch was that they had to raise $10 million to foot the bill.

But far from being discouraged, they helped rally one of the poorest areas in the country to the cause. A local high school donated the proceeds from a junior class play. Preachers held "Smoky Mountain Sunday" services and encouraged their congregations to donate. Local businesses chipped in. And students from every grade in the city of Asheville—which was still segregated at the time—made a contribution.[43]

In 2022 the North Carolina Department of Natural and Cultural Resources (NCDCR) erected a historical marker in downtown Asheville's Pack Square to honor George Masa. It reads, "Japanese photographer. Born Masahara Iizuka [n.b., based on the research described in *George Masa: A Life Reimagined*, this is incorrect]. Advocate of Great Smoky Mountains National Park and Appalachian Trail. His studio was nearby."[44] It is a simple but fitting tribute to a man who lived simply and in concert with nature. That same year, the George Masa Foundation (georgemasafoundation.org) was established in Asheville to support youth engagement in environmental and conservation initiatives, much like George Masa had done during his lifetime.

In 2023 the East Tennessee Development District, based in Knoxville, in collaboration with the Land of the Sky Regional Council and High Country Council of Governments of North Carolina, awarded the inaugural George Masa Environmental Stewardship Award to honor Masa's legacy of commitment to the region. The award is given to an individual or organization within the region who has contributed significantly to environmentalism, conservation, and outdoor recreation.

Finally, it all seemed to come full circle: On May 20, 2023, during Bryson City's annual Horace Kephart Days celebration, the Horace Kephart Foundation, directed by his great-granddaughter Libby Kephart Hargrave, completed Project Reunite by unveiling two markers by Kephart's grave. The first honors the enduring love and devotion of his wife, Laura, who had wished for her ashes to be placed beside her husband's grave following her death in 1954 (sadly, this was not to be, as the ashes were lost many years ago). The second memorializes Kephart's deep friendship with George Masa, who had asked to be buried next to Kep. Perhaps these three souls have now been reunited in both spirit and memory.

James "Jim" Thompson

> Thompson . . . was a Great Smokies enthusiast. He went into remote sections of the area and brought back pictorial evidence of the charm and majesty that was later to be enjoyed firsthand by millions of people. . . . It requires no stretch of one's imagination to realize that without the help of these magnificent views there might have been no national park in the Great Smokies.—Carlos Campbell, *Birth of a National Park in the Great Smoky Mountains*, 1978

James "Jim" Thompson was a fixture in Knoxville, Tennessee, for nearly three-quarters of a century. While he was a respected commercial photographer, business leader, and dedicated Rotarian, Thompson was undoubtedly best remembered for his love of hiking, exploring, and photographing the Great Smoky Mountains. His images of the rugged landscapes, rushing streams, and lush coves were shared around the nation, proving invaluable in the efforts to establish a national park in those beloved mountains. Despite his many contributions, Thompson's work, though well known in the region, has received less national attention than the images produced by his friend and contemporary George Masa.

Jim Thompson was born in 1880 in Morristown, Tennessee, to Charles "Mortimer" and Cora Thompson. The family moved to Knoxville when Jim was a child. There Mortimer, a gifted artist and musician, studied painting under local artist Lloyd Branson, who was noted for his portraits of local politicians and scenes of pioneer life in Tennessee. Mortimer also served as bandleader for a musical group that performed at the 1896 Tennessee Centennial celebration.

When the family relocated to Knoxville, they moved into an old house owned by former mayor Samuel Boyd. The frame structure, locally known as the Blount House, was originally constructed in 1792 for William Blount, the signer of the U.S. Constitution who President George Washington had appointed to serve as the first governor of the Southwest Territory. Under Blount's leadership, the territory would be admitted to the Union in 1796 as the state of Tennessee. By the 1920s the house was nearly in ruins and at risk of being demolished, but a local group raised the funds needed to save and restore it. Today the restored Blount Mansion is a National Historic Landmark.

In addition to his other roles, Mortimer worked as an architectural draftsman and, in 1909, was appointed by the mayor as Knoxville's first building inspector. In that capacity, he developed the city's early building codes and ordinances. Outside his day job, he also painted the official portraits of mayors John E. Brooks (1908–9) and John H. McMillan (1916–19). Meanwhile, Cora Thompson was active in local social and charitable causes. The Knoxville Police Department employed her as a matron who helped young women escape poverty, crime, and prostitution. Cora would eventually open a shelter that provided housing for many of her wards, for which she was affectionately dubbed Mother Thompson by many in Knoxville.

When Jim Thompson was a teen, his father introduced him to art, drafting, and photography. Following high school, he worked in Knoxville and then briefly in Chattanooga. On returning home, he set up a darkroom in his parents' house and became an active hobbyist. He gained local recognition when his photographs of a fire that swept through downtown Knoxville on April 6, 1897, were published in the local newspaper. According to historian Paul James, who wrote about Thompson for the book *Knoxville Lives II*, the fire "was a decisive event that propelled his photography career."[45]

In 1900 Jim Thompson began working as a technician for O. C. Wiley, a local dealer in optical equipment and supplies that was also one of Knoxville's first commercial photography businesses. Thompson immersed himself in both the creative and technical details of the craft and was promoted to manager of the company's picture department.

Still uncertain about a photography career, he studied drafting in the studio of local architect George Barber. While there he developed a keen eye for detail but realized that his passion was photography. Determined to earn a living in the field, he opened his first commercial photography studio, Thompson Photo, Inc., in 1902. The business prospered, and he moved to larger facilities with space to create photo murals up to thirty feet in length, which proved popular in auditoriums, restaurants, and other large spaces. During his career, Thompson provided images for businesses, summer camps, and charitable organizations; he also produced catalog illustrations and photographs for government projects and local social events.

In 1902 Jim Thompson married Emily Boyd, a Connecticut native and longtime Knoxvillian. They had three children, Emily, Margaret, and Charles Ethelbert, whom they called Bert. In a newspaper interview years later, Bert's son, Ed Thompson, noted that his grandfather "was really one of the first photographers of the area to make a living making pictures of things and places instead of people."[46]

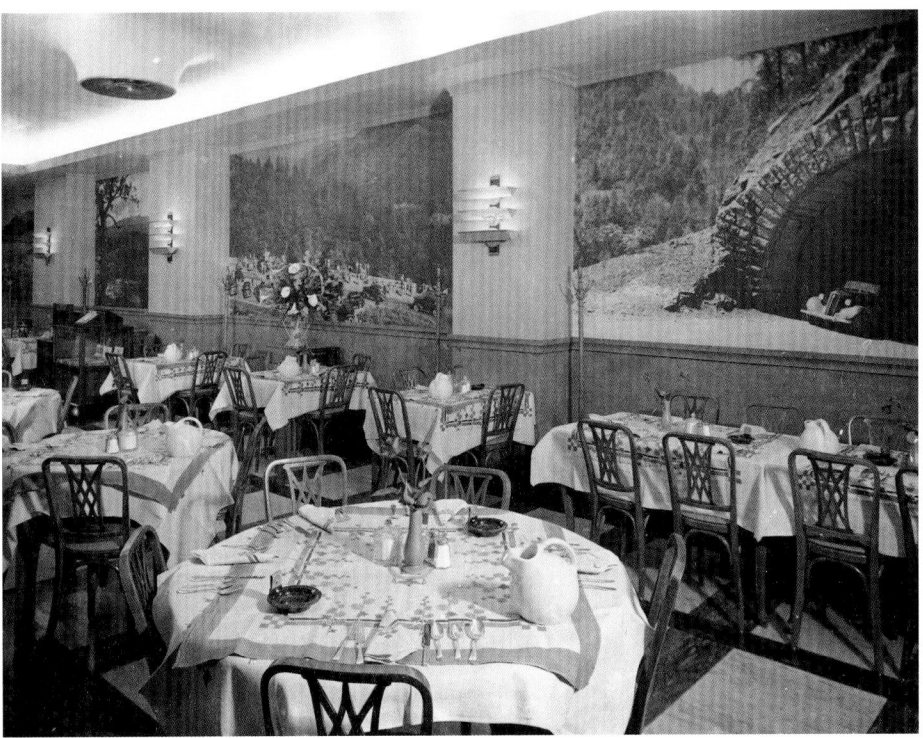

Mural photographs by Jim Thompson in the Farragut Hotel, Knoxville. Photograph by Jim Thompson. McClung Historical Collection, Knox County Public Library, Smoky Mountains Photograph Collection, Thompson Brothers.

In 1903 Thompson captured a Knoxville milestone event when he photographed local inventor Cowan Rodgers as he departed by automobile for a 123-mile trip to Chattanooga, hoping to become the first person to make the arduous journey by car. Thompson's image of Rodgers, decked out in captain's hat and bow tie, at the tiller of his home-built vehicle, is reputed to be the first photograph ever taken of a car in Knoxville (Rodgers successfully completed the journey in nine hours and forty minutes). Cowan Rodgers would later become an outspoken advocate for improved roads

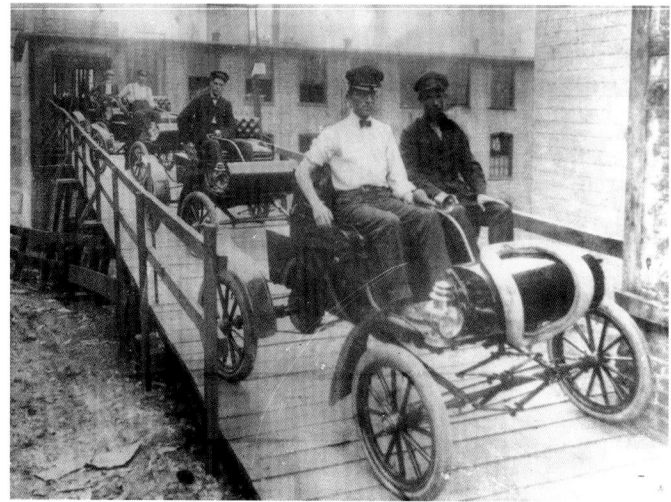

Cowan Rodgers departing Knoxville on the first automobile trip from Knoxville to Chattanooga, 1903. Photograph by Jim Thompson. McClung Historical Collection, Knox County Public Library, Jim Thompson, Smoky Mountains Photograph Collection, Thompson Brothers.

from Knoxville to Gatlinburg and into the Great Smoky Mountains, making the area more accessible to tourists and cross-mountain travelers.

The following year, Thompson's photographs were back in the news as he captured stunning images of the wreckage from the tragic New Market railroad accident, when two trains collided just outside Knoxville. While the local papers did not publish the photographs, Thompson placed them in the windows of a downtown store where hundreds of people could view them. Unfortunately, these images have been lost.

Jim Thompson's reputation grew, and in 1913, he served as the official photographer for the National Conservation Exposition, a fair celebrating the environmental ideals espoused by former president Theodore Roosevelt, who had established the National Conservation Commission in 1908. Knoxville was chosen as host due to its location and status as one of the largest cities in the Southern Appalachian Mountains. The fair, lasting from September to November, opened with a telegram of welcome from President Woodrow Wilson. More than one million visitors toured exhibits and heard speeches from such notables as Booker T. Washington, Helen Keller, Gifford Pinchot, and Secretary of State William Jennings Bryan.

Thompson's younger brother Robin joined the business in 1919, following his military service in World War I, and the studio's name was changed to the Thompson Brothers. The two men differed in the skills that they brought to their work. Jim Thompson's strength was composing outdoor scenes, ranging from cityscapes to construction sites and mountain landscapes (including close-ups of wildflowers that he shared with his invalid mother). Robin excelled in portraiture work and aerial photography, which he had learned while training in reconnaissance during the war. He demonstrated these skills when, on August 16, 1919, flying over Knoxville with a U.S. Army pilot, he produced the first known aerial photographs of the city. The images created quite a sensation when published on the front page of the *Knoxville Sentinel*. Aerial photography would later become an important part of his work on behalf of the Great Smoky Mountains National Park. Jim and Robin Thompson remained in business together for several years, but disagreements led Robin to open his own studio in the mid-1920s. Biographer Paul James states, "The brothers had a sometimes-challenging relationship, with Robin's gentle nature in sharp contrast to Jim's sometimes overbearing personality."[47]

Despite their differences, the brothers were actively involved and occasionally collaborated in efforts to promote the national park. Many of their photographs from

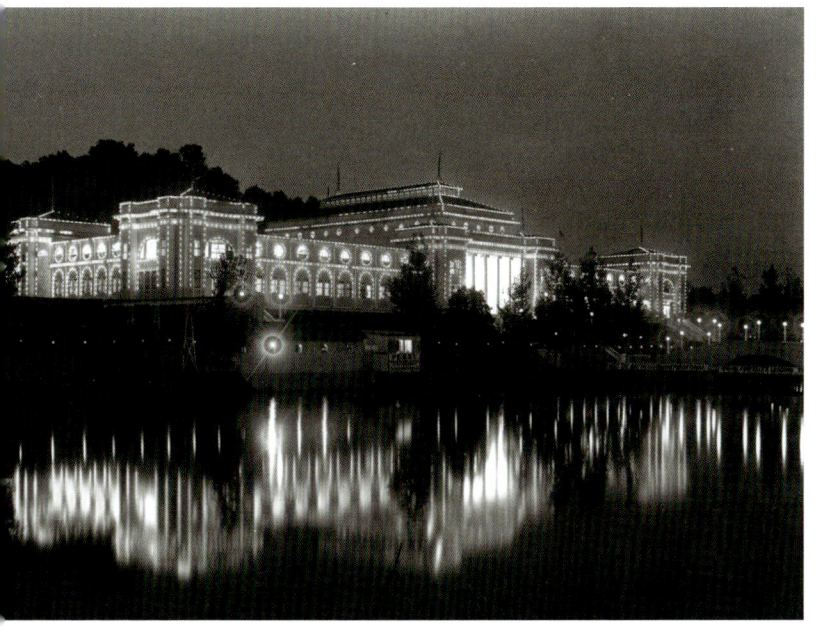

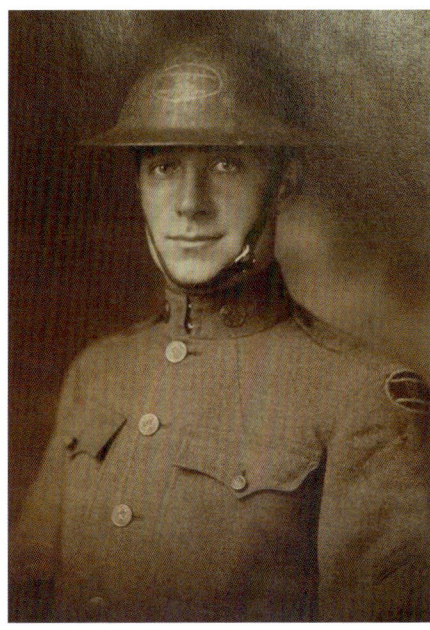

the 1920s were simply credited to the Thompson Brothers, leaving viewers to ponder who took which images. Today many credit Jim Thompson with producing most of the iconic landscape images, while Robin often snapped group photographs and aerial shots. In 1933 the brothers reconciled and reunited under the name Thompsons, Inc., which was considered to be "one of the most complete studios in the South" at the time.[48] Additionally, Jim Thompson was widely respected in his profession, serving as president of the Southeastern Photographers Association in 1924 and, in 1946, as president of the National Photographers Association of America (now the Professional Photographers of America).

A third brother, Mortimer Thompson, born in 1889, served as a sergeant in the U.S. Army infantry during World War I and was later active in the American Legion. He briefly worked with Jim and Robin at Thompson Brothers before starting his own business. Then he accepted a position with the photography department of the Tennessee Valley Authority (TVA). However, he would die unexpectedly of a heart attack in 1935.

Jim Thompson expanded the studio and opened his first retail camera store, the Snap Shop, in 1930, offering camera equipment, film, and processing services. He expanded the business to include stores in Oak Ridge and Gatlinburg, Tennessee, as well as in Lexington and Frankfort, Kentucky. His son, Bert, would later manage one of the stores, and today, the family still operates the remaining Thompson Photo Products store in Knoxville.

While Jim Thompson's occupation was commercial photography, his passion was the Great Smoky Mountains. He often traveled deep into the remote wilderness to hike, camp, and capture stunning photographs of the landscape. In the early days, roads were poor or nonexistent, and an

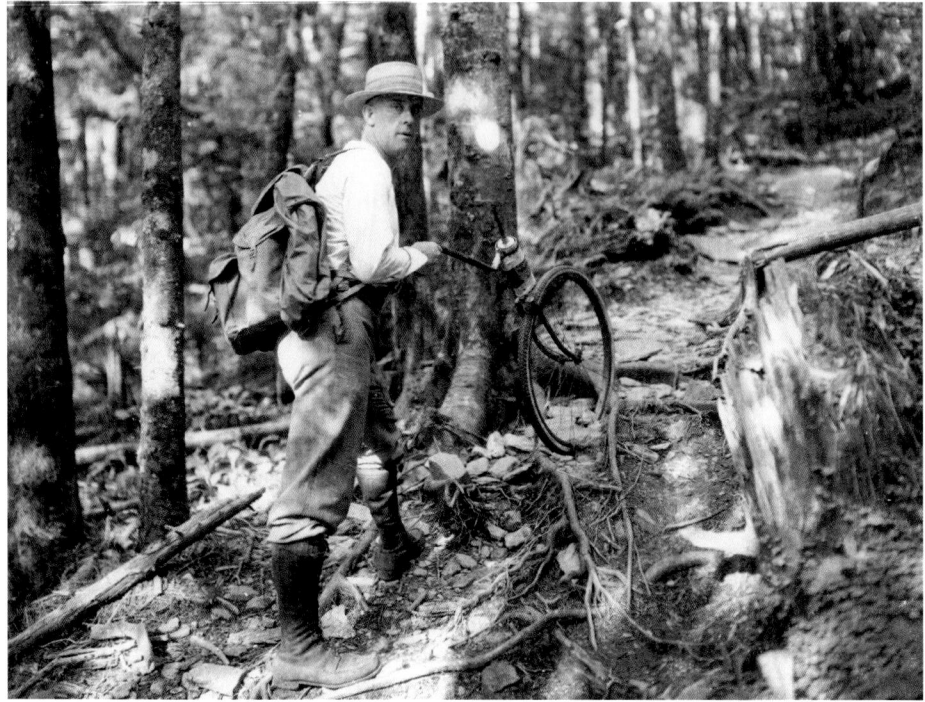

Jim Thompson measuring trail distance with a cyclometer somewhere in the
Great Smoky Mountains, year unknown. Photograph by Albert "Dutch" Roth.
McClung Historical Collection, Knox County Public Library, Jim Thompson,
Smoky Mountains Photograph Collection, Thompson Brothers.

automobile trip to Gatlinburg could take two days. An alternative was a daylong railroad trip to Townsend, Tennessee, followed by a brief ride on the Little River Lumber Company's train to the resort community of Elkmont. From there, the mountains beckoned.

OFFICIAL PHOTOGRAPHER FOR THE
PARK MOVEMENT

Thompson's images were well known to William P. Davis, Colonel David Chapman, and the other local leaders who had begun the campaign for a national park by forming the Great Smoky Mountains Conservation Association (GSMCA) in 1924. Thompson enthusiastically joined this effort, serving as the GSMCA's official photographer, providing many images to support the work. He also accompanied survey trips to the mountains for government officials, local civic leaders, and business executives to win their support. One example was a railroad trip taken by state legislators in March 1925 to Townsend, Cades Cove, and Elkmont, sponsored by the Association and the Knoxville Chamber of Commerce. Despite being impressed with the landscape's beauty, the legislature failed to approve funding to purchase land for a park. Undeterred, Thompson continued to utilize every opportunity to illustrate the beauty of the Great Smokies in promotional documents, magazine articles, and print displays. Thompson also created scrapbooks of prints that were provided to political leaders, including Interior Secretary Hubert Work.

Jim Thompson was actively involved in founding the Smoky Mountains Hiking Club (SMHC) in 1924, serving as club president from 1928 to 1930. The club began under the leadership of Marshall Wilson and George Barber from the Gatlinburg YMCA Camp. For October 19–20, 1924, the club organized an overnight hike to the summit of Mount LeConte. Thompson joined the trek and took photographs, including one of the hikers atop the summit. His note on the back of the print reads, "Group on main top of Mt. LeConte, Oct. 1924. It was this trip that crystallized interest in the formation of a hiking club organized as the Smoky Mountains Hiking Club."[49] (The back of the photo lists the name of each hiker.)

Jim Thompson's friends and hiking companions—notably, Albert "Dutch" Roth, Carlos Campbell, and Brockway Crouch—were often "enlisted" to help carry his heavy camera equipment on many of the club's hikes. While each was a talented photographer in his own right (and Jim Thompson frequently printed their photos), they endearingly referred to themselves as Thompson's "porters."[50] In 1960 Campbell wrote *Birth of a National Park in the Great Smoky Mountains*, a detailed account of the effort to create the national park.

In an article titled "The Smoky Mountains Hiking Club: The Early Years," published by the University of Tennessee Libraries in their Spring 2003 issue of *Great Smoky Mountains*

Colloquy, the editors noted, "Among the membership in the earliest years are distinguished individuals whose respect for the wilderness and whose boundless energies were instrumental in promoting both Anne Davis's vision of 'a national park in the East,' and Benton MacKaye's proposal for a long trail over the full length of the Appalachian skyline, from the highest peak in the north to the highest peak in the south."[51] Jim Thompson would be at the forefront of both endeavors.

Thompson generously provided images for both local and national publications—exposure that garnered attention

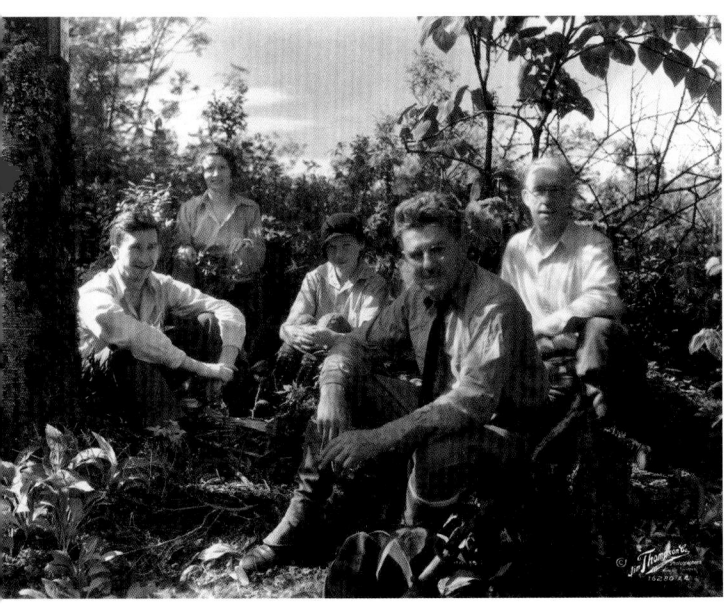

Colonel David Chapman (center) and group on the summit of Mount Chapman. Harvey Broome is on the left and Jim Thompson, on the right. Other hikers are Mrs. Charles Myers and Miss Mildred Query, year unknown. Photograph by Jim Thompson. McClung Historical Collection, Knox County Public Library, Smoky Mountains Photograph Collection, Thompson Brothers.

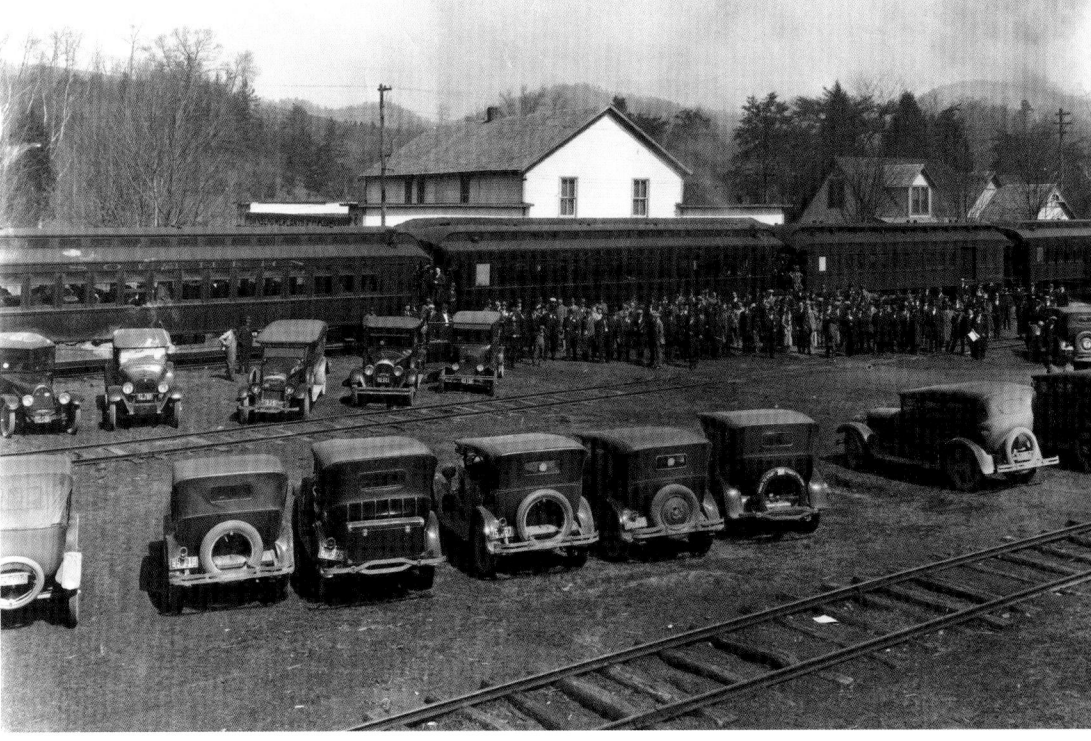

Tennessee legislators exiting trains in Townsend, Tennessee, for tour of Elkmont area of proposed Great Smoky Mountains National Park, 1925. Photograph by Jim Thompson. McClung Historical Collection, Knox County Public Library, Smoky Mountains Photograph Collection, Thompson Brothers.

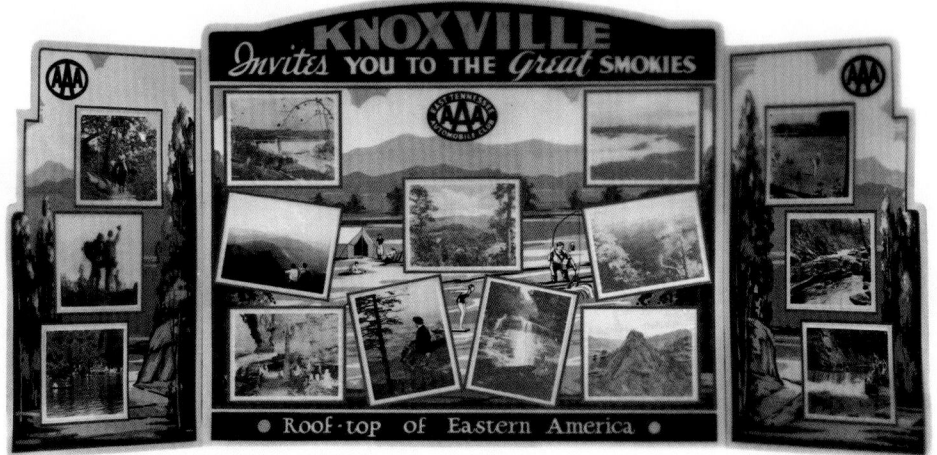

Jim Thompson's photographs illustrated the Knoxville Automobile Club's (AAA) promotion of travel to the Great Smoky Mountains "Rooftop of Eastern America," year unknown. Photograph by Jim Thompson. McClung Historical Collection, Knox County Public Library, Smoky Mountains Photograph Collection, Thompson Brothers.

from North Carolina outdoor writer and park supporter Horace Kephart. To illustrate his powerful piece "Last of the Eastern Wilderness," published in 1926 for the magazine *World's Work*, Kephart chose photographs taken by Jim Thompson. The essay, with its accompanying photographs, proved so compelling that it was reproduced in other guides and periodicals during the ongoing effort to create the park.

NAMING NATURE

In addition to his photographic work, Jim Thompson had a deep knowledge of the Smokies, which led to his appointment to the Tennessee Nomenclature Committee. Led by Paul Fink, the committee was charged by the U.S. Board of Geographic Names with determining the appropriate names for mountains, streams, and other natural features within the Tennessee boundaries of the planned national park. An entry in the 1929 SMHC handbook noted that "the United States Geological Survey is engaged in the work of accurately mapping the area of the Great Smoky Mountains

National Park ...It is suggested that members of the Club hand to the Secretary lists of such names as they now know and may obtain on future trips in the mountains."[52] Members were urged to send their information to SMHC president Jim Thompson. In a 1931 letter to Arno Cammerer, Paul Fink wrote, "Jim Thompson has done a monumental piece of work in transcribing every place name in the park area, arranging them alphabetically, with location, so that we can decide on elimination of duplications, unsuitable names, and the like."[53]

Nomenclature work was also well underway across the state line. Forester Verne Rhoades chaired the North Carolina Nomenclature Committee, with Horace Kephart also serving alongside him. Kephart was aided by George Masa, who provided images, trip notes, and detailed maps. Following Kephart's death in 1931, Masa continued to assist the committees, working with Rhoades, Thompson, Fink (who oversaw both committees), and others to finalize place-names throughout the Great Smokies.

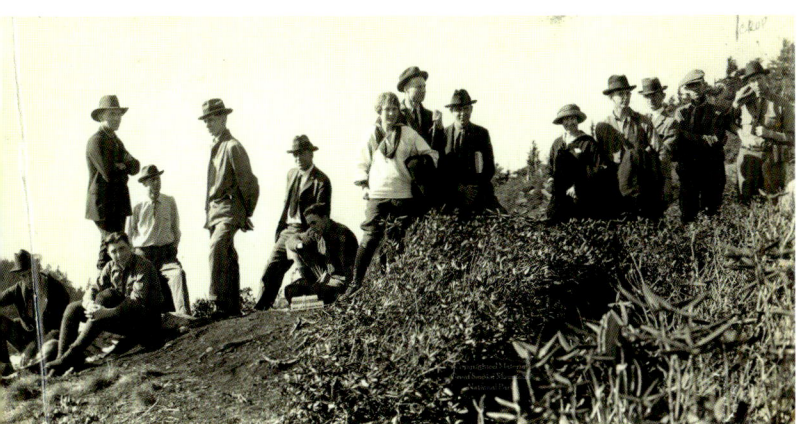

Hikers on the summit of Mount LeConte, October 1924. This trip prompted the establishment of the Smoky Mountains Hiking Club. Photograph by Jim Thompson. Western Carolina University, Hunter Library Special Collections.

PUTTING HIS STAMP ON THE NATIONAL PARK

To celebrate the establishment of the new Great Smoky Mountains National Park and to promote visitation to all the national parks, President Franklin D. Roosevelt declared 1934 to be National Parks Year. In support of the initiative, Roosevelt instructed Interior Secretary Harold Ickes and Postmaster General James Farley to produce ten unique postage stamps depicting scenes from the various national parks to be released during the year. Of the ten stamps, five were based on images by NPS chief photographer George Grant, and two were by landscape photographer Ansel Adams. The Great Smoky Mountains stamp, featuring Mount LeConte, was adapted from a photograph by Jim Thompson.

For many years Thompson would continue his photography on behalf of GSMCA and, later, the park service. He often accompanied groups on treks into the mountains

so that they could see firsthand the beauty they were being asked to preserve. In 1933 Thompson's image of Little Bald Mountain was featured in the booklet *The National Parks and Emergency Conservation*, published to highlight the work of the New Deal–era Civilian Conservation Corps' work in the national parks. On September 2, 1940, President Franklin D. Roosevelt officially dedicated Great

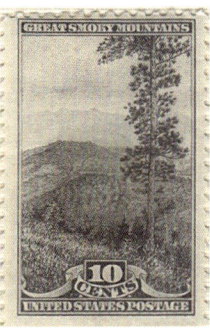

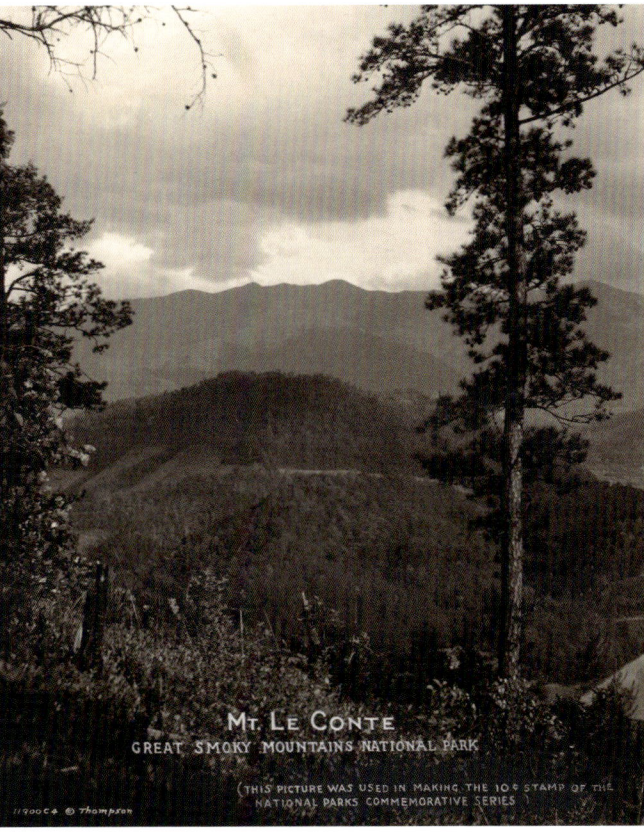

Jim Thompson's photograph of Mount LeConte that was adapted for use as a U.S. postage stamp, 1934. National Park Service, Great Smoky Mountains National Park Collections Preservation Center, Jim Thompson Collection. Postage Stamp image from the Ren and Helen Davis Collection.

Smoky Mountains National Park at a ceremony held at the Rockefeller Memorial in Newfound Gap. Thompson attended the event and took photographs of the crowds gathered to celebrate the long-sought accomplishment.

In addition to his work in support of the national park, Jim Thompson served on the ATC Board of Managers. As a leader of the SMHC, Thompson led many treks in the Smokies and organized sing-alongs at club gatherings. For many years his photographs were prominently featured in the SMHC annual handbook. In a brief biography of Thompson on the Knoxville History Project website Smoky Mountain Explorers, it was noted that "Jim's photography inspired millions of people over the years."[54]

In his AT work, Thompson and other club members conferred with Masa, Kephart, and others, including ATC leaders, to resolve disagreements and finalize a route for the trail through the Great Smokies. Where no trail existed, club members constructed the path by hand and marked it with distinctive AT signs. Beyond the Great Smokies, Thompson also worked closely with ATC chairman Myron Avery, among others, to survey and photograph potential AT routes across other Tennessee mountains.

In addition to his widely respected work as a commercial photographer, Jim Thompson was also a skilled newsreel filmmaker. In the mid-1920s, he befriended Robert Neyland, a new football coach at the University of Tennessee (UT). A West Point graduate and World War I veteran, Brigadier General Neyland had played football and later coached at the military academy before he accepted a faculty position at Tennessee in 1925, where he would teach military science. The following year, he was named head football coach and athletic director. This began his nearly three-decade-long, highly successful career

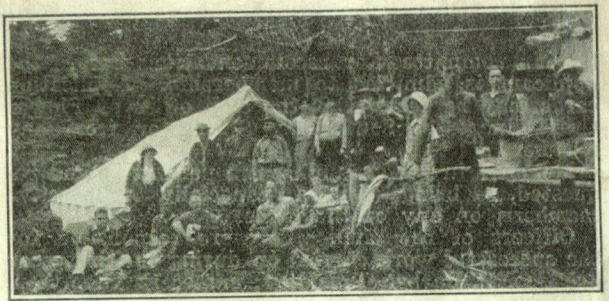

Members of Smoky Mountains Hiking Club on Mt. Le Conte, one of the most interesting and most distinctive mountains in America. This is in the heart of the proposed Great Smoky Mountains National Park.

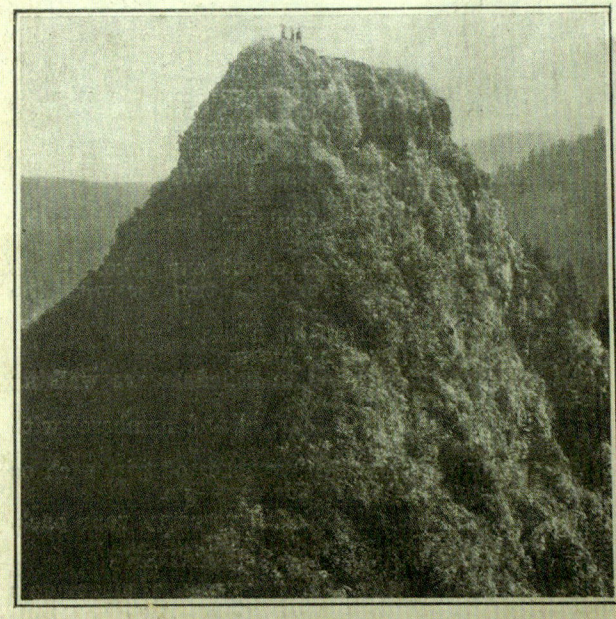

Three daring members of the Smoky Mountains Hiking Club on one of the "Chimneys". The photographer, another member of our club, was balancing himself on the other "Chimney top".

Photographs by Jim Thompson were frequently used to illustrate the Smoky Mountains Hiking Club annual handbook, ca. 1926. University of Tennessee–Knoxville, Hodges Library, Betsy B. Creekmore Special Collections and University Archives, Smoky Mountains Hiking Club Collection.

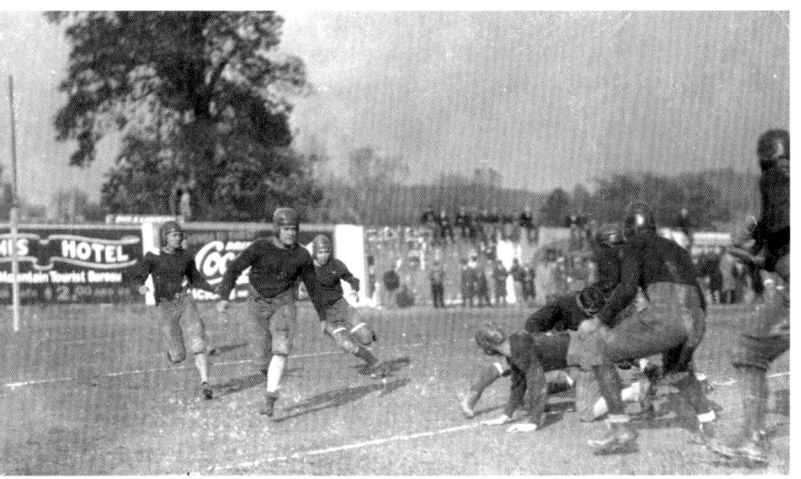

The University of Tennessee Volunteers football team in action during the mid-1920s. Photograph by Jim Thompson. McClung Historical Collection, Knox County Public Library, Jim Thompson, Thompson Brothers.

at the university, though he was also twice interrupted for military service—first, in the Panama Canal Zone in the 1930s and, again, during World War II.

General Neyland recognized the value of film study for analyzing past games and preparing for upcoming contests. He asked Thompson to serve as the athletic department's official photographer, filming Tennessee football games for review during the upcoming week. In the beginning Thompson worked from the stands, with the opposing teams and fans objecting to his filming the contests. In an interview on August 3, 1975, published in the *Knoxville News Sentinel*, Thompson recalled, "The Georgia people got very upset at the thought of it. They had people try to stand in front of my camera."[55] As a consequence, there were threats to cancel future games, and the use of cameras was banned for several years. Thompson began filming home games in the 1920s,

later adding road contests until the early 1960s. Notably, he accompanied the football team and its supporters to the 1940 Rose Bowl in Pasadena, California, where he shot color films of both the Rose Parade and the game against the University of Southern California (Tennessee lost 14–0). His son, Bert, also filmed UT basketball games for many years.

A MEETING WITH MARGARET BOURKE-WHITE?

Given his knowledge of the region, Jim Thompson was occasionally asked to assist journalists and photographers traveling on assignments to the area. According to Thompson's grandson, also James Thompson, this may have been the case when the elder Thompson escorted renowned photojournalist Margaret Bourke-White on a trip into the mountains. The younger Thompson recalled his grandfather talking about the experience but was uncertain of the date of the meeting. Research conducted in Knoxville newspaper archives reveals that Bourke-White traveled to Knoxville on at least two occasions, in 1935 and again in 1941.

It is possible that Thompson and Bourke-White met during her 1935 visit, when she was on assignment for Eastern Air Transport (later, Eastern Air Lines) and the Newspaper Enterprise Service (NEA) to produce photographs in the Tennessee Valley area. At the time, she was working with writer Erskine Caldwell (her future husband) on the book *You Have Seen Their Faces*, published in 1937. Bourke-White spent eighteen months crisscrossing the South, capturing images of impoverished people's living conditions during the depths of the Great Depression. Jim Thompson's grandson's clearest recollection of the meeting was his grandfather's humorous comment on first meeting Bourke-White, when he said he had "never before seen so much camera equipment loaded into an automobile!"[56]

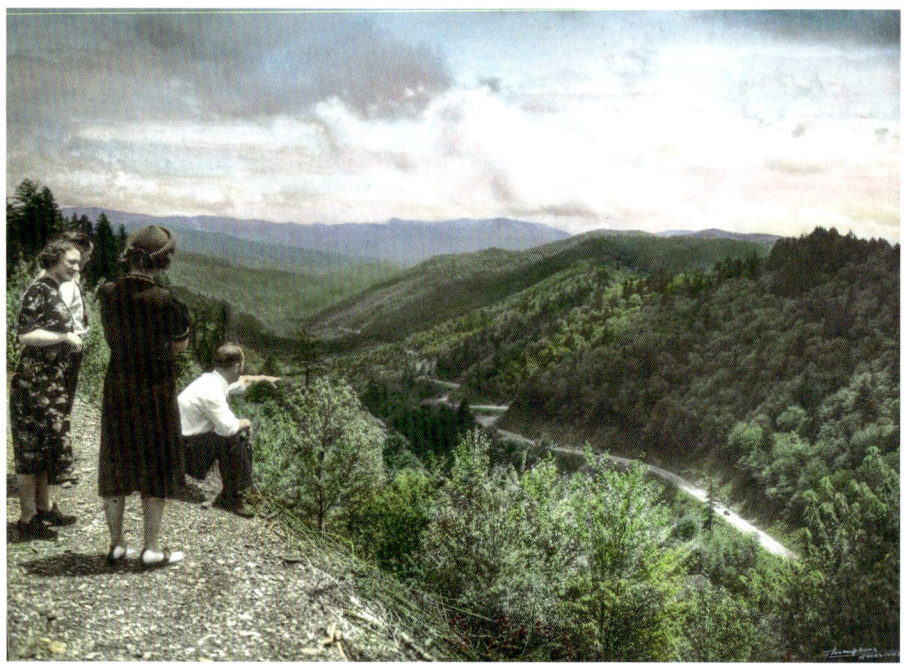

A colorized photograph of visitors enjoying the view from Newfound Gap in the Great Smoky Mountains National Park, ca. 1940. Photograph by Jim Thompson. National Park Service, Great Smoky Mountains National Park Collections Preservation Center, Jim Thompson Collection.

In addition to managing the camera stores and commercial studio, Jim Thompson continued to hike and photograph in the Smokies, producing perhaps the largest individual collection of images of the park in existence at the time. Many of his iconic black-and-white landscape prints were colored by hand by a cadre of "colorers," including his wife Emily, whom he employed to tackle this tedious work. Such "colorized" prints and postcards proved popular with tourists until the 1950s, when color film became readily available for general use.

THE MASTER PHOTOGRAPHER

Jim Thompson earned several honors during his working career. In the 1950s the National Photographers Association of America named him a Master Photographer. He was also a dedicated Rotarian, receiving an award for twenty-one years of perfect attendance in 1938. However, Thompson did not rest on his laurels, and he extended his perfect attendance record to more than forty years. His commitment to Rotary was noted by Paul James who wrote, "Following a mishap, Thompson had colleagues bring him to a meeting on a stretcher rather than blot his record."[57]

Thompson and Emily built a vacation cabin in Gatlinburg, which provided a retreat from work and easy access to the mountains. They dubbed it Shangri-la and spent much of their time there as they grew older. In 1952, shortly after the couple celebrated their fiftieth wedding anniversary, Emily died during a visit to the cabin. Twelve years later, Jim Thompson remarried, choosing his longtime friend and store employee, Margaret Arning, as his spouse.

In the 1960s, shortly after retiring, Thompson sold five hundred of his Great Smoky Mountains negatives to Mildred Kite, who later resold them to Gene Walker, a local entrepreneur planning to print and sell copies. Walker was not an expert photographer and lacked the skills and equipment needed to print high-quality images. He eventually abandoned the venture and moved to Puerto Rico. Unfortunately, the whereabouts of the negatives once in his possession remains unknown.

As Jim Thompson approached his ninetieth birthday, he received a request from Pollyanna Creedmore, the librarian of the Calvin M. McClung Historical Collection at Knoxville's Lawson McGhee Library, to donate his extensive portfolio of images of Knoxville, the Great Smokies, and the surrounding region to the library's archives. Thompson readily agreed, and his collection of nearly seventy thousand prints and negatives now resides in the library's Special Collections. Images from the two Thompson collections, the Thompson Photograph Collection and the Great Smoky Mountains Photograph Collection—Thompson Brothers, are accessible to researchers, with portions viewable on the library's website. Today the collections represent an unsurpassed legacy of the beauty of the nearby Smoky Mountains, as well as the city's and region's growth during the twentieth century.

Of Thompson's commitment to the Smokies, Paul James wrote, "[His] photographs of the Smoky Mountains featured in national newspapers and publications helped boost a movement to create a national park beyond his hometown. More than a few of his photographs are considered iconic. Outside of photography, he worked to build trails and determine lasting place names that still inform visitors' experiences in the Smokies today."[58]

Jim Thompson died in 1976 at the age of ninety-four and is buried at Berry Highland Cemetery in Knoxville. To the nation's great benefit, many of his photographs of the Great Smoky Mountains endure, delighting those who seek to appreciate the beauty of the mountains he so lovingly worked to save and the national park he helped to create.

Notes

1. Carroll McMahan, "Man of the Mountains: George Masa's Pivotal Role in Preserving Mountain Landscapes," *Smoky Mountain Living Magazine*, August 1, 2014, www.smliv.com/stories/man-of-the-mountains.

2. *The Mystery of George Masa*, "Interview with Gil Leebrick," directed by Paul Bonesteel, written by Paul Bonesteel and Trent Bouts (Bonesteel Films, 2002; PBS North Carolina Presents, aired 2003), 58 min., 2 sec.

3. Susan Miles, "A Photographic Memory: George Masa's Life Journey Carried Him across an Ocean and Landed Him in Asheville, Where His Passion for Photography Drove Him to Explore WNC's Roughest Wilderness," *WNC Magazine: Mountain Living in Western North Carolina*, July 2009, https://wncmagazine.com/feature/photographic_memory.

4. Janet McCue and Paul Bonesteel, *George Masa: A Life Reimagined* (Gatlinburg, Tenn.: Smokies Life, 2024), 175.

5. Ibid., 175.

6. Ibid., 185–6.

7. July 1915 journal entry, shared by author Susan Shumaker, *George Masa: A Report for America's Best Idea: Our National Parks*, April 2005, 2, research report for Florentine Films, hereafter cited as FF.

8. July 11, 1915, journal entry in FF, 2.

9. July 12, 1915, journal entry in FF, 2.

10. Immigration Act of 1917, Pub. L. No. 64-301, 39 Stat. 874 (1917): An act to regulate the immigration of aliens to, as well as the residence of aliens in, the United States, enacted February 5, 1917.

11. George Masa to Miss L. Scott (Fred Seely's secretary), May 4, 1917, FF, 3.

12. George Masa to Fred Seely, July 4, 1917, FF, 3.

13. McCue and Bonesteel, *George Masa,* 38.

14. George Masa to Fred Seely, February 25, 1919, FF, 4.

15. George Masa to Fred Seely, December 13, 1919. FF, 4.

16. McCue and Bonesteel, *George Masa,* 59.

17. Ibid., 59.

18. Ibid., 63.

19. Ibid., 64.

20. *The Mystery of George Masa*, directed by Paul Bonesteel (Asheville: Bonesteel Films, 2003).

21. Tom Alexander Jr. and Jane D. Alexander, eds., *Mountain Fever: Tom Alexander* (Asheville, N.C.: Bright Mountain Books, 1995), 57.

22. Arno Cammerer to George Masa, April 6, 1931, Pack Memorial Library, Asheville, N.C., hereafter cited as PML.

23. Virginia Lathrop, "The Little Jap," *The State* 21, no. 14 (September 1953): 4.

24. Horace Kephart to Paul Fink, January 28, 1920, in George Ellison and Janet McCue, *Back of Beyond* (Gatlinburg, Tenn.: Great Smoky Mountains Association, 2019), 270.

25. Arno Cammerer to George Masa, March 21, 1930, Hunter Library Special Collections, Western Carolina University, Cullowhee, N.C.

26. Ellison and McCue, *Back of Beyond*, 305.

27. Paul Fink to George Masa, March 15, 1931, *Masa Report*, FF, 6.

28. Mrs. Barbara A. Thorne, "George Masa: The Best Mountaineer," June 3, 1996, interview by William A. Hart Jr., in Robert S. Brunk, ed., *May We All Remember Well: A Journal of the History & Cultures of Western North Carolina*, vol. 1 (Asheville, N.C.: Robert S. Brunk Auction Services, 1997), 257.

29. George Masa to Margaret Gooch, March 2, 1931, *Masa Report*, FF, 10.

30. McCue and Bonesteel, *George Masa*, 152–53.

31. Thorne, "George Masa: The Best Mountaineer," interview by Hart, *May We All Remember Well*, 268.

32. George Masa to Margaret Gooch, April 3, 1931, *Masa Report*, FF, 13.

33. George Masa to Paul Fink, April 19, 1931, *Masa Report*, FF, 14.

34. George Masa to Myron Avery, April 10, 1931, Appalachian Trail Conservancy Records, Myron Avery Collection, George Mason University Special Collections and Archives, Fairfax, Va.

35. *The Mystery of George Masa*.

36. George Masa to Margaret Gooch, October 20, 1931, *Masa Report*, FF, 15.

37. Avery to Appalachian Trail Conference Board of Managers, February 15, 1932, PML.

38. *Carolina Mountain Club Bulletin*, vol. 3, no. 7, July 1933, PML.

39. George McCoy to I. K. Stearns, August 5, 1933, PML.

40. Paul Bonesteel to Ren and Helen Davis, October 16, 2023, *Masa Report*, FF, 16–17.

41. Carolina Mountain Club Collection, Box 38, Documents Related to George Masa, University of North Carolina Asheville Special Collections and Archives.

42. Arno Cammerer to George Masa, February 16, 1933, PML.

43. President Barack Obama, "Remarks by the President on America's Great Outdoors Initiative," The White House, released February 16, 2011, https://obamawhitehouse.archives.gov/the-press-office/2011/02/16/remarks-president-americas-great-outdoors-initiative.

44. North Carolina Department of Natural and Cultural Resources, "George Masa d. 1933 (P-99)," Historical Markers, published January 23, 2024, https://www.dncr.nc.gov/blog/2024/01/23/george-masa-d-1933-p-99.

45. Paul James, "The Photographic Conservationist: The Surprising Legacy of Jim Thompson," *Knoxville Lives II* (Knoxville, Tenn.: Knoxville History Project, 2020), 46.

46. Jesse Fox Mayshark, "Photographer Jim Thompson Started His Business in Downtown Knoxville 100 Years Ago. It's Still There and So Are His Pictures," *Metro Pulse Online*, June 27, 2002.

47. James, "The Photographic Conservationist," 51.

48. Ibid., 61.

49. Thompson photography collection, Great Smoky Mountains National Park (GRSM) 24106, Great Smoky Mountains National Park Library and Archives.

50. James, "The Photographic Conservationist," 59.

51. Editors, "The Smoky Mountains Hiking Club: The Early Years," *Great Smoky Mountains Colloquy* 4, no. 1 (Spring 2003): 1–3.

52. 1929 SMHC Handbook, UTK Libraries Special Collections, Smoky Mountains Hiking Club Collection.

53. James, "The Photographic Conservationist," 57.

54. "Birth of a National Park in the Smokies," Knoxville History Project, last modified July 2024, https://knoxvillehistoryproject.org/smokies.

55. Marvin West, "Pictures from the Past: Fans Made Cameraman 'Shutter,'" *Knoxville News Sentinel*, August 3, 1975, D2–3.

56. Ren and Helen Davis, telephone conversation with Jim Thompson (grandson), April 19, 2021.

57. James, "The Photographic Conservationist," 64.

58. Ibid., 43.

PHOTOGRAPHS

George Masa

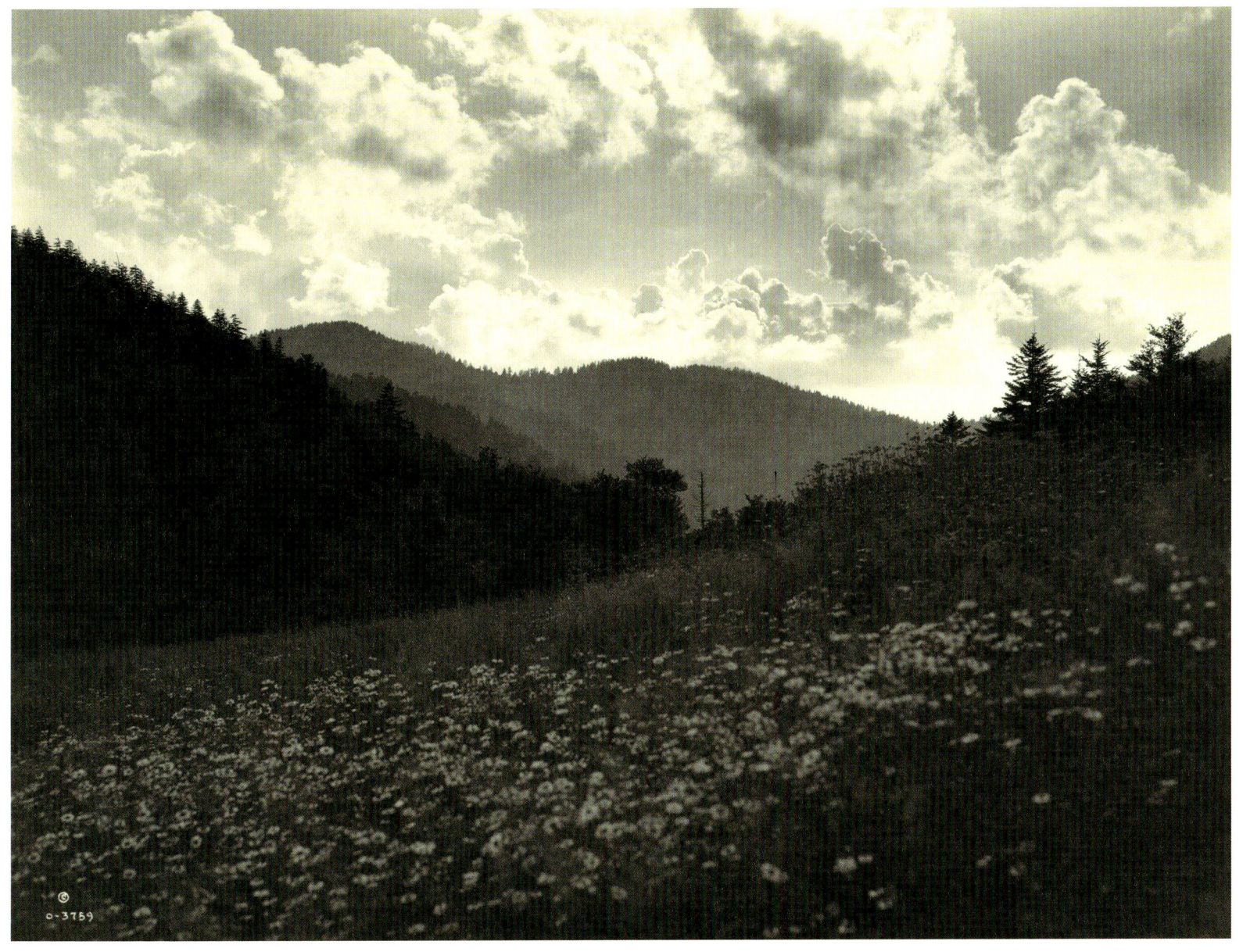

1   A sunset scene in Indian Gap. Courtesy of Smokies Life.

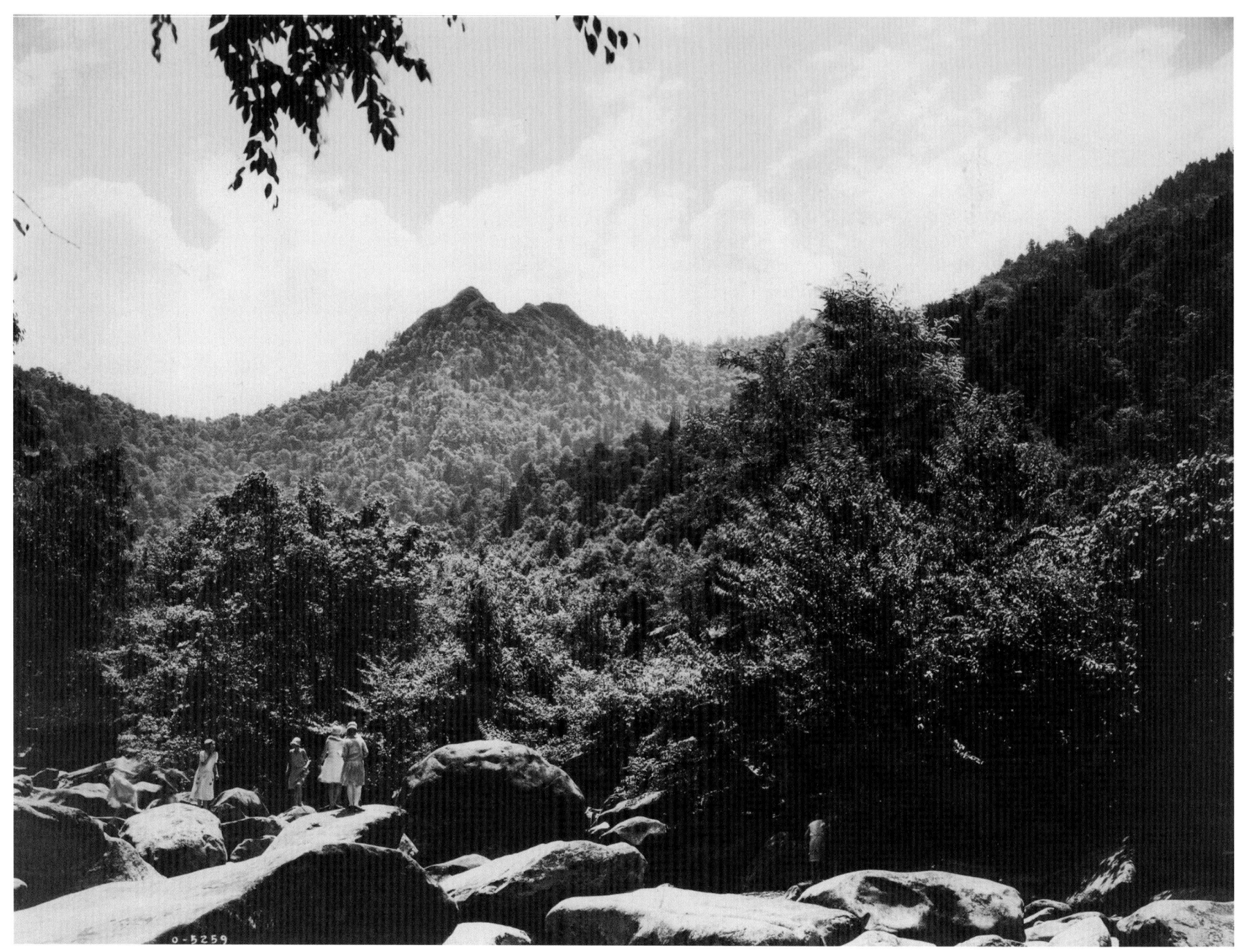

2 Chimney Tops and people in the Great Smokies. Courtesy of Pack Memorial Library.

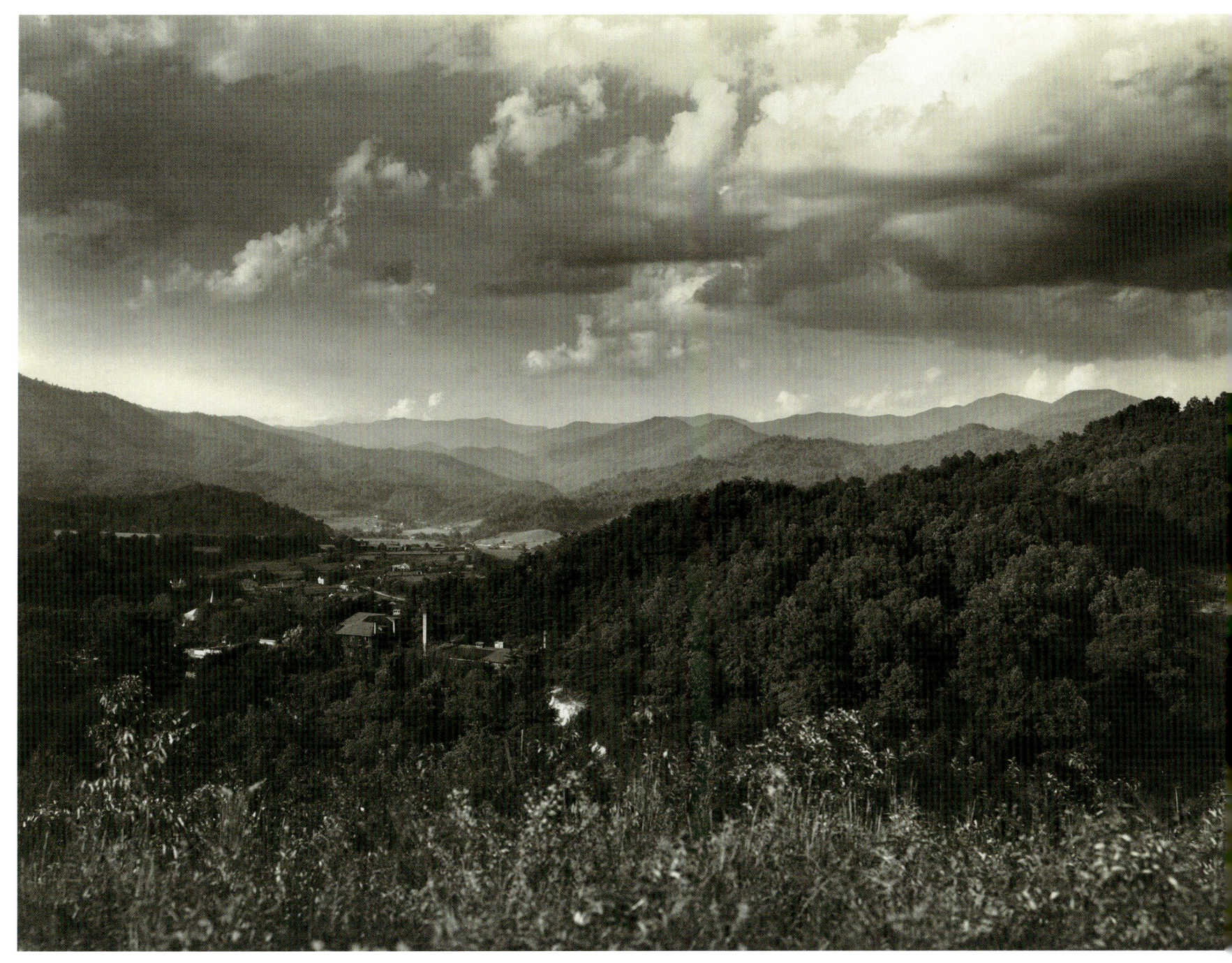

3   Bryson City with clouds over the mountains. Courtesy of Smokies Life.

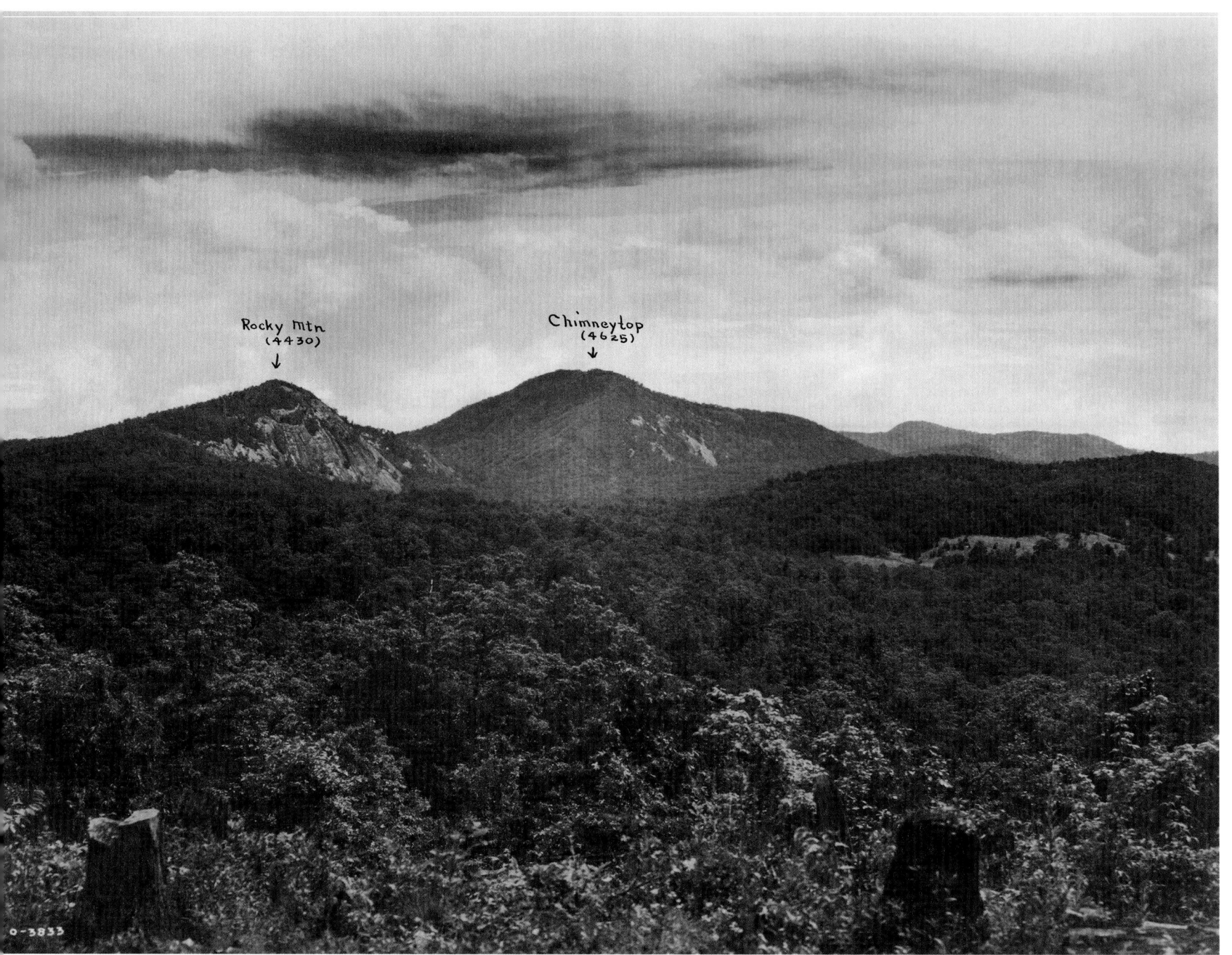

Rocky Mtn
(4430)

Chimneytop
(4625)

O-3833

4   Chimney Tops and Rocky Mountain, with notations. Courtesy of Smokies Life.

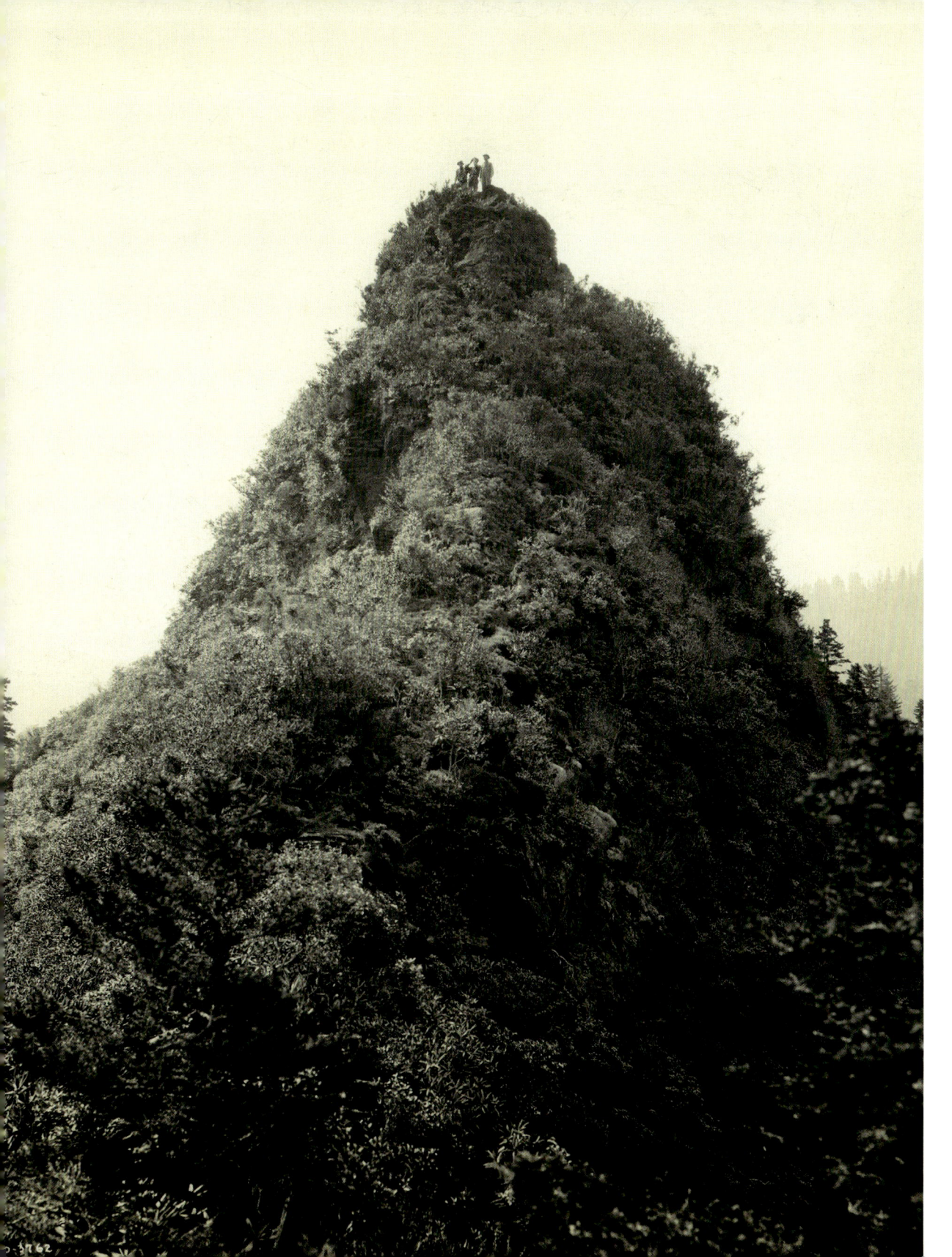

5 Chimney Tops with people on the summit. Courtesy of Smokies Life.

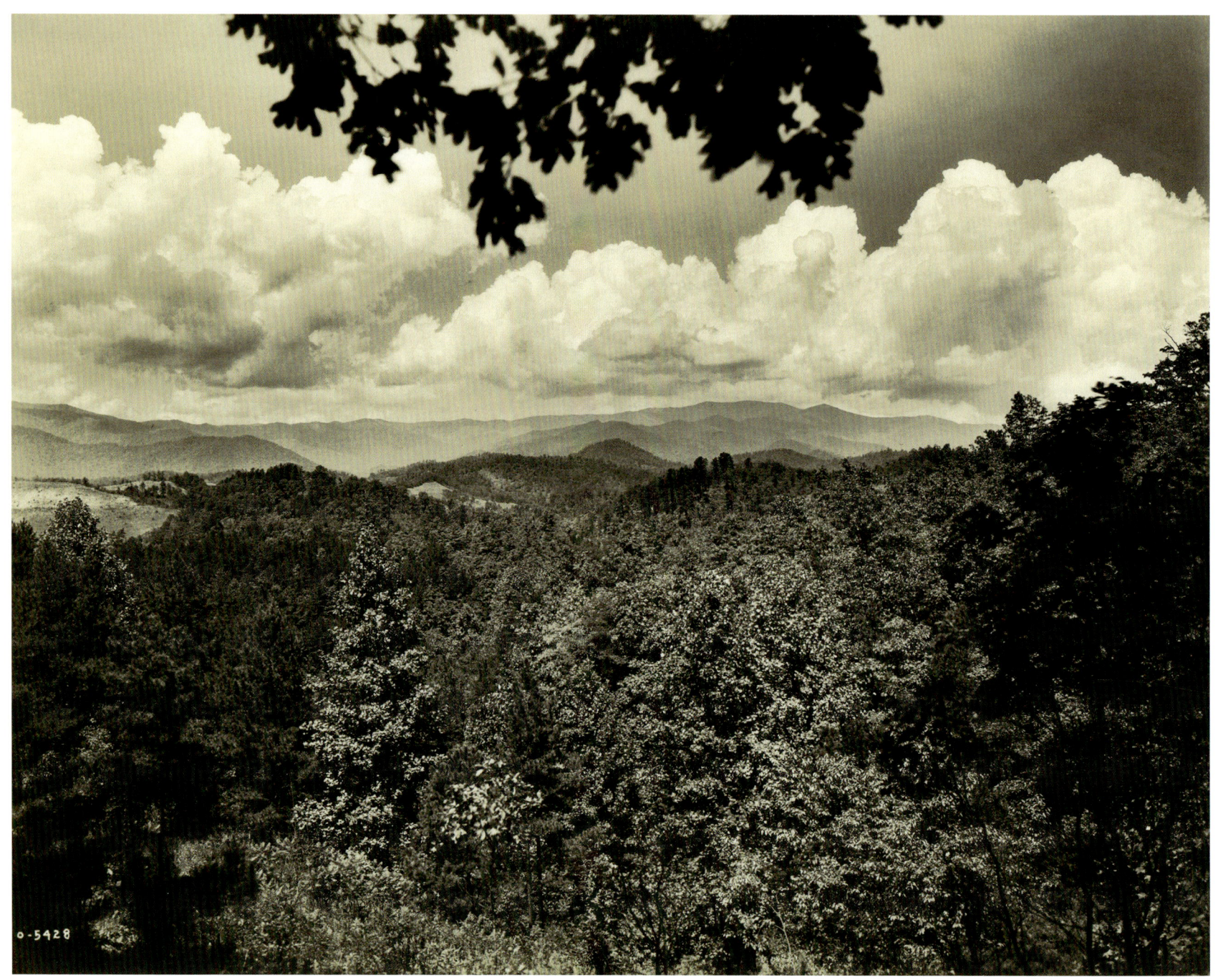

6   View westward to Kuwohi, formerly Clingmans Dome. Courtesy of Smokies Life.

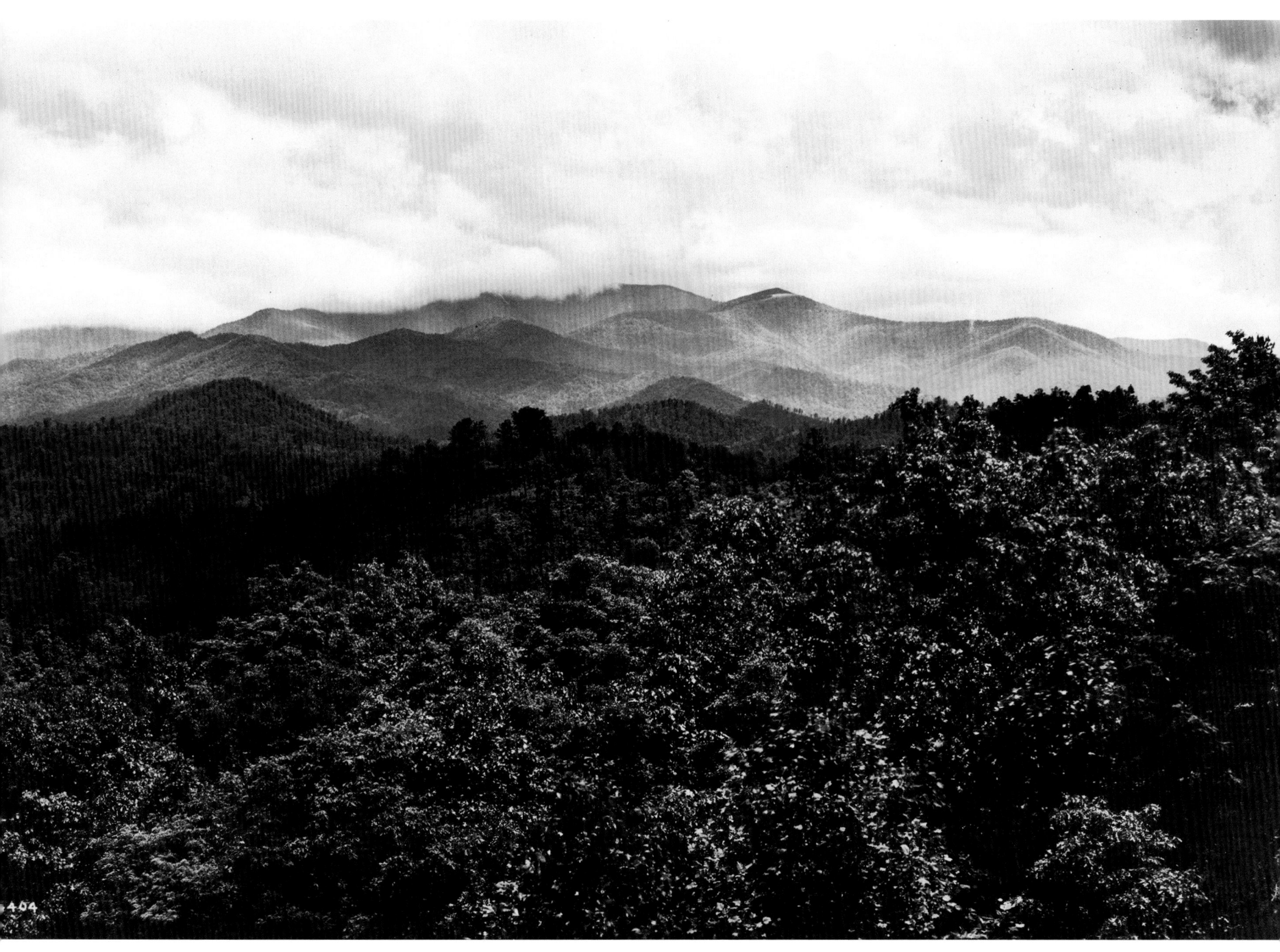

7   Kuwohi shrouded in clouds. Courtesy of Smokies Life.

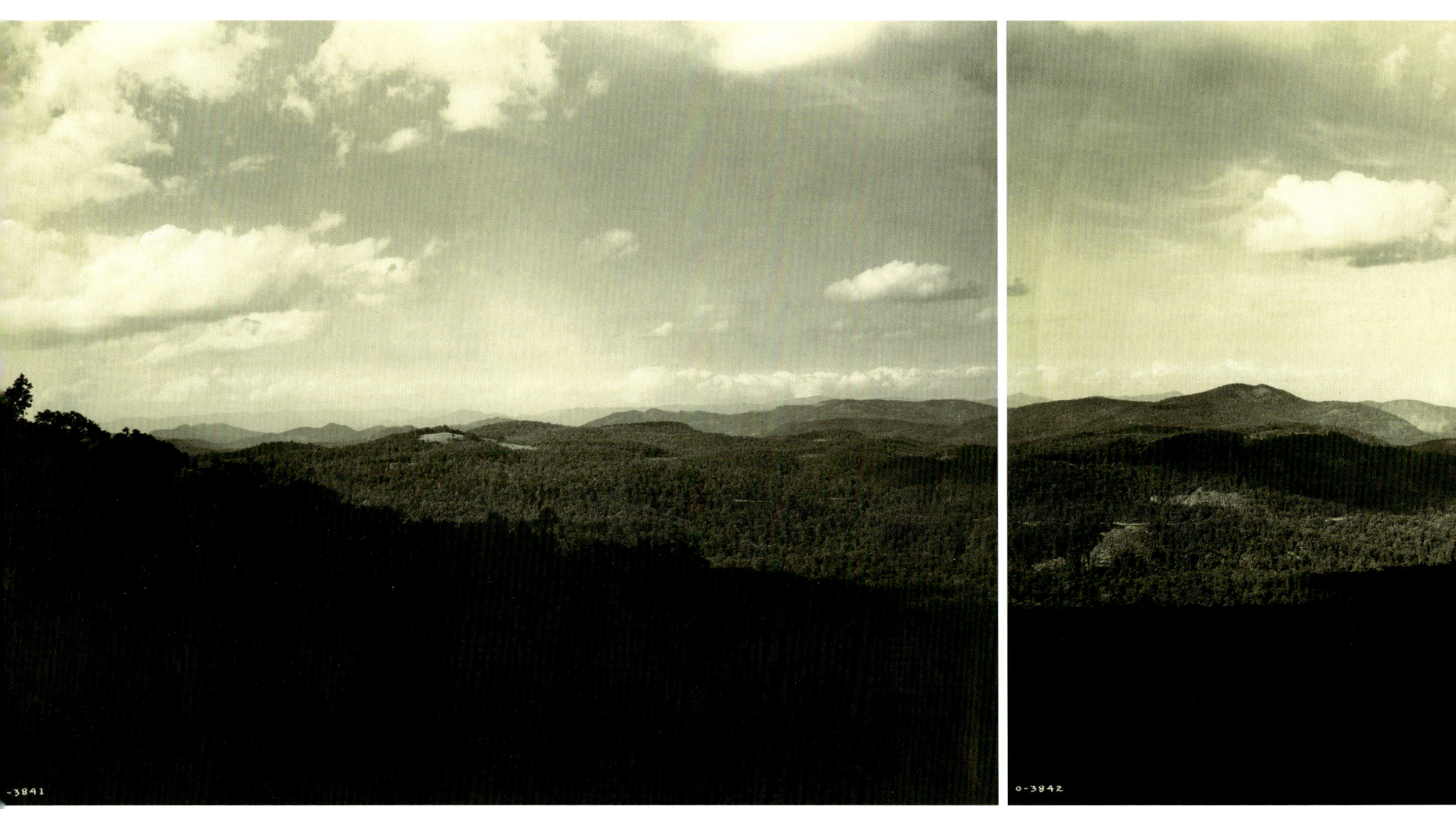

8   Highway 28 panorama, left image. Courtesy of Smokies Life.

9   Highway 28 panorama, center image. Courtesy of Smokies Life.

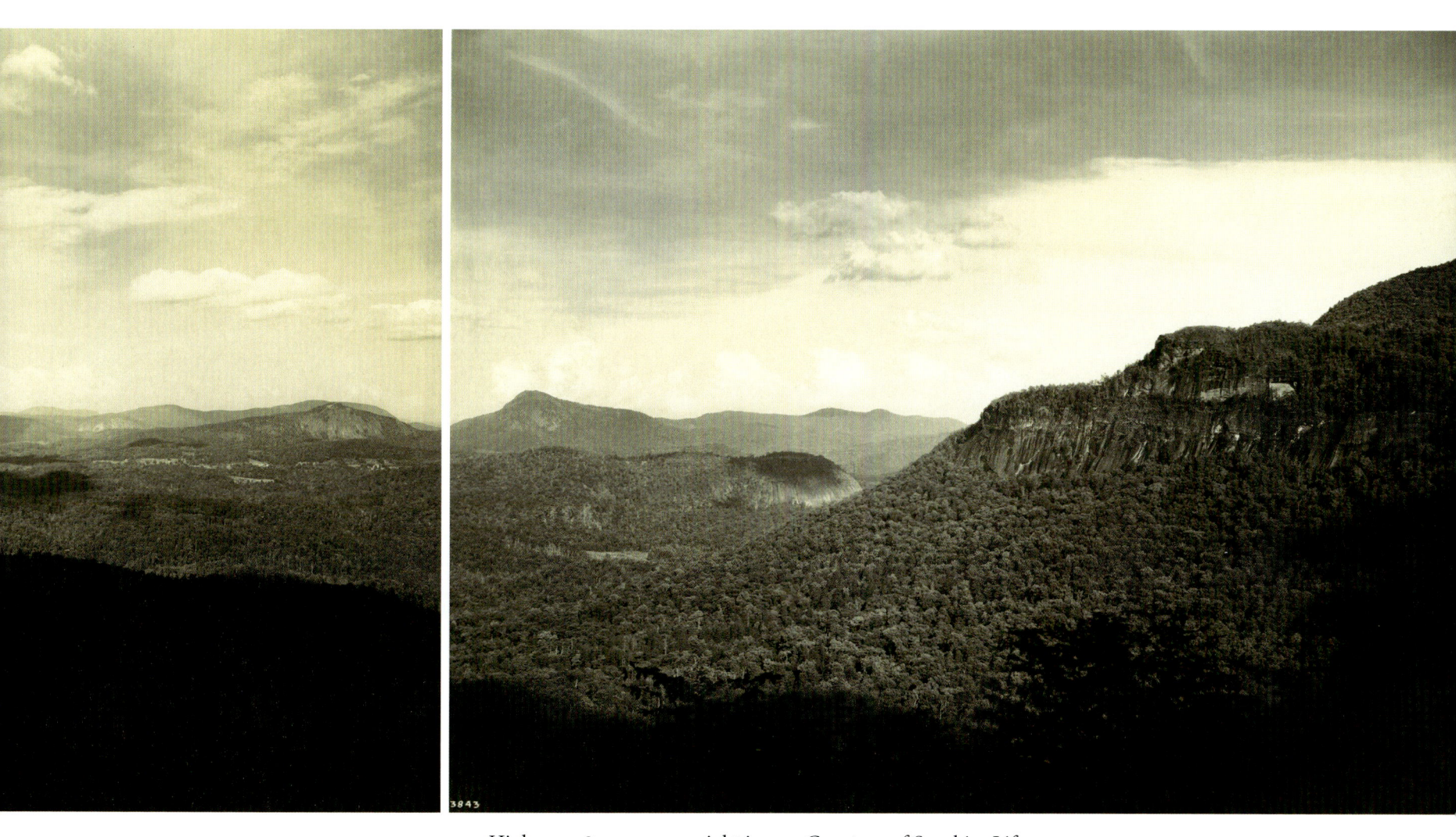

10   Highway 28 panorama, right image. Courtesy of Smokies Life.

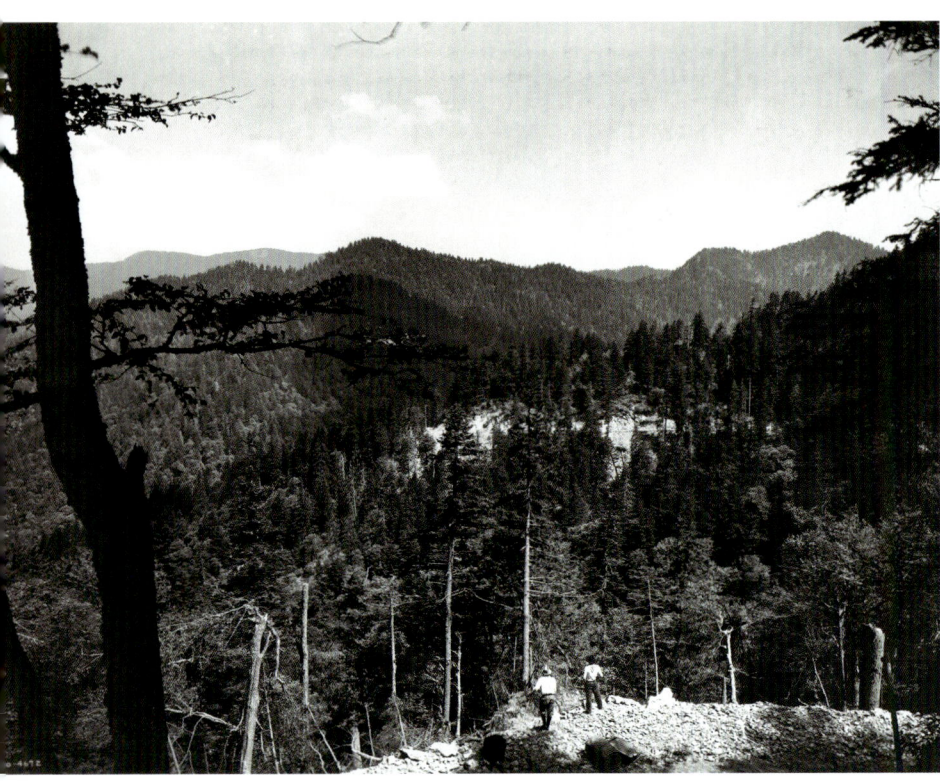

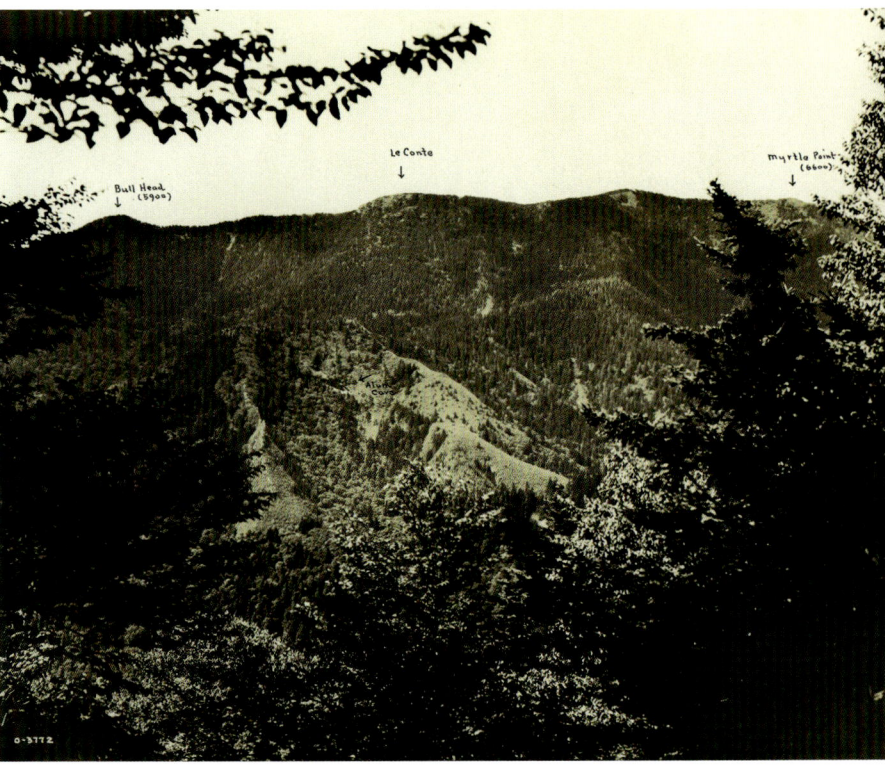

11   View from Newfound Gap. Courtesy of Smokies Life.

12   Mount LeConte and Alum Cave area, with handwritten notations. Courtesy of Smokies Life.

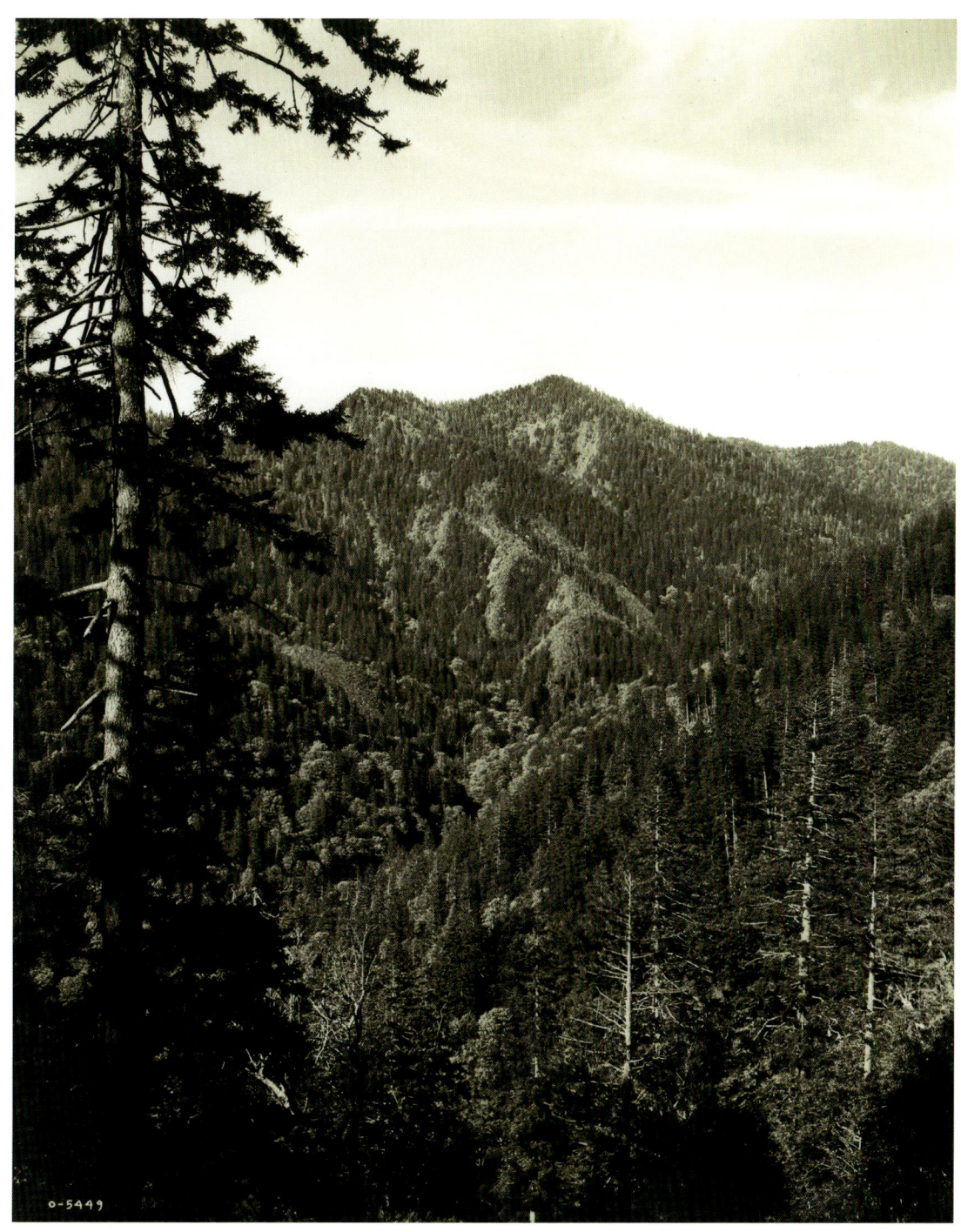

13   A mountain view with tree in the
      foreground. Courtesy of Smokies Life.

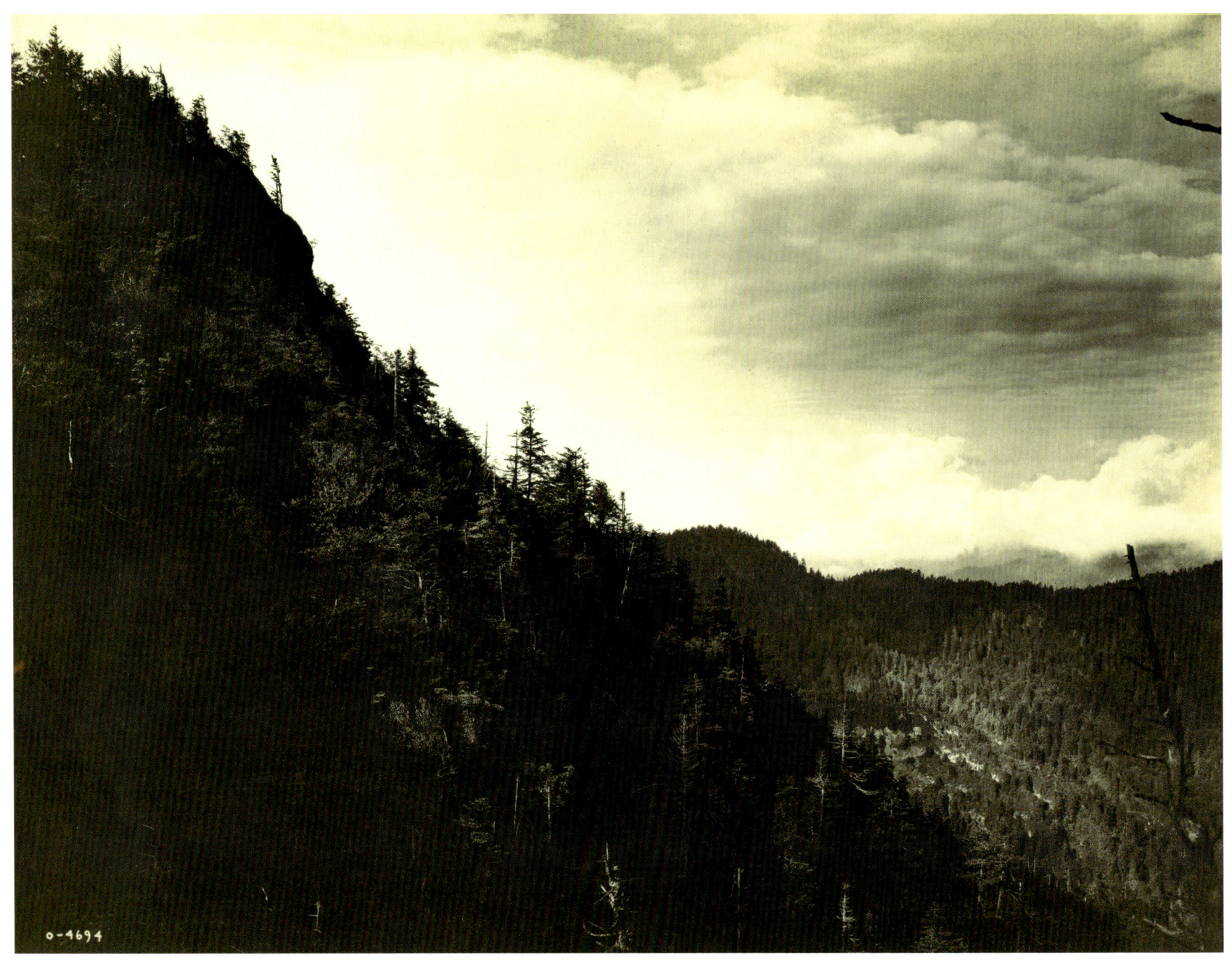

14   A view of mountains from the state line east of Hughes Ridge. Courtesy of Smokies Life.

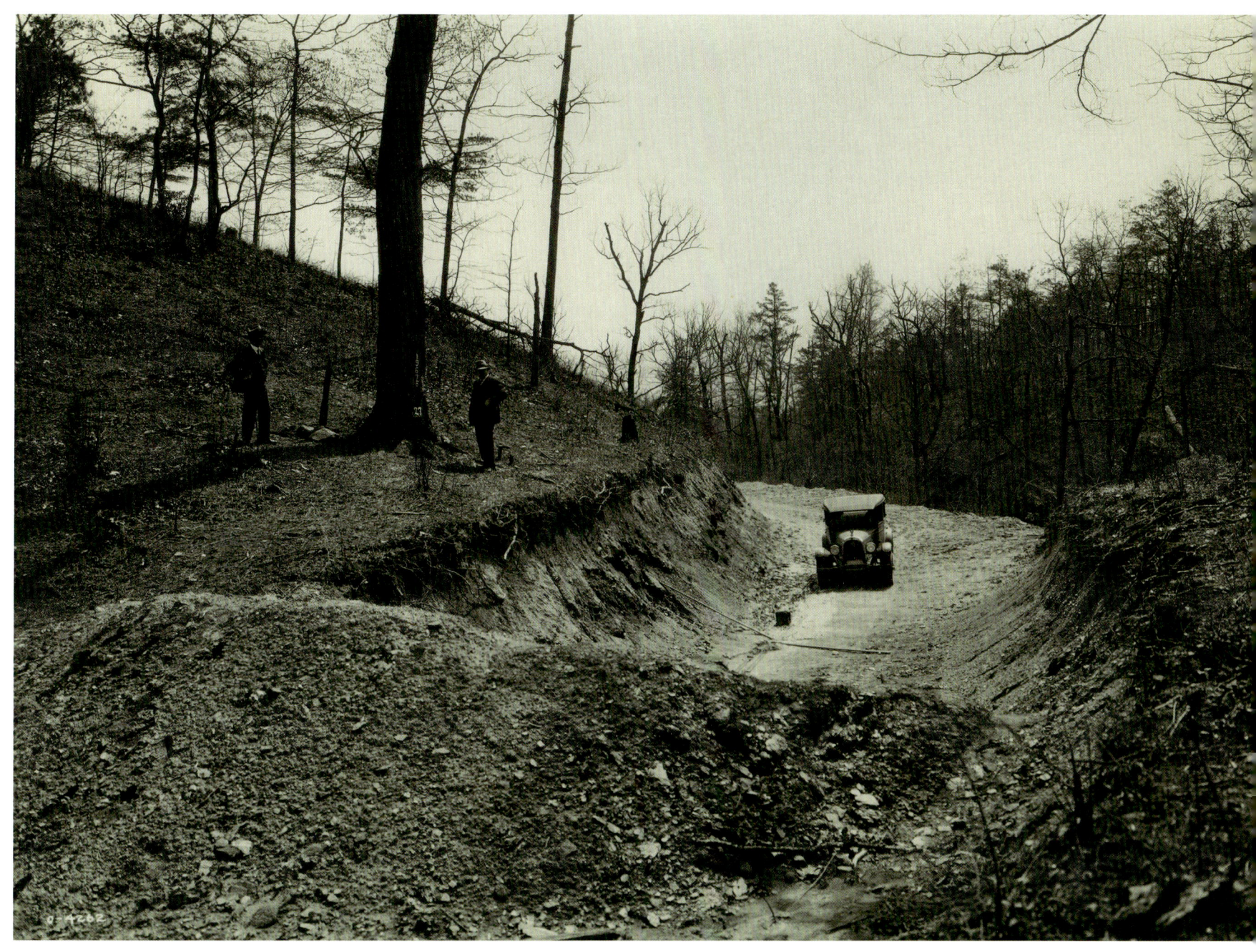

15 An automobile at the end of unfinished N.C. Highway 28, near Deals Gap, North Carolina, 1929.
Courtesy of Smokies Life.

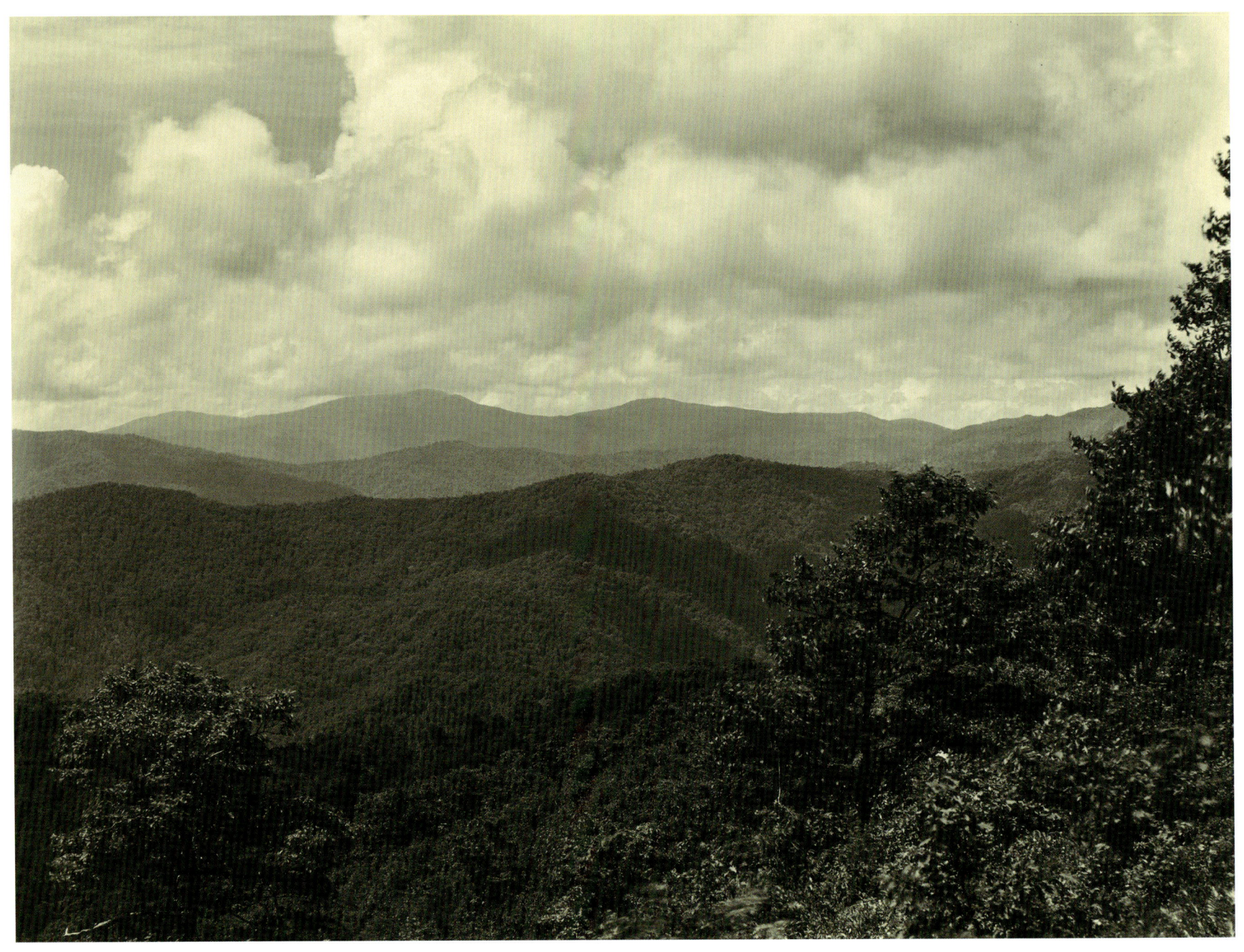

16   Mount Kephart and Kuwohi. Courtesy of Smokies Life.

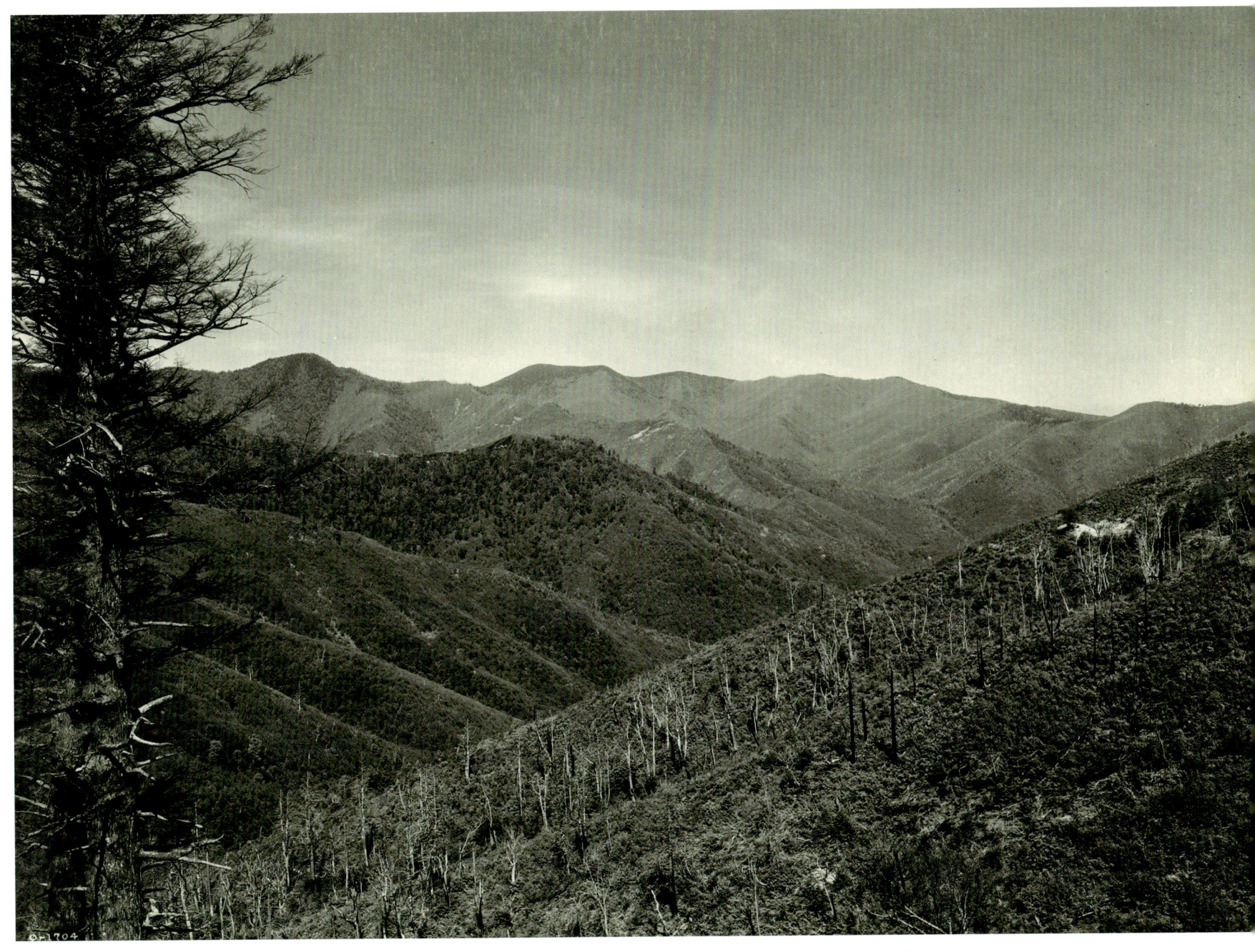

17   A view of Mount Guyot from Swallow Creek. An annotated version of this image was given to ATC president

Myron Avery to show results of timber cutting. See page 10. Courtesy of Smokies Life.

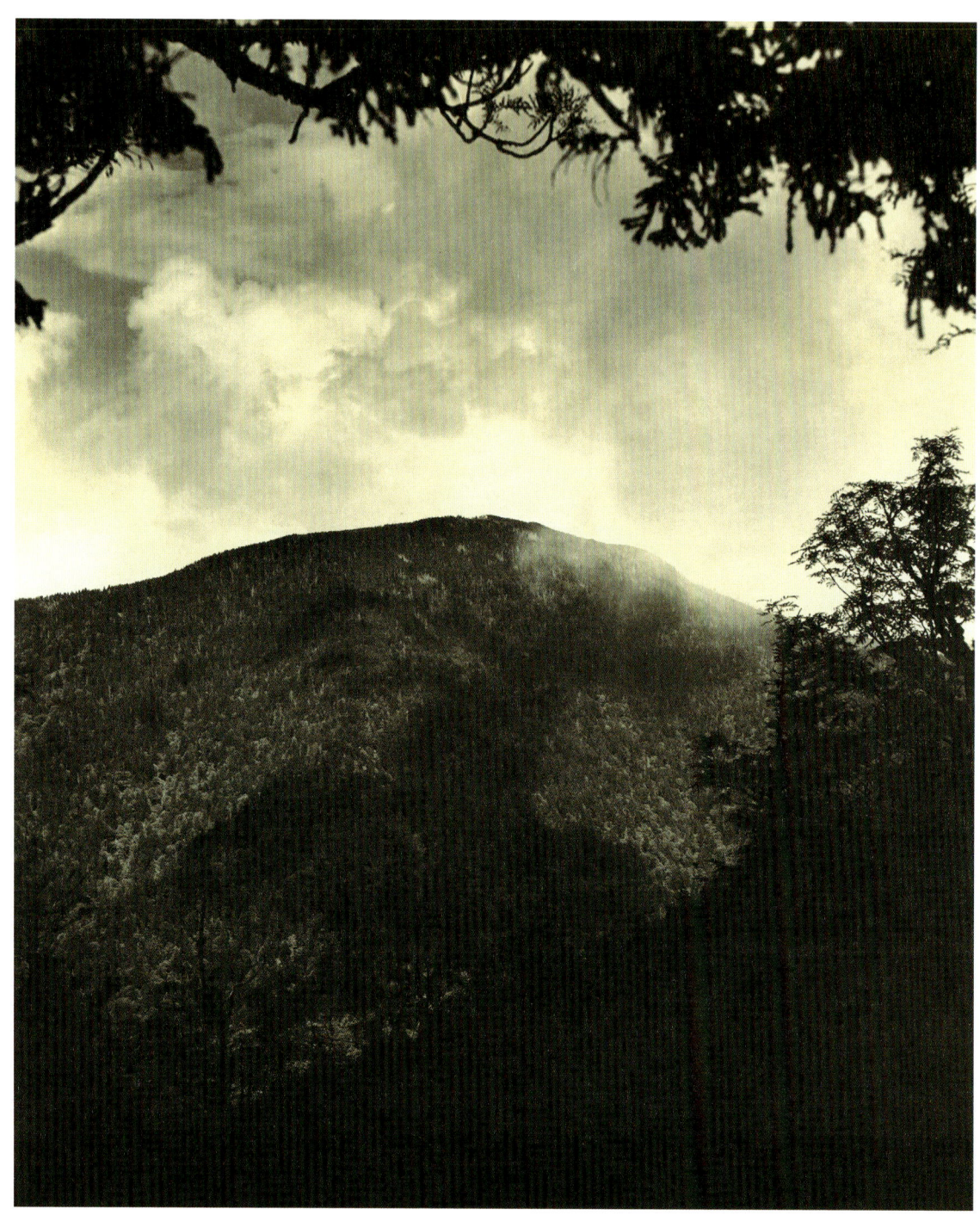

18   Mount Guyot from the Old Black
Mountain. Courtesy of
Smokies Life.

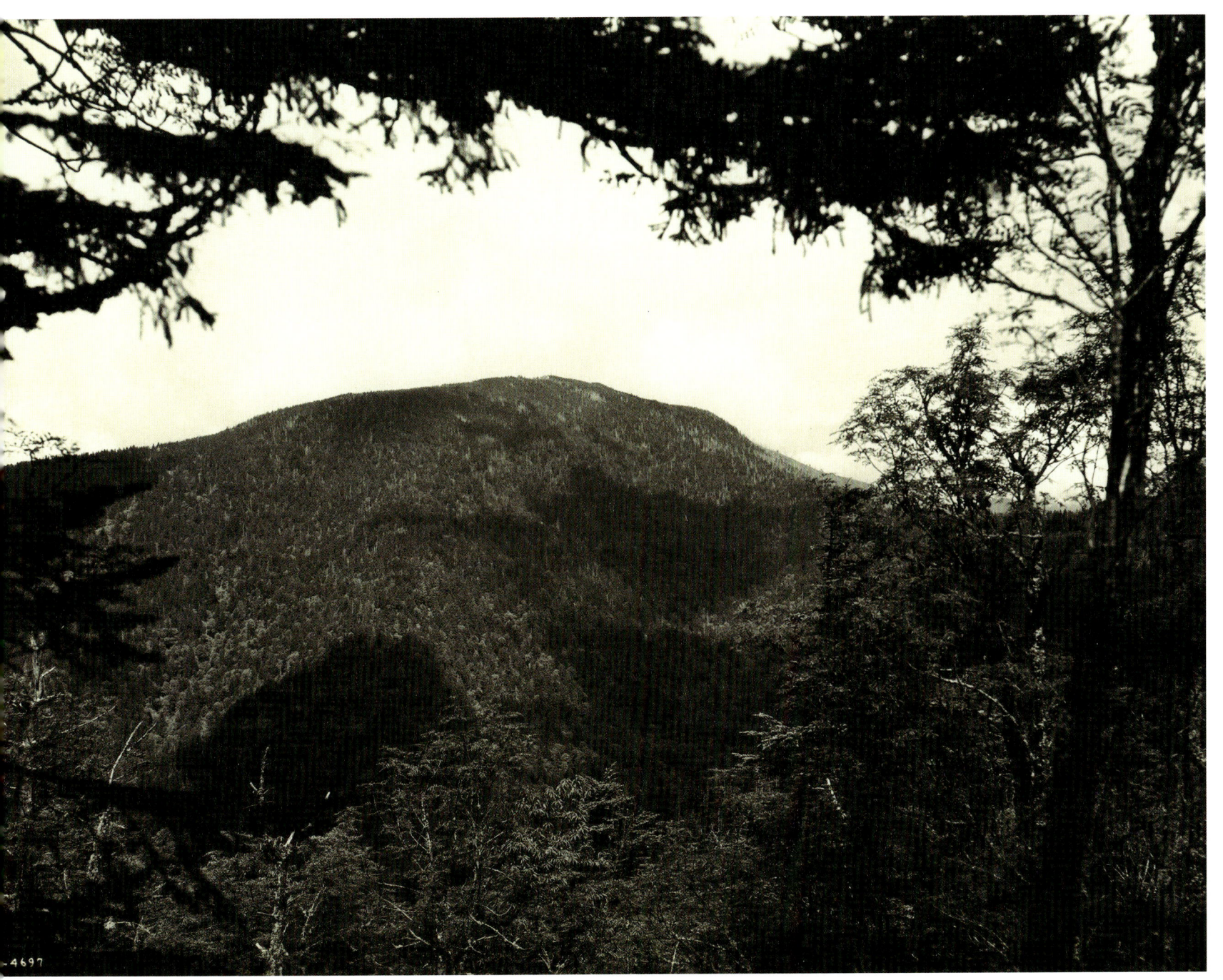

19   Mount Guyot from the Old Black Mountain. Courtesy of Smokies Life.

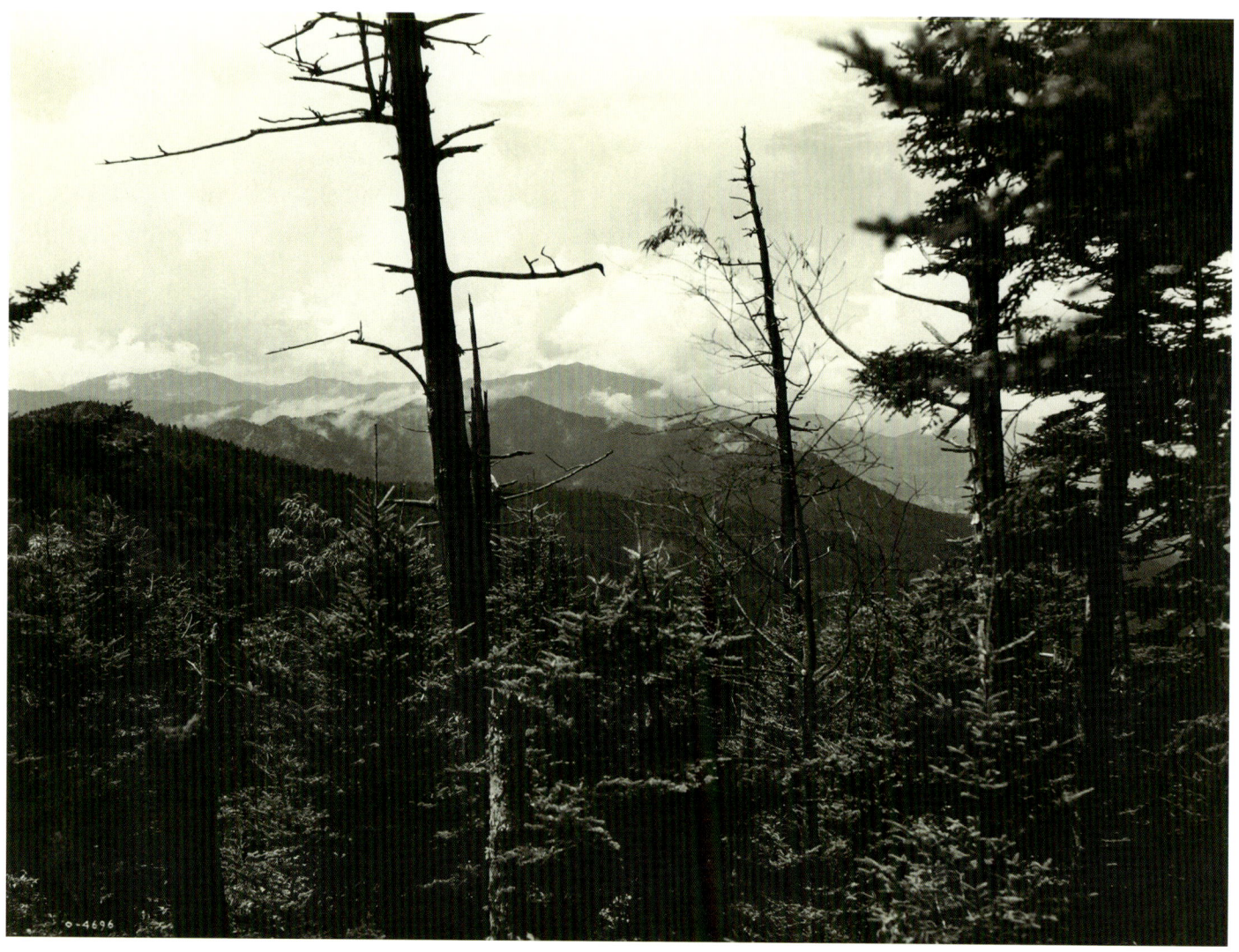

20 Mount LeConte from state line near Hughes Ridge. Courtesy of Smokies Life.

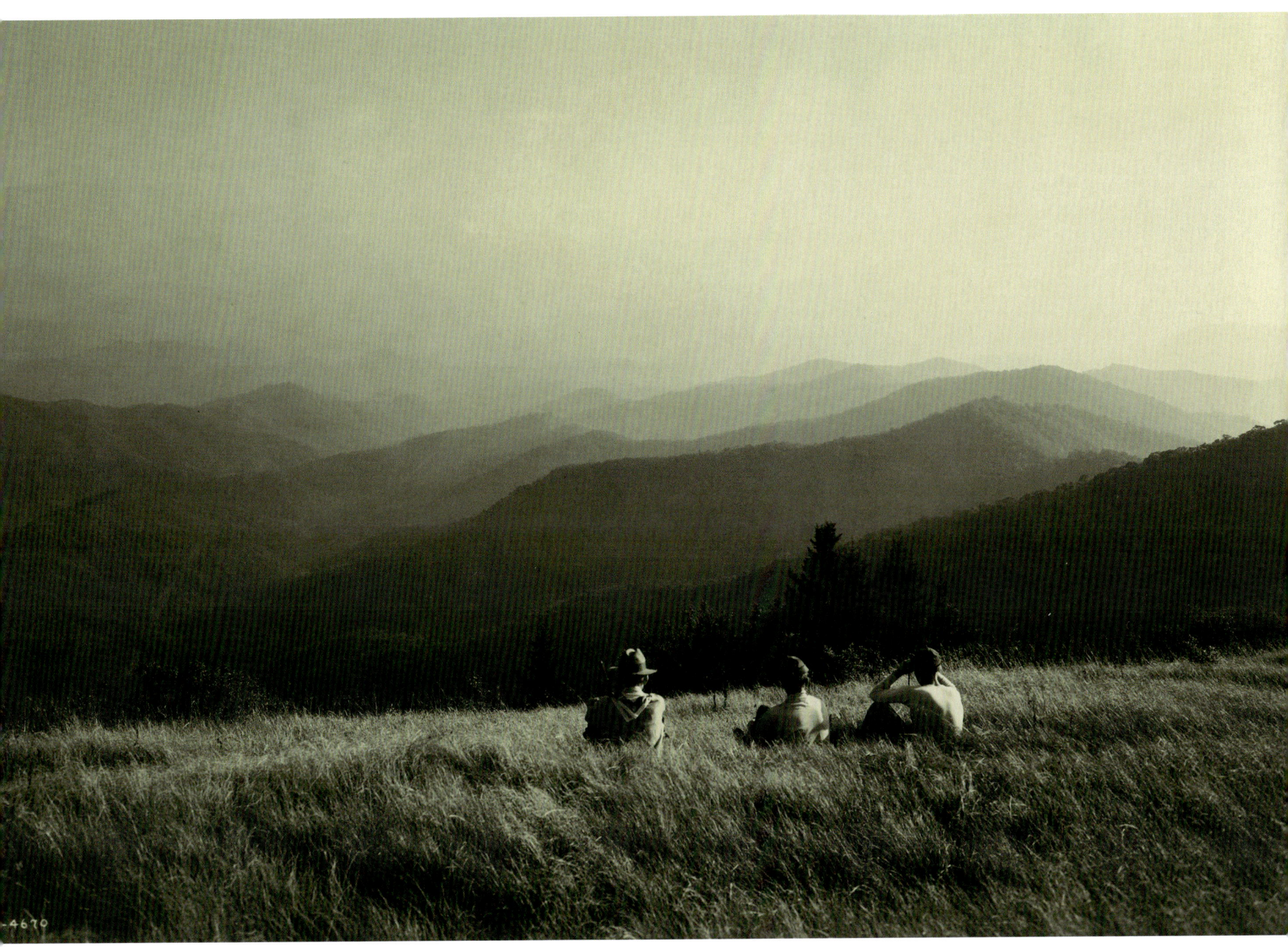

21   Noland Creek Valley from Andrew's Bald. Courtesy of Smokies Life.

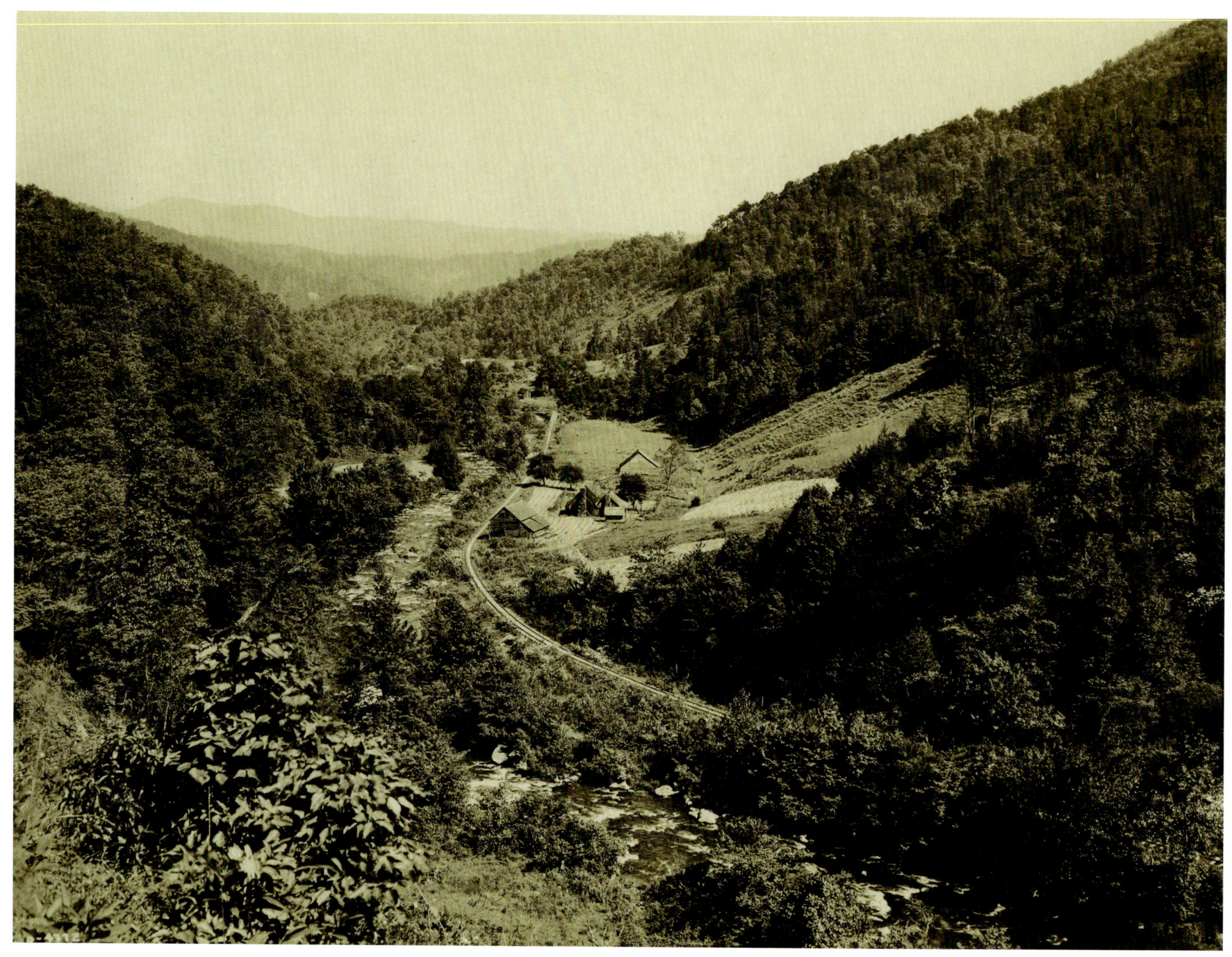

22   A view looking down into the Smokemont area. Courtesy of Smokies Life.

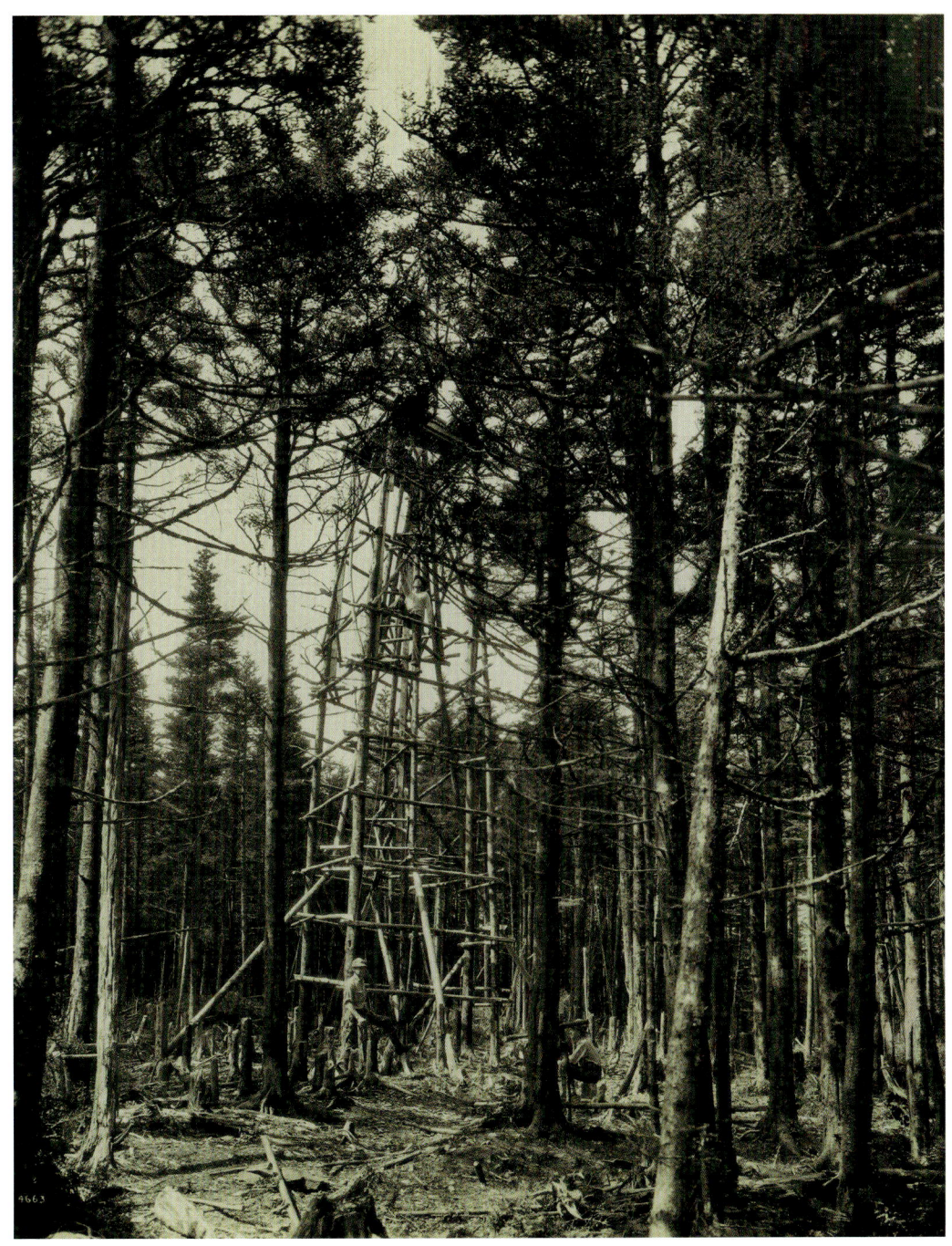

23 A wooden tower on summit of Kuwohi.
Courtesy of Smokies Life.

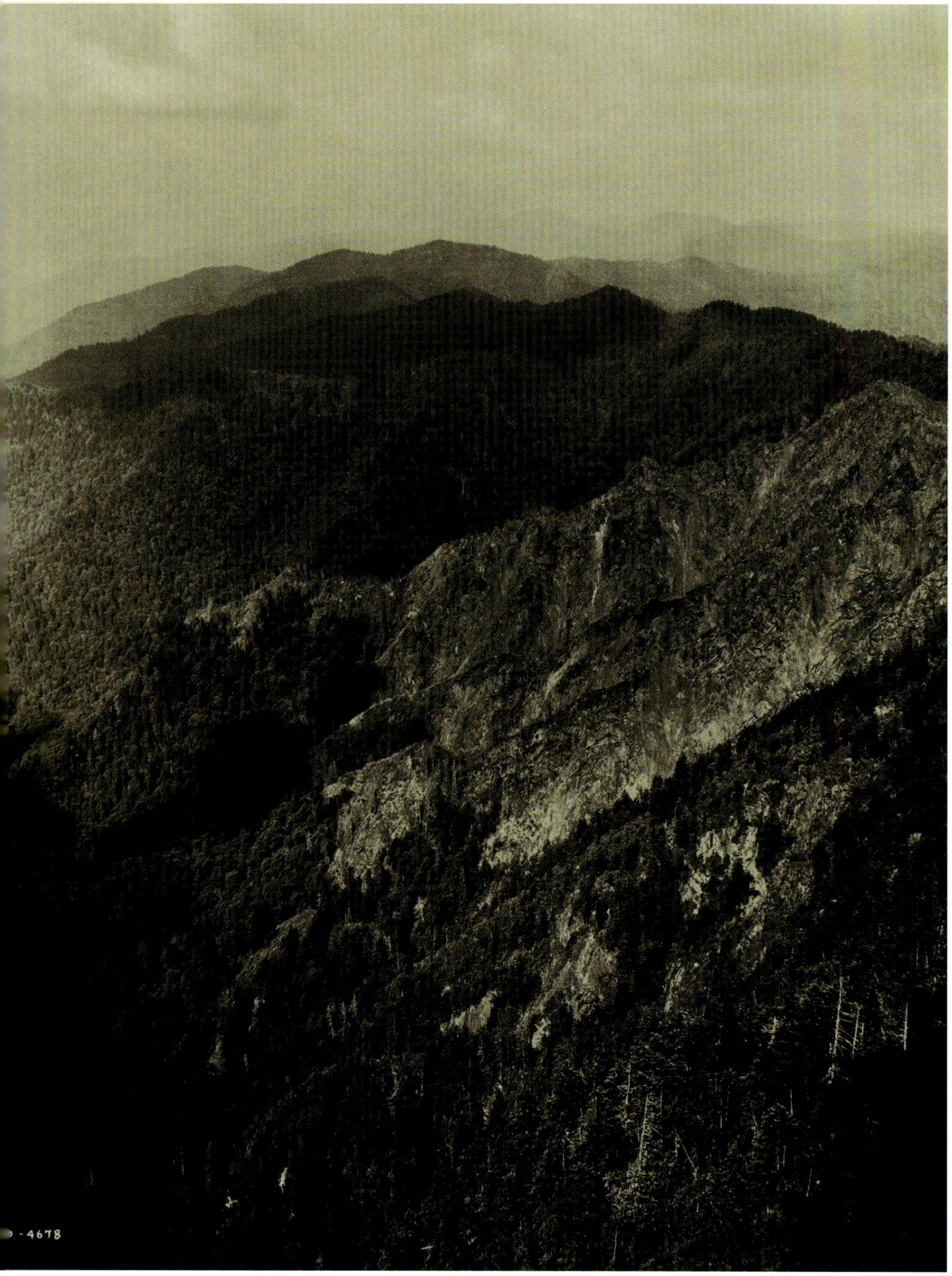

24 View from Jump Off. Courtesy of Smokies Life.

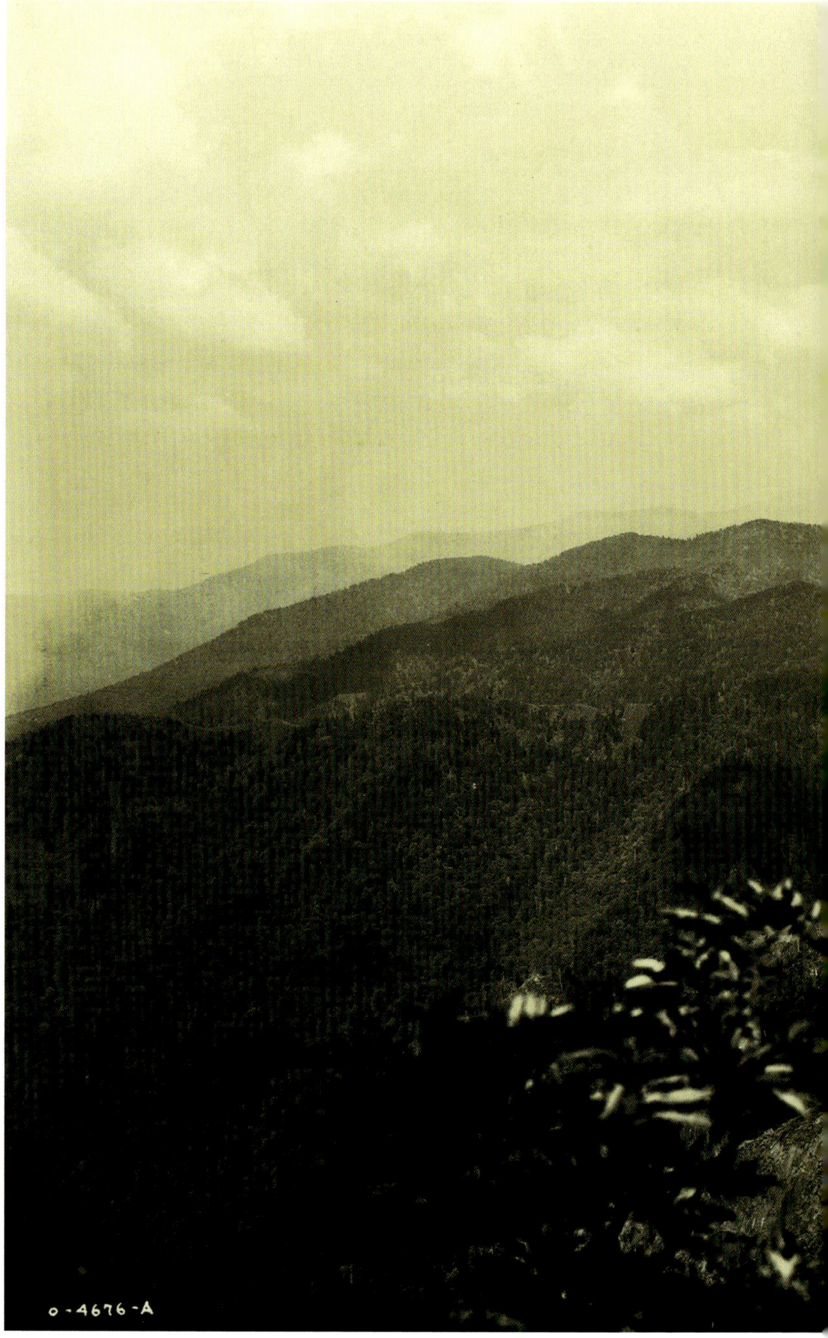

25 View from Jump Off. Courtesy of Smokies Life.

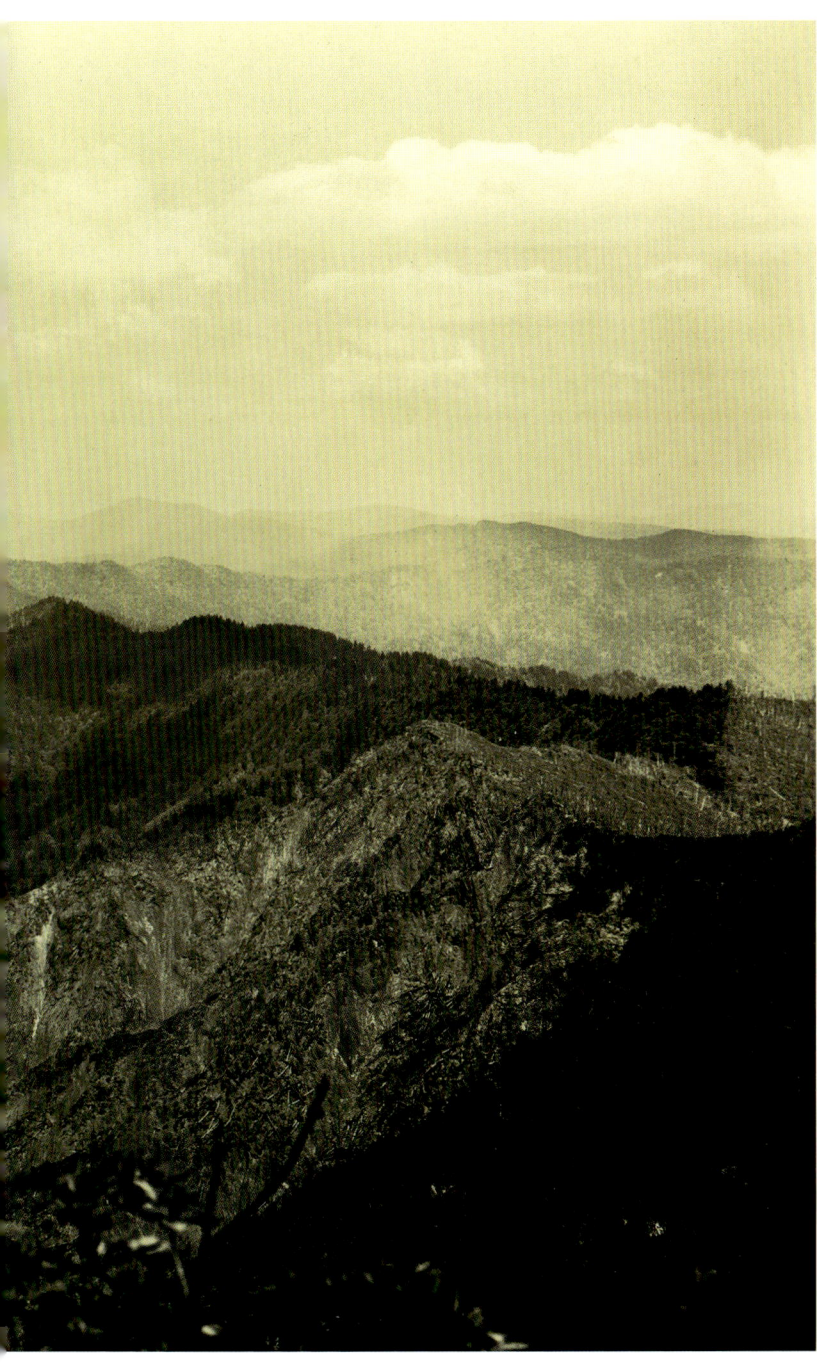

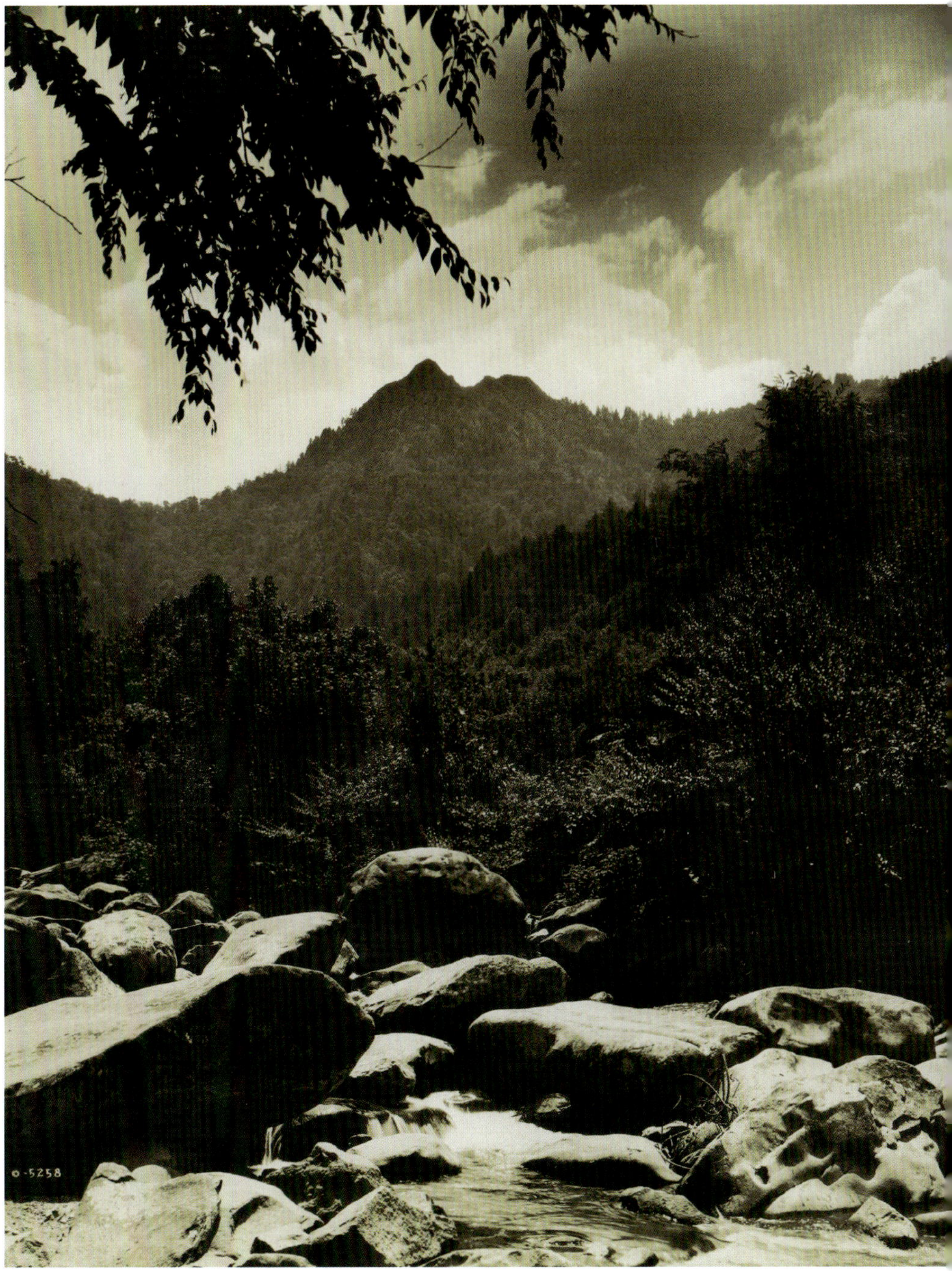

26   View of Chimney Tops. Courtesy of Smokies Life.

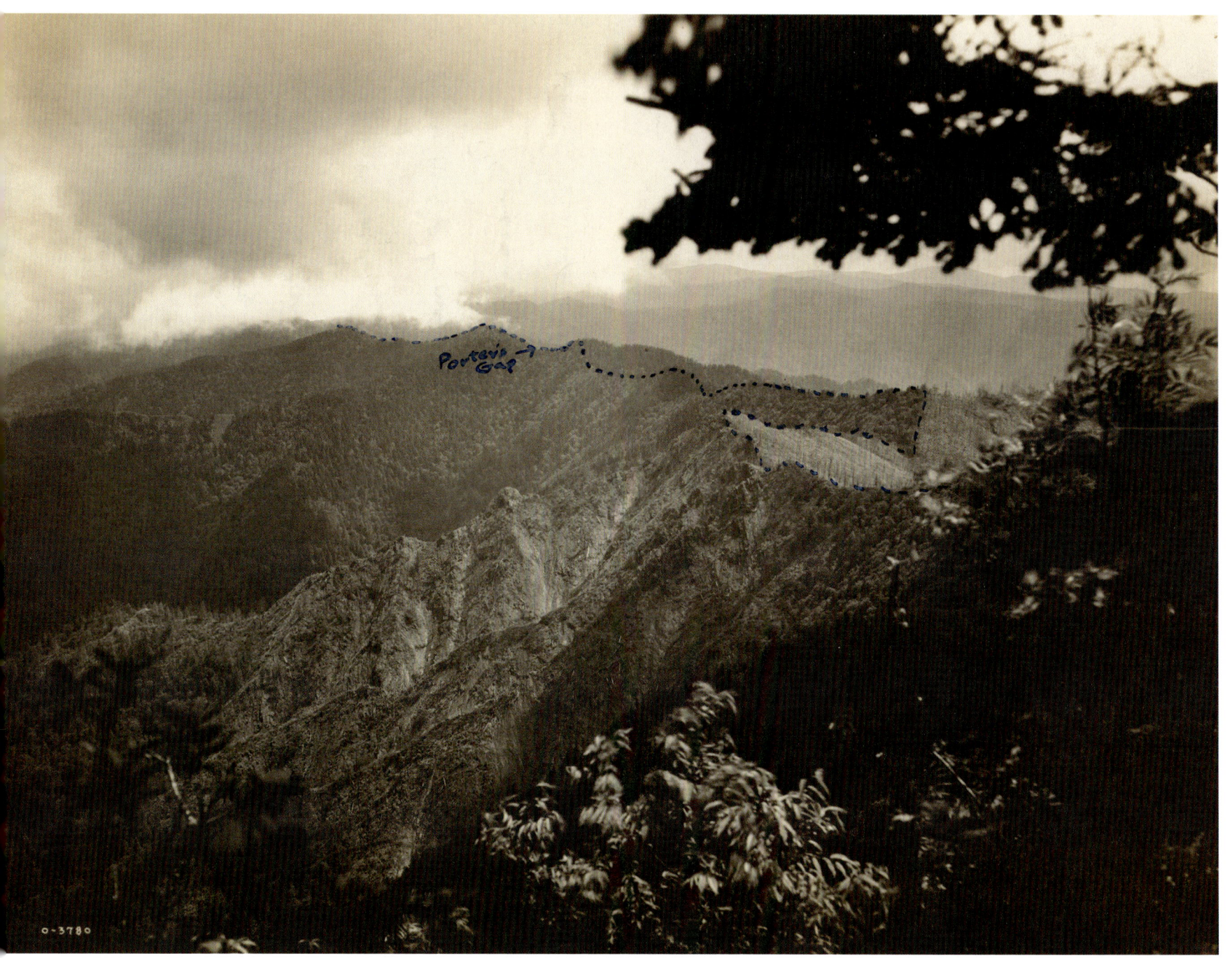

27   View from below Mount Collins along the state line, with Masa's hand-drawn notations. Courtesy of the National Park Service.

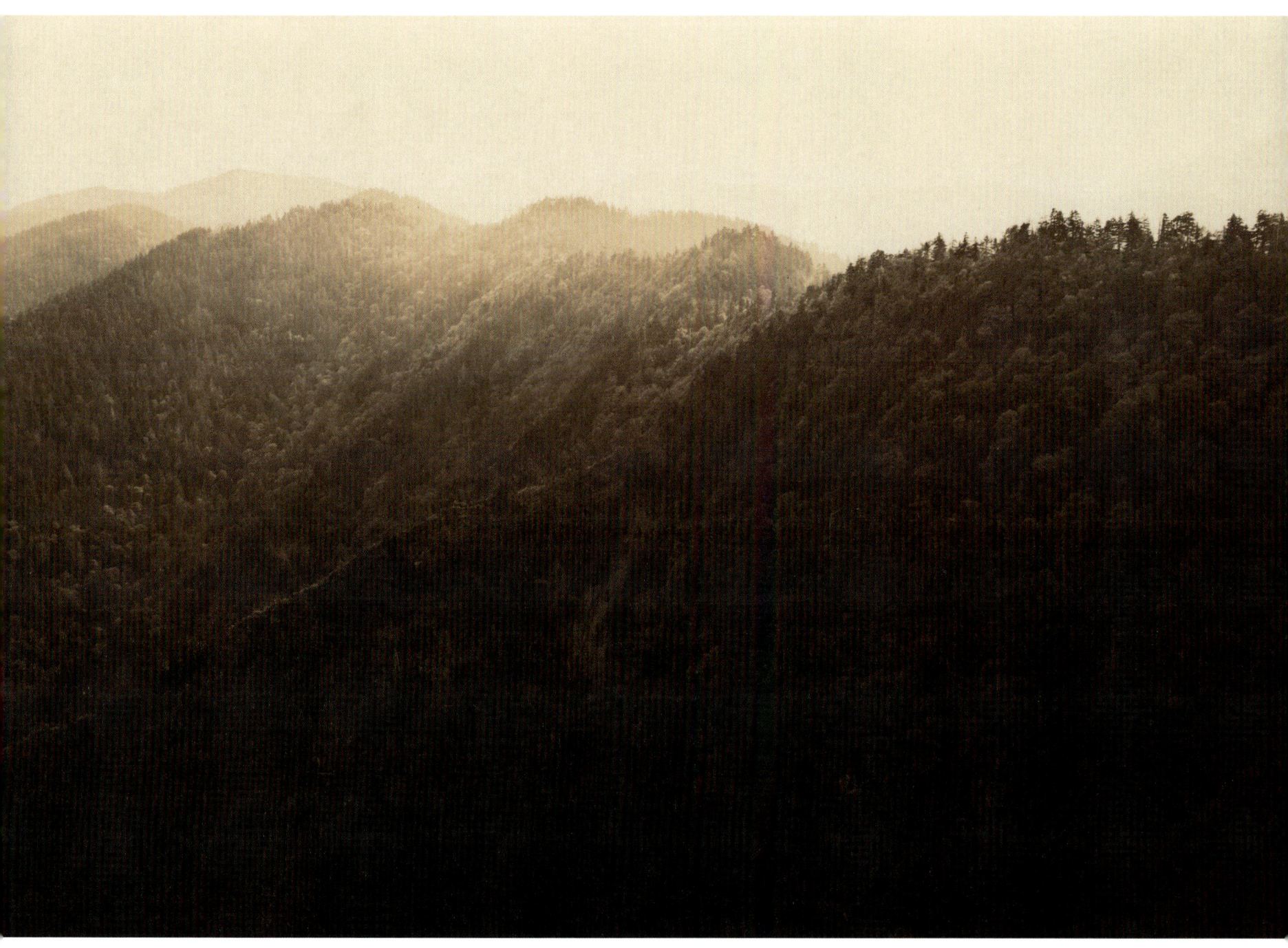

28 View from Charlies Bunion, looking east. Courtesy of the National Park Service.

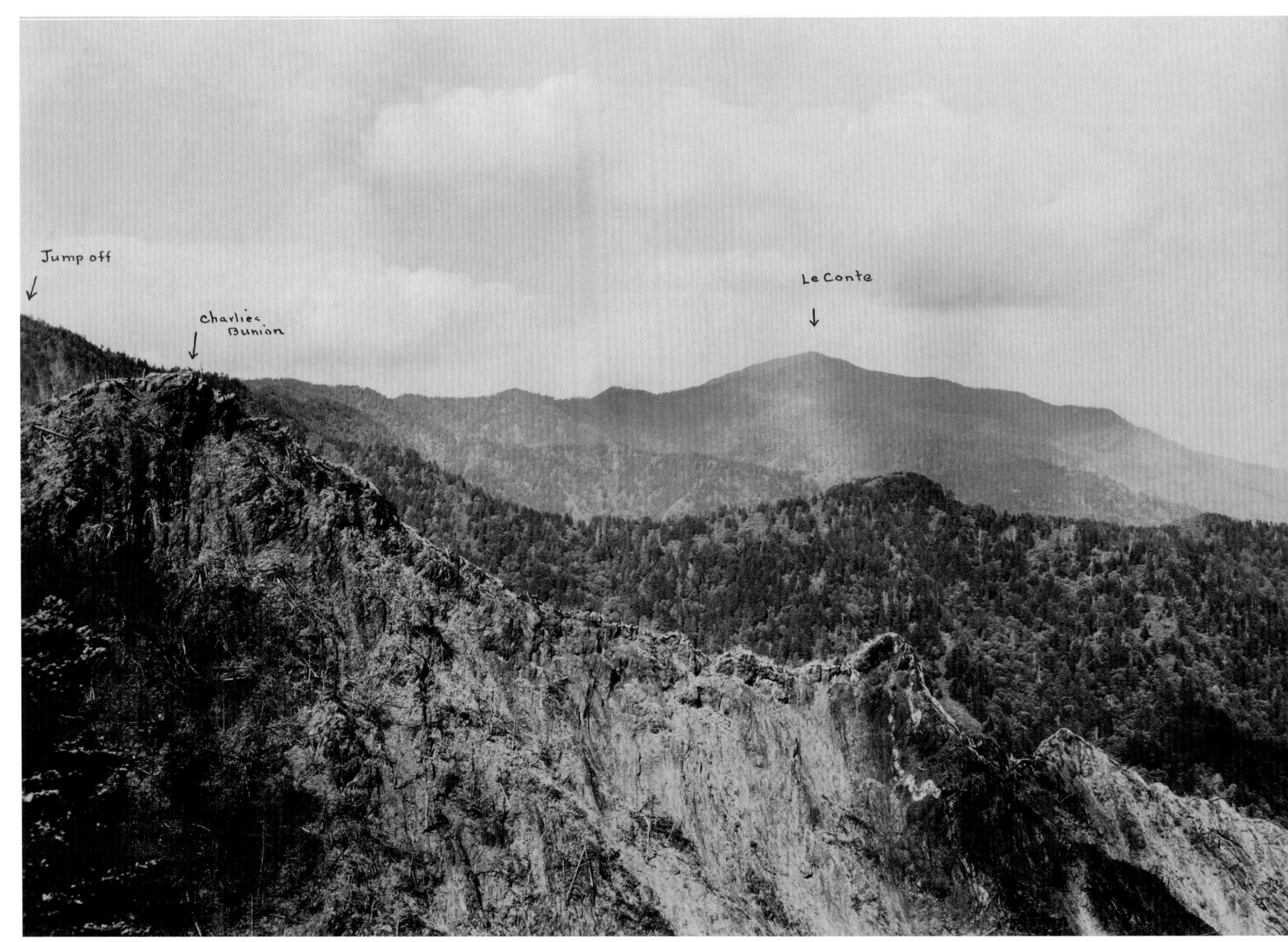

29   View of the main ridge of the Smokies from Jump Off to Mount LeConte, with handwritten notations.
       Courtesy of the National Park Service.

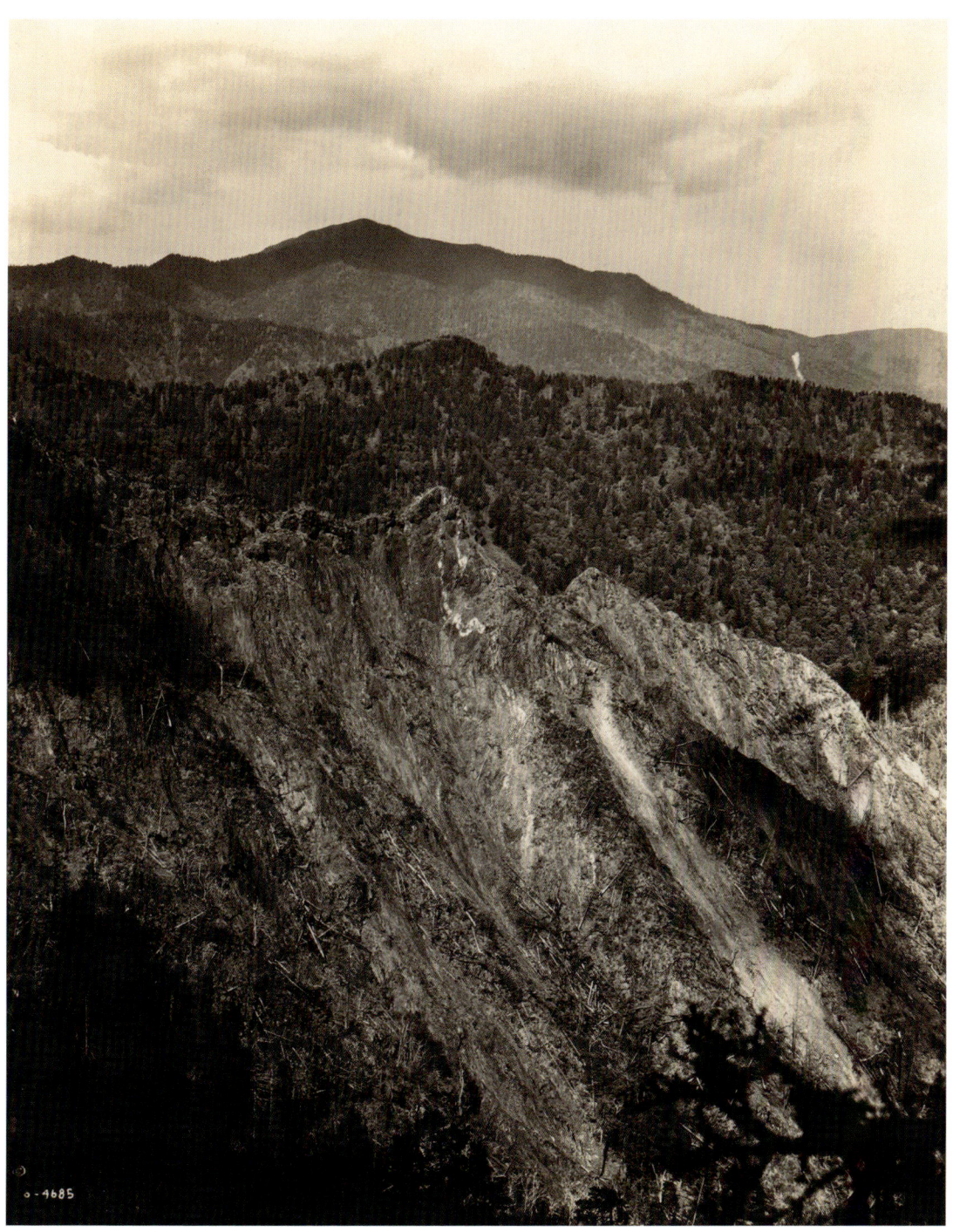

30 View looking west from the high
knob, above Dry Sluice Gap.
Courtesy of the National
Park Service.

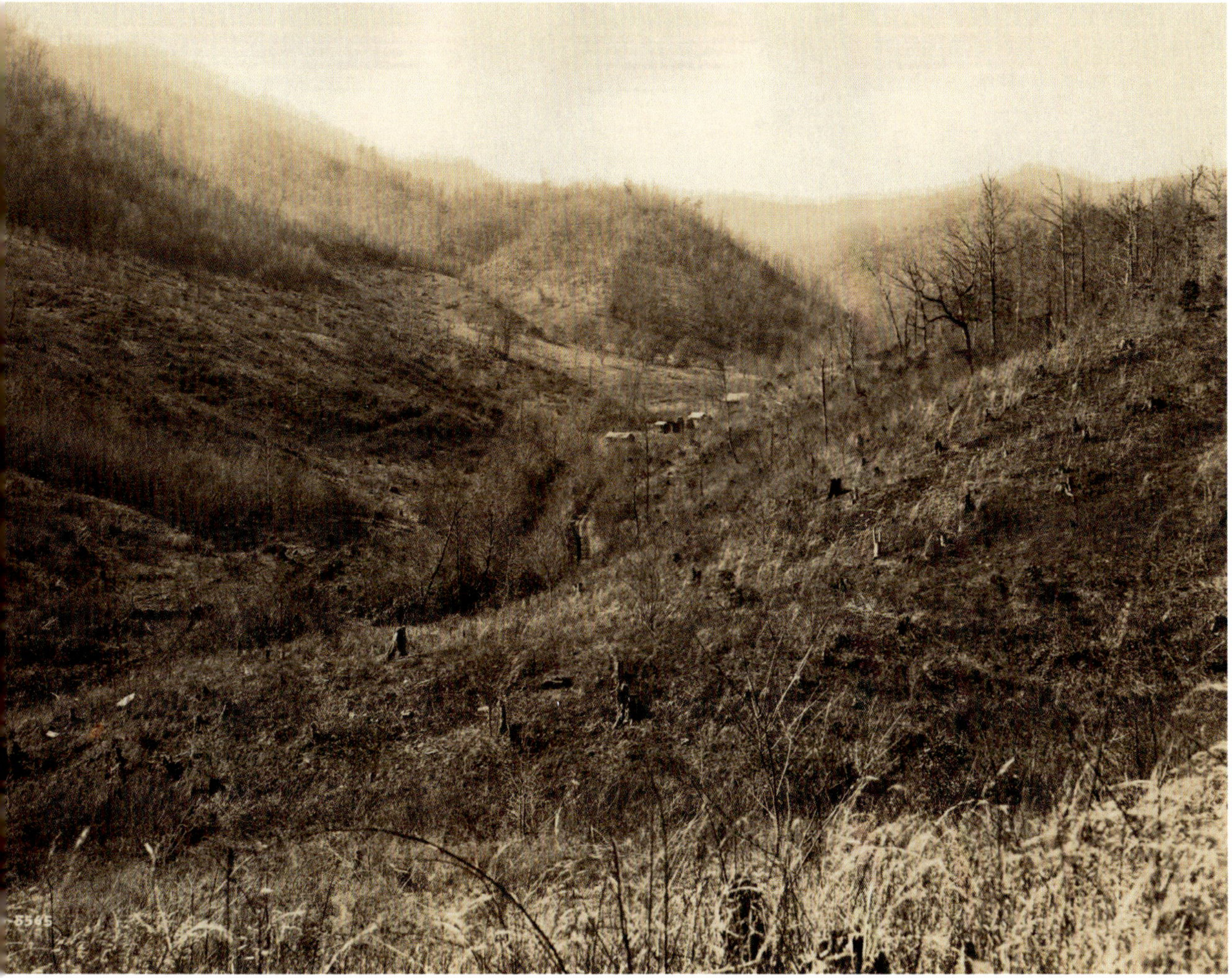

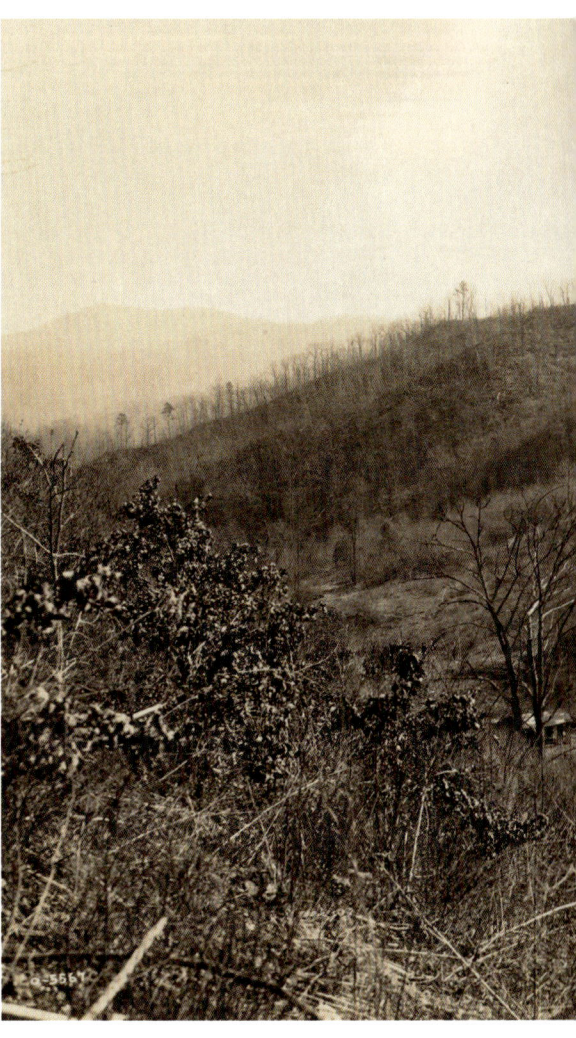

31   View looking up Mingus Creek.
Courtesy of the National Park Service.

32   View looking down Mingus Creek.
Courtesy of the National Park Service.

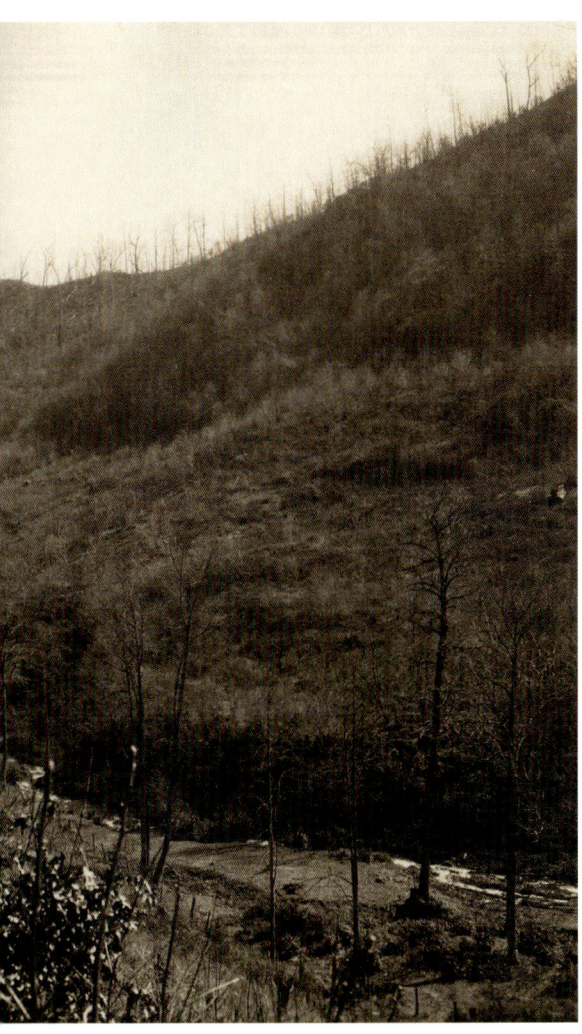

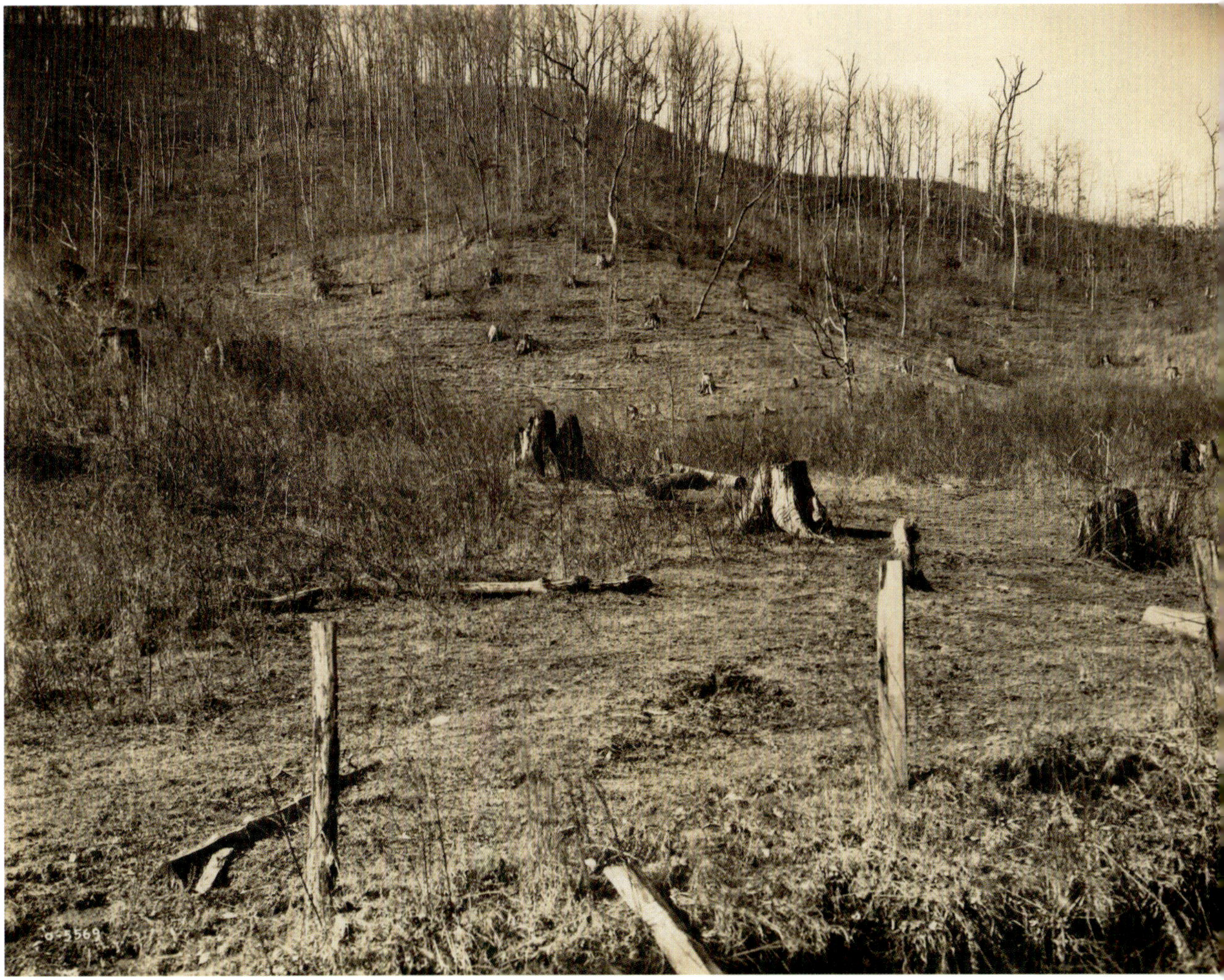

33   View of landscape near Mingus Creek after commercial logging.
      Courtesy of the National Park Service.

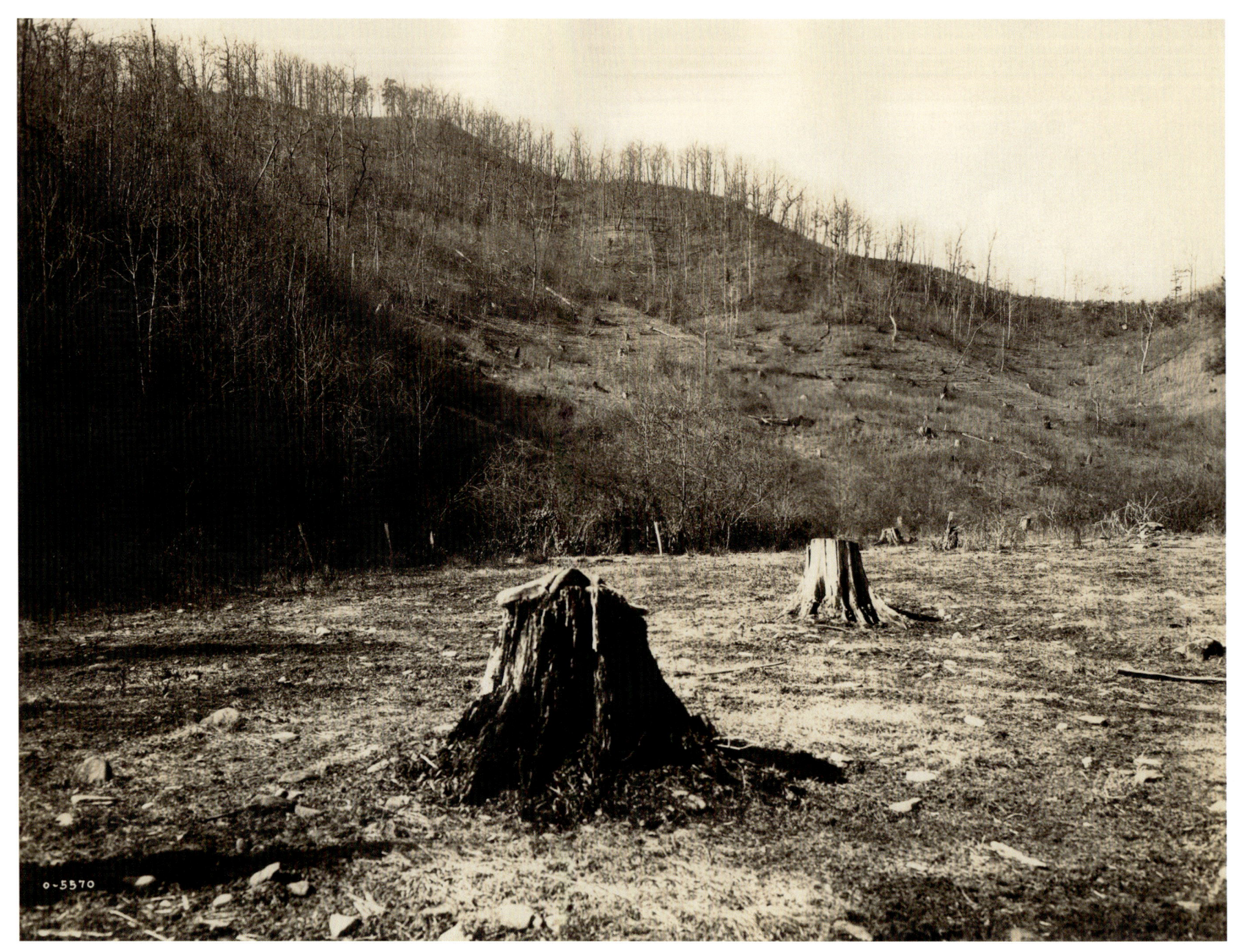

34   Tree stumps near Mingus Creek after the area was commercially logged. Courtesy of the National Park Service.

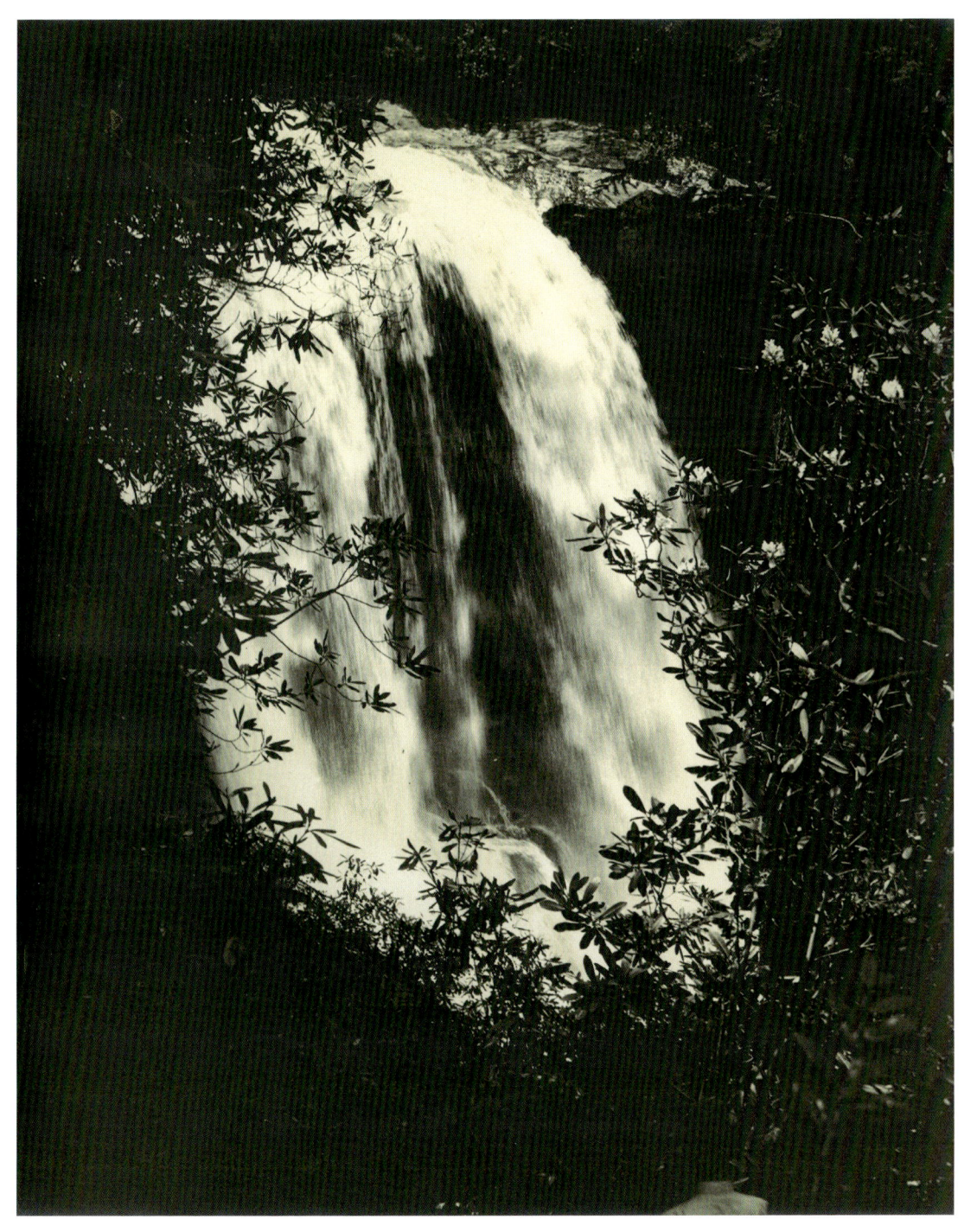

35   A waterfall with a person.
Courtesy of Smokies Life.

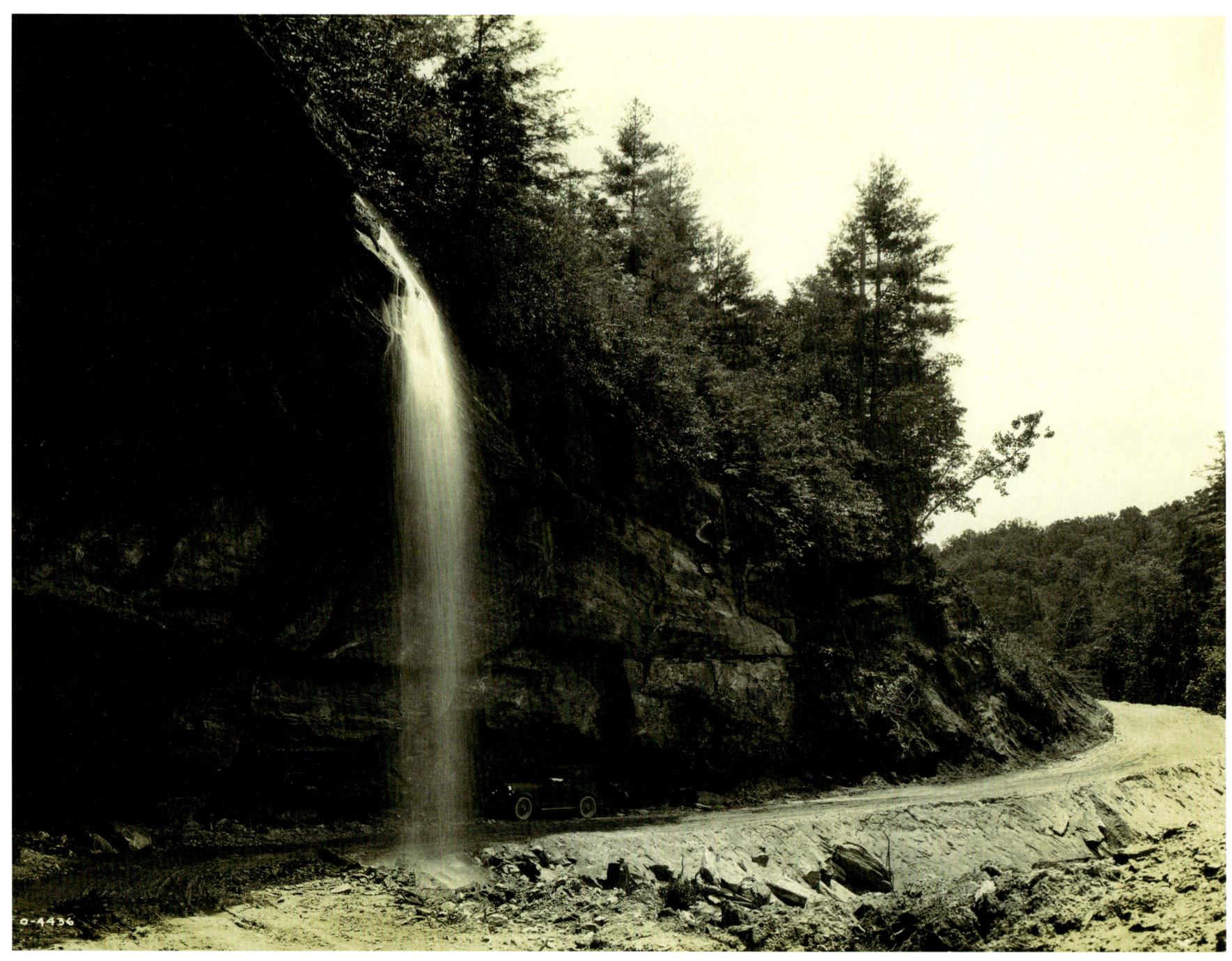

36   Bridal Veil Falls, near Highlands, North Carolina. Courtesy of Smokies Life.

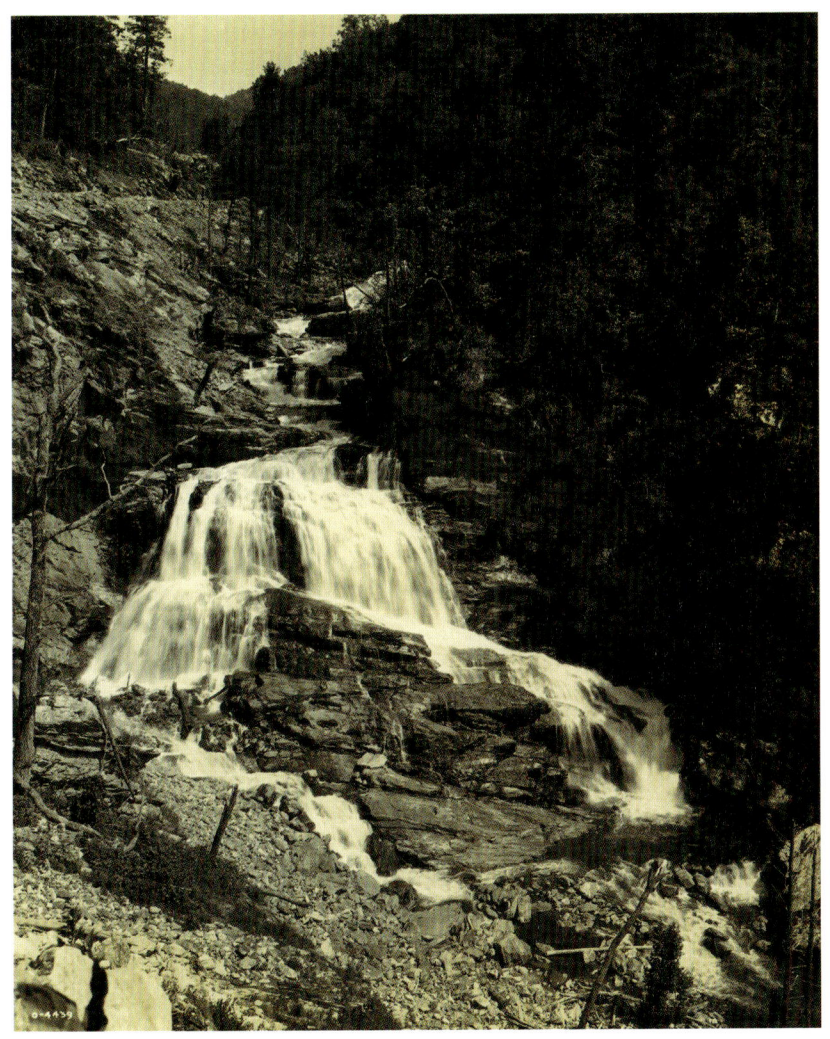

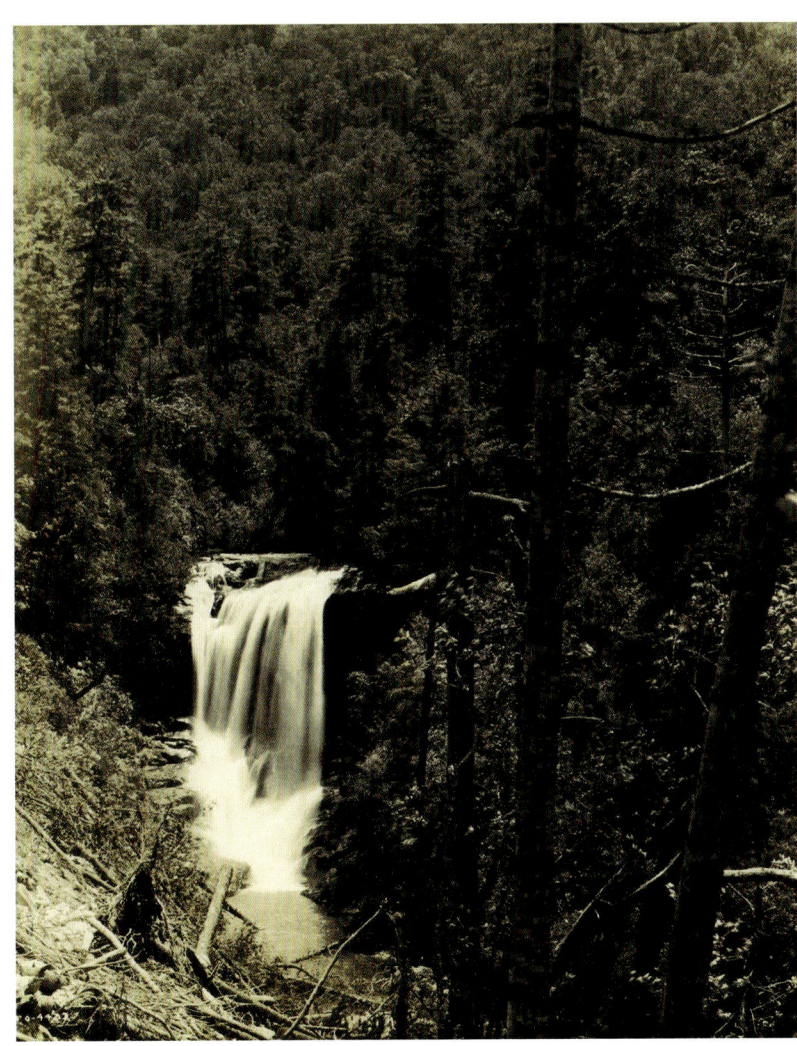

37 View of Cullasaja Falls. Courtesy of Smokies Life.

38 View of Dry Falls. Courtesy of Smokies Life.

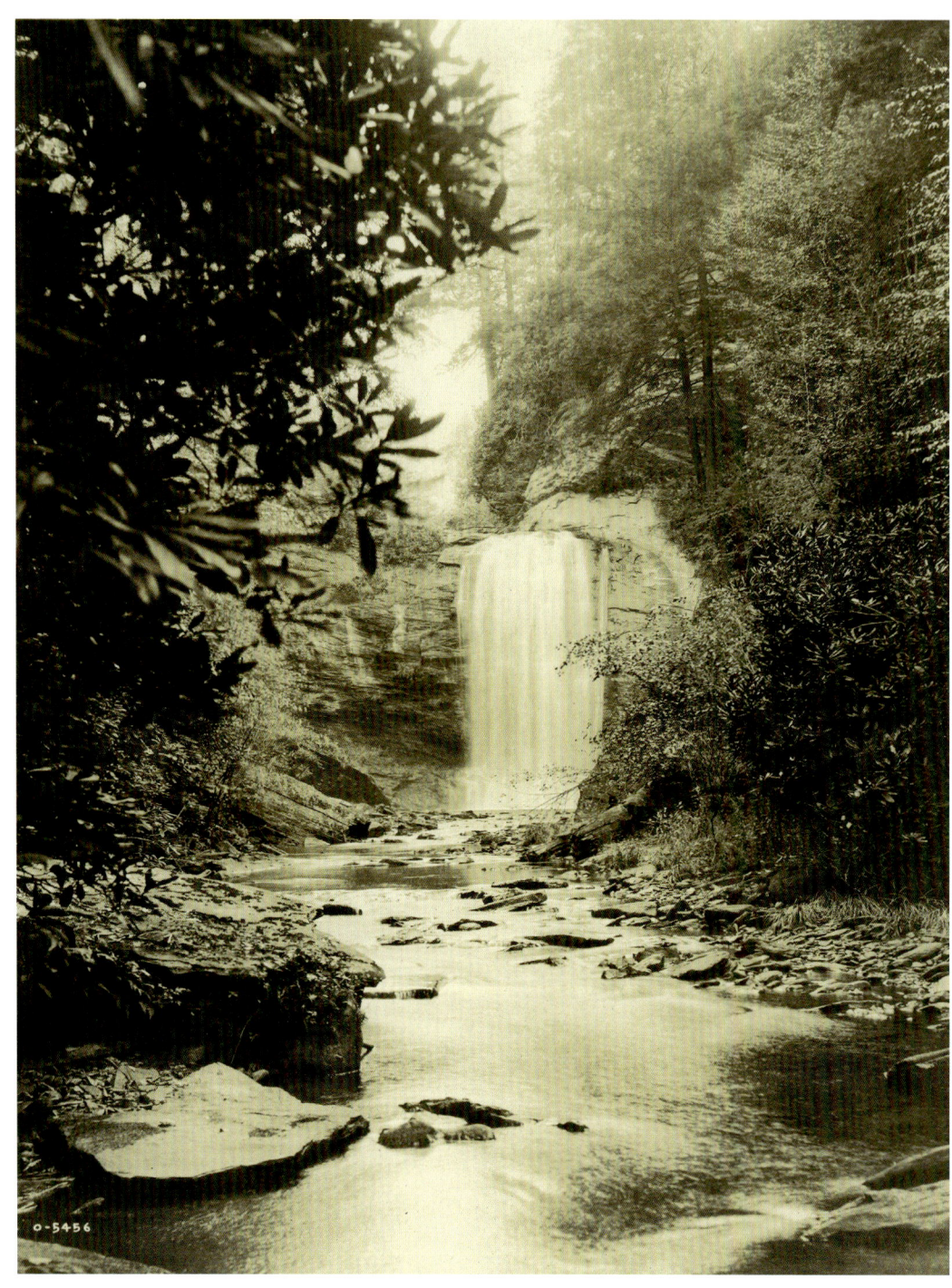

39   View of Looking Glass Falls near Lake Lure.
Courtesy of Pack Memorial Library.

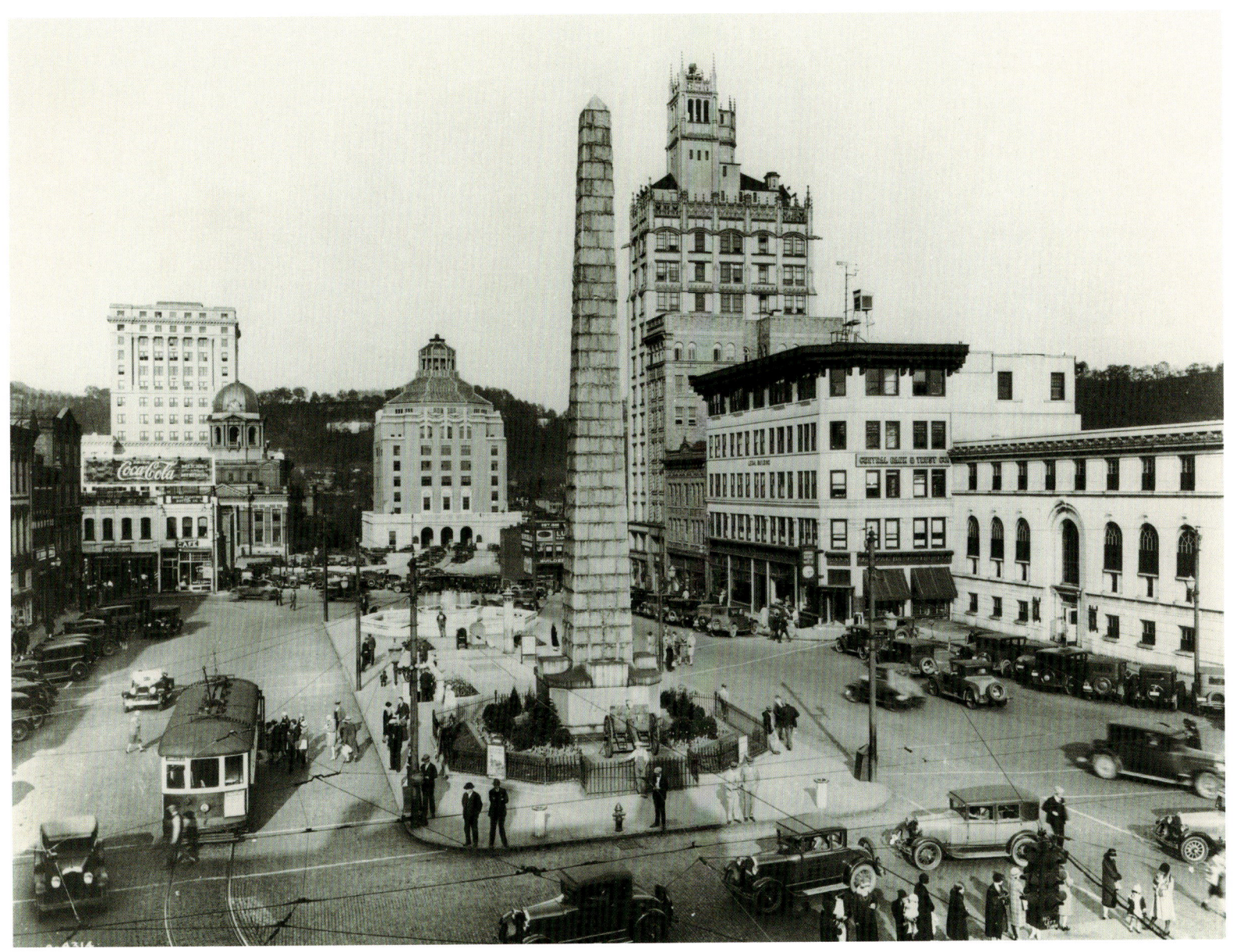

40   Pack Square in downtown Asheville, 1930. Courtesy of Pack Memorial Library.

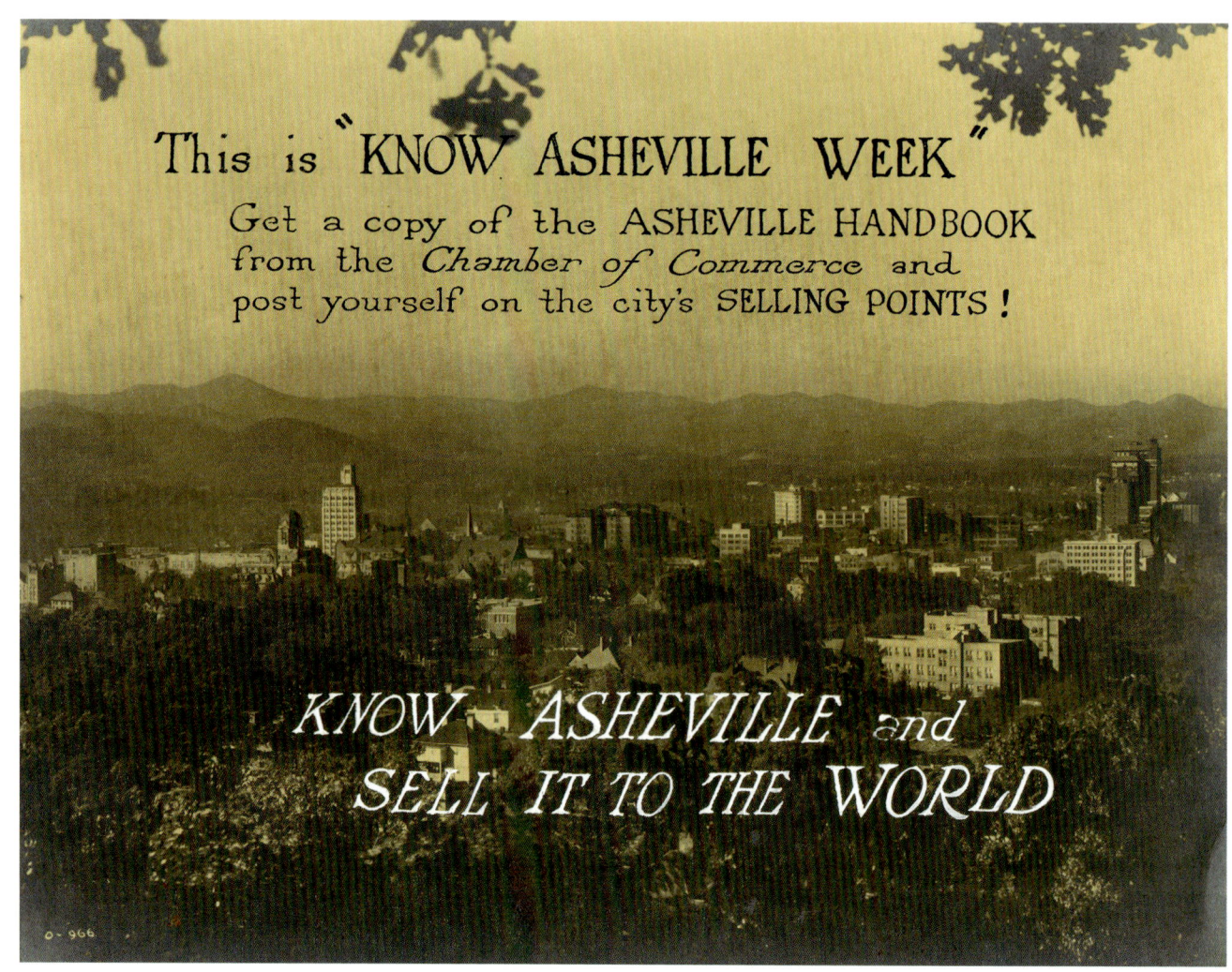

This is "KNOW ASHEVILLE WEEK"

Get a copy of the ASHEVILLE HANDBOOK from the *Chamber of Commerce* and post yourself on the city's SELLING POINTS!

KNOW ASHEVILLE and SELL IT TO THE WORLD

41 Asheville tourism brochure featuring George Masa's photograph of the city skyline, ca. 1926–27. Courtesy of Pack Memorial Library.

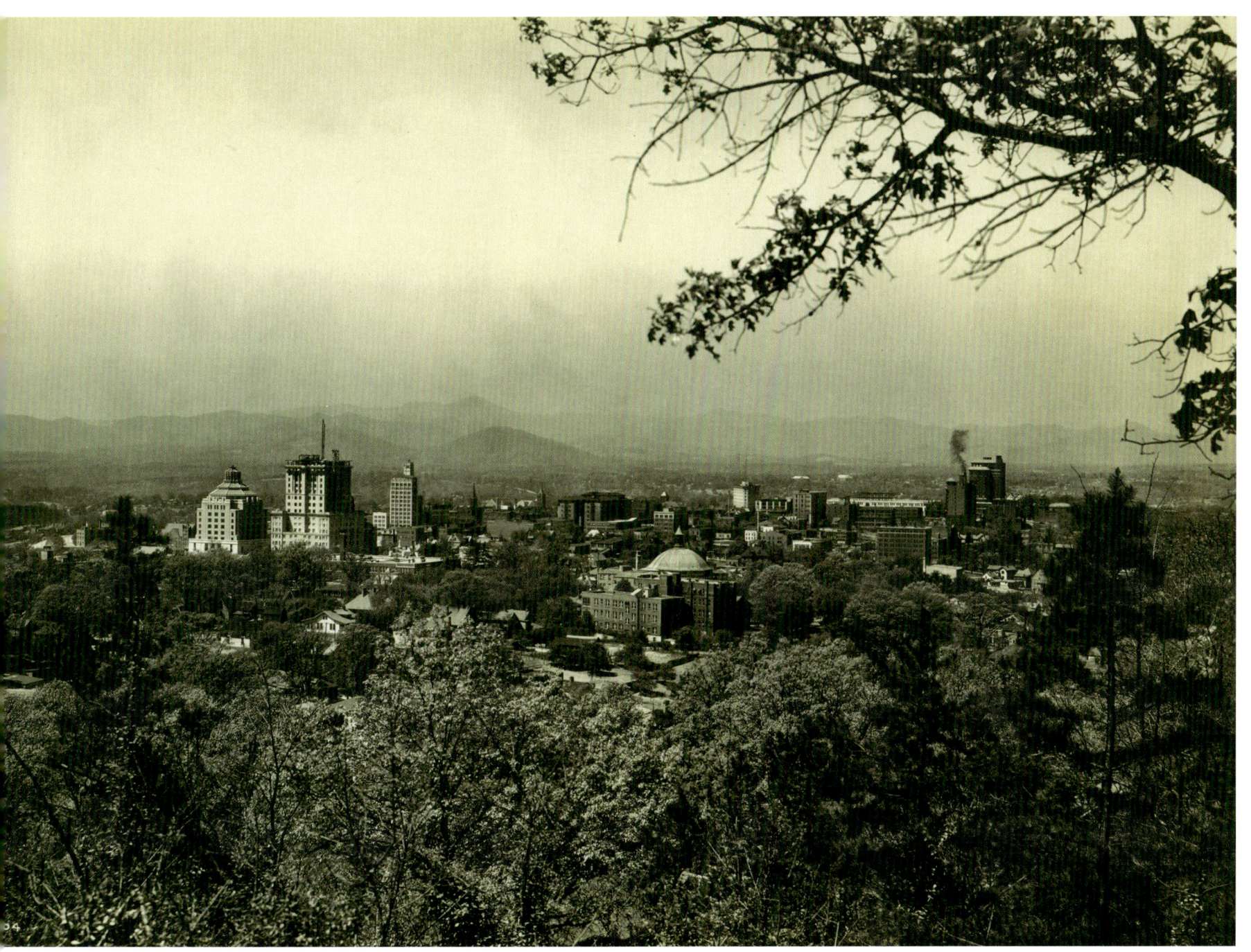

42   Asheville skyline from Sunset Mountain, ca. 1928. Courtesy of Pack Memorial Library.

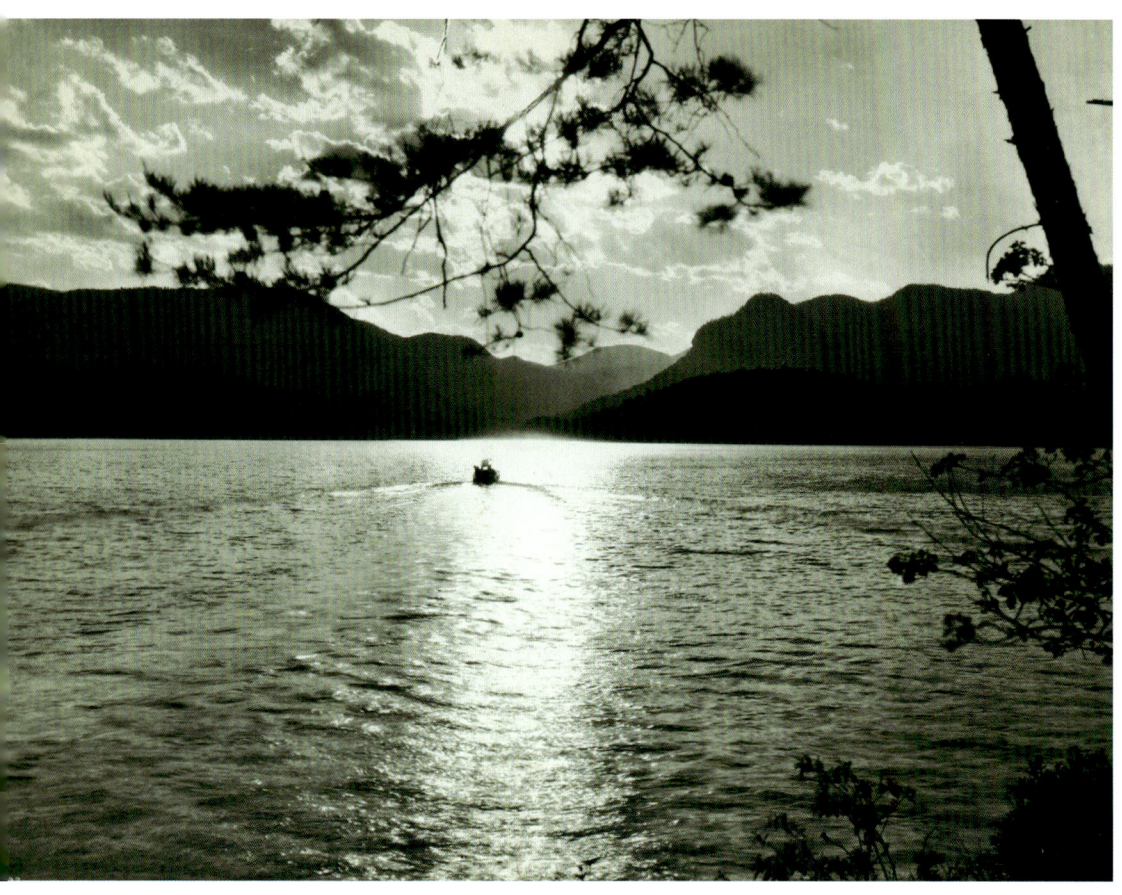

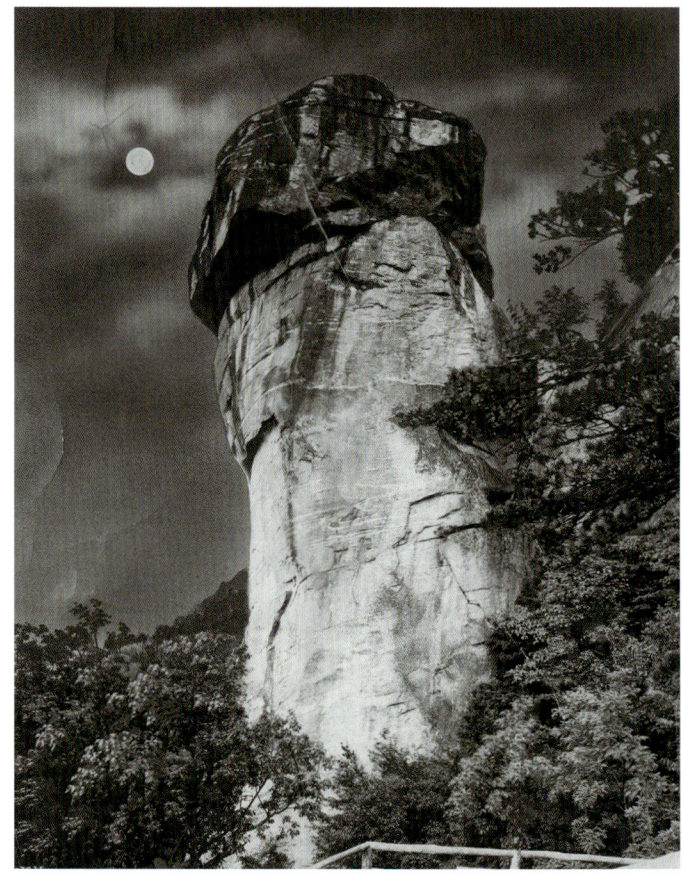

43   A boat on Lake Lure at sunset. Courtesy of Pack Memorial Library.

44   Chimney Rock by moonlight.
Courtesy of Pack Memorial Library.

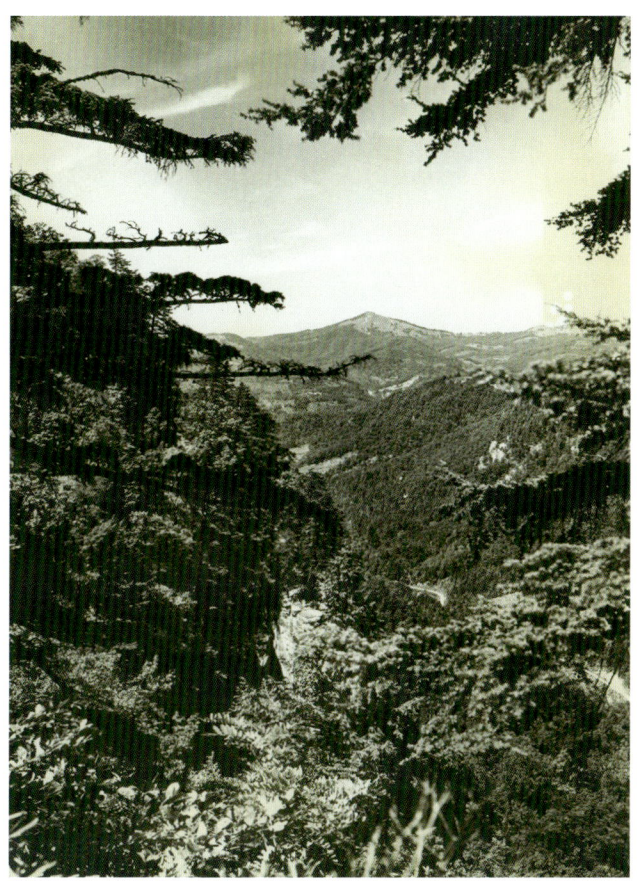

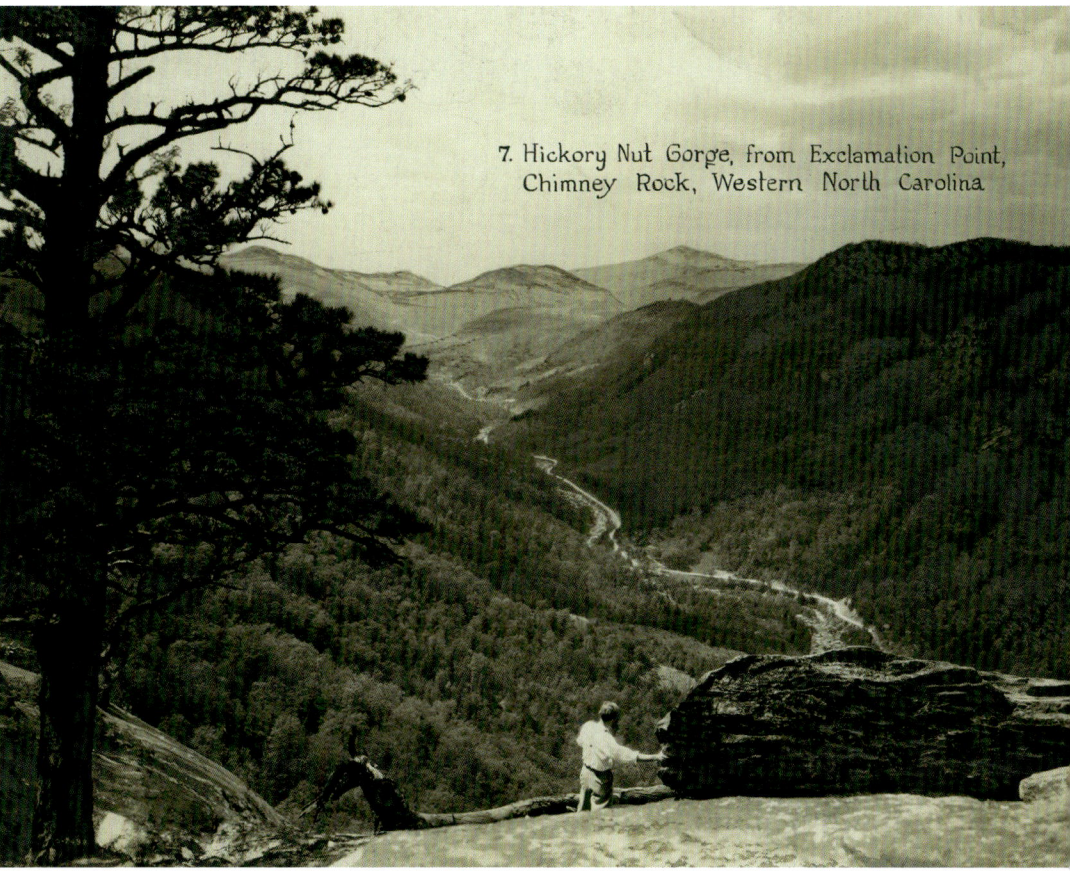

7. Hickory Nut Gorge, from Exclamation Point,
Chimney Rock, Western North Carolina

45   Hickory Nut Gap and Little Pisgah Mountain, as seen from Chimney Rock. Courtesy of Pack Memorial Library.

46   Hickory Nut Gorge, as seen from Exclamation Point on Chimney Rock. Courtesy of Pack Memorial Library.

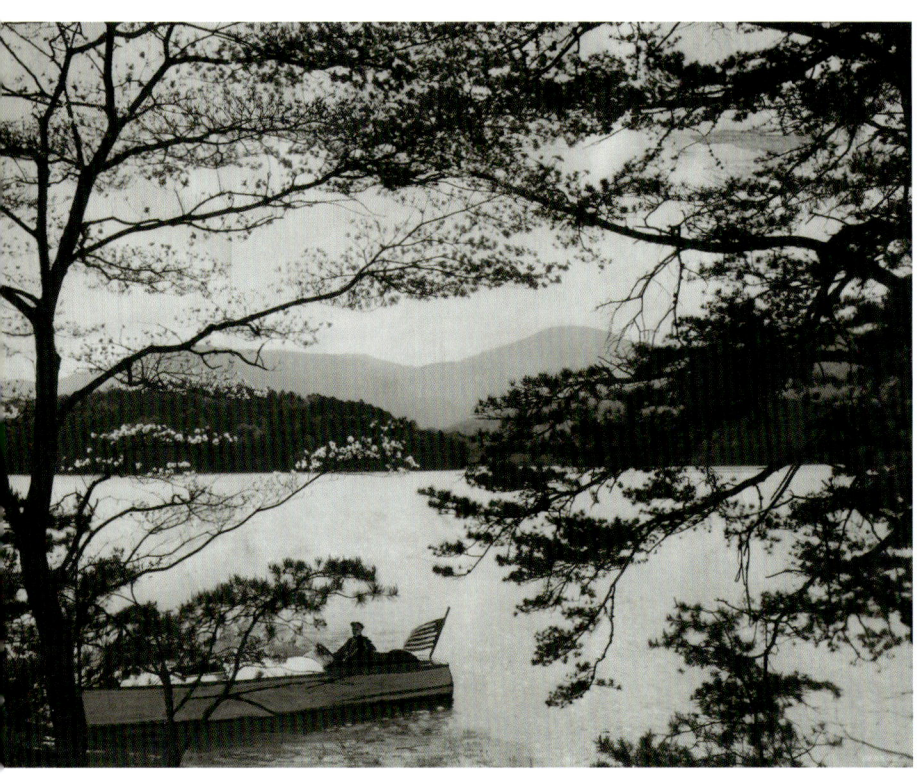

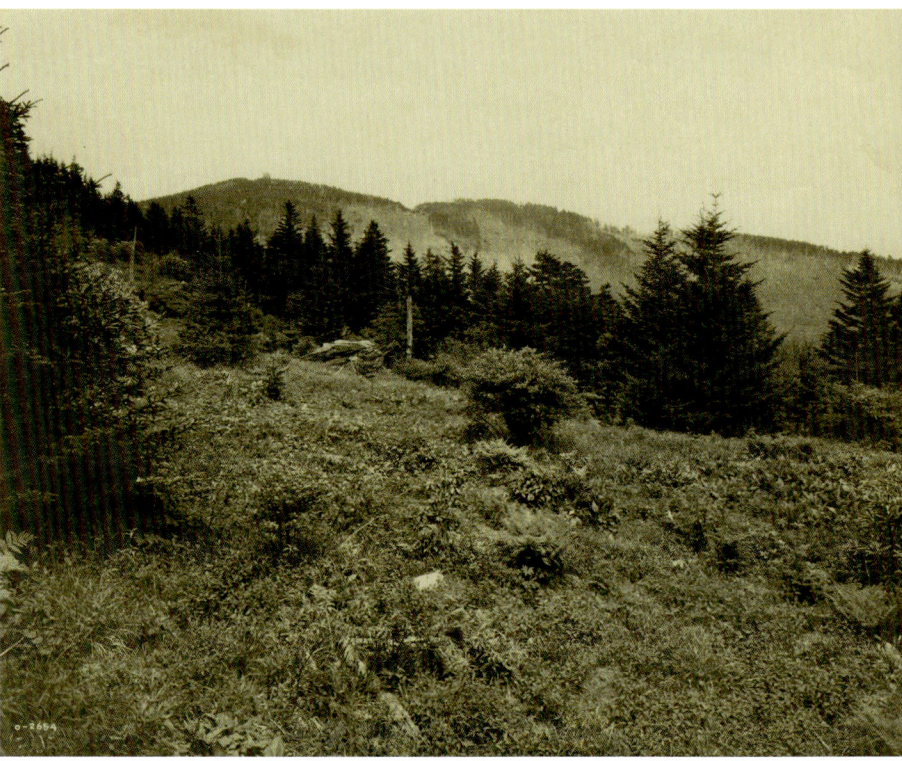

47   A man in speedboat on Lake Lure.
Courtesy of Pack Memorial Library.

48   Mount Mitchell from Stepps Gap.
Courtesy of Pack Memorial Library.

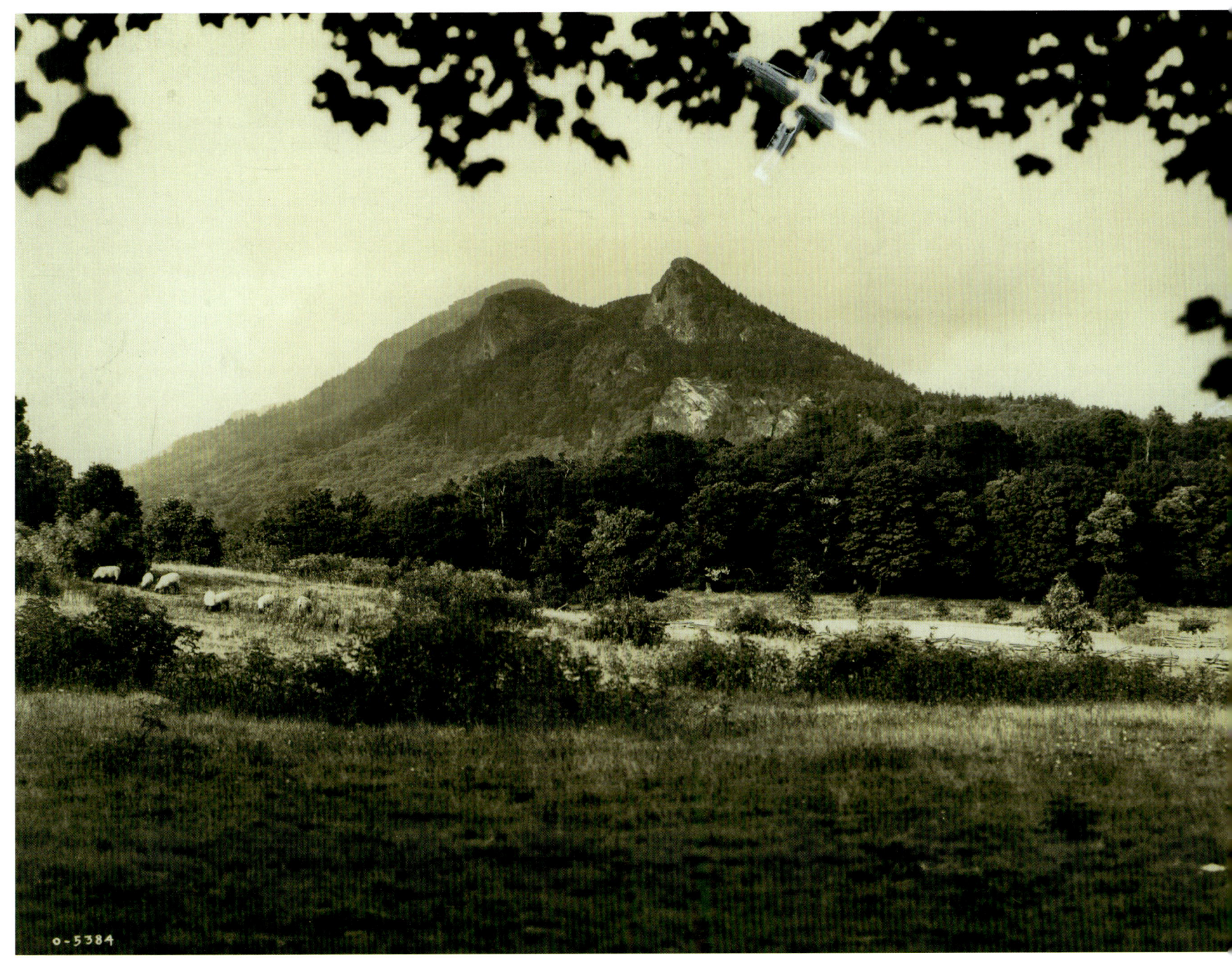

49   Photograph of Grandfather Mountain. Courtesy of Pack Memorial Library.

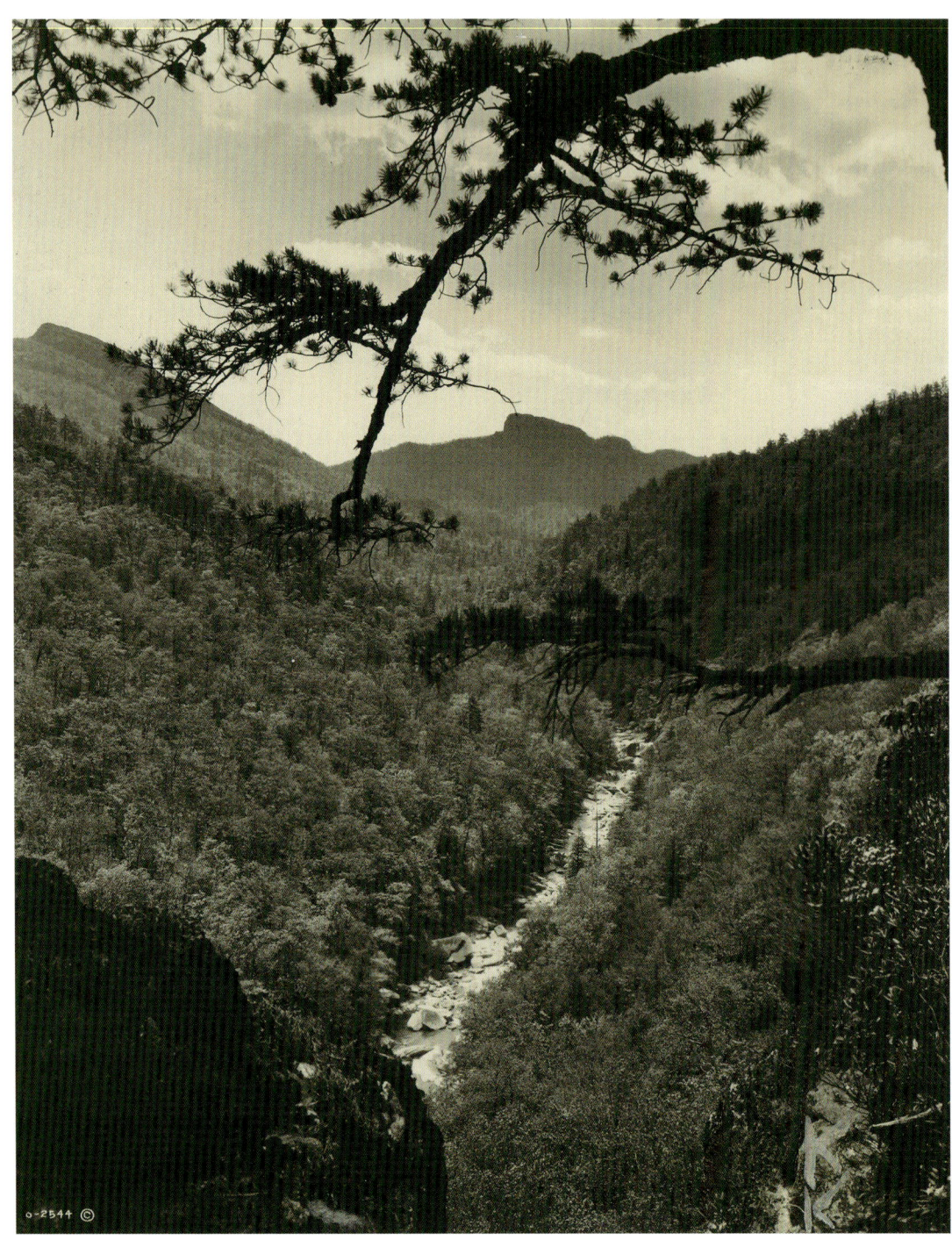

50 View looking up the Linville River with Hawksbill and Table Rock Mountains. Courtesy of Pack Memorial Library.

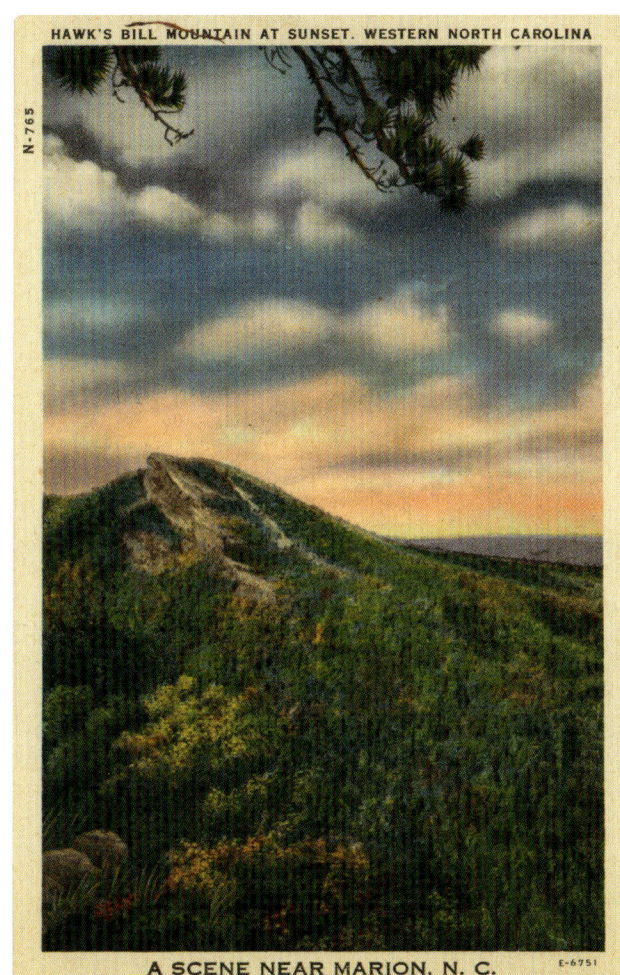

HAWK'S BILL MOUNTAIN AT SUNSET. WESTERN NORTH CAROLINA

N-765

A SCENE NEAR MARION, N. C.

E-6751

51   Color postcard image of Hawksbill Mountain
       at sunset. Courtesy of Pack Memorial Library.

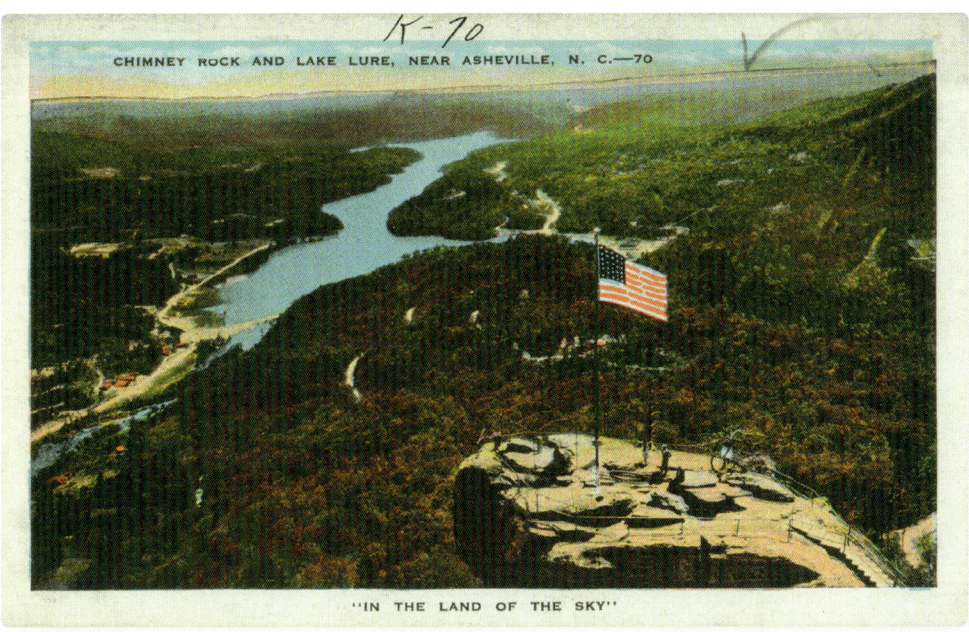

CHIMNEY ROCK AND LAKE LURE, NEAR ASHEVILLE, N. C.—70

"IN THE LAND OF THE SKY"

52   Chimney Rock and Lake Lure—"In the Land of the Sky"
       color postcard. Courtesy of Pack Memorial Library.

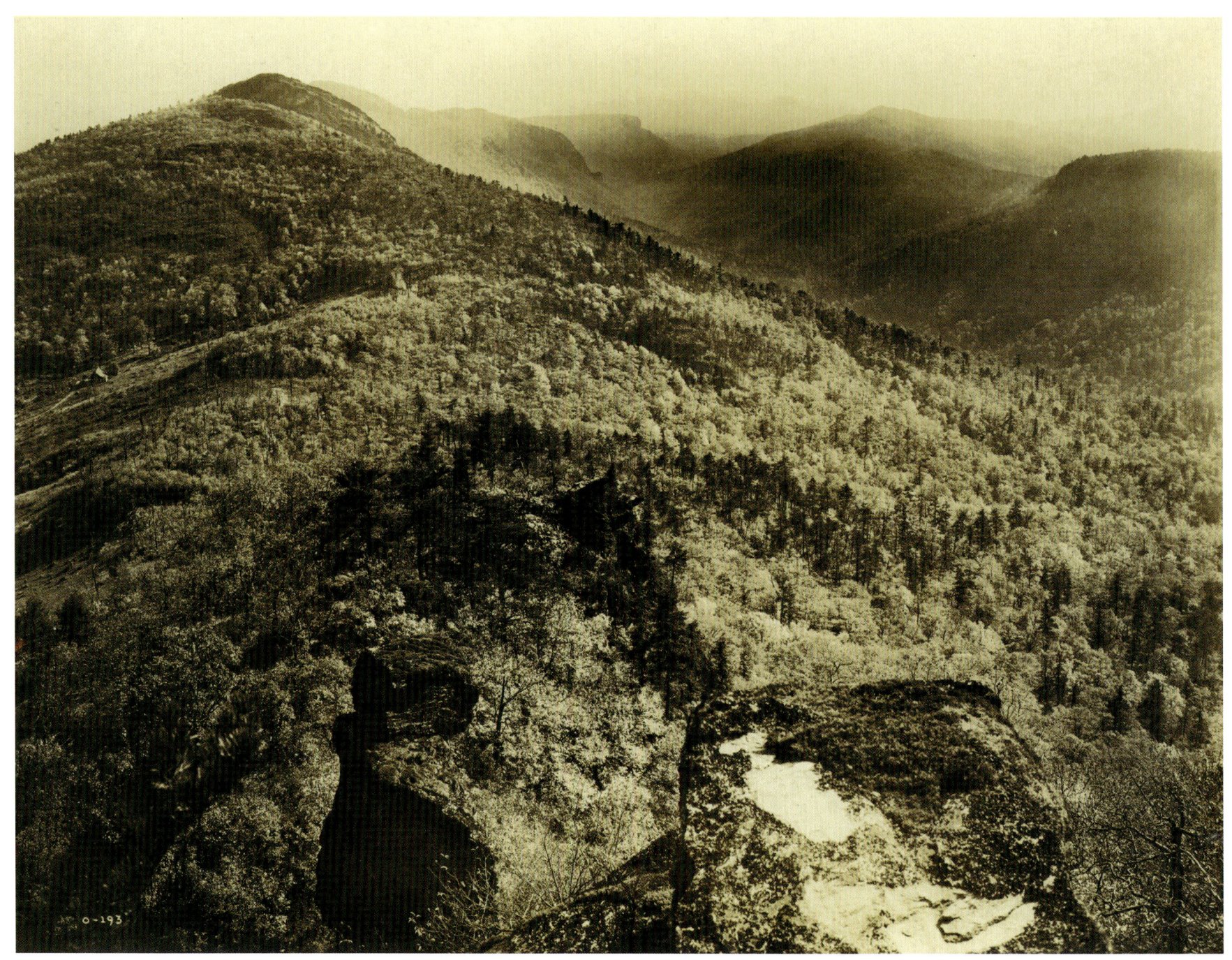

53   View looking down on Sitting Bear Rock, Burke County, North Carolina. Courtesy of Pack Memorial Library.

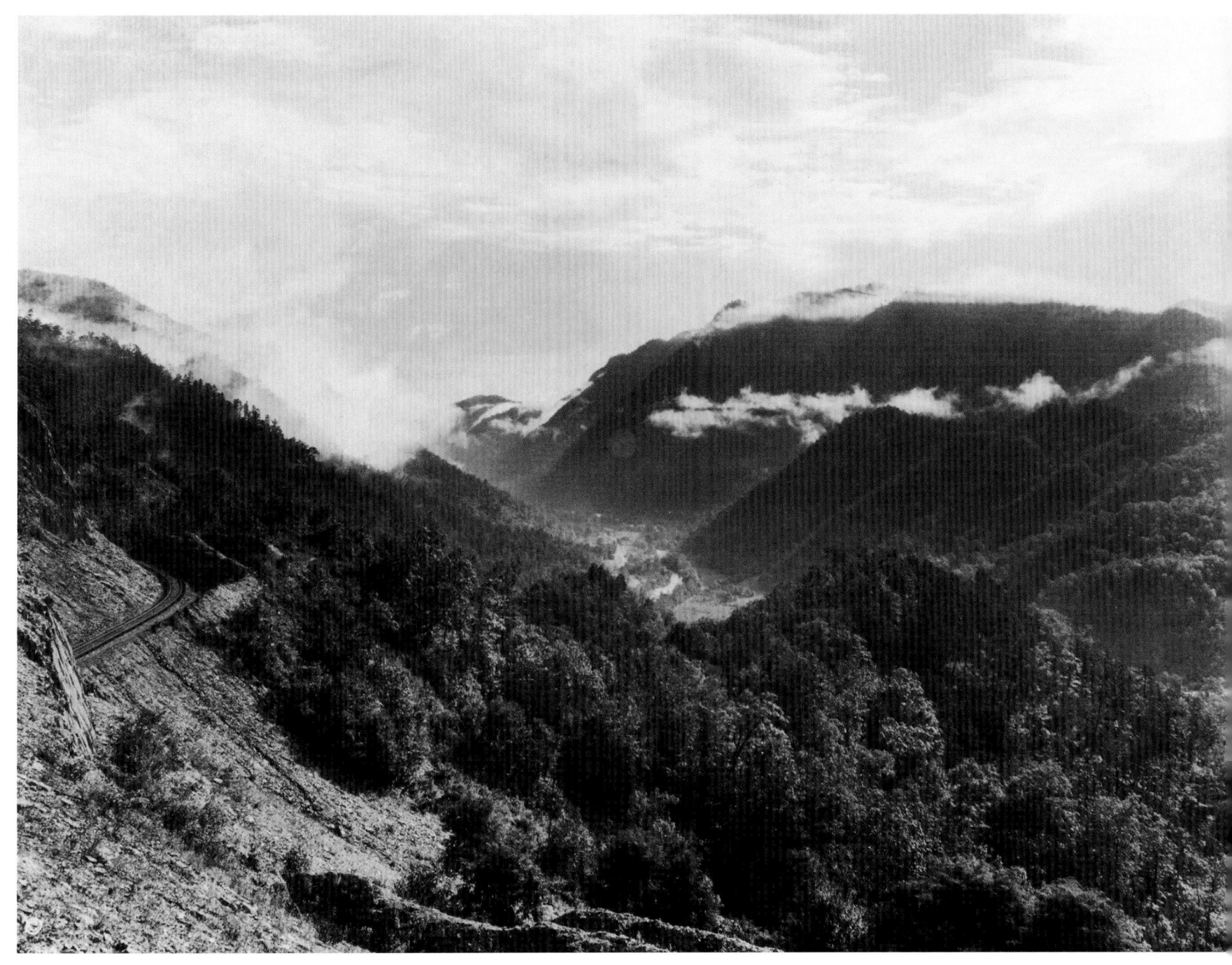

54   Nantahala Gorge, with railroad tracks on the left. Courtesy of Pack Memorial Library.

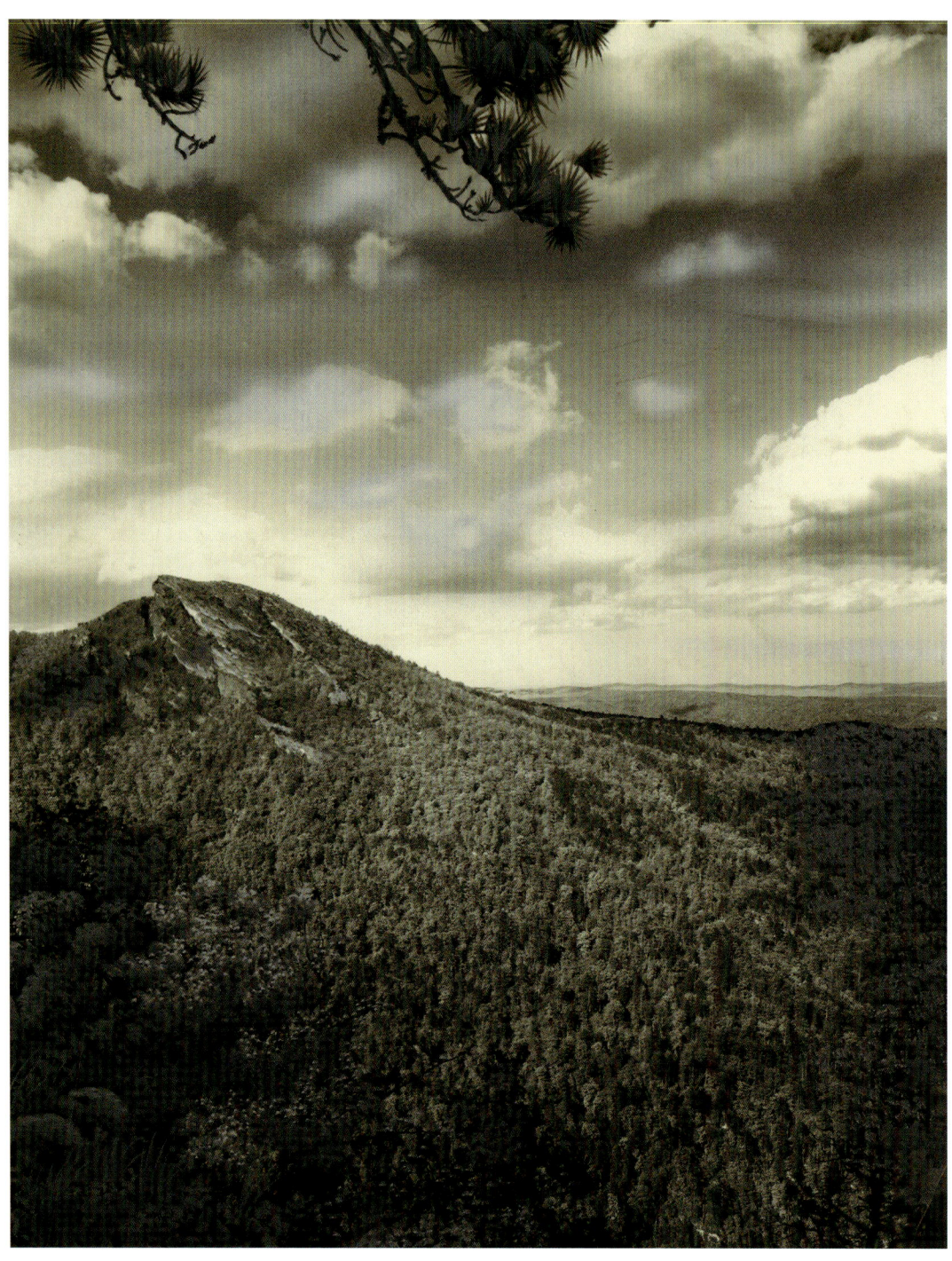

55   Hawksbill Mountain near Linville,
      North Carolina. Courtesy of Pack
      Memorial Library.

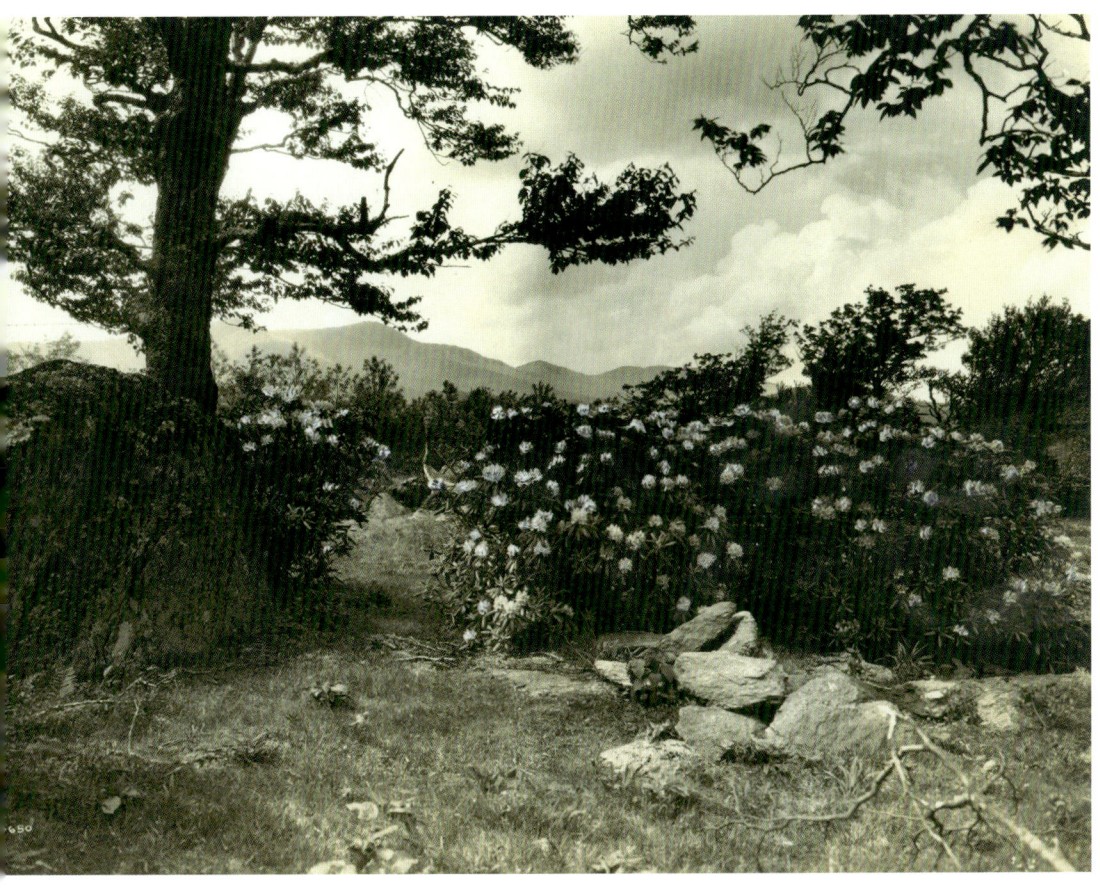

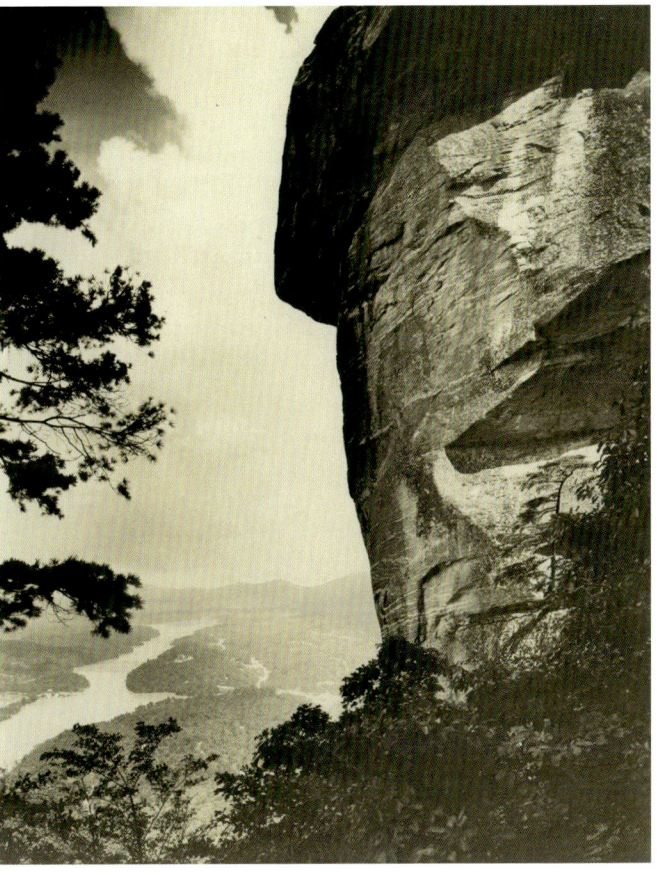

56   Rhododendrons on the Craggies. Courtesy of Pack Memorial Library.

57   Chimney Rock and Lake Lure.
Courtesy of Pack Memorial Library.

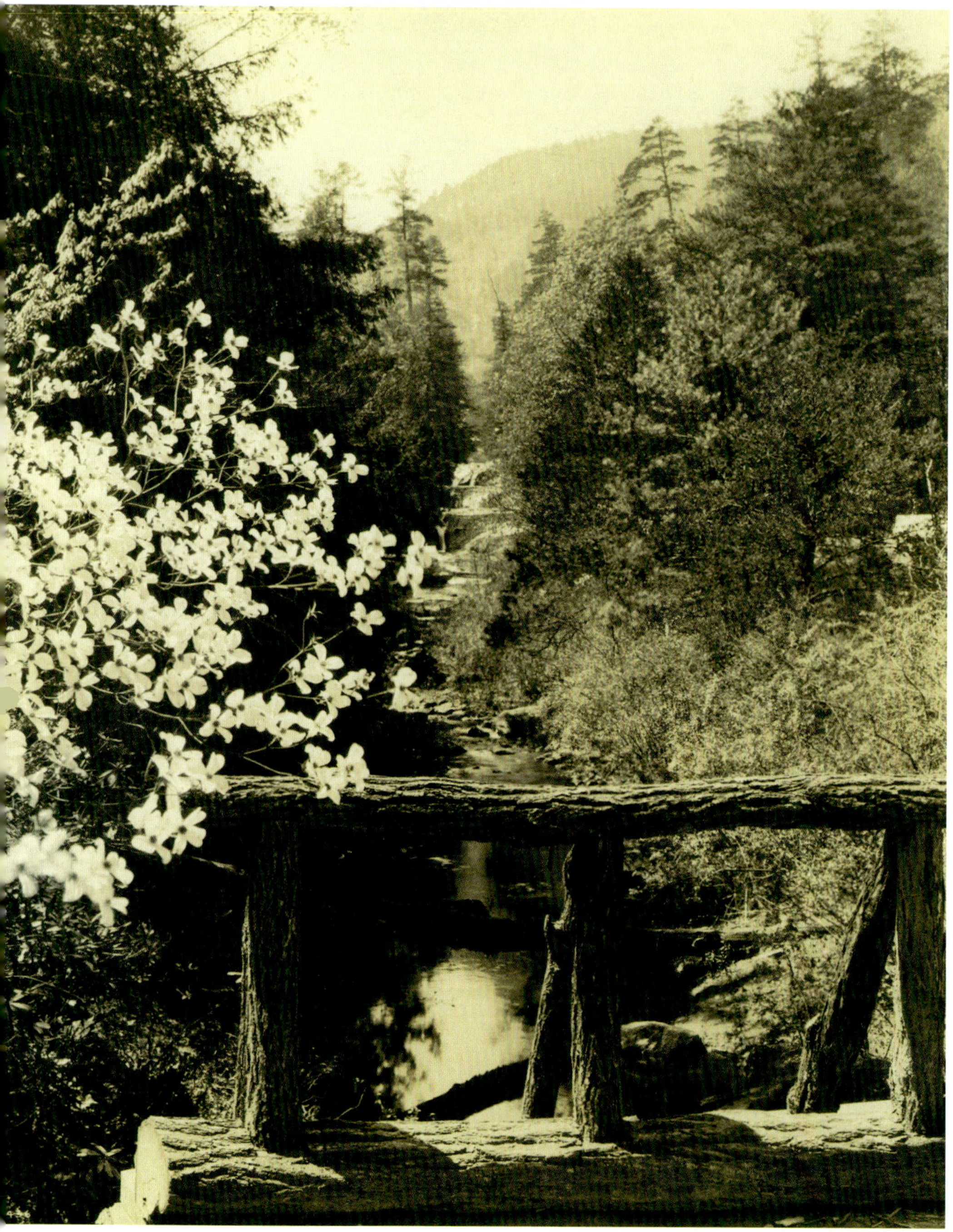

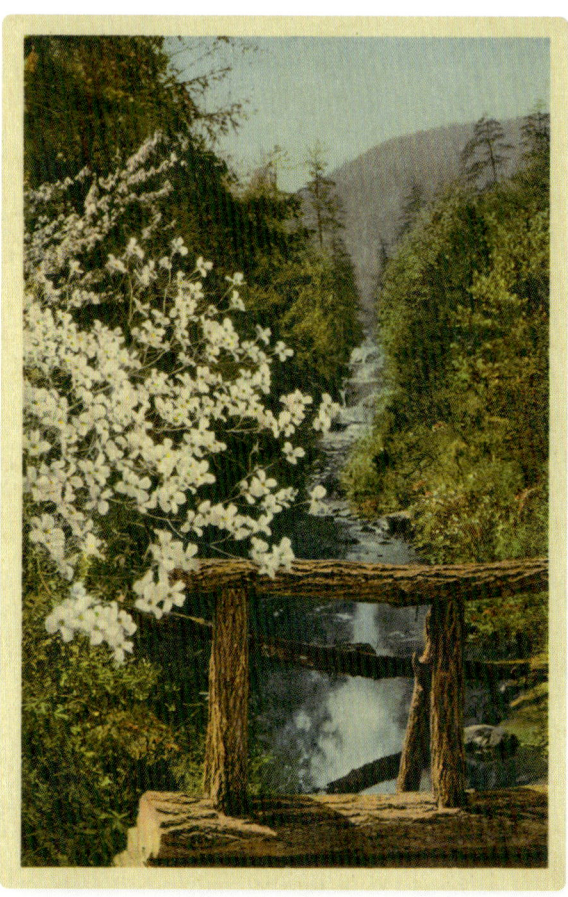

59   A rustic log footbridge.
Courtesy of Pack Memorial Library.

58   A rustic log footbridge. Courtesy of Pack Memorial Library.

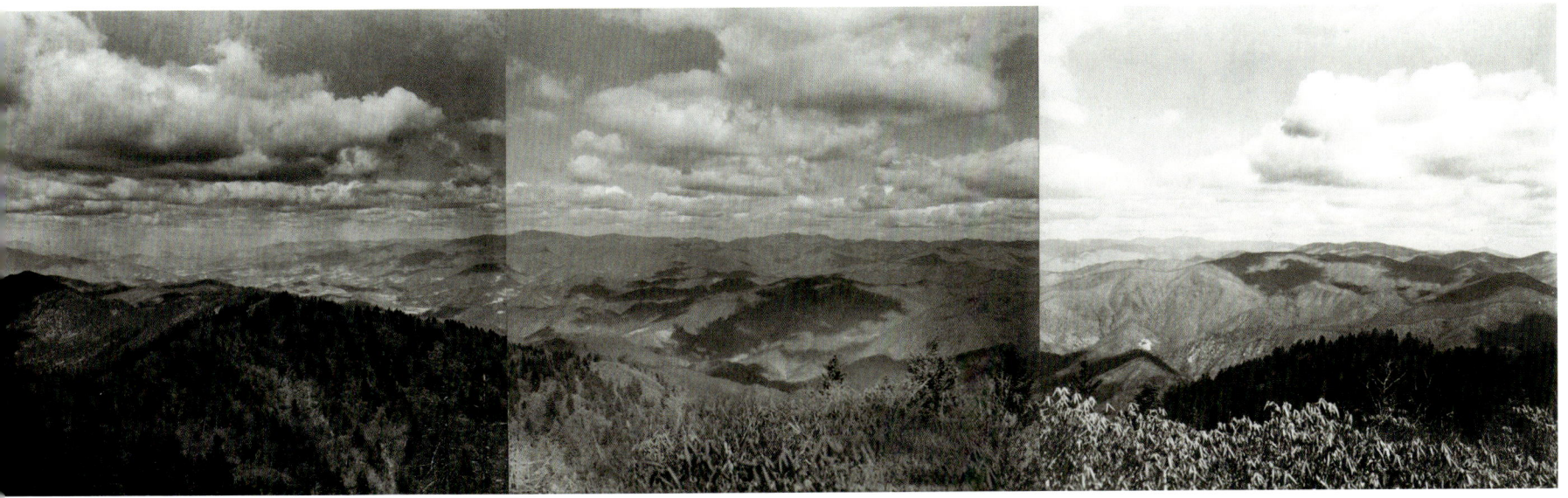

60   Panoramic view of the northern half of the Great Smokies taken from Table Rock. Courtesy of Pack Memorial Library.

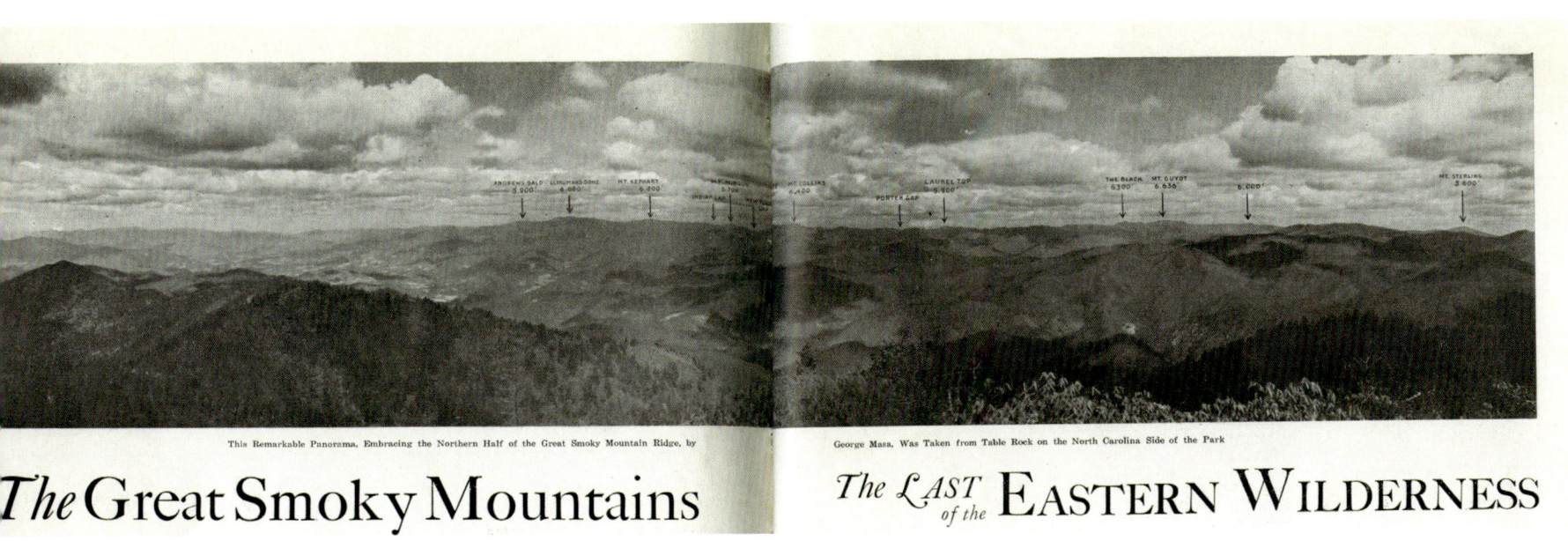

This Remarkable Panorama, Embracing the Northern Half of the Great Smoky Mountain Ridge, by   George Masa, Was Taken from Table Rock on the North Carolina Side of the Park

The Great Smoky Mountains   *The* LAST *of the* EASTERN WILDERNESS

61   Panoramic view of the northern half of the Great Smokies used on the title page of two articles. Courtesy of Pack Memorial Library.

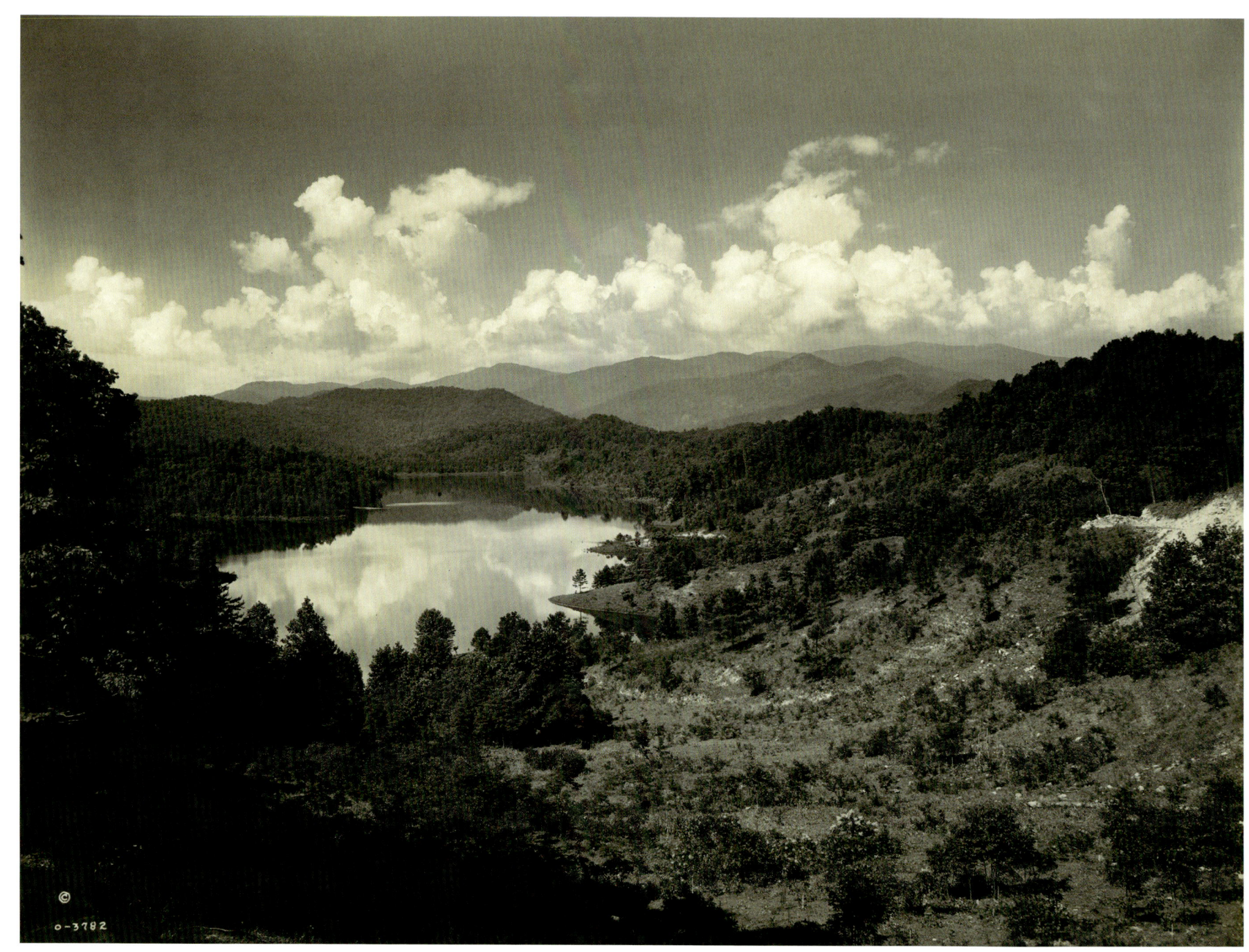

62   View of Lake Santeetlah. Courtesy of Smokies Life.

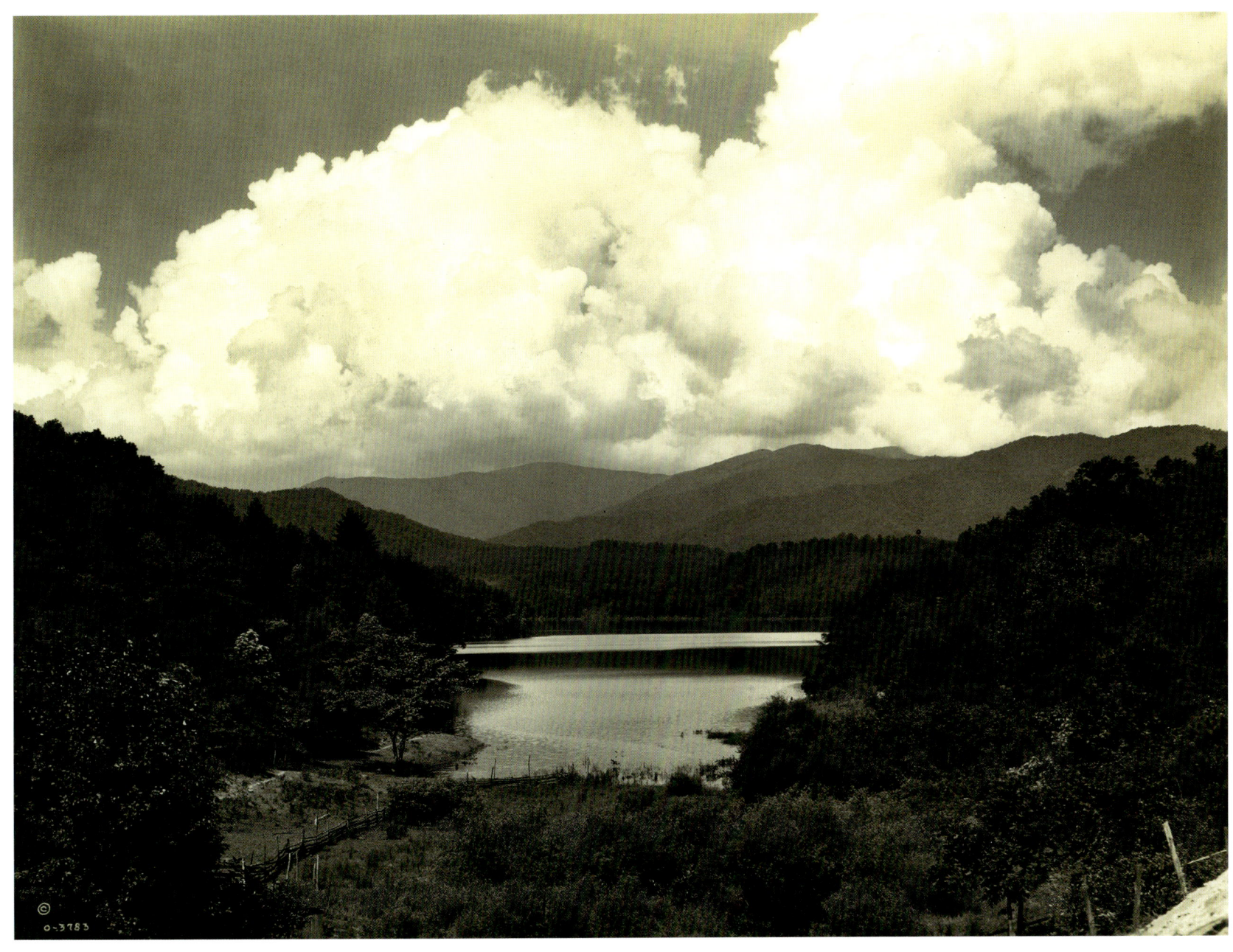

63   View of Lake Santeetlah. Courtesy of Smokies Life.

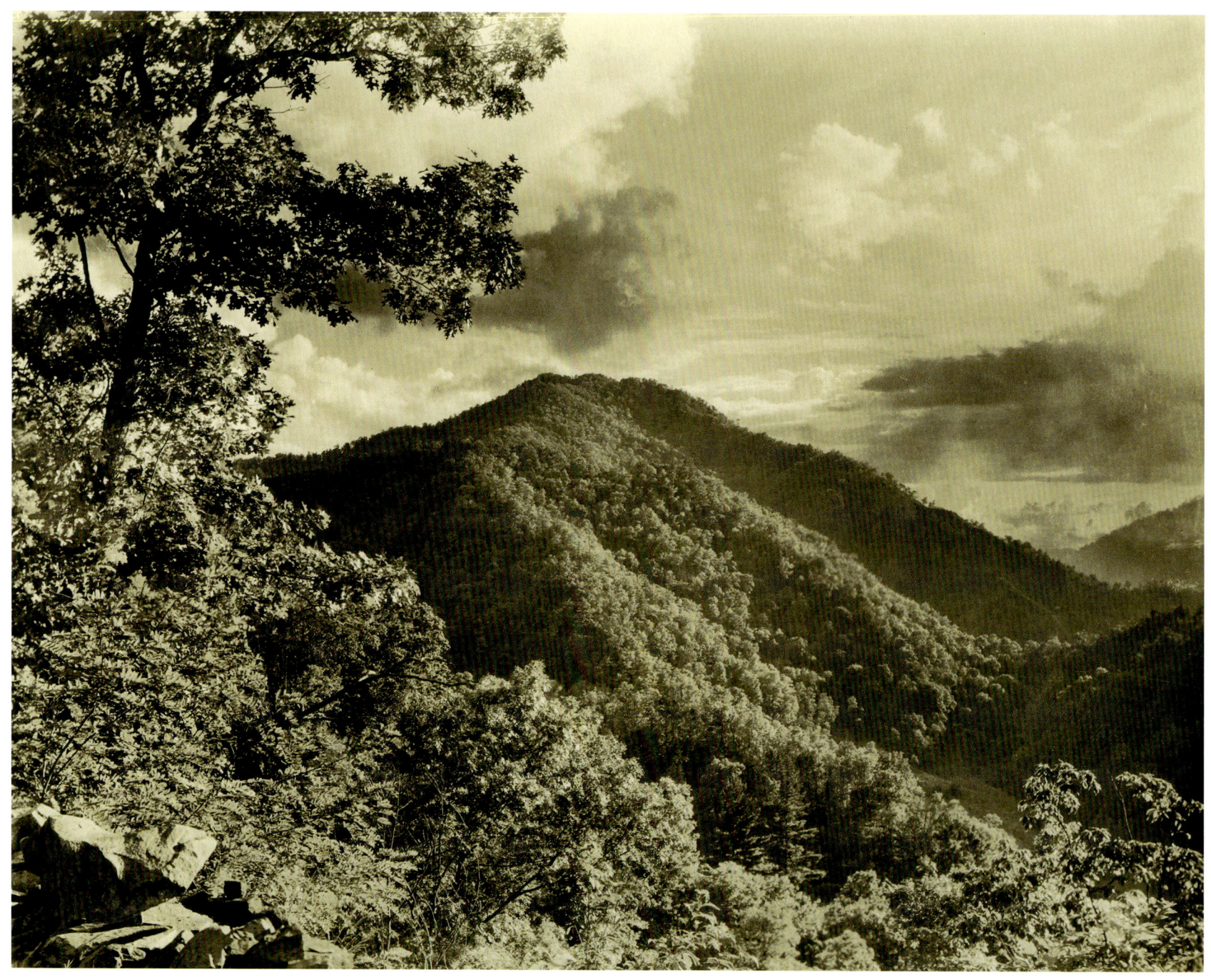

64   One of the Snowbird Mountains, south of the Great Smoky Mountains National Park. Courtesy of Smokies Life.

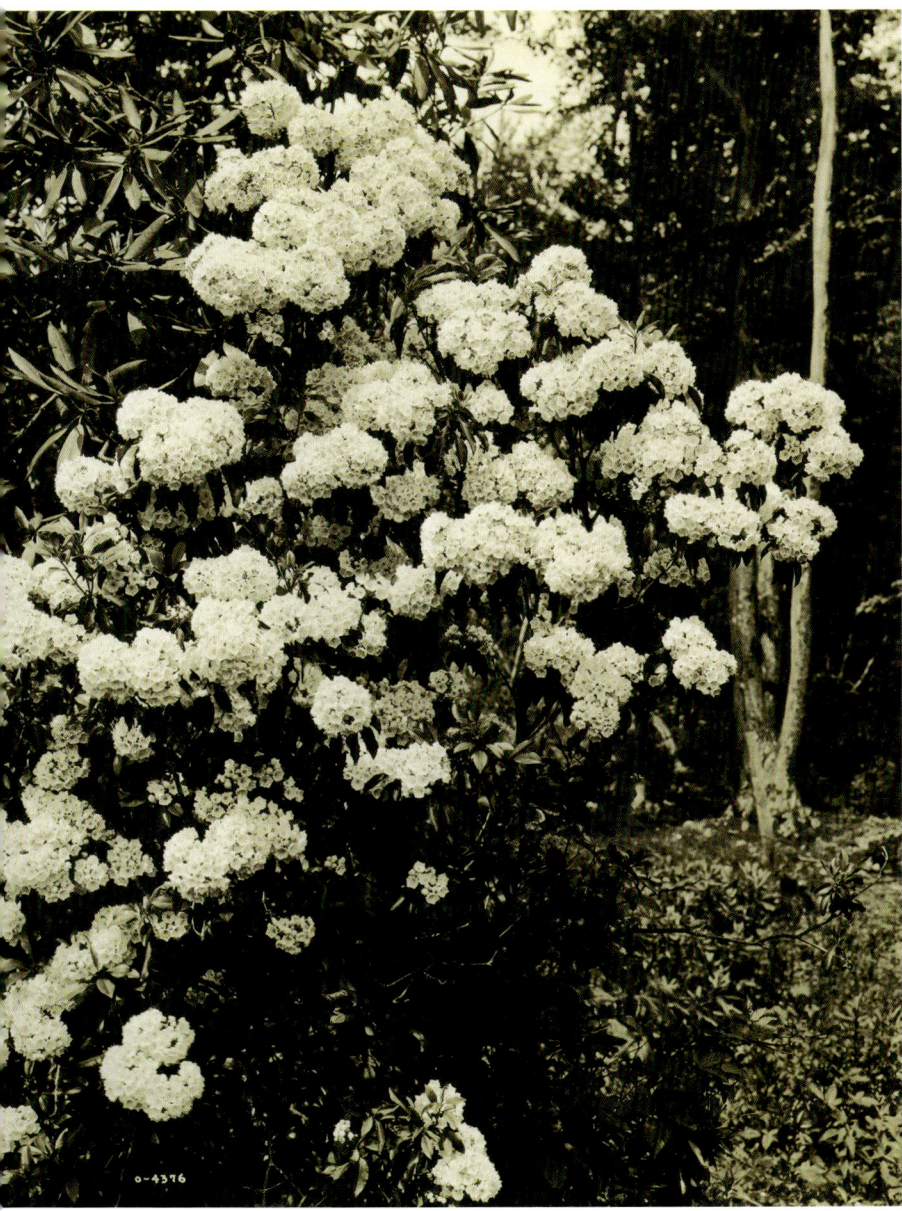

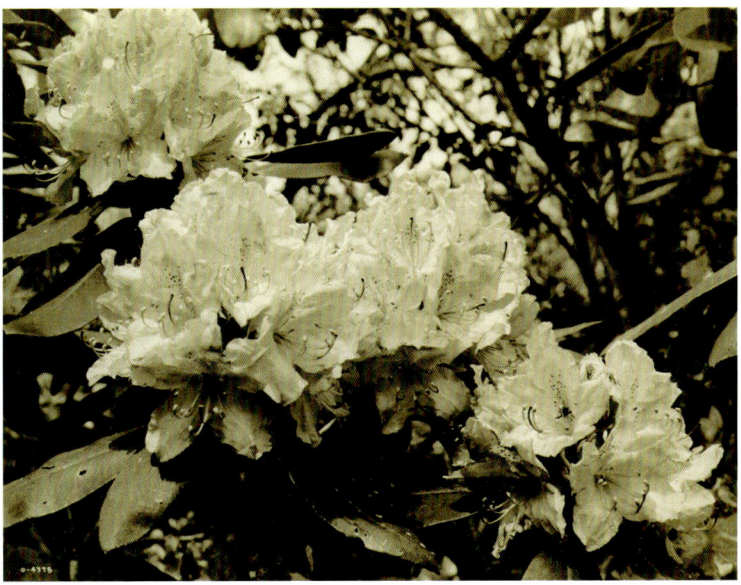

66   A close-up of a rhododendron cluster.
Courtesy of Smokies Life.

65   A close-up view of mountain laurel.
Courtesy of Smokies Life.

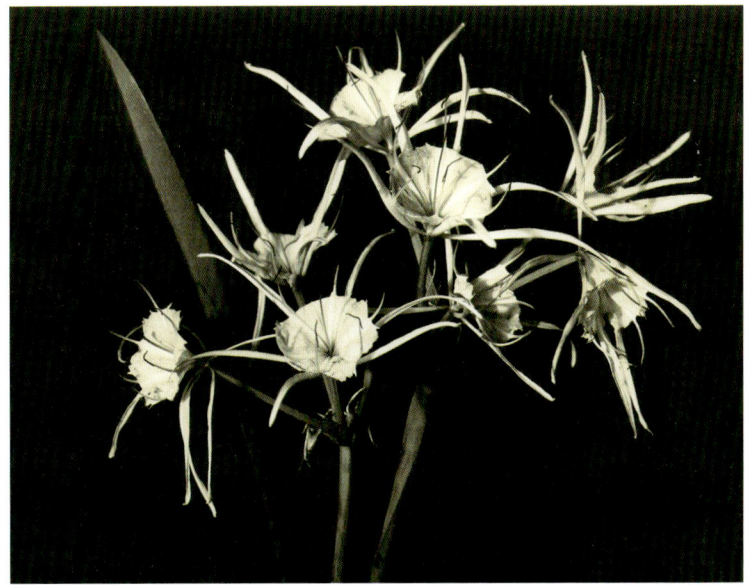

67   Spider lilies. Courtesy of Smokies Life.

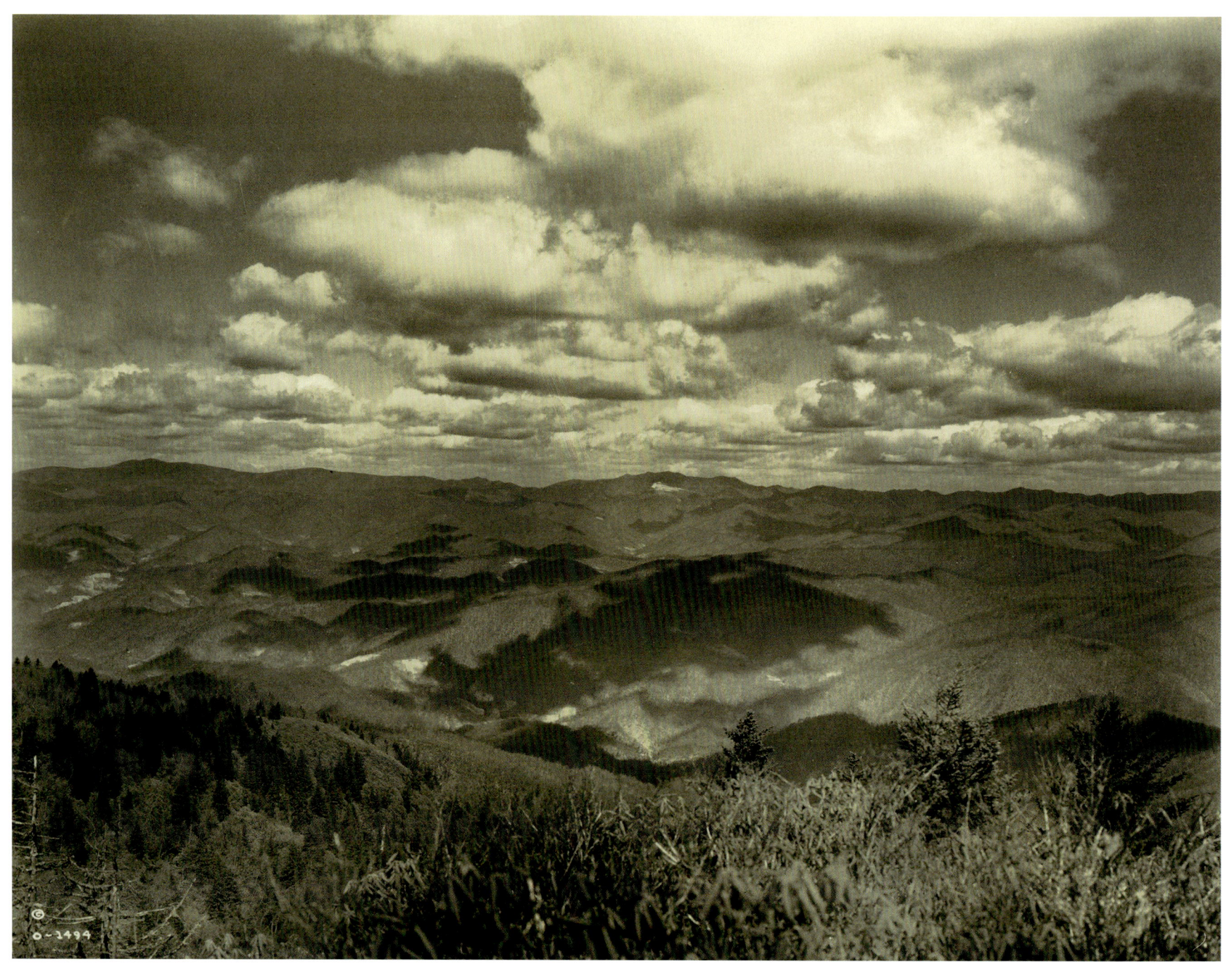

68   View from Black Rock on Plott Balsams, east of Great Smoky Mountains National Park. Courtesy of Smokies Life.

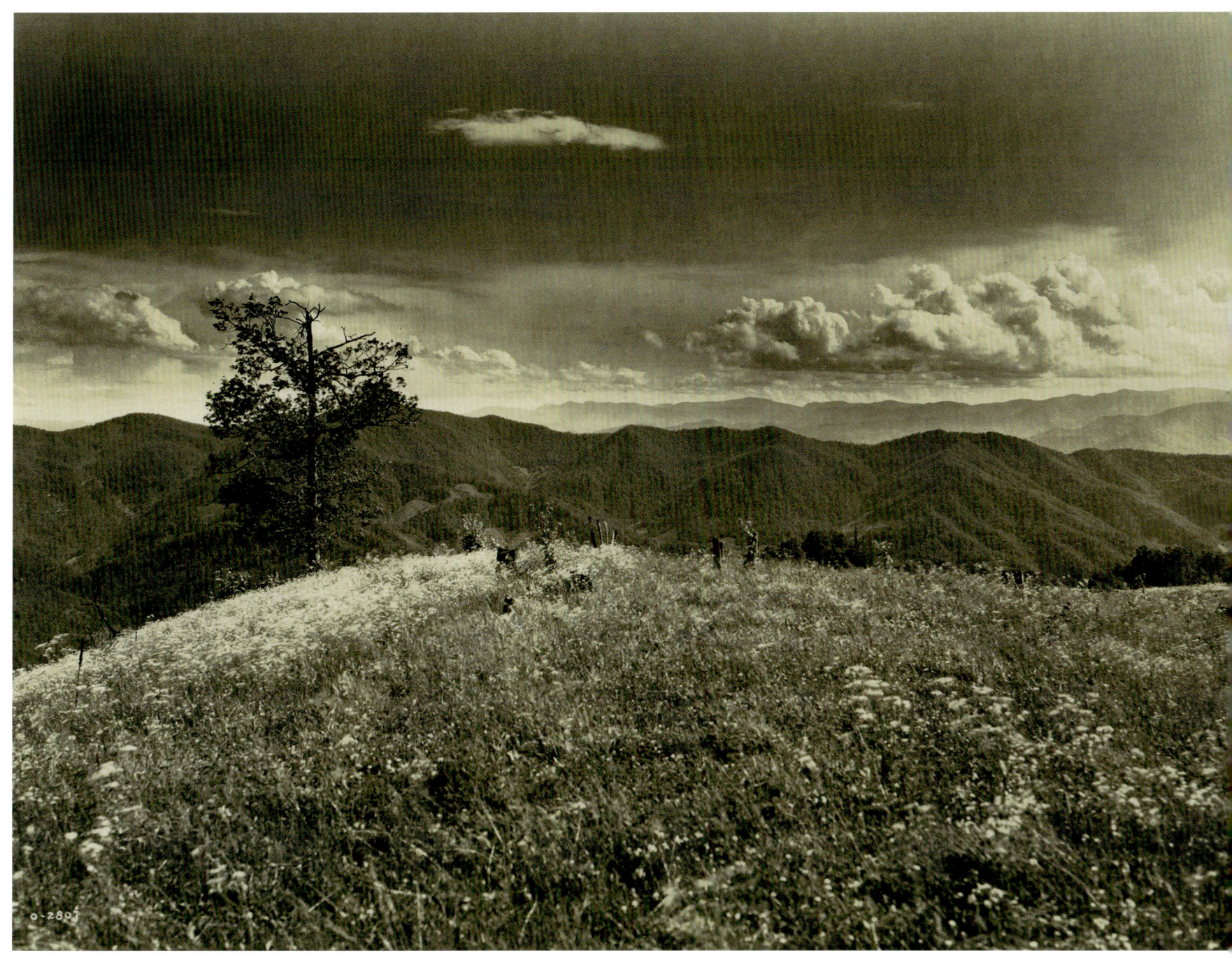

69   View of Rich Mountain, near Boone, North Carolina. Courtesy of Smokies Life.

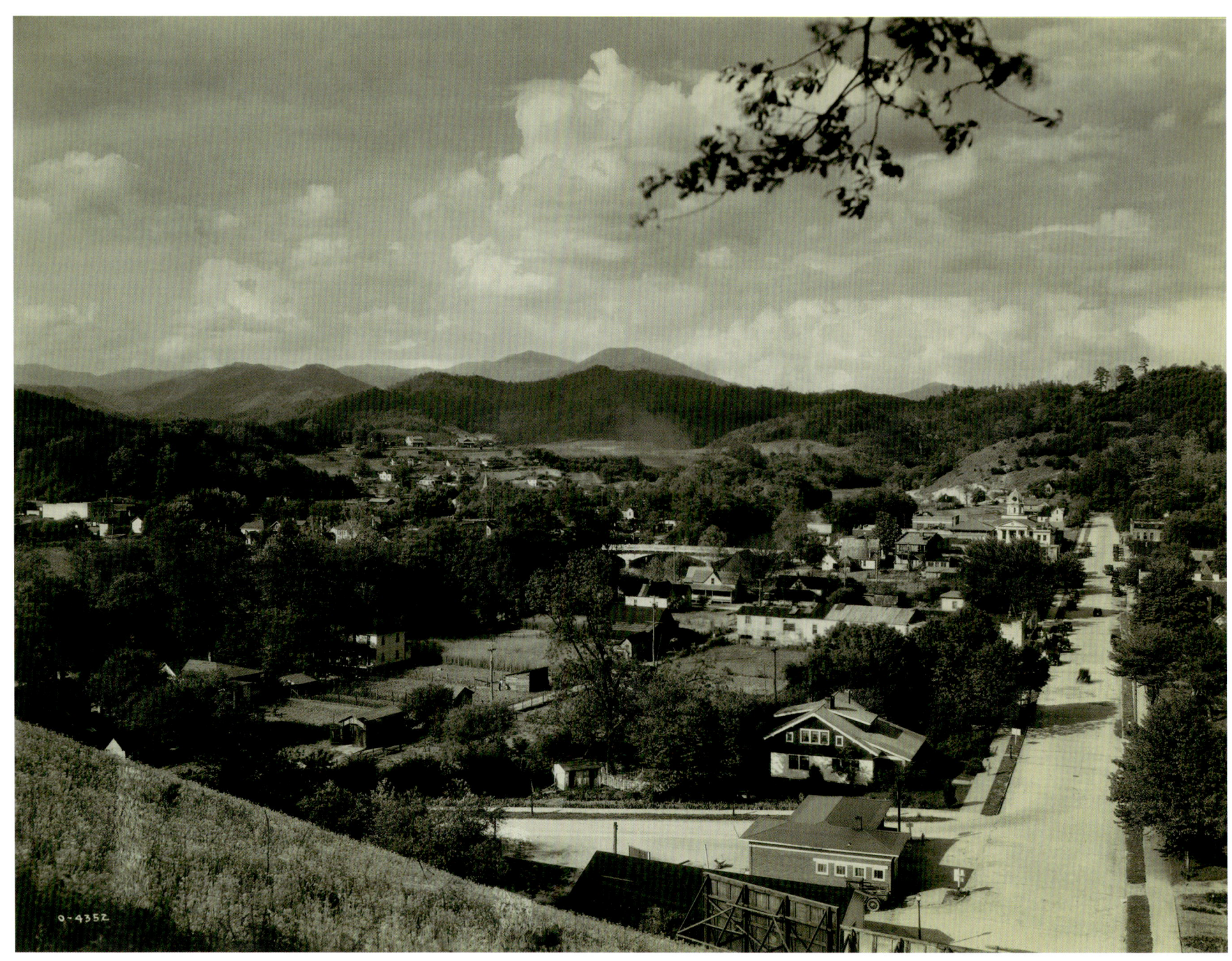

70 View of Bryson City. Courtesy of Smokies Life.

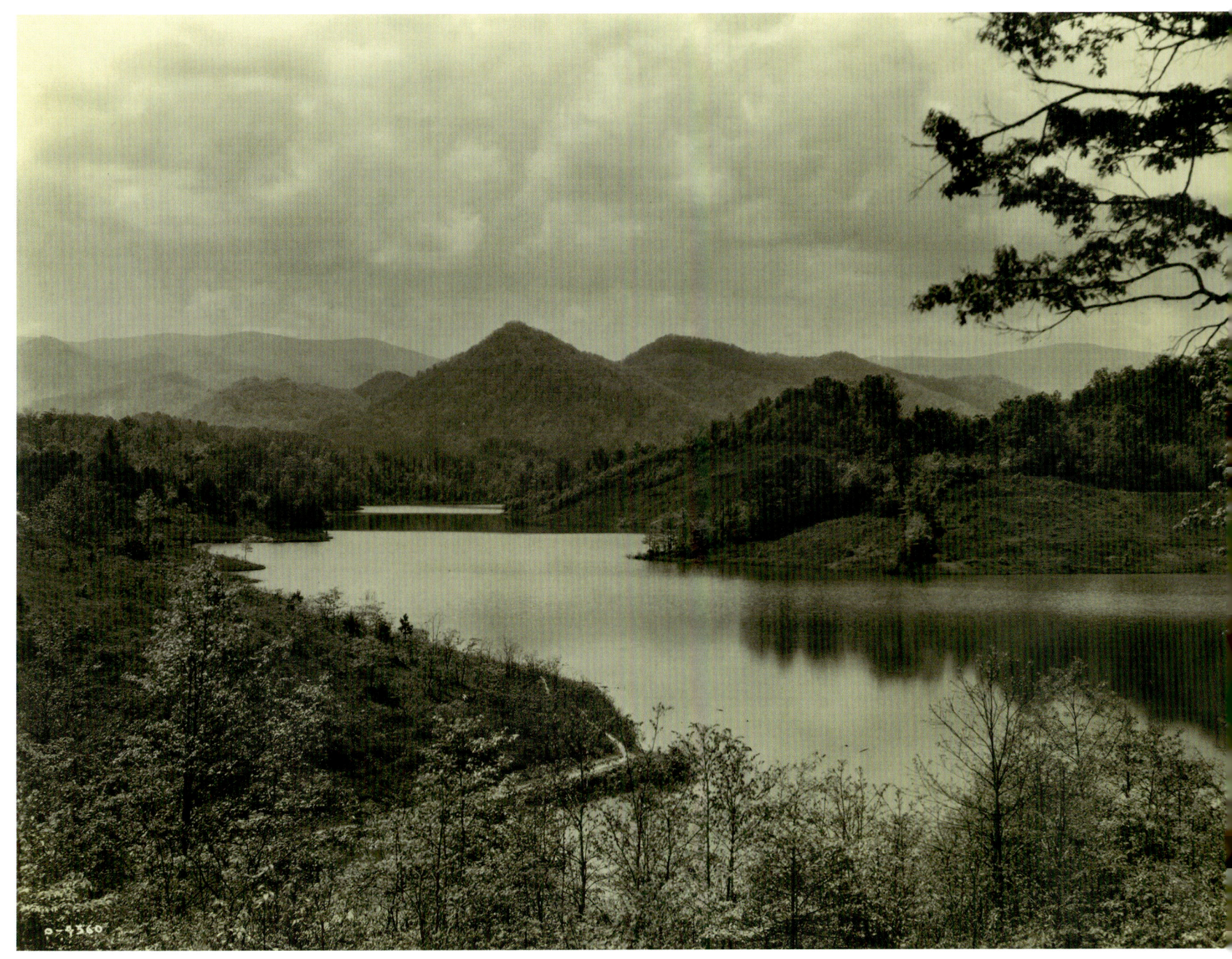

71 View of lake with sharp-peaked mountains. Courtesy of Smokies Life.

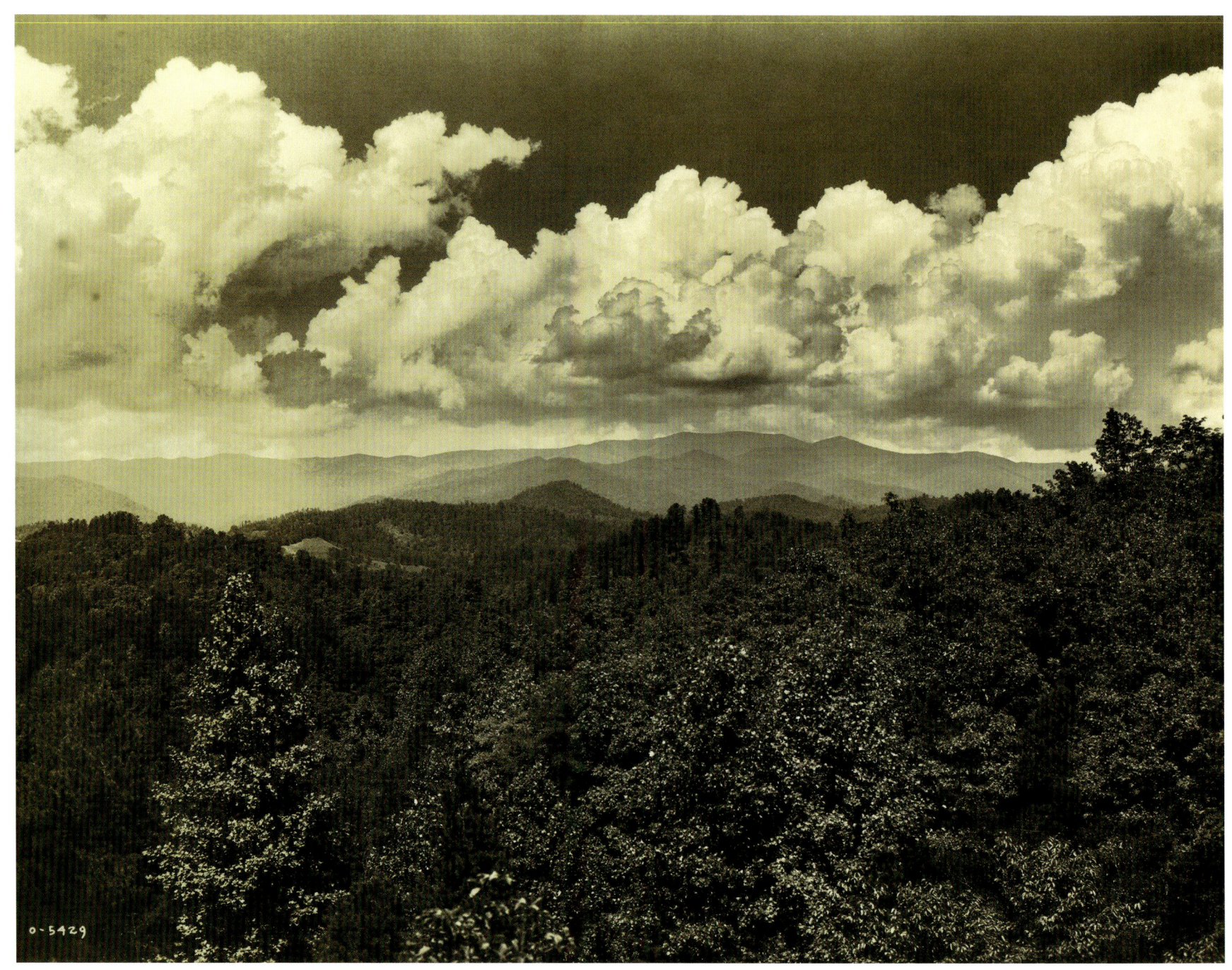

72　View of distant mountains and clouds. Courtesy of Smokies Life.

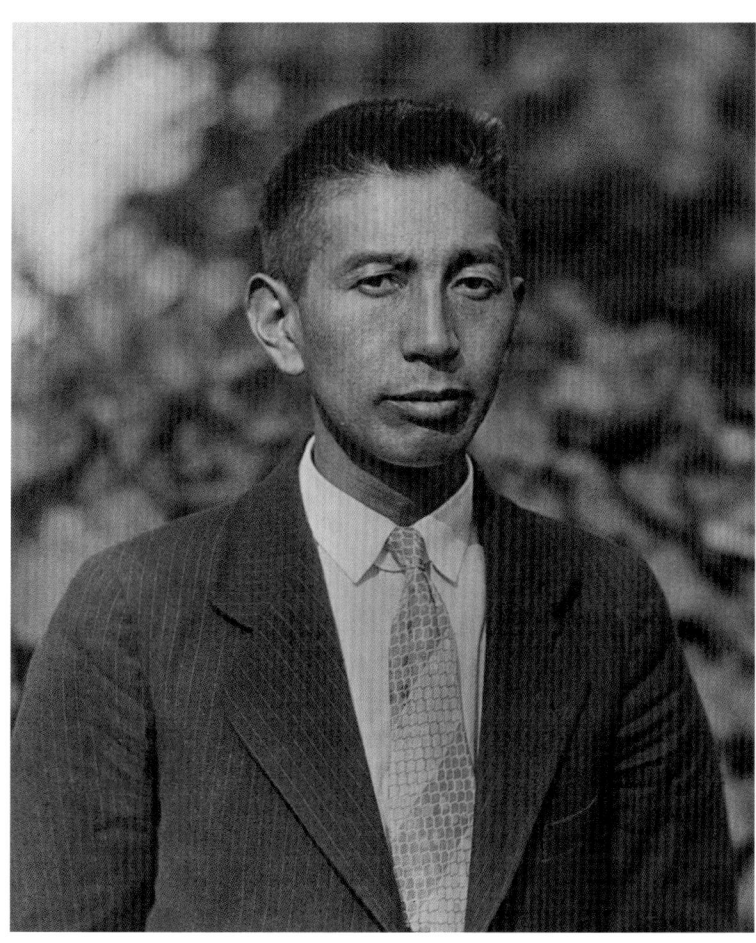

73 A portrait of George Masa. Courtesy of
Western Carolina University.

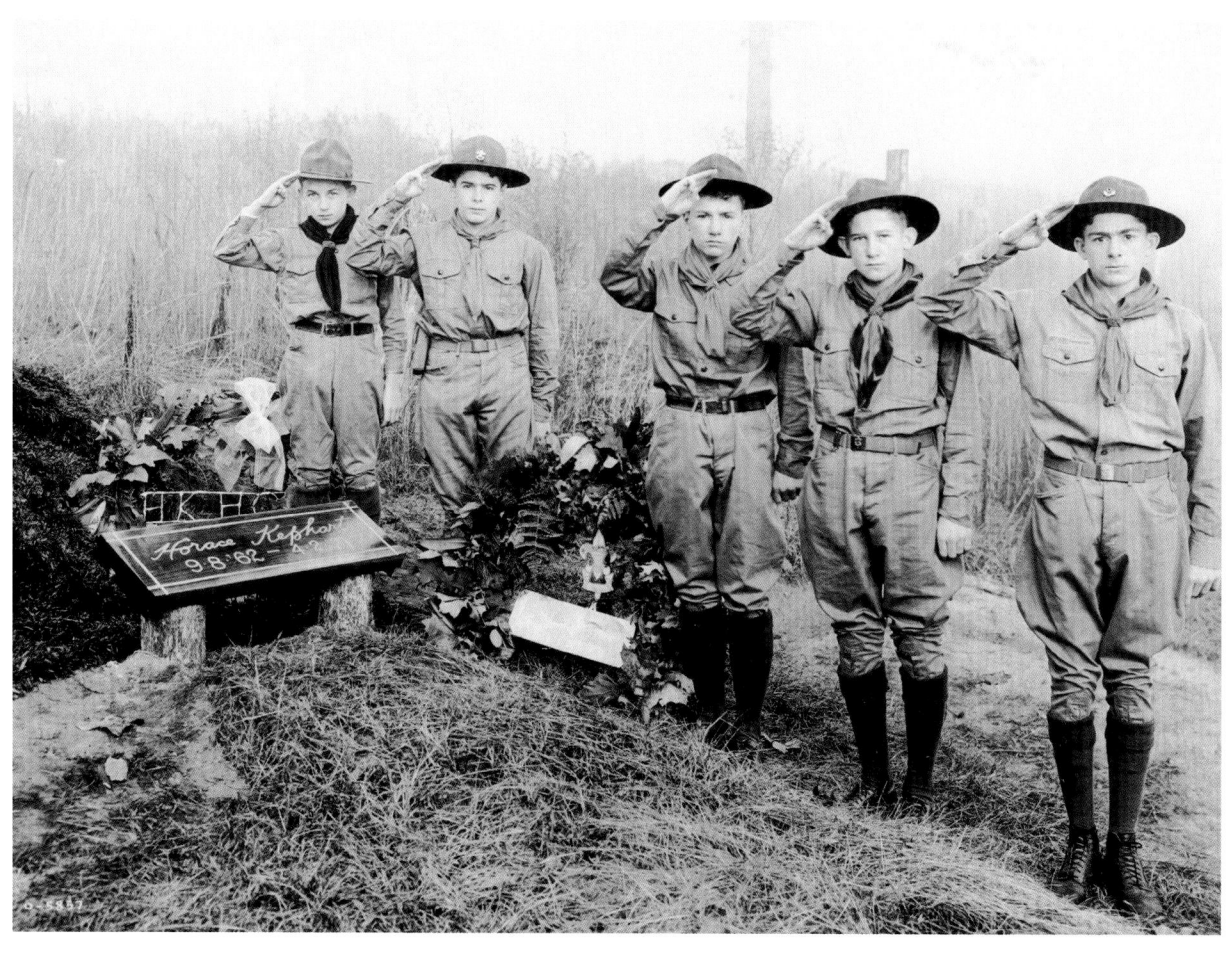

74　Boy Scouts salute during the memorial service for Horace Kephart, November 15, 1931.
Courtesy of Pack Memorial Library.

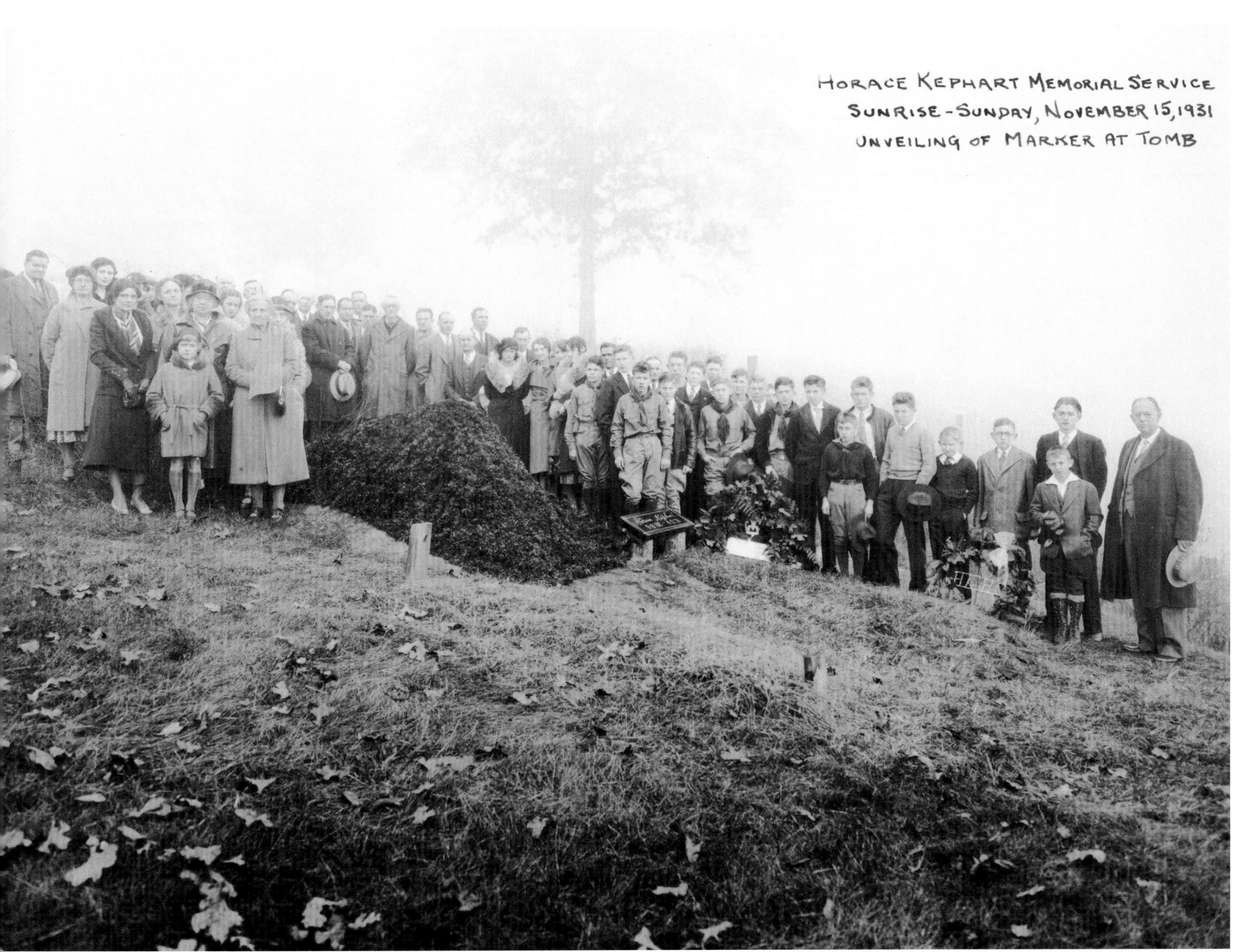

HORACE KEPHART MEMORIAL SERVICE
SUNRISE - SUNDAY, NOVEMBER 15, 1931
UNVEILING OF MARKER AT TOMB

75   Group attending the memorial service for Horace Kephart, November 15, 1931. Courtesy of Pack Memorial Library.

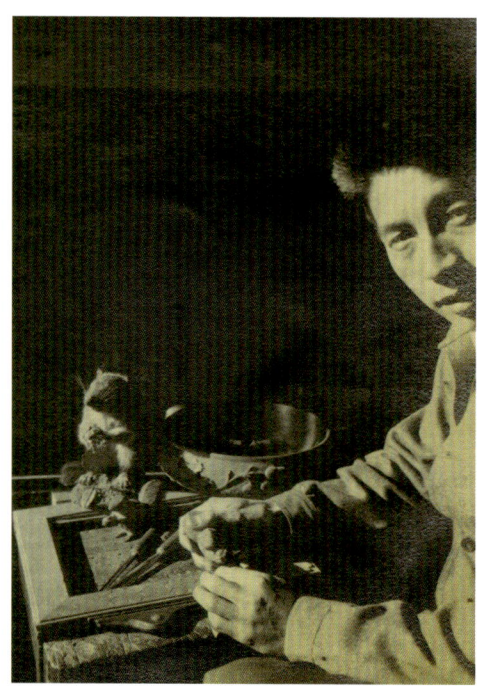

76   George Masa with a carved
      squirrel in the Biltmore Industries
      wood carving shop, ca. 1917.
      Photograph by Julia E. Brookshire.
      Courtesy of Pack Memorial
      Library.

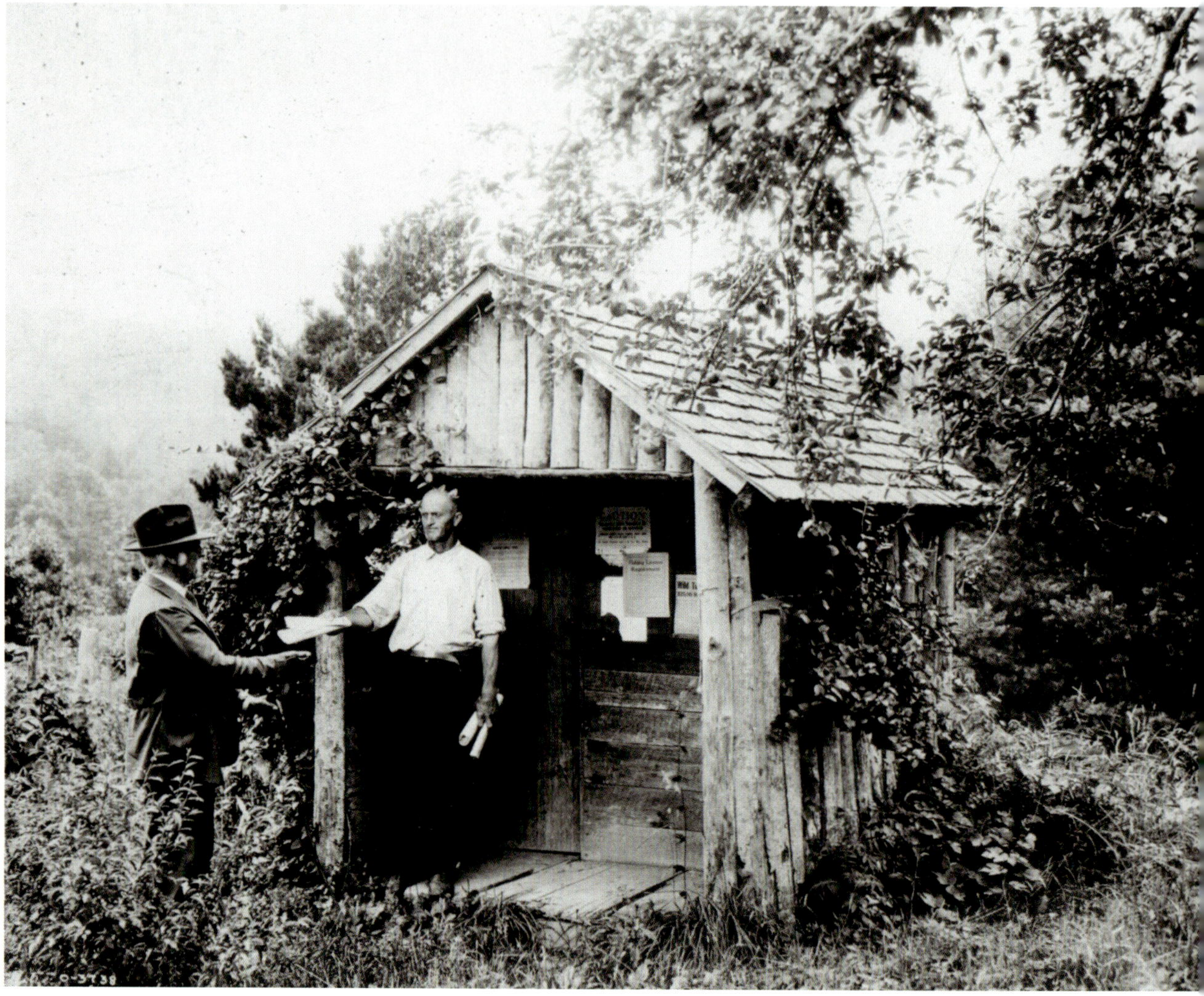

77   Warren Alexander dispensing mail at Grimshawes.
      Courtesy of Pack Memorial Library.

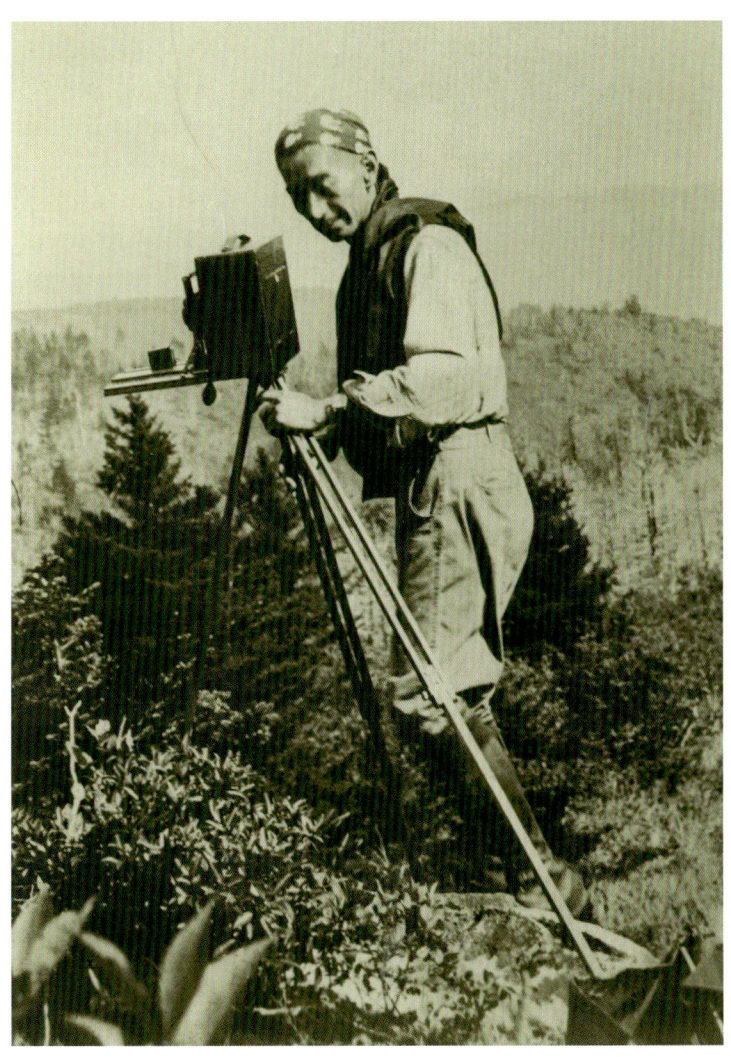

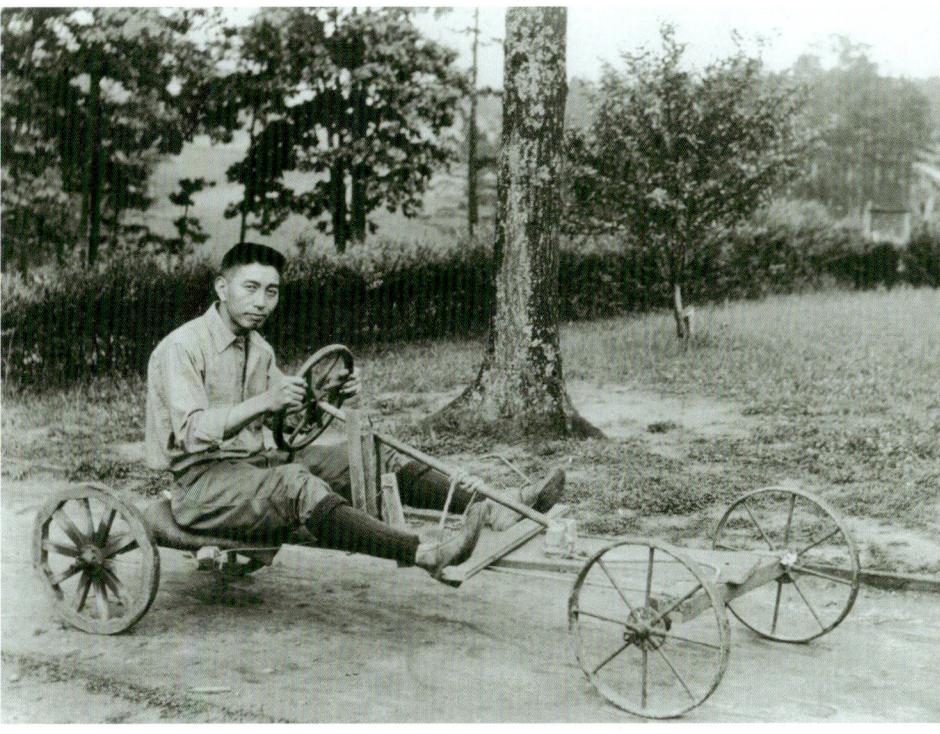

79   George Masa in a cart in front of Creasman house in Asheville,
      North Carolina. Courtesy of Pack Memorial Library.

78   George Masa on location with his camera on a tripod.
      Courtesy of Pack Memorial Library.

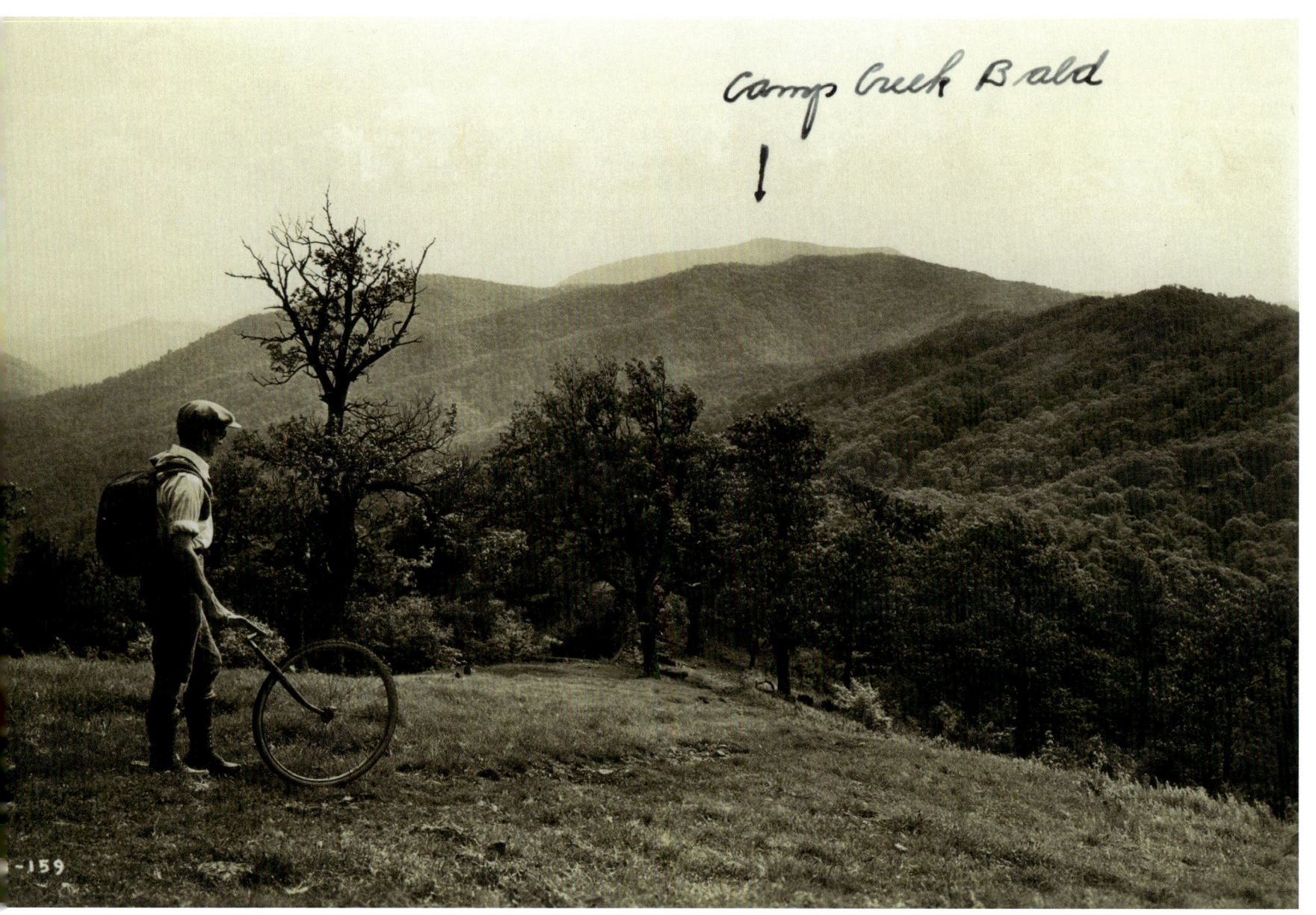

Camp Creek Bald

80   Hiker on the Appalachian Trail with a measuring wheel. Appalachian Trail Conference Collection,
     Myron Avery Collection, Special Collections and Archives, George Mason University Libraries.

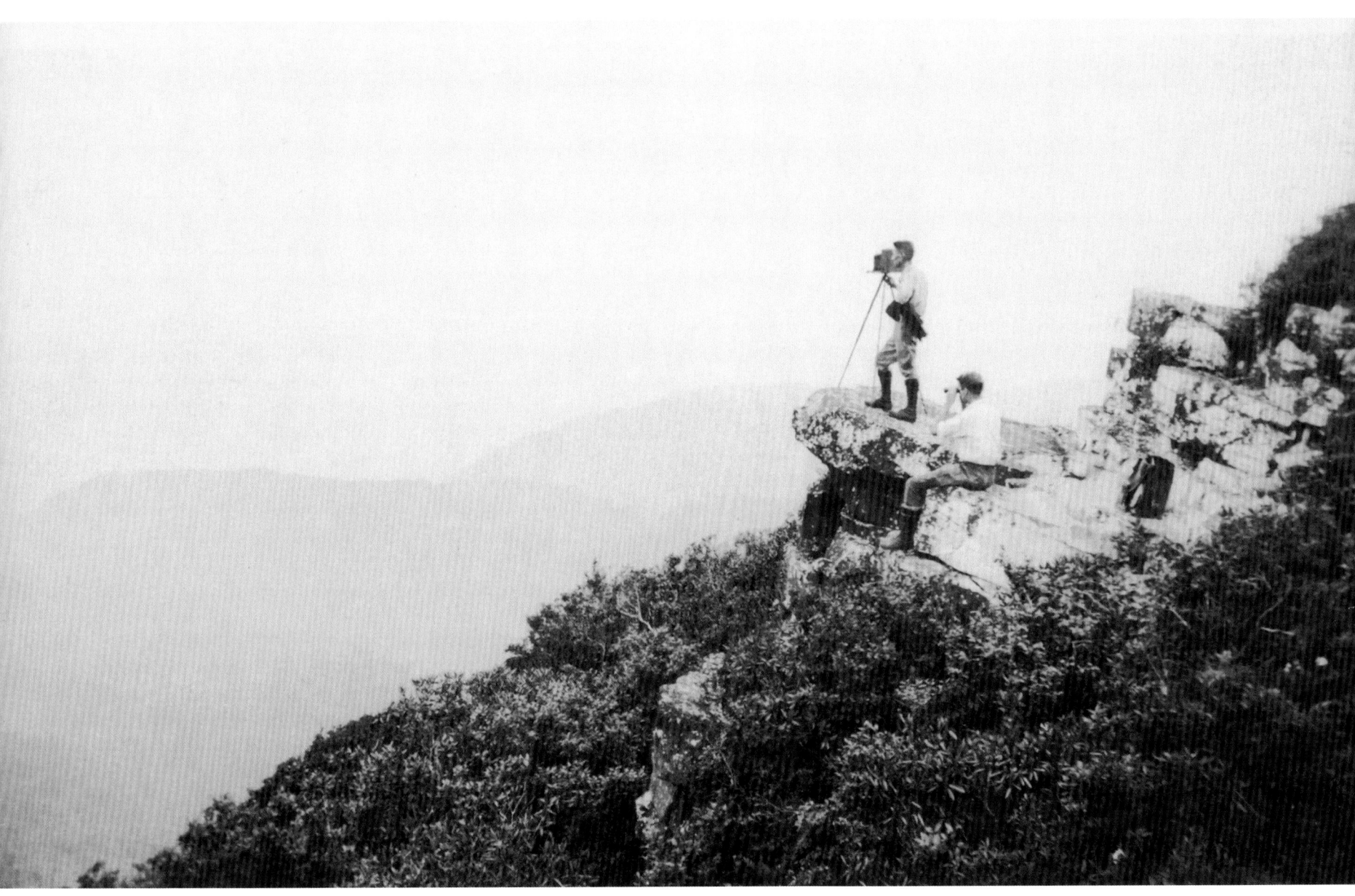

81   George Masa with a camera and an unidentified companion in the field with a camera.
      Recent research identifies the location of the photograph to be Blackstack Cliffs
      in the Cherokee National Forest. Courtesy of Pack Memorial Library.

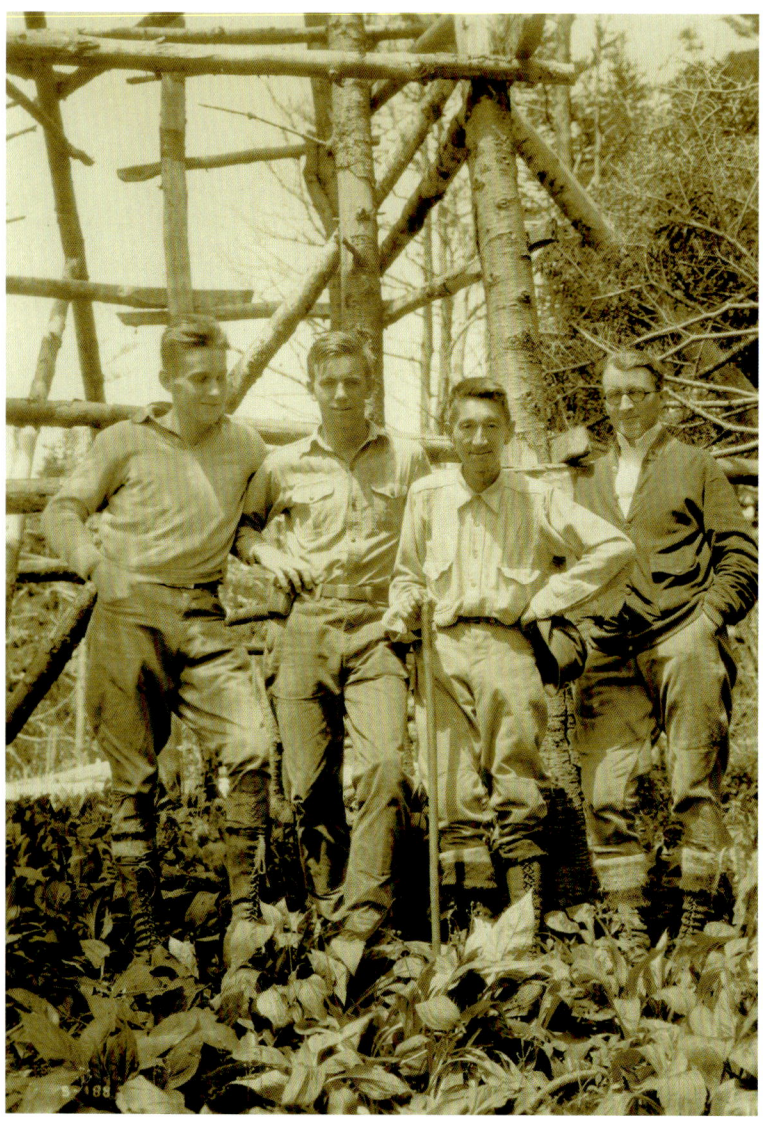

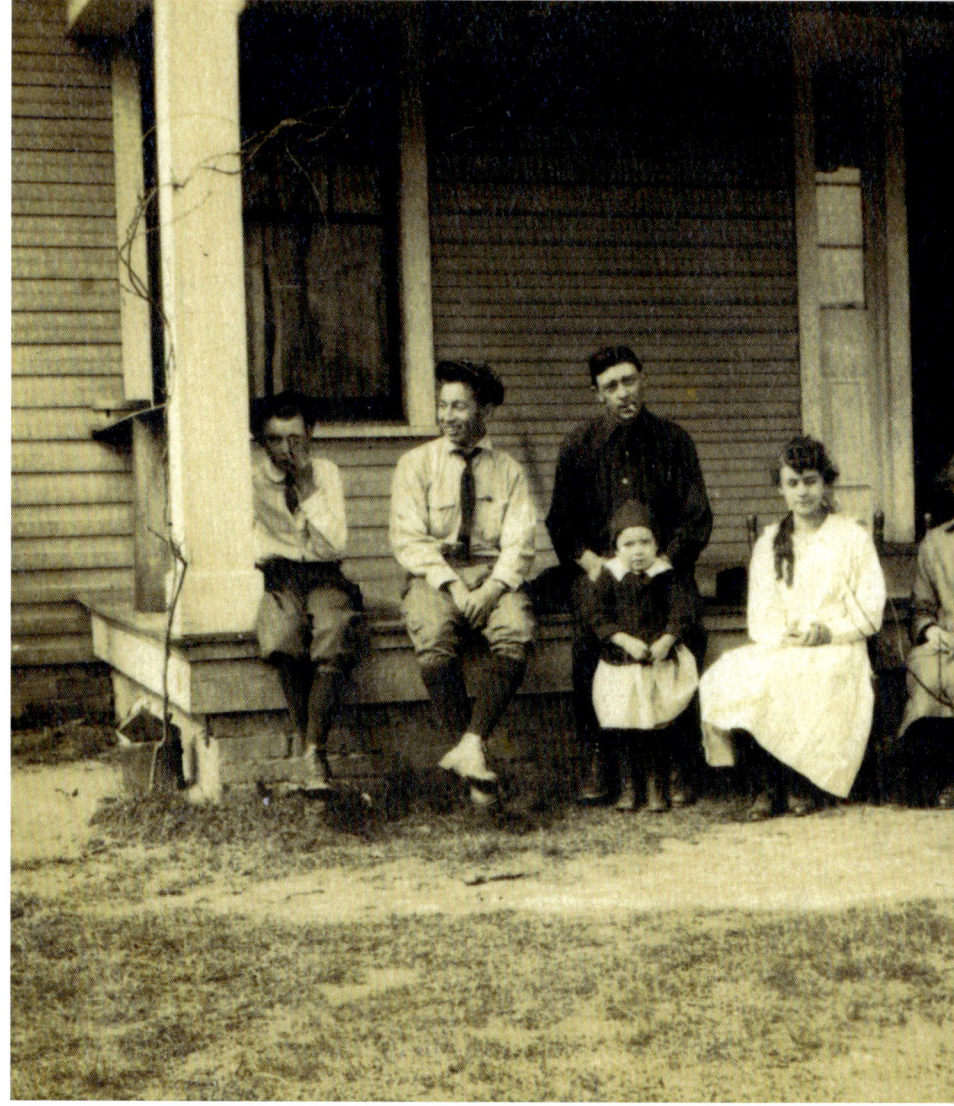

82   George Masa with unidentified hiking companions beside
     a wooden tower, possibly on the summit of Kuwohi.
     Courtesy of Pack Memorial Library.

83   George Masa with Creasman family on the porch of their home.
     Left to right: Blake Creasman, George Masa, Oscar Creasman,
     Doris Creasman, Blanche Creasman, Leila Pressly (cousin),
     and Ruby Creasman. Courtesy of Pack Memorial Library.

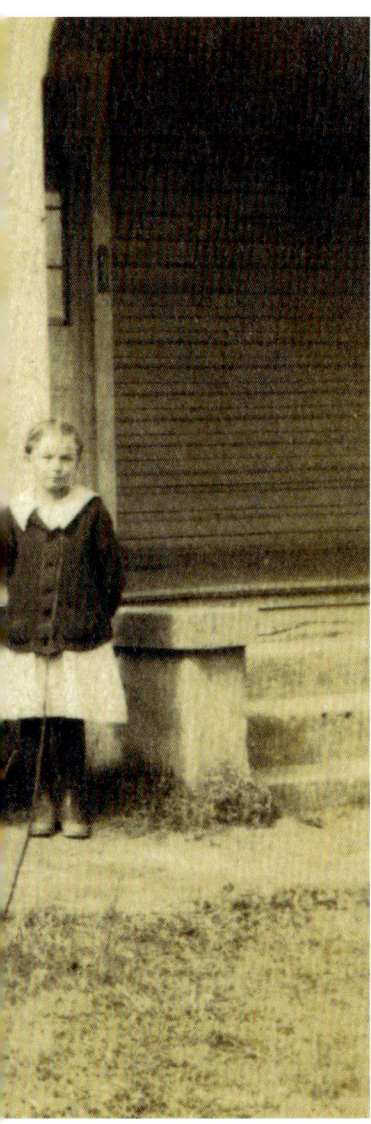
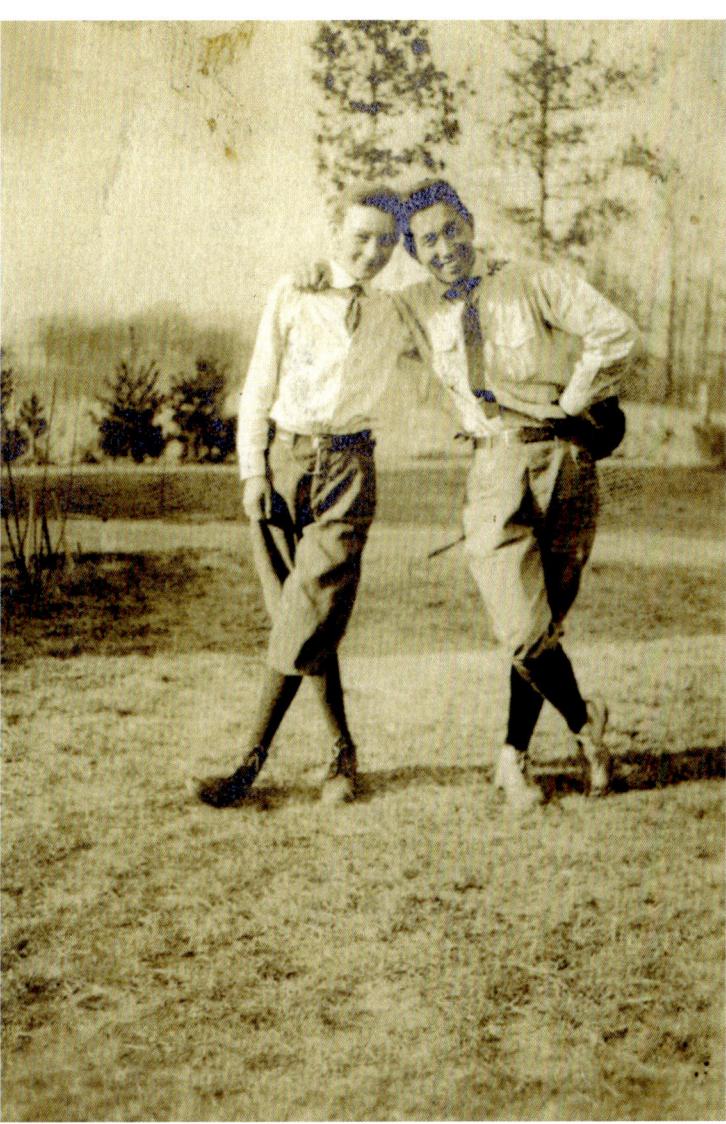

84 Blake Creasman and George Masa in front of Creasman house. Courtesy of Pack Memorial Library.

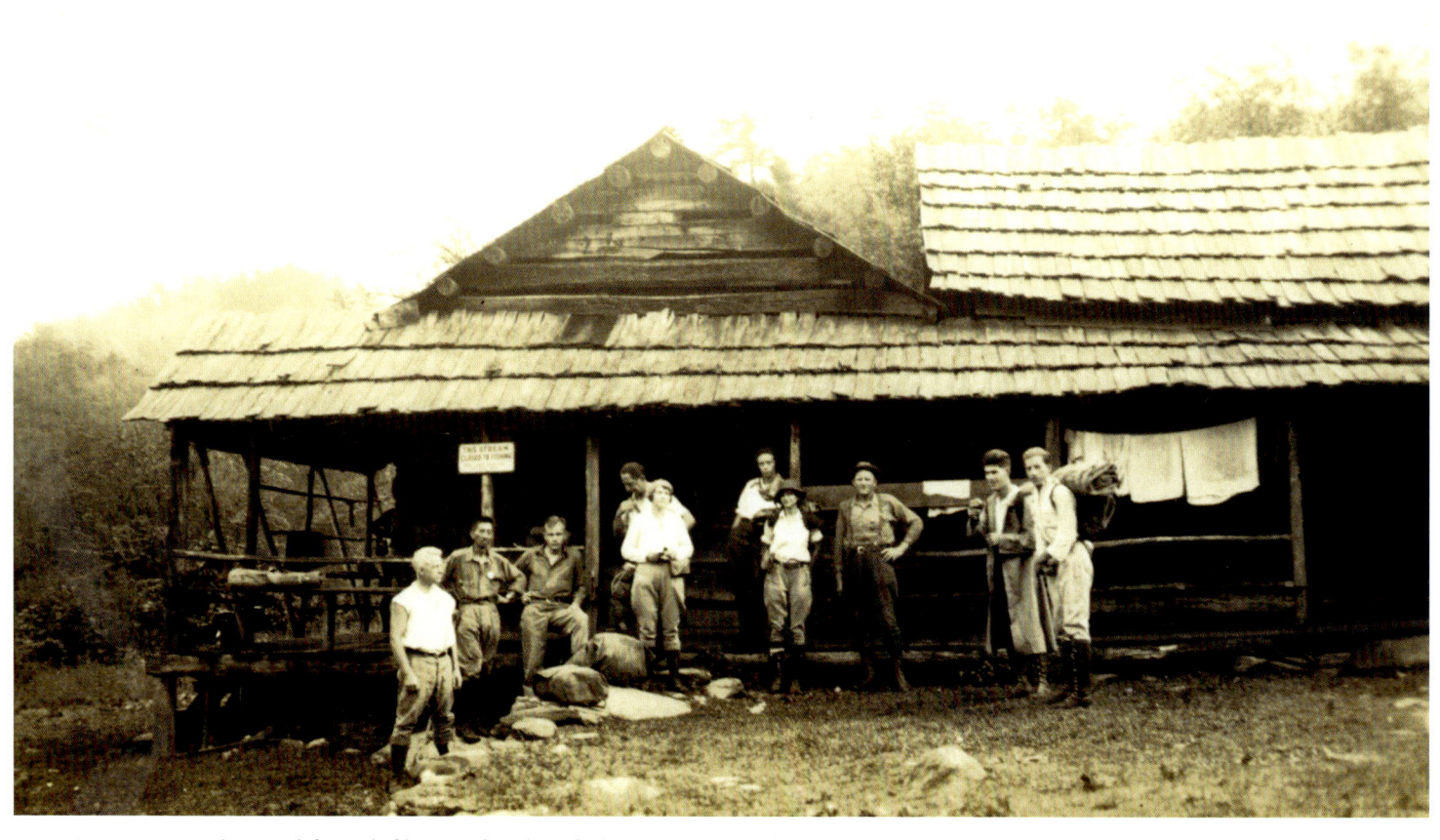

85   George Masa (second from left) outside a log shelter. Courtesy of Pack Memorial Library.

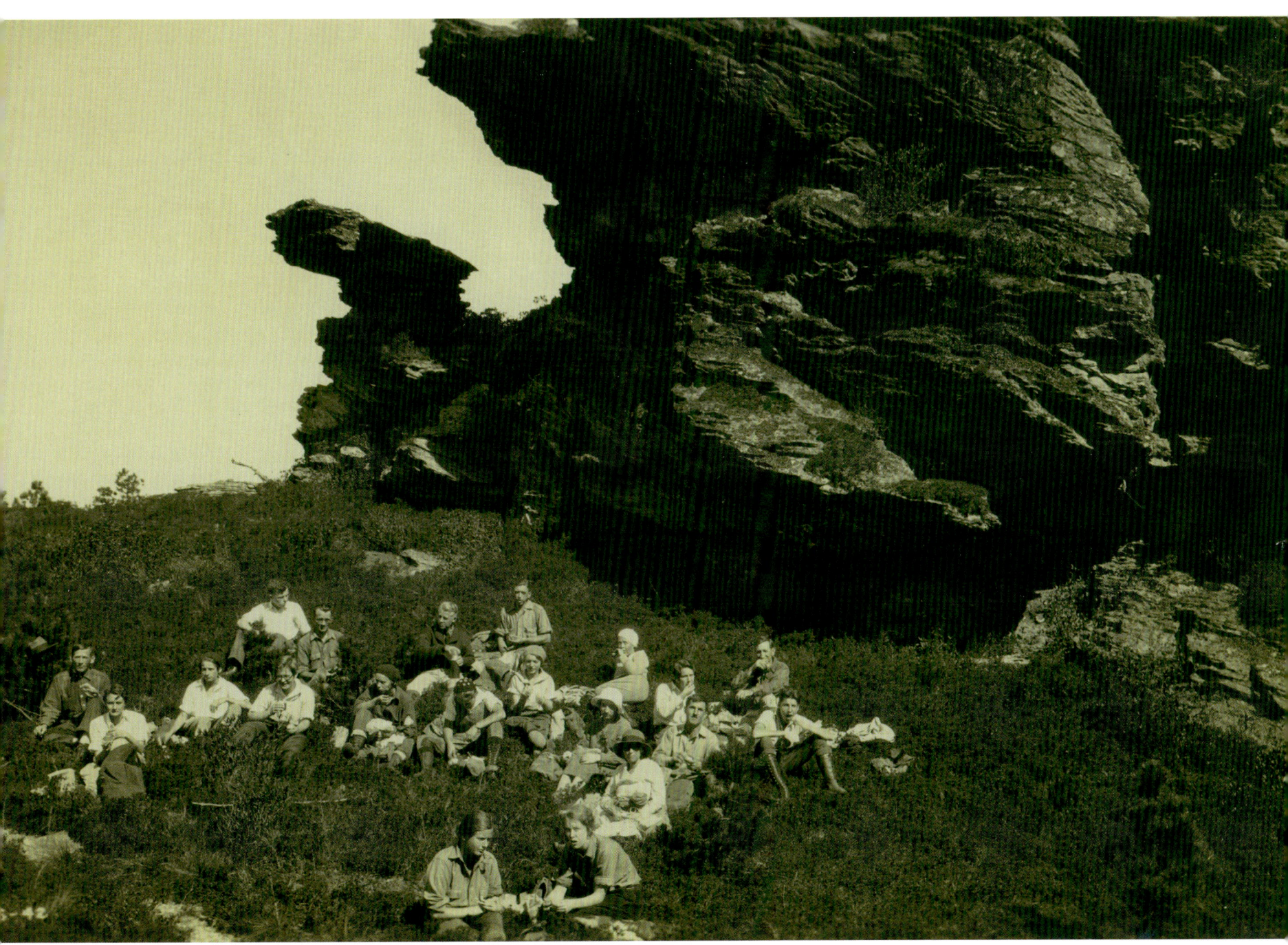

86   Hikers in a field beneath Table Rock formation. Courtesy of Pack Memorial Library.

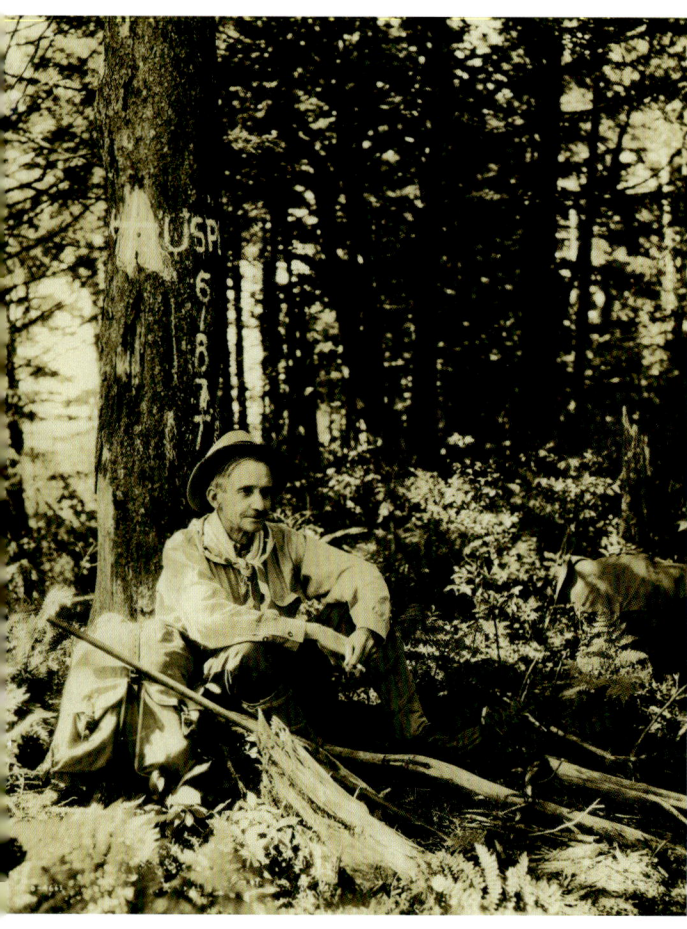

87   Horace Kephart resting beneath a tree near
      the summit of the original Mount Kephart.
      Courtesy of Pack Memorial Library.

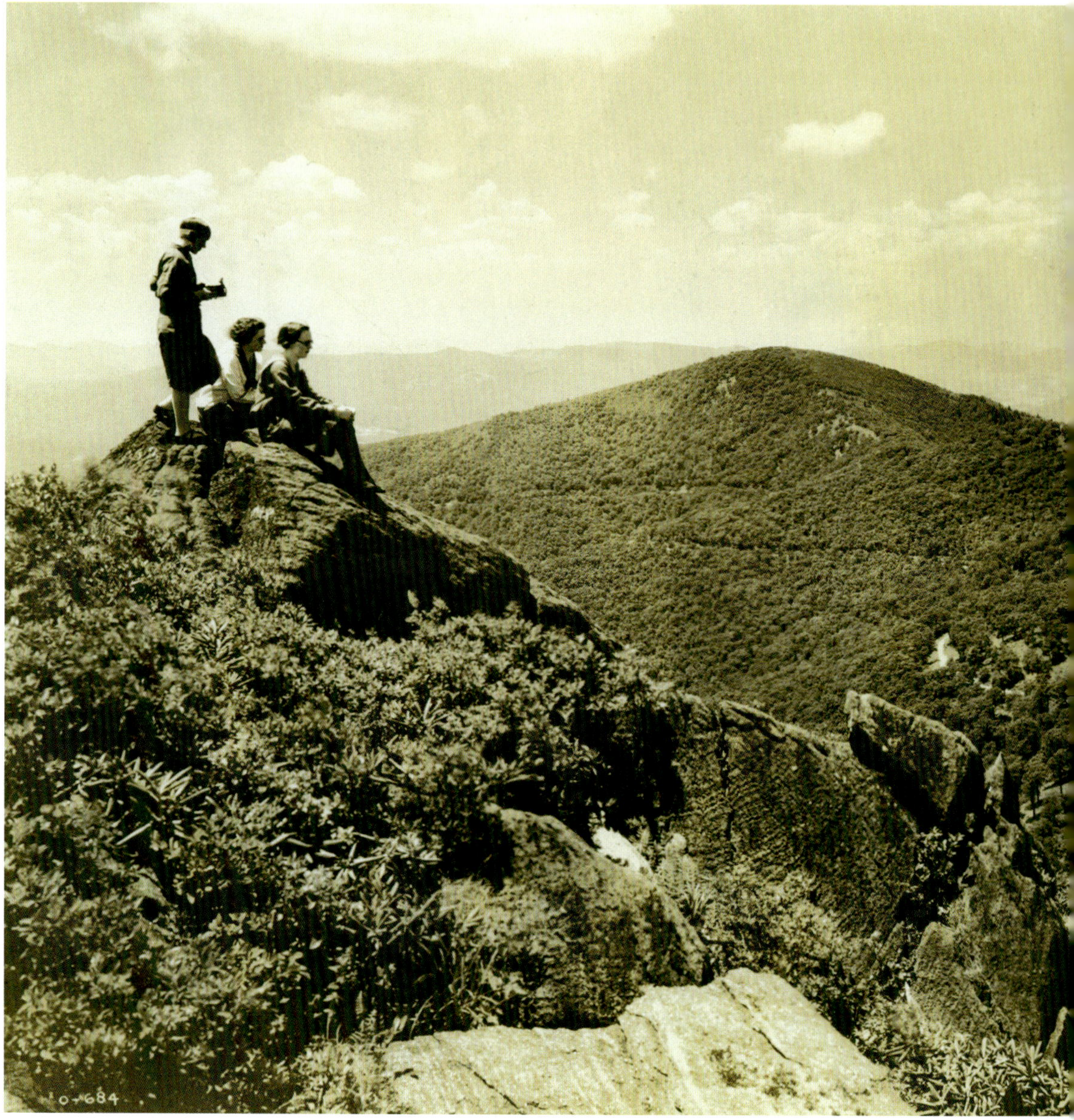

88   Hikers viewing Mount Mitchell from the Pinnacle.
      Courtesy of Pack Memorial Library.

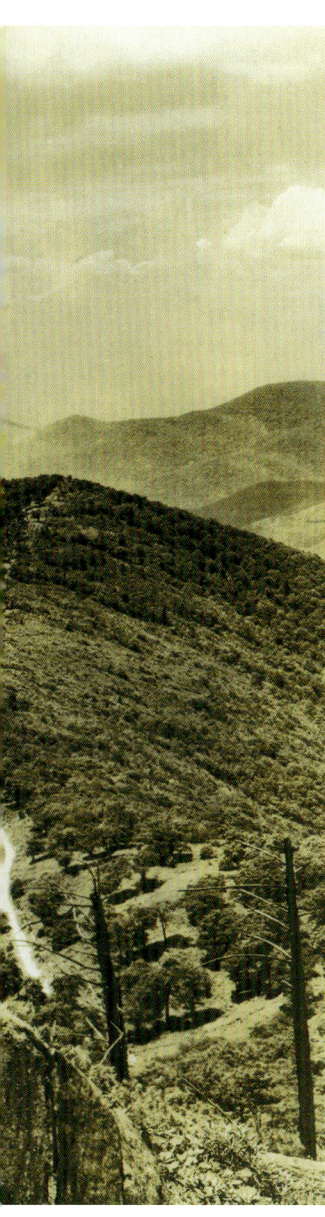

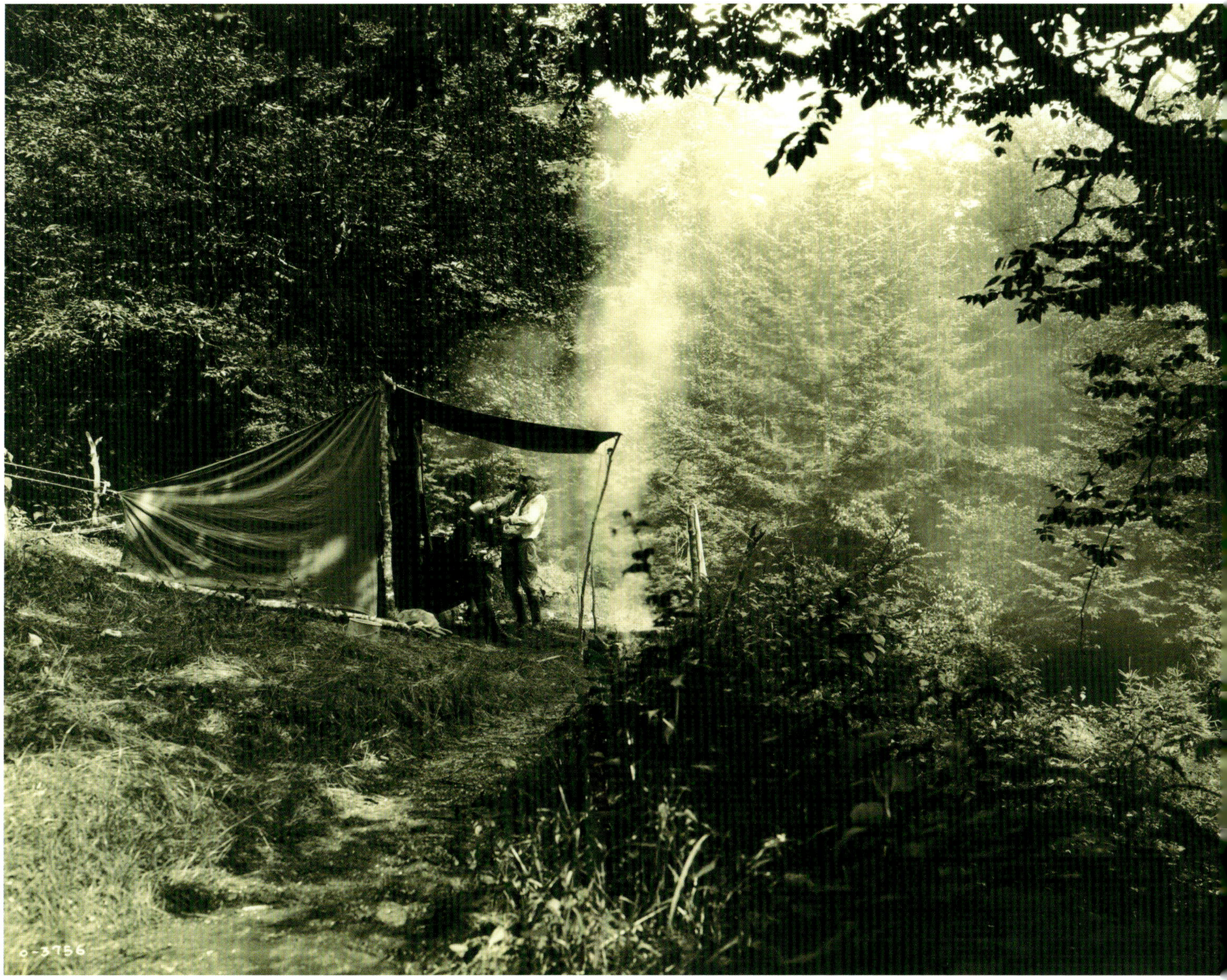

89　Horace Kephart in camp near Indian Gap. Courtesy of Pack Memorial Library.

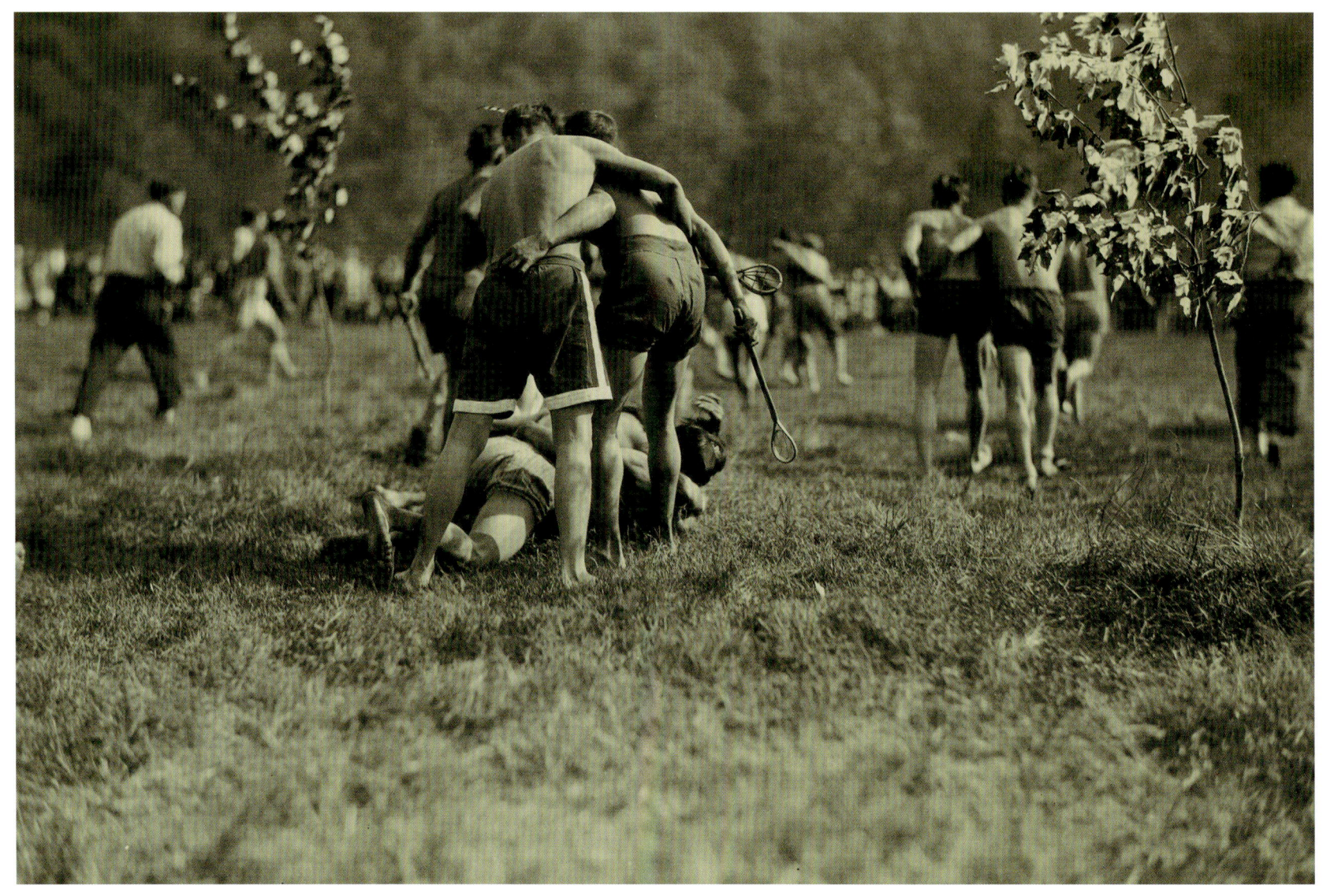

90   Native Americans playing a ball game at a Cherokee festival. Courtesy of Smokies Life.

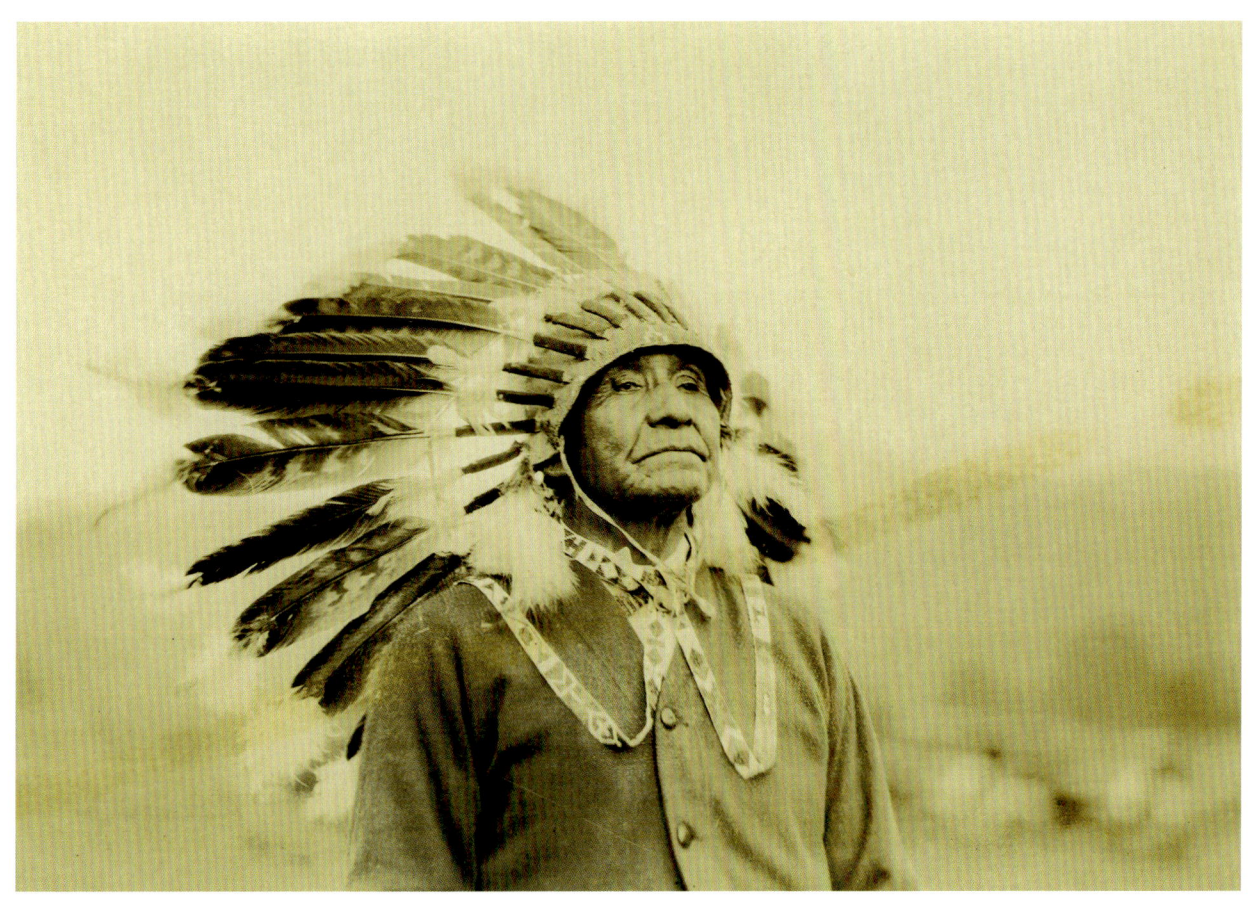

91   Cherokee Chief Owl in full headdress during a festival. Courtesy of Smokies Life.

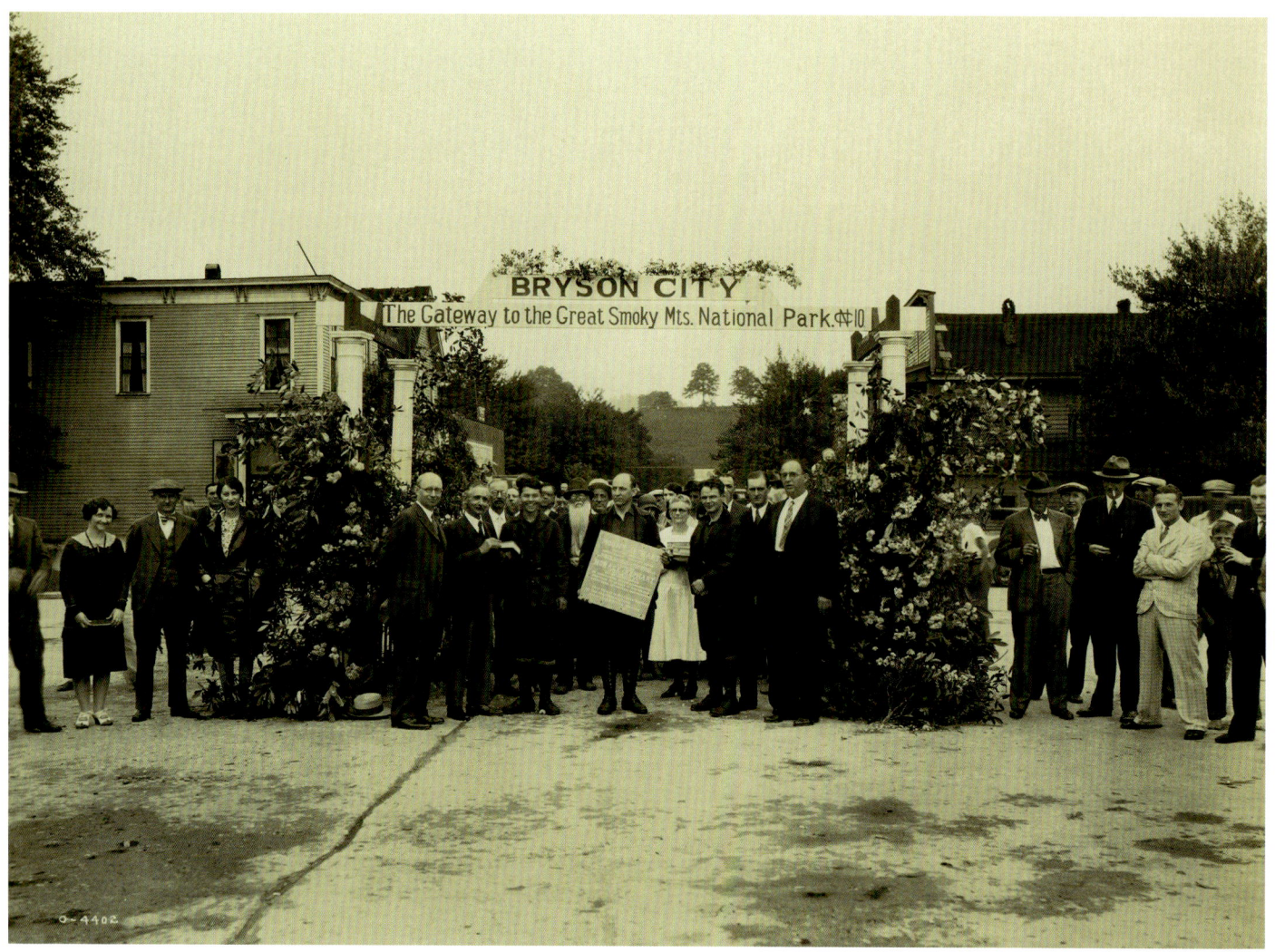

92   A group gathering in Bryson City prior to placing memorial tablet on Mount Kephart. Courtesy of Smokies Life.

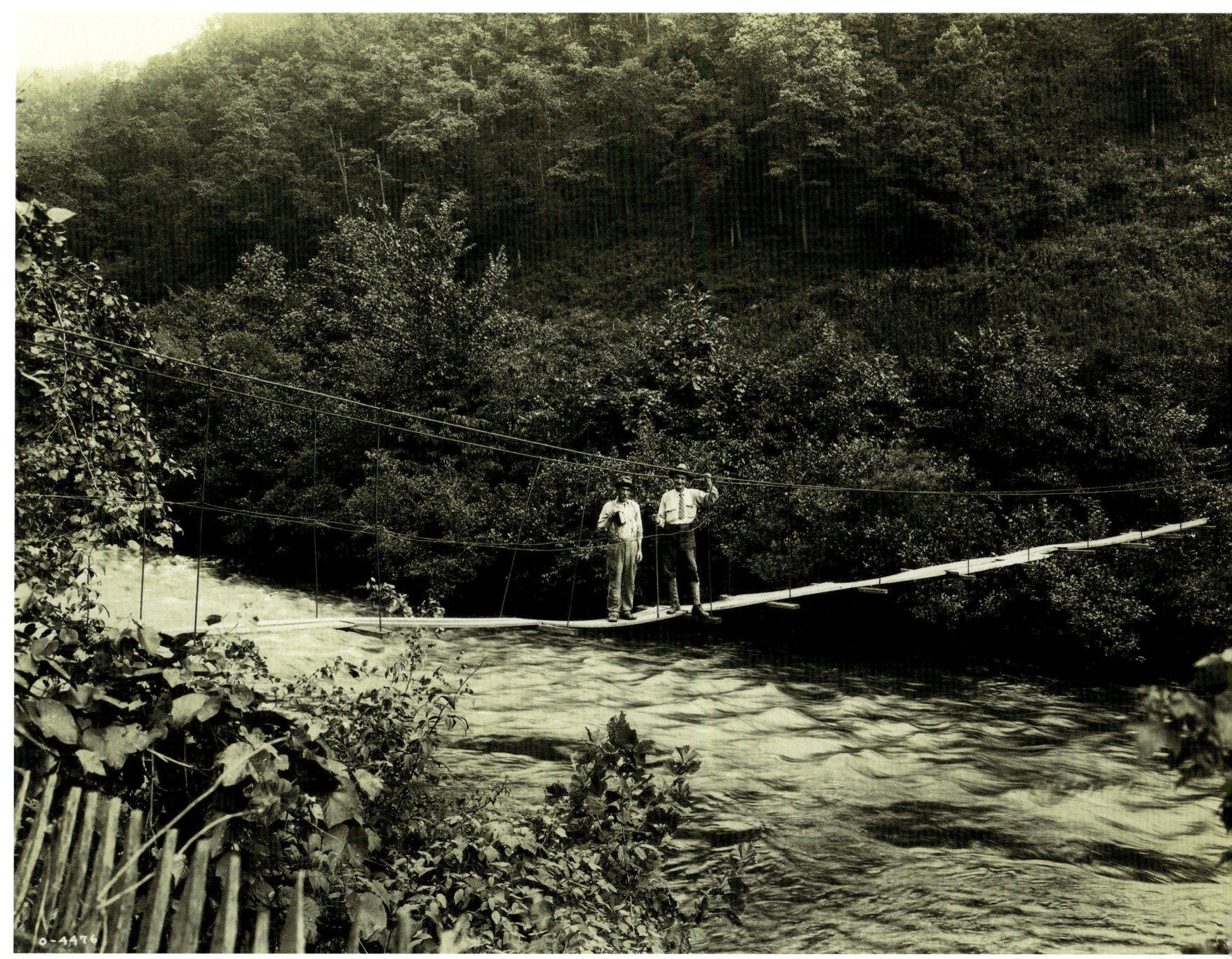

93   Horace Kephart (right) with an unidentified man on footbridge. Courtesy of Smokies Life.

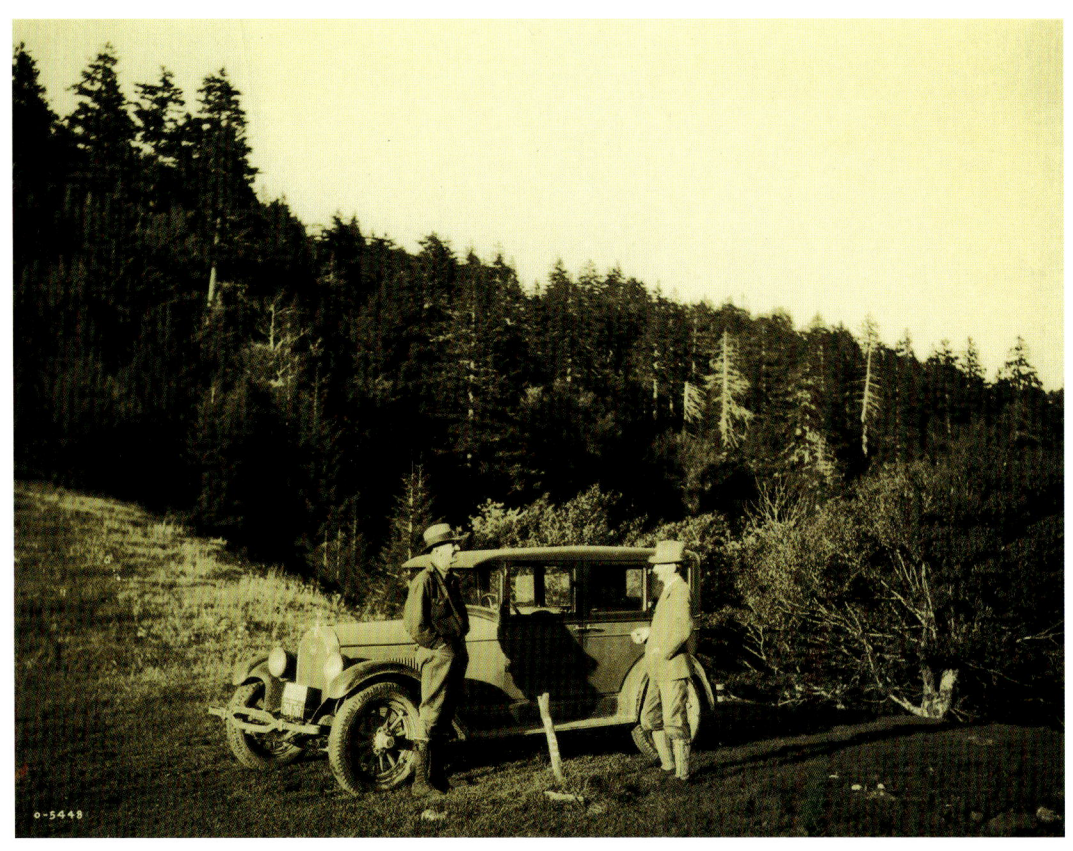

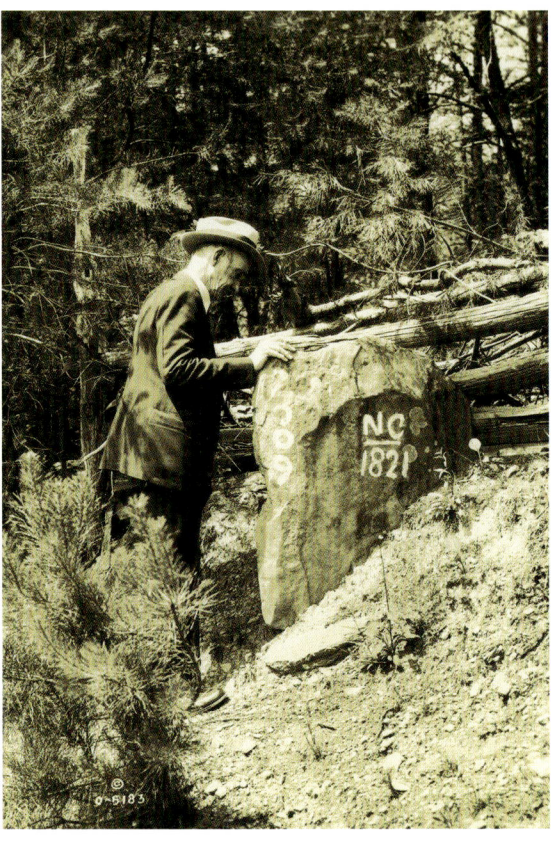

94　Horace Kephart (right) and an unidentified person standing by an automobile. Courtesy of Smokies Life.

95　Horace Kephart examining the North Carolina–Tennessee boundary marker in the Smokies. Courtesy of Smokies Life.

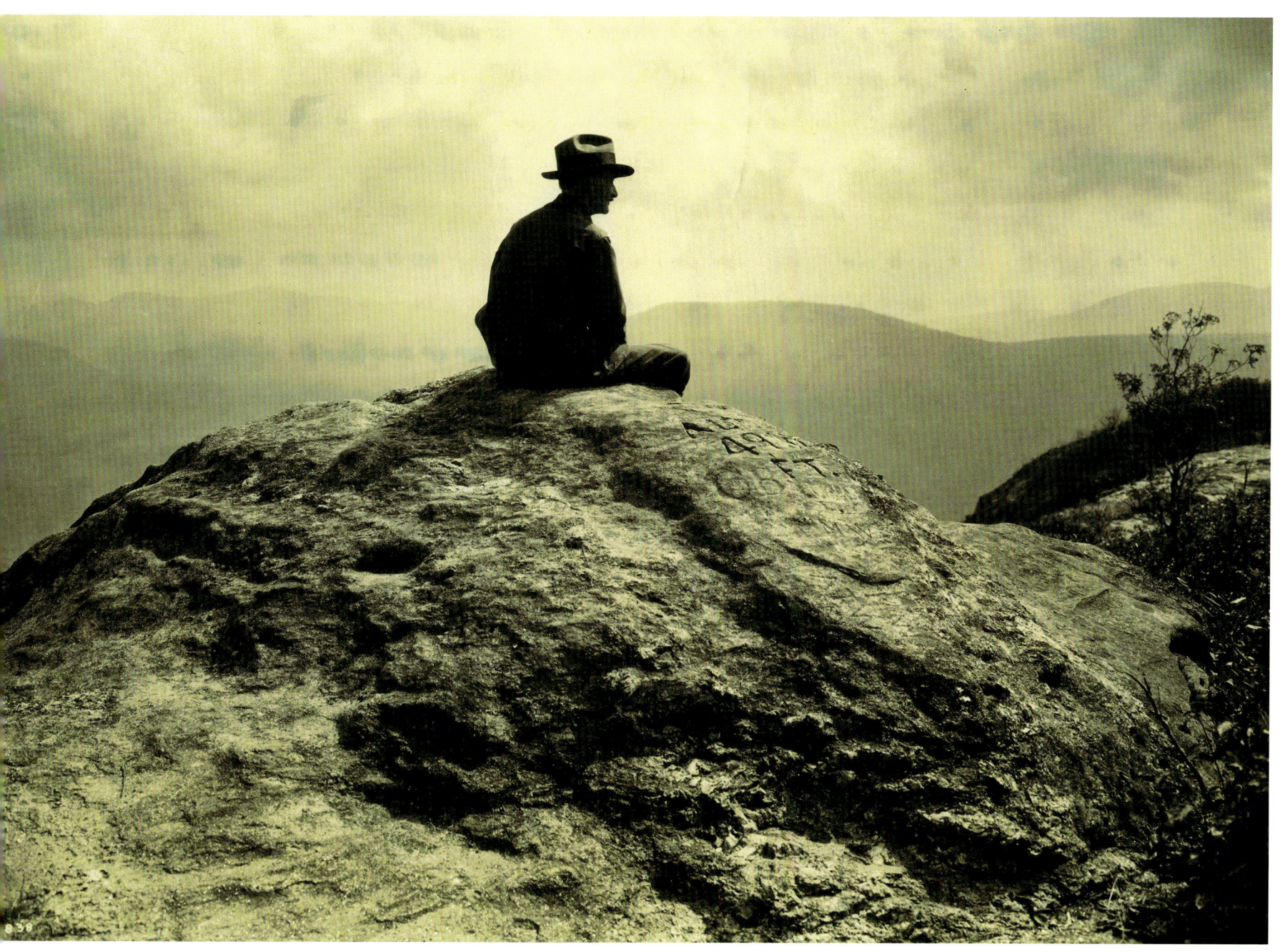

96   Horace Kephart resting on a rock outcrop on Whiteside Mountain, near Cashiers.
      Courtesy of Smokies Life.

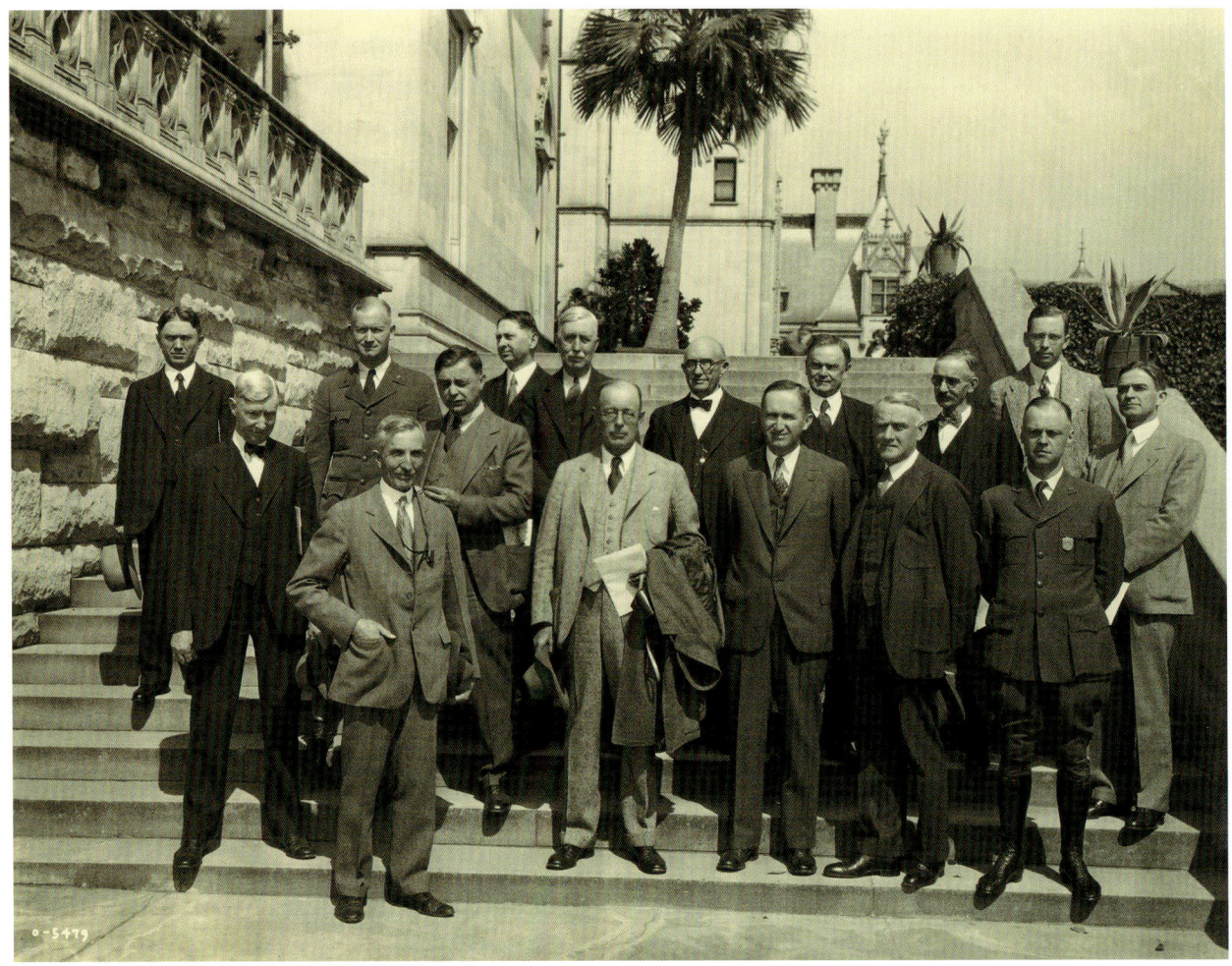

97   National Park supporters at Biltmore Estate. Arno Cammerer is second from left in the second row;
      Horace Albright is third from right in the second row; and Horace Kephart is third from right in the
      third row. Courtesy of Smokies Life.

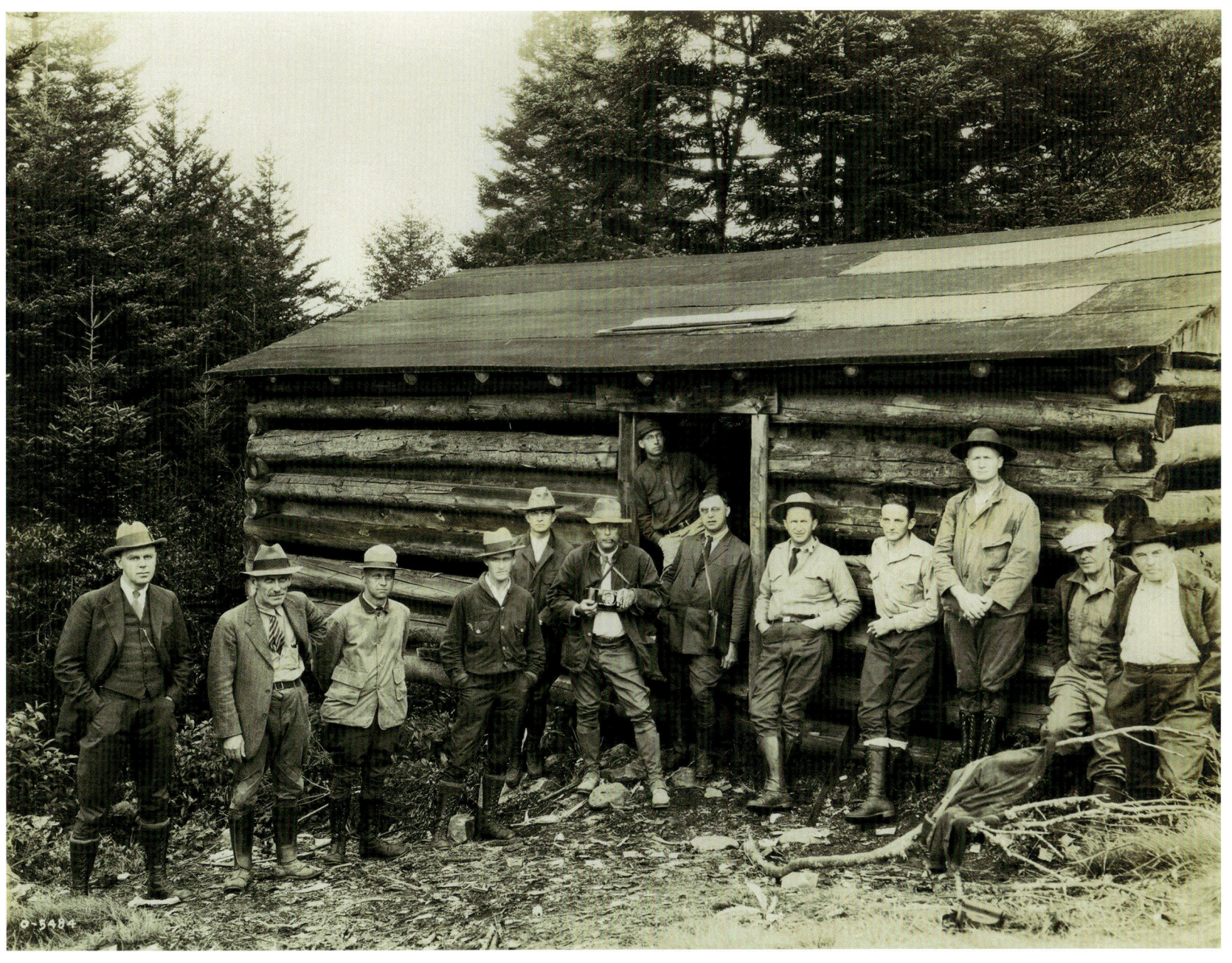

98   Thirteen National Park Service officials and others at a shelter in the Great Smoky Mountains National Park, 1930. Arno Cammerer is below the doorway, and Horace Albright is to the right of the doorway. Courtesy of Smokies Life.

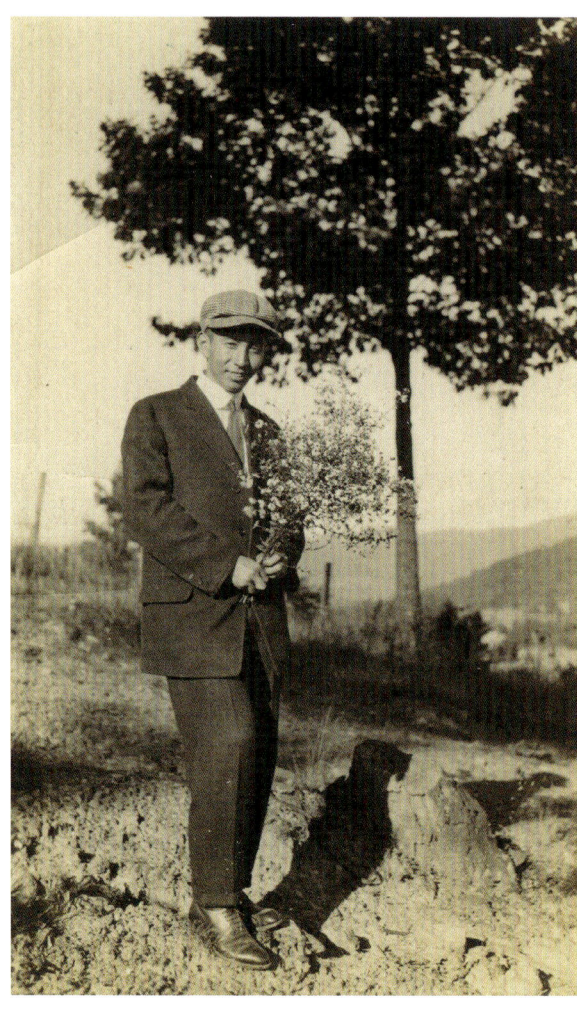

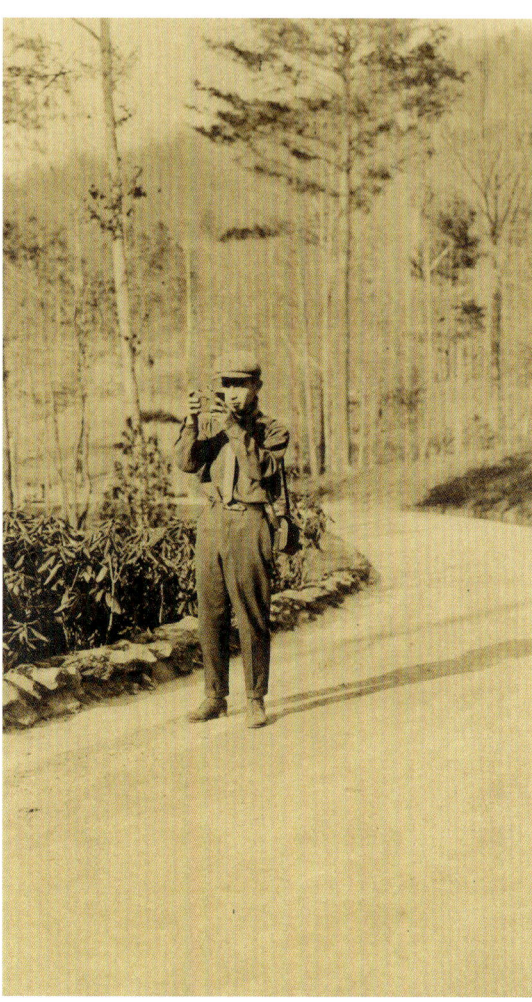

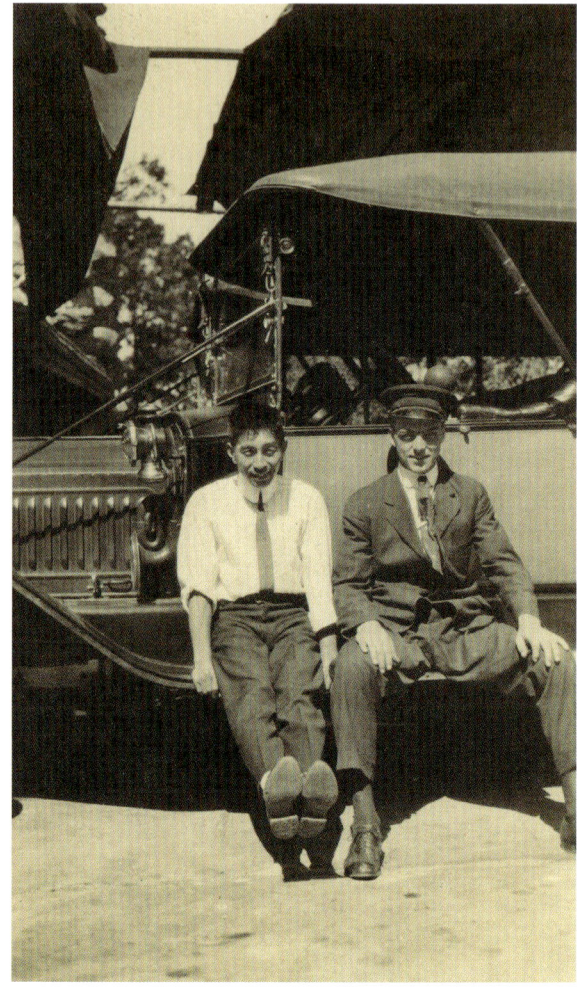

99   George Masa with flowers.
      By George Masa or Blake Creasman.
      Courtesy of Western Carolina University.

100   George Masa holding a small camera.
      Courtesy of Western Carolina
      University.

101   George Masa and a coworker serving
      as valets at the Grove Park Inn, ca. 1915.
      Courtesy of Western Carolina
      University.

Jim Thompson

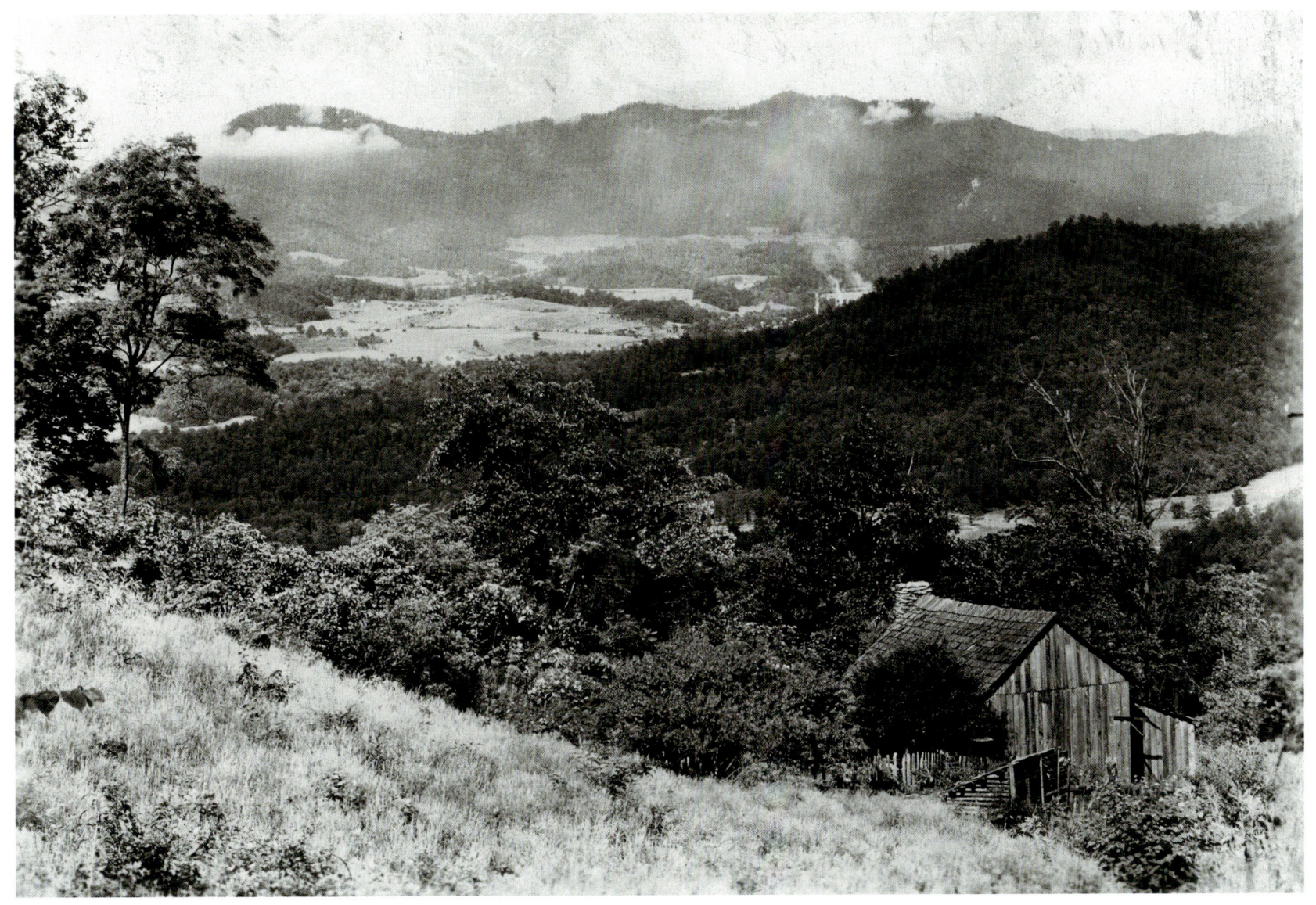

102   A view into Cades Cove. Courtesy of Knox County Public Library.

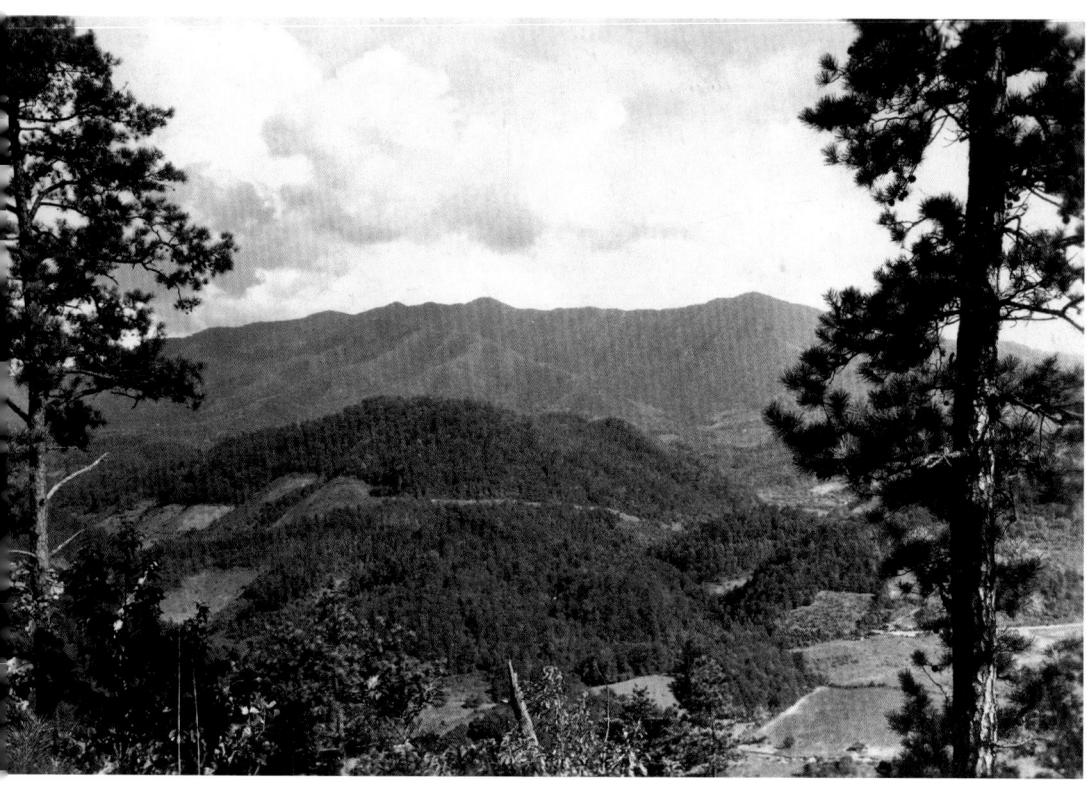

103   Mount LeConte with trees and valley. Courtesy of Knox County Public Library.

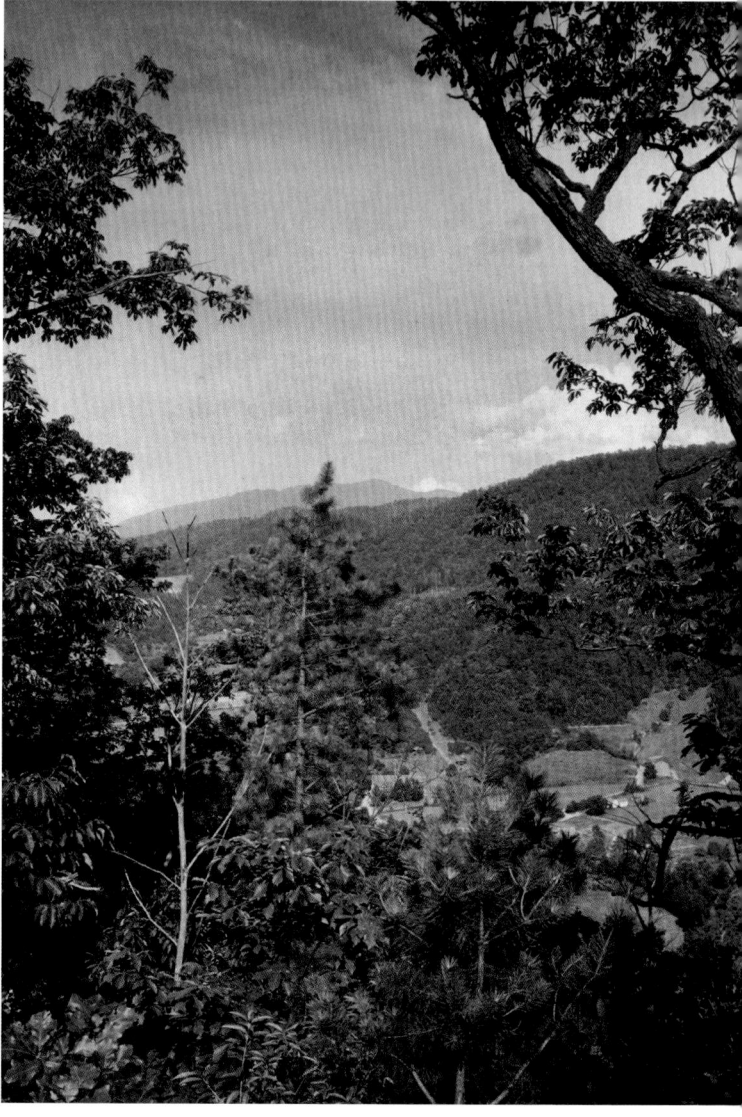

104   Panoramic view of Round Top,
Mount LeConte, and Balsam, with Gatlinburg
in the foreground. Courtesy of Knox County
Public Library.

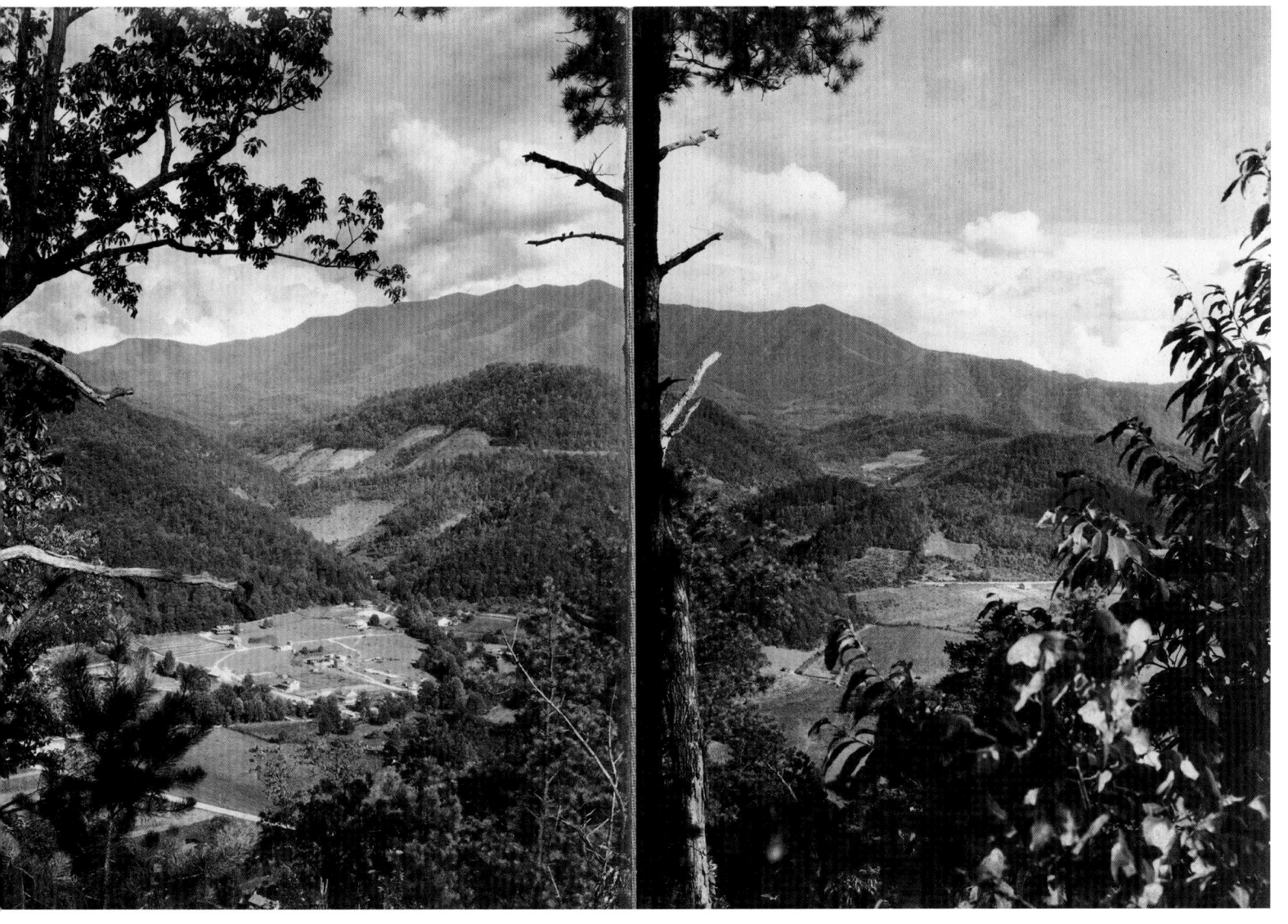

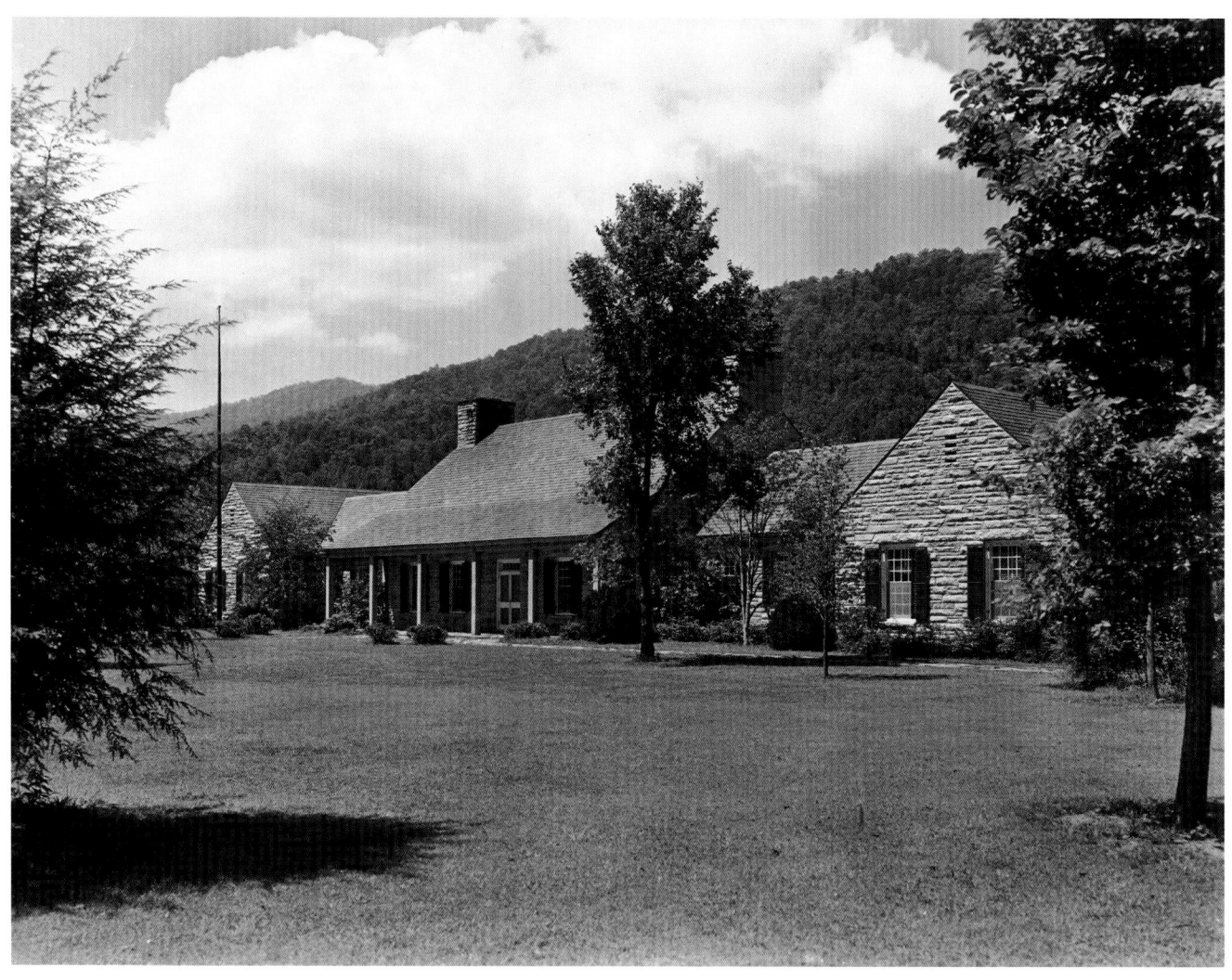

105   New Great Smoky Mountains National Park Headquarters
at Sugarland, ca. 1940. Courtesy of Knox County Public Library.

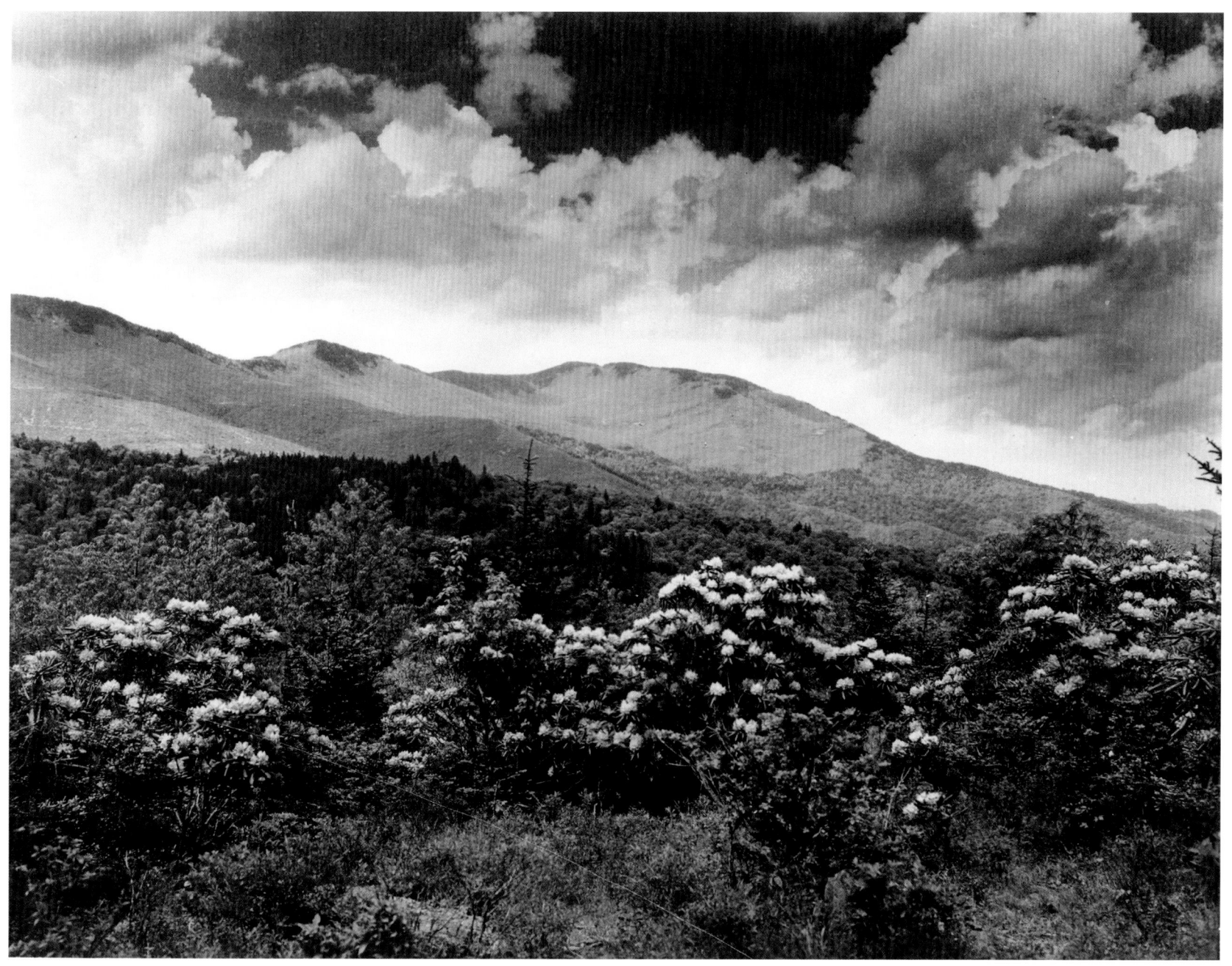

106   View of the Great Smoky Mountains with commercially logged areas clearly visible.

Courtesy of Knox County Public Library.

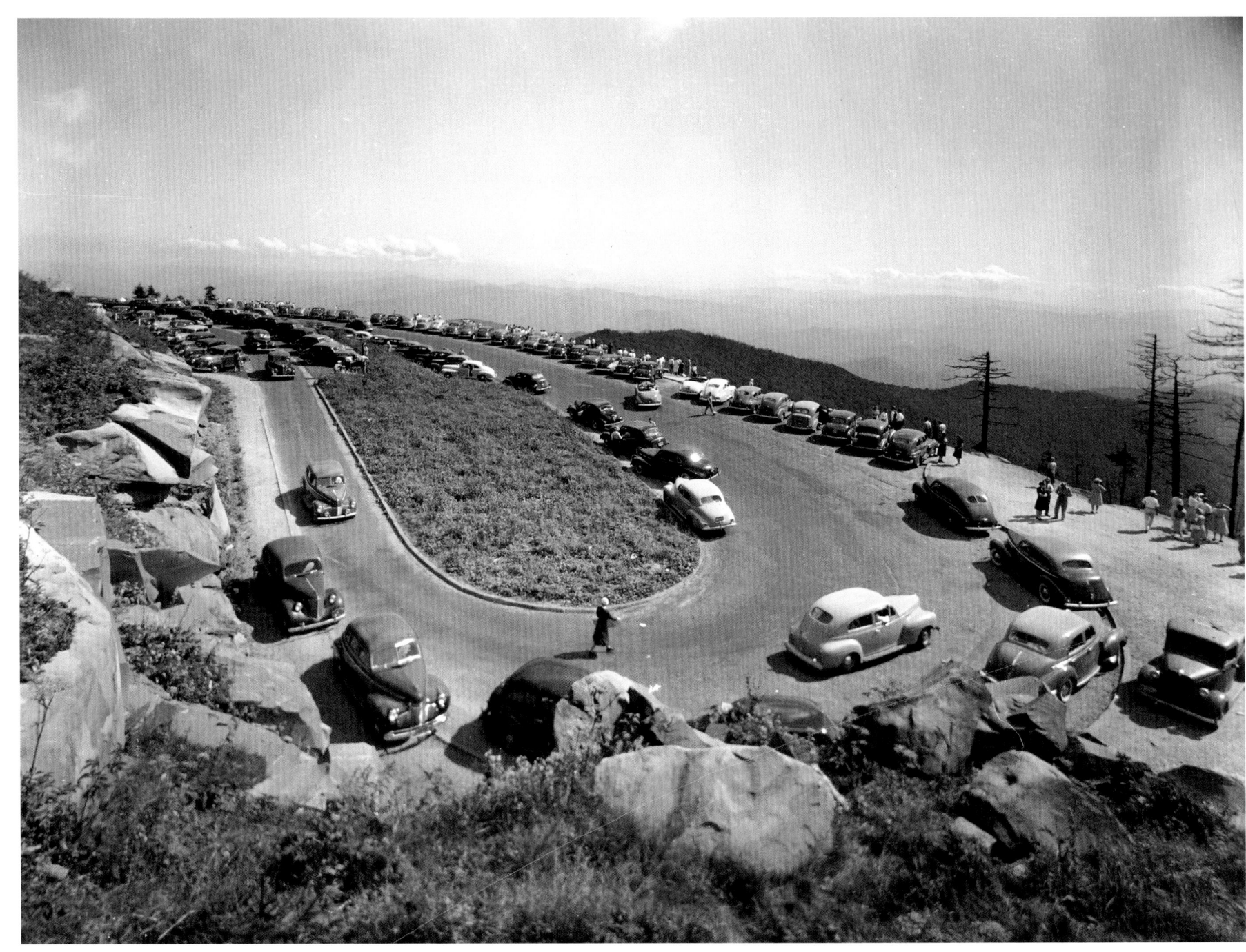

107   Parking area of Kuwohi, formerly Clingmans Dome, ca. 1940. Courtesy of Knox County Public Library.

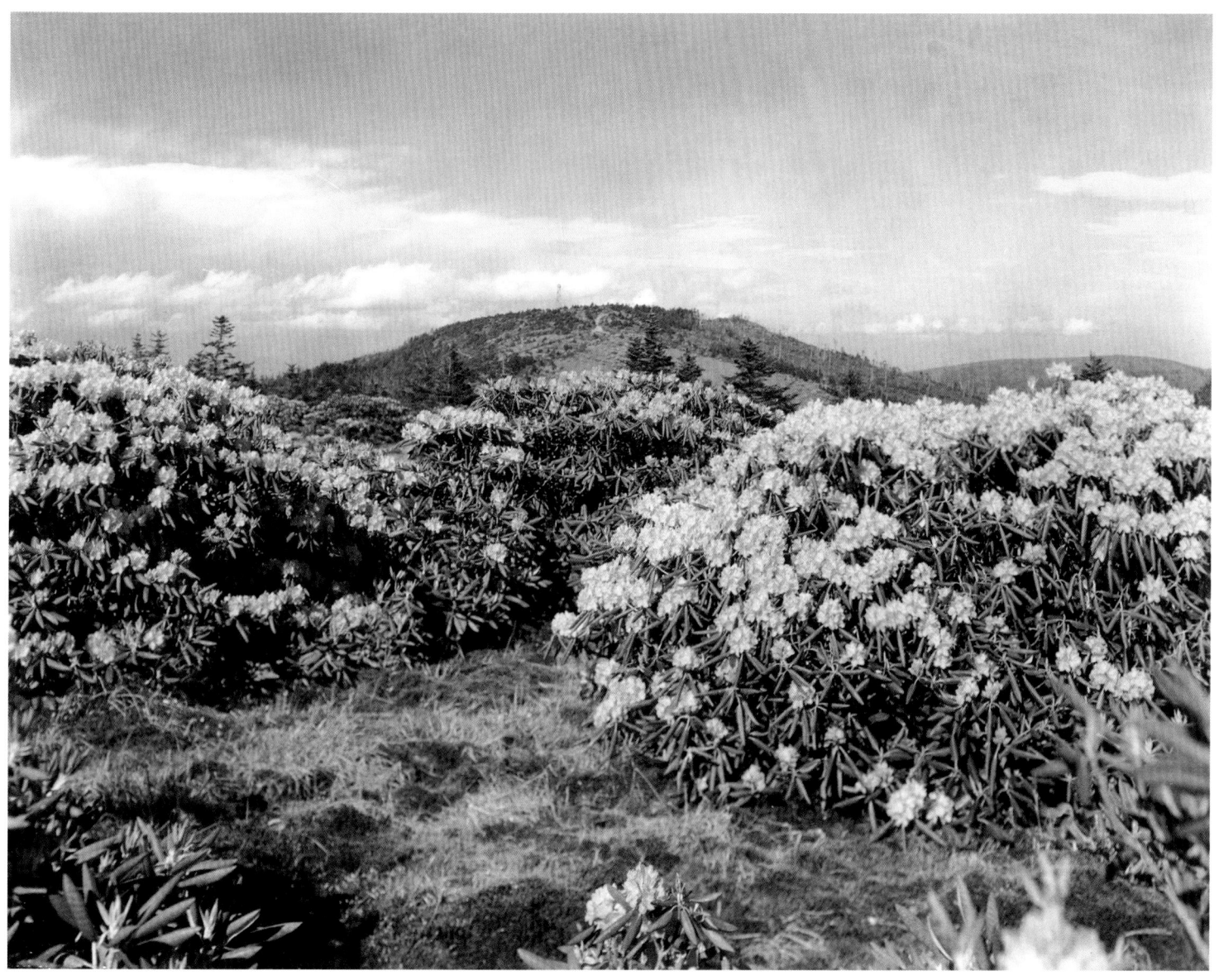

108   Blooming rhododendron with tower in the distance. Courtesy of Knox County Public Library.

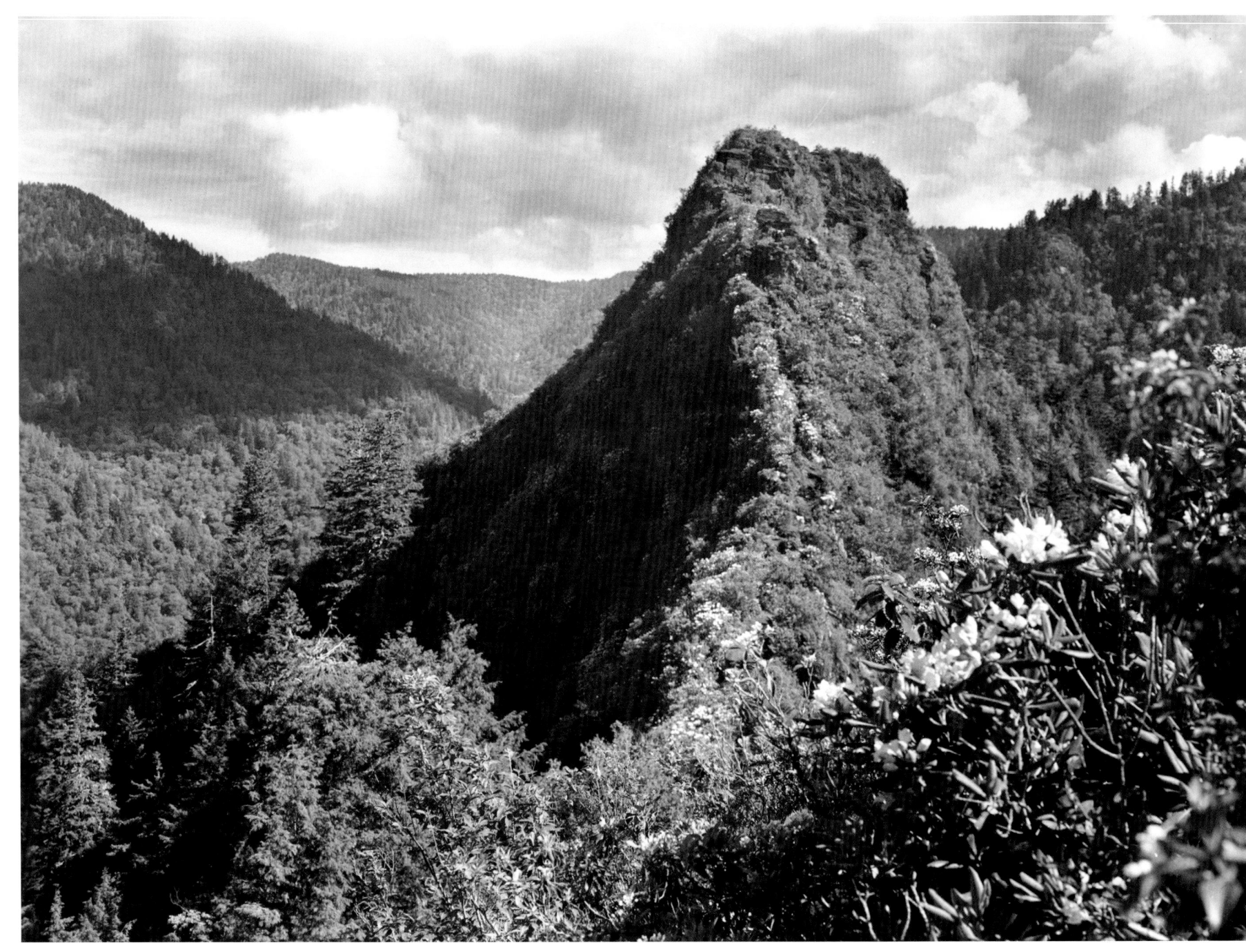

109   A close-up of Chimney Tops. Courtesy of Knox County Public Library.

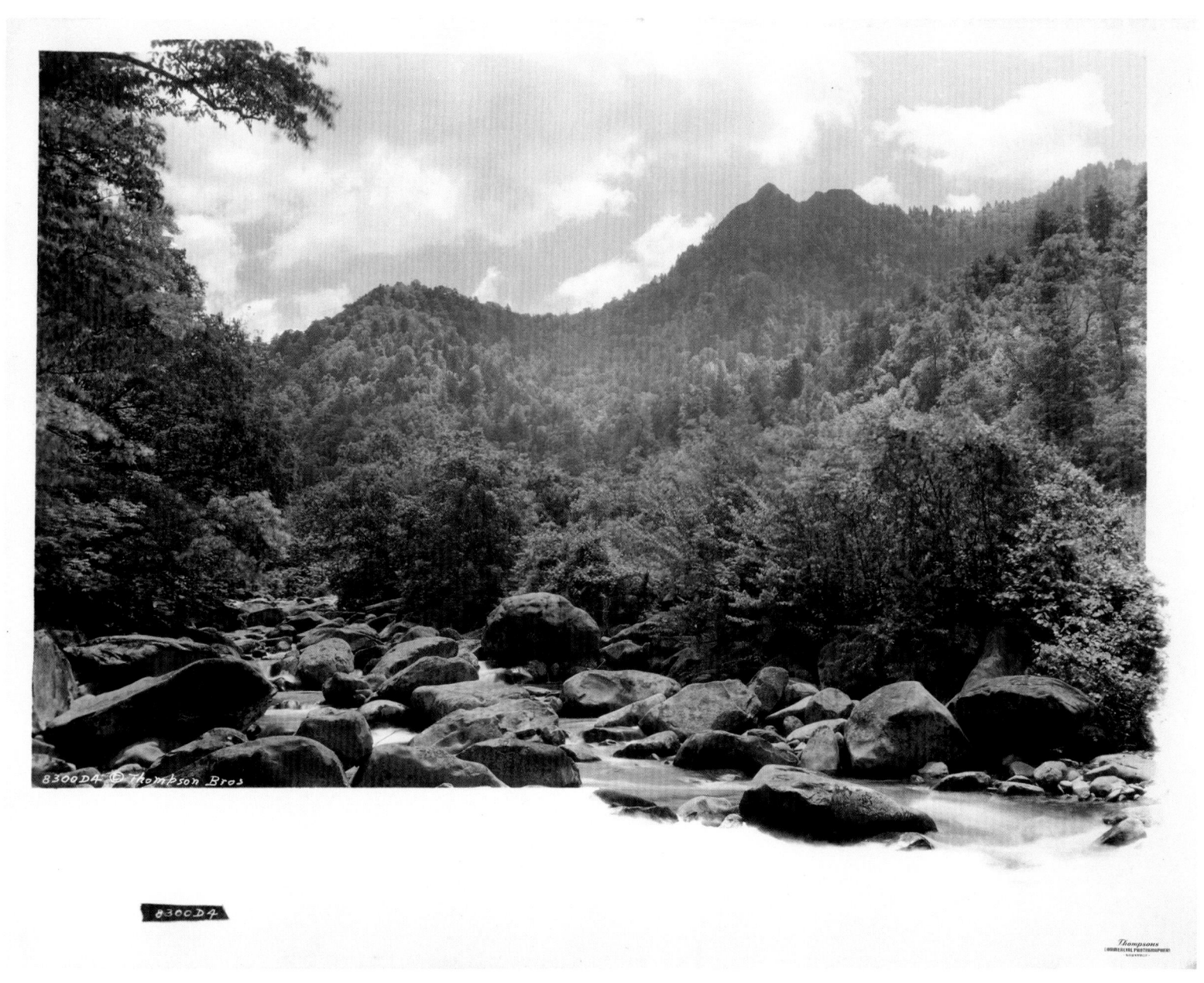

110   Chimney Tops from Indian Gap Trail. Courtesy of Knox County Public Library.

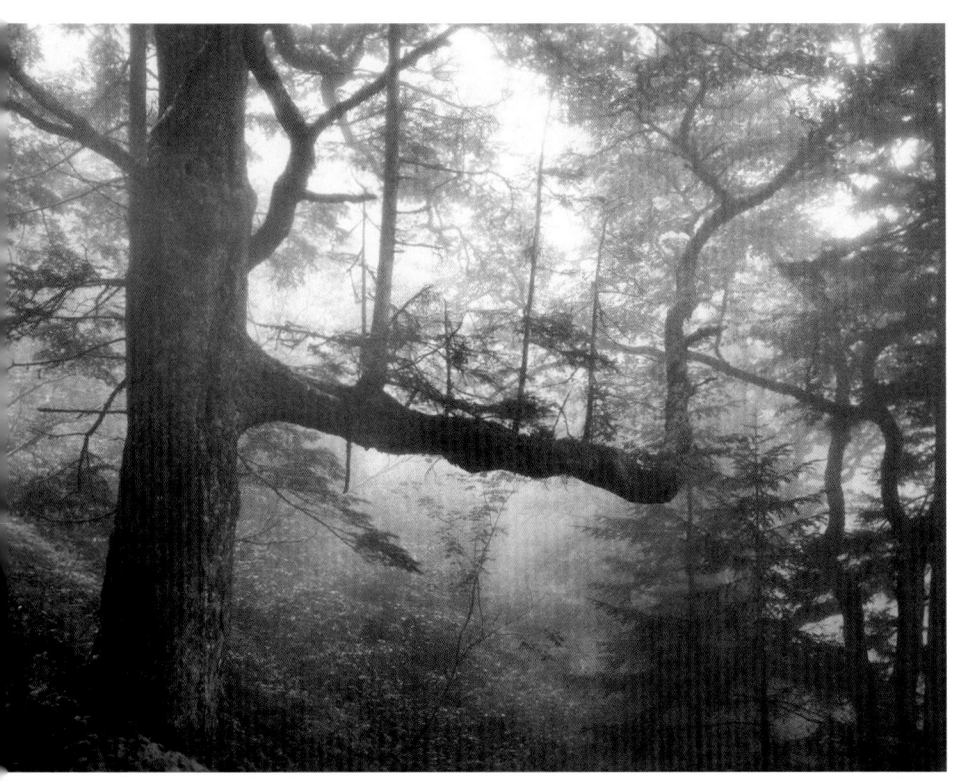

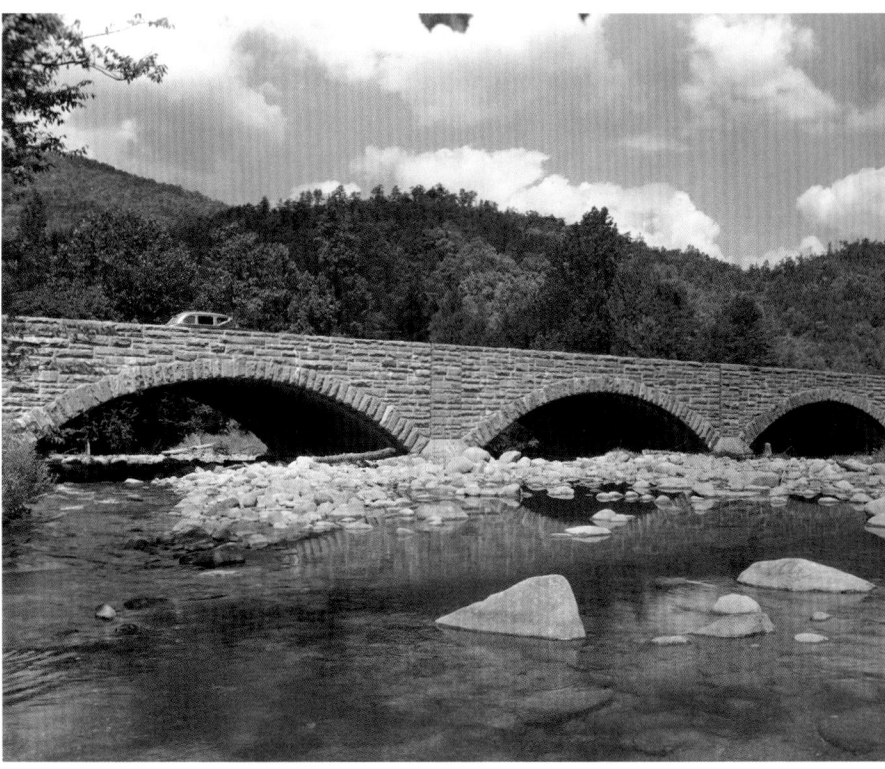

111   A tree in fog. Courtesy of
      Knox County Public Library.

112   Triple Arch Stone Bridge over a stream in the national park,
      near Sugarland. Courtesy of Knox County Public Library.

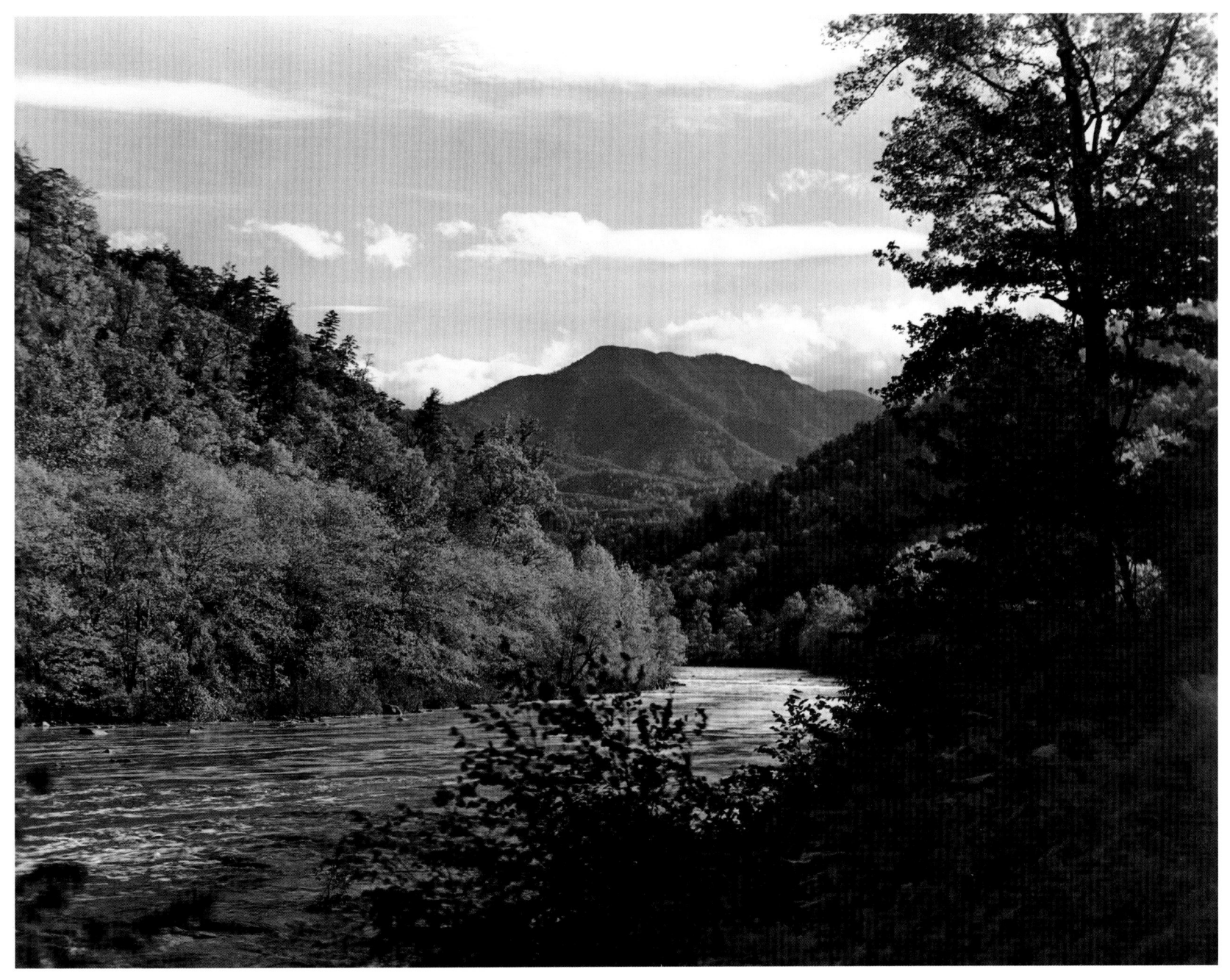

113   Mount Cammerer, named for National Park Service Director Arno Cammerer.
Courtesy of Knox County Public Library.

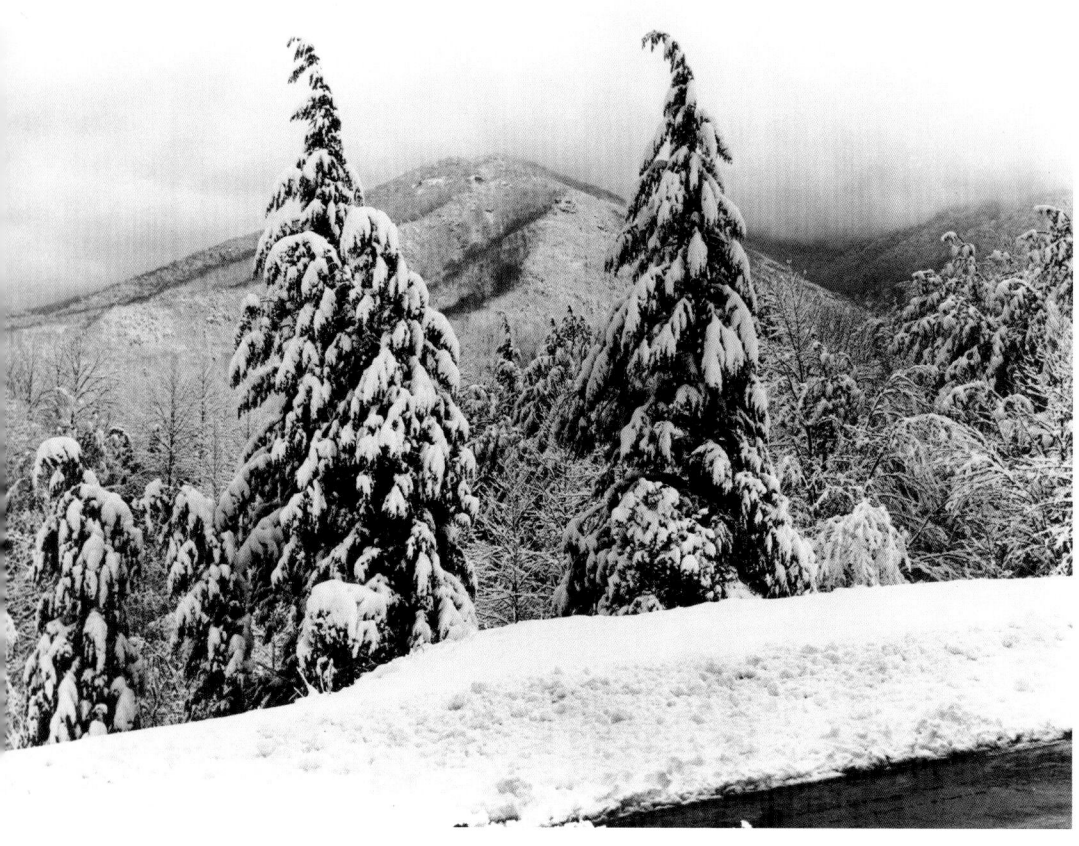

114   Heavy snow in the Smokies. Courtesy of Knox County Public Library.

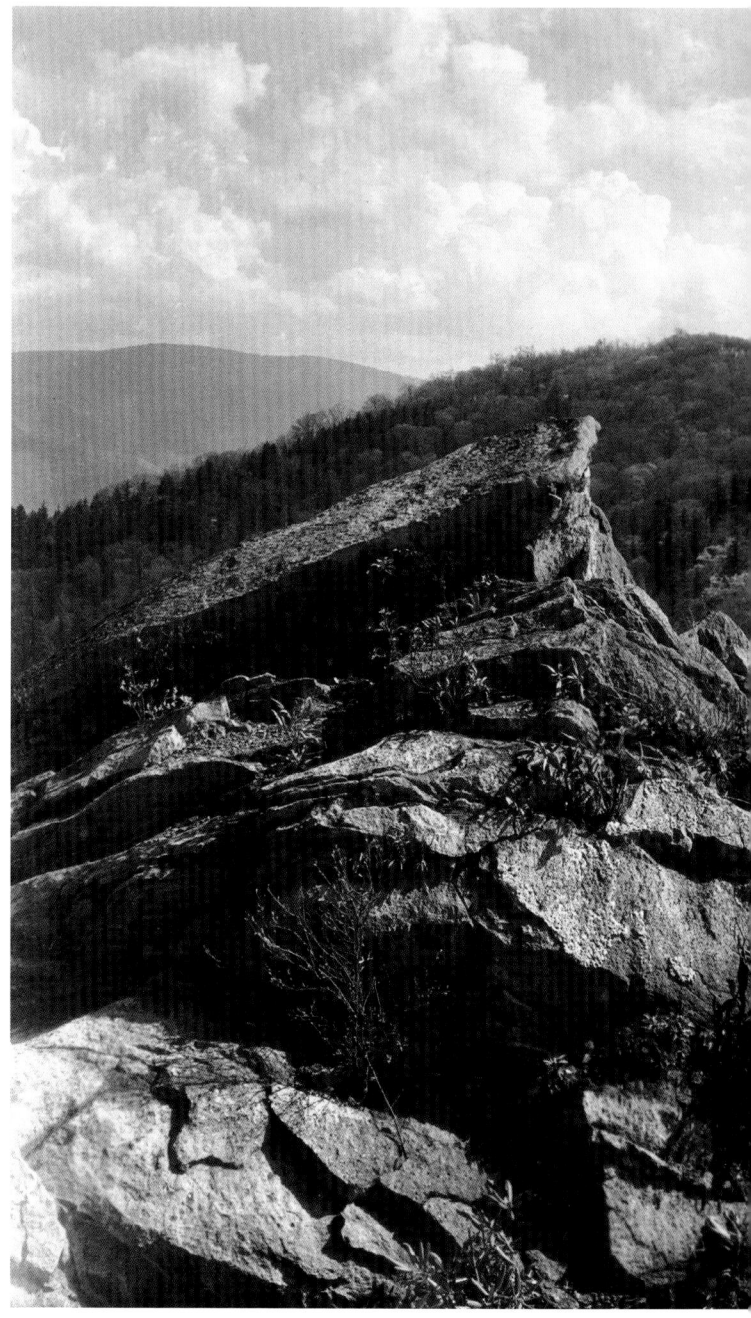

115   White Rock, formerly called Sharp Rock, in the northeastern Smokies, with Mt. Sterling in the distance. White Rock was the future site of the Mt. Cammerer fire tower constructed by the Civilian Conservation Corps in the 1930s. Courtesy of Knox County Public Library.

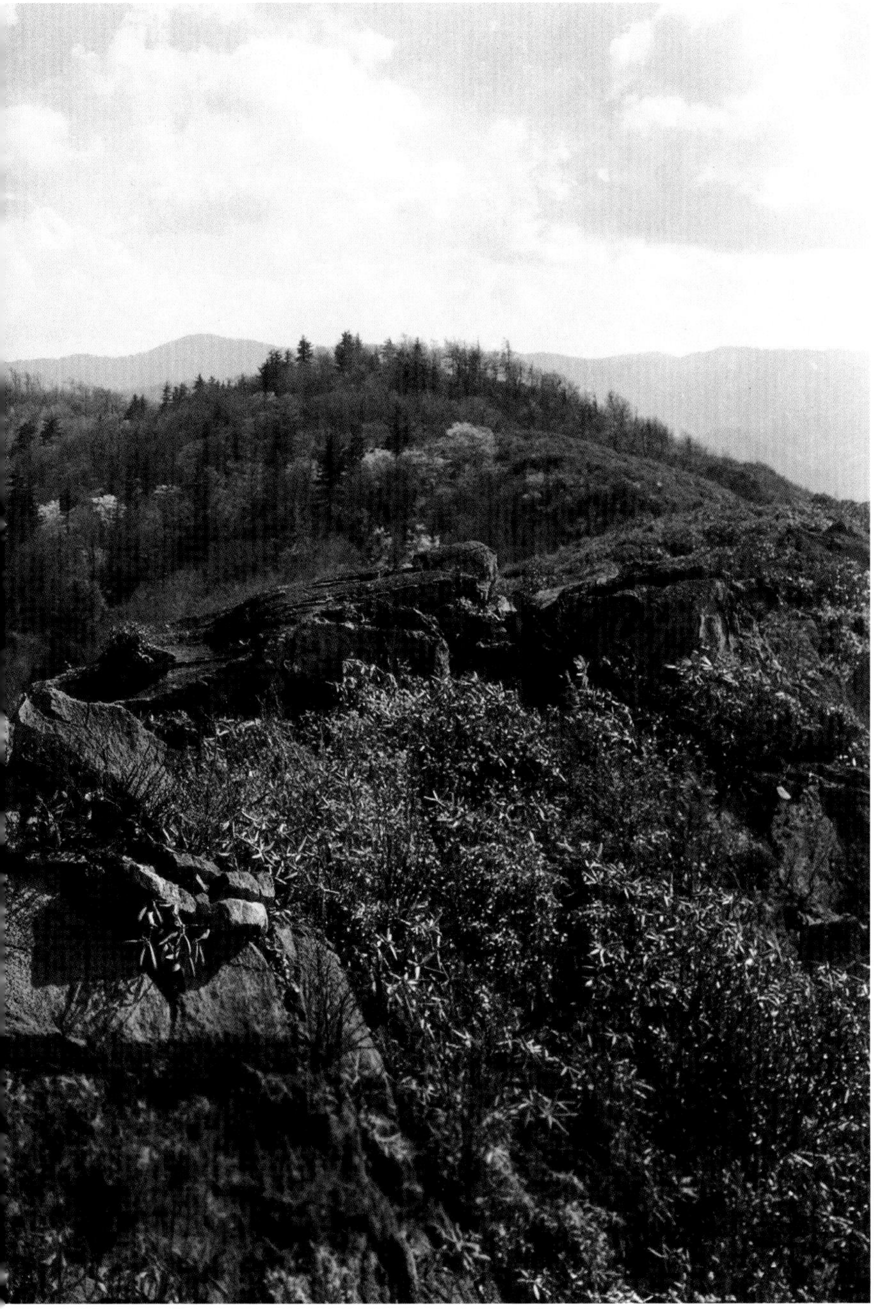

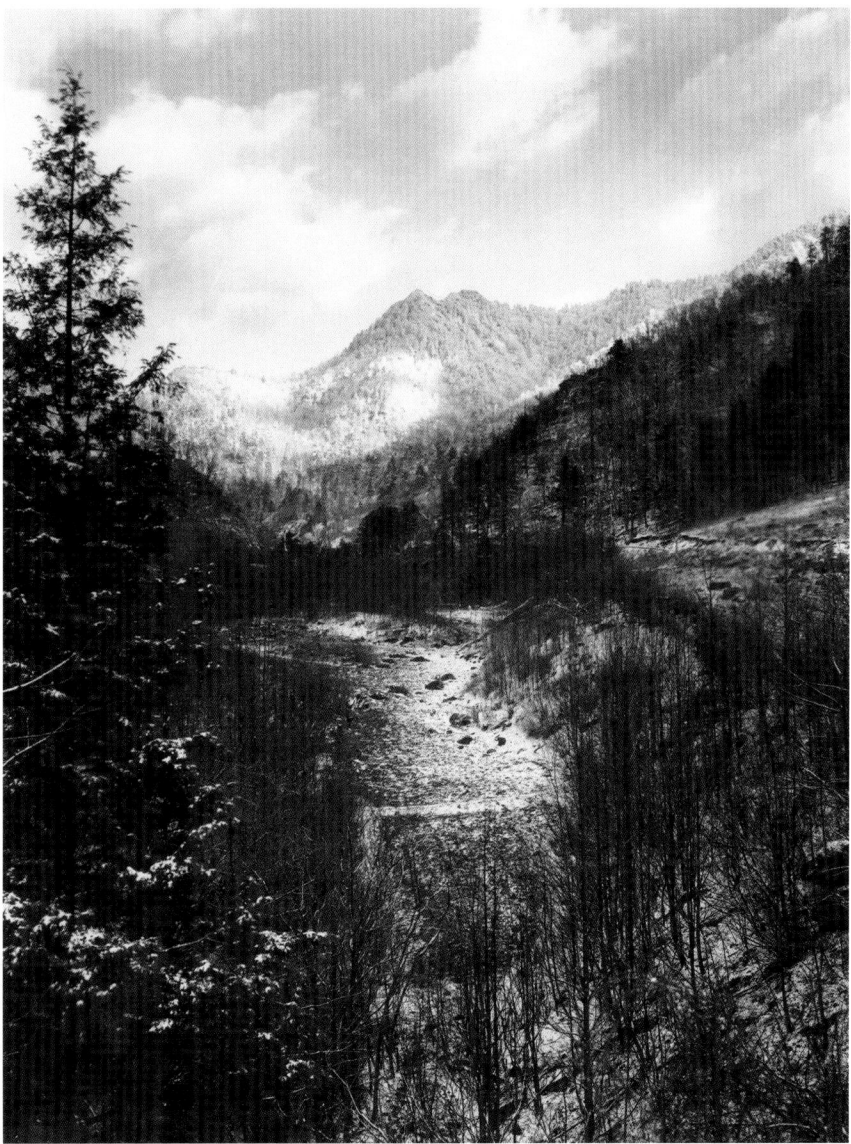

116   Snow-covered Chimneys. Courtesy of Knox County Public Library.

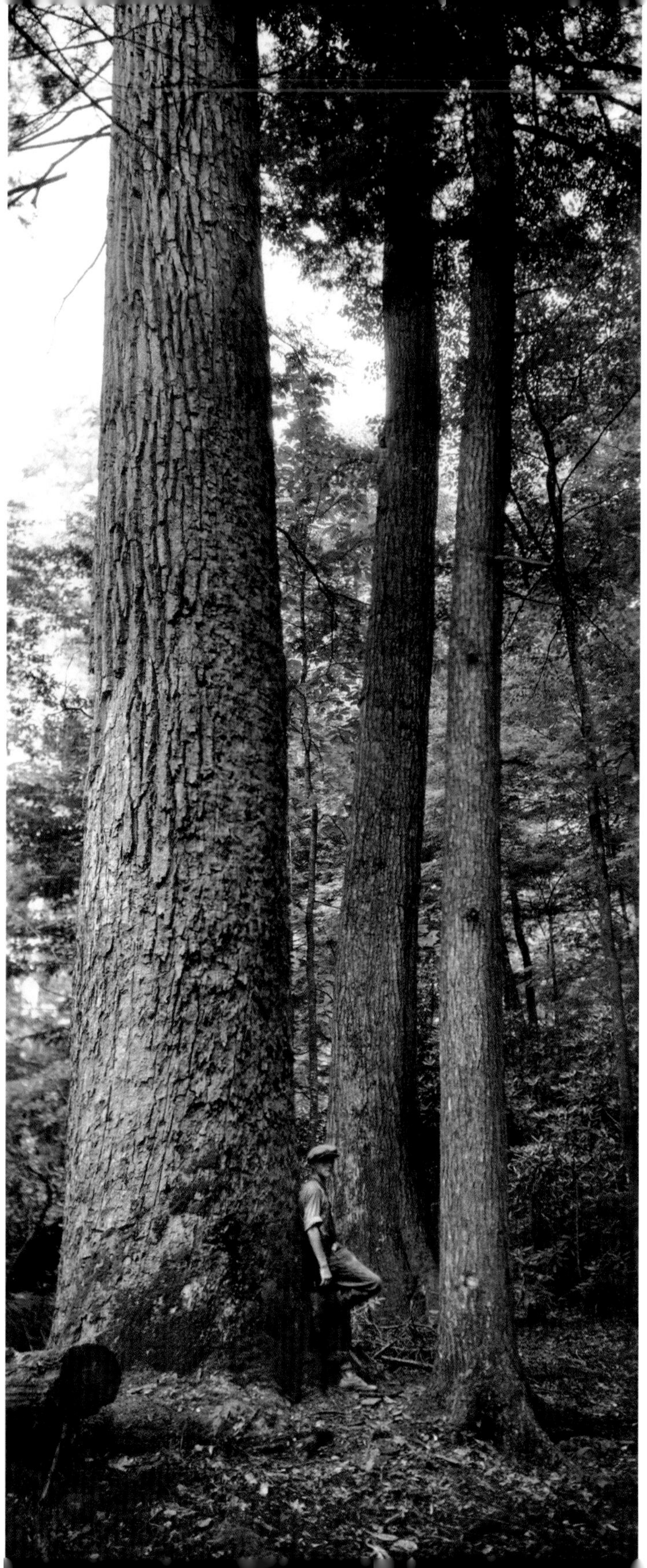

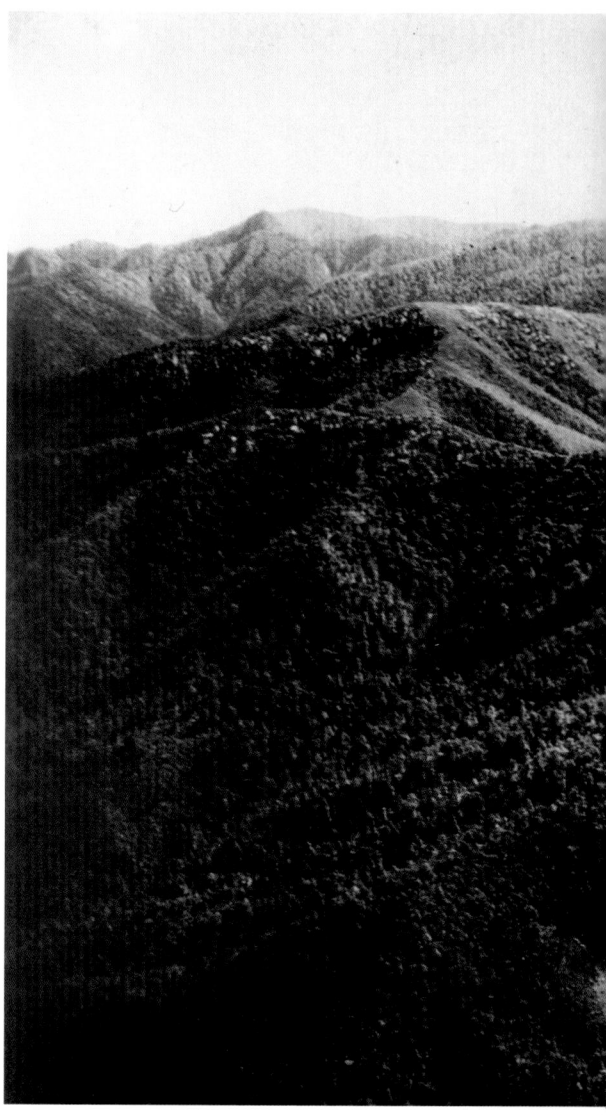

117 A man standing beneath a giant tulip poplar in the
Smokies. Courtesy of Knox County Public Library.

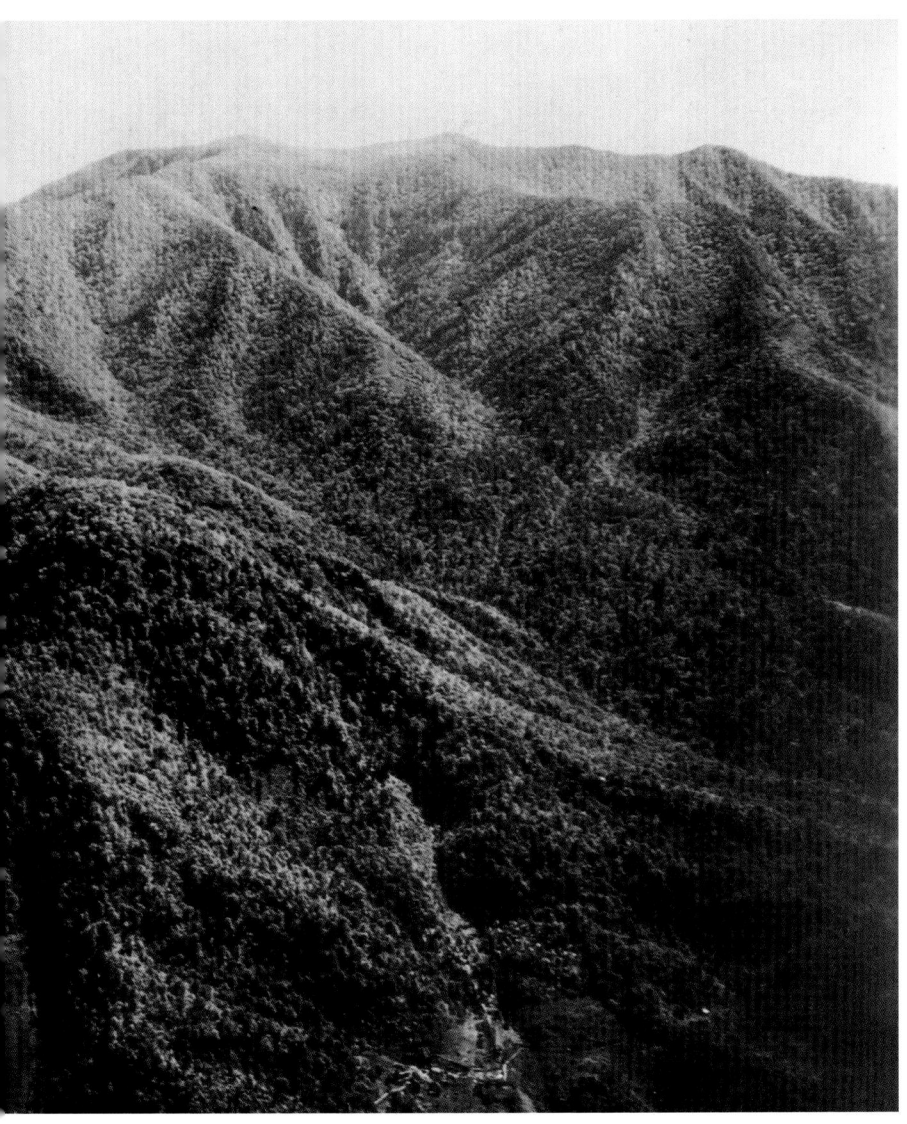

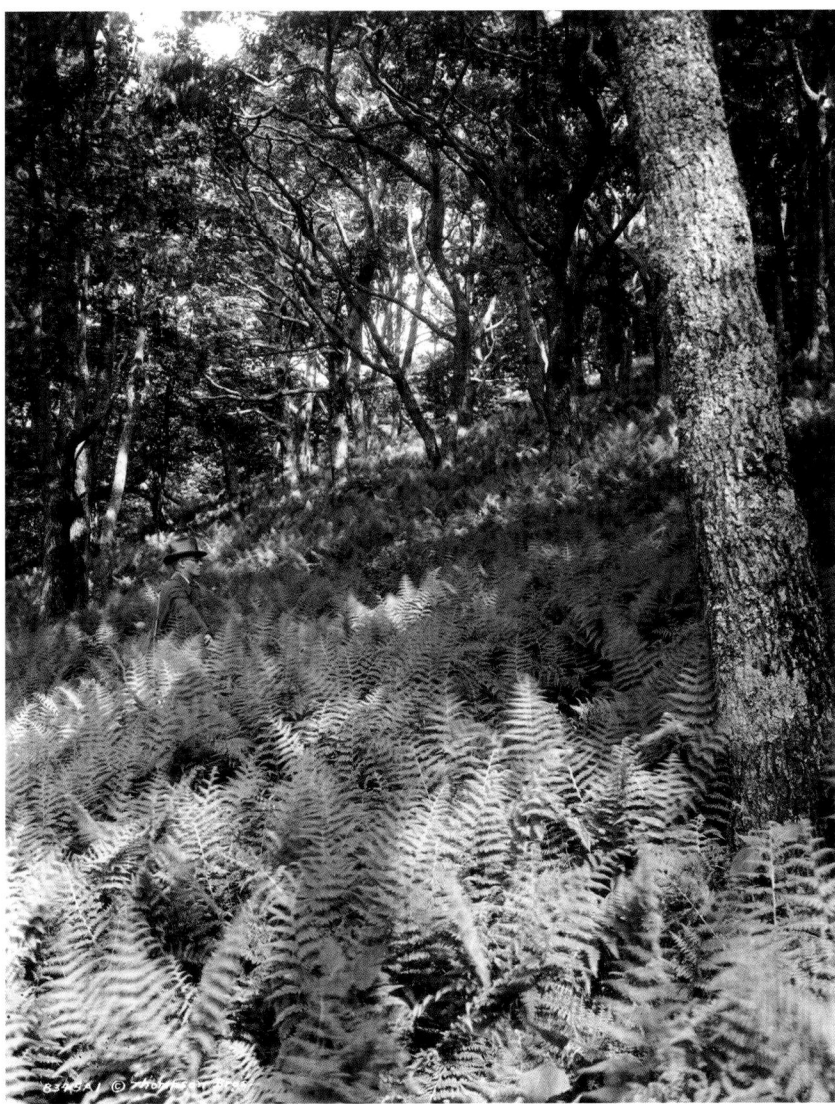

118   An aerial view of the Great Smokies. Photograph by Jim Thompson or Robin Thompson. Courtesy of Knox County Public Library.

119   Ferns on the side of trail to Gregory Bald. Courtesy of Knox County Public Library.

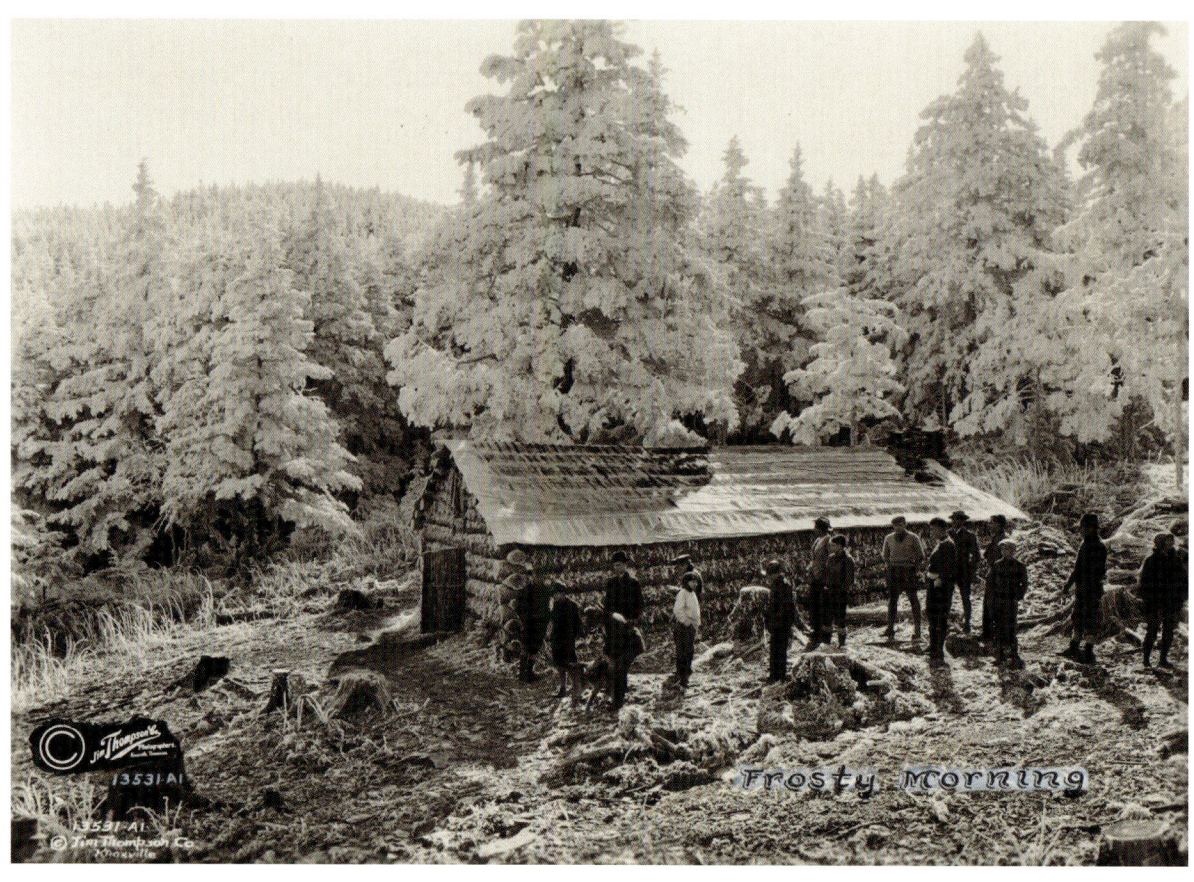

120   Frosty morning on trees around Jack Huff's cabin with
Smoky Mountain Hiking Club (SMHC) hikers.
Courtesy of Knox County Public Library.

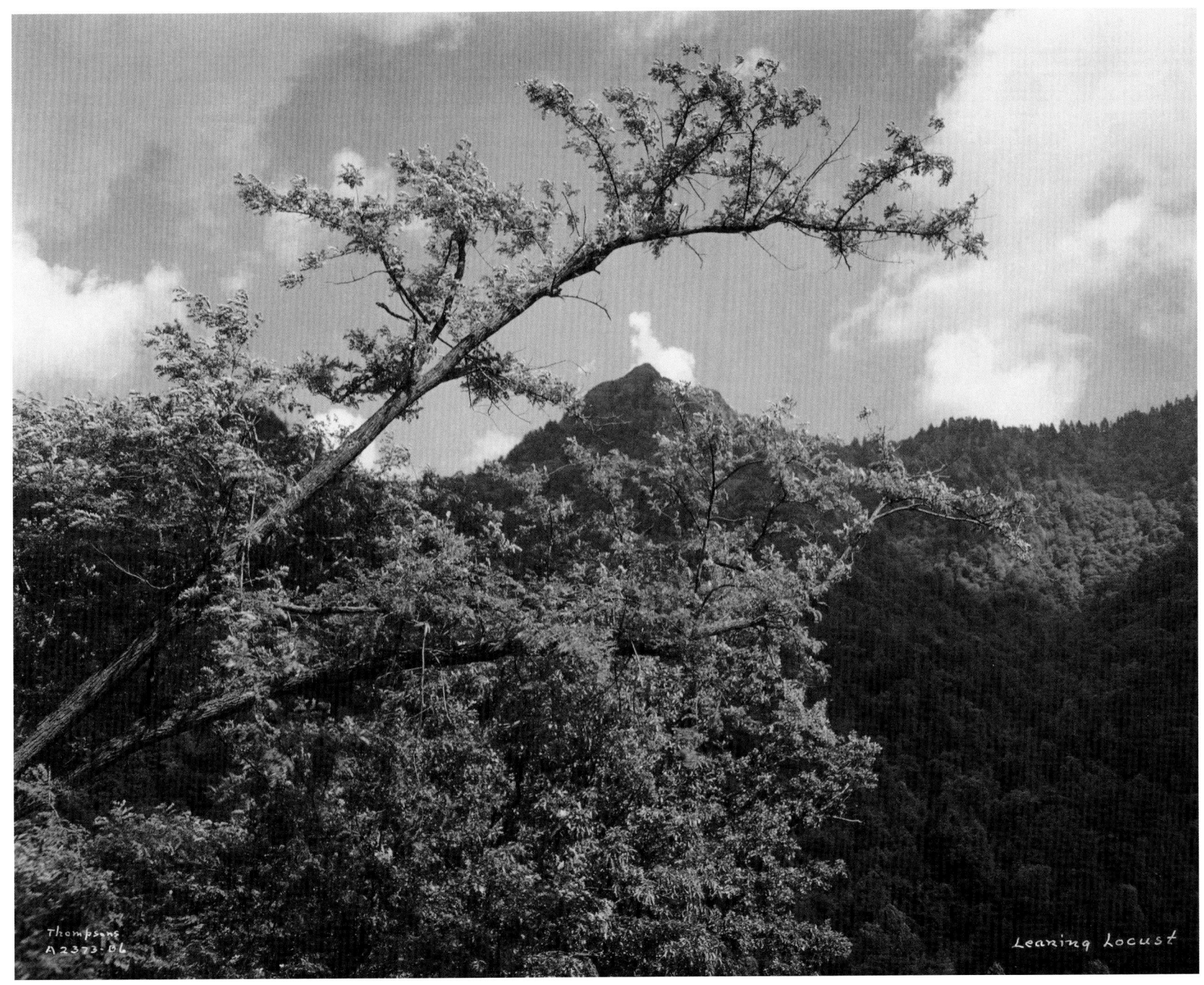

121   Leaning locust tree in the Great Smokies. Courtesy of National Park Service.

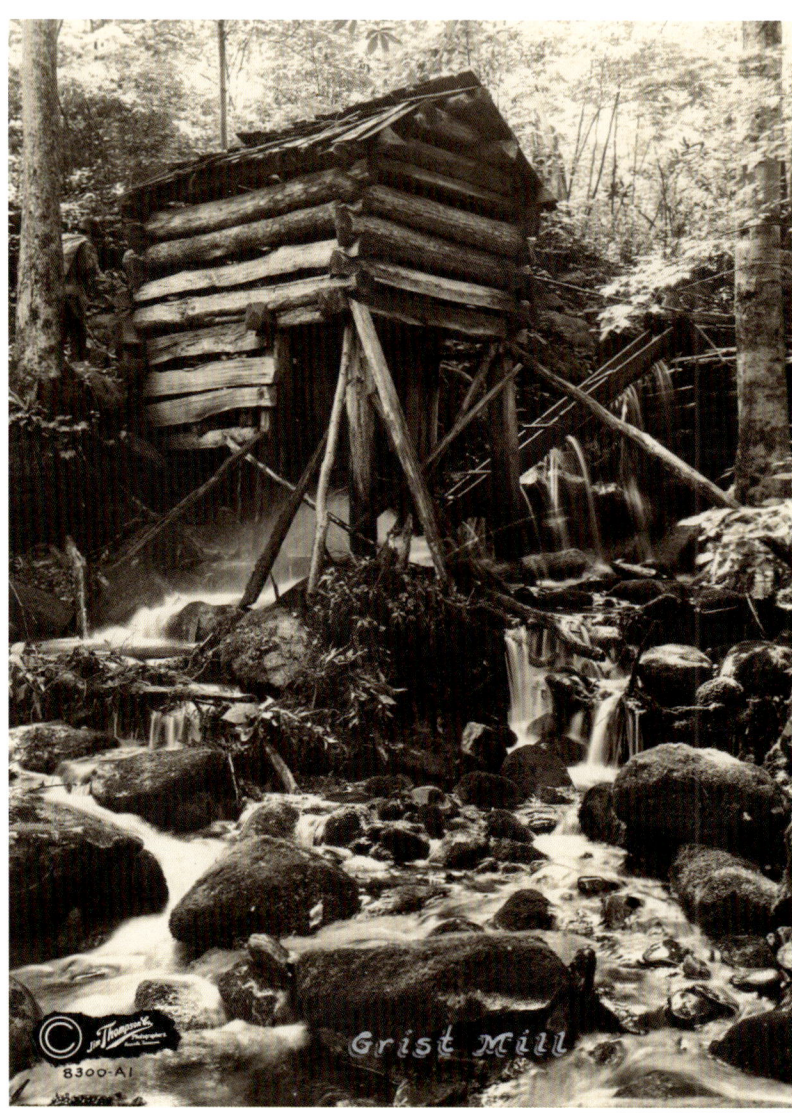

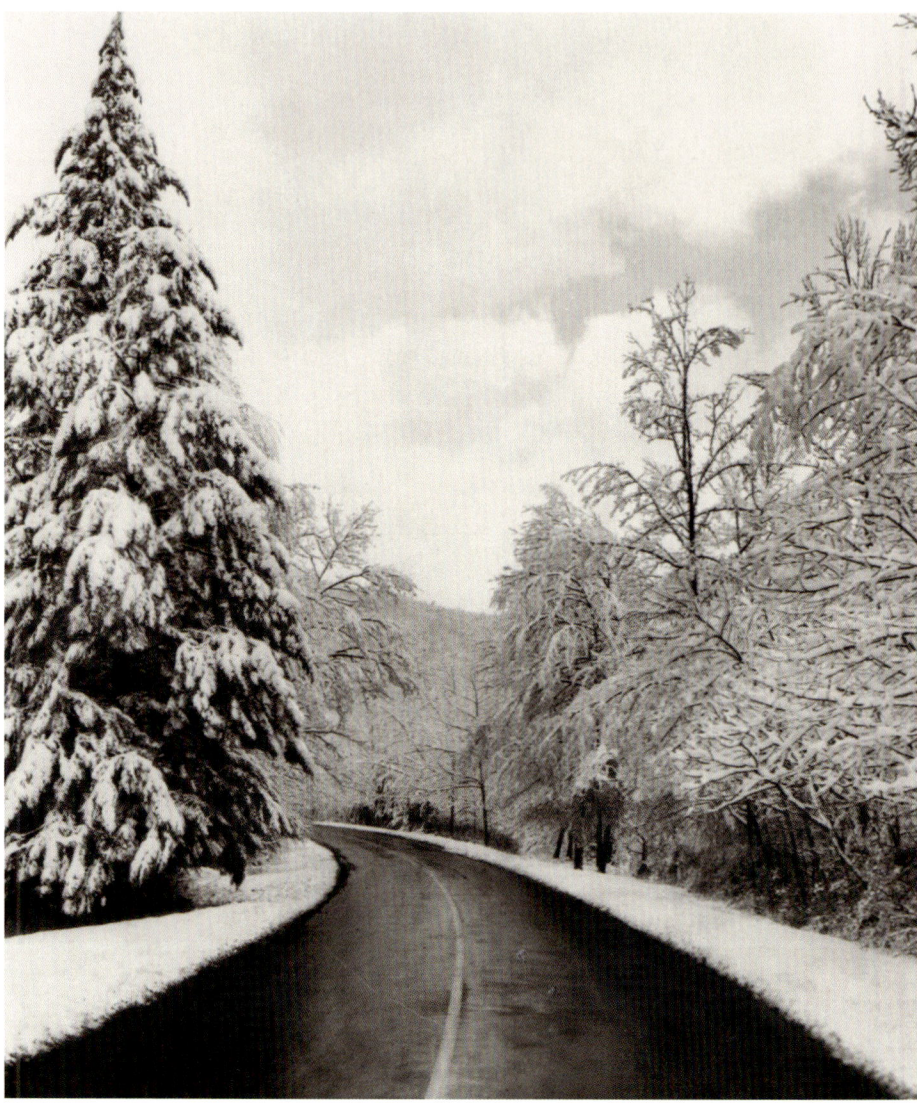

122   Primitive grist mill, or tub mill, in the Great Smokies.
Courtesy of National Park Service.

123   The Road to Fairyland in the Great Smoky Mountains
National Park. Courtesy of National Park Service.

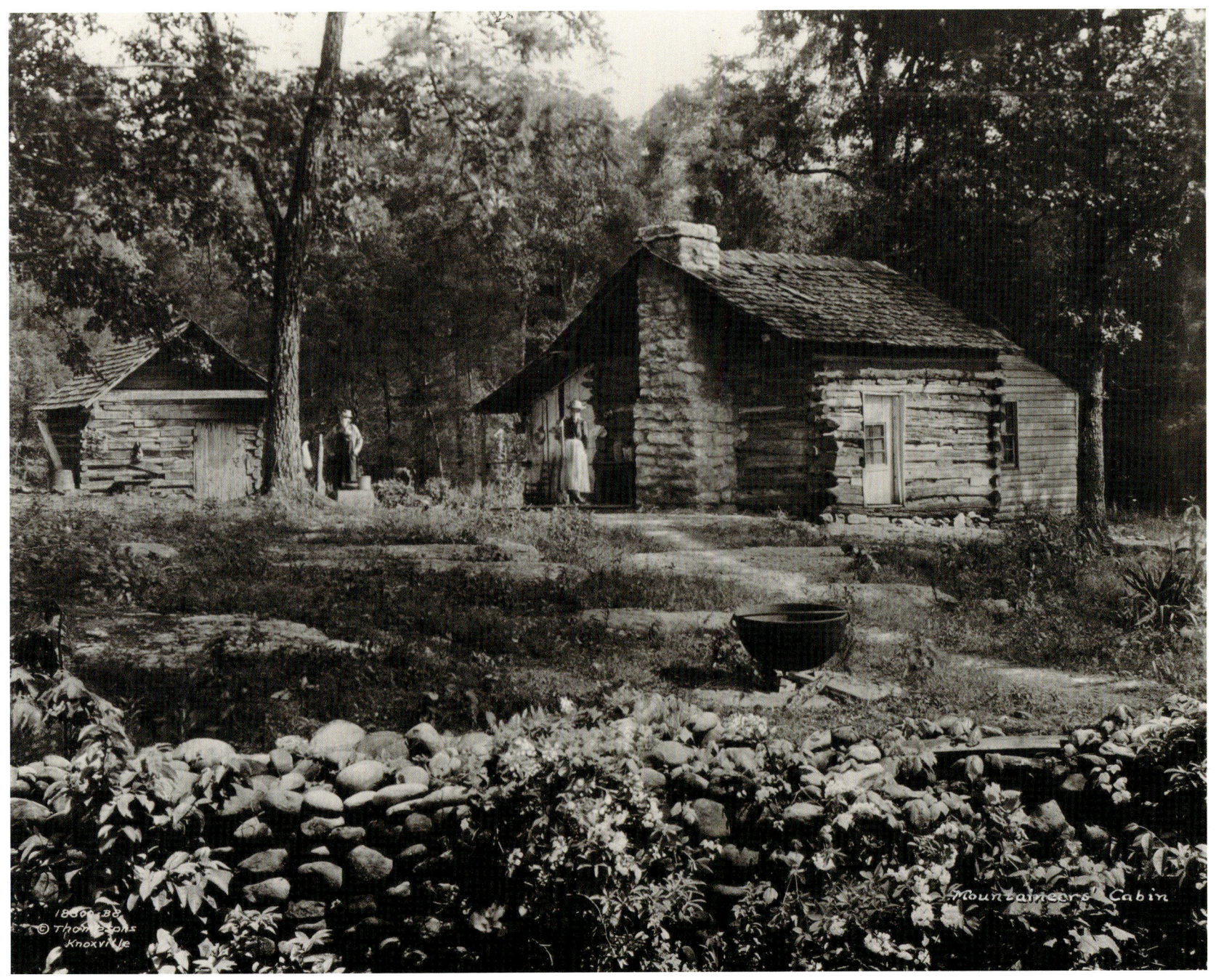

124   Tom and Sophie Campbell outside their cabin near Gatlinburg. Courtesy of National Park Service.

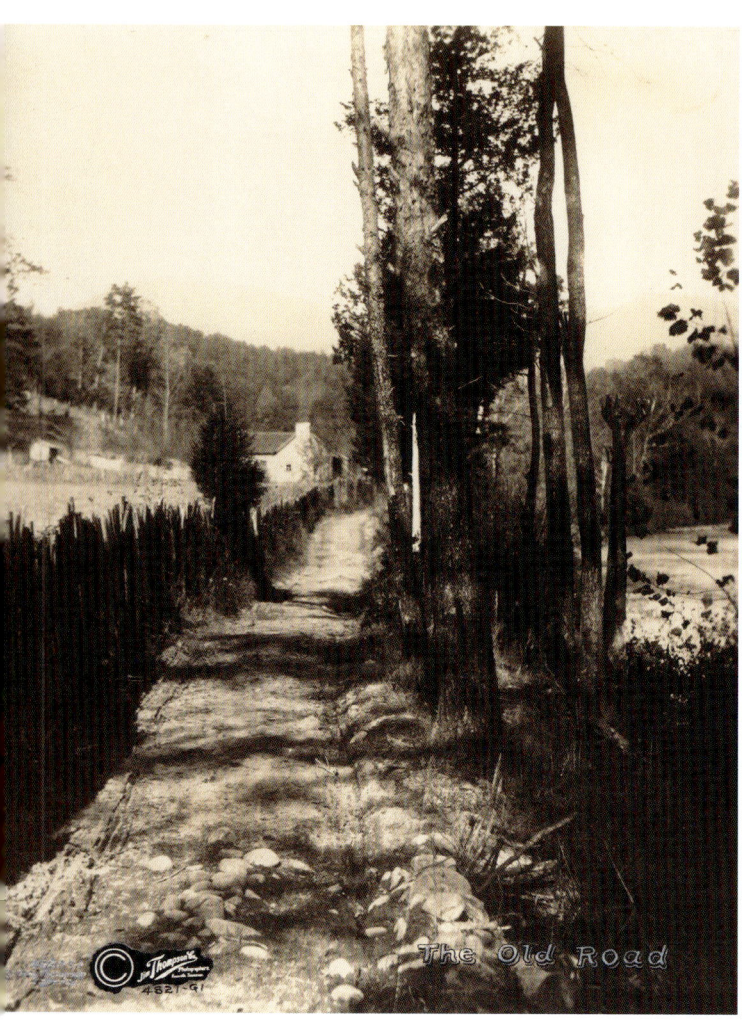

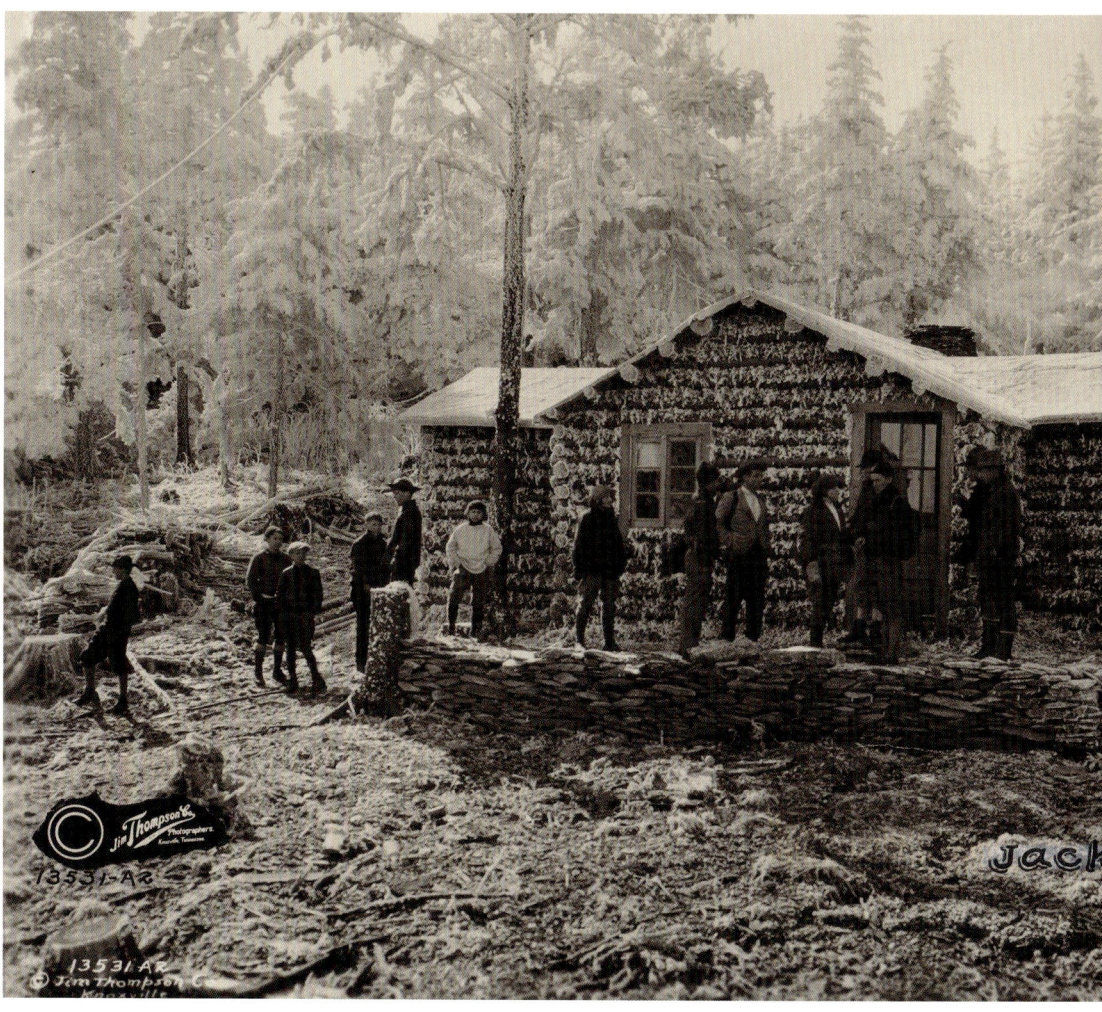

125   An old road in the Great Smokies.
       Courtesy of National Park Service.

126   Jack Huff's cabin in snow. Courtesy of National Park Service.

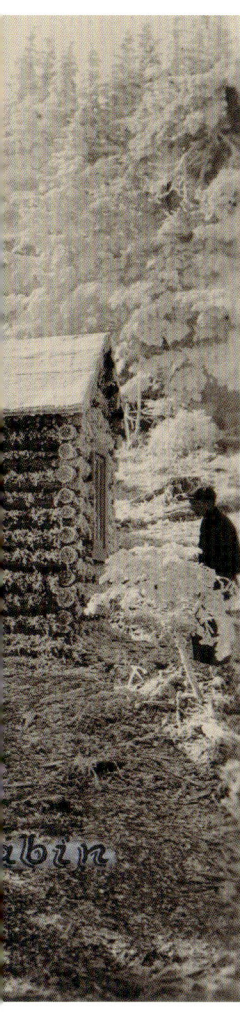

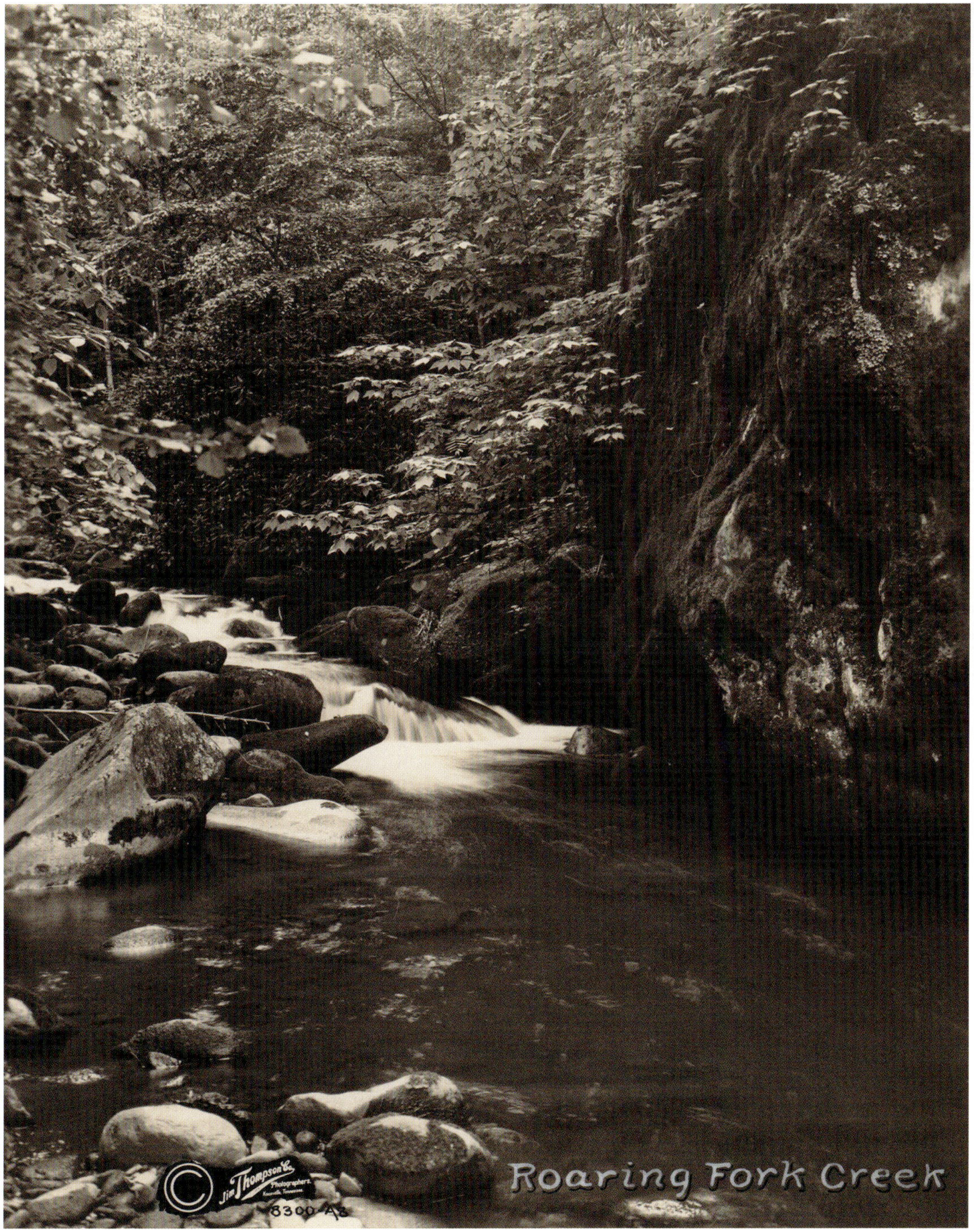

ubin

Roaring Fork Creek

127   Roaring Fork Creek.
       Courtesy of National
       Park Service.

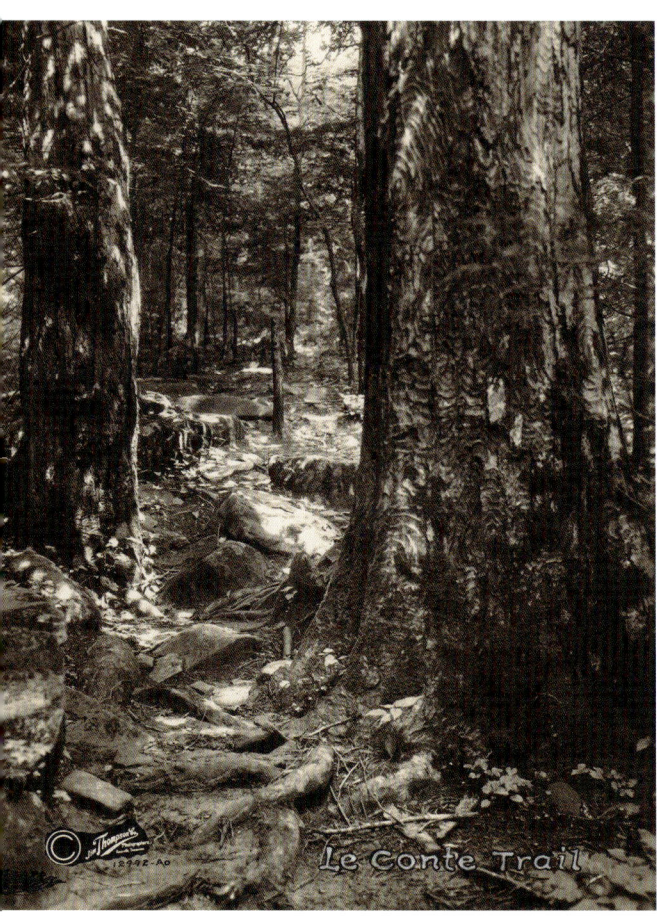

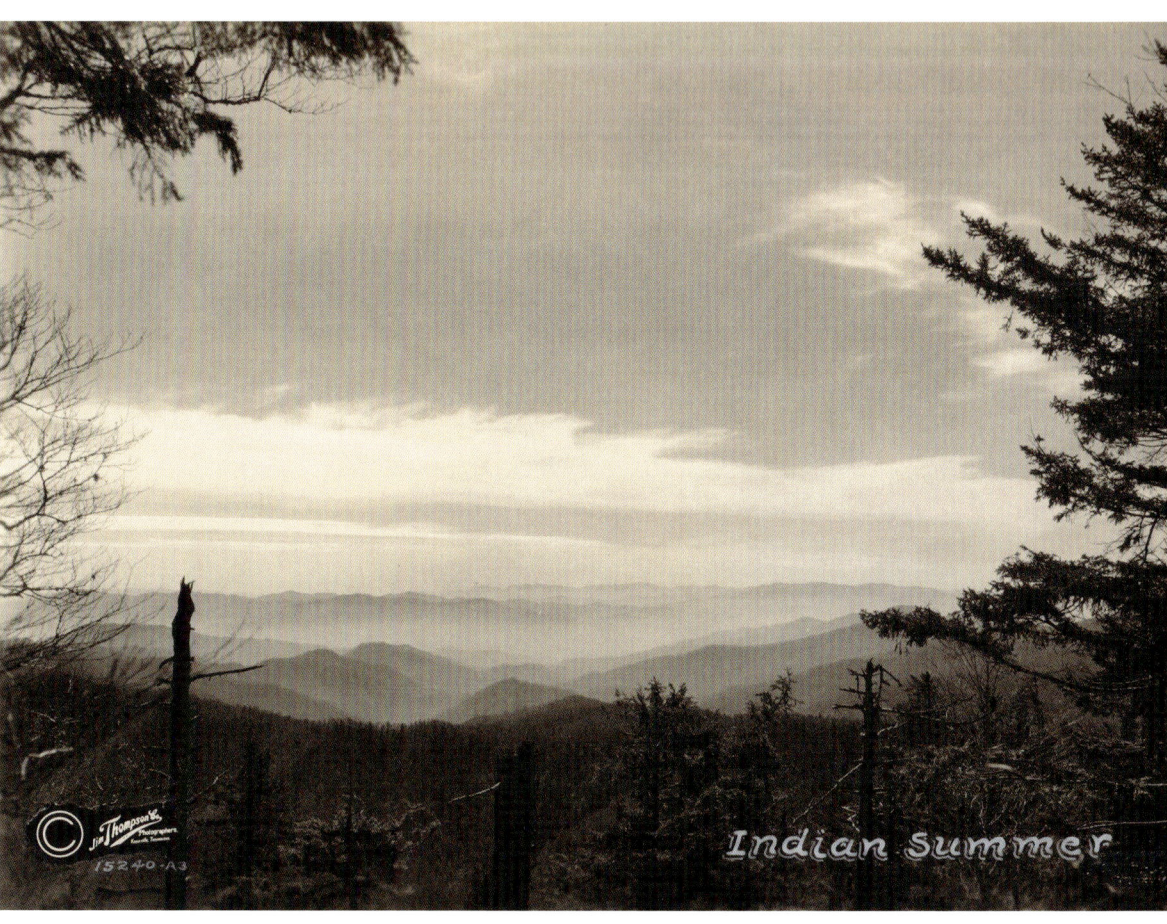

128   LeConte Mountain Trail. Courtesy of
        National Park Service.

129   Indian Summer. Courtesy of National Park Service.

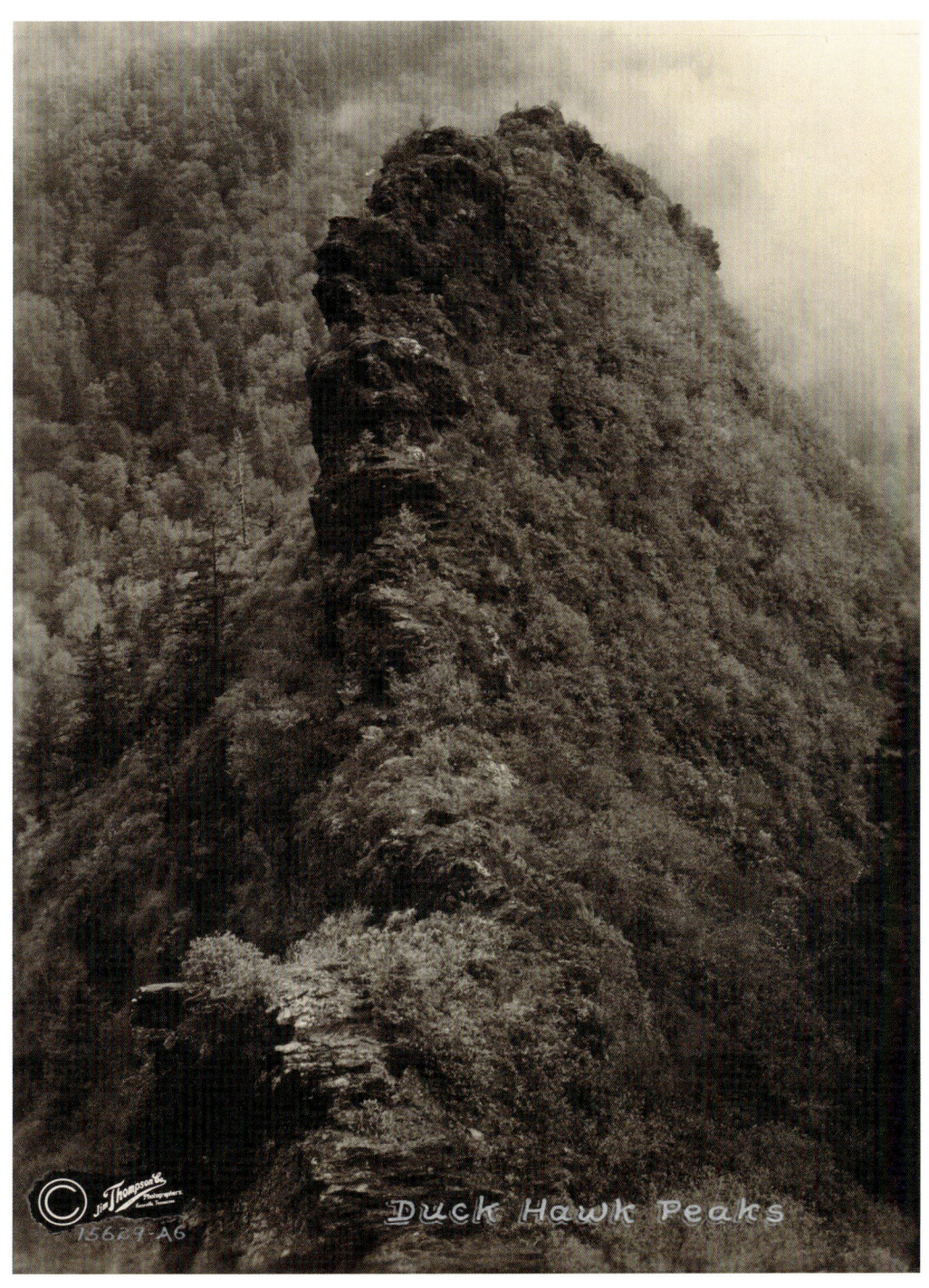

130 Duck Hawk Peaks.
Courtesy of National Park Service.

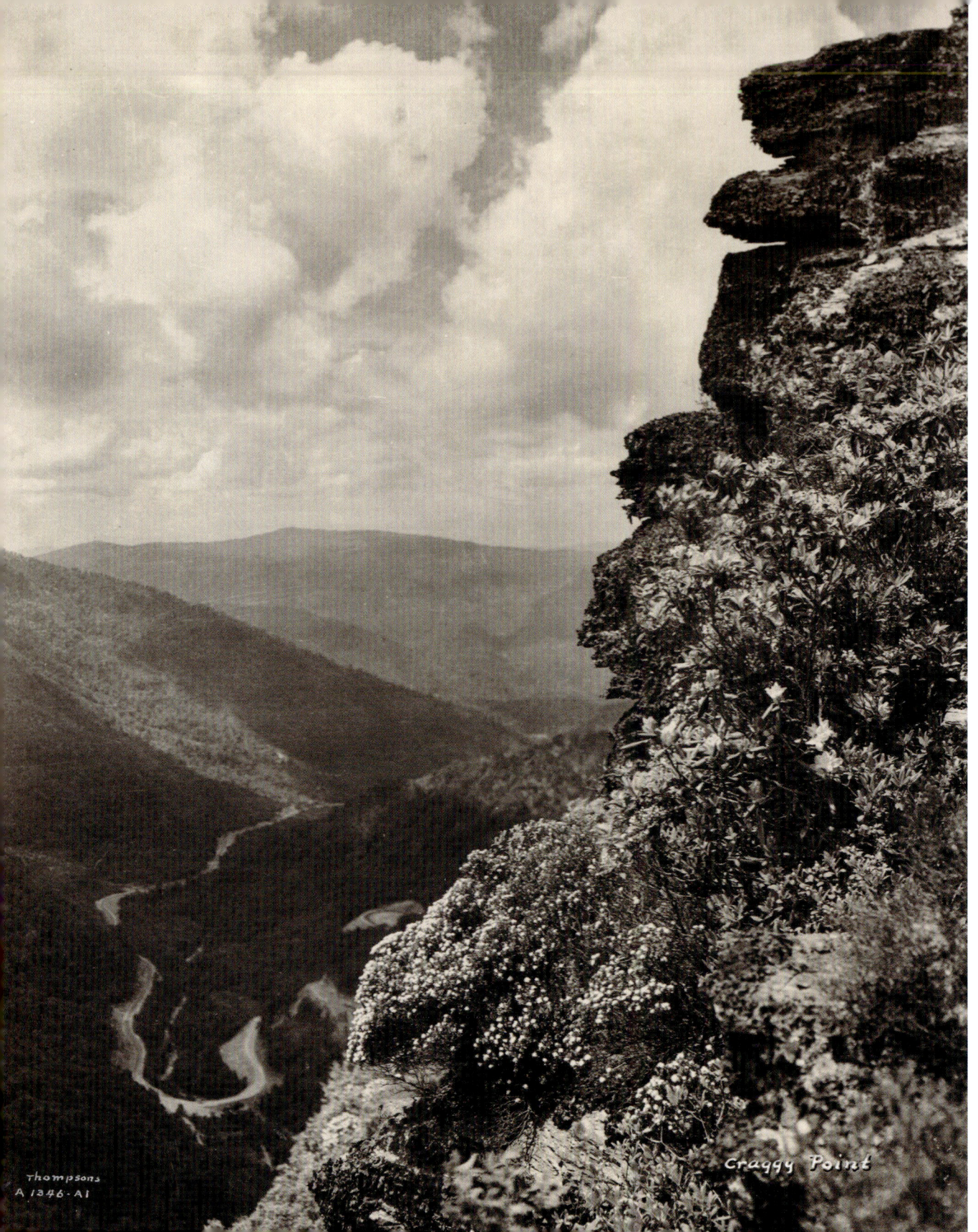

Thompsons
A 1346-A1

Craggy Point

131   Craggy Point.
      Courtesy of National
      Park Service.

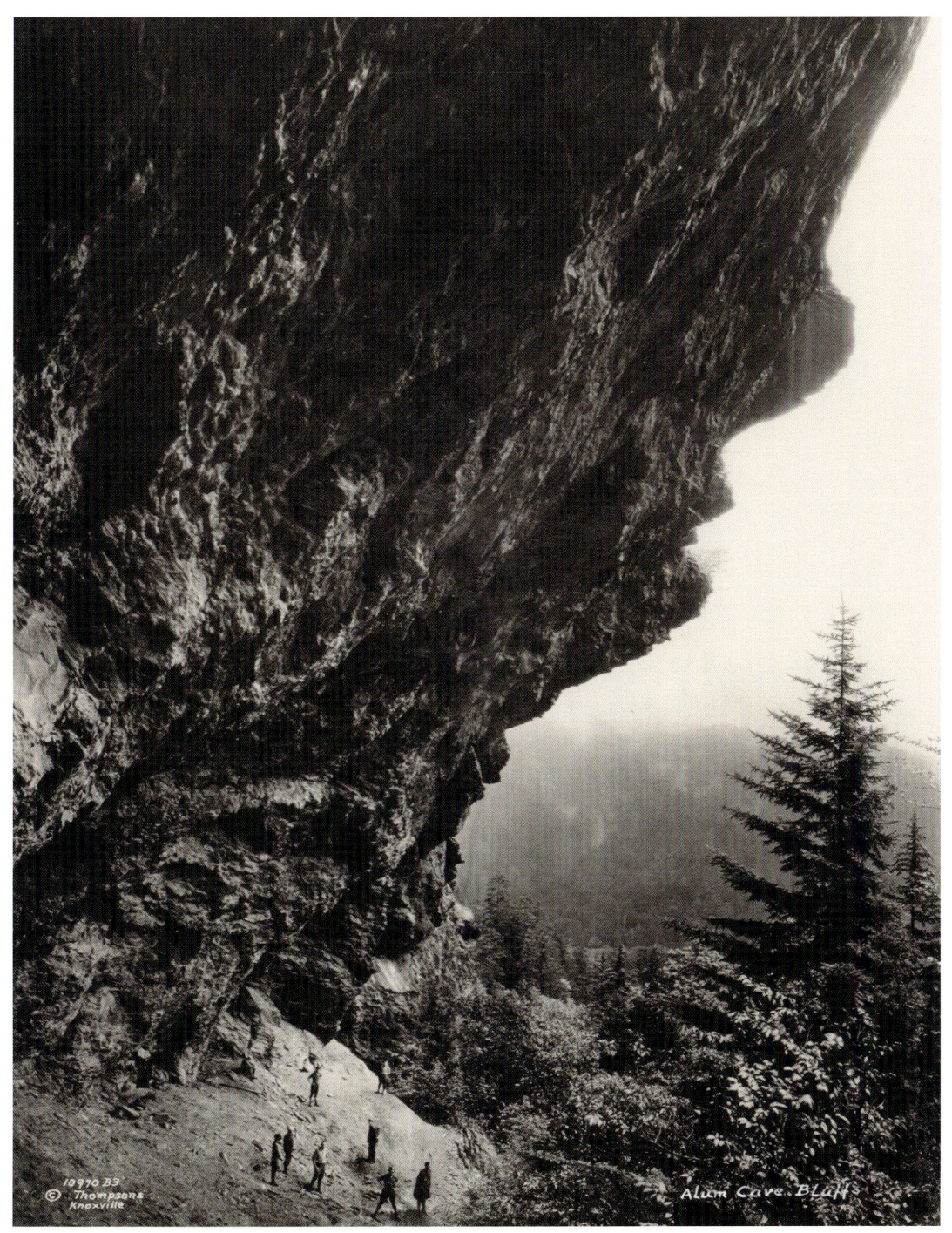

132 Alum Cave Bluffs.

Courtesy of National Park Service.

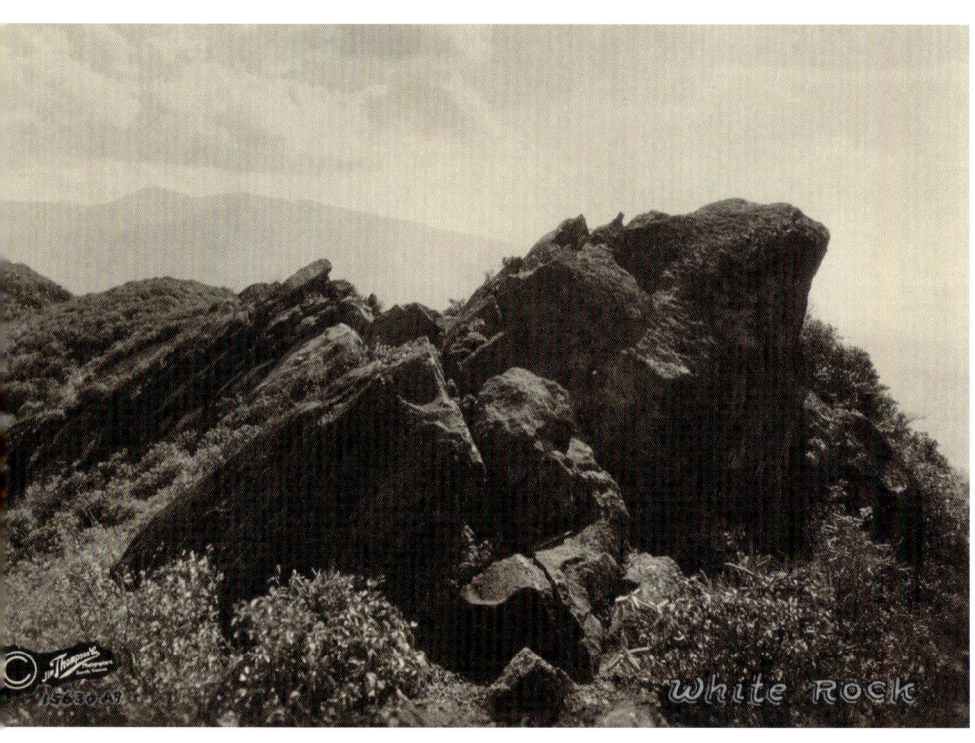

133   White Rock. Courtesy of National Park Service.

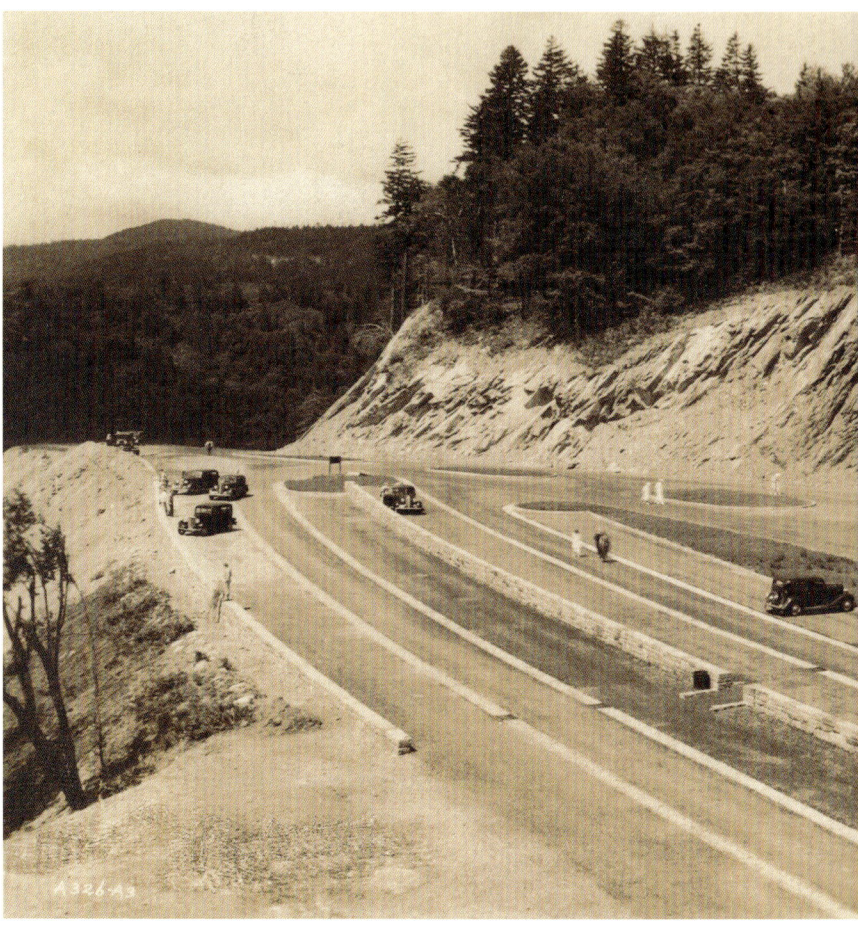

134   Newfound Gap parking area with road to Kuwohi
       on right. Courtesy of National Park Service.

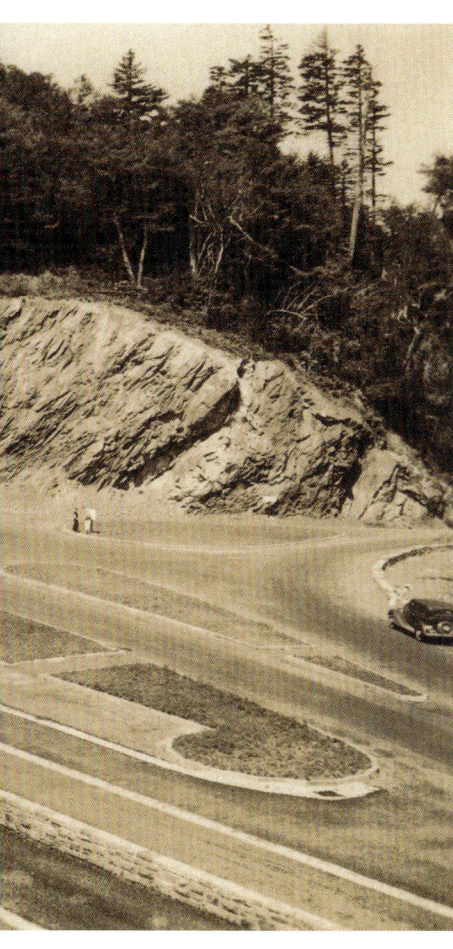

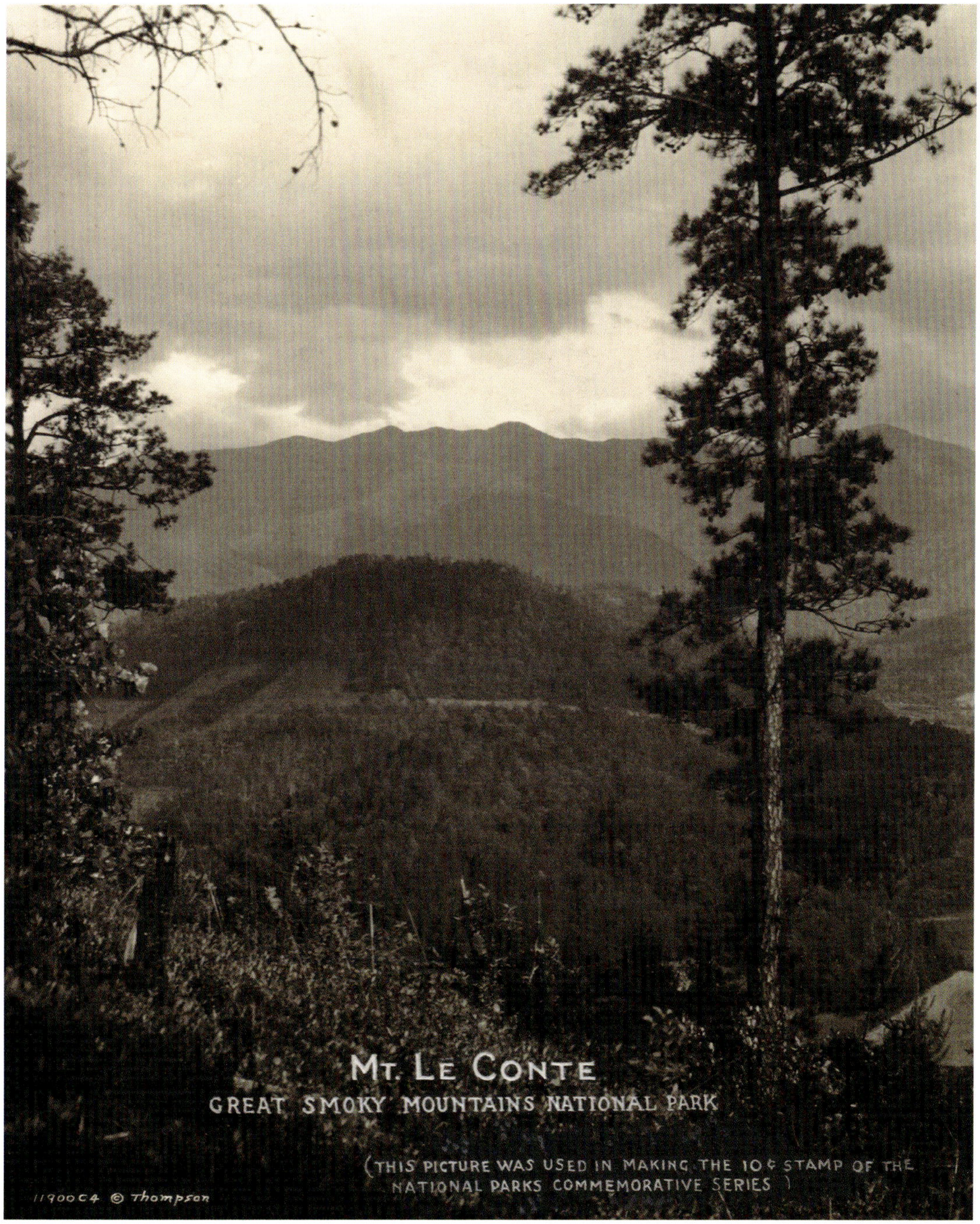

135   Mount LeConte. Courtesy of National Park Service.

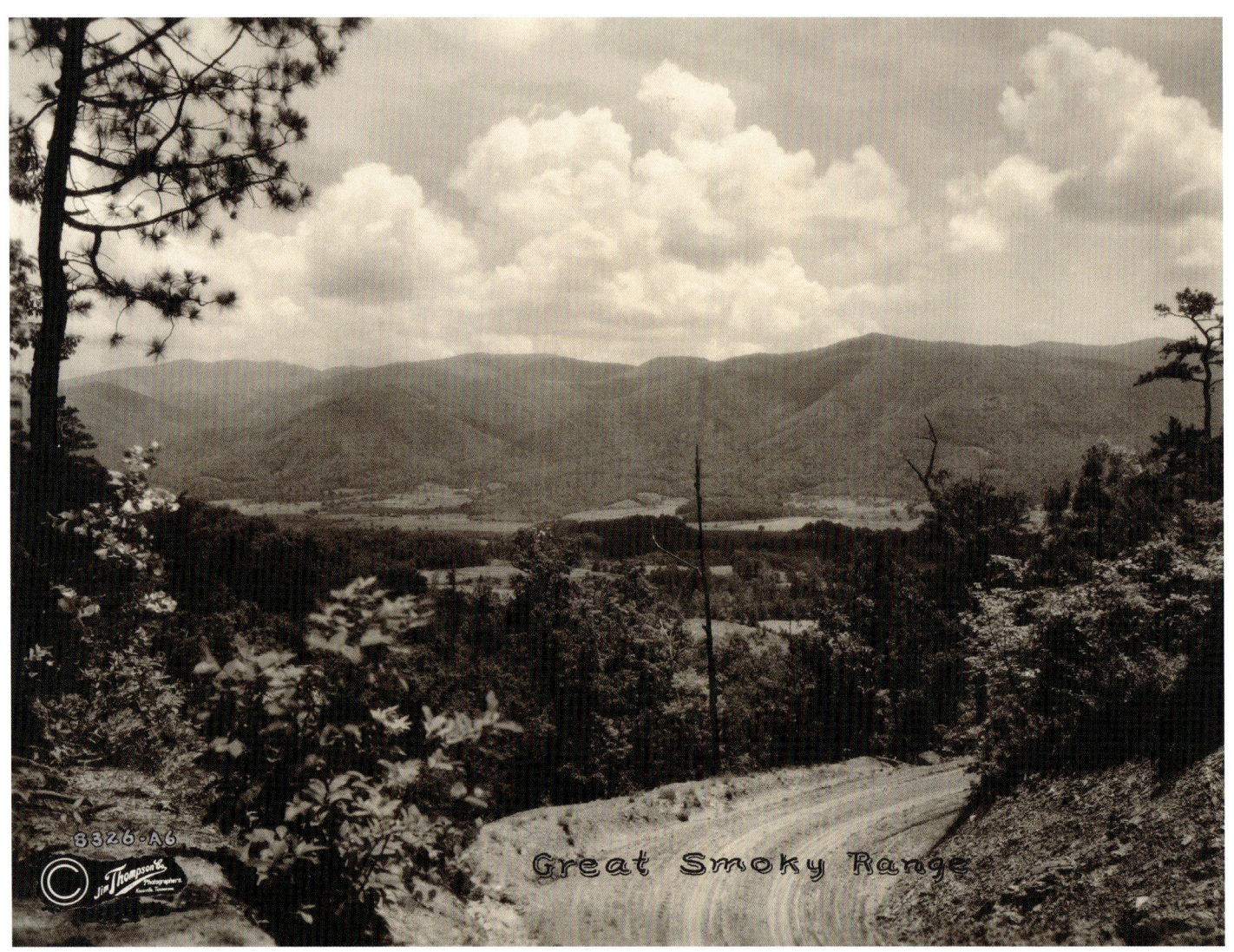

Great Smoky Range

136   Great Smoky Range. Courtesy of National Park Service.

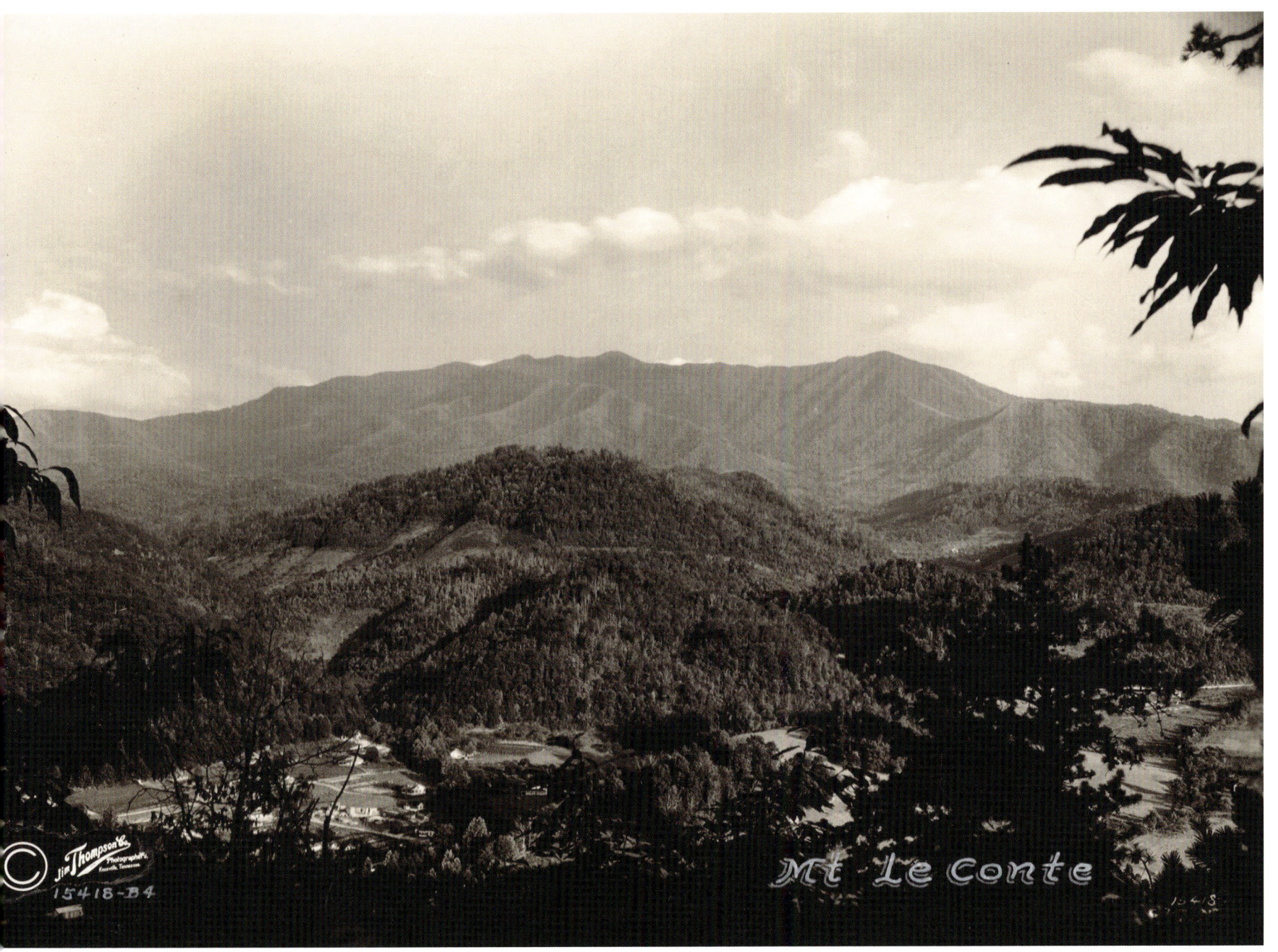

137   Mount LeConte with Gatlinburg in the foreground. Courtesy of National Park Service.

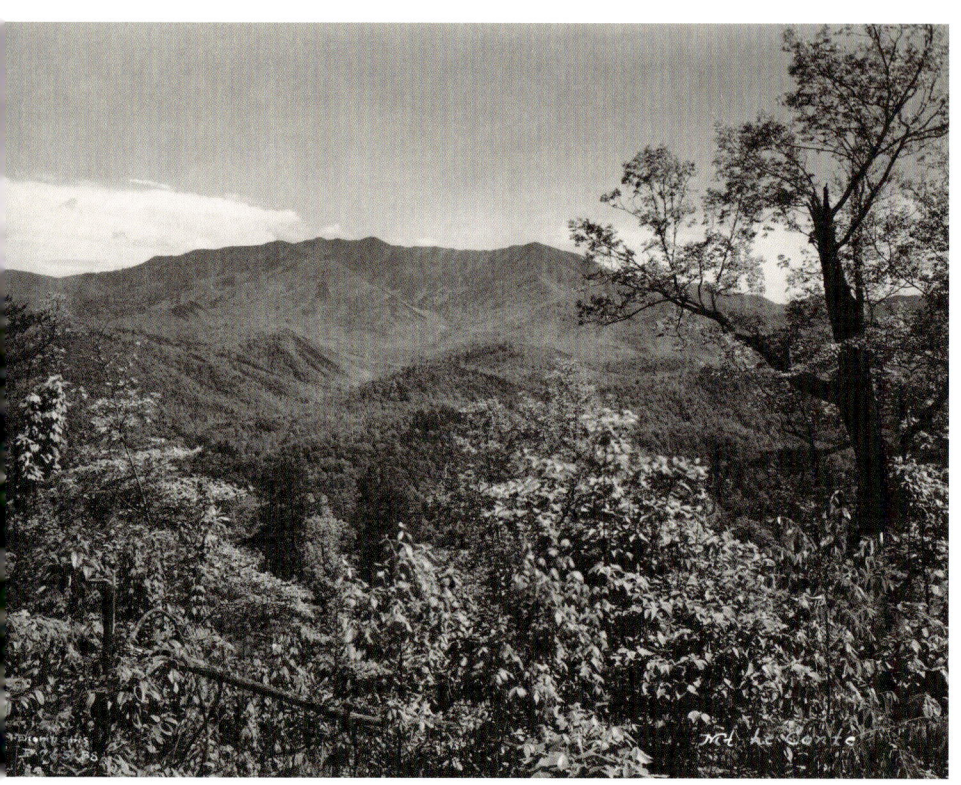

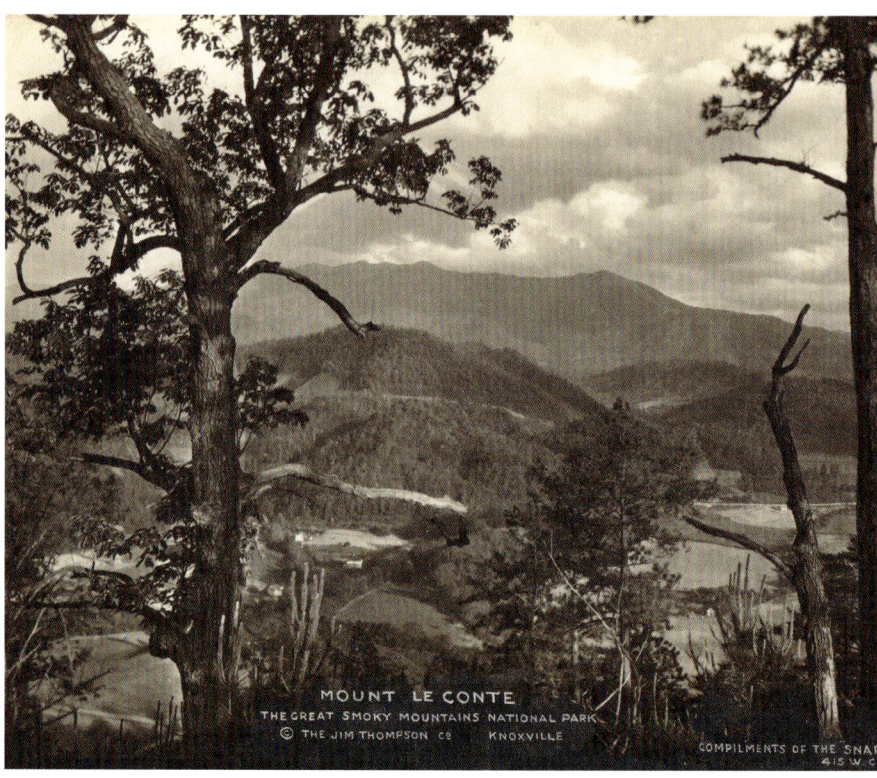

138   A distant view of Mount LeConte. Courtesy of National Park Service.

139   Mount LeConte in the distance.

Courtesy of National Park Service.

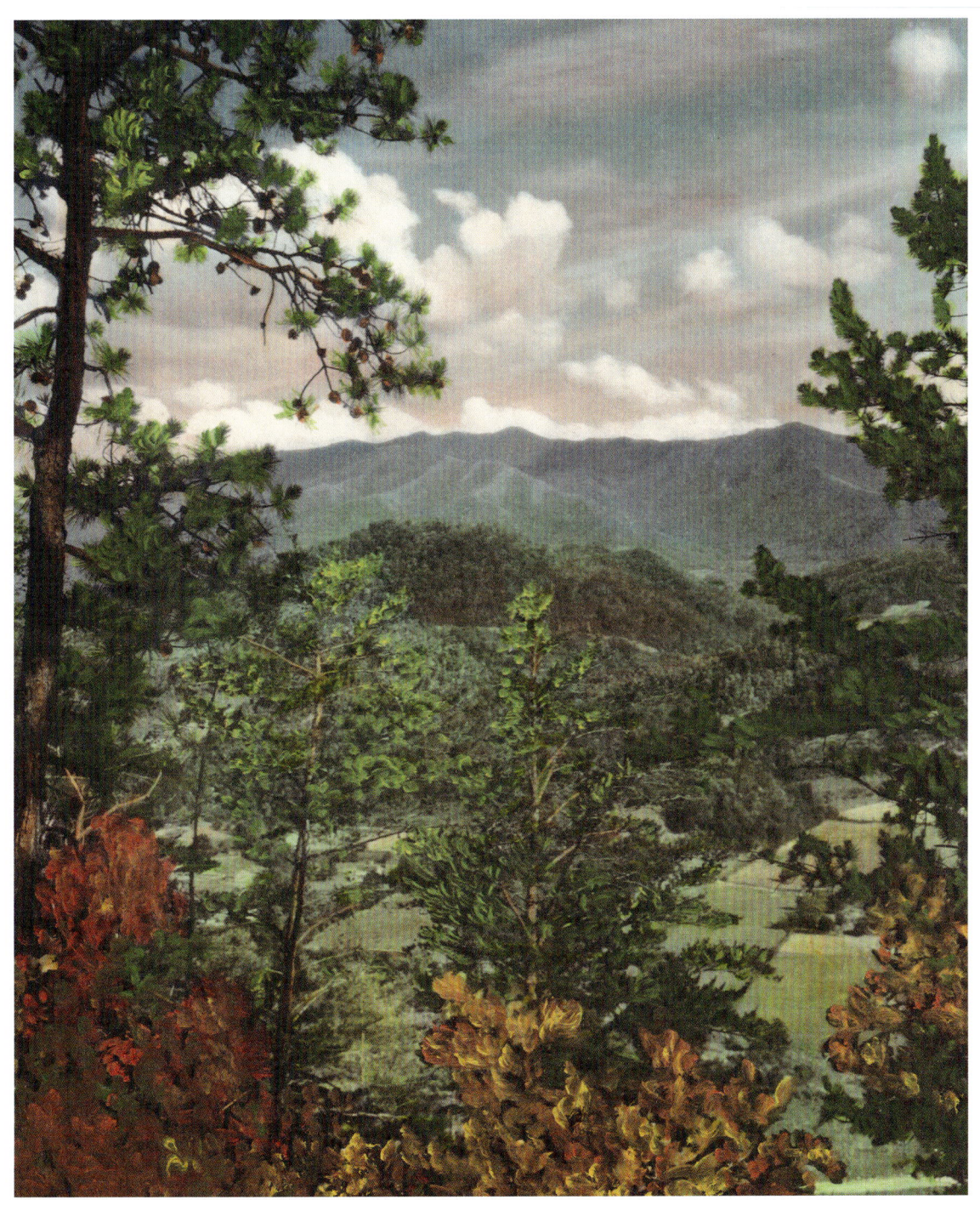

140   Hand-colorized image of Mount LeConte. Courtesy of National Park Service.

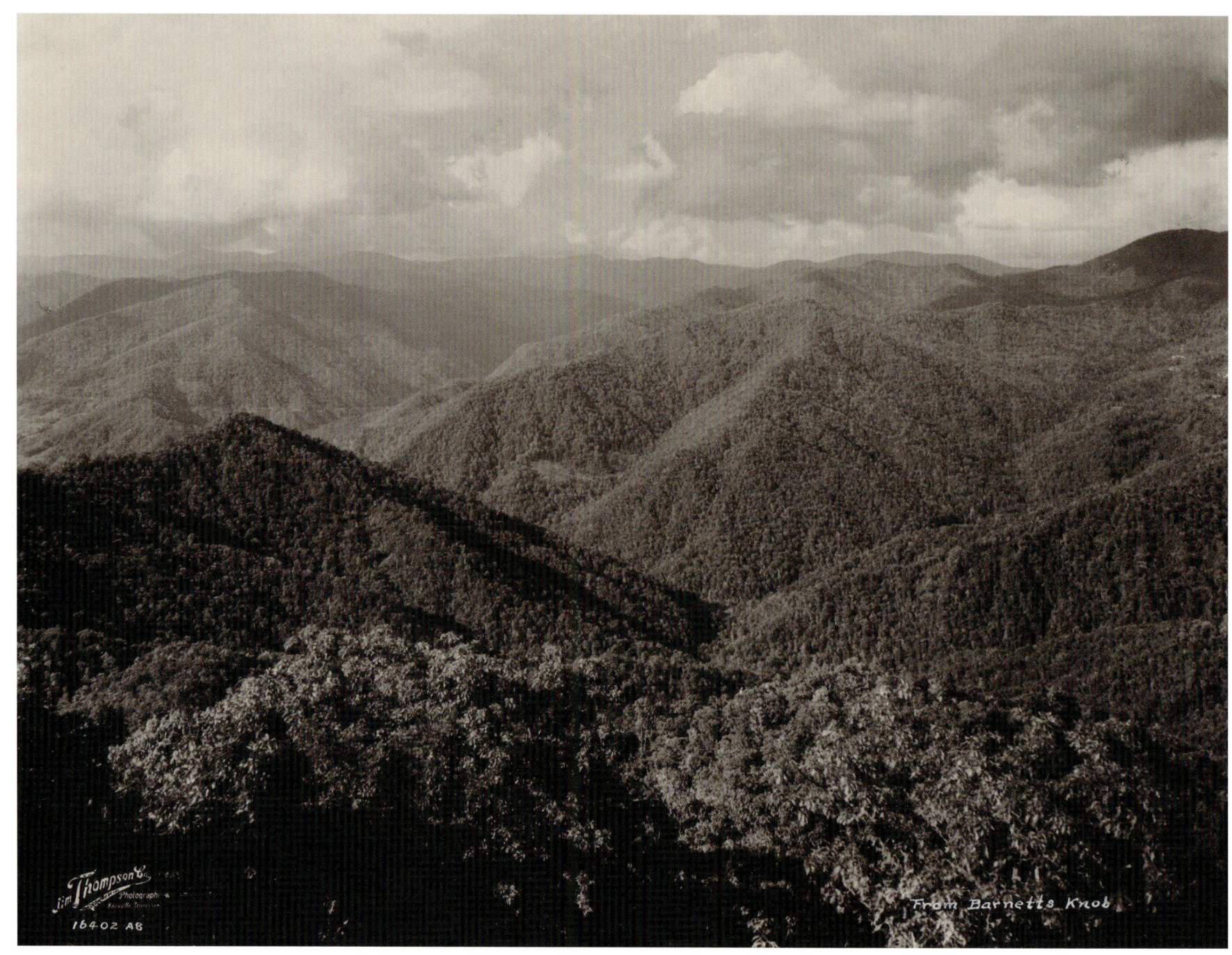

141   View from Barnett's Knob, north of Cherokee, North Carolina. Courtesy of National Park Service.

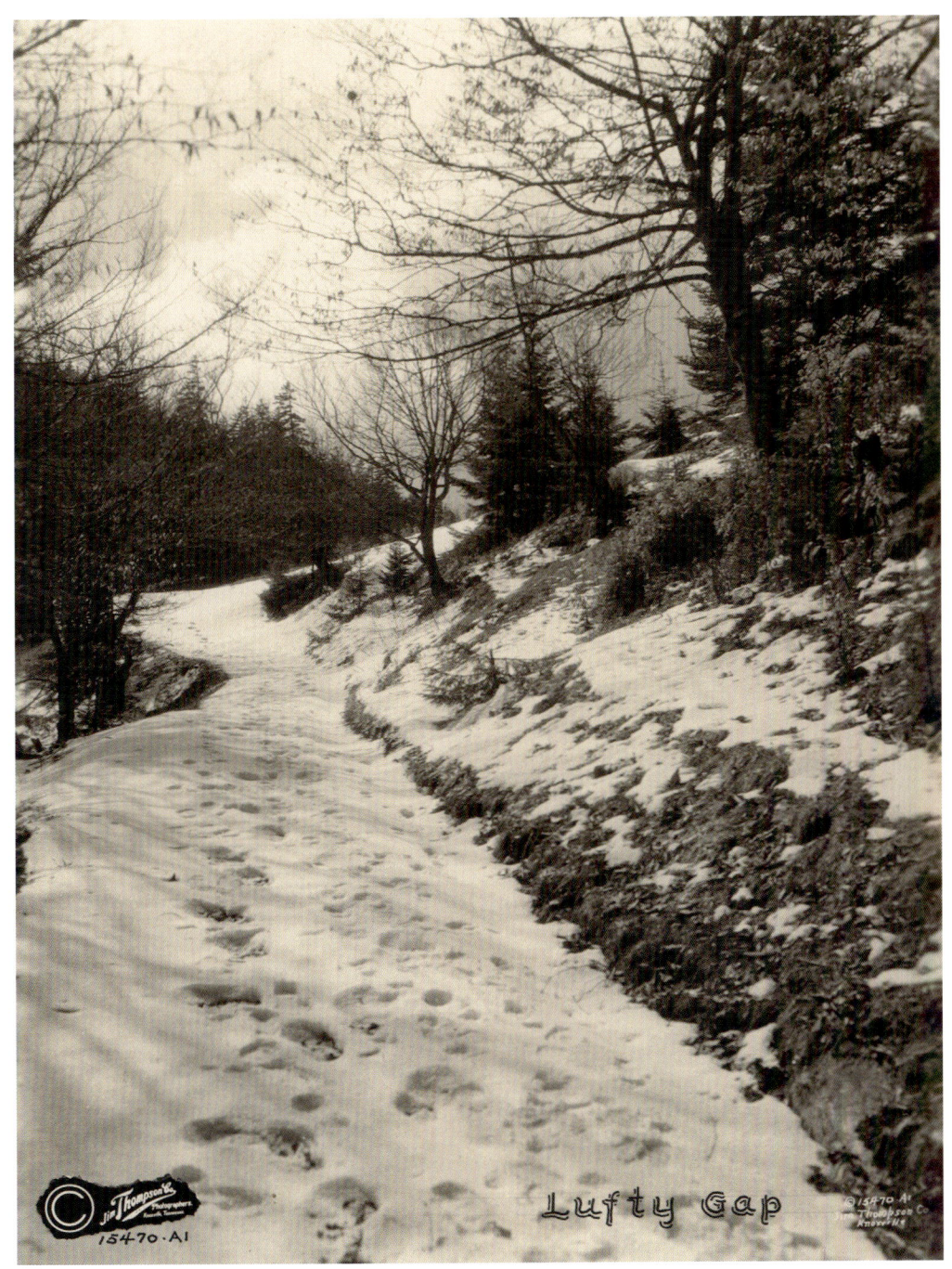

Lufty Gap

142 Scene in Lufty Gap.
Courtesy of National Park Service.

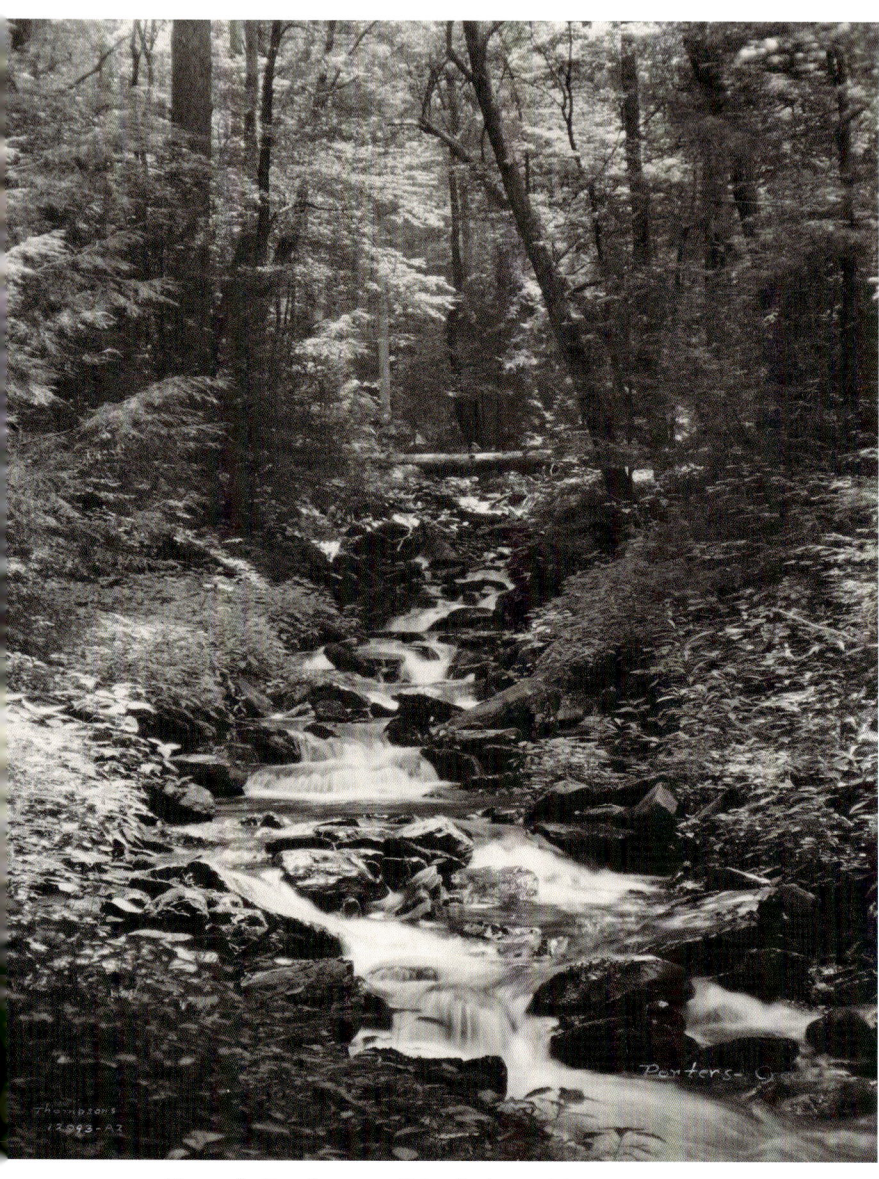

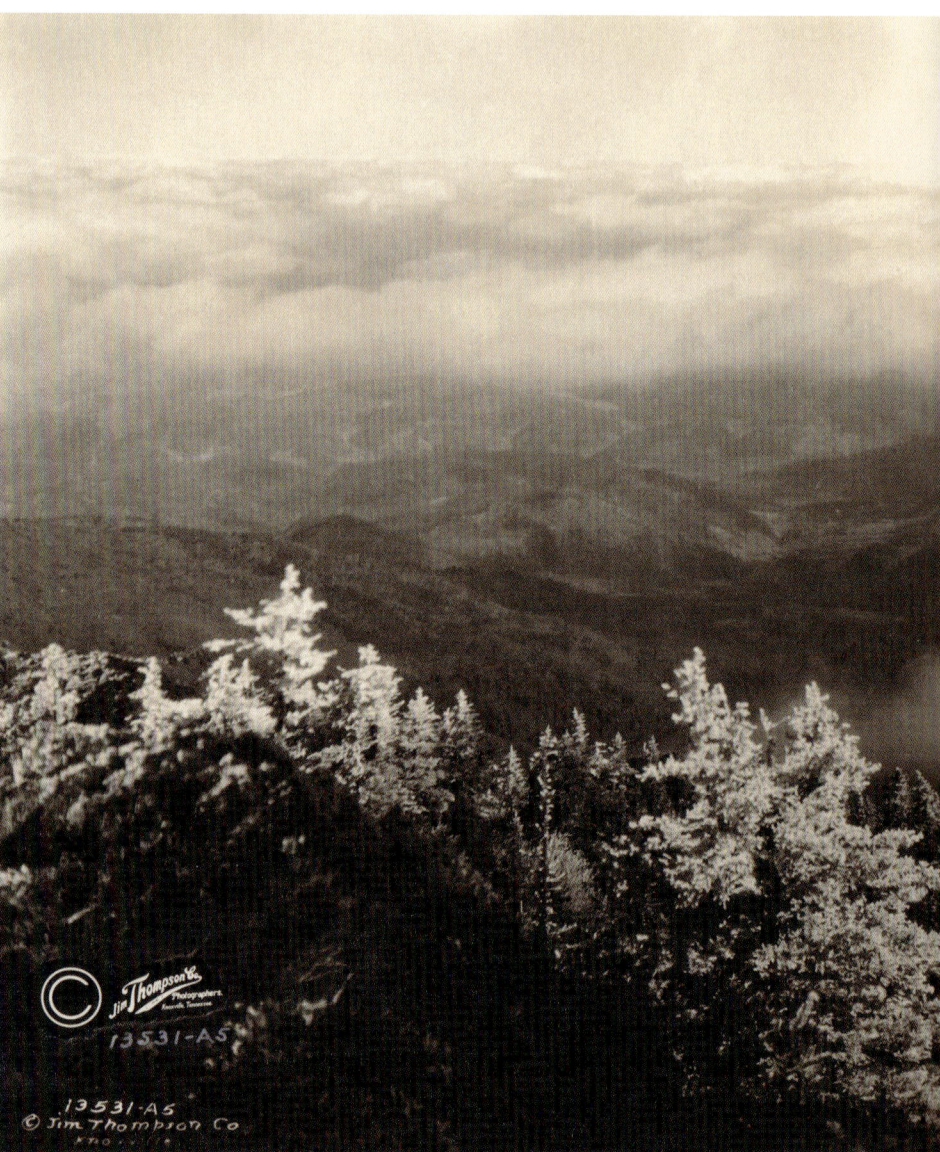

143 Porter's Creek, east of Gatlinburg, Tennessee.
Courtesy of National Park Service.

144 Frost and clouds. Courtesy of National Park Service.

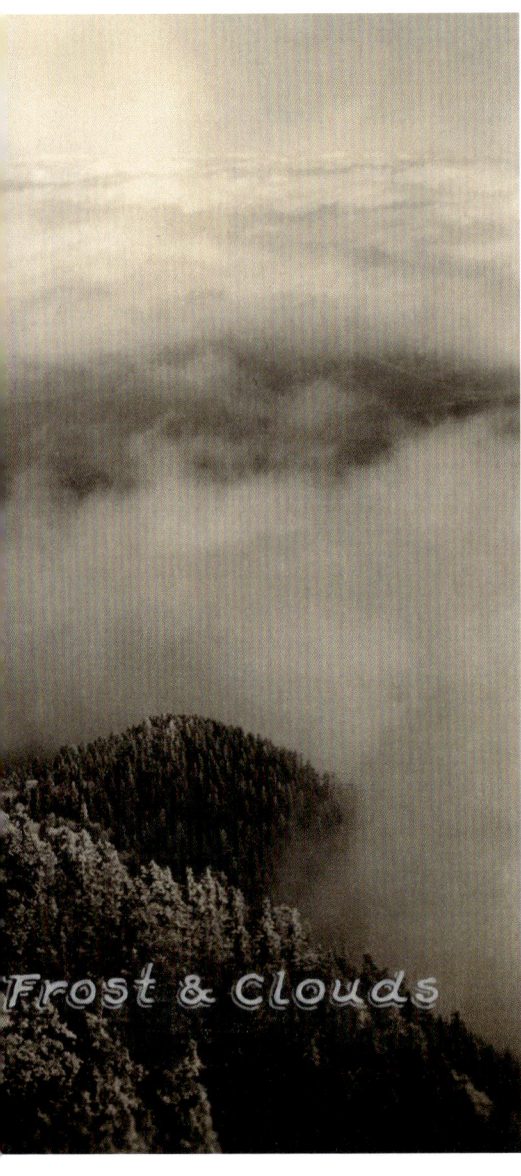

Frost & Clouds

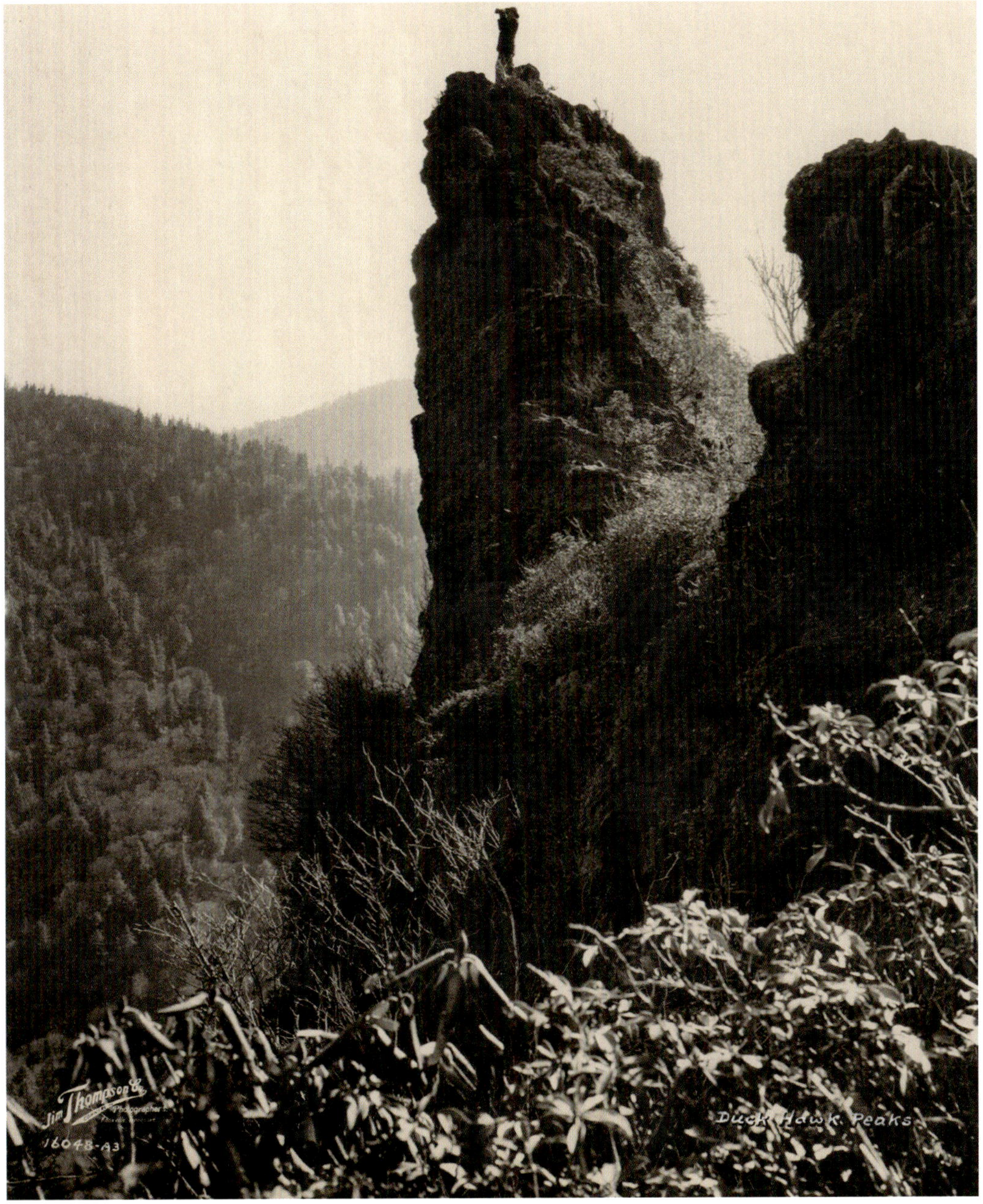

145   A person standing atop one of the Duck Hawk Peaks
       located near Alum Cave in the Great Smoky Mountains
       National Park. Courtesy of National Park Service.

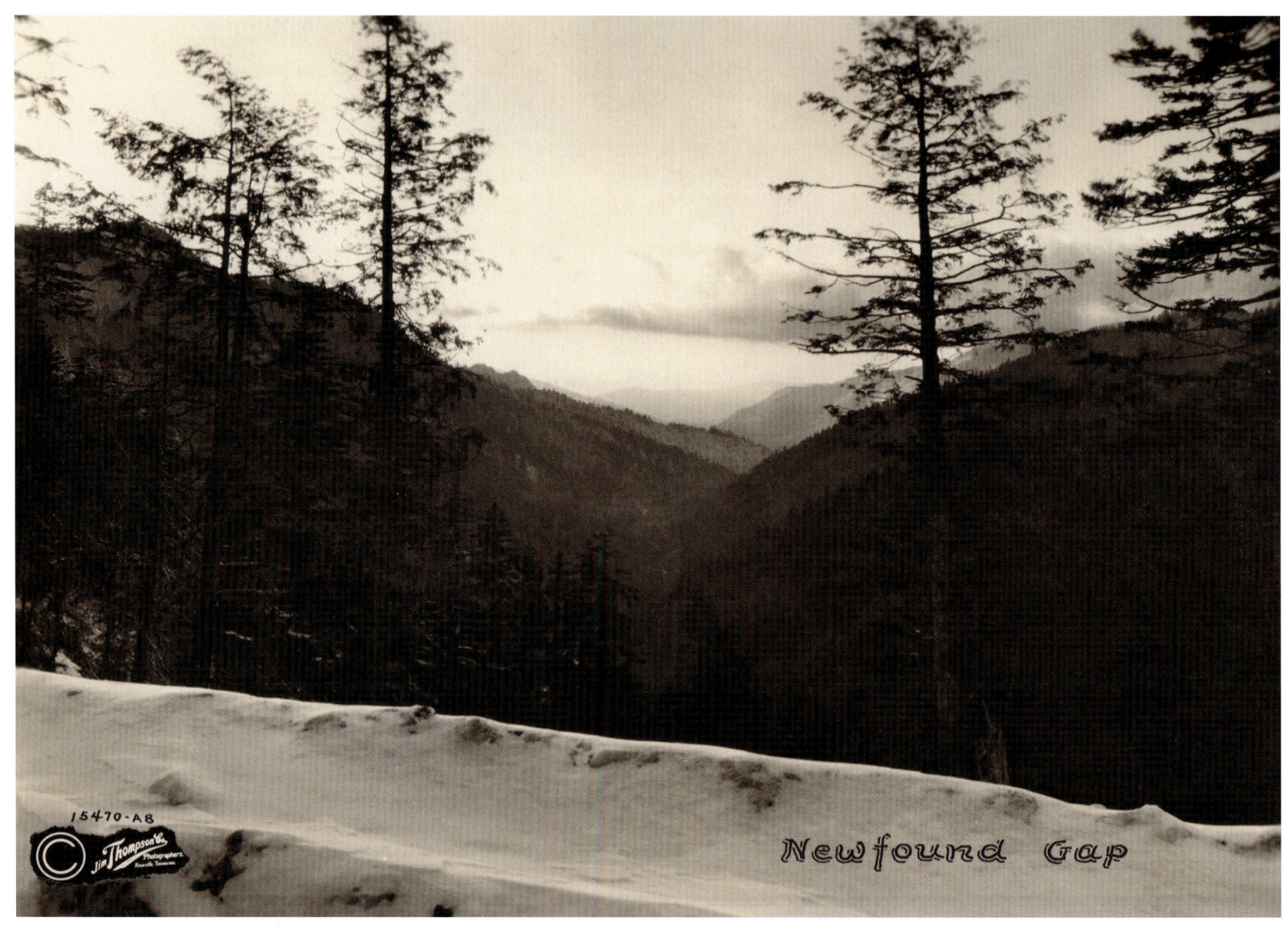

146   Snow at Newfound Gap. Courtesy of National Park Service.

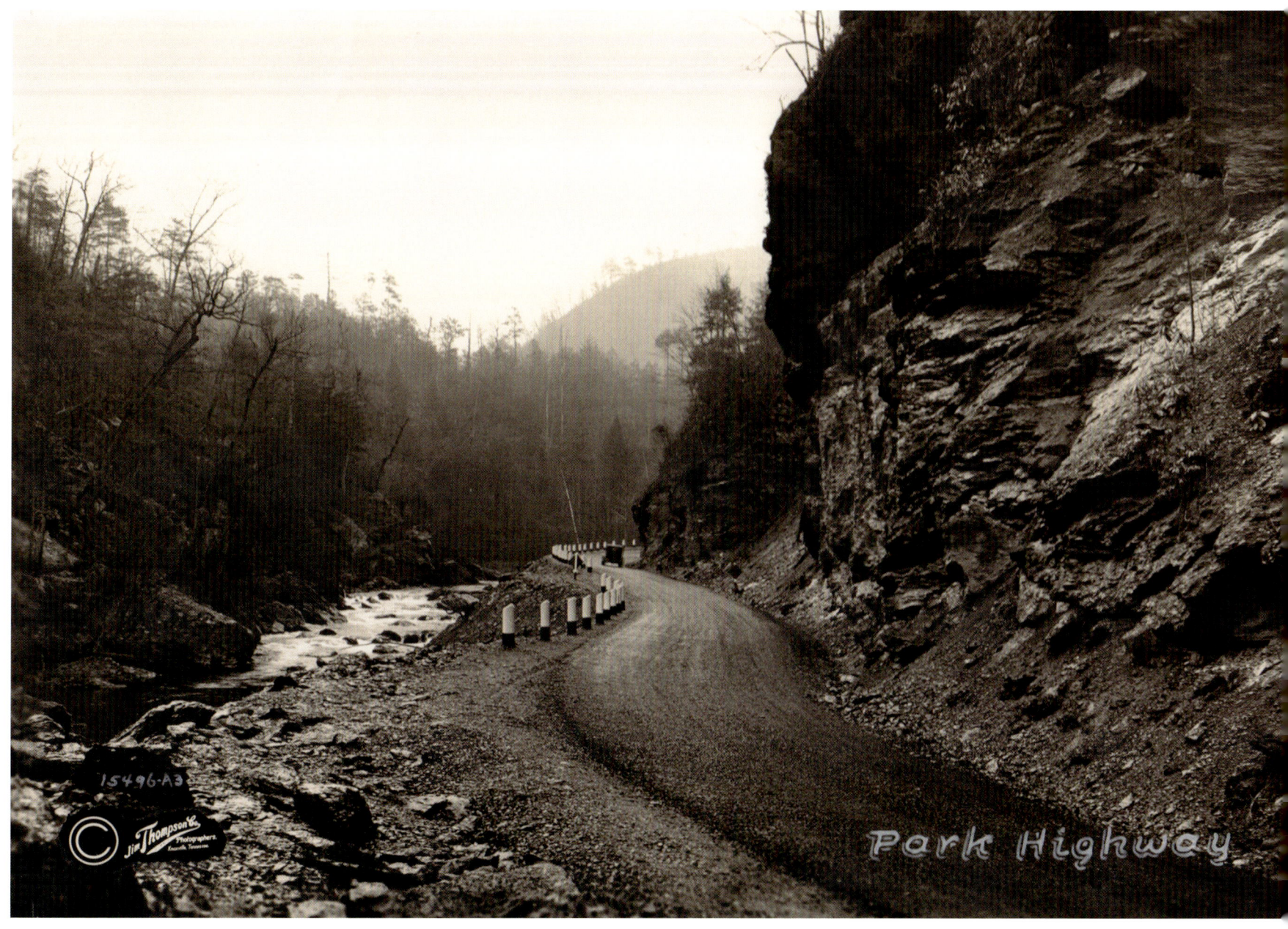

Park Highway

147   Park Highway. Courtesy of National Park Service.

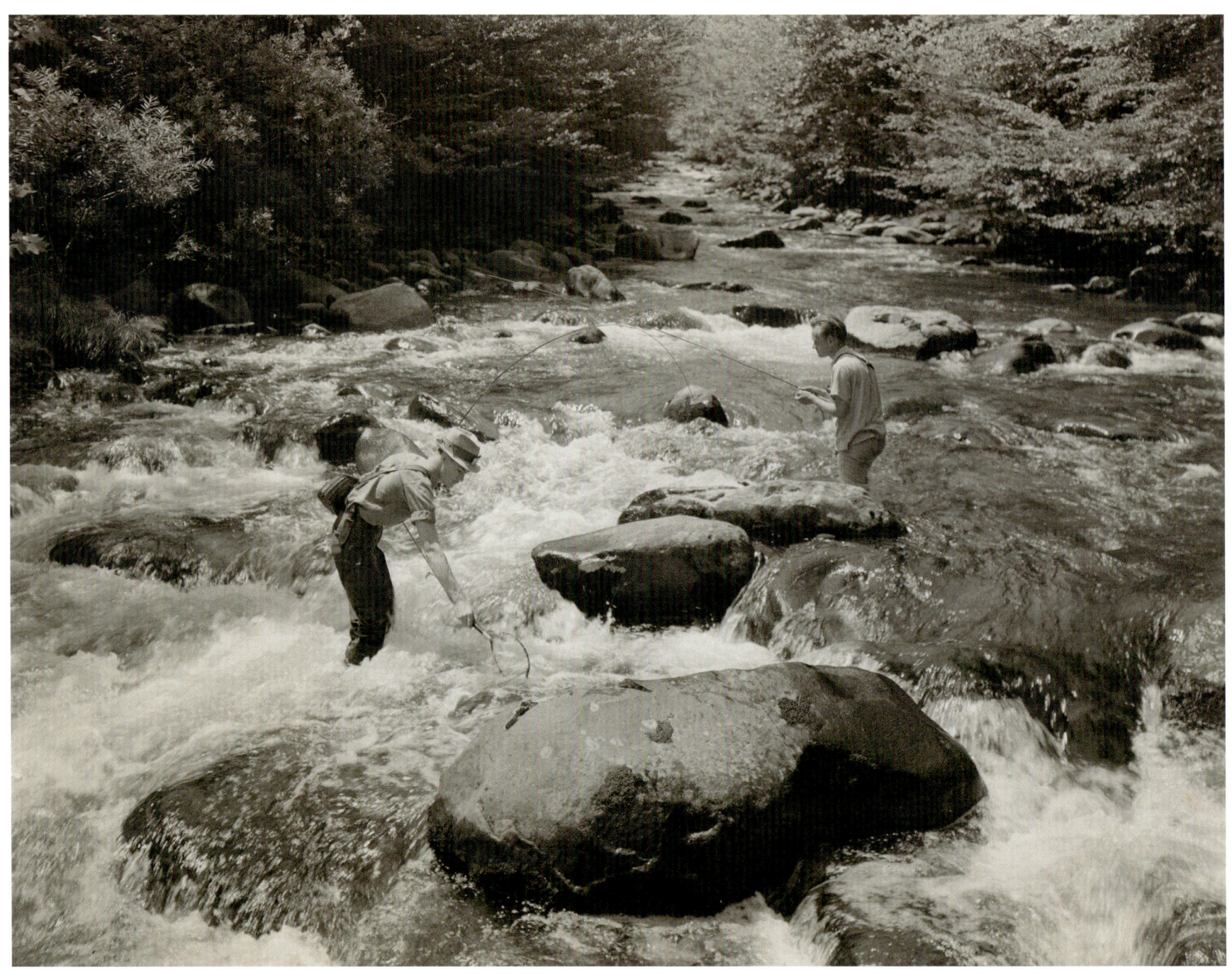

148   Anglers fishing on a stream in the Great Smoky Mountains. Courtesy of National Park Service.

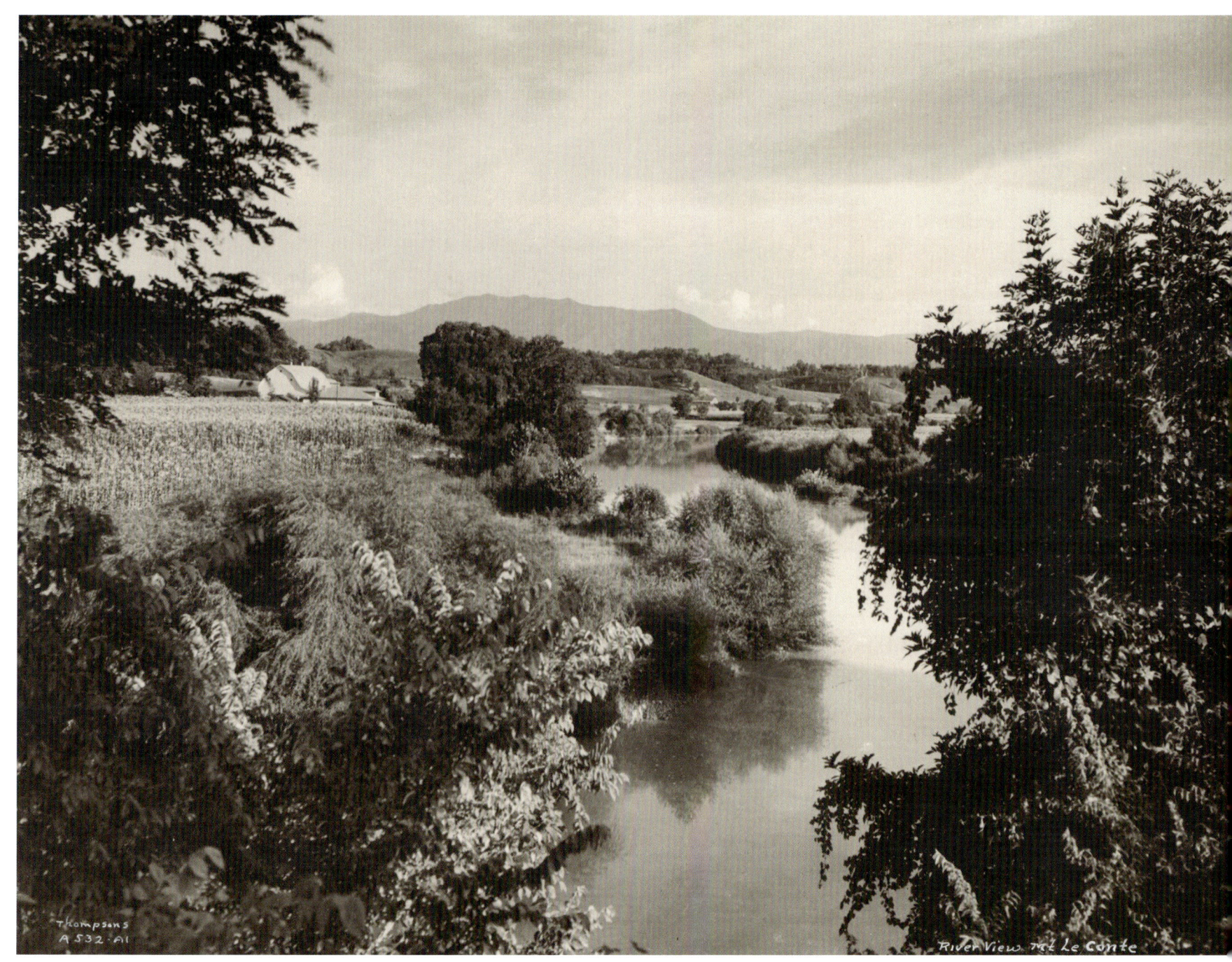

149   River view of Mount LeConte. Courtesy of National Park Service.

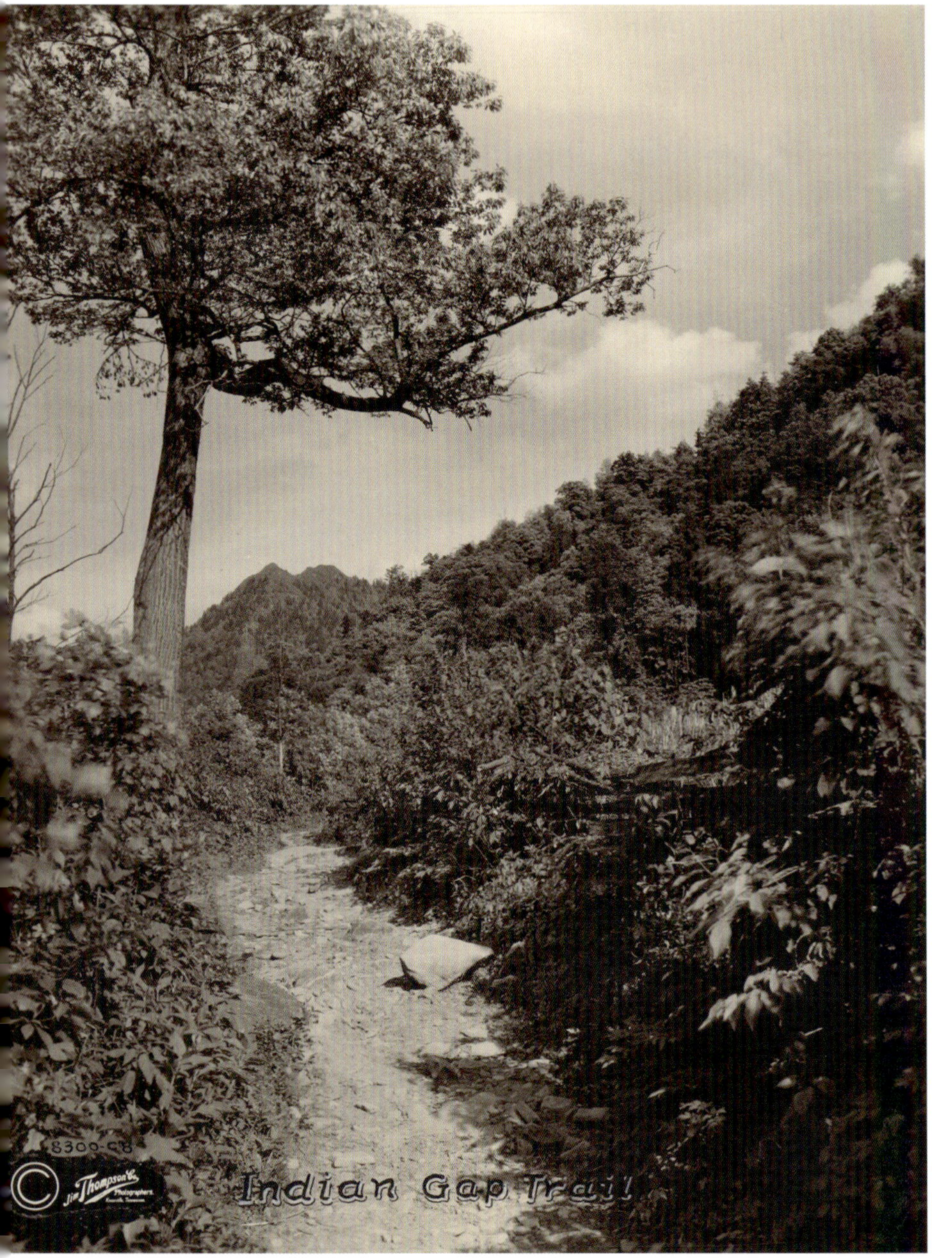

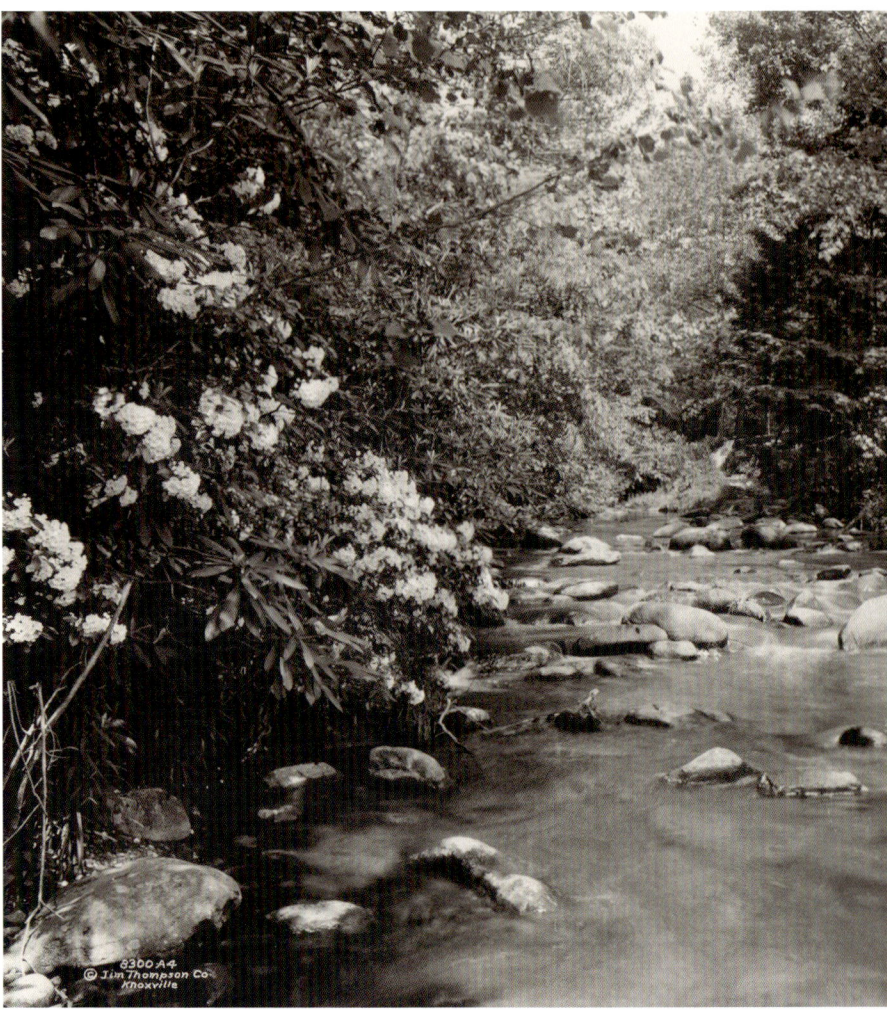

151   Laurel Creek in Great Smoky Mountains National Park. Courtesy of National Park Service.

150   Indian Gap Trail in Great Smoky Mountains National Park. Courtesy of National Park Service.

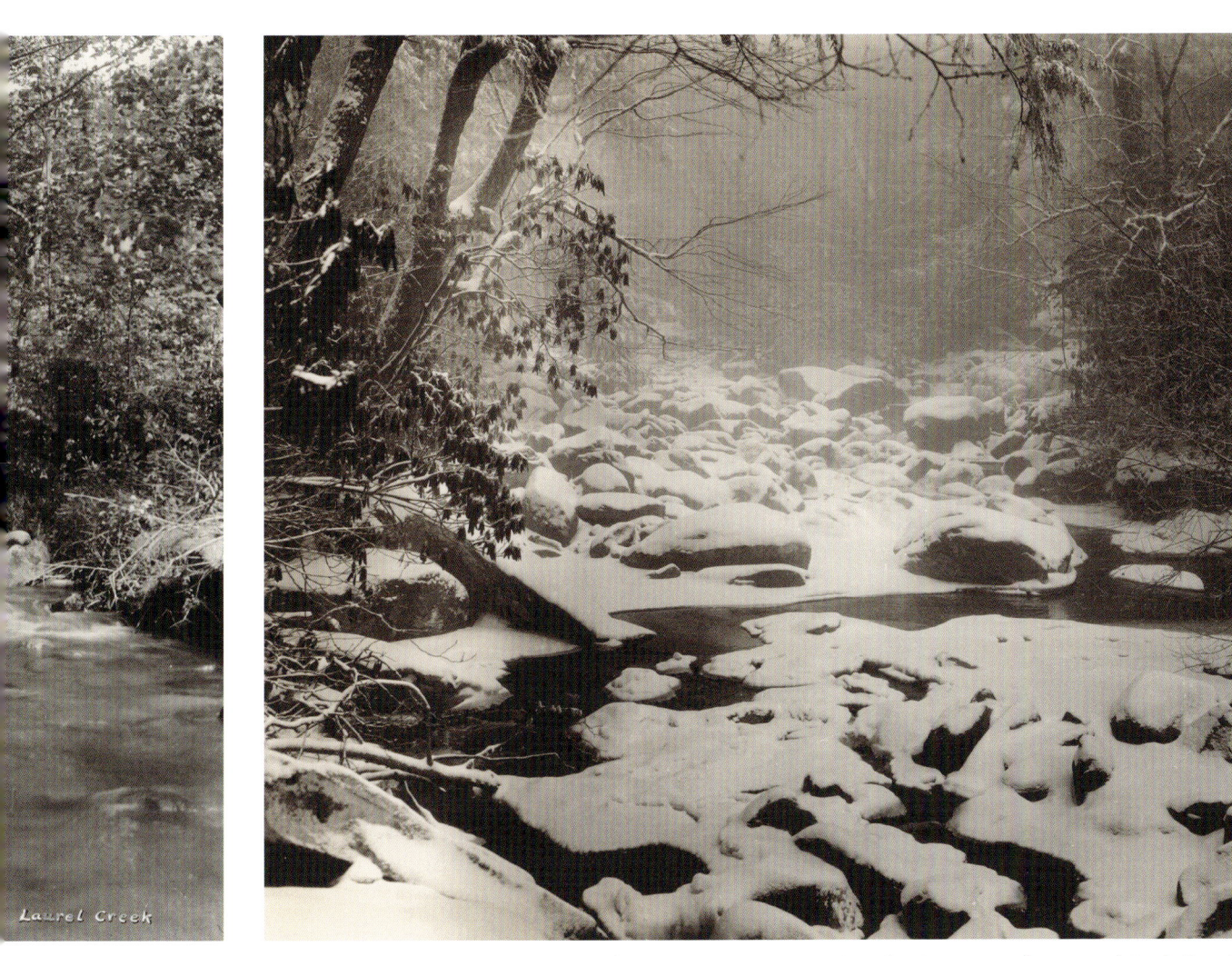

152 Winter stream in Great Smoky Mountains National Park. Courtesy of National Park Service.

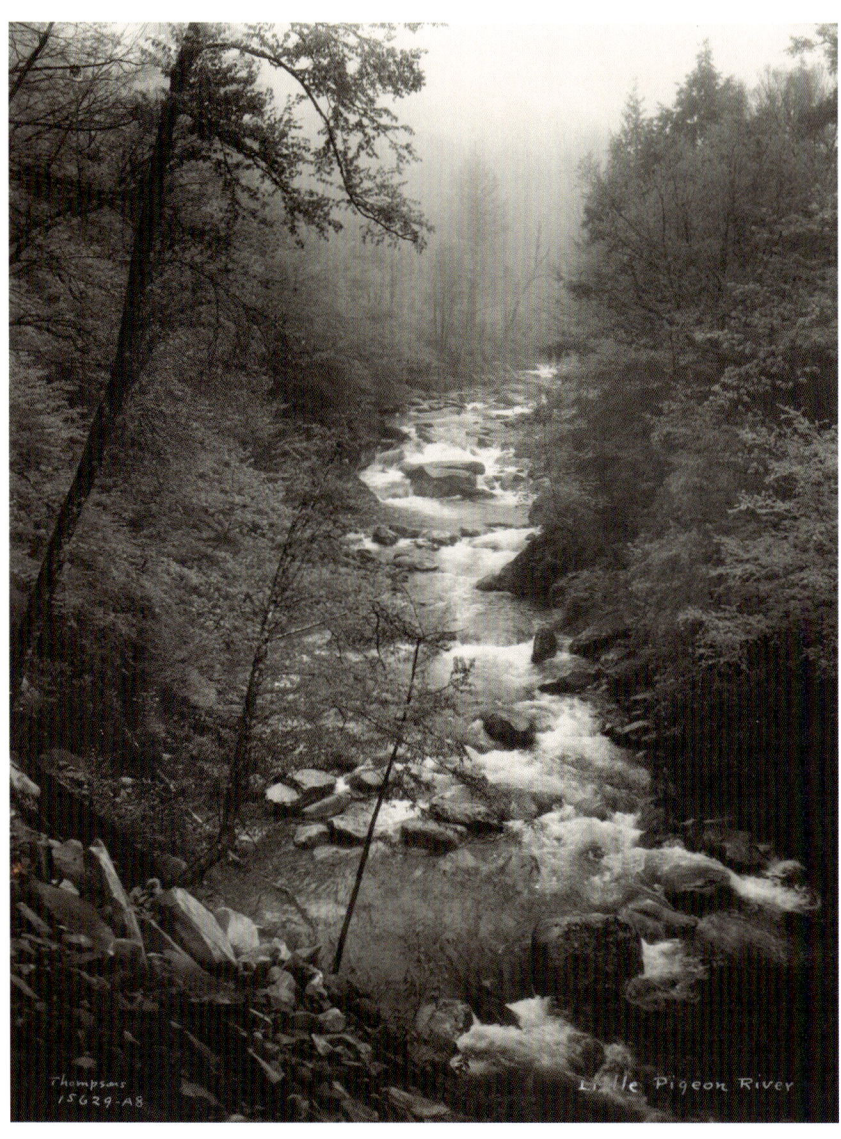

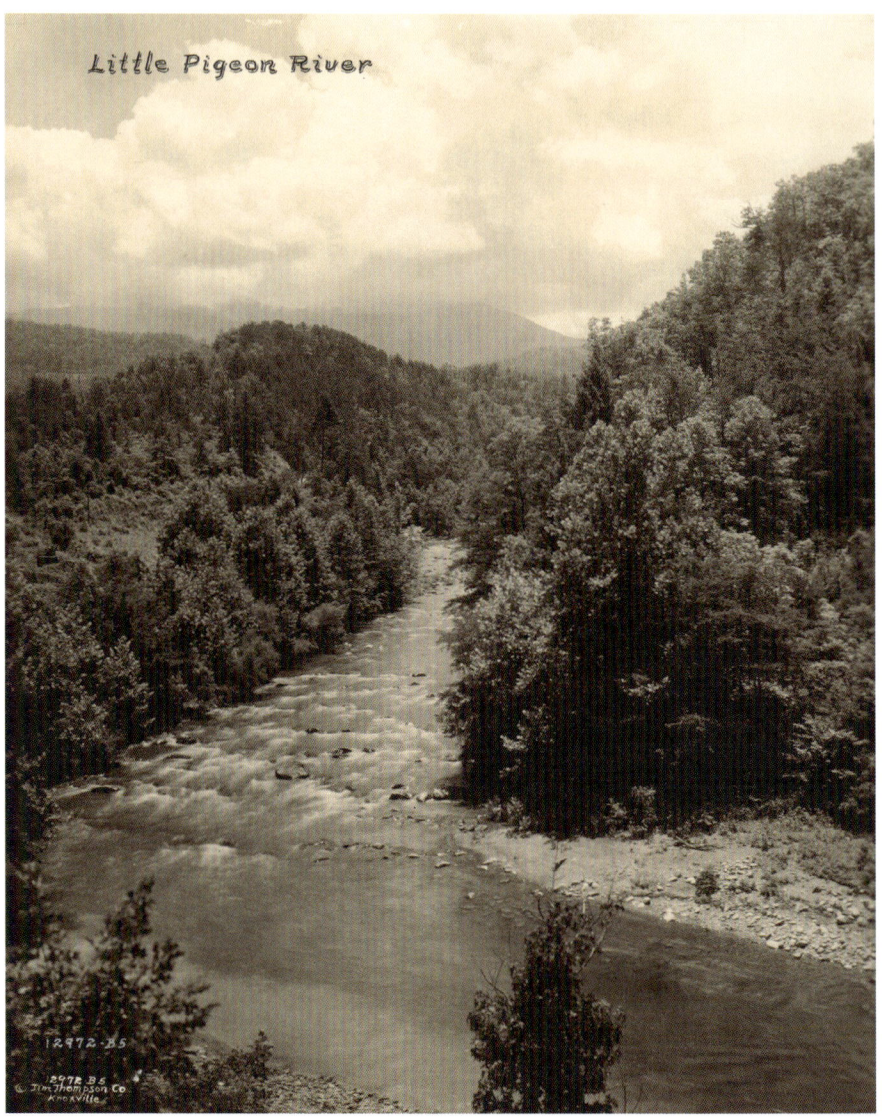

153   Little Pigeon River east of Gatlinburg in the Great Smoky Mountains National Park. Courtesy of National Park Service.

154   Little Pigeon River in Great Smoky Mountains National Park. Courtesy of National Park Service.

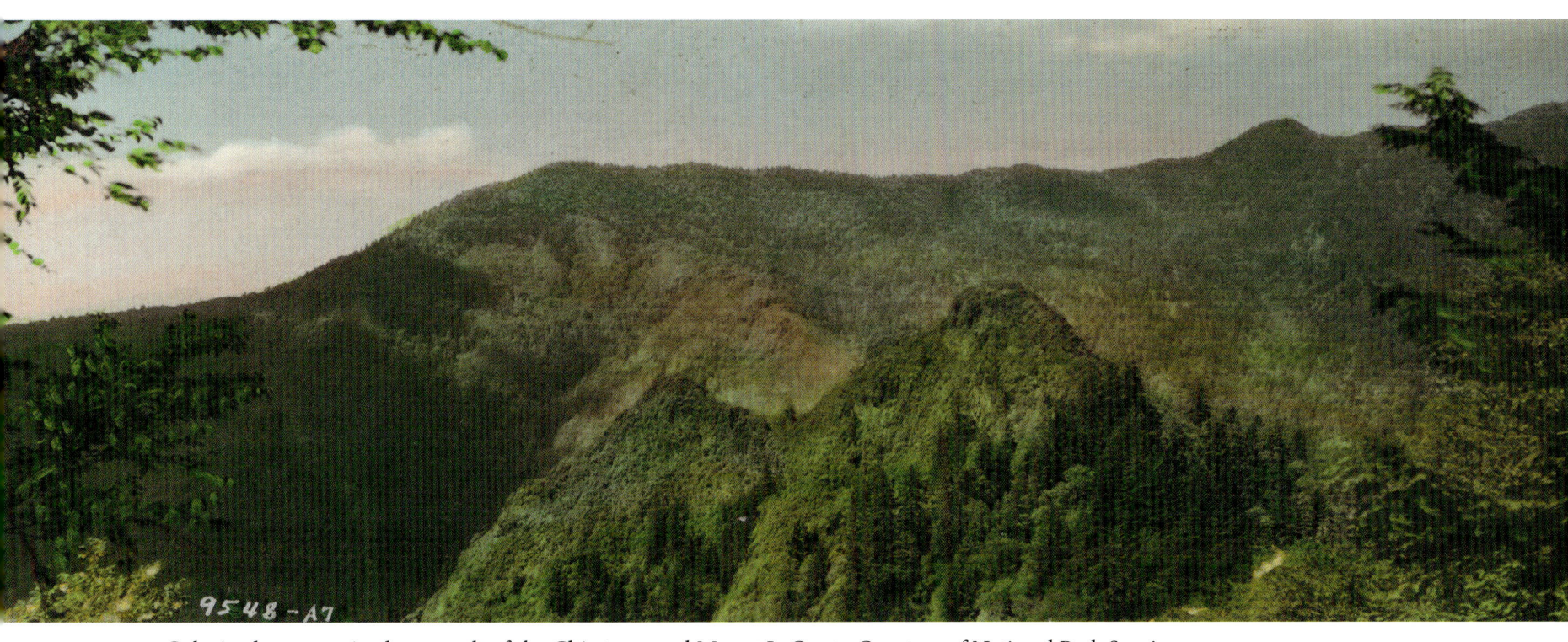

155   Colorized panoramic photograph of the Chimneys and Mount LeConte. Courtesy of National Park Service.

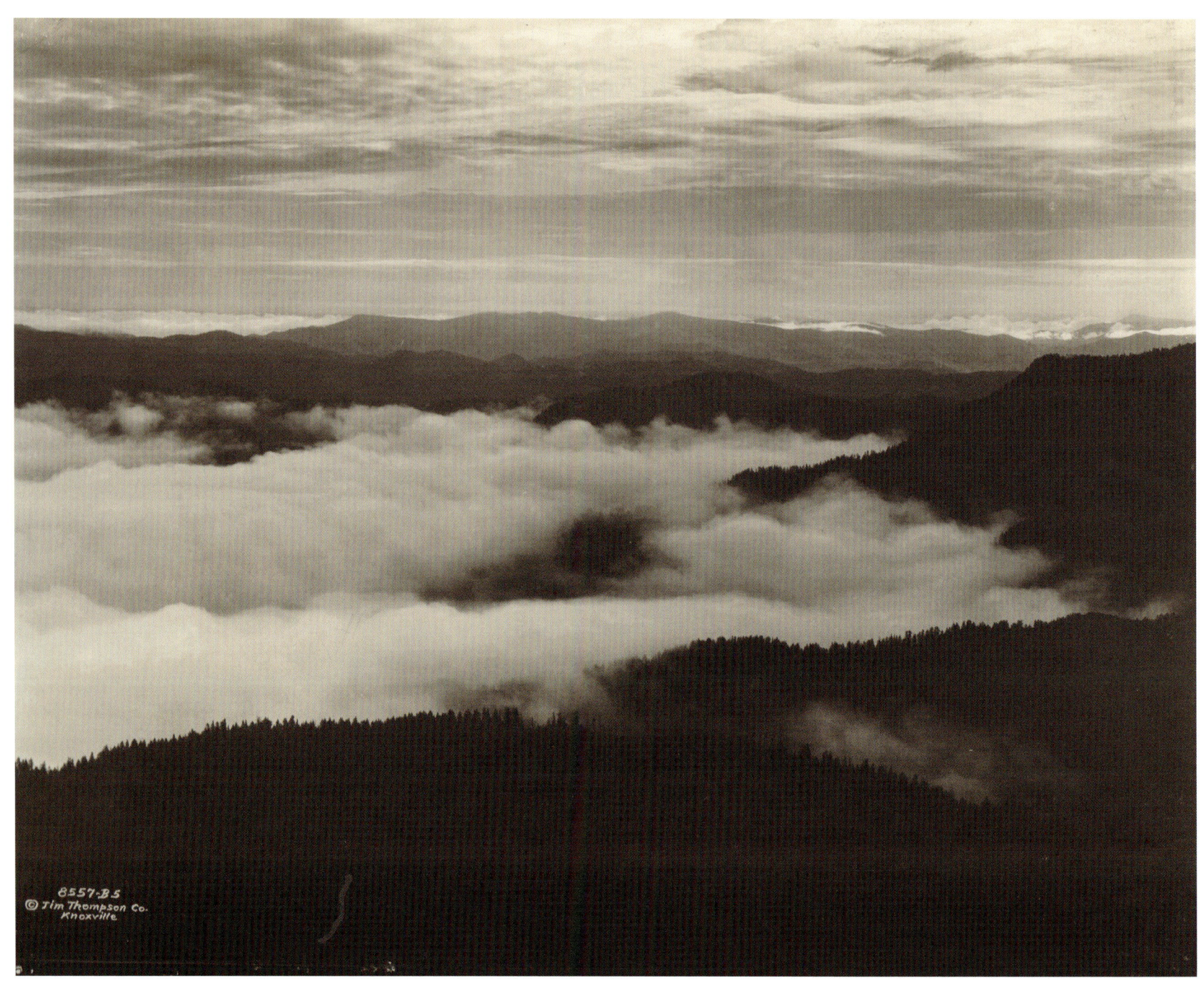

156   Early morning fog in Great Smoky Mountains National Park. Courtesy of National Park Service.

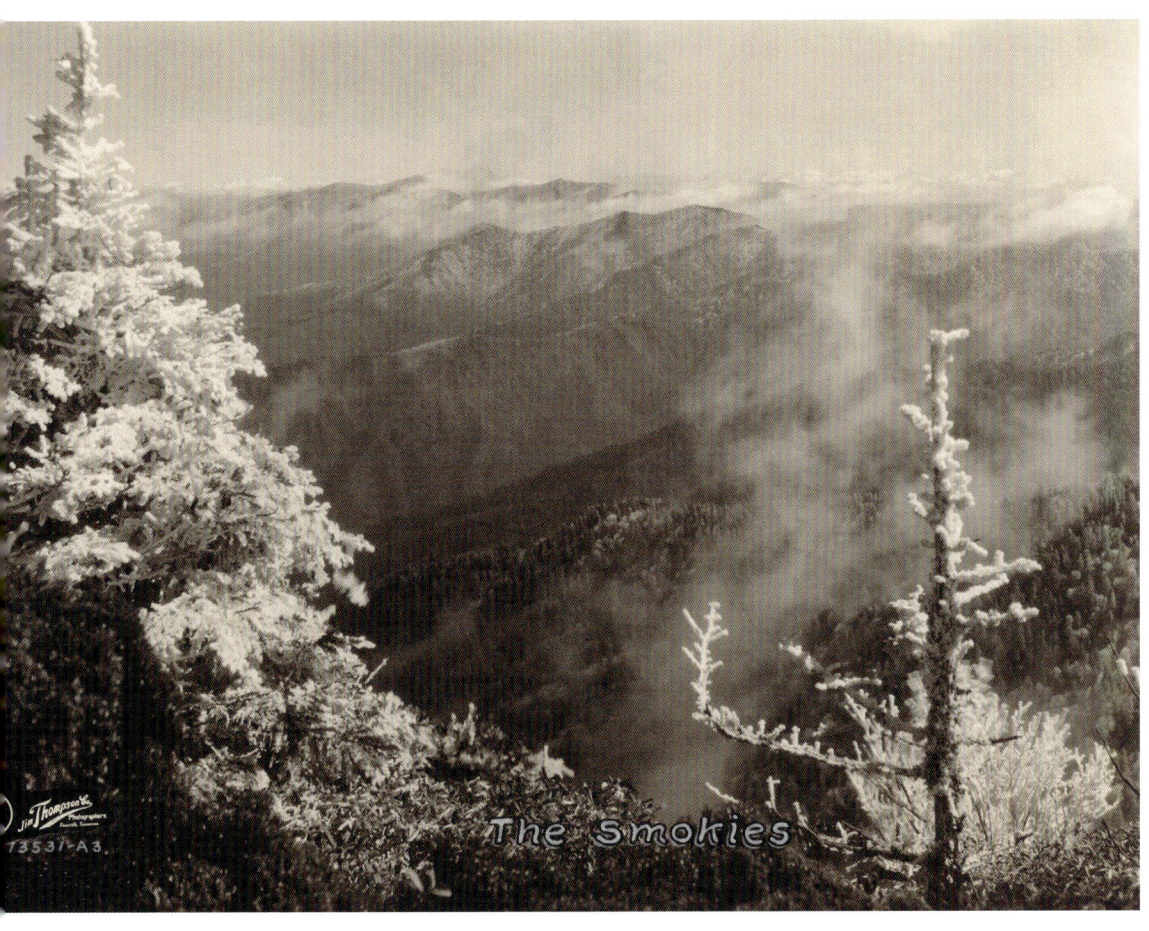

157   Snow in the Smokies.

Courtesy of National Park Service.

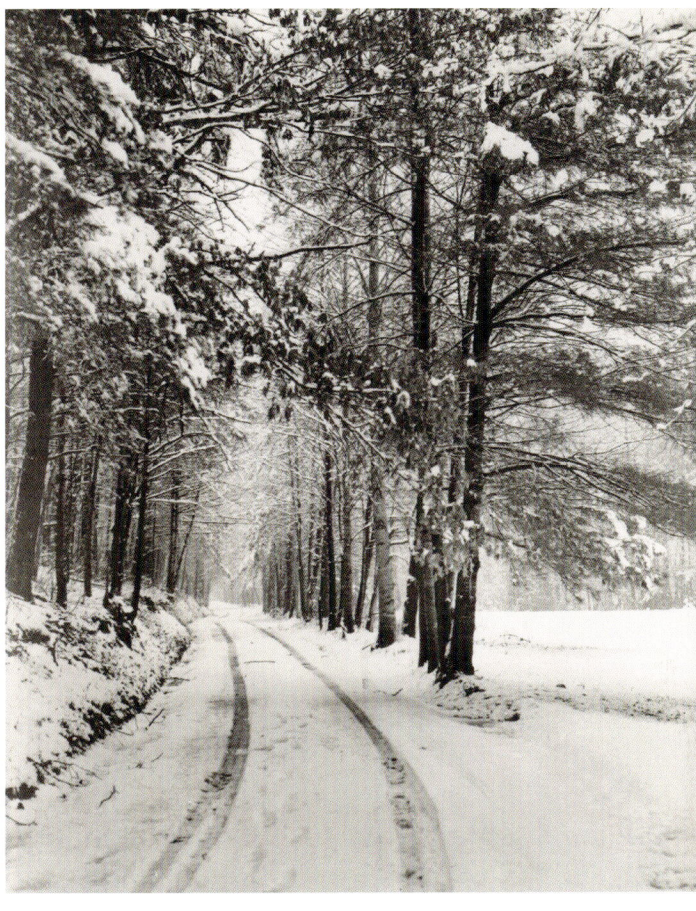

158   Roadway in Caves Cove in winter snow.

Courtesy of National Park Service.

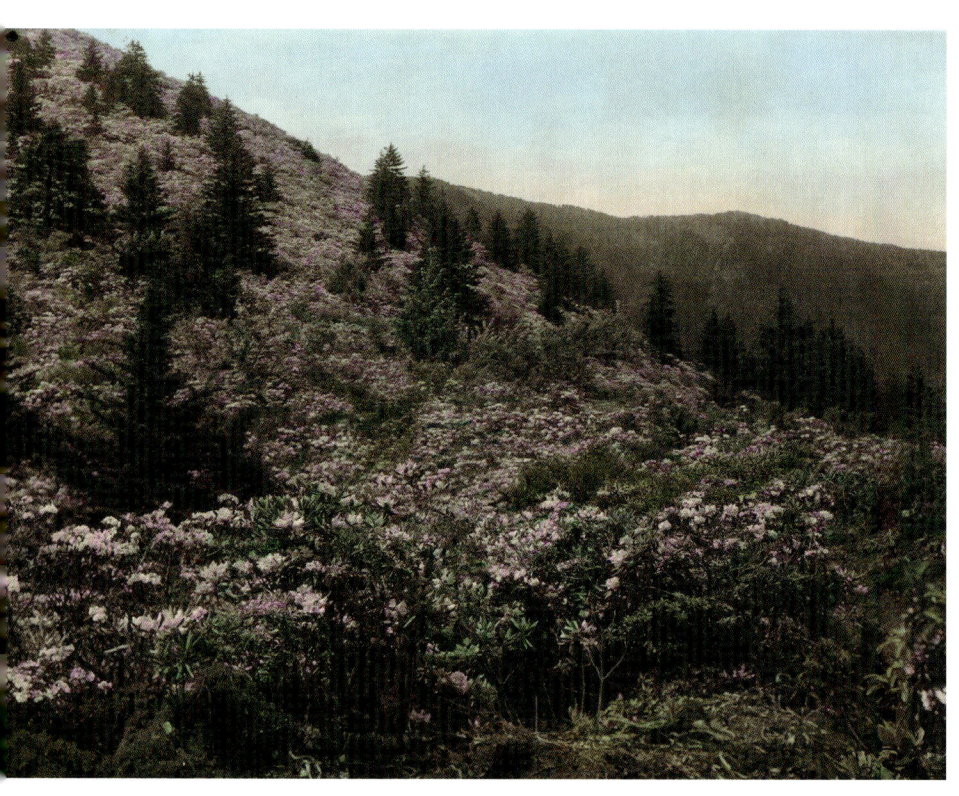

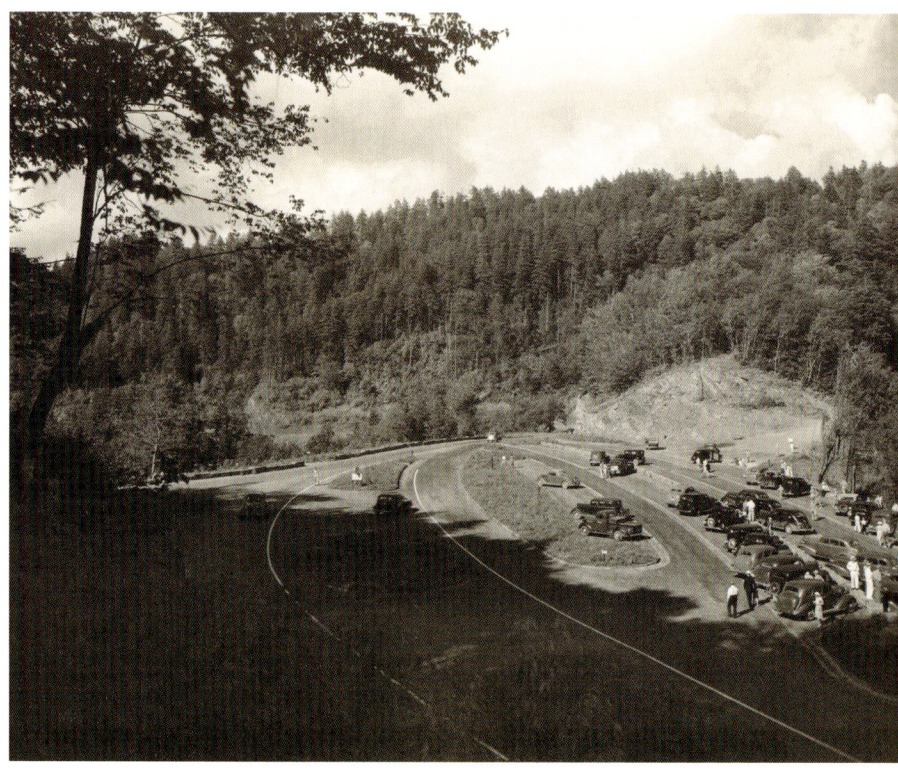

159   Heath Bald on Alum Cave Bluffs in Great Smoky Mountains National Park. Courtesy of National Park Service.

160   Newfound Gap parking area, with the future site of the Rockefeller Memorial in the cleared area on the right. Courtesy of National Park Service.

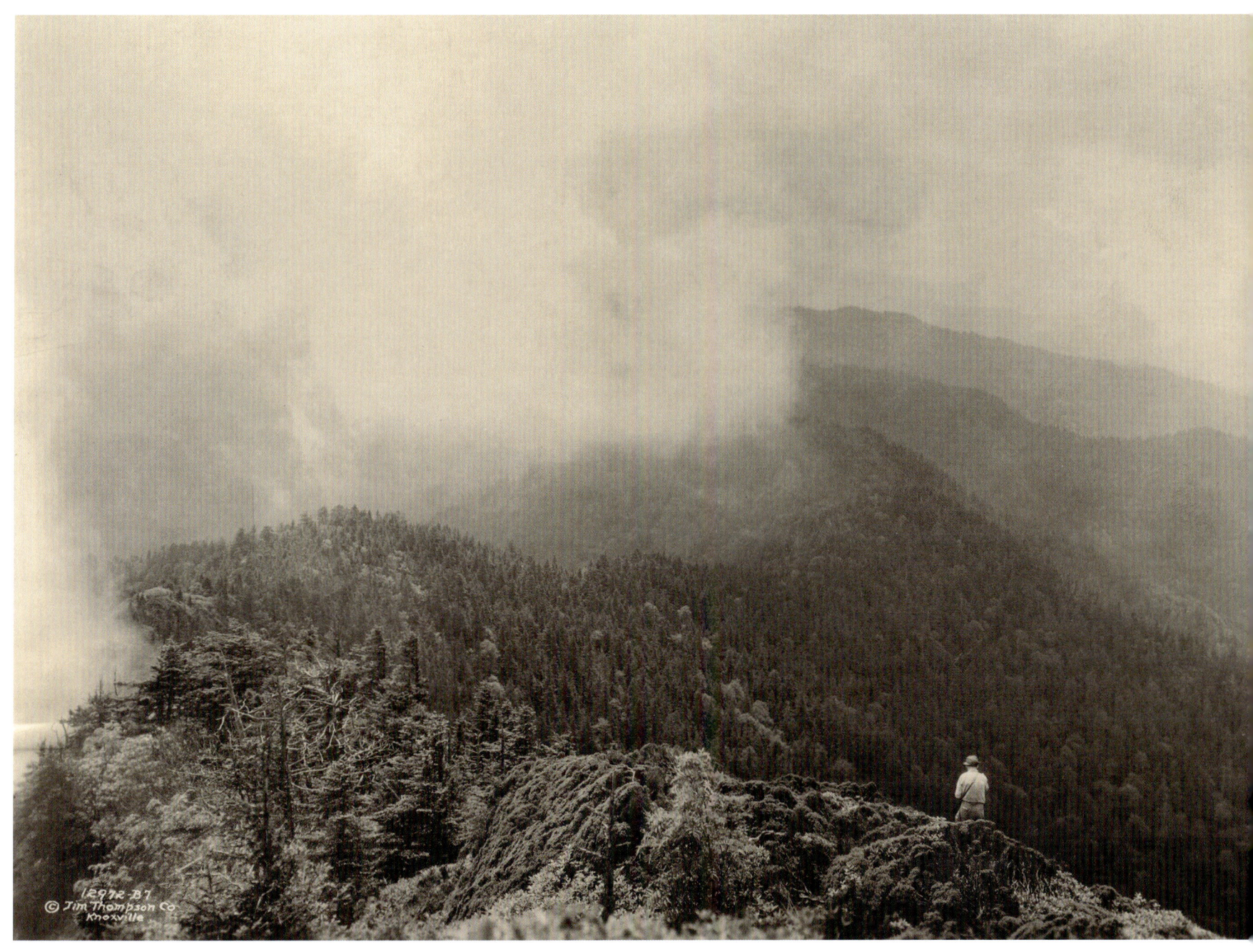

161   Playground of the clouds in Great Smoky Mountains National Park.
Courtesy of National Park Service.

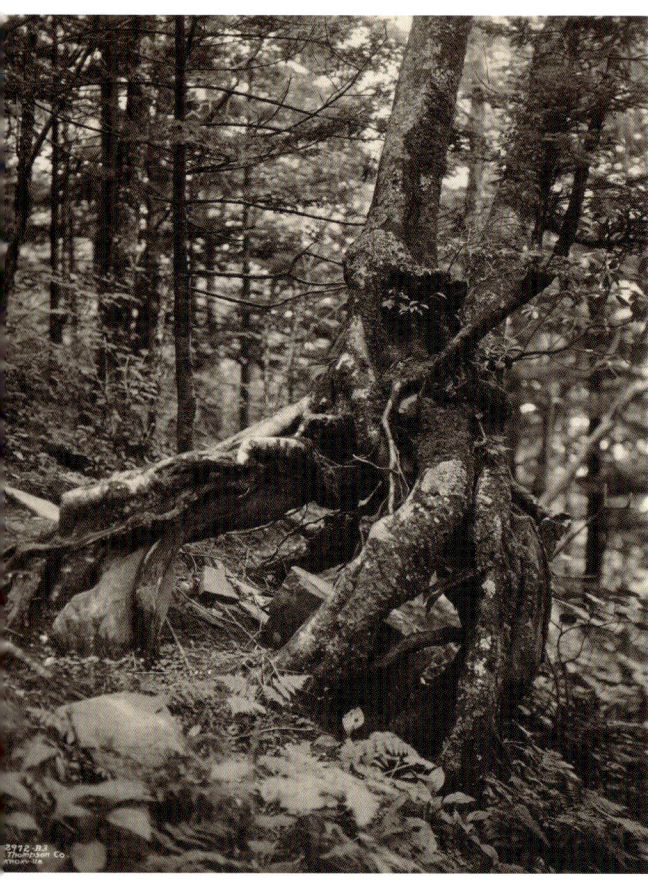

162   Large tree roots on Alum Cave Trail in
       Great Smoky Mountains National Park.
       Courtesy of National Park Service.

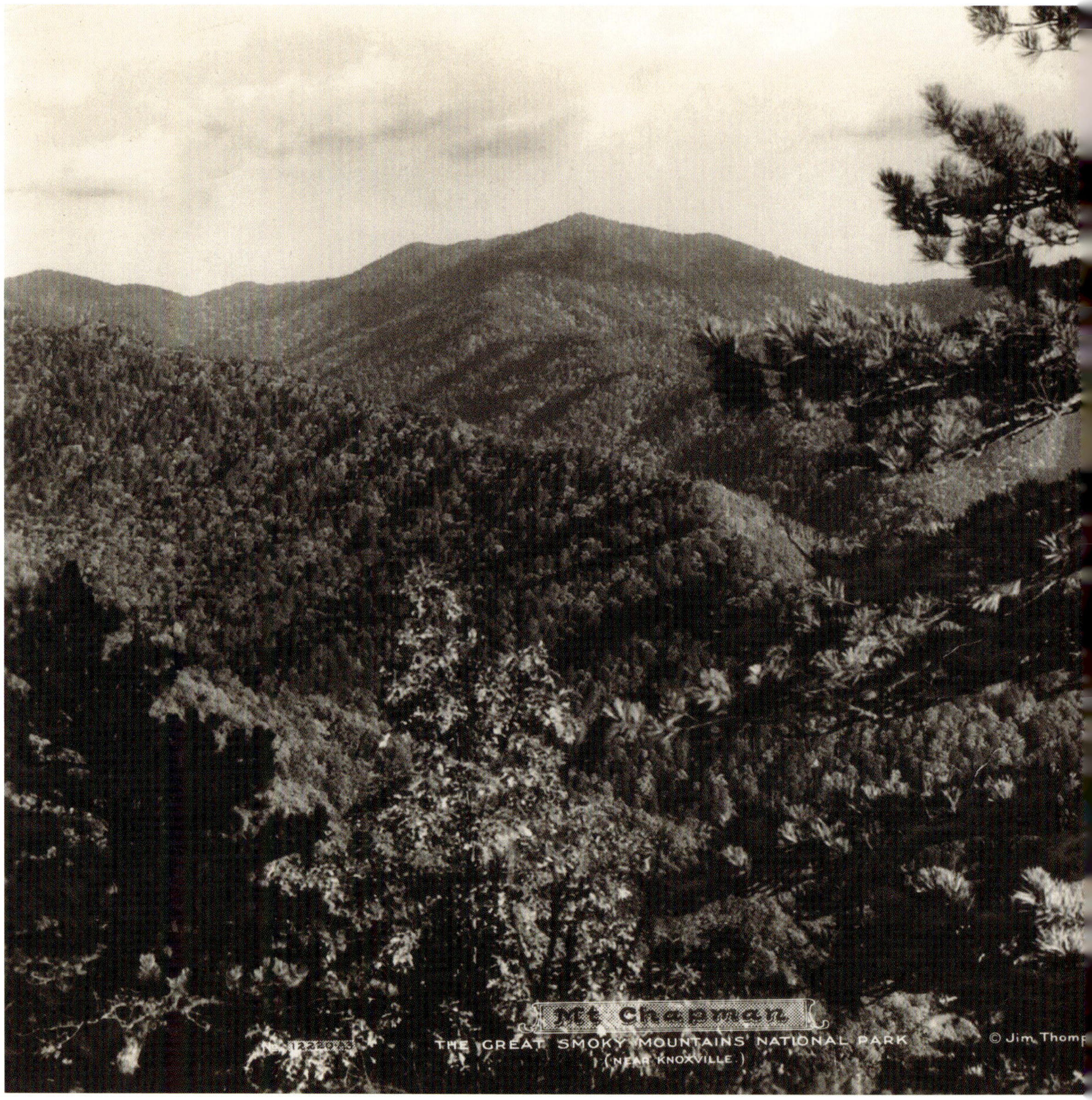

163   Mount Chapman in Great Smoky Mountains National Park.
       Courtesy of National Park Service.

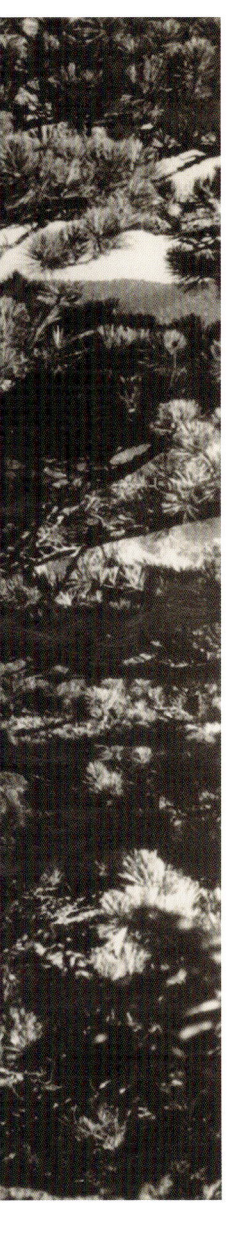

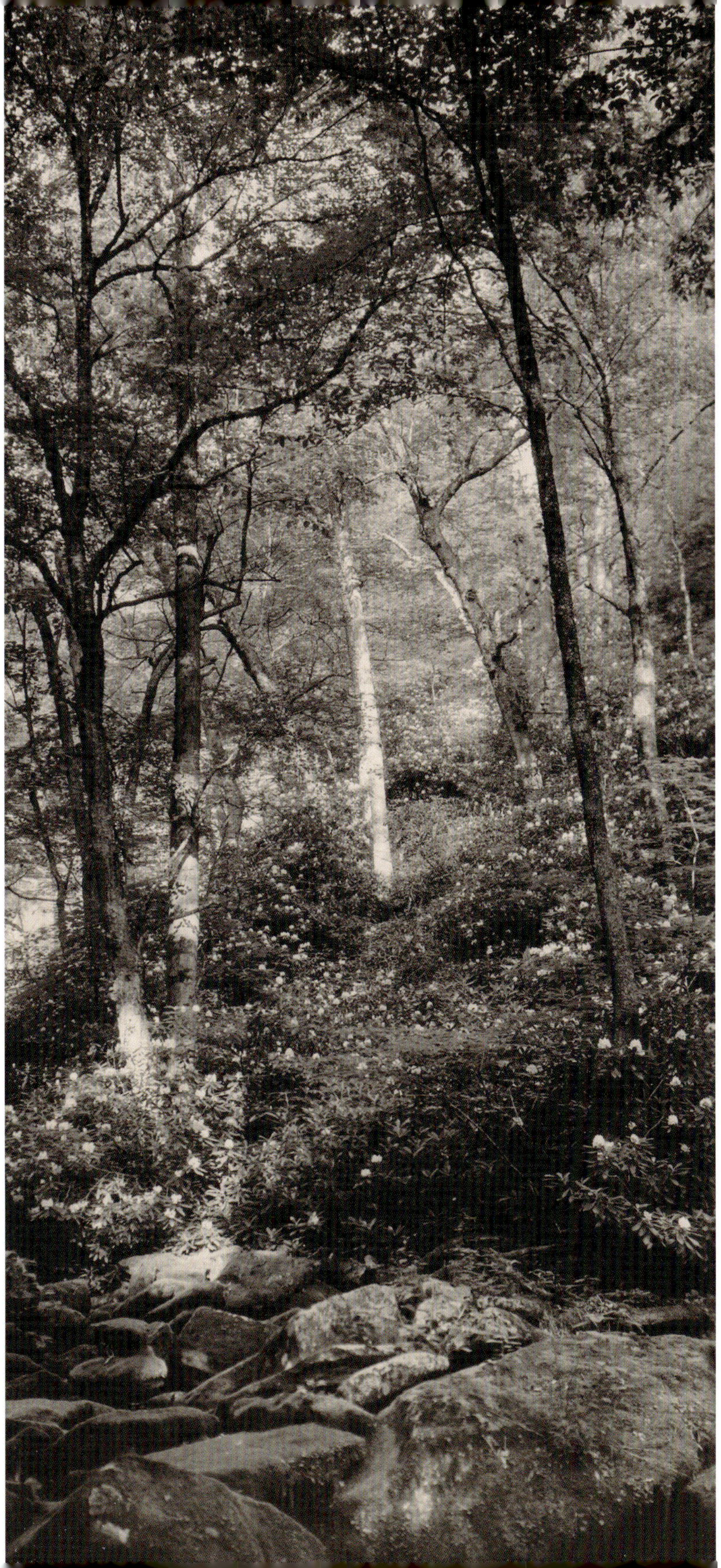

164　A rhododendron on Mill Creek in Great Smoky
Mountains National Park. Courtesy of National
Park Service.

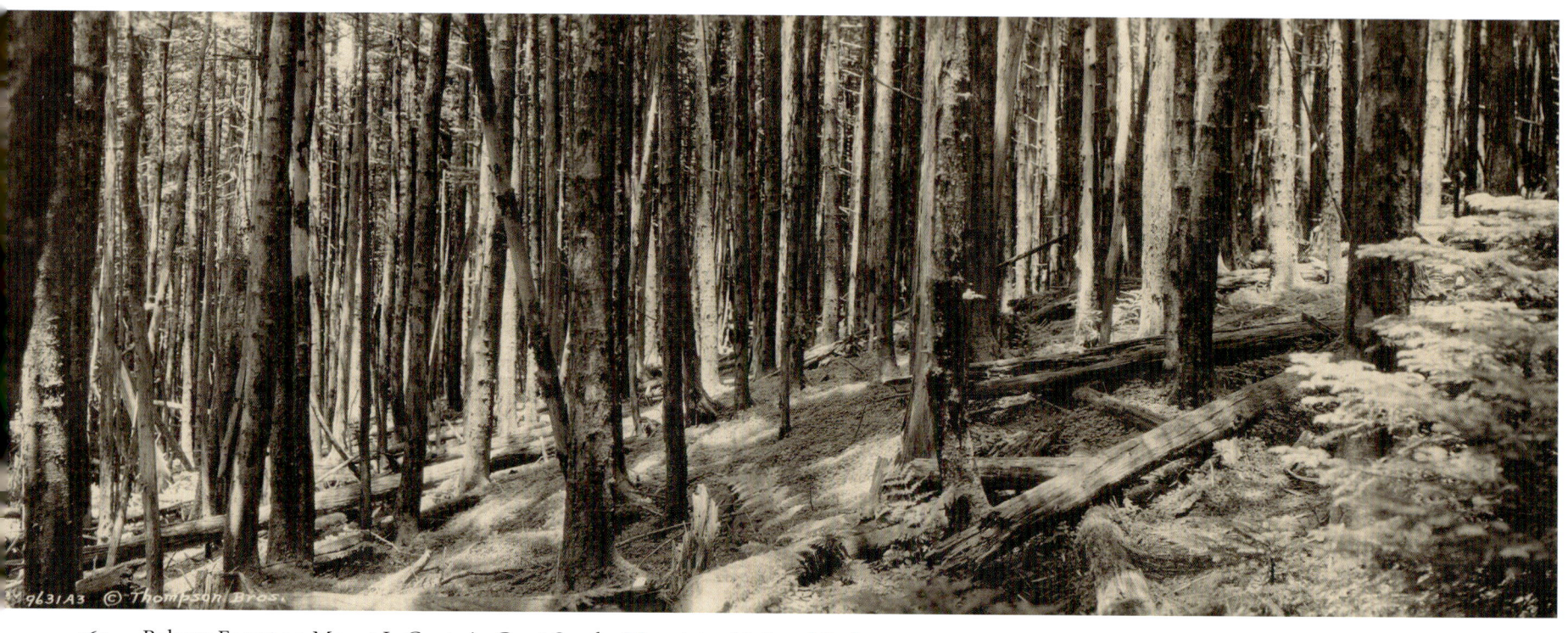

165   Balsam Forest on Mount LeConte in Great Smoky Mountains National Park.
Courtesy of National Park Service.

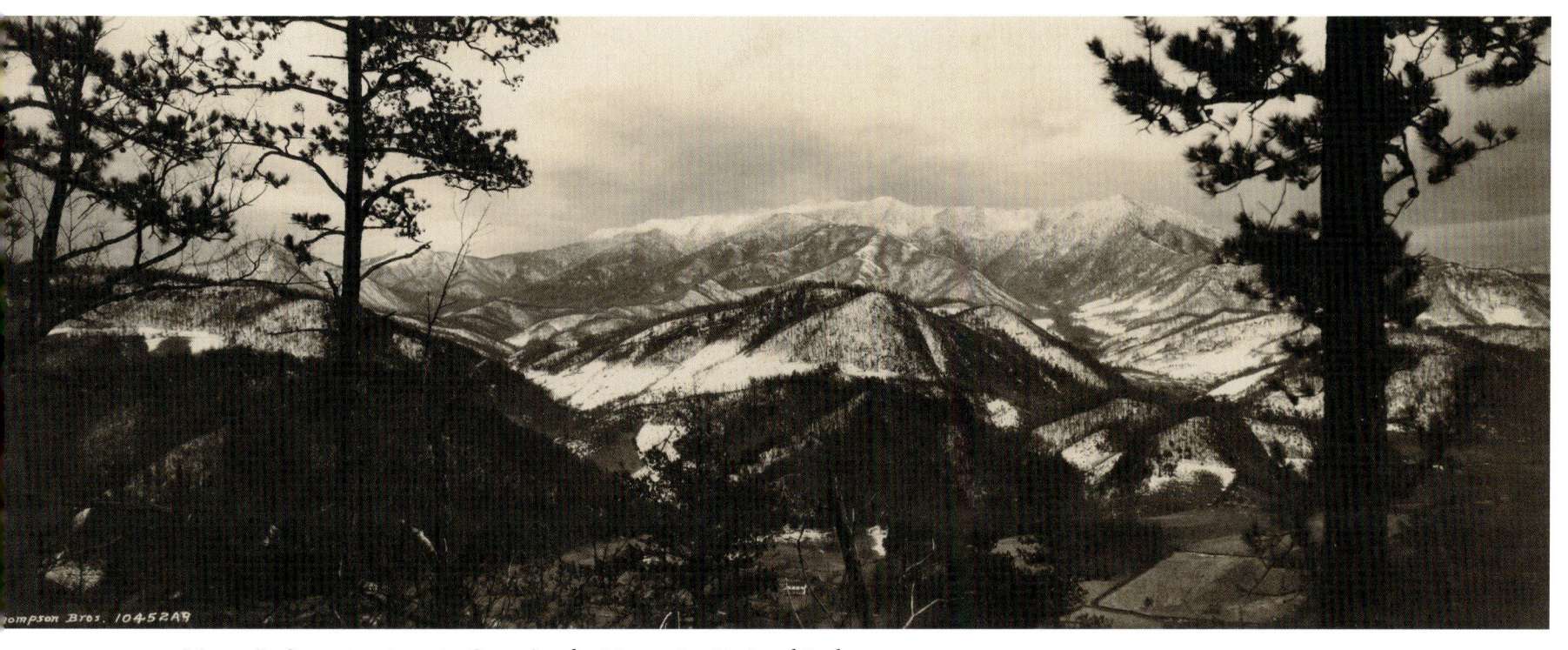

166   Mount LeConte in winter in Great Smoky Mountains National Park.
        Courtesy of National Park Service.

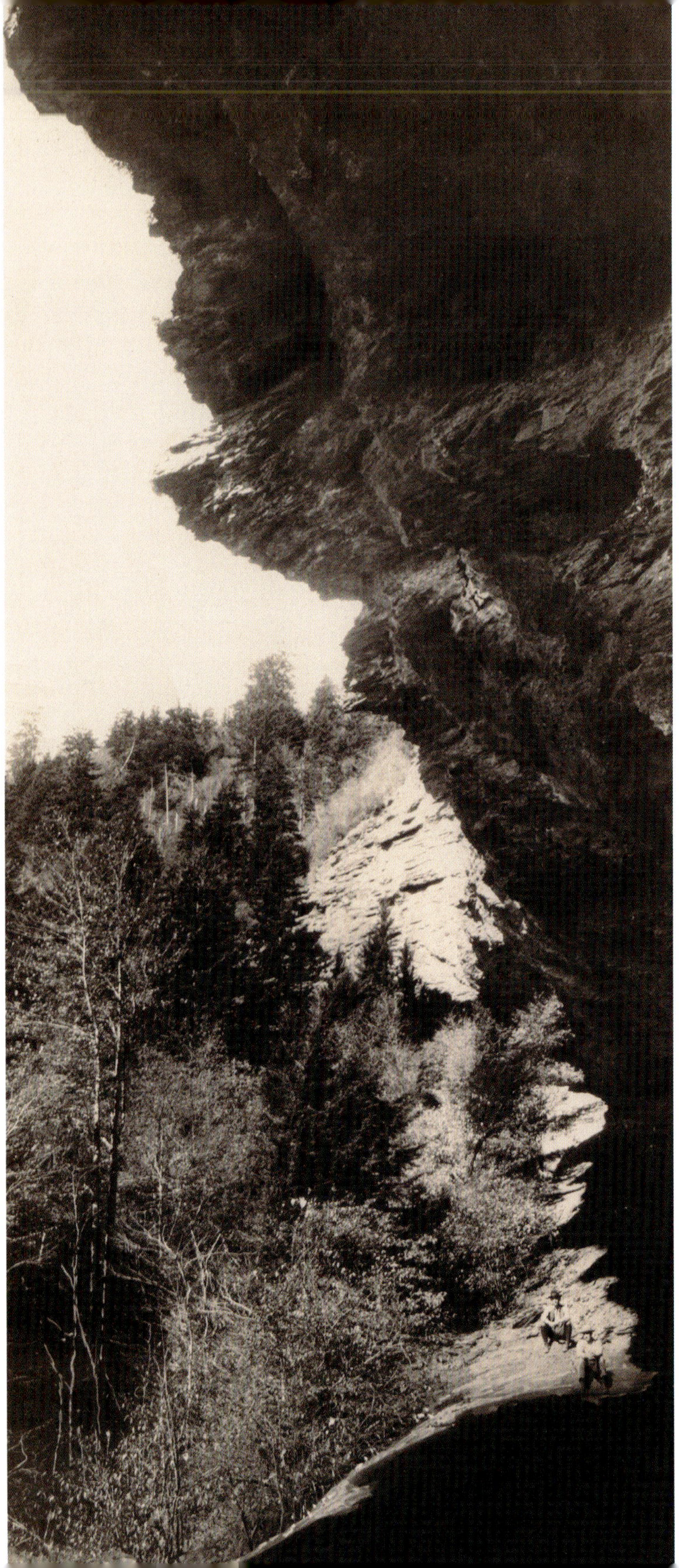

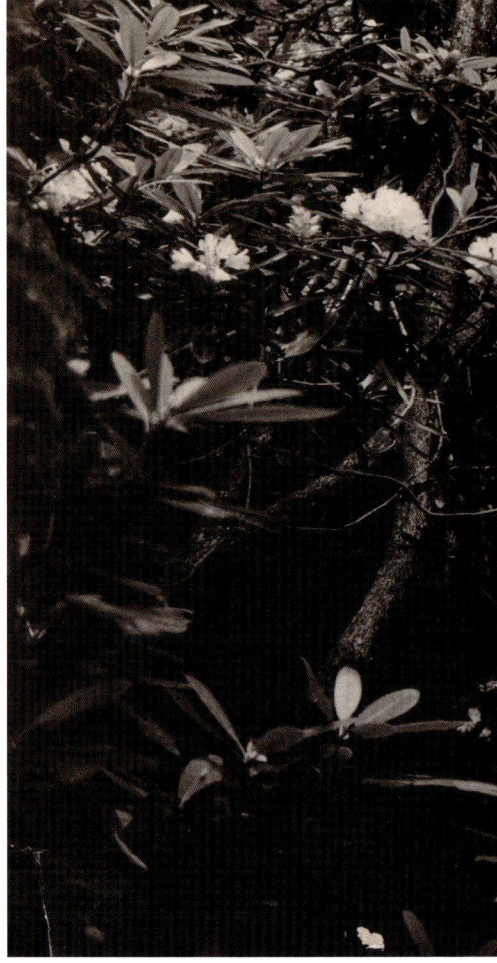

168   Rhododendron thicket
      on Rocky Spur in Great
      Smoky Mountains
      National Park. Courtesy
      of National Park Service.

167   Alum Cave Trail on Mt. LeConte in Great Smoky Mountains
      National Park. Courtesy of National Park Service.

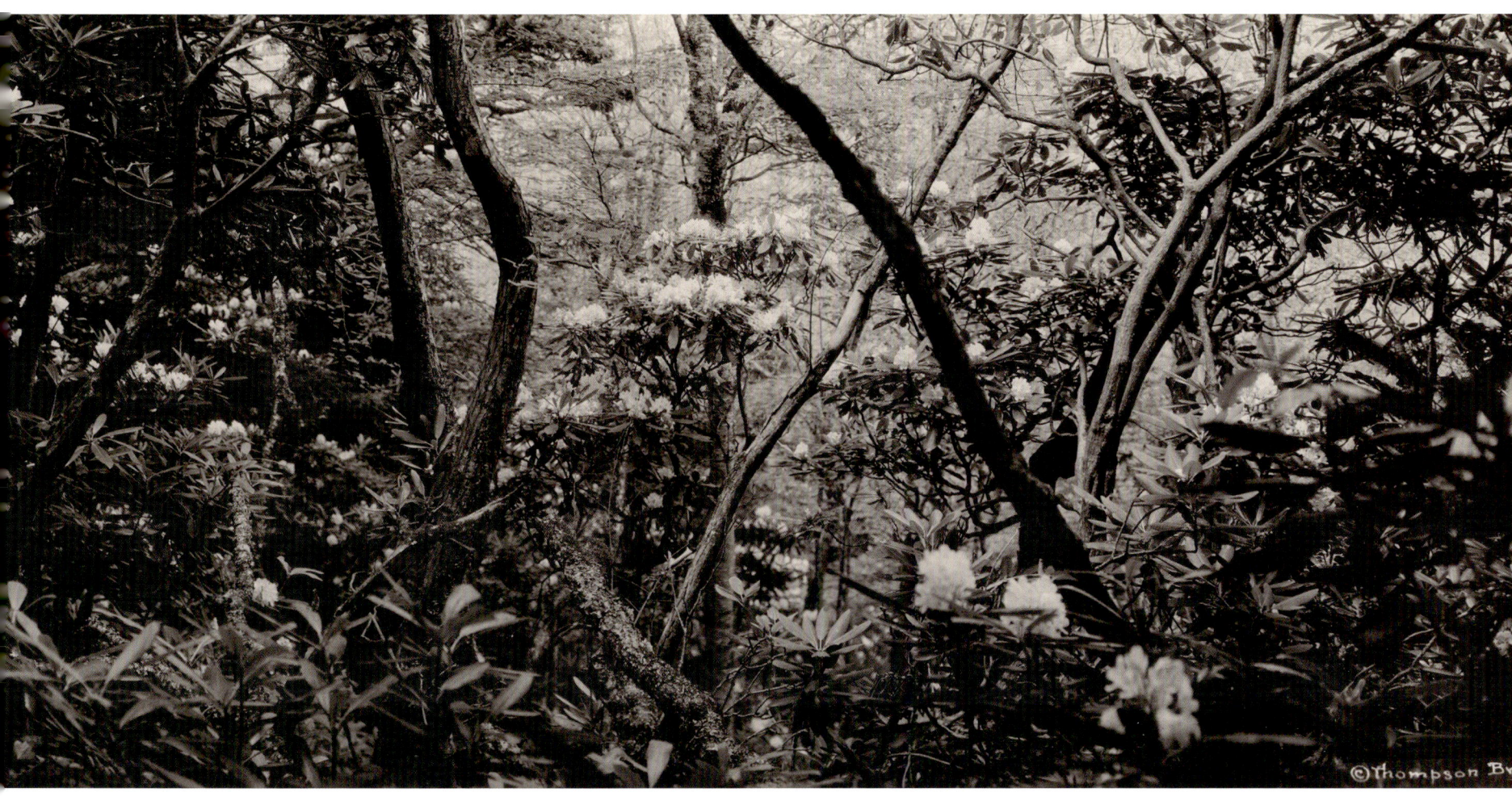

205

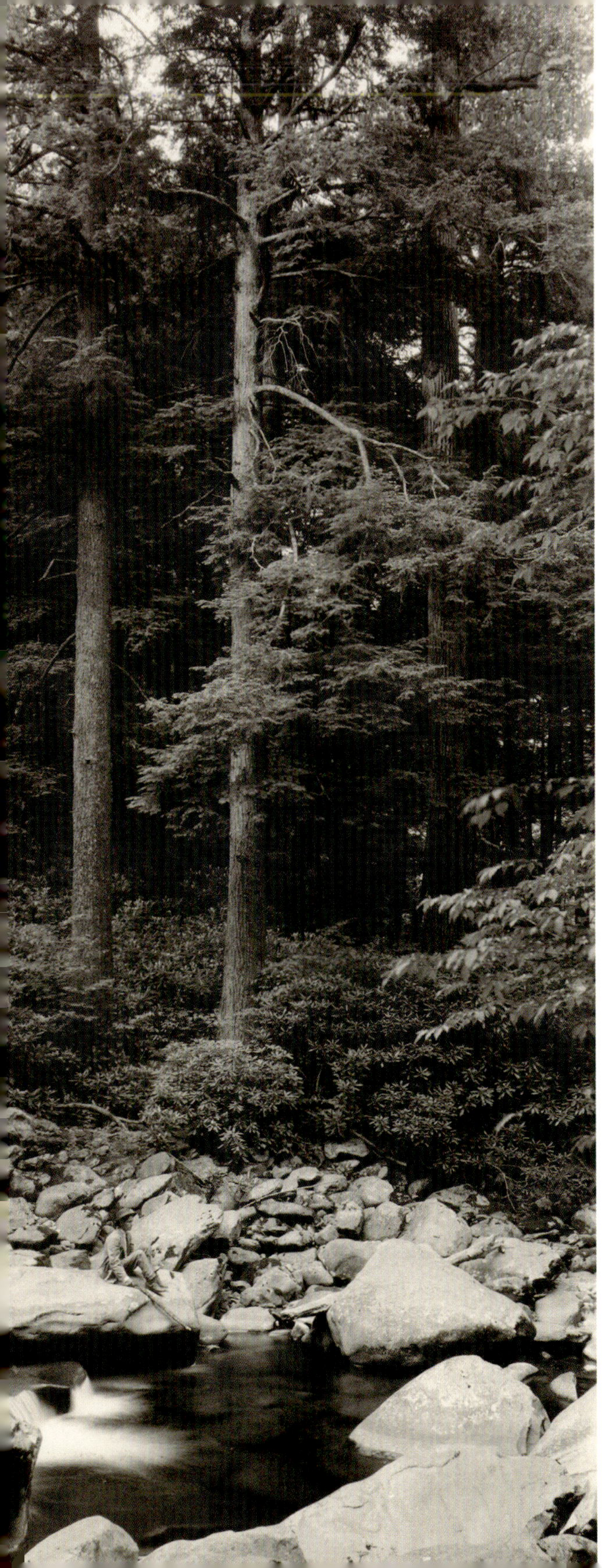

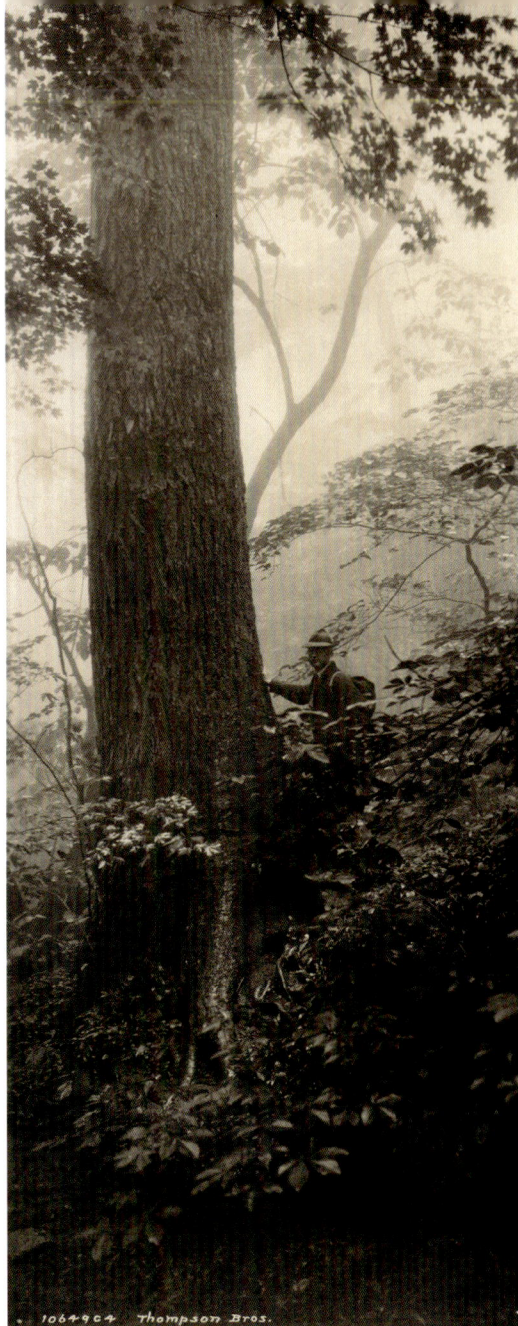

170   A man nearly hidden by a tree in Great Smoky Mountains National Park. Courtesy of National Park Service.

169   Hemlock tree by a creek in Great Smoky Mountains National Park. Courtesy of National Park Service.

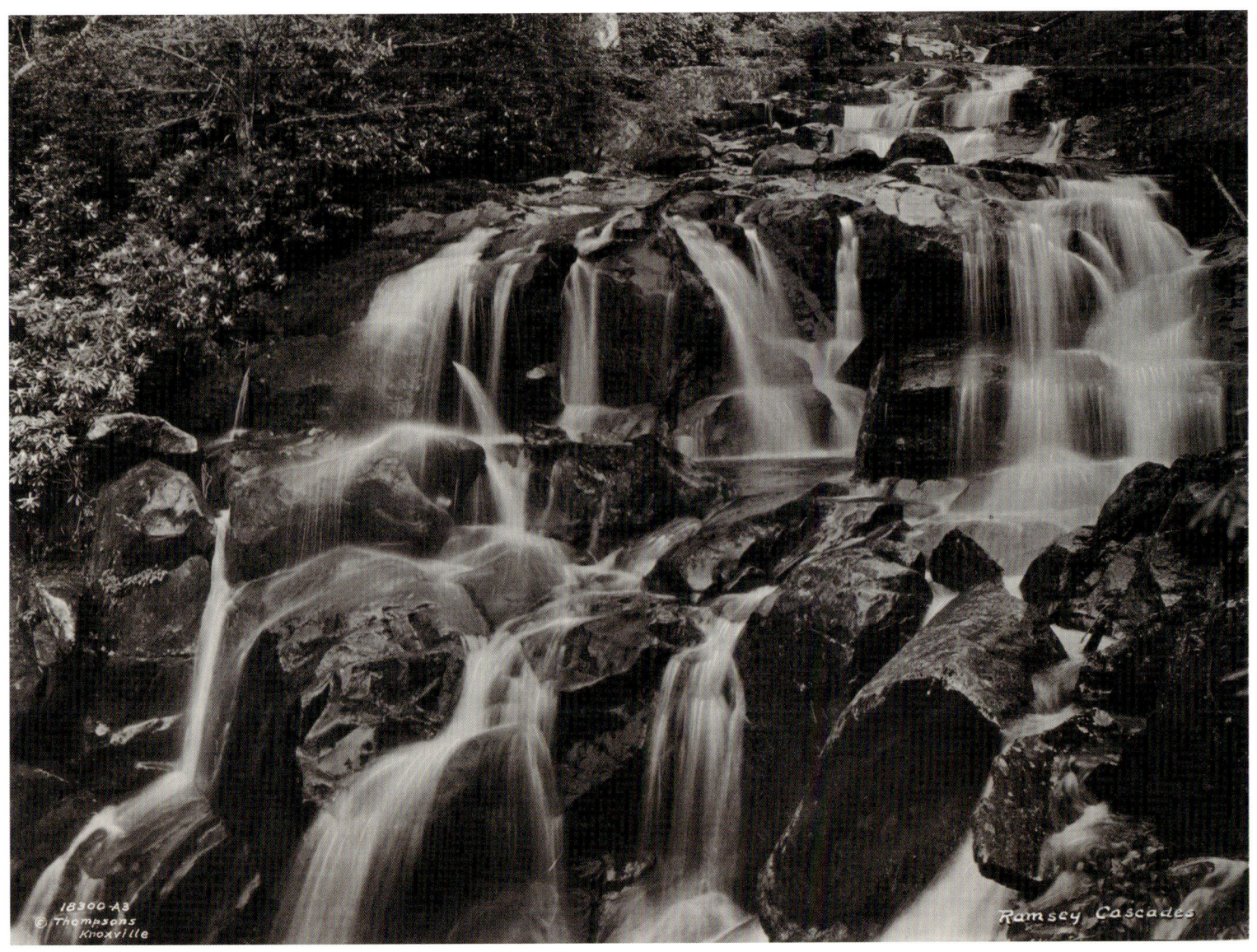

171   Ramsey Cascades along Ramsey Prong in Great Smoky Mountains National Park.
Courtesy of National Park Service.

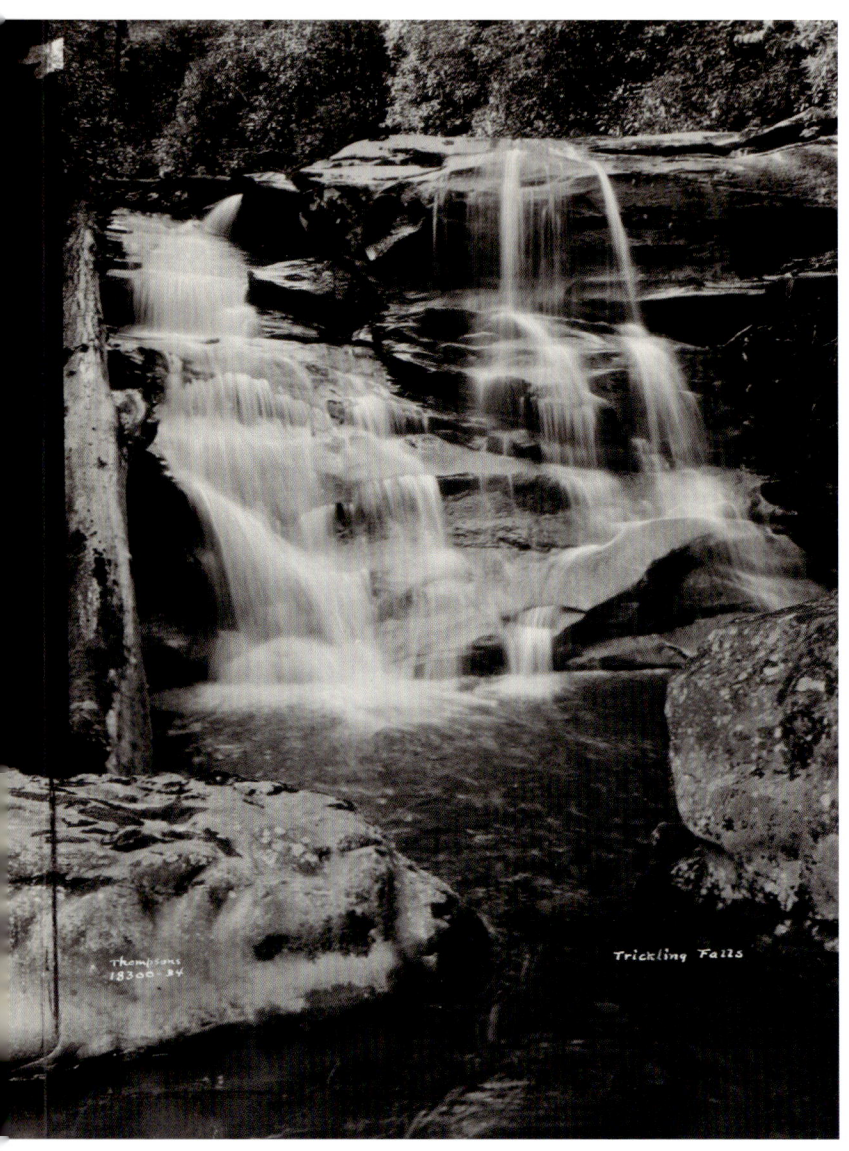

172   Trickling Falls near Chimney Tops in Great Smoky Mountains National Park. Courtesy of National Park Service.

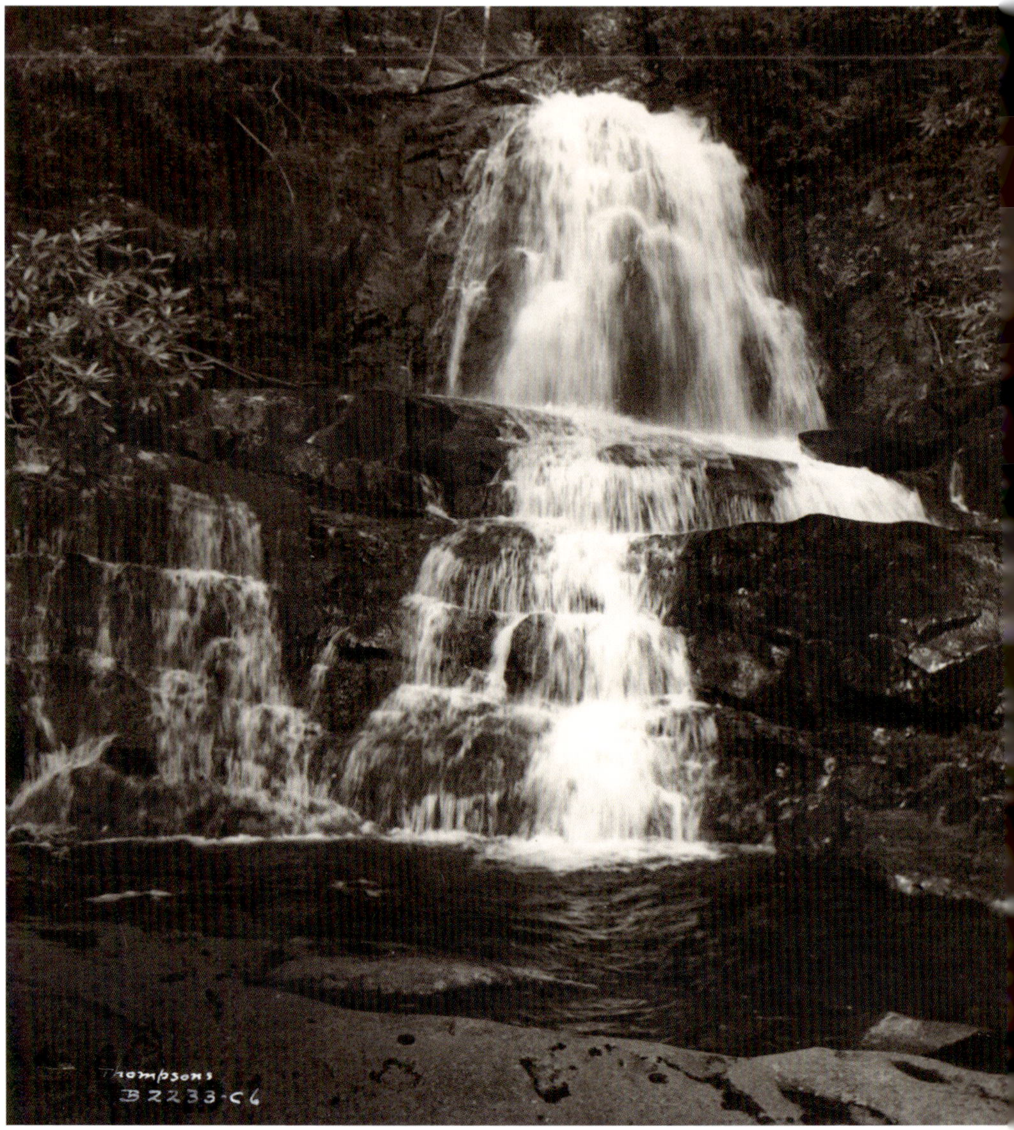

173   Laurel Falls on Laurel Branch in Great Smoky Mountains National Park. Courtesy of National Park Service.

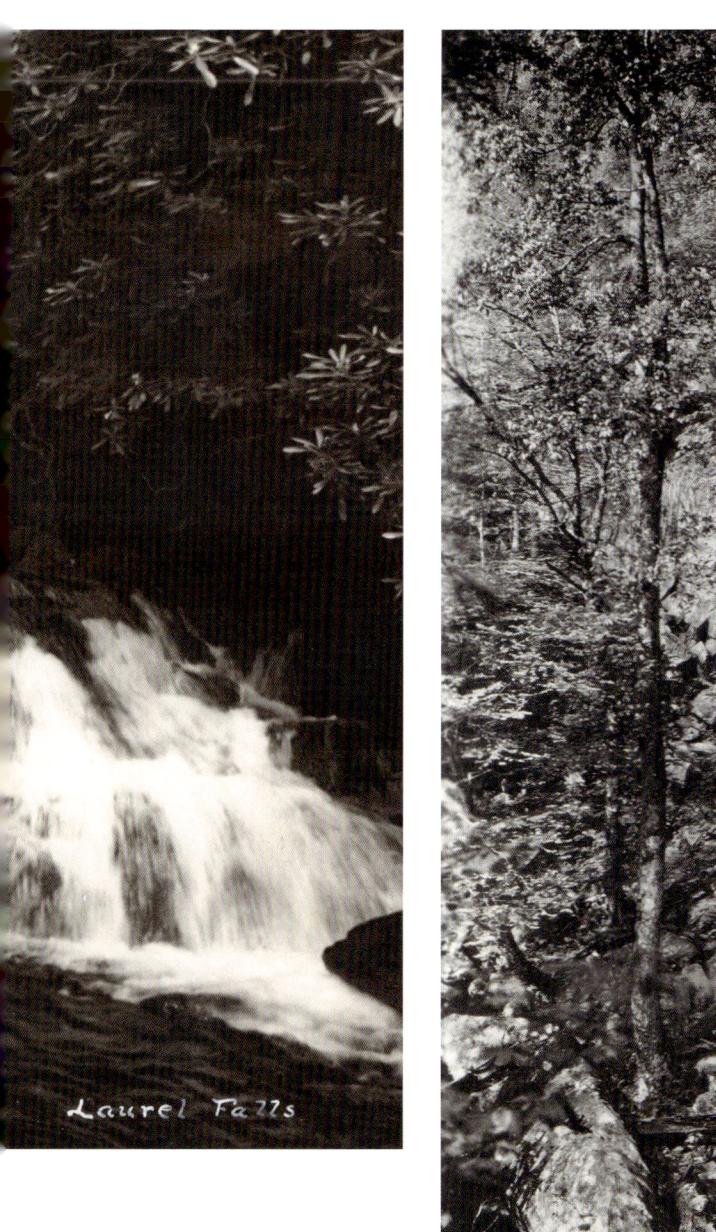

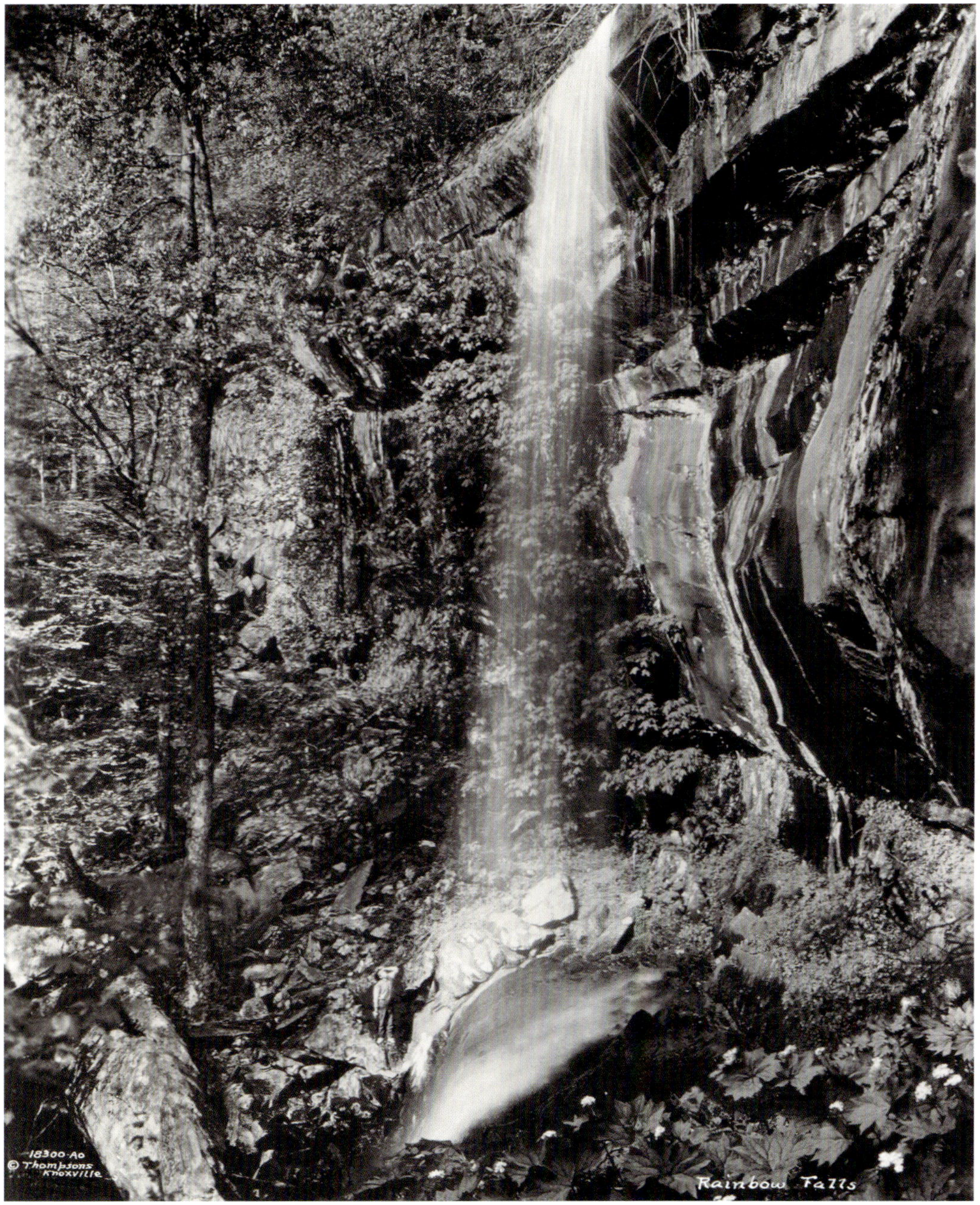

174   Rainbow Falls on LeConte Creek in Great Smoky Mountains National Park.
Courtesy of National Park Service.

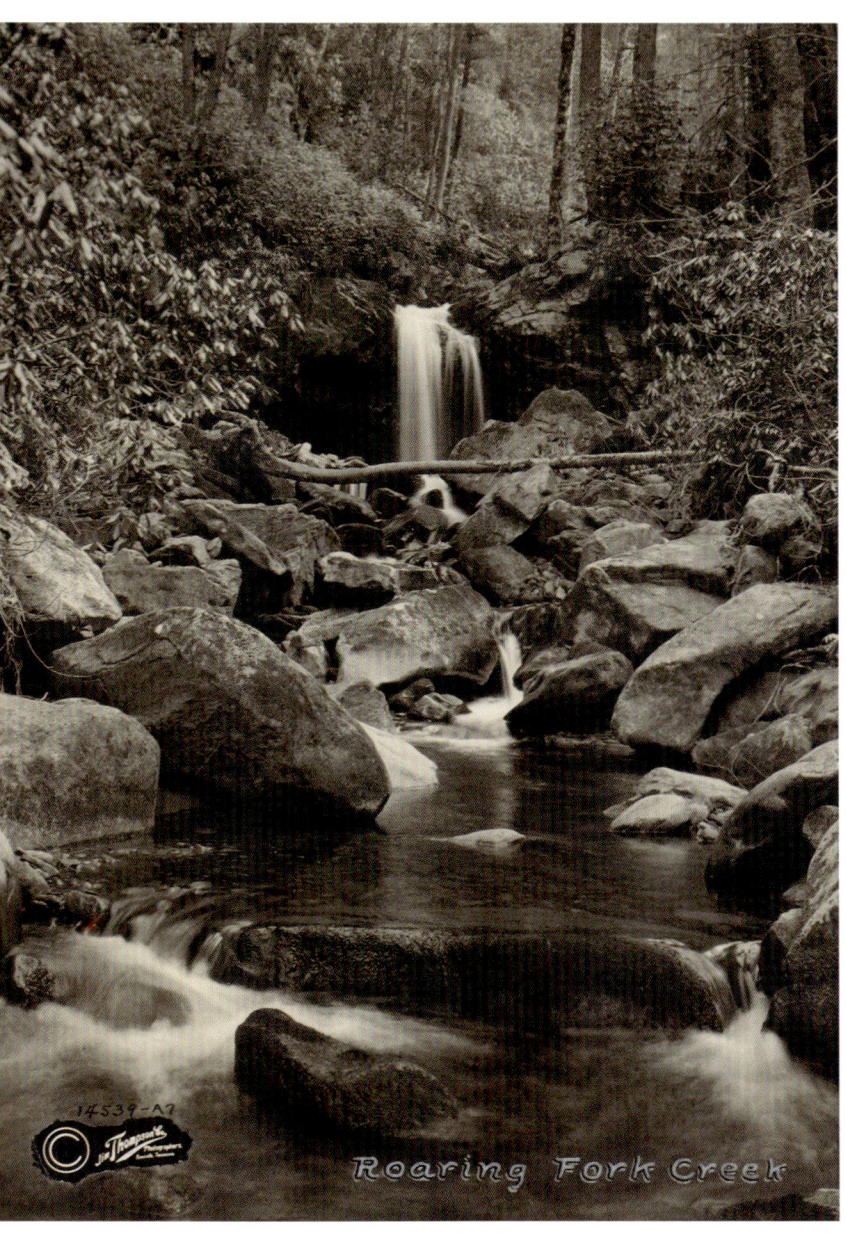

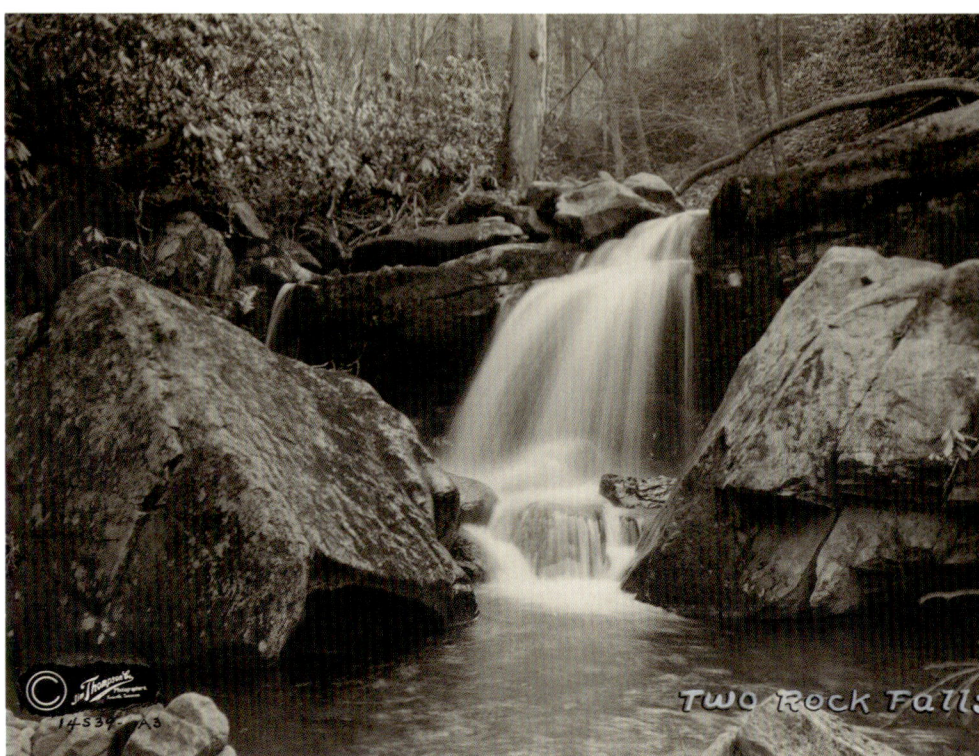

176   Two Rock Falls in Great Smoky Mountains National Park.
Courtesy of National Park Service.

175   Falls on Roaring Fork Creek outside Gatlinburg in
Great Smoky Mountains National Park. Courtesy of
National Park Service.

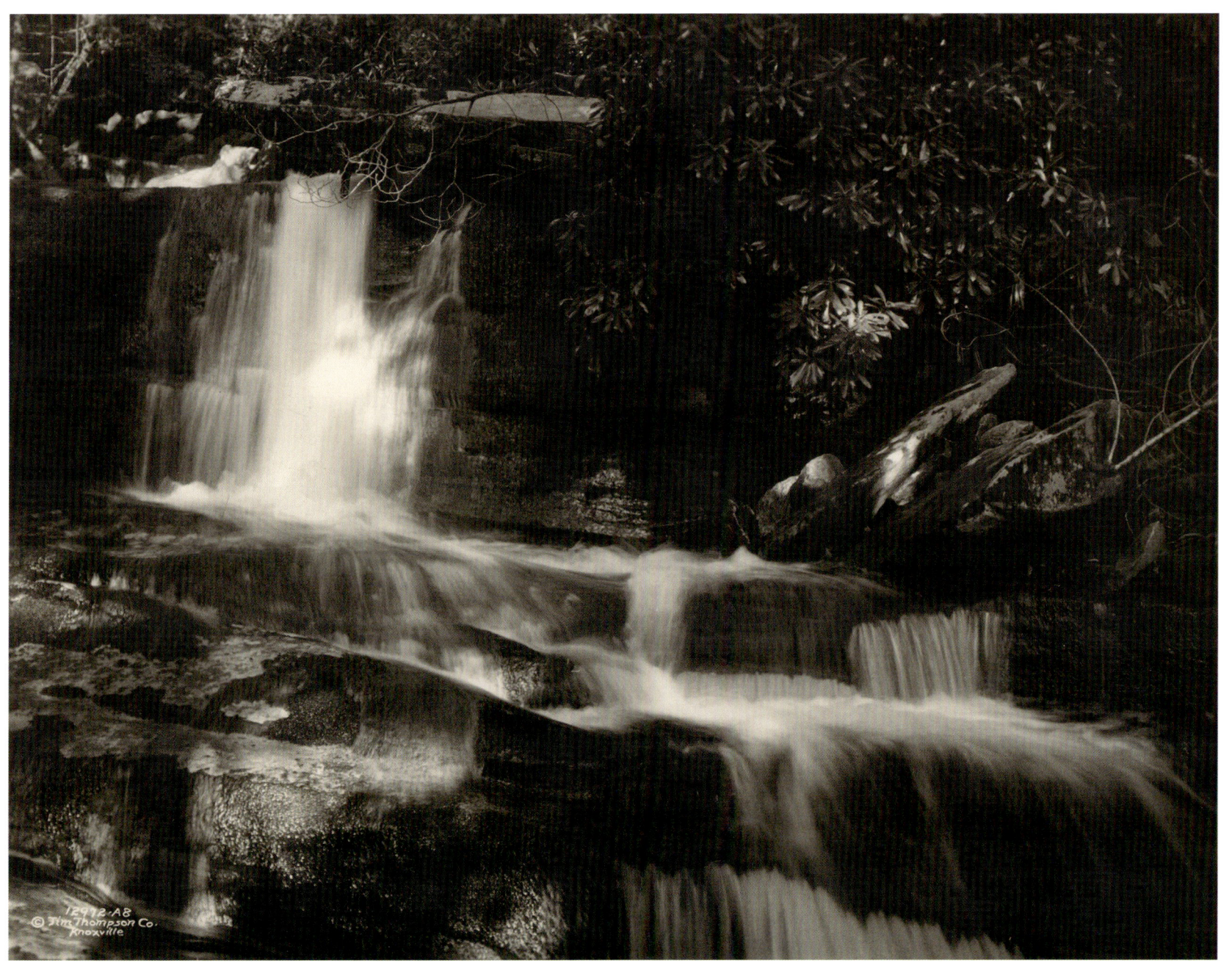

177   Falls and Cascades in Great Smoky Mountains National Park. Courtesy of National Park Service.

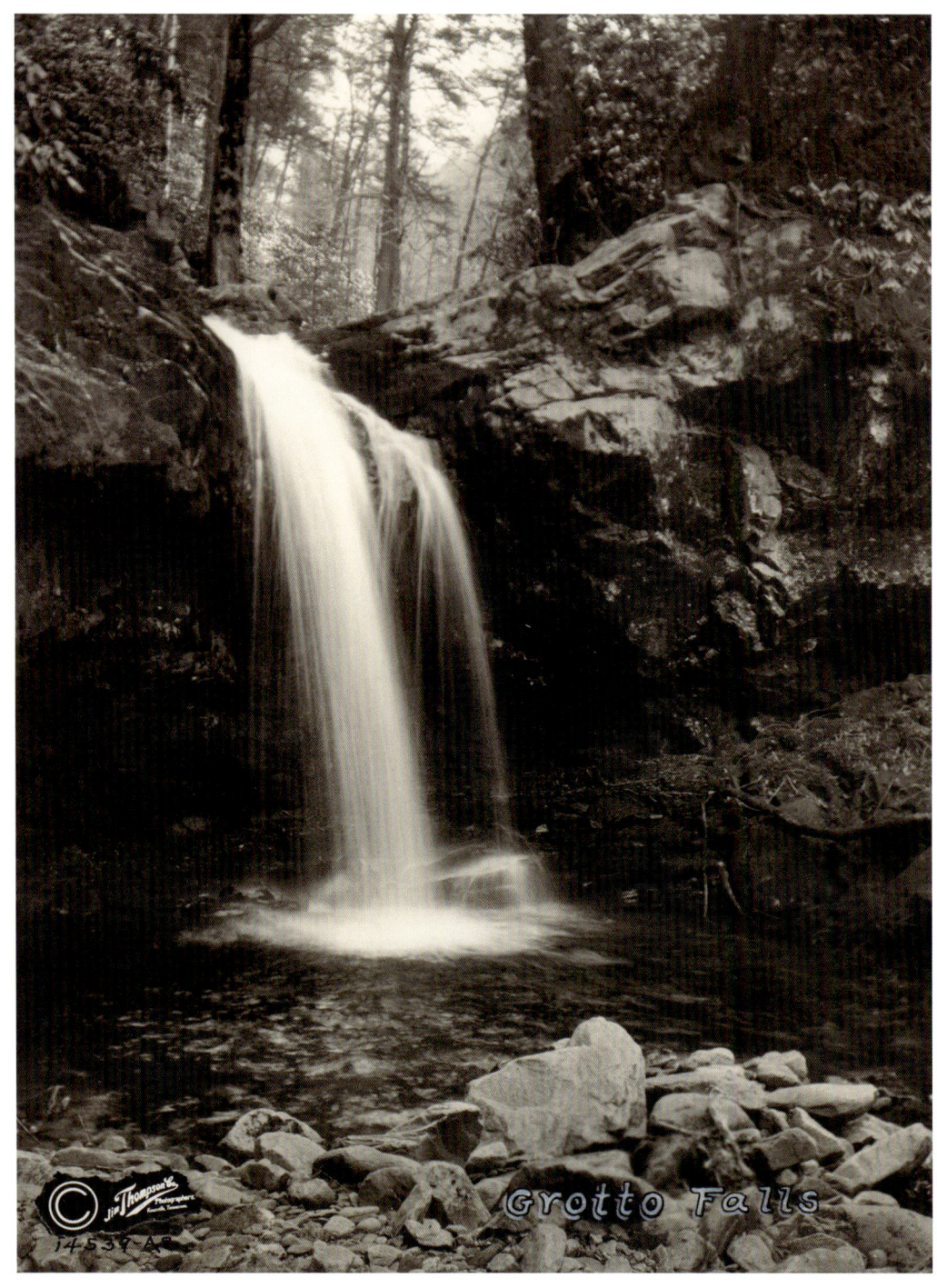

Grotto Falls

178 Grotto Falls on Roaring Fork Creek in
Great Smoky Mountains National Park.
Courtesy of National Park Service.

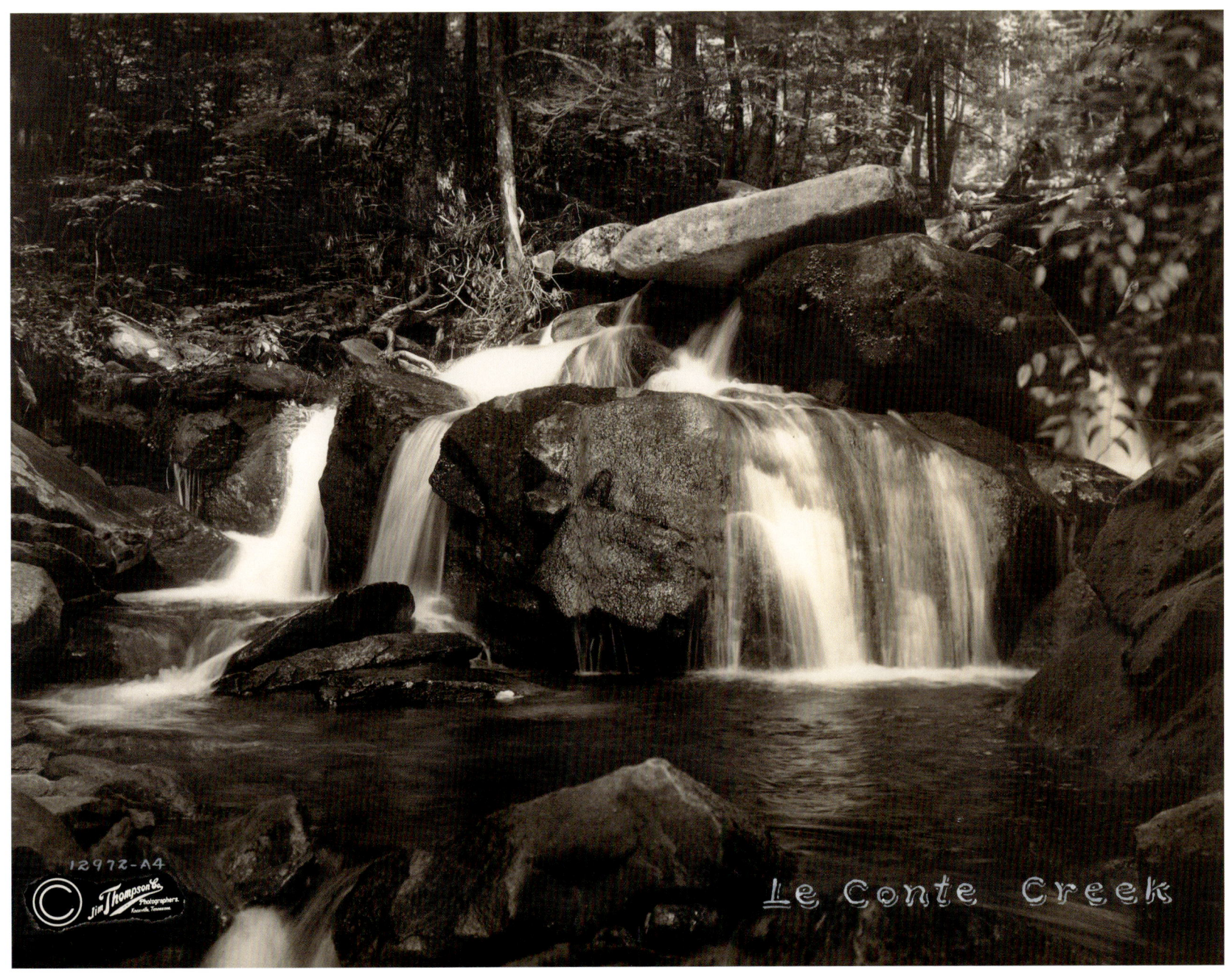

179   Photograph of LeConte Creek in Great Smoky Mountains National Park.
Courtesy of National Park Service.

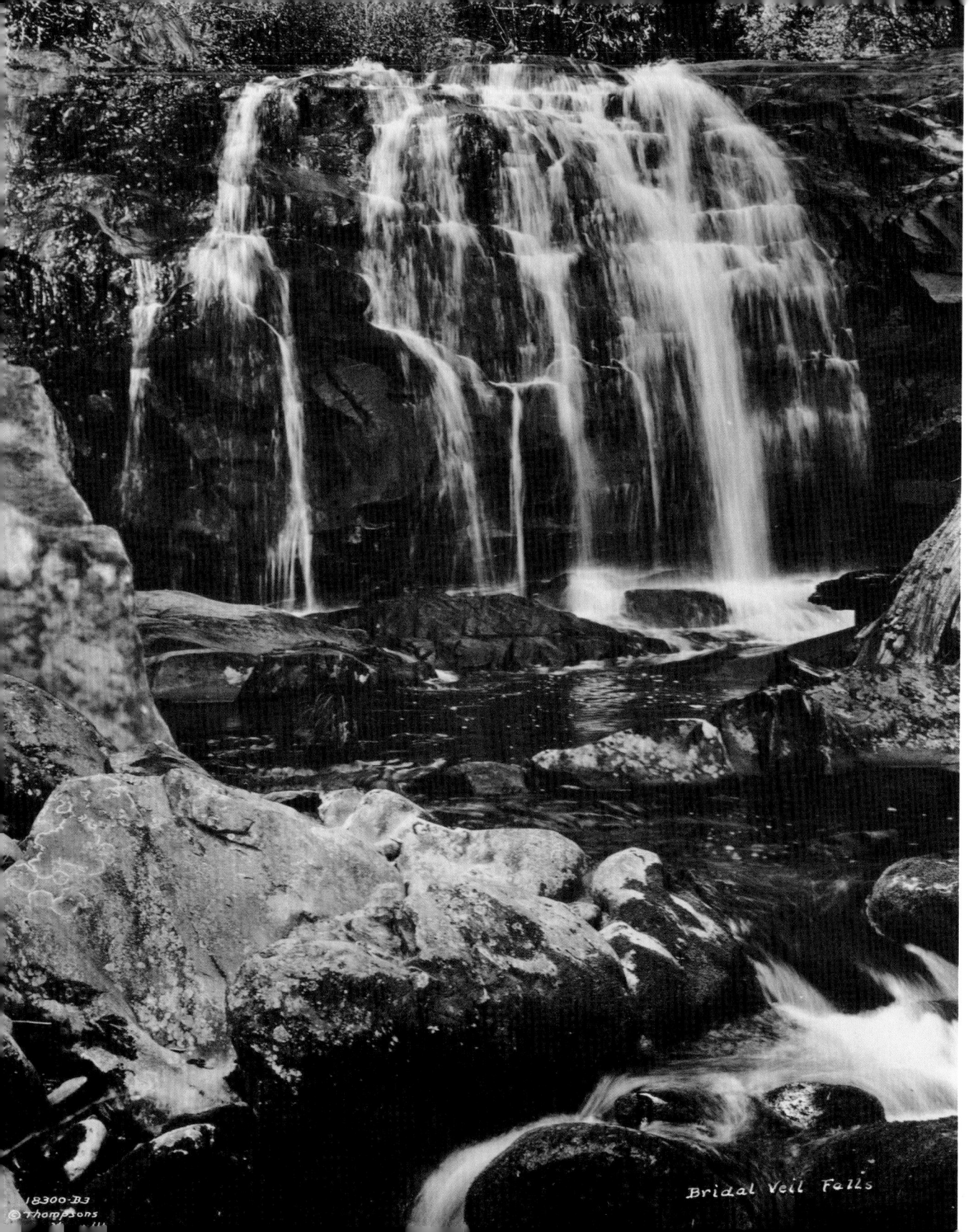

180　Bridal Veil Falls
in Great Smoky
Mountains National
Park. Courtesy of
National Park Service.

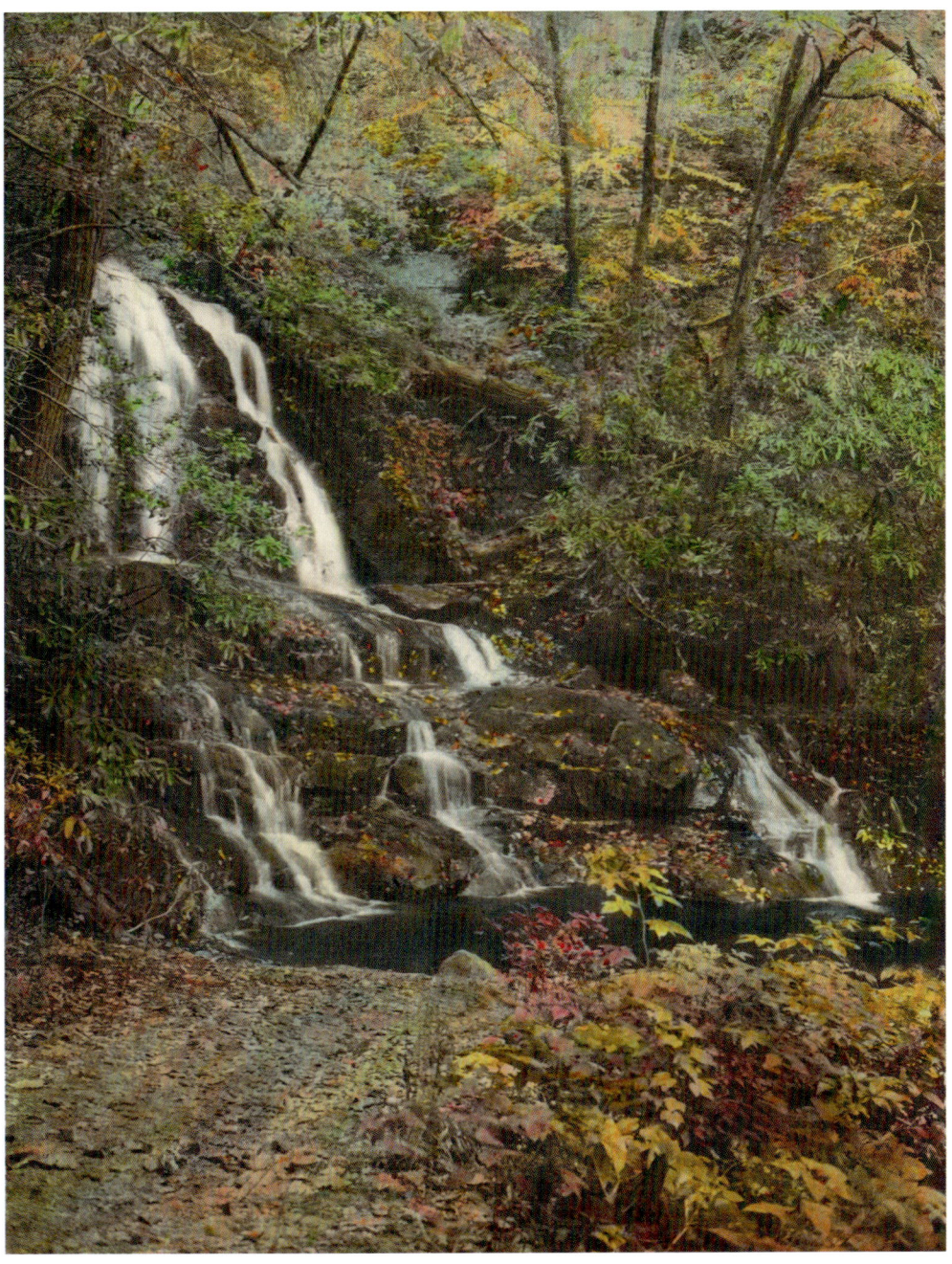

181   Colorized photograph of Laurel Falls on Laurel Branch in Great Smoky
        Mountains National Park. Courtesy of National Park Service.

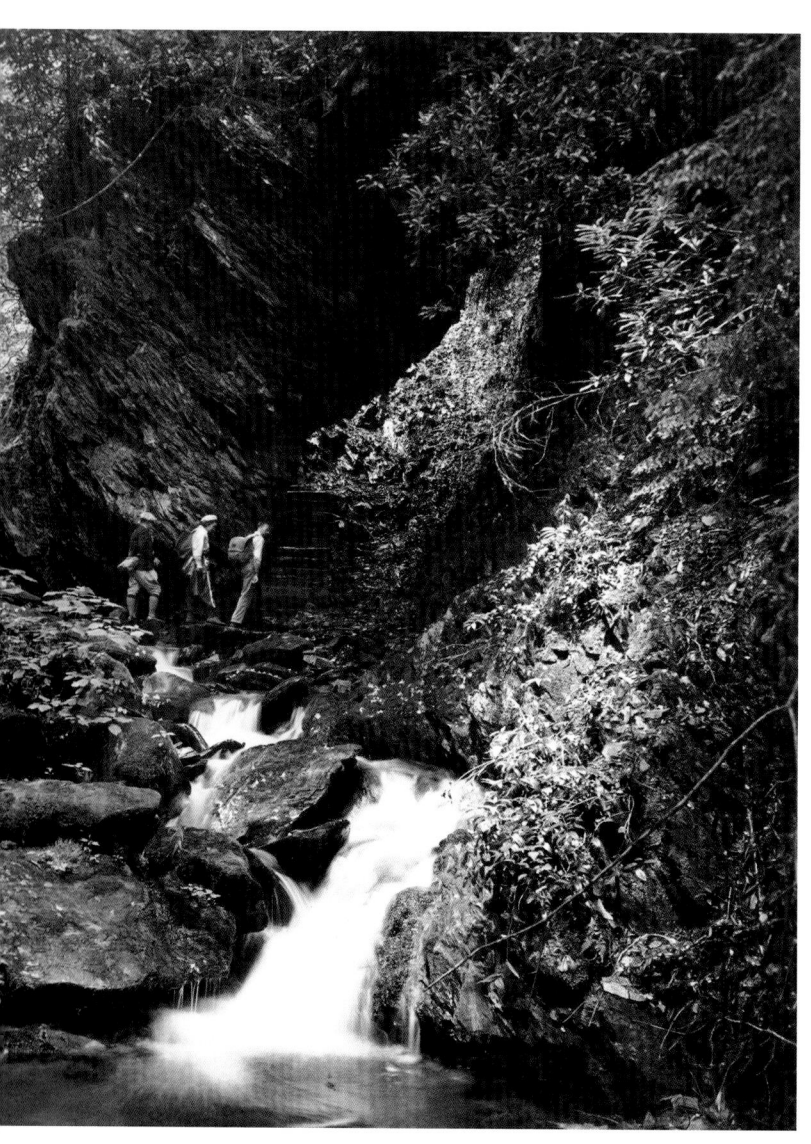

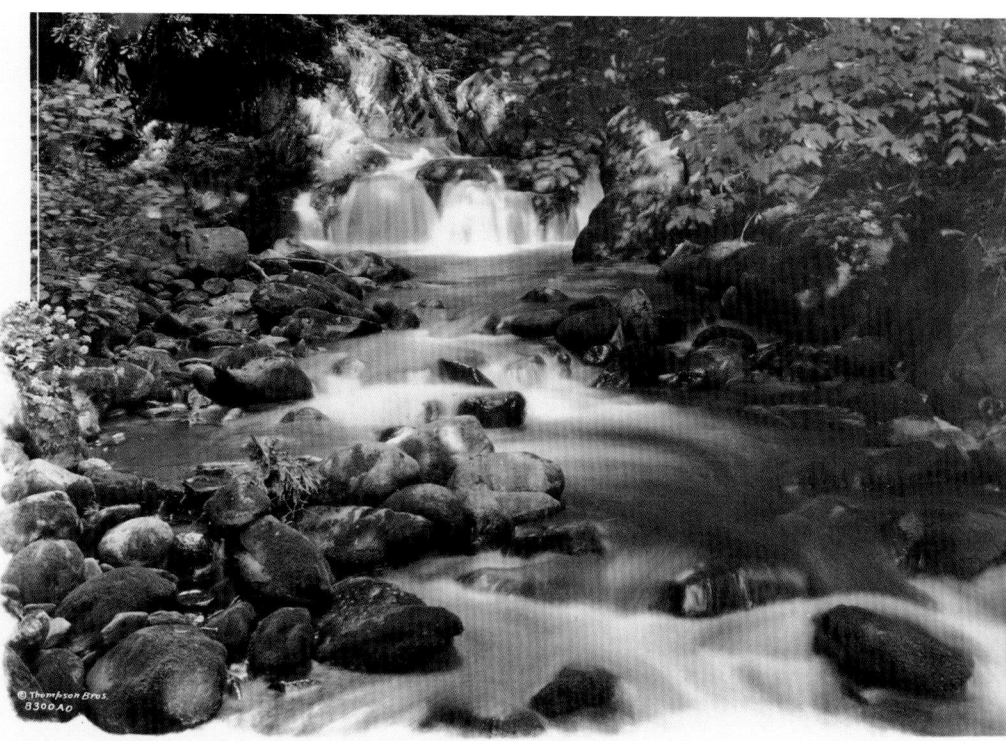

183   Arch Rock on Styx Branch near Huggins Hell in Great Smoky
Mountains National Park. Courtesy of National Park Service.

182   LeConte Creek cascades in Great Smoky
Mountains National Park. Courtesy of
National Park Service.

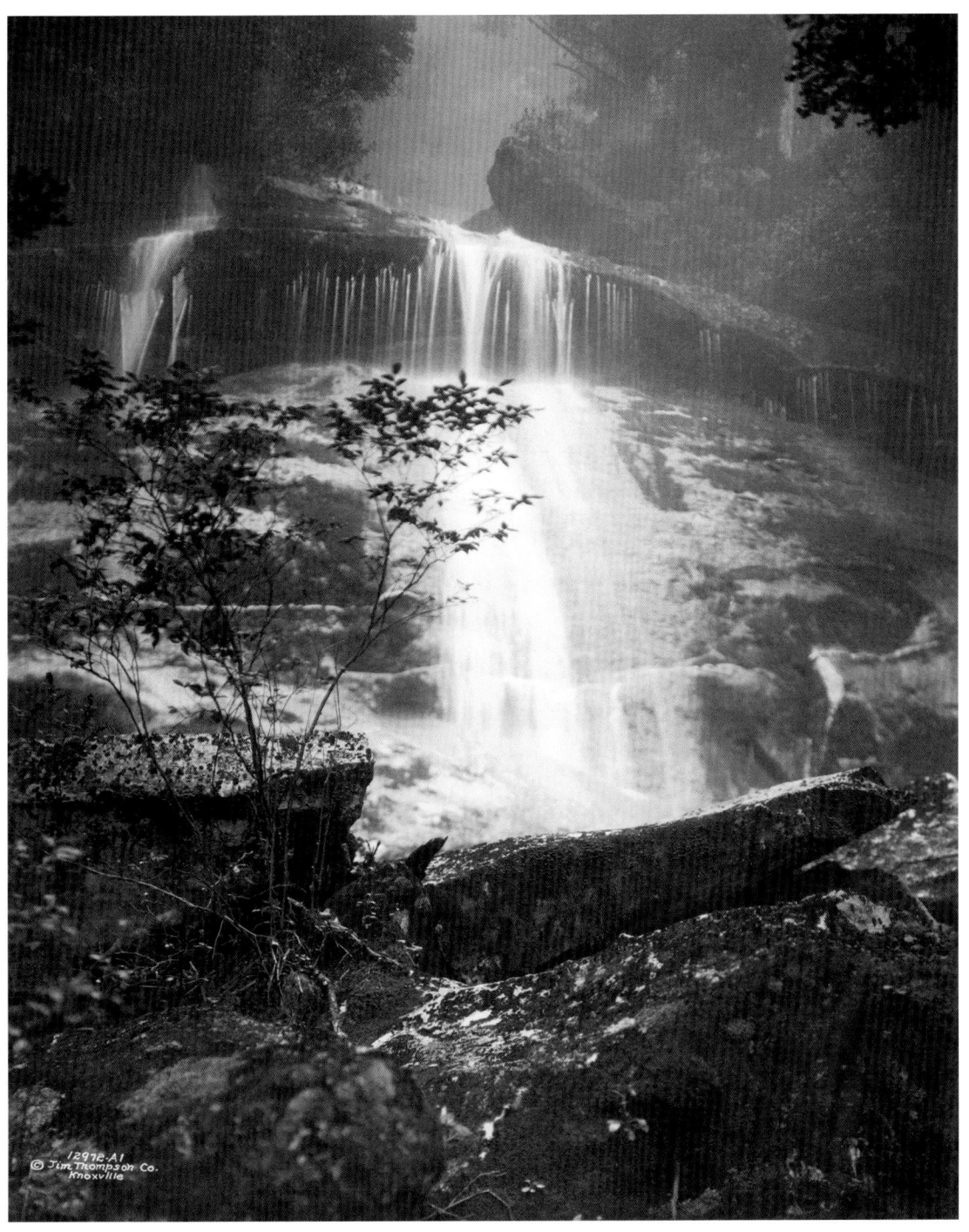

184   Dome Falls on Mount LeConte
       in Great Smoky Mountains National
       Park. Courtesy of National Park
       Service.

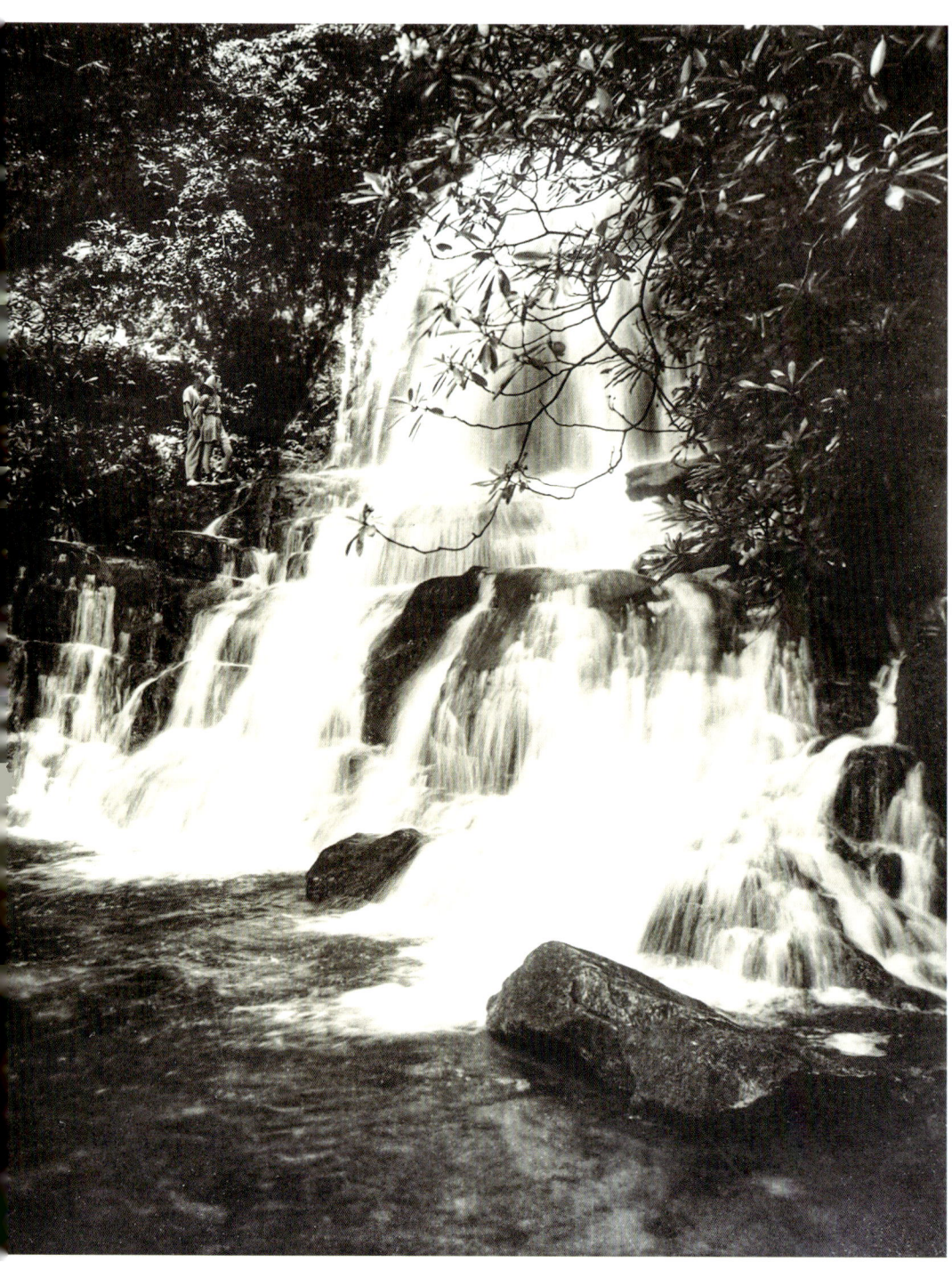

185   Laurel Falls on Laurel Branch in
Great Smoky Mountains National Park.
Courtesy of National Park Service.

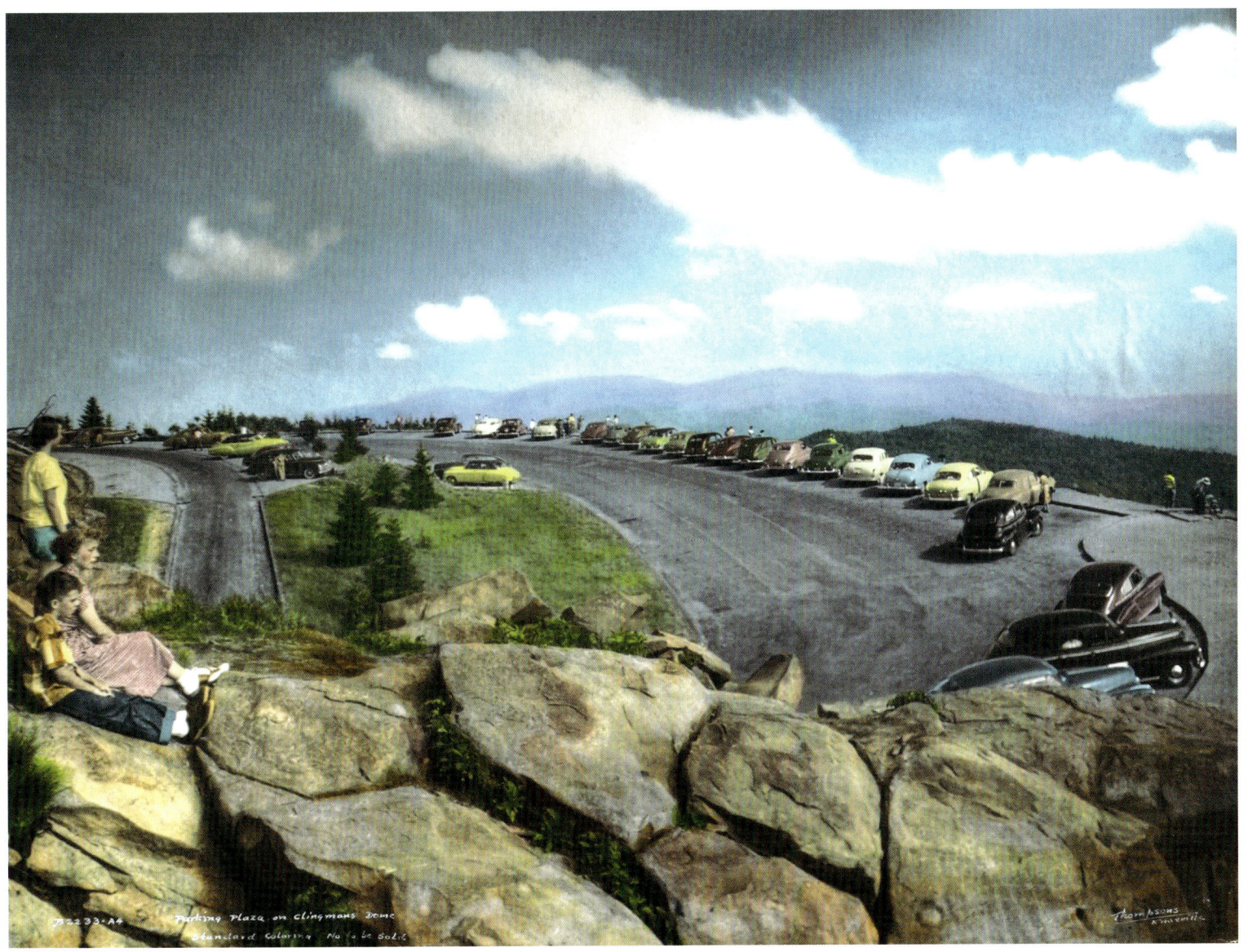

186 Colorized photograph of parking plaza at Kuwohi, formerly Clingmans Dome.
Courtesy of National Park Service.

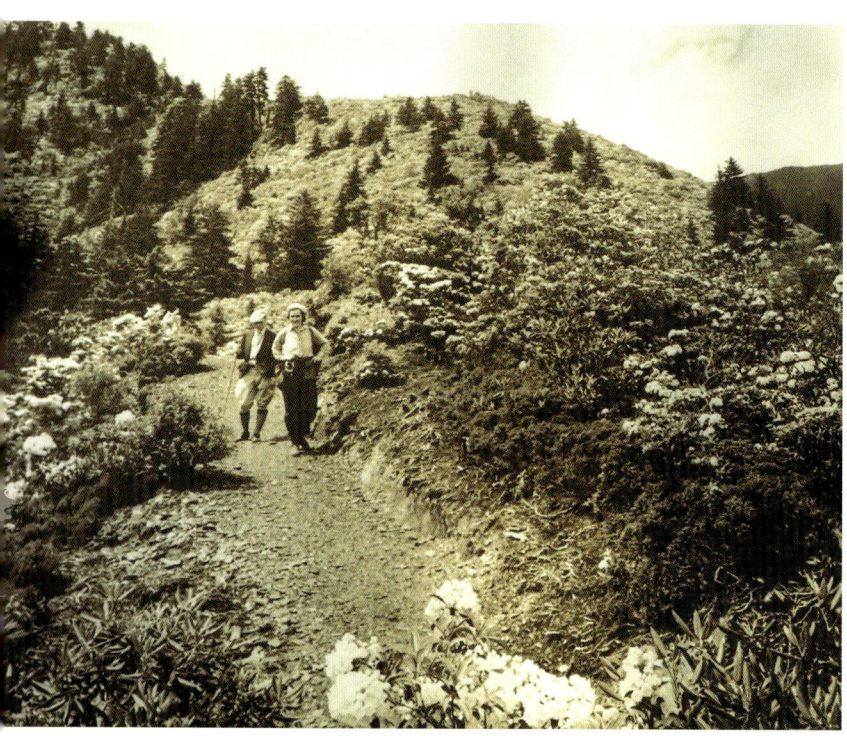

187   Bluff Gardens in Great Smoky Mountains National Park.
Courtesy of National Park Service.

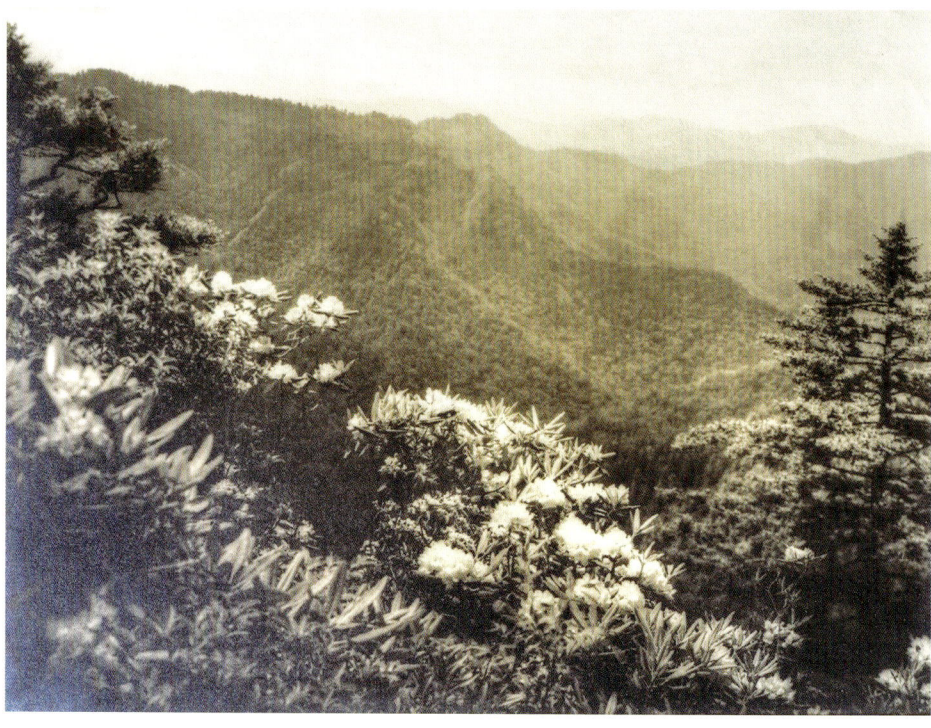

188   Pulpit Point in Great Smoky Mountains National Park.
Courtesy of National Park Service.

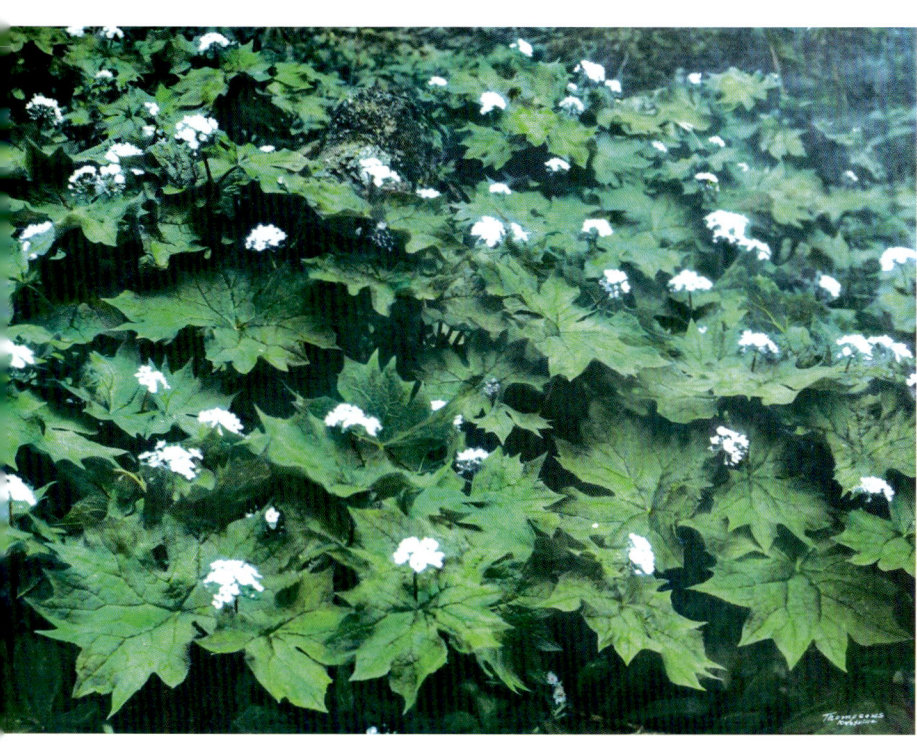

189   Umbrella leaves in Great Smoky Mountains
National Park. Courtesy of National Park Service.

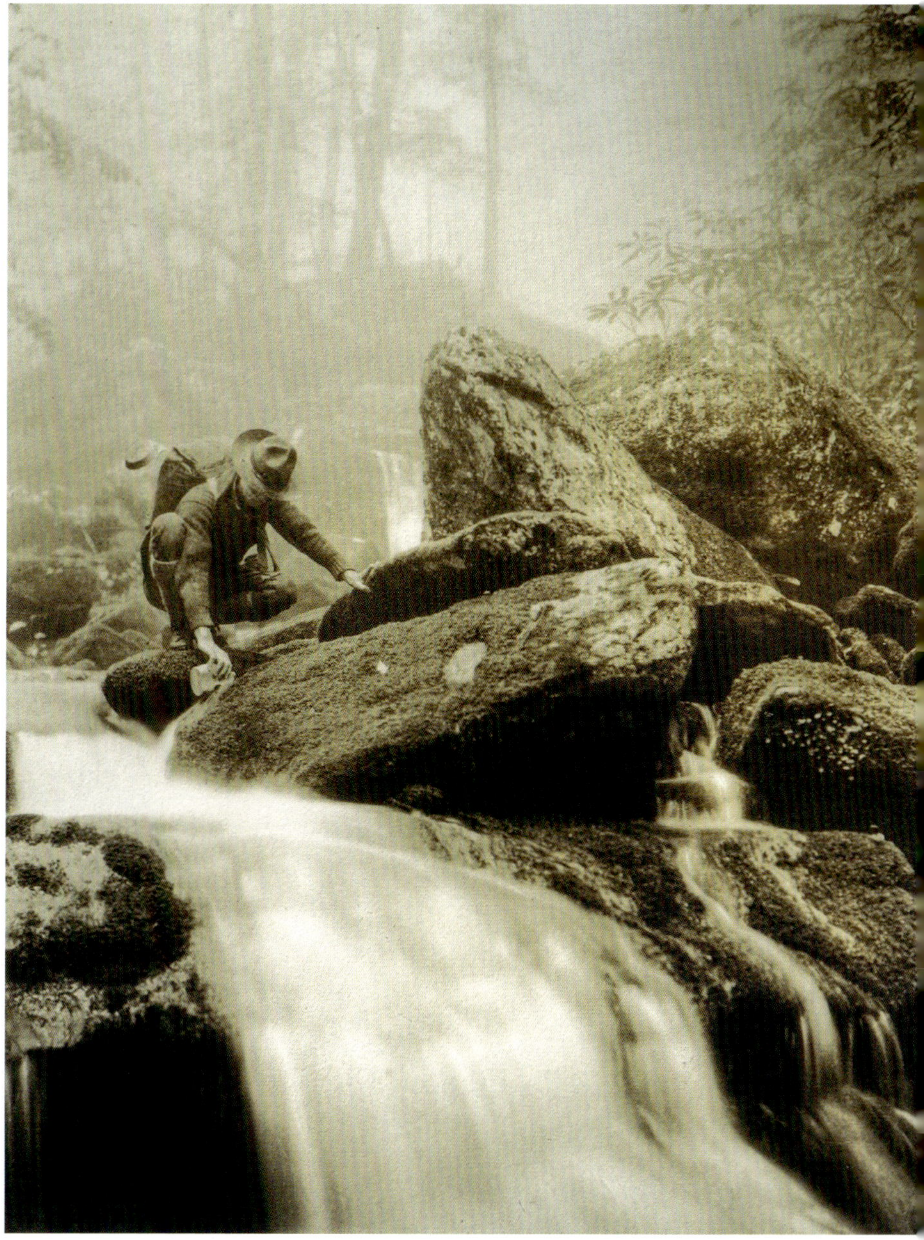

190   Fresh water. A hiker dips his cup into a fast-flowing stream
in Great Smoky Mountains National Park. Courtesy of National
Park Service.

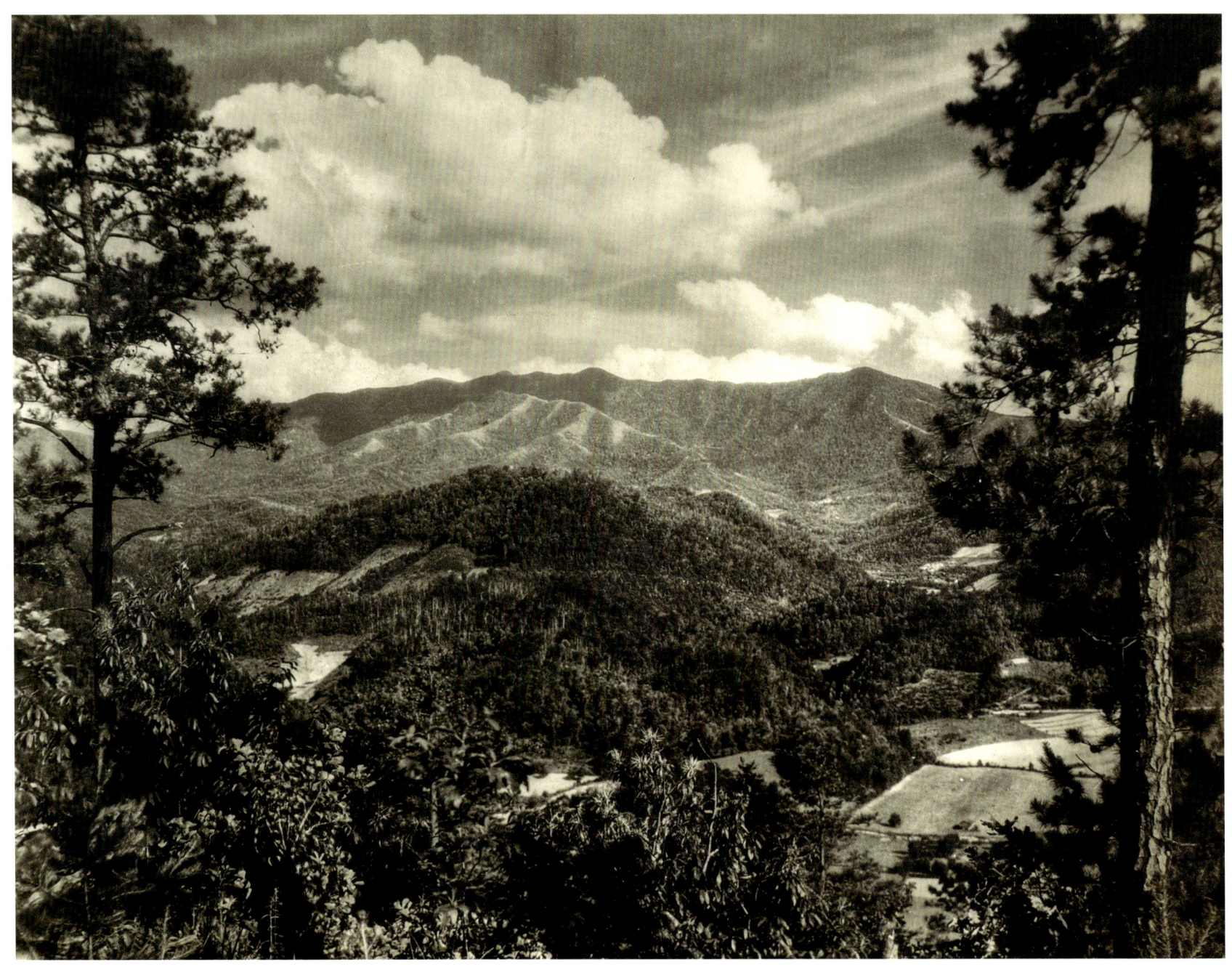

191   Mount LeConte beneath the clouds in Great Smoky Mountains National Park.
Courtesy of National Park Service.

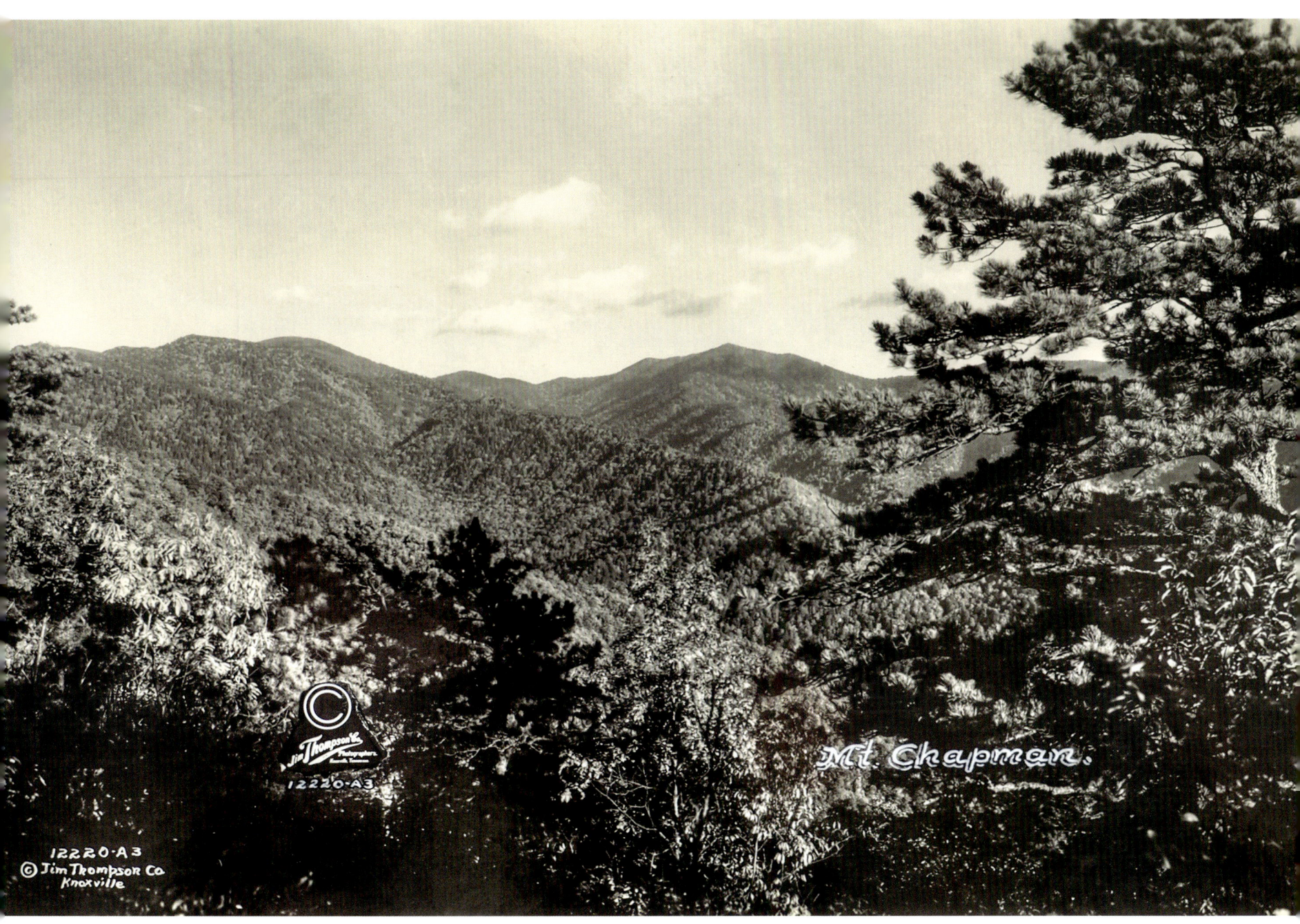

192   Mount Chapman in Great Smoky Mountains National Park.
Courtesy of National Park Service.

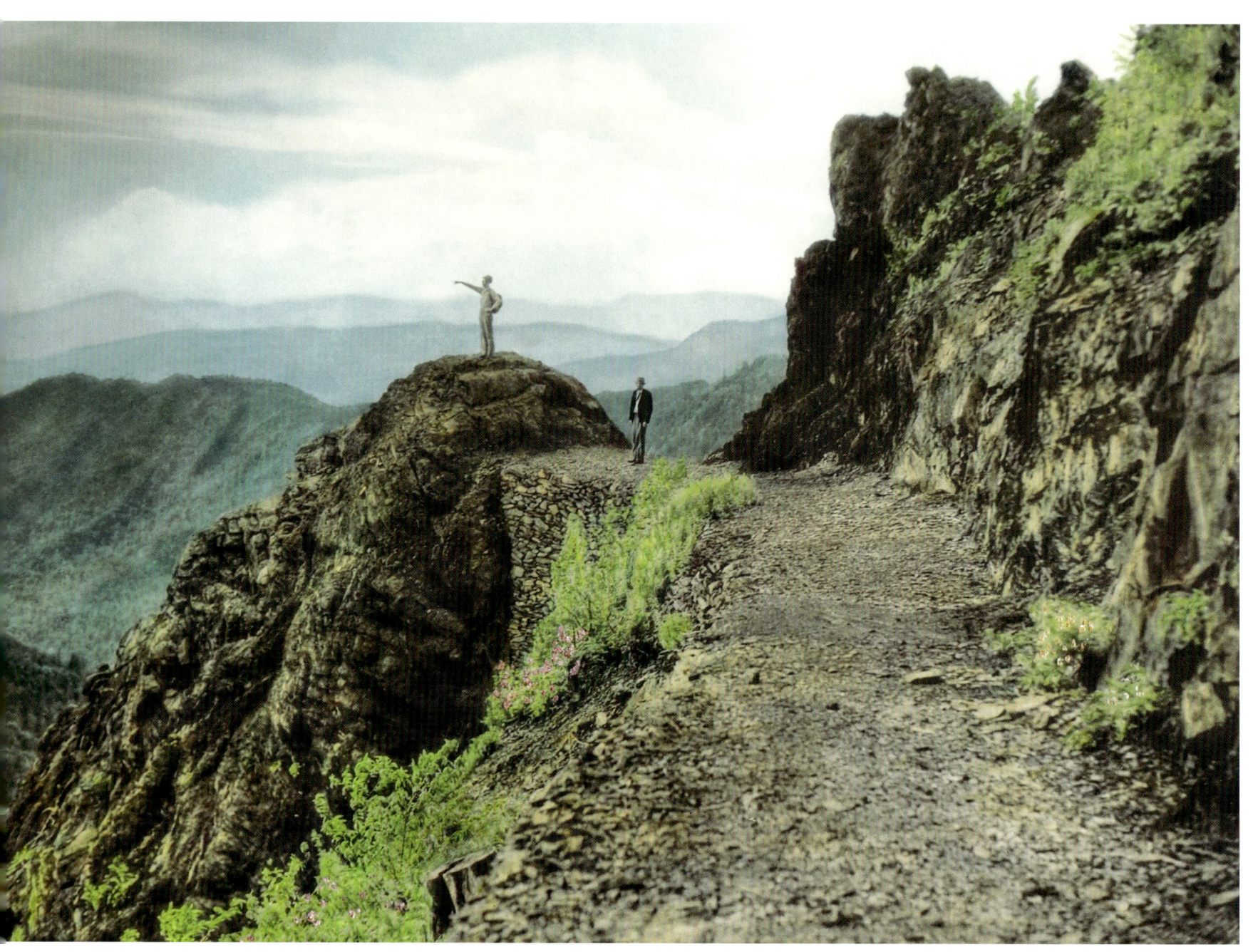

193   Charlies Bunion along the Appalachian Trail in Great Smoky Mountains National Park.
Courtesy of National Park Service.

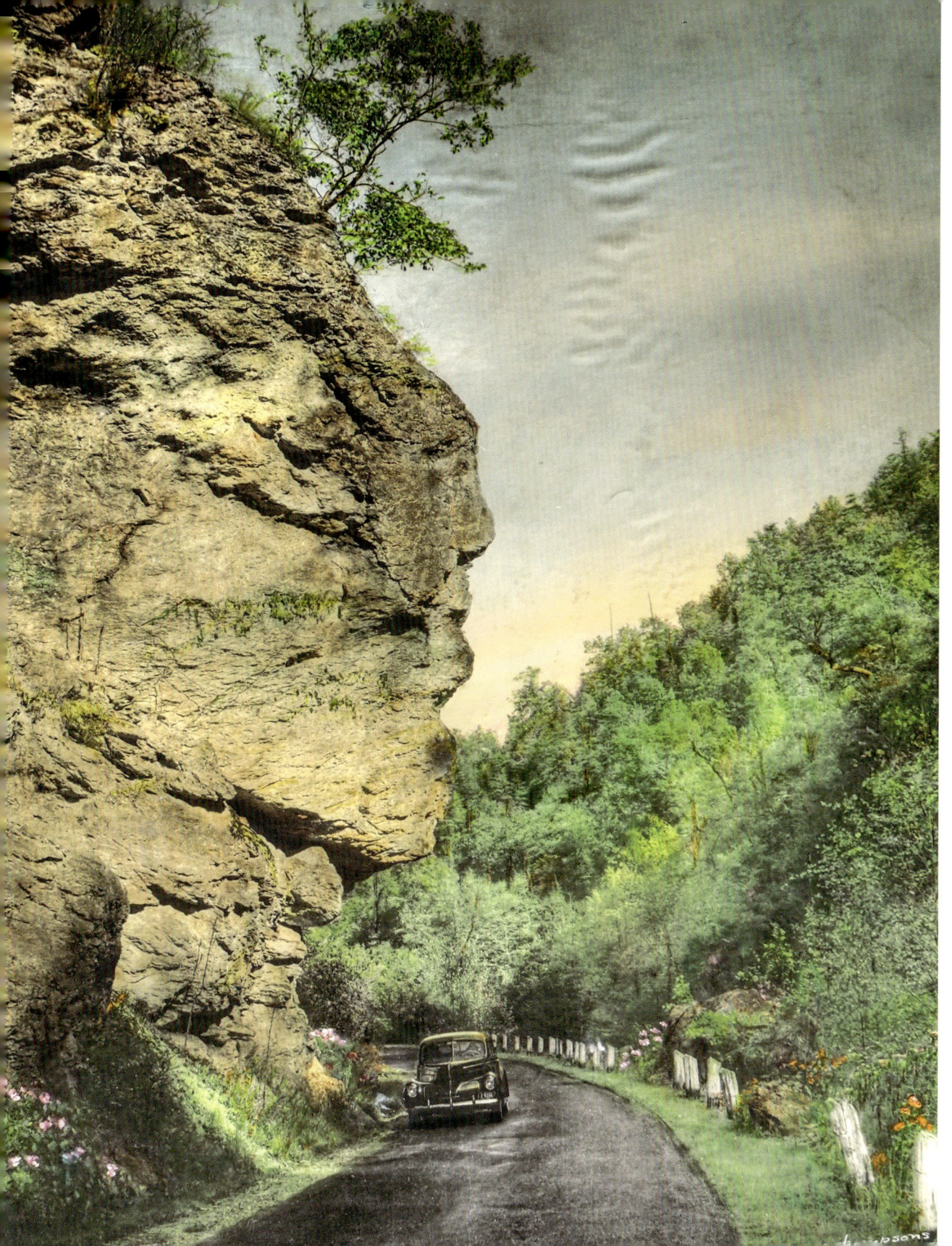

194   Indian Head Rock on the Circle
Loop on Highway 73 between
Townsend and Gatlinburg.
Courtesy of National
Park Service.

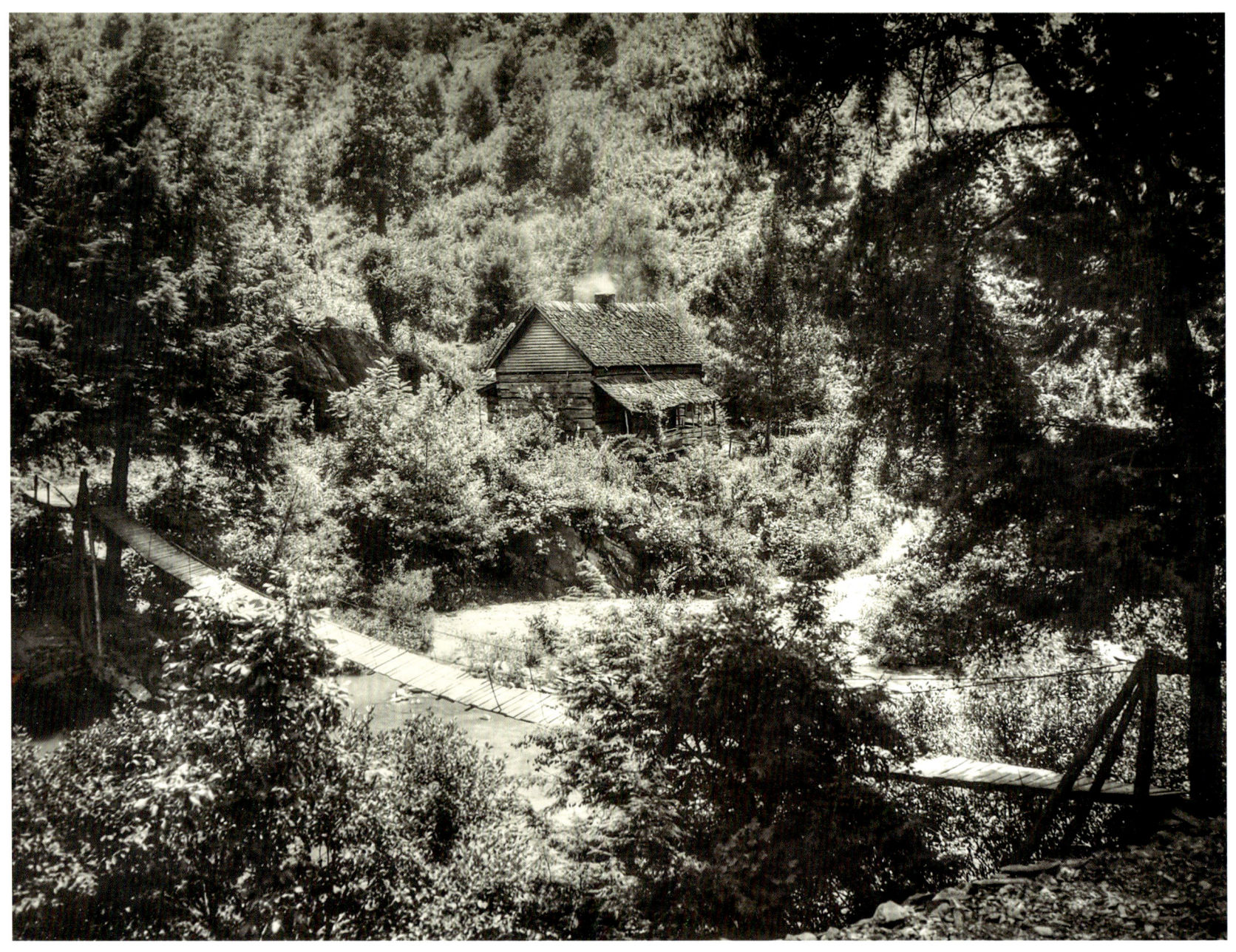

195   Booger Town east of Gatlinburg on the border of Great Smoky Mountains National Park.

Courtesy of National Park Service.

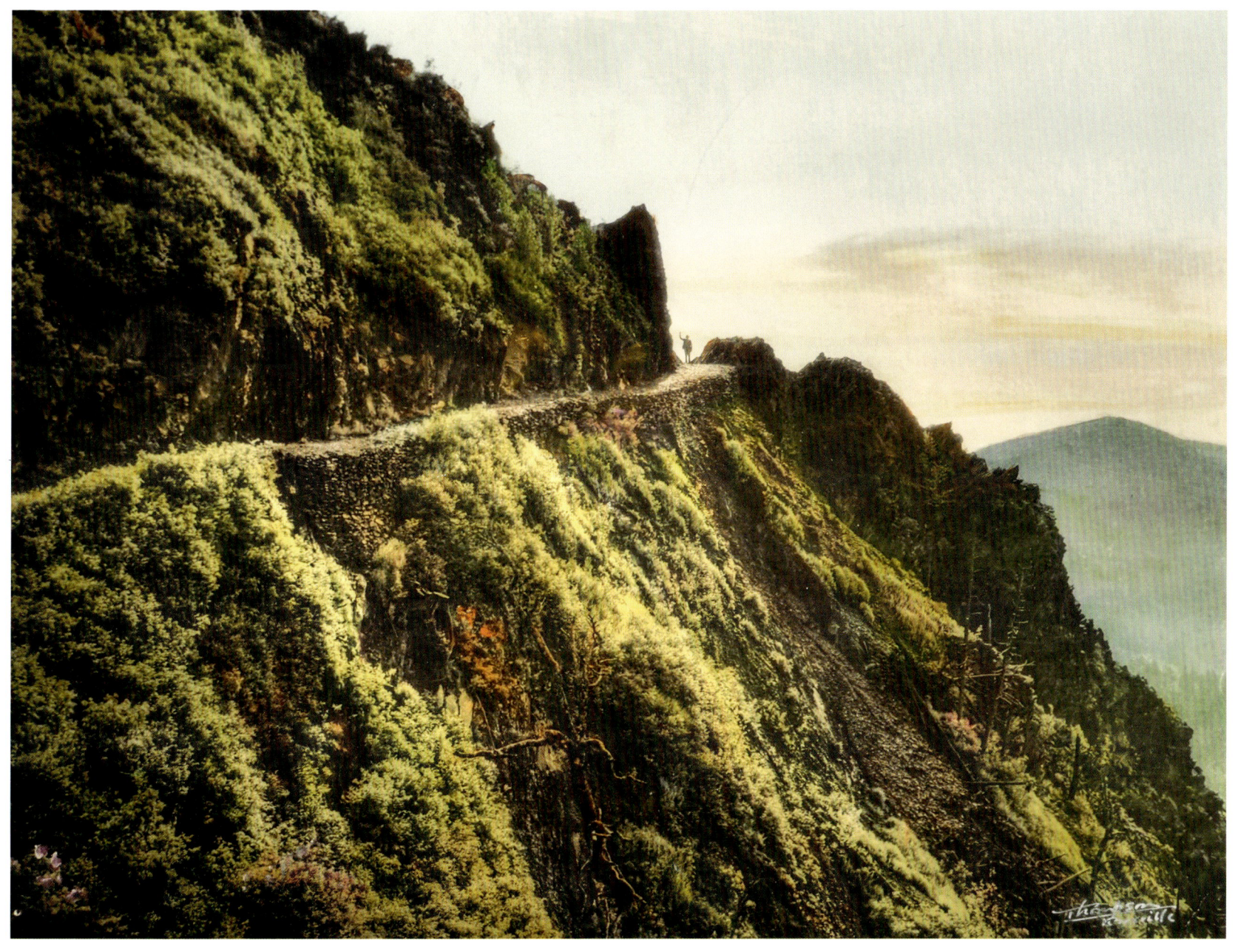

196 Charlies Bunion on the Appalachian Trail in Great Smoky Mountains National Park.
Courtesy of National Park Service.

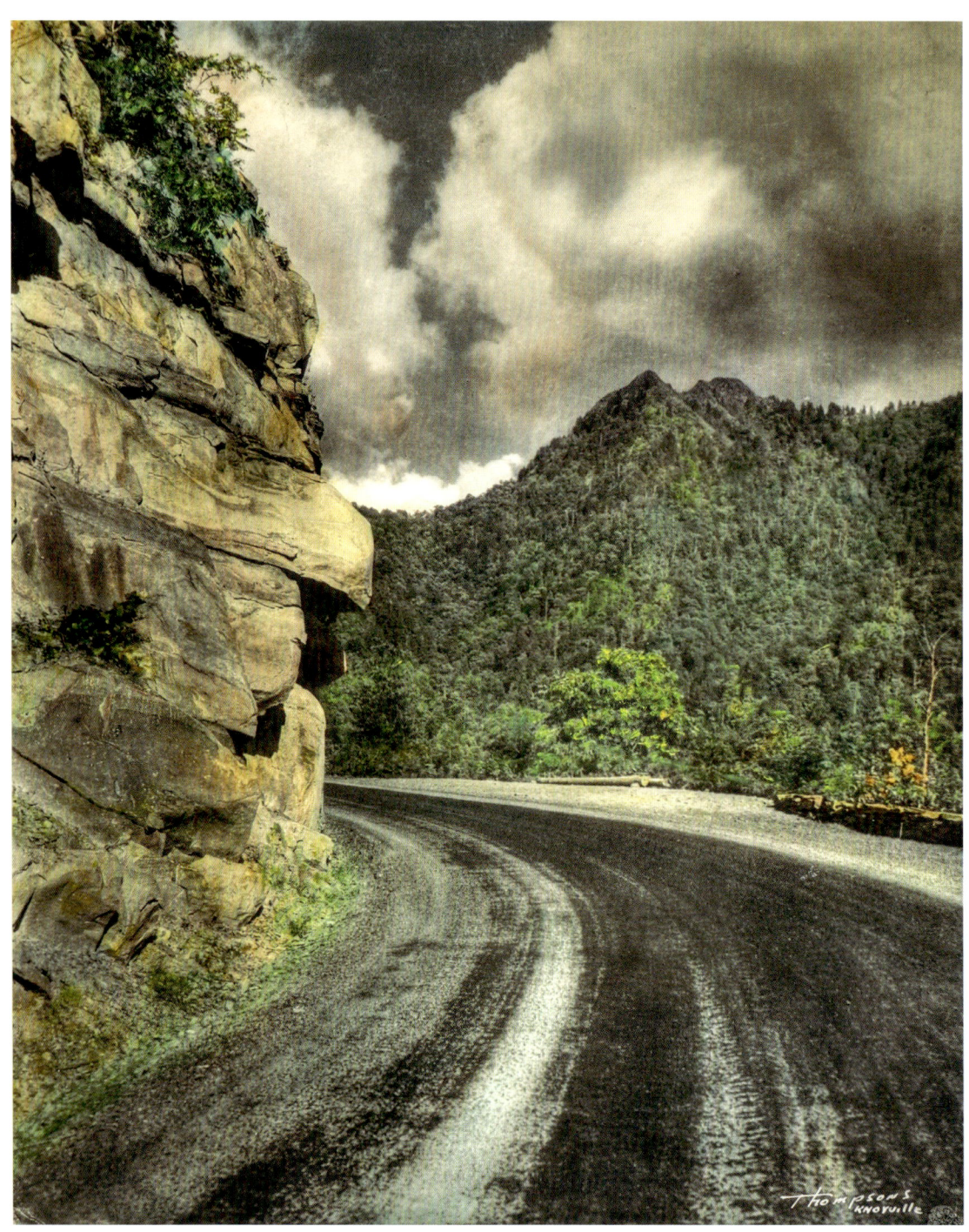

197   Chimney Tops from the Newfound
       Gap Road in Great Smoky
       Mountains National Park.
       Courtesy of National Park Service.

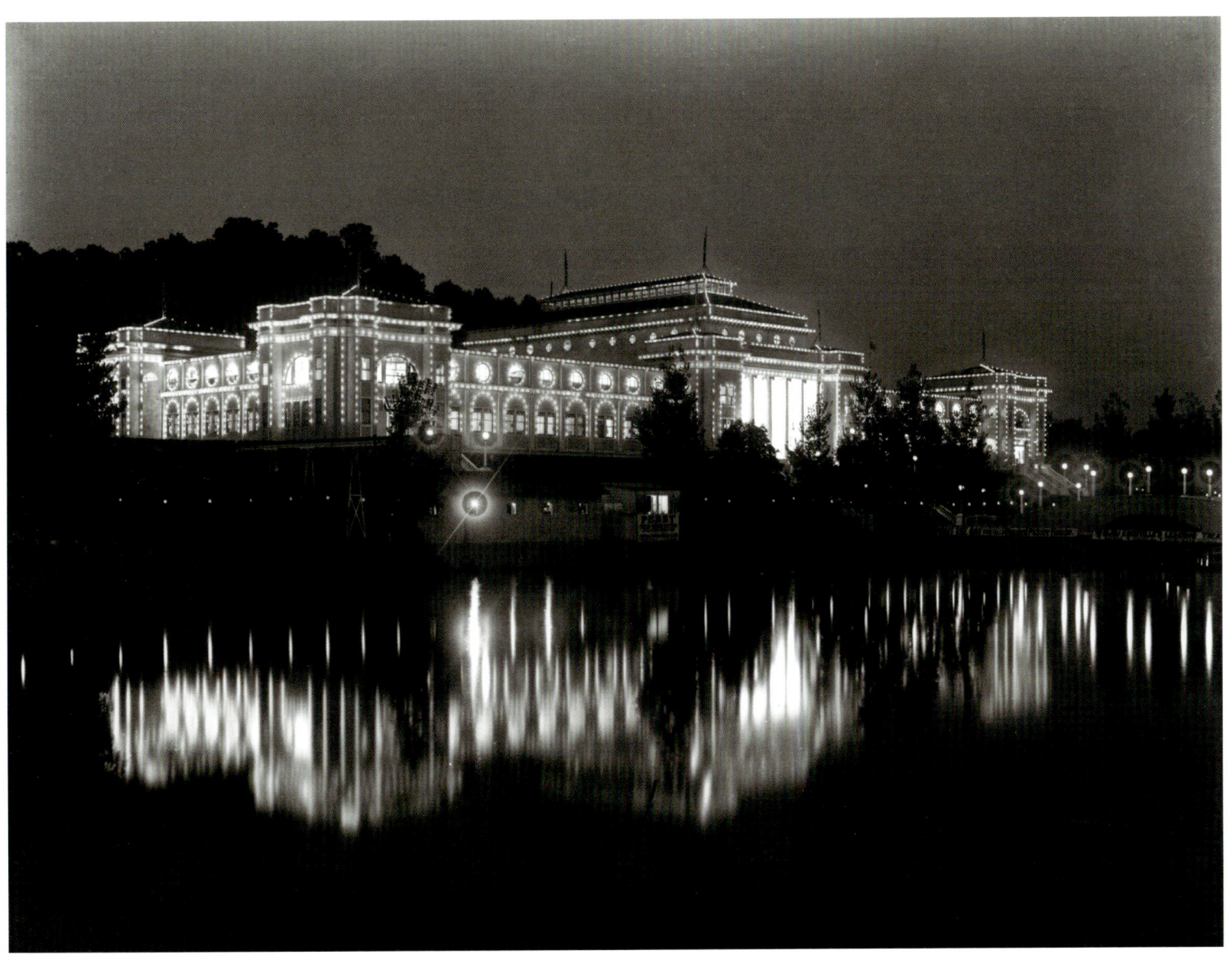

198   Photograph of illuminated buildings at the National Conservation Exposition in Knoxville, 1913.
       Courtesy of Knox County Public Library.

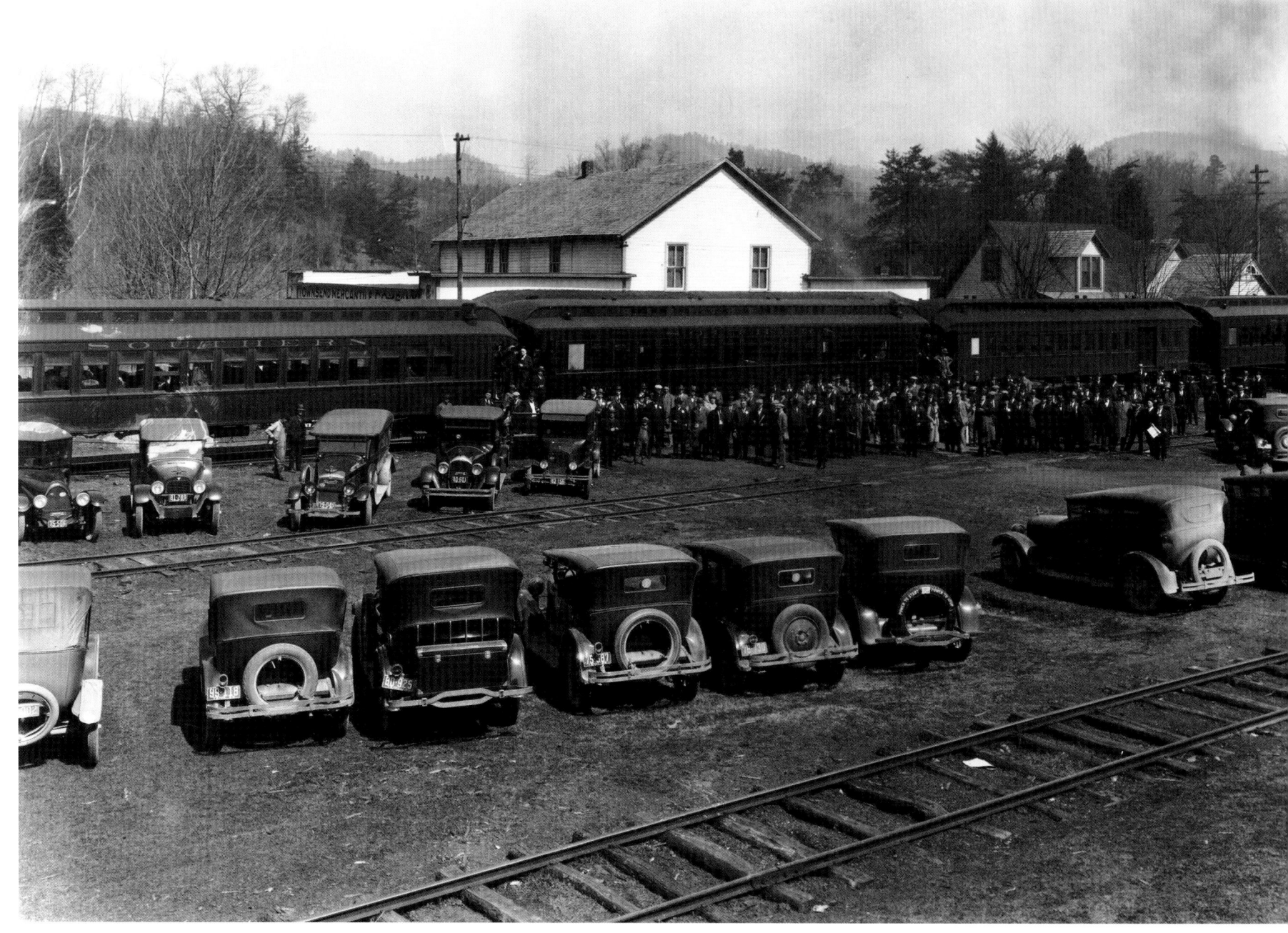

199   Tennessee legislators exiting trains in Townsend, Tennessee, for tour of Elkmont area of proposed
       Great Smoky Mountains National Park, 1925. Courtesy of Knox County Public Library.

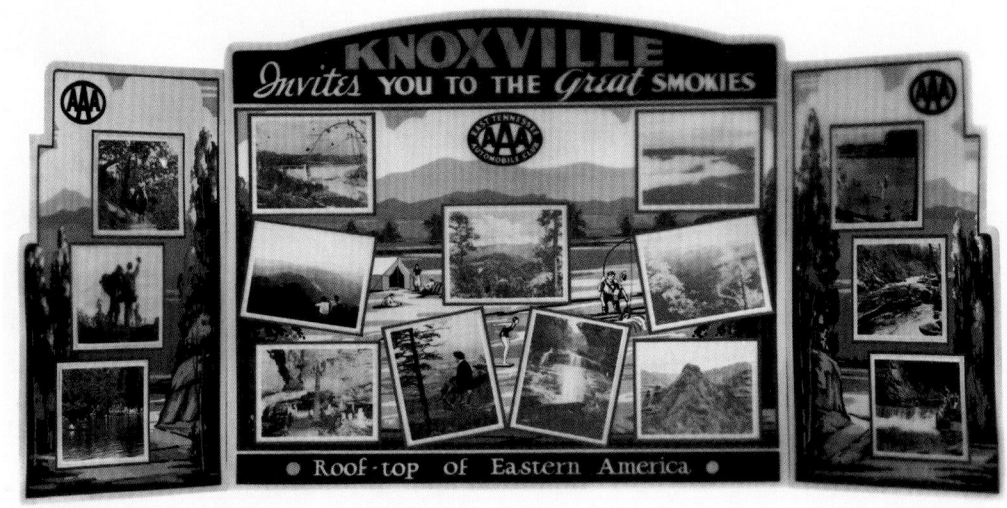

200 Jim Thompson's photographs illustrated the Knoxville Automobile Club's (AAA) promotion of travel to the Great Smoky Mountains "Rooftop of Eastern America." Courtesy of Knox County Public Library.

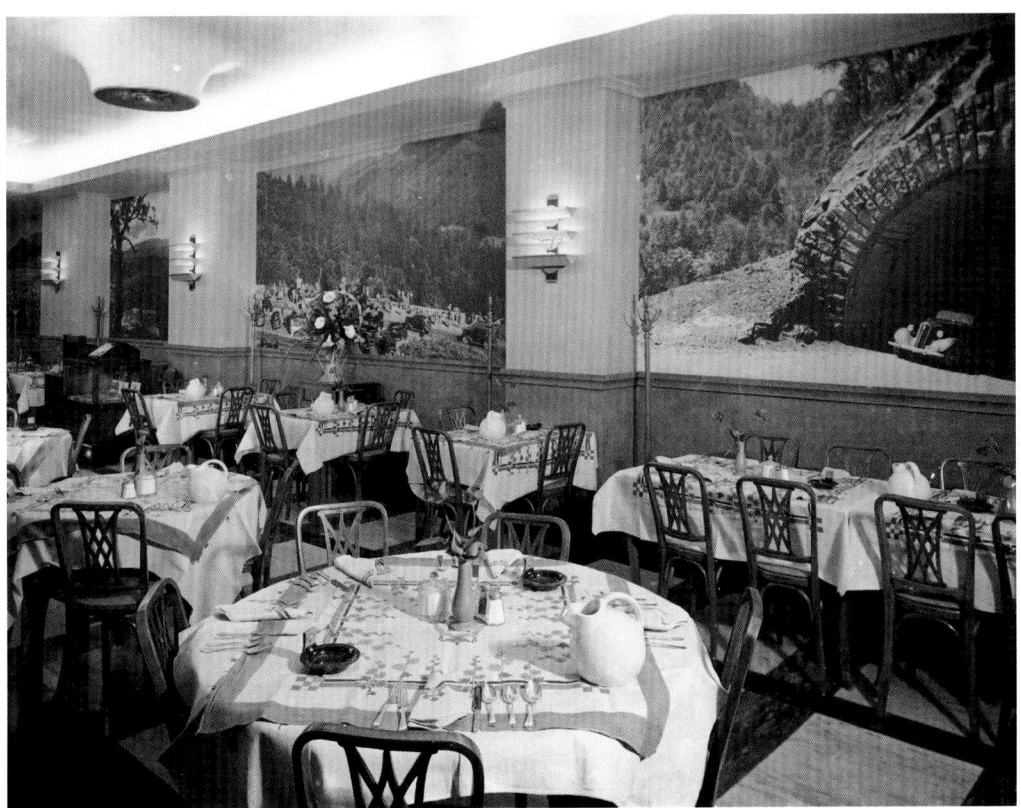

201 Jim Thompson's mural photographs on the wall of a dining room at the Farragut Hotel, Knoxville. Courtesy of McClung Historical Collection, Thompson Brothers Collection.

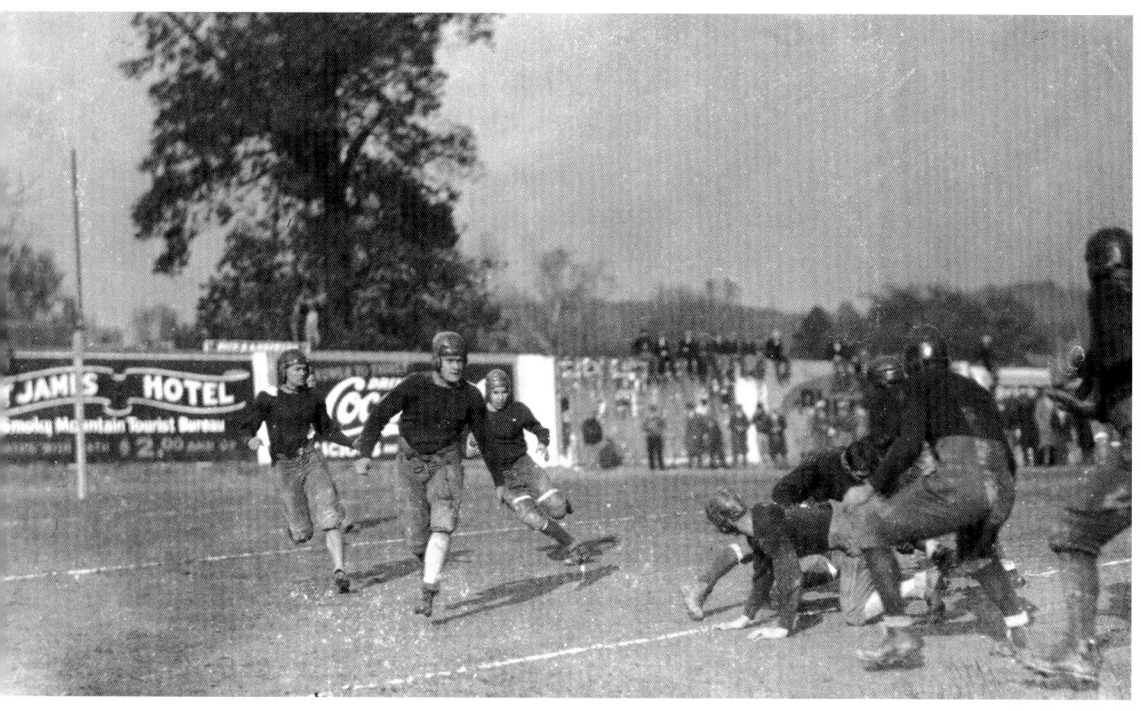

202   The University of Tennessee Volunteers football team in action
       during the mid-1920s. Courtesy of Knox County Public Library.

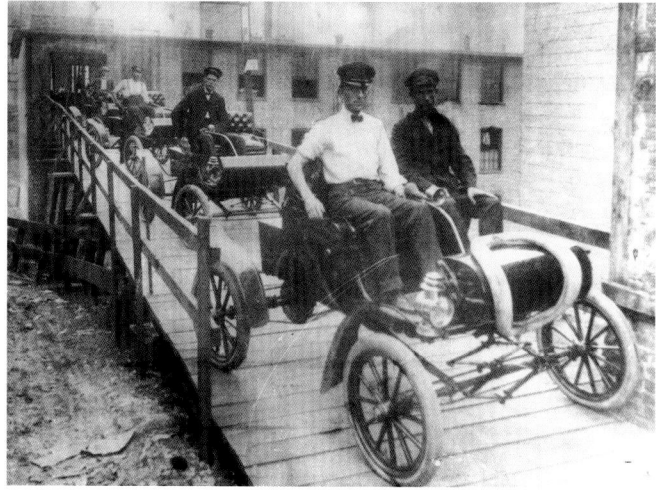

203   Cowan Rodgers departing
       Knoxville on the first automobile
       trip from Knoxville to
       Chattanooga, 1903. Courtesy of
       Knox County Public Library.

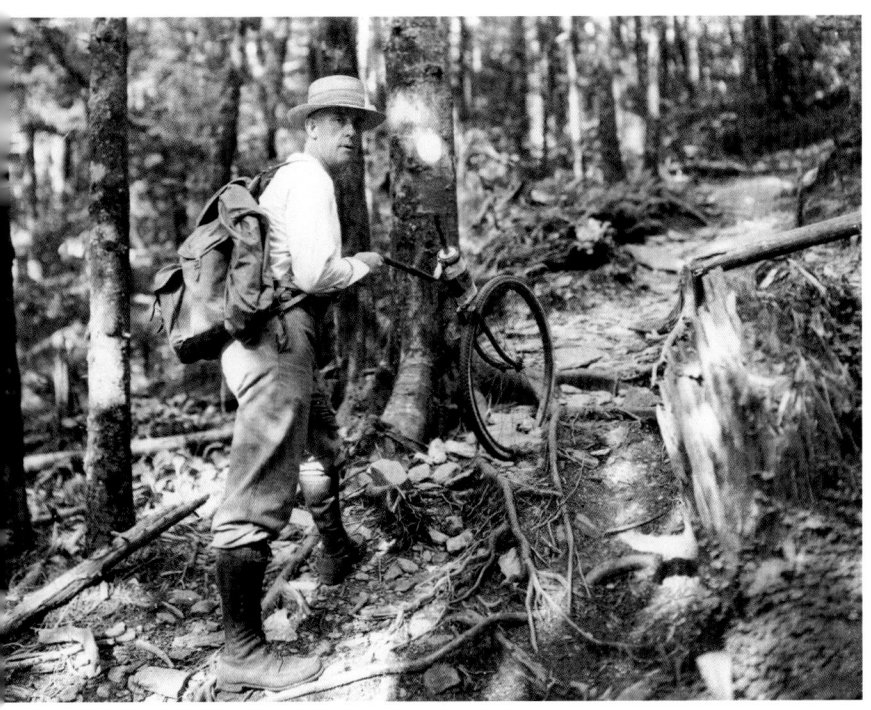

204   Jim Thompson measuring trail distance with a cyclometer somewhere in the Great Smoky Mountains. Courtesy of Knox County Public Library.

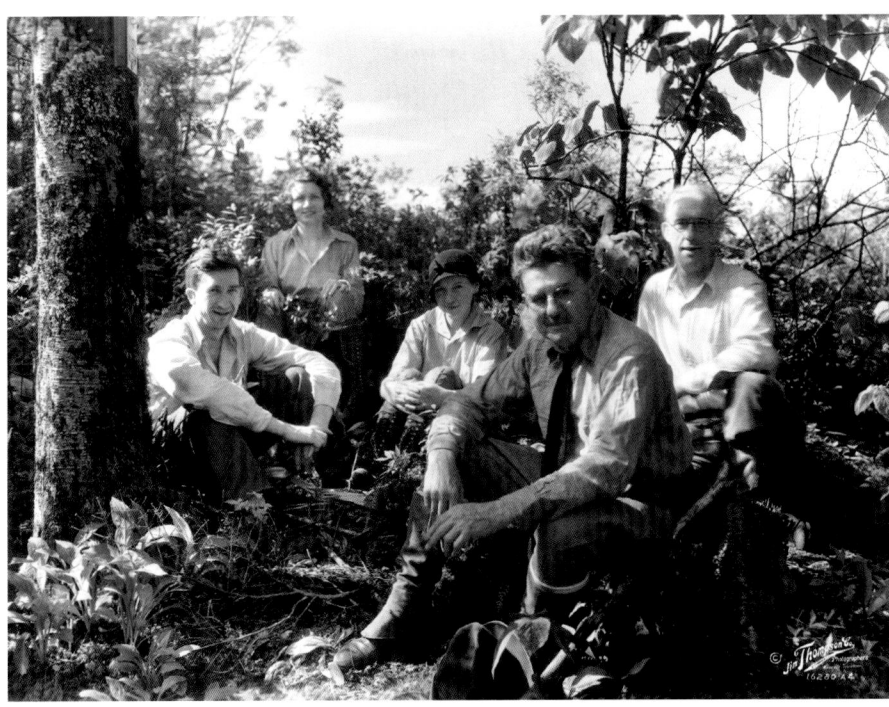

205   Colonel David Chapman (center) and group on the summit of Mount Chapman. Harvey Broome is on left and Jim Thompson, on the right. Back left is Mrs. Charles Myers and in center is Miss Mildred Query. Courtesy of Knox County Public Library.

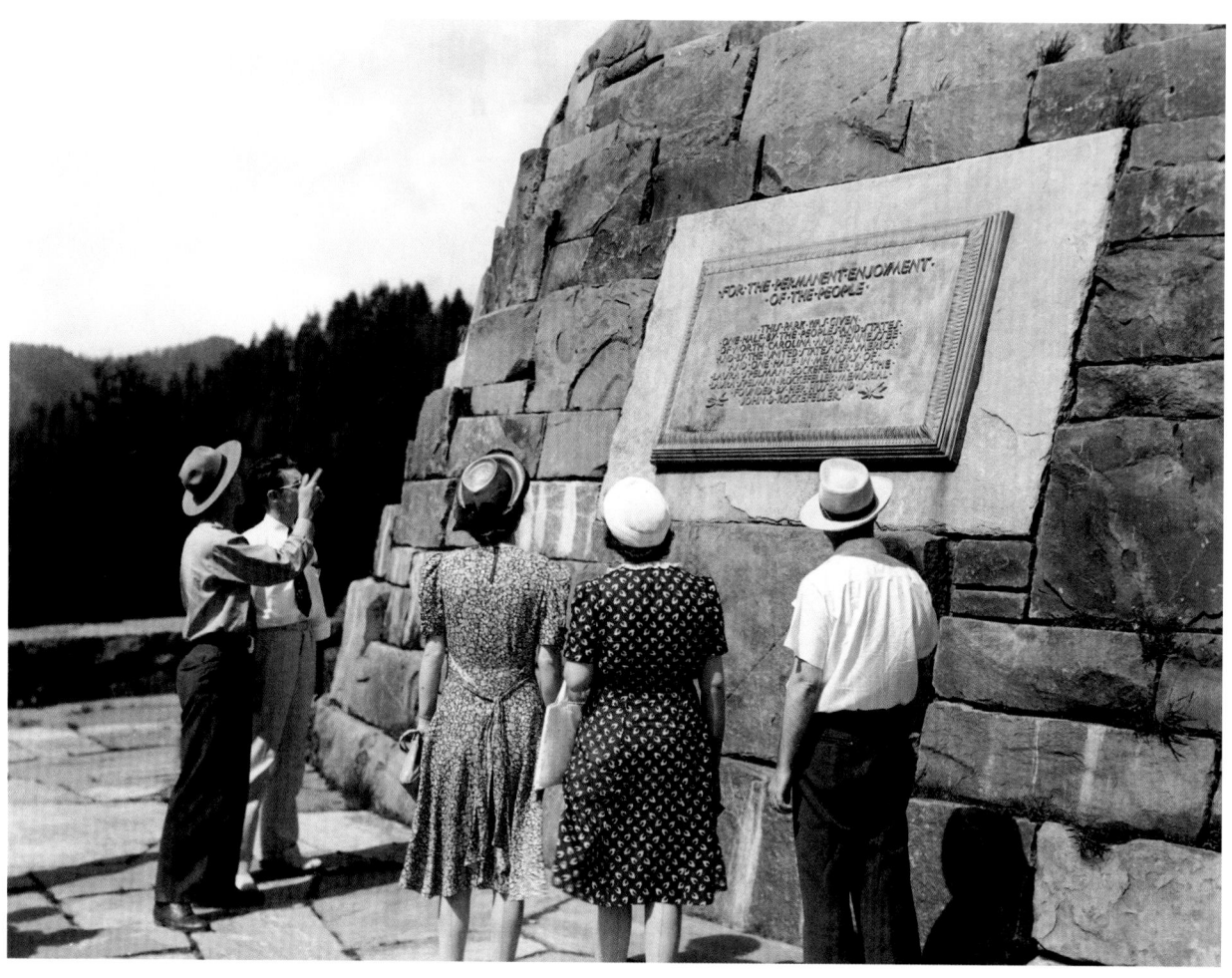

206   Visitors reading the plaque at the Rockefeller Memorial at Newfound Gap.
       Courtesy of Knox County Public Library.

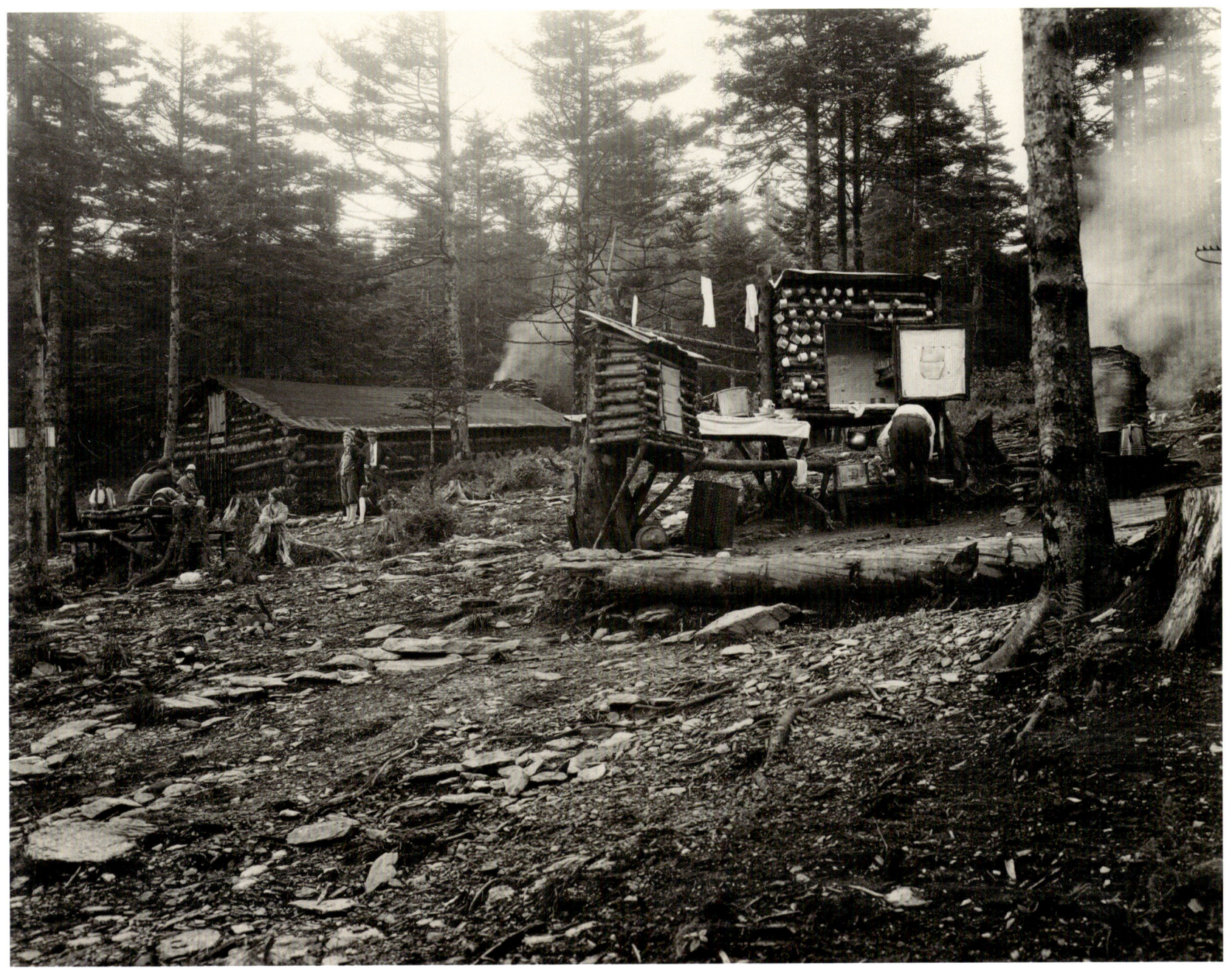

207   Preparing breakfast at the LeConte Lodge. Courtesy of the National Park Service.

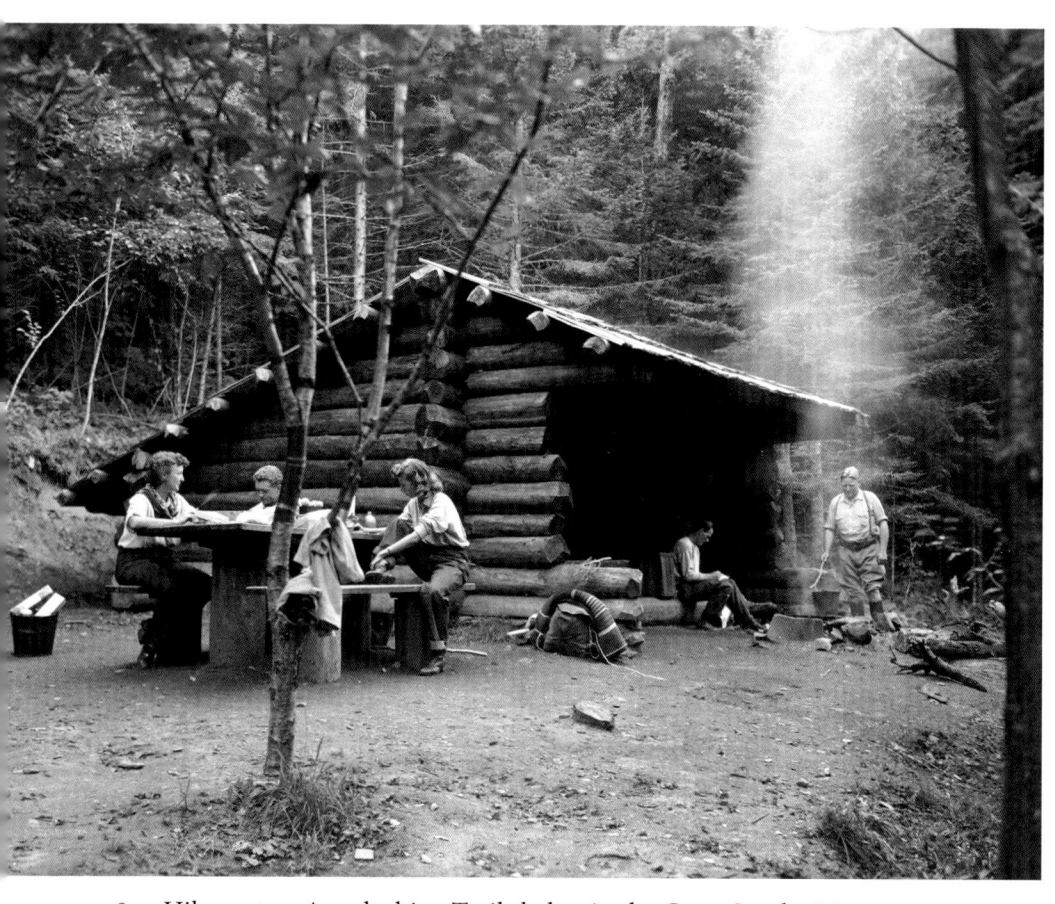

208   Hikers at an Appalachian Trail shelter in the Great Smoky Mountains
       National Park. Courtesy of Knox County Public Library.

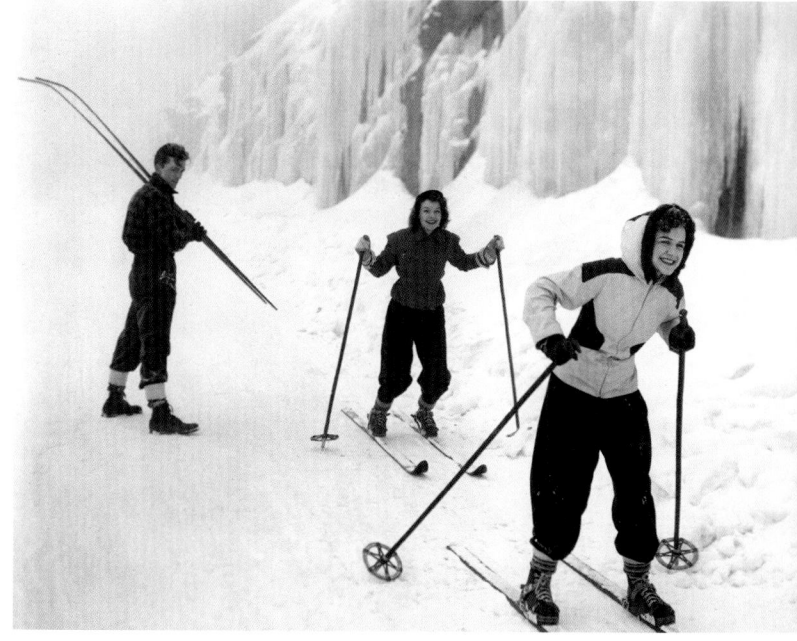

209   Skiers in the Smokies. Courtesy of Knox County
       Public Library.

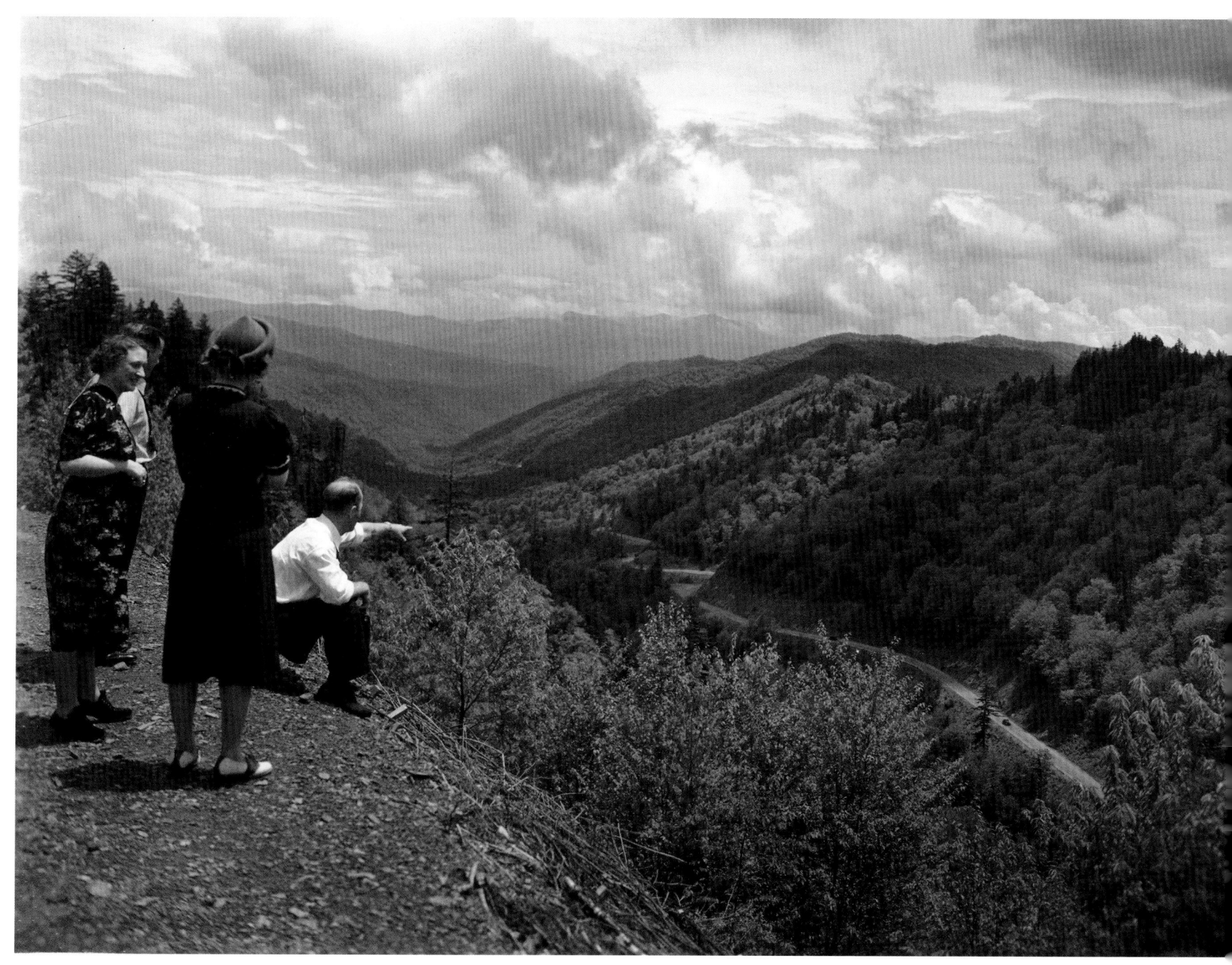

210   View looking into Oconaluftee Gorge. Courtesy of Knox County Public Library.

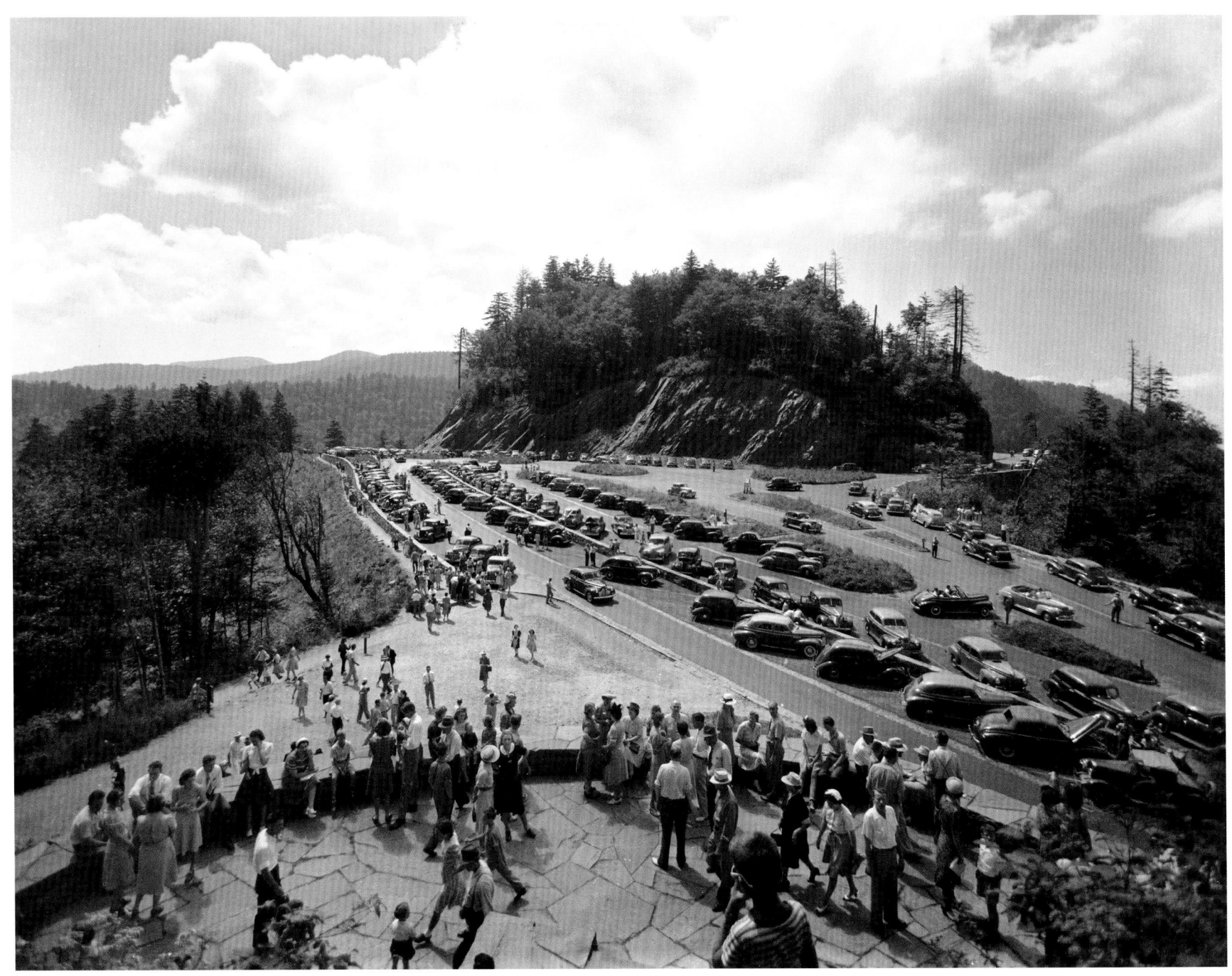

211   A busy day at Newfound Gap. View from Rockefeller Memorial. Courtesy of Knox County Public Library.

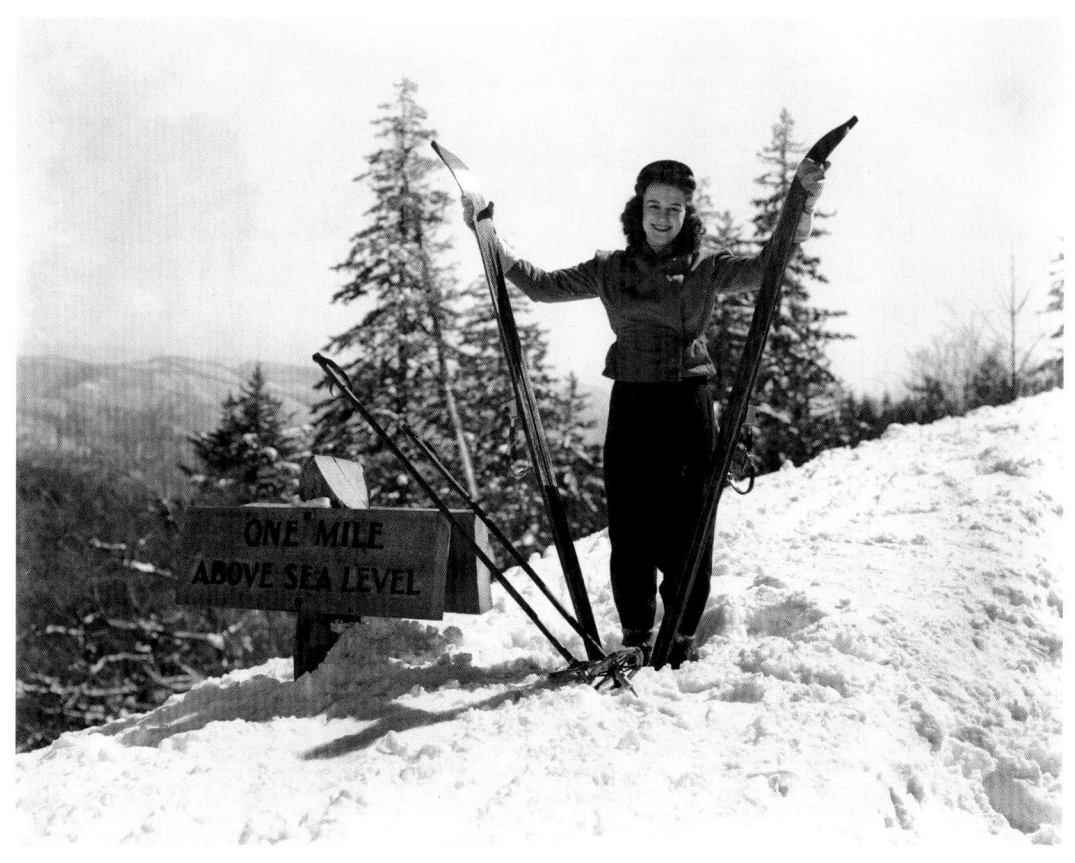

212   A skier in the Smokies at a mile above sea level.

       Courtesy of Knox County Public Library.

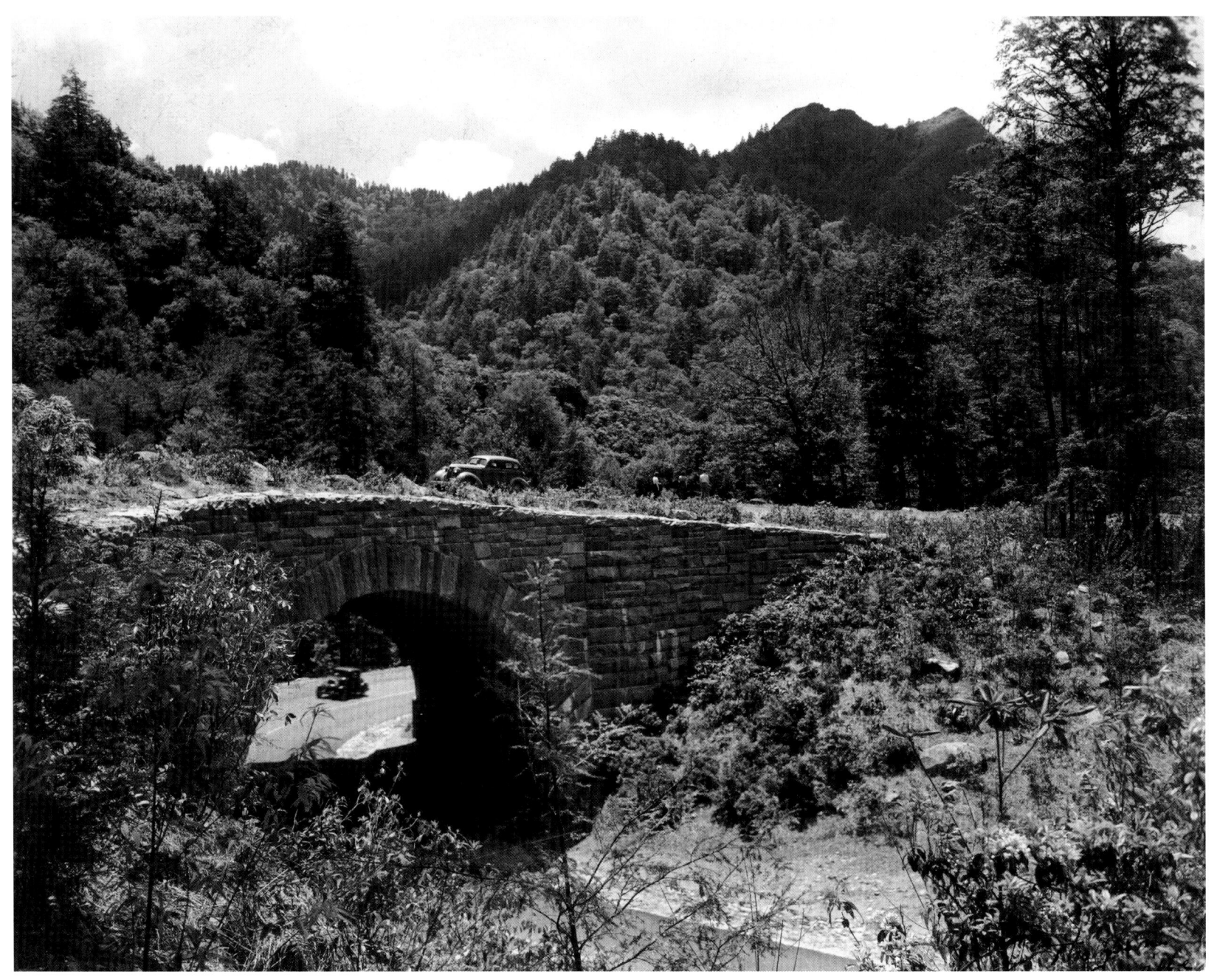

213   Automobiles on the Loop Bridge on the Newfound Gap Road. Courtesy of Knox County Public Library.

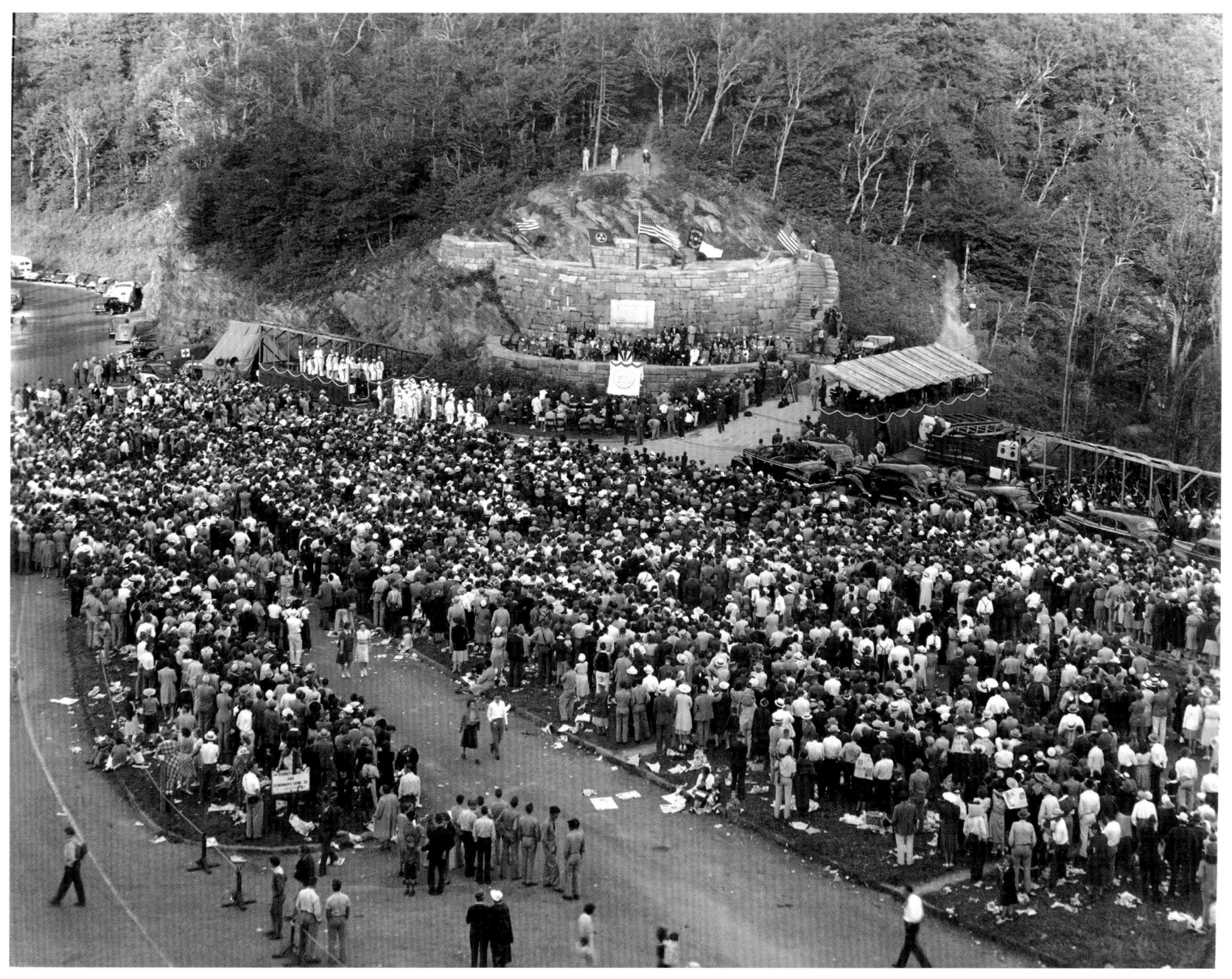

214   A crowd gathered to hear President Roosevelt dedicate Great Smoky Mountains National Park,
       September 2, 1940. Courtesy of Knox County Public Library.

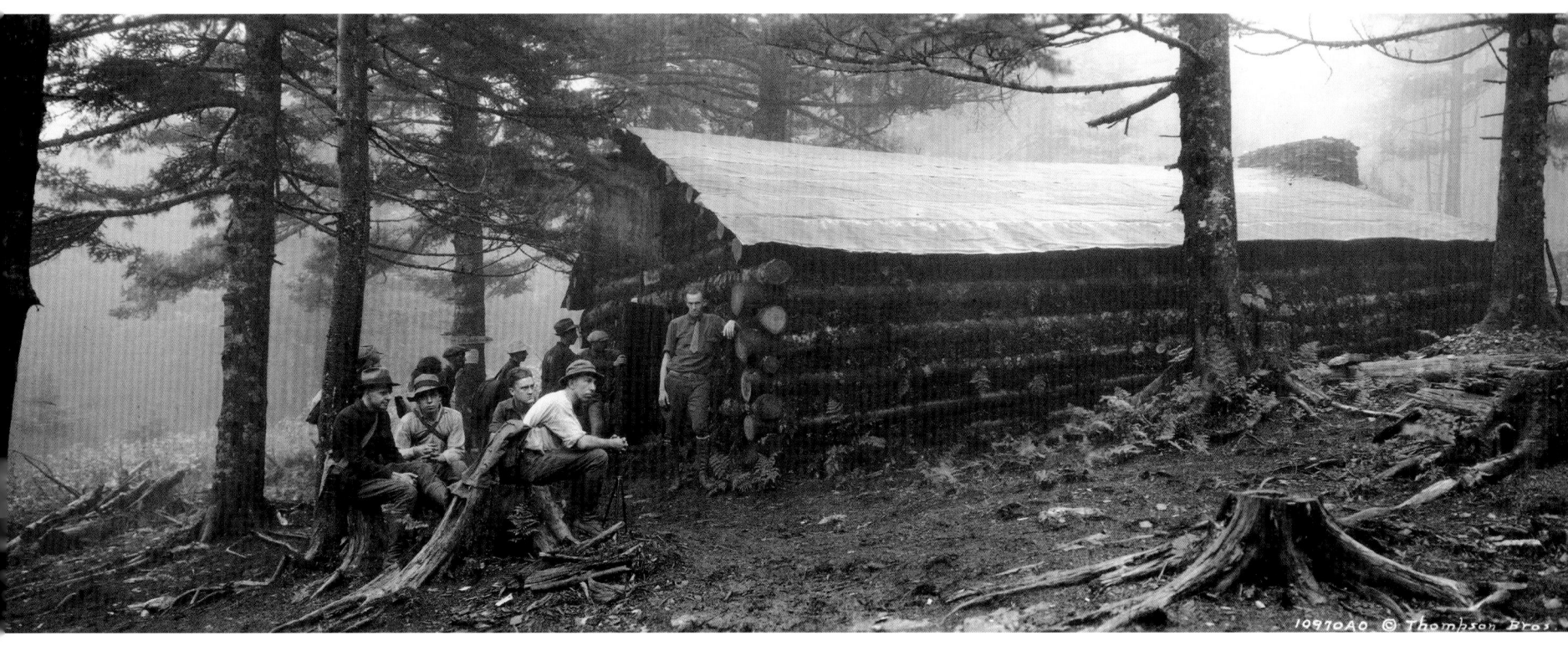

215   Hikers from the Smoky Mountains Hiking Club at LeConte Lodge in 1926.
Courtesy of Knox County Public Library.

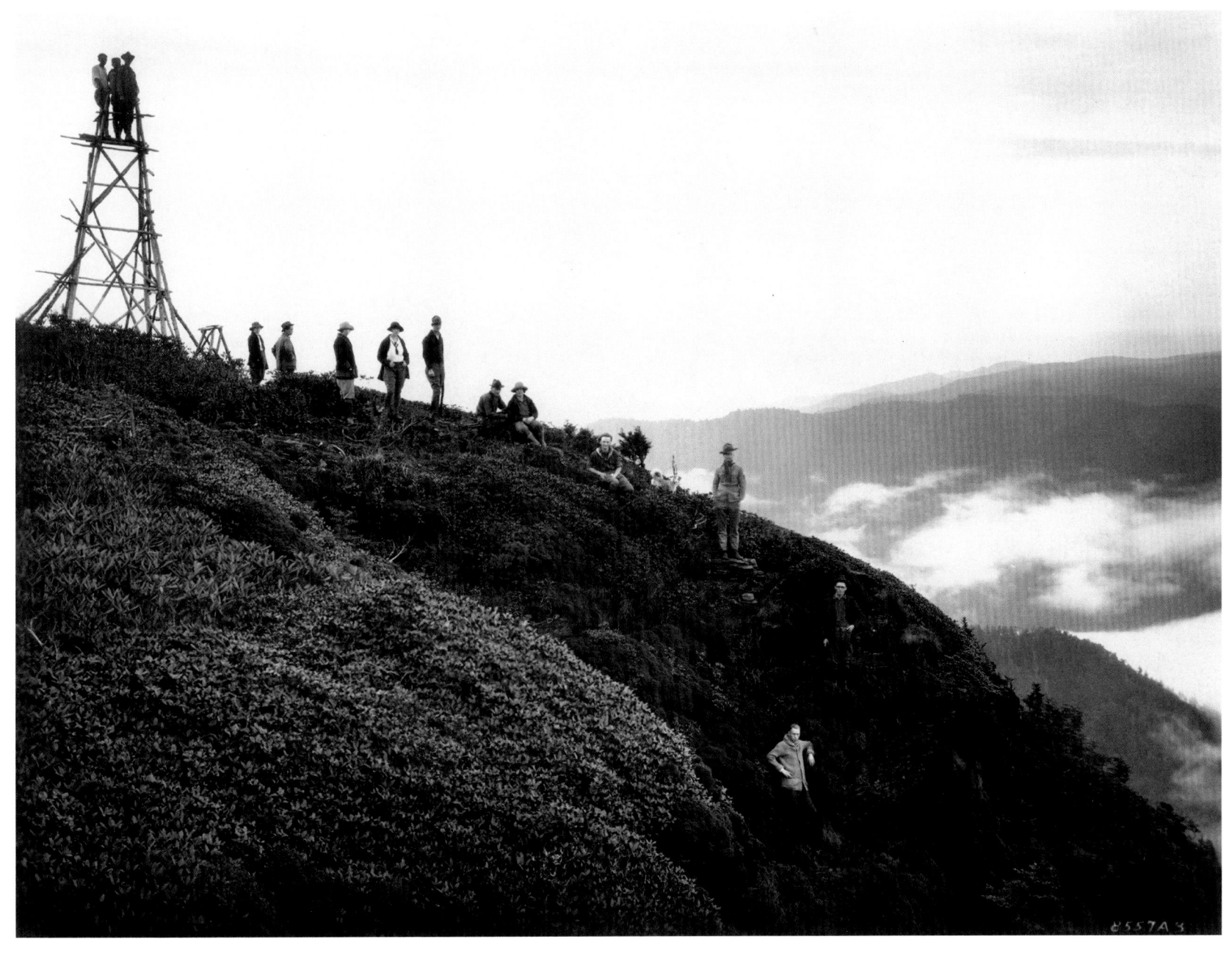

216   Hikers at tower on Mount LeConte in Great Smoky Mountains National Park.
Courtesy of Knox County Public Library.

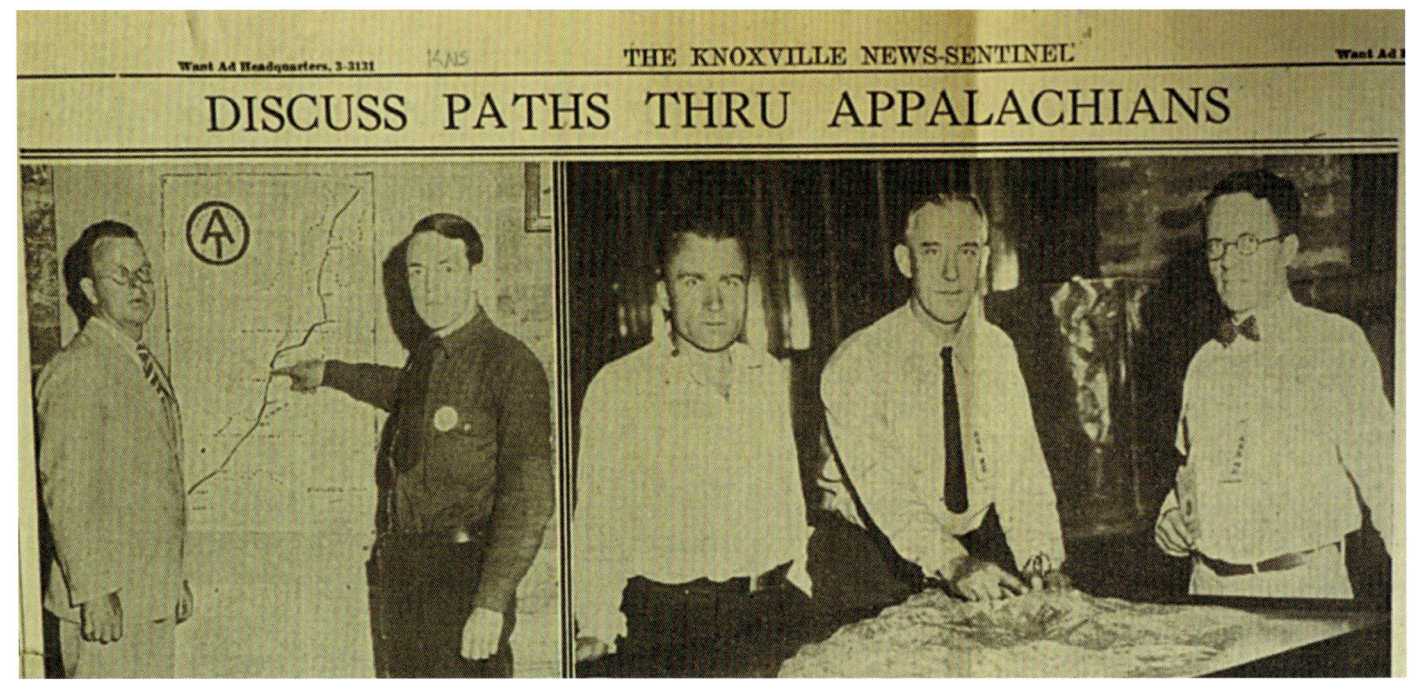

DISCUSS PATHS THRU APPALACHIANS

217   Attendees at the Appalachian Trail Conference meeting in Gatlinburg in
      June 1931 discussing paths through the Appalachians. The left image features
      Reid Russell and George Stephens; the right image features Myron Avery,
      Jim Thompson, and Dr. H. M. Jemmison.Courtesy of Knox County
      Public Library.

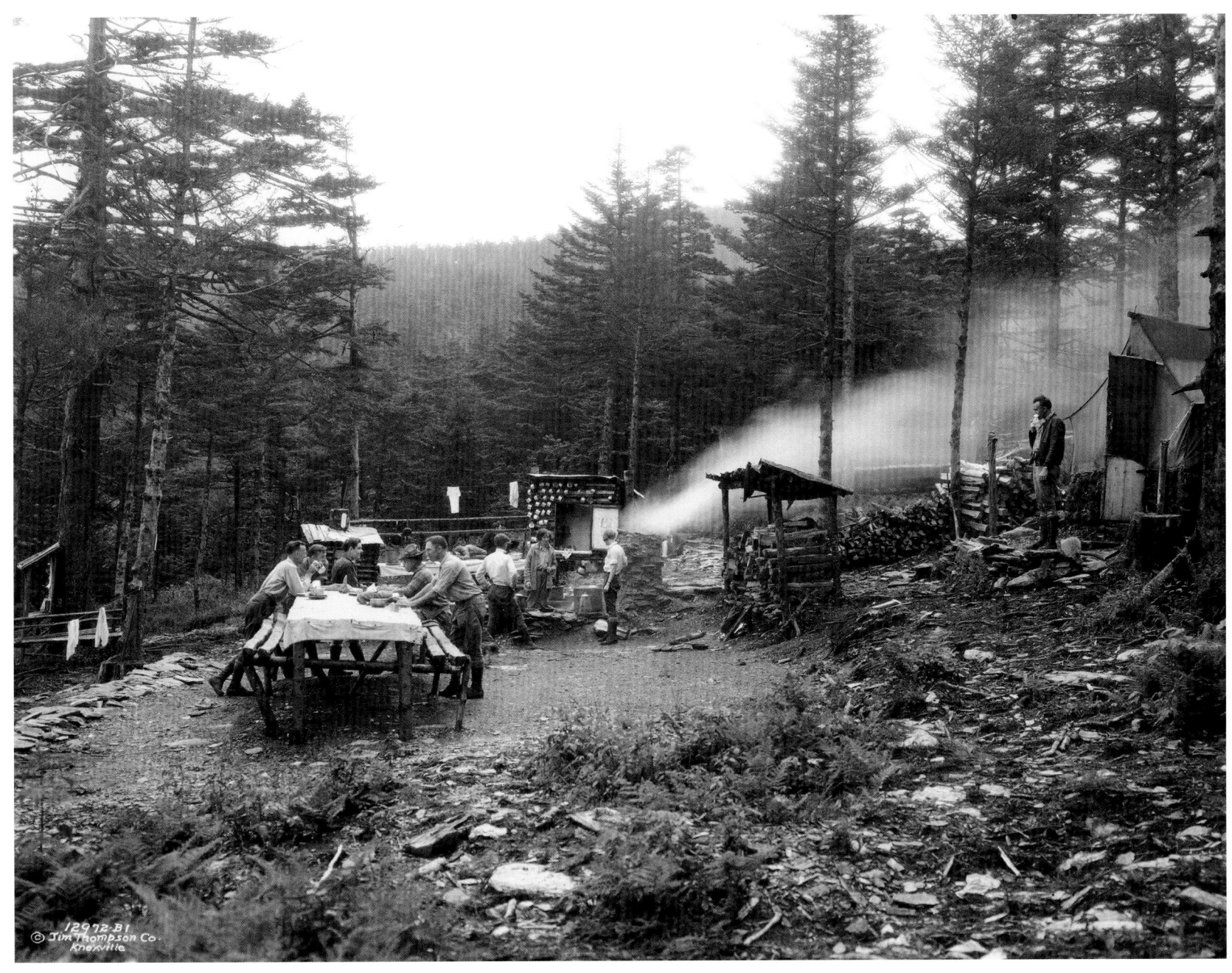

218   Mealtime at camp on Mount LeConte in Great Smokies. Courtesy of Knox County Public Library.

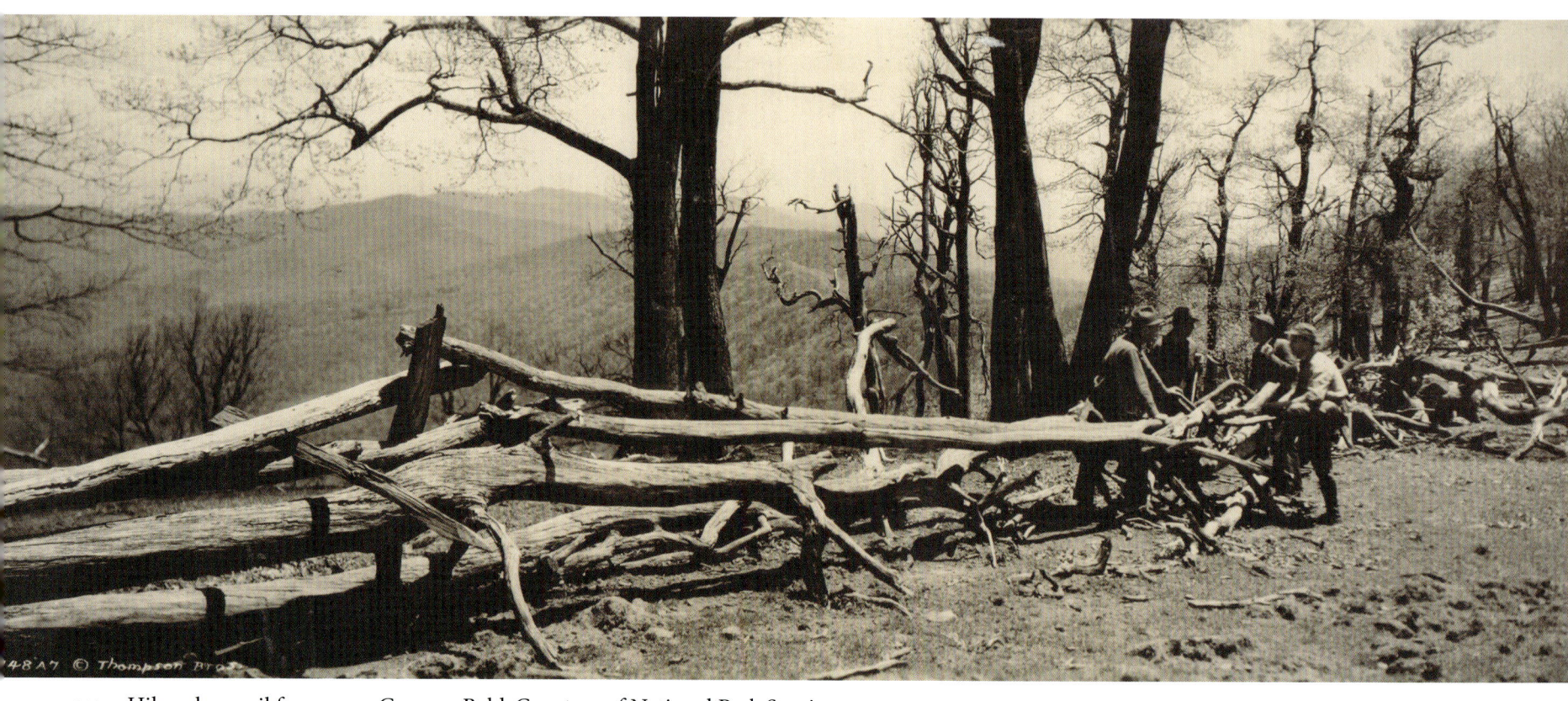

219   Hikers by a rail fence near Gregory Bald. Courtesy of National Park Service.

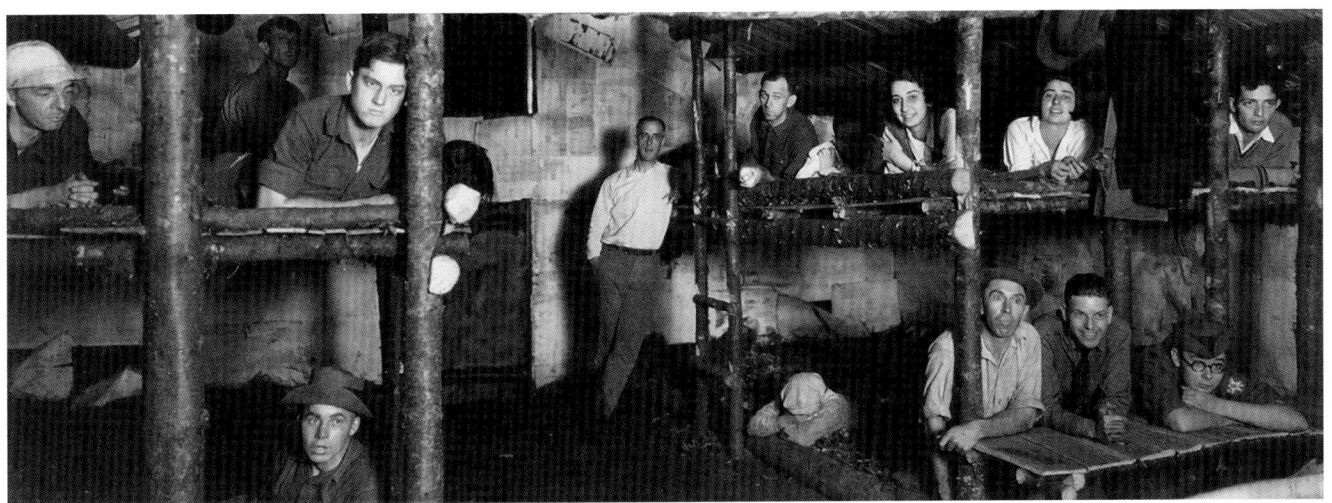

220   Smoky Mountain Hiking Club hikers at LeConte Lodge, with Jim Thompson standing in center.
       Courtesy of University of Tennessee–Knoxville, Hodges Library.

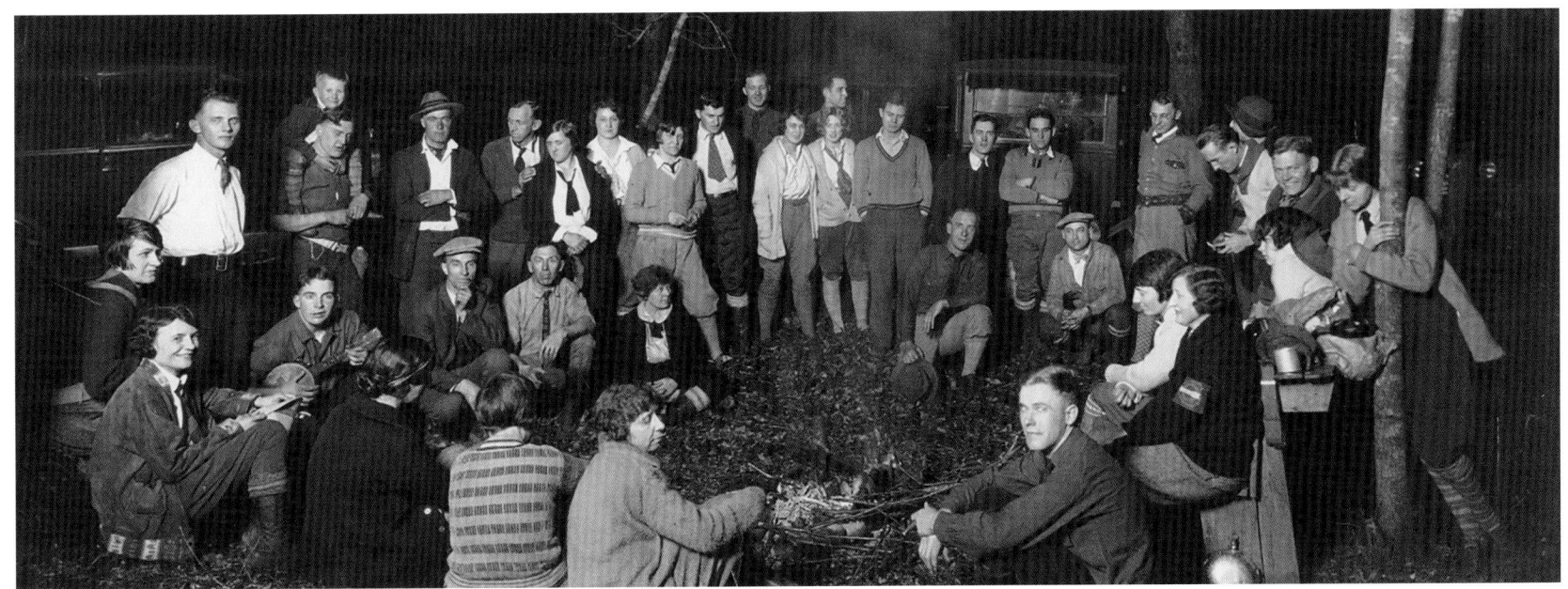

221   Smoky Mountain Hiking Club hikers at LeConte Lodge. Courtesy of University of Tennessee Library Special Collections.

Tools of Their Craft

Cameras Used by George Masa and Jim Thompson

The scene is a familiar one today. An automobile pulls into a park's scenic overlook; a passenger steps out, snaps a few pictures with a cell phone camera, returns to the car, and leaves. Or, perhaps, a photography enthusiast sets up a tripod with a digital single lens reflex (SLR) camera and uses a remote shutter button to shoot multiple images that will later be edited on a computer. It is difficult to imagine what great landscape photographers from the past, like William Henry Jackson, Ansel Adams, Eliot Porter, George Grant, George Masa, and Jim Thompson, would have made of this.

These artists dedicated their careers to capturing powerful landscape images, carrying large, heavy view cameras, film holders, tripods, and other accessories to shooting locations, often in remote areas. There they waited, sometimes for hours, for the ideal lighting to capture a photograph they may have visualized in their mind beforehand. For them, clicking the shutter was the culmination of careful planning, research, and deep immersion in the natural landscape. In many ways, these photographers' cameras were more than a tool. They were an extension of themselves.

Like many of their contemporaries, George Masa and Jim Thompson used two types of cameras for much of their landscape work. Their primary tool was an Eastman View 2 camera in 5×7 or 8×10 format or a Follmer & Schwing 8×10 camera. (The numbers represent the dimensions in inches of the film sheet.) A 5×7 camera was lighter for use in more remote destinations, while the 8×10 was better suited to studios or locations close to roads or trails.

Developed in the late nineteenth century, these cameras remain popular with dedicated enthusiasts. Their design is simple, featuring a front section that holds an interchangeable lens and a rear section with a focusing screen and a slot for a sheet of film in a light-tight holder. The sections are joined by flexible bellows, which may be adjusted or tilted for perspective. The cameras frequently include a hood so that the photographer can clearly see the focusing screen and adjust the lens setting accordingly. Unlike with modern cameras, these images would appear upside down and backward, requiring the artist's skill and experience to compose the scene and determine the proper exposure of the final image. (In modern reflex cameras, a pentaprism corrects the image so that it appears in the viewfinder as the eye sees it.) To take a second photograph, the photographer would seal the exposed negative in the light-tight holder and then remove it so that another sheet of film could be inserted and the process repeated.

In addition to these "workhorse" cameras, photographers occasionally used other types of equipment. Thompson

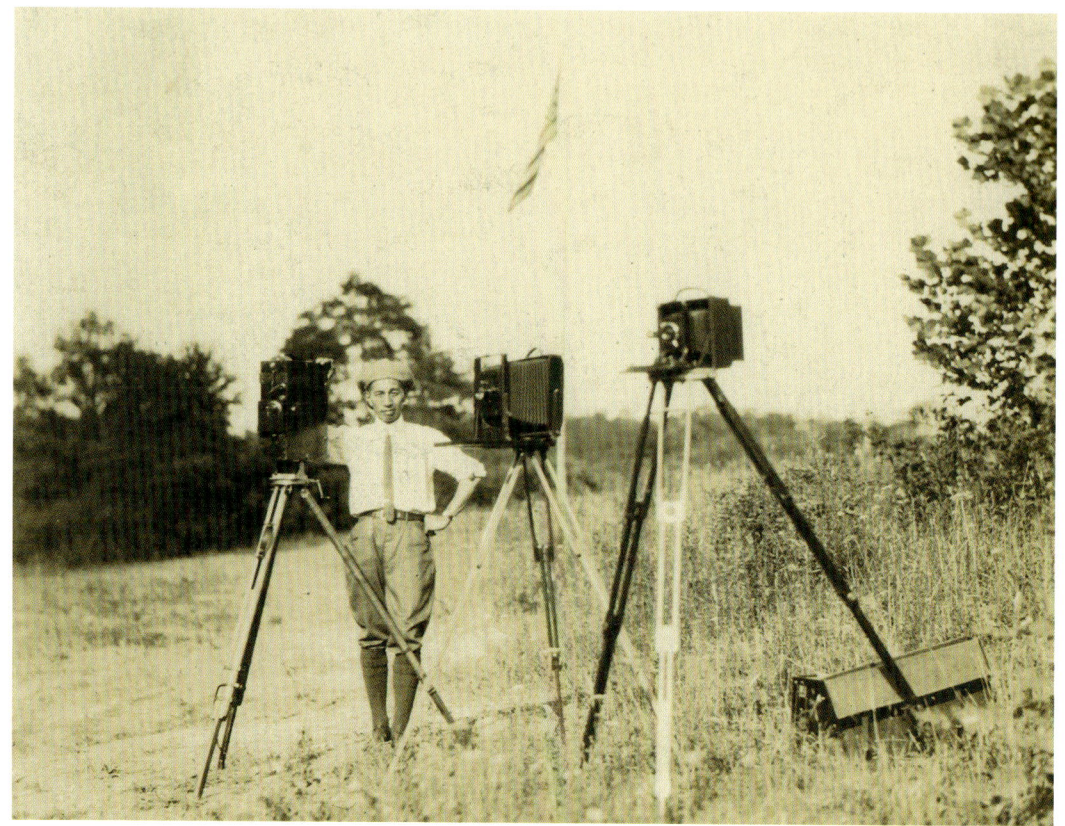

George Masa with his cameras: a Cirkut 10 camera, an 8×10 camera, and a 5×7 camera, ca. 1920s. Photographer unconfirmed; likely by Masa using tripod, but potentially by Blake Creasman. Buncombe County Special Collections, Pack Memorial Library.

was known to use a Leica 35 mm camera, while both he and Masa employed a specialized Eastman Cirkut 10 camera. First developed in 1904, the Cirkut camera was a sophisticated device designed to produce panoramic images. The camera body rested on a gear-driven clockwork motor attached to a tripod, which could rotate the camera up to 360 degrees. The camera utilized rolls of film at the desired width (for a Cirkut 10, the film would be ten inches wide and could be several feet in length). After loading the film, the photographer would adjust the motor to the desired number of degrees, set the aperture, and click the

shutter, activating the rotation. The resulting image would be a long, narrow photograph displaying a wide view of the subject. While Masa and Thompson utilized their Cirkut cameras principally for landscapes, these types of cameras were also popular for producing photographs of large groups.

Capturing an image in the field was only the first step a photographer would take to create a finished print. After returning to the studio, he or she would process the exposed film in a darkroom, using water and photo chemicals to produce a negative that could then be made into a contact print in its native dimension (5×7, 8×10, etc.) or enlarged to the desired size. The photographer would follow a similar development process to produce the final images from the panoramic rolls, while production of the final prints required specialized trays, negative holders, and enlargers.

The long, often tedious, and difficult tasks undertaken by George Masa and Jim Thompson yielded extraordinary works of art that captured both singular moments in time in the Appalachian Mountains and the timeless beauty of the landscape. A century later, they remain powerful visual testaments to the power of imagery to "move mountains."

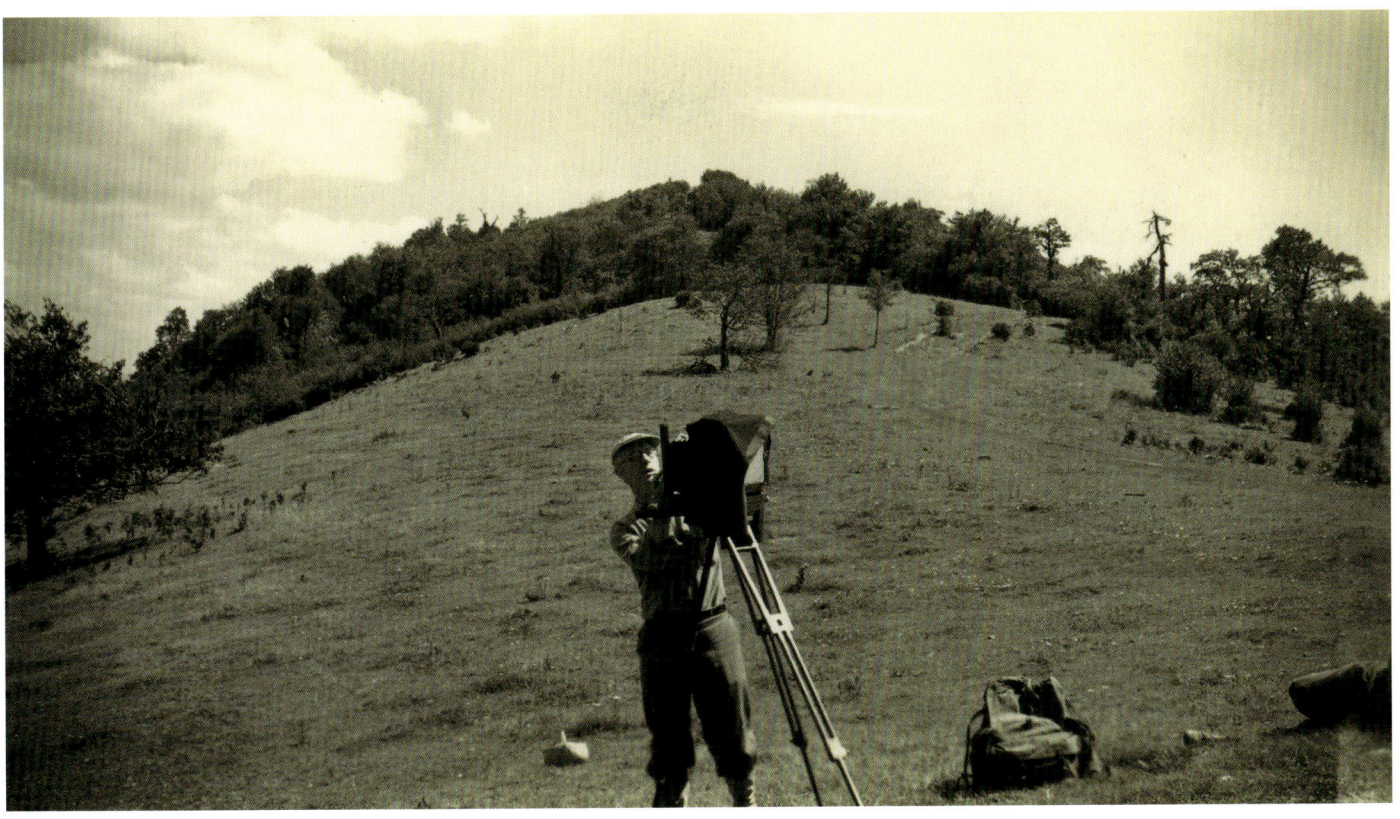

Jim Thompson sets up his field camera on Cold Springs Mountain, September 10, 1934. Photograph by Carlos Campbell. National Park Service, Great Smoky Mountains National Park Collections Preservation Center, Jim Thompson Collection.

George Masa

Master Mapmaker

George Masa may be best remembered for his evocative photographs that influenced the efforts to create Great Smoky Mountains National Park and blaze the Appalachian Trail through the southern mountains. Yet the meticulous attention to detail and accuracy of the maps he created from his mountain treks proved equally indispensable to achieving these goals. Beginning with careful notations of distances (calculated with his measuring wheel) and topographic line drawings sketched in his hiking notebooks, George Masa was obsessed with exploring the many contours of the landscape and recording the information necessary for finishing maps that would be used by park advocates, the state nomenclature committees, the Appalachian Trail Conference, and the National Park Service.

Below are selected examples of the maps and field notes George Masa produced.

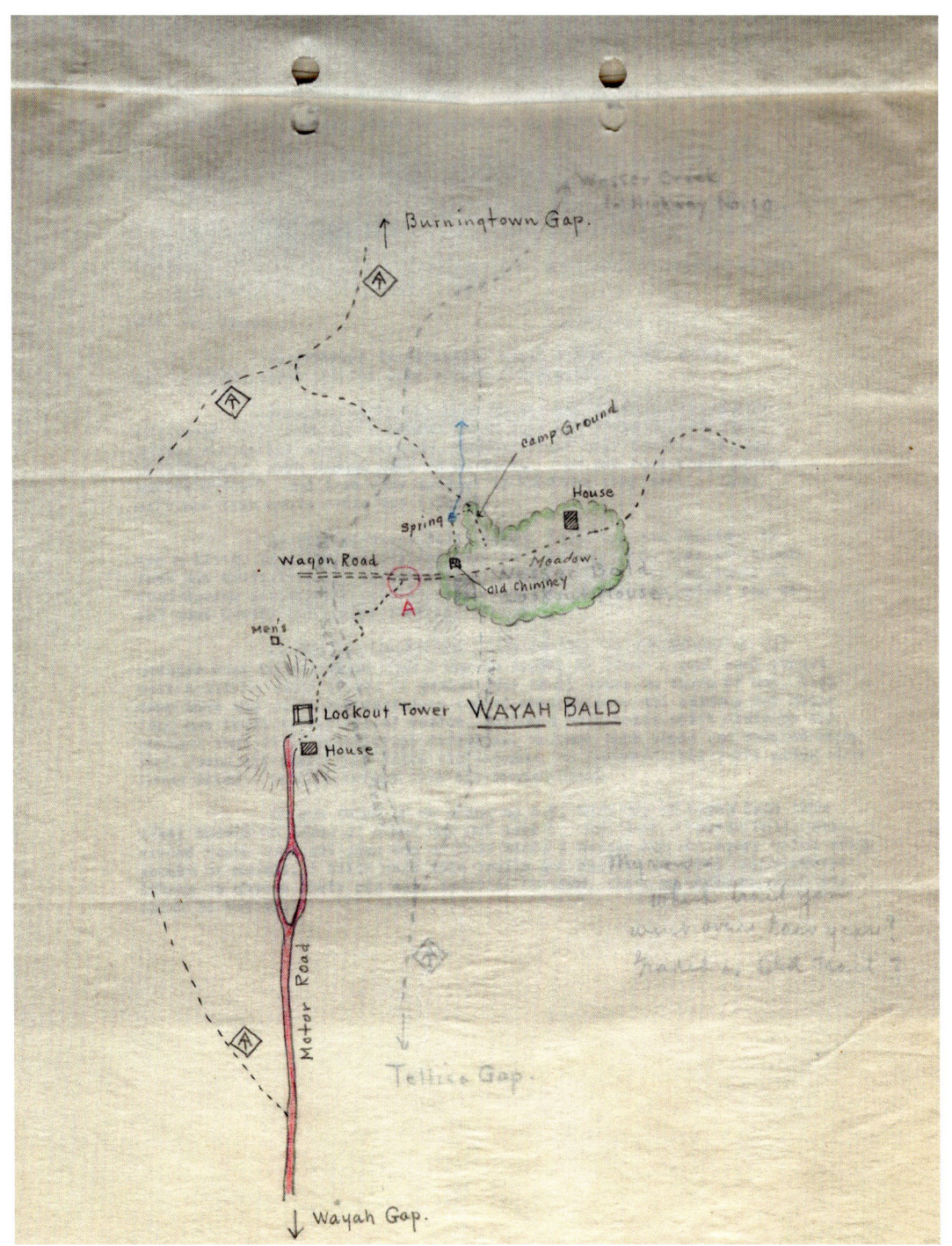

George Masa's hand-drawn map of the AT near Wayah Bald. Scanned by Ren and Helen Davis. Buncombe County Special Collections, Pack Memorial Library.

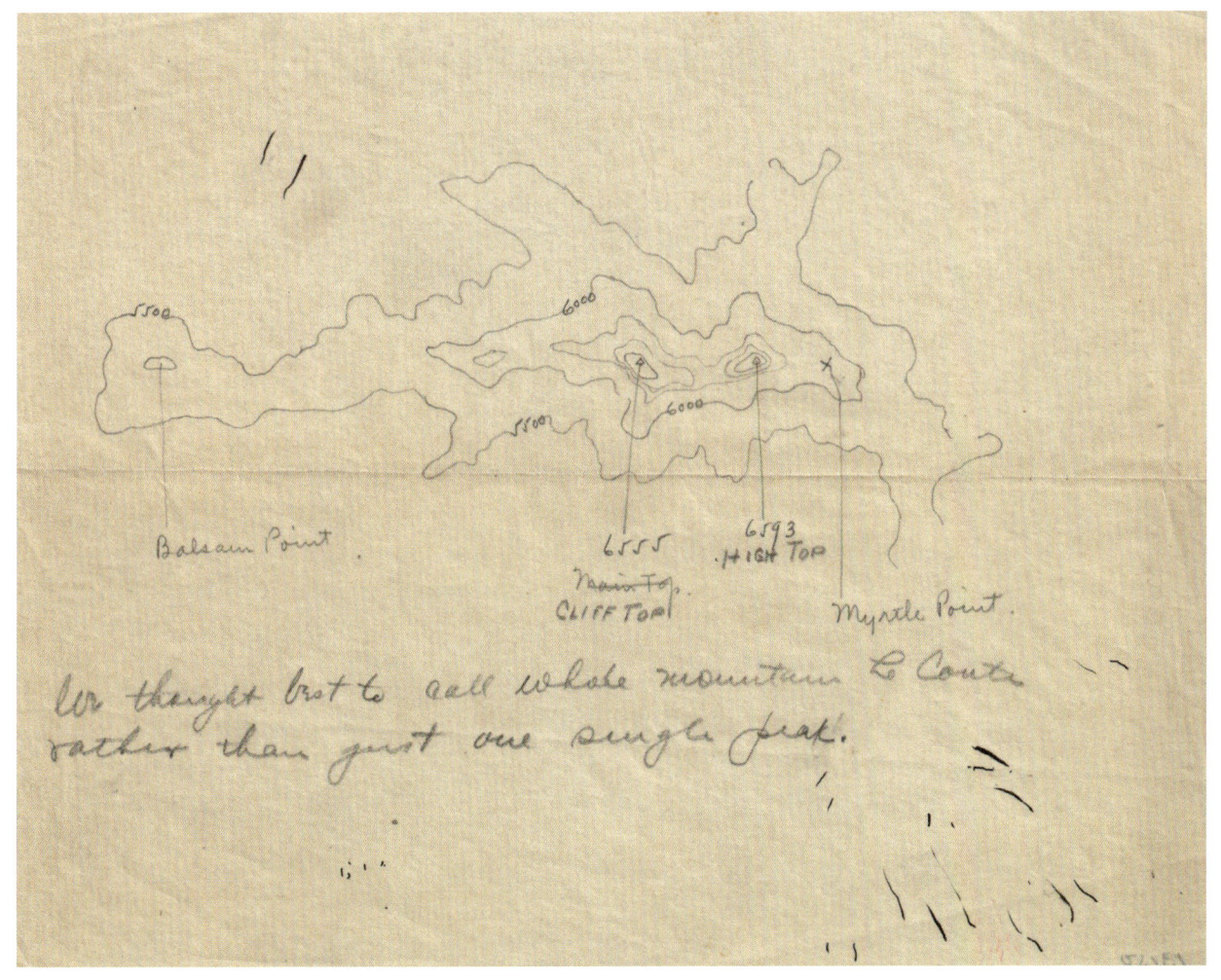

George Masa's hand-drawn map of the Mount LeConte area in Great Smoky Mountains National Park. Scanned by Ren and Helen Davis. National Park Service, Great Smoky Mountains National Park Collections Preservation Center, George Masa Collection.

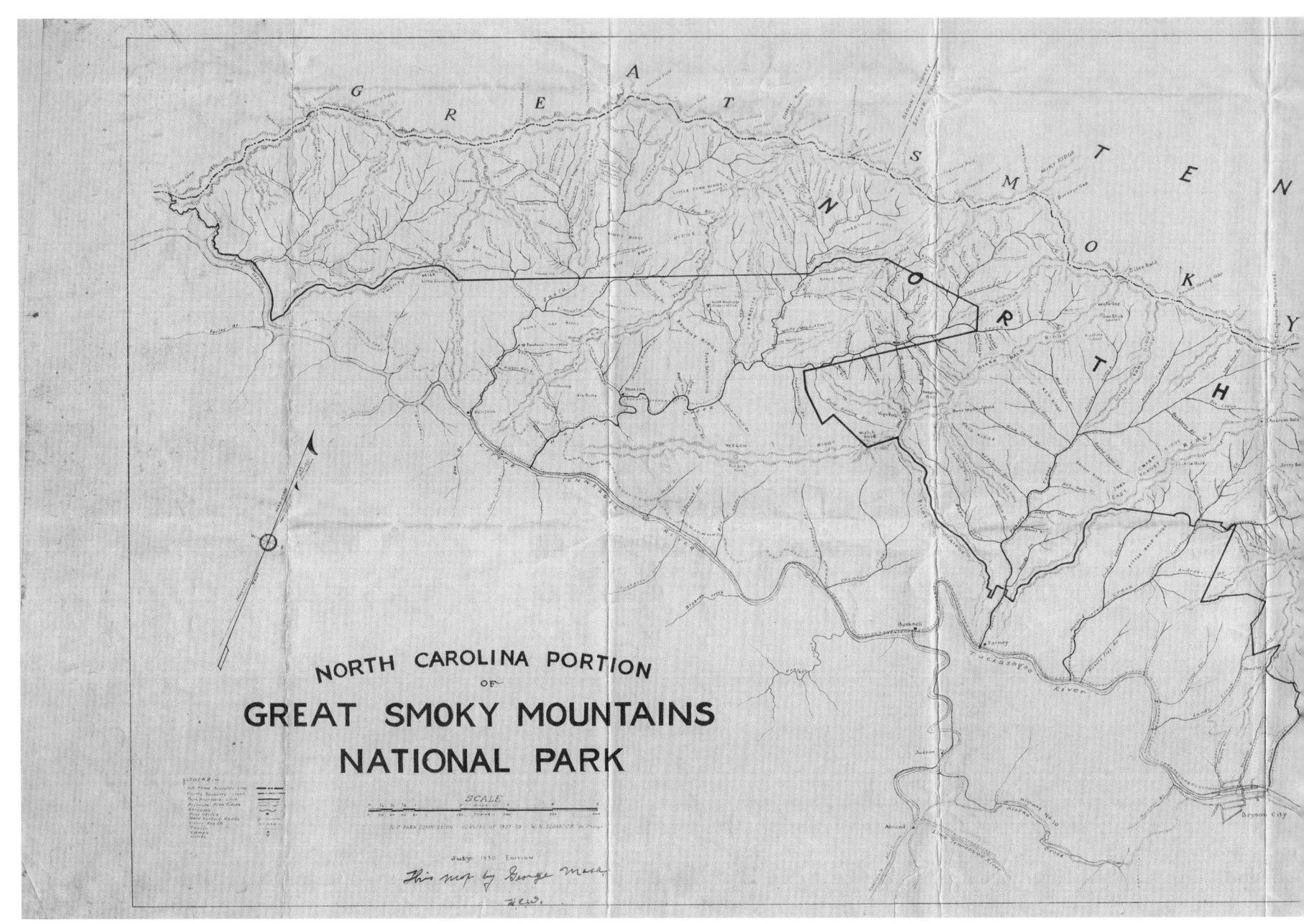

A map of the North Carolina section of the Great Smoky Mountains National Park, 1930 (based on 1927–28 survey by N.C. Park Commission). Buncombe County Special Collections, Pack Memorial Library.

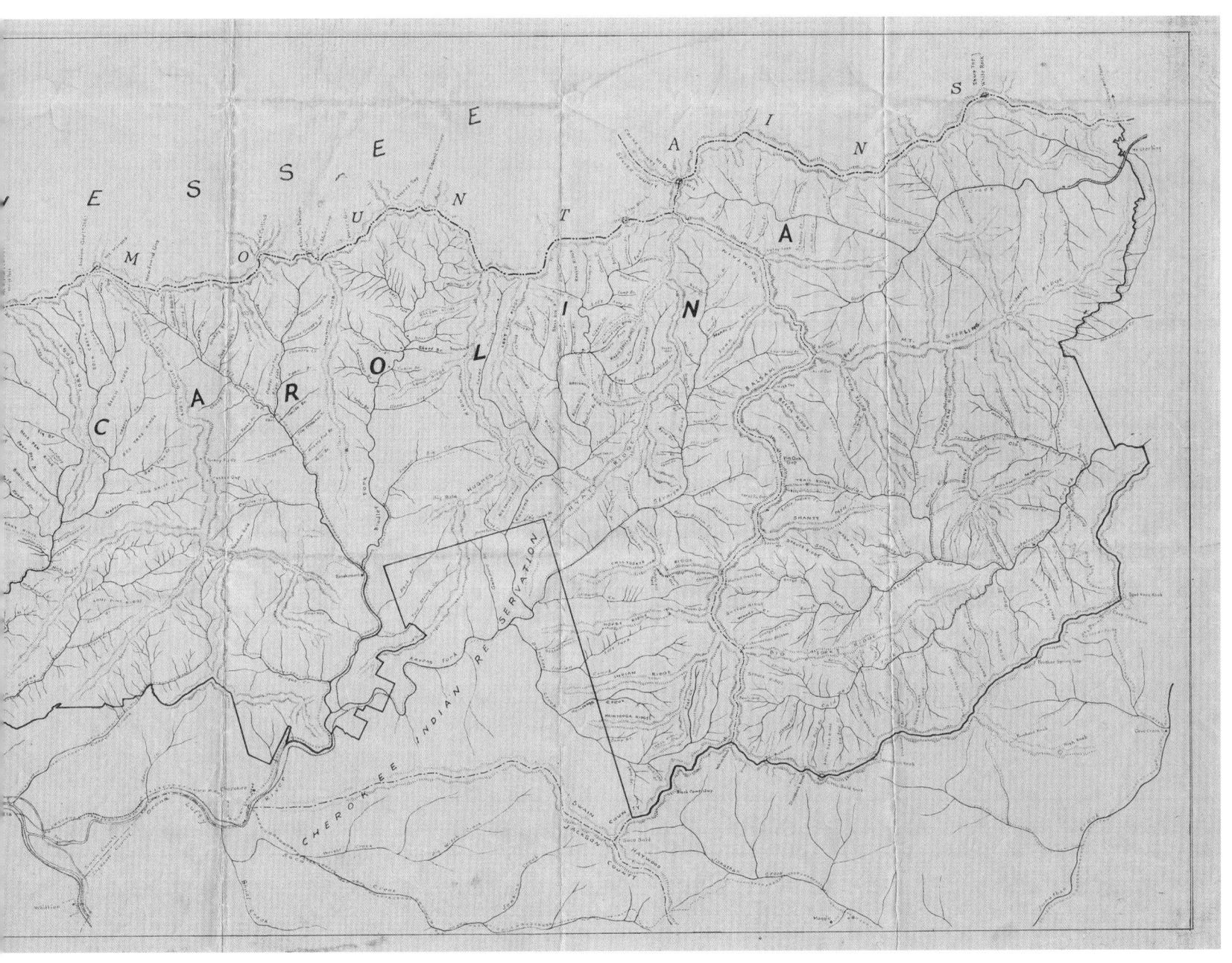

257

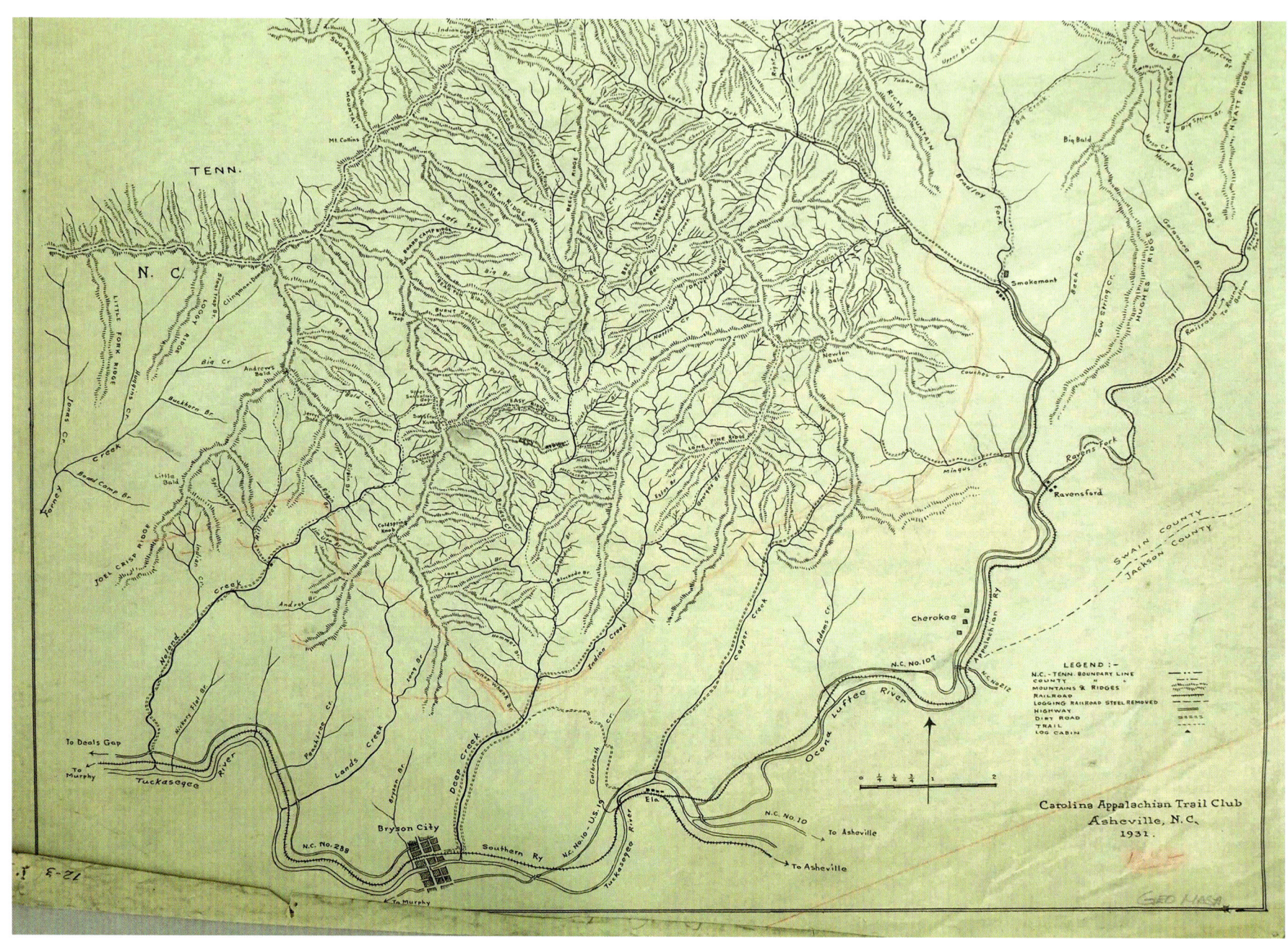

Hand-drawn map created for the Carolina Appalachian Trail Club of a section of Great Smoky Mountains National Park, near Bryson City, 1931. Likely drawn by George Masa, scanned by Ren and Helen Davis. National Park Service, Great Smoky Mountains National Park Collections Preservation Center, George Masa Collection.

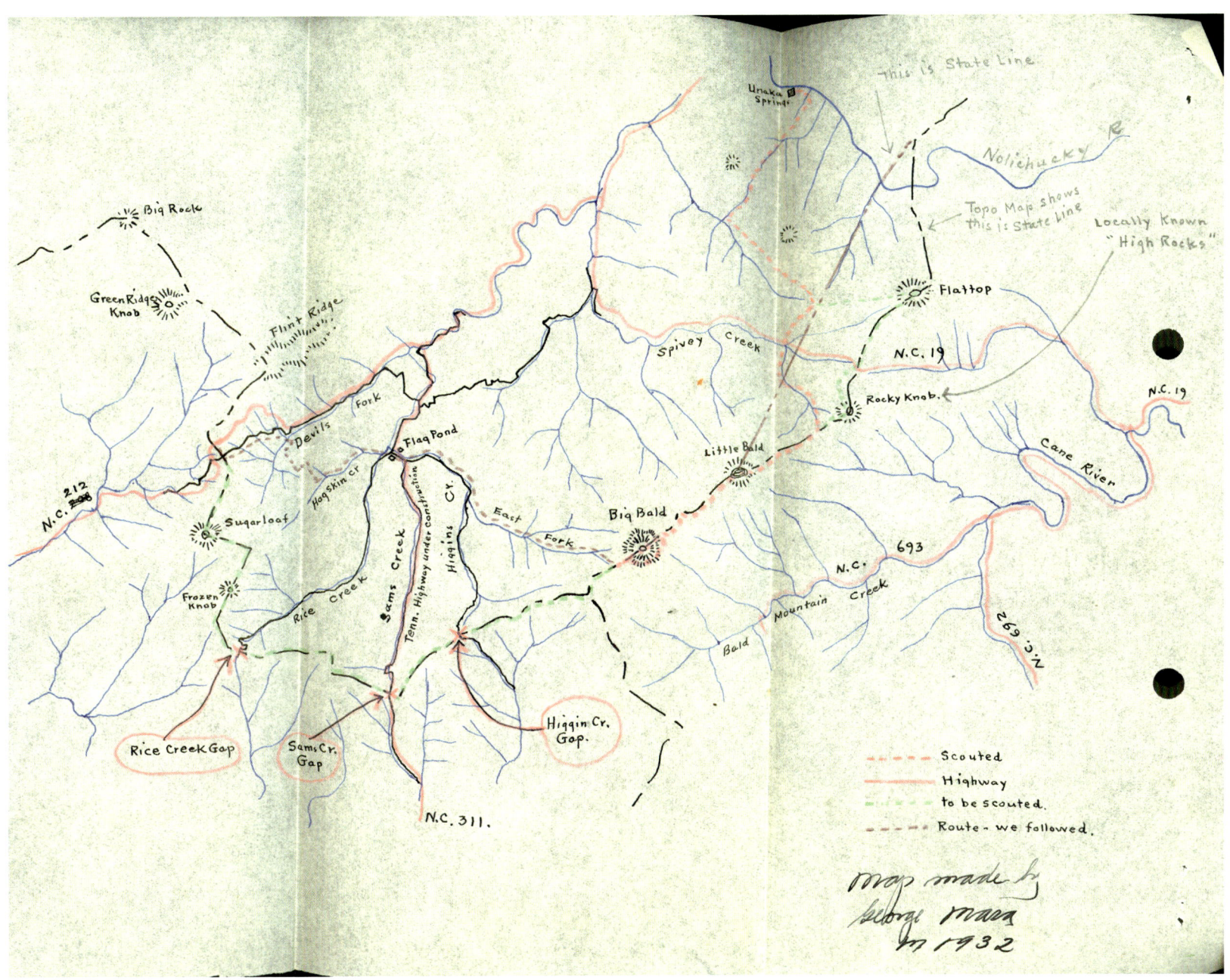

George Masa's scouting map of the Big Bald area for the ATC, created 1932. Appalachian Trail
Conference Collection, Myron Avery Collection, Special Collections and Archives,
George Mason University Libraries.

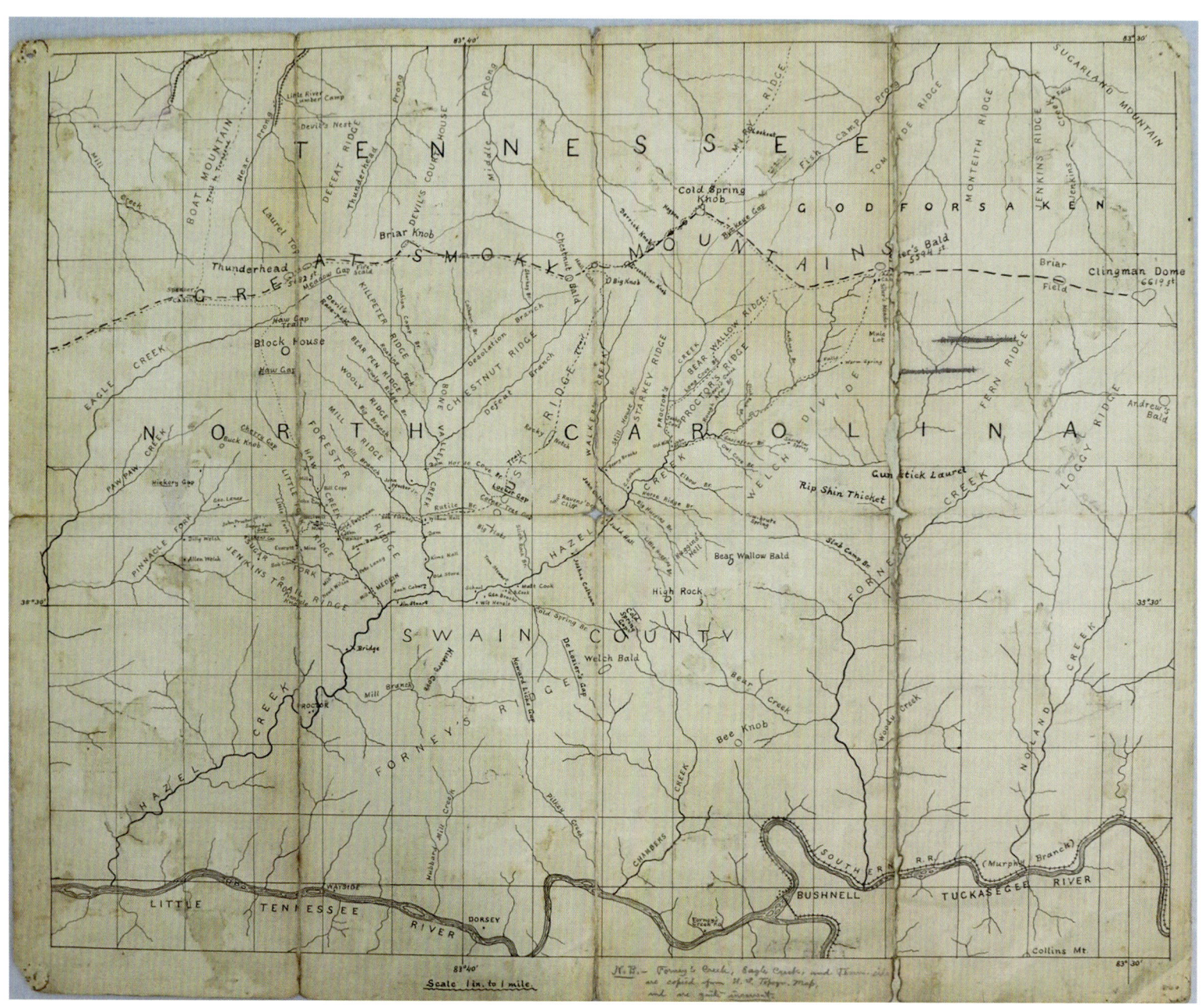

George Masa's hand-drawn map of the Hazel Creek area of Great Smoky Mountains National Park, 1930.
Scanned by Ren and Helen Davis. National Park Service, Great Smoky Mountains National Park
Collections Preservation Center, George Masa Collection.

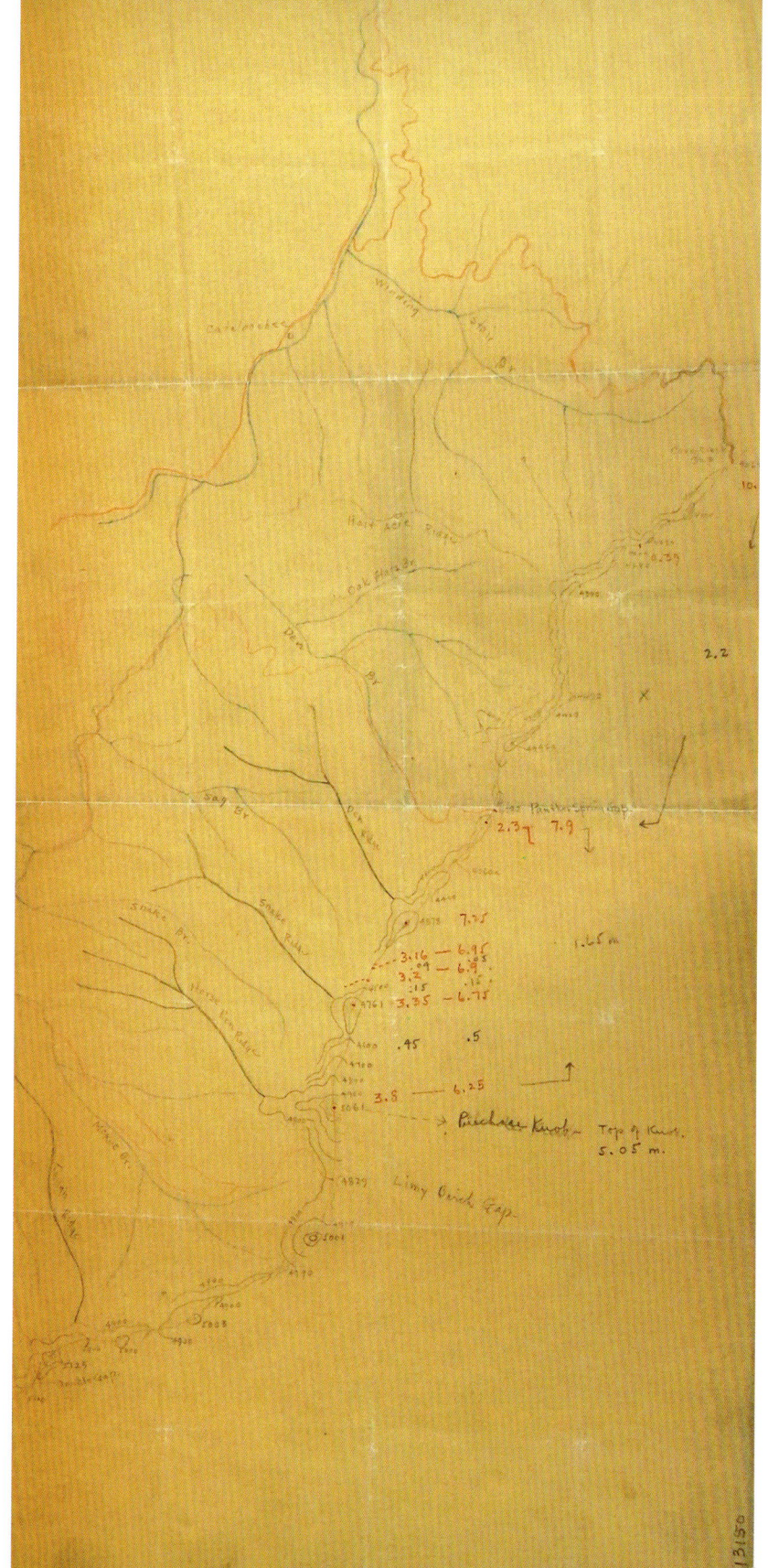

Map of Purchase Gap area with detailed notes on topography, landscape, and distances, year unknown. Scanned by Ren and Helen Davis. National Park Service, Great Smoky Mountains National Park Collections Preservation Center, George Masa Collection.

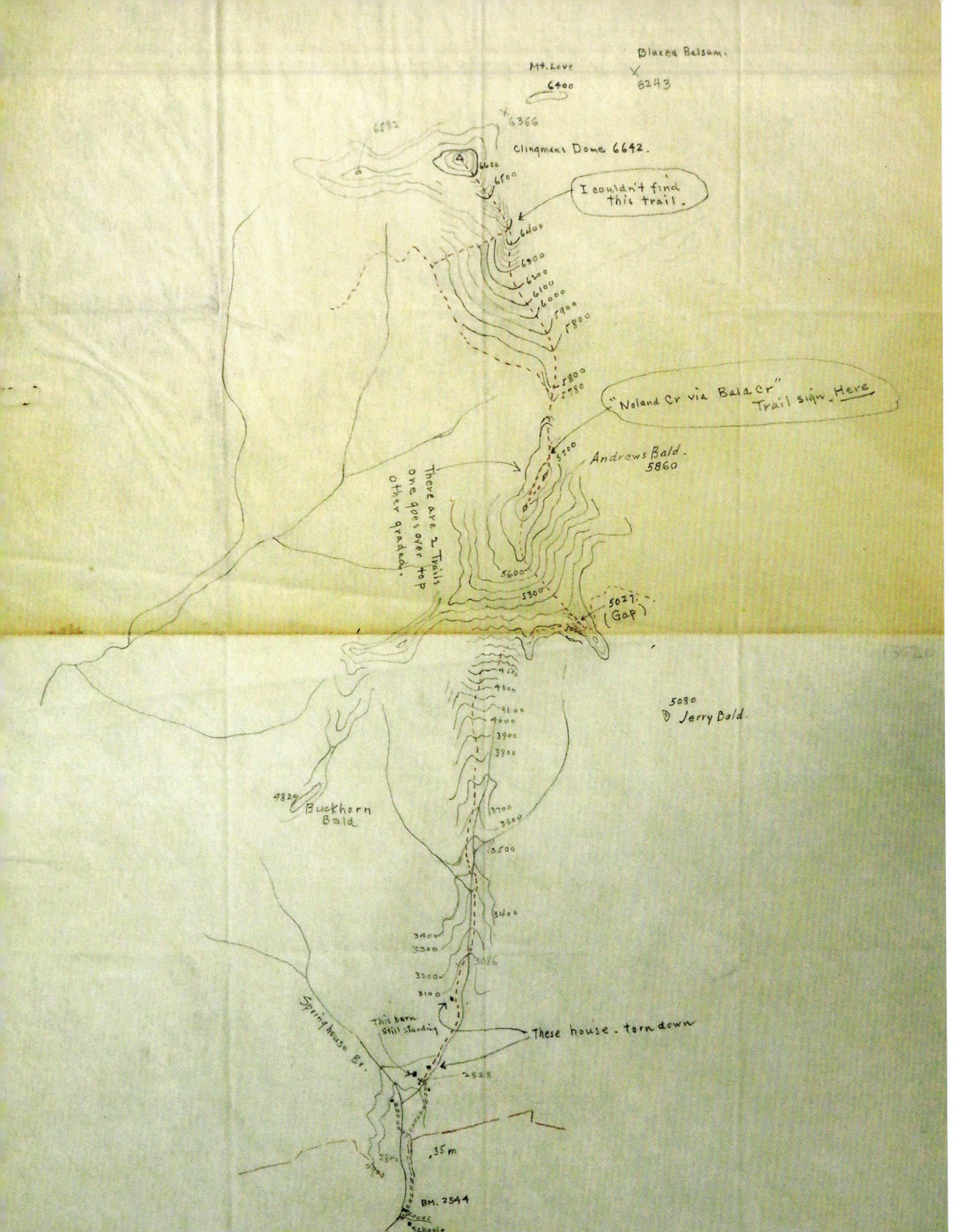

Map of Kuwohi, formerly Clingmans Dome, area with detailed notes on landscape and topography, year unknown. Drawn by George Masa, scanned by Ren and Helen Davis. National Park Service, Great Smoky Mountains National Park Collections Preservation Center, George Masa Collection.

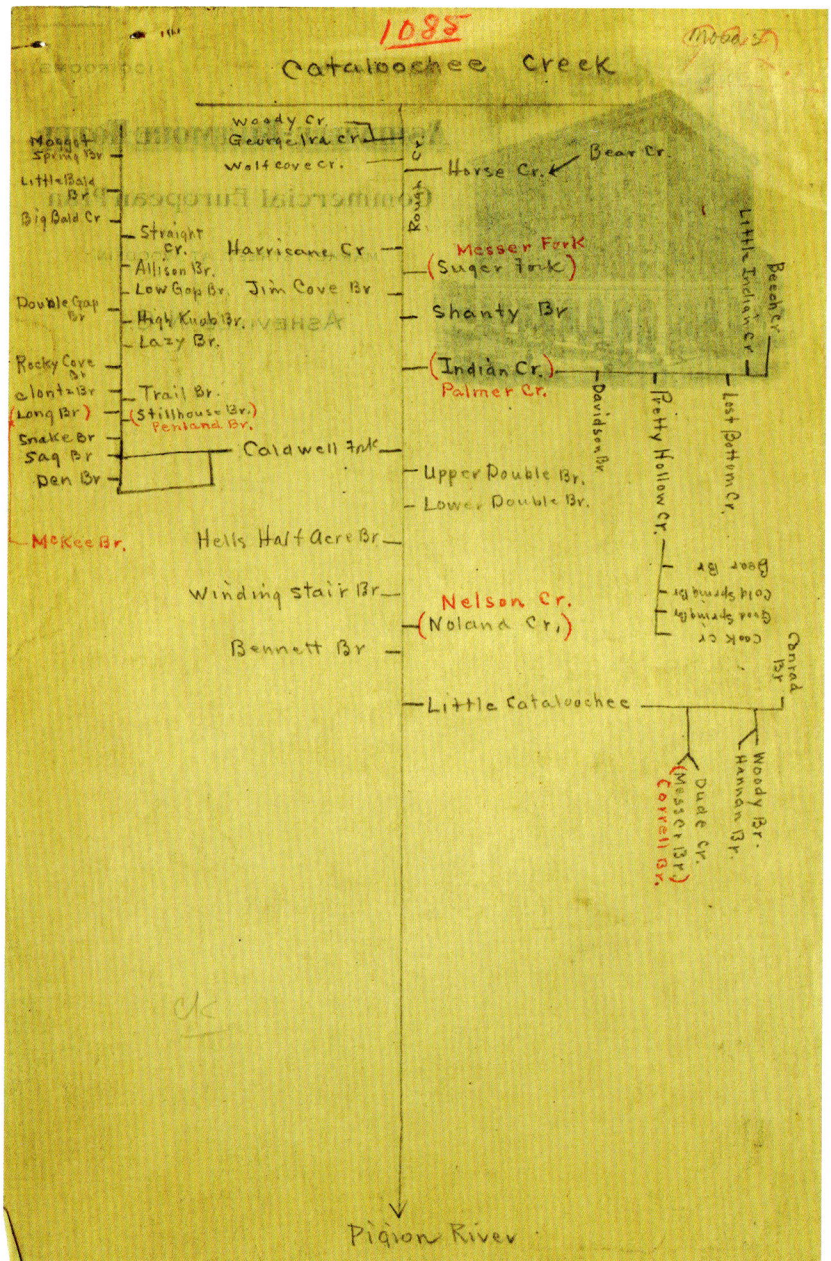

Drawing of Cataloochee Creek and tributaries flowing to Pigeon River, year unknown. Drawn by George Masa, scanned by Ren and Helen Davis. Western Carolina University, Hunter Library Special Collections.

George Masa's notes on hiking club outing from Curtis Creek to Green Knob, May 1, 1932. Scanned by Ren and Helen Davis. Western Carolina University, Hunter Library Special Collections.

Bibliography

Alexander, Tom, Jr., and Jane Alexander, ed. *Mountain Fever: Tom Alexander*. Asheville: Bright Mountain Books, 1995.

Anderson, Ben. "A Closer Look at Some Prominent Place Names in Great Smokies: Is There Need to Change Some?" *National Parks Traveler Magazine*, June 1, 2021. https://nationalparkstraveler.org/2021/06/op-ed-it-time-reconsider-some-place-names-great-smokies.

Anderson, Emily. "Anti-Japanese Exclusion Movement." *Densho Encyclopedia*. Accessed June 20, 2024. https://encyclopedia.densho.org/Anti-Japanese%20exclusion%20movement.

Beadle, Michael. "An Eye for the Mountains: An Ansel Adams of the Smokies, George Masa Was One of the Greatest Photographers of His Era. So Why Have So Many People Never Heard of Him?" *Smoky Mountain News* (Waynesville, N.C.), August 12, 2009.

"Birth of a National Park in the Smokies." Knoxville History Project. Published July 2024. https://knoxvillehistoryproject.org/smokies/.

Bonesteel, Paul, dir. *The Mystery of George Masa*. Asheville, N.C.: Bonesteel Films. Aired 2003.

Bonesteel, Paul, and Janet McCue. *George Masa: A Life Reimagined*. Gatlinburg: Smokies Life, 2024.

Bridges, Anne. "God Alone Can Make a National Park: NPS Officials Visit the Smokies in 1930." *Smokies Life* 18, no. 1 (Spring 2024): 48–51.

Bridges, Anne, Russell Clement, and Ken Wise, eds. *Terra Incognita: An Annotated Bibliography of the Great Smoky Mountains, 1544–1934*. Knoxville: University of Tennessee Press, 2014.

Brinkley, Douglas. *Rightful Heritage: Franklin D. Roosevelt and the Land of America*. New York: Harper Collins, 2016.

———. *The Wilderness Warrior: Theodore Roosevelt and the Crusade for America*. New York: Harper Collins, 2009.

Brown, Margaret Lynn. *The Wild East: A Biography of the Great Smoky Mountains*. Gainesville: University Press of Florida, 2000.

California Department of Parks and Recreation. *Five Views: An Ethnic Historic Site Survey for California*. Sacramento, Calif.: National Park Service online book, 1988. Modified 2004. http://www.cr.nps.gov/history/online_books/5views/5views.htm.

Campbell, Carlos. *Birth of a National Park in the Great Smoky Mountains*. Knoxville: University of Tennessee Press, 1960. Reprint, 1978.

Casada, Jim. "George Masa." *Dictionary of North Carolina Biography*. Reprinted University of North Carolina Press, 1991. www.ncpedia.org/biography/masa-george.

Clement, Russell, Ken Wise, and Anne Bridges, eds. *Great Smoky Mountains Colloquy* 4, no. 1 (Spring 2003). https://utk.primo.exlibrisgroup.com /permalink/01UTN_KNOXVILLE/bcmt7h/alma9926506864202311.

———, eds. *Great Smoky Mountains Colloquy* 11, no. 2 (Fall 2010). https://utk.primo.exlibrisgroup.com /permalink/01UTN_KNOXVILLE/bcmt7h/alma9926506866502311.

———, eds. *Great Smoky Mountains Colloquy* 12, no. 1 (Spring 2011). https://utk.primo.exlibrisgroup.com/permalink/01UTN_KNOXVILLE/bcmt7h/alma9926506866402311.

———, eds. *Great Smoky Mountains Colloquy* 14, no. 2 (Fall 2013). https://utk.primo.exlibrisgroup.com/permalink/01UTN_KNOXVILLE/bcmt7h/alma9926506865902311.

———, eds. *Great Smoky Mountains Colloquy* 15, no. 2 (Fall 2014). https://utk.primo.exlibrisgroup.com/permalink/01UTN_KNOXVILLE/bcmt7h/alma9926506865702311.

Coffey, Thomas M. *Imperial Tragedy: Japan in World War II, the First Days and the Last.* New York: The World, 1970.

Currin, Grant. "Meet George Masa, the Photographer Whose Work Helped Protect the Great Smoky Mountains." *Audubon Magazine*, January 19, 2021.

Davis, Timothy. *National Park Roads: A Legacy in the American Landscape.* Charlottesville: University of Virginia Press, 2016.

Decker, Sarah Jones. "Coming into Focus: George Masa's Legacy." *Appalachian Trail Magazine* (blog), April 8, 2022. https://appalachiantrail.org/official-blog/coming-into-focus-george-masa-legacy.

Dilsaver, Larry, ed. *America's National Park System: The Critical Documents.* Lanham, Md.: Rowman and Littlefield, 1994.

Duncan, Dayton. *The National Parks: America's Best Idea.* New York: Alfred Knopf, 2009.

Dunn, Durwood. *Cades Cove: The Life and Death of a Southern Appalachian Community—1818–1937.* Knoxville: University of Tennessee Press, 1988.

Ellison, George. "Nature Journal: 'Less Talk, More Walk.'" *Asheville Citizen Times* (Asheville, N.C.), April 25, 2018.

Ellison, George, and Janet McCue. *Back of Beyond: A Horace Kephart Biography.* Gatlinburg, Tenn.: Great Smoky Mountains Association, 2019.

Frizzell, George, and Mae Miller Claxton, eds. *Horace Kephart: Writings.* Knoxville: University of Tennessee Press, 2020.

Gatewood, Willard Badgette. "North Carolina's Role in the Establishment of the Great Smoky Mountains National Park." *North Carolina Historical Review* 37, no. 2 (1960): 165–84. http://www.jstor.org/stable/23526724.

Georgia Appalachian Trail Club. *Friendships of the Trail: The History of the Georgia Appalachian Trail Club, 1930–1980.* Marietta, Ga.: Cherokee, 1995.

Great Smoky Mountains National Park: Land of the Everlasting Hills. Knoxville, Tenn.: J. L. Caton, 1941.

Hart, William A., Jr. "A Voice in the Wilderness: The Miracle of Harvey Broome." *Smokies Life* 8, no. 1 (2014): 40–51, 249–75.

Hart, William A., Jr. "George Masa: The Best Mountaineer." In *May We All Remember Well: A Journal of the History & Cultures of Western North Carolina*, edited by Robert S. Brunk. Asheville, N.C.: Robert S. Brunk Auction Services, 1997.

Hill, Eliza. "The Photos That Saved the Smokies: George Masa's Photos Shed Light on the Importance of the Smoky Mountains." *Blue Banner* (University of North Carolina Asheville), April 20, 2020. https://thebluebanner.net/11330/arts-features-2/the-photos-that-saved-the-smokies-george-masas-photos-shed-light-on-the-importance-of-the-smoky-mountains/.

Hunt, Max. "George Masa and the Birth of Great Smoky Mountains National Park." *Mountain XPress*, April 16, 2020. https://mountainx.com/news/george-masa-and-the-birth-of-great-smoky-mountains-national-park/.

James, Paul. *Knoxville Lives II.* Knoxville, Tenn.: Knoxville History Project, 2020.

"Japanese Immigrants." Immigrant Groups. Published September 14, 2015. https://immigrationtounitedstates.org/663-japanese-immigrants.html.

Johnson, Becky. "Judging Kephart: Legacy of Author, Outdoorsman Still Debated." *Smoky Mountain News* (Waynesville, N.C.), April 29, 2009.

Juniper, Andrew. *Wabi Sabi: The Japanese Art of Impermanence.* North Clarendon, Vt.: Tuttle, 2003.

Kemp, Steve. "Lost in the Smokies: Park Service Top Brass Experience Horrible, Awful, Very Bad, No Good Hike." *Smokies Life* 18, no. 1 (Spring 2024): 44–7.

Kephart, Horace. *The Cherokees of the Great Smoky Mountains.* Original Copyright Laura Mack Kephart, 1936. Reprinted Gatlinburg, Tenn.: Great Smoky Mountains Association, 2010.

Lance, Jeanne Creasman. Interview by Peggy Gardner and Bill Hart. March 25, 2000, Asheville, N.C., Pack Library Oral History Project.

Maynard, Charles. "Dutch Roth—A Smoky Mountain Amateur." *Tennessee Conservationist* 75, no. 3 (May/June 2009): 10–14.

Mayshark, Jesse Fox. "Photographer Jim Thompson Started His Business in Downtown Knoxville 100 Years Ago. It's Still There and So Are His Pictures." *Metro Pulse* 12, no. 26 (June 2002).

McCoy, George. *Brief History of the Great Smoky Mountains National Park Movement in North Carolina.* Asheville, N.C.: Inland Press, 1940.

McMahan, Carroll. "Man of the Mountains: George Masa's Pivotal Role in Preserving Mountain Landscapes." *Smoky Mountain Living Magazine*, August 1, 2014.

Miles, Susan Smith. "A Photographic Memory: George Masa's Life Journey Carried Him across an Ocean and Landed Him in Asheville, Where His Passion for Photography Drove Him to Explore WNC's Roughest Wilderness." *WNC Magazine: Mountain Living in Western North Carolina*, July 2009. https://wncmagazine.com/feature/photographic_memory.

National Park Service. *Great Smoky Mountains National Park: Historic Resource Study, Vol. 1.* Washington, D.C.: Department of the Interior, 2016.

NeSmith, Eric. "George Masa's Terra Incognita: There's a Tremendous Sacrifice in Making a Photograph a Work of Art." *The Bitter Southerner*, October 26, 2021. https://bittersoutherner.com/feature/2021/george-masas-terra-incognita.

Pierce, Daniel S. *The Great Smokies: From Natural Habitat to National Park.* Knoxville: University of Tennessee Press, 2000.

Priestly, Kent. "Light and Shadow: The Mystery and Legacy of George Masa." *Mountain XPress*, August 26, 2009. https://mountainx.com/arts/art-news/082609light_and_shadow/.

Public Archaeology Laboratory. *Great Smoky Mountains National Park Historic Resource Study, GRSM 133/134404/A.* National Park Service, Southeast Region: 2016. https://irma.nps.gov/DataStore/DownloadFile/570834

Seagrave, Sterling and Peggy. *The Yamato Dynasty: The Secret History of Japan's Imperial Family.* New York: Broadway Books, 1999.

Searcy, Aaron. "Saving the Great Smoky Mountains Supercut: How the Tennessee Archives of Moving Pictures and Sound Is Preserving, and Sharing the First Moving Pictures of the People's Park." *Smokies Life* 16, no. 2 (Fall 2022): 60–9.

Shaffner, Randall. "Allowing the Soul to Bloom." *Plateau Magazine: Mountain Living in Highlands-Cashiers North Carolina*, February/March 2021. https://theplateaumag.com/allowing-the-soul-to-bloom.

Shumaker, Susan. *A Report for America's Best Idea: Our National Parks: George Masa.* Gatlinburg, Tenn.: National Park Service, 2005.

Shumaker, Susan. *A Report for America's Best Idea: Our National Parks: Horace Kephart.* Gatlinburg, Tenn.: National Park Service, 2005.

Simpson-Ehrenclou, Susan. "Crossing the Mountain: The Newfound Gap Road Yesterday and Today." *Smokies Life* 8, no. 1 (2014).

Streip, Drew. "Thompson's Photos Helped Sway Congress." *Knoxville Sentinel*, April 26, 2009.

Thompson, James. Interview by Vic Weals in 1975. Tennessee Archive of Moving Image and Sound (TAMIS), Knoxville.

U.S. Board on Geographic Names. "Domestic Names Committee: Research and Decision Files, 1890–2023." North Carolina Nomenclature Committee.

———. "Domestic Names Committee: Research and Decision Files, 1890–2023." Tennessee Nomenclature Committee.

White House Office of the Press Secretary. "Remarks by the President on America's Great Outdoors Initiative." The White House, President Barack Obama. Published February 16, 2011. https://obamawhitehouse.archives.gov/the-press-office/2011/02/16/remarks-president-americas-great-outdoors-initiative.

Collections of Documents and Photographs

GEORGE MASON UNIVERSITY, SPECIAL COLLECTIONS
RESEARCH CENTER, FENWICK LIBRARY

Appalachian Trail Conservancy Archives, Myron Avery
　　Collection

GREAT SMOKY MOUNTAINS NATIONAL PARK ARCHIVES /
GREAT SMOKY MOUNTAINS ASSOCIATION COLLECTIONS

Carlos Campbell Collection
George Masa Collection
Horace Kephart Family Collection (with permission from
　　Smokies Life)
James Thompson Collection

KNOX COUNTY LIBRARY, CALVIN MCCLUNG HISTORICAL
COLLECTION

James Thompson Collection
Thompson Brothers Collection

NATIONAL ARCHIVES AND RECORDS ADMINISTRATION.

Record Group 57, still photography

NATIONAL PARK SERVICE

Yellowstone's Photo Collection (nps.gov)

PACK MEMORIAL LIBRARY, BUNCOMBE COUNTY
SPECIAL COLLECTIONS

Carolina Mountain Club Collection
George Masa Collection
Horace Kephart Collection

UNIVERSITY OF NORTH CAROLINA AT ASHEVILLE,
RAMSEY LIBRARY SPECIAL COLLECTIONS

Carolina Mountain Club Collection
George Masa Collection
Verne Rhodes Collection

UNIVERSITY OF NORTH CAROLINA AT CHAPEL HILL,
LOUIS ROUND WILSON SPECIAL COLLECTIONS LIBRARY

Carolina Mountain Club of Asheville Collection

UNIVERSITY OF TENNESSEE HODGES LIBRARY
SPECIAL COLLECTIONS

James Casada Collection
James Thompson Collection
Smoky Mountains Hiking Club Collection

WESTERN CAROLINA UNIVERSITY HUNTER LIBRARY
SPECIAL COLLECTIONS

George Masa Collection
Hart Masa Collection
Horace Kephart Collection

Index